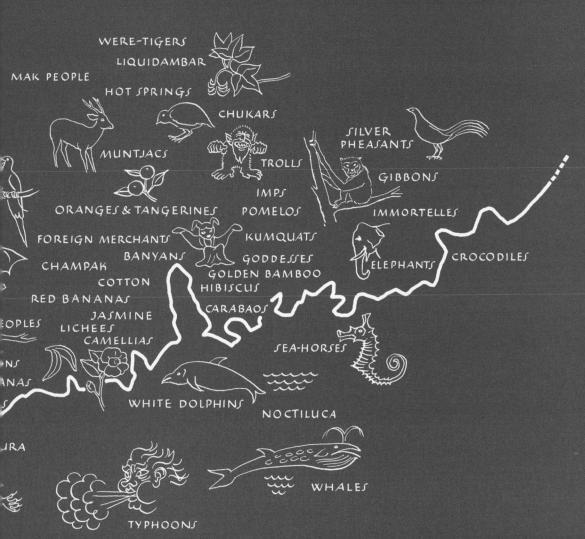

MT CHIU-I

WERE-TIGERS
LIQUIDAMBAR
MAK PEOPLE
HOT SPRINGS

CHUKARS

SILVER
PHEASANTS

MUNTJACS

TROLLS

GIBBONS

IMPS

ORANGES & TANGERINES   POMELOS

IMMORTELLES

FOREIGN MERCHANTS   KUMQUATS

BANYANS   GODDESSES

CHAMPAK   GOLDEN BAMBOO   ELEPHANTS   CROCODILES

COTTON   HIBISCUS

RED BANANAS   CARABAOS

EOPLES   JASMINE

LICHEES

NS   CAMELLIAS

ANAS   SEA-HORSES

URA   WHITE DOLPHINS

NOCTILUCA

WHALES

TYPHOONS

THE SWOLLEN SEA

NAM-VIET

The Vermilion Bird

The Vermilion Bird

T'ANG IMAGES OF THE SOUTH

EDWARD H. SCHAFER

UNIVERSITY OF CALIFORNIA PRESS · BERKELEY AND LOS ANGELES · 1967

University of California Press
Berkeley and Los Angeles, California
Cambridge University Press
London, England
Copyright © 1967, by
The Regents of the University of California

Library of Congress Catalog Card Number: 67-10463
Designed by Theo Jung
Printed in the United States of America

TO PETER ALEXIS BOODBERG

CONTENTS

vii

Contents

LIST OF PLATES

Dates at Which Chinese Dynasties Began

ca.	1500	B.C.	SHANG
ca.	1000	B.C.	CHOU
	221		CH'IN
	206		HAN
A.D.	220		Three Kingdoms
	265		CHIN (TSIN)
	317		Northern (non-Chinese) and Southern (Chinese) Dynasties
	589		SUI
	618		T'ANG
	907		Five Dynasties (North) Ten Kingdoms (South)
	960		SUNG LIAO (Khitan) and CHIN (KIN) (Jurchen) in North
	1260		YÜAN (Mongol)
	1368		MING
	1644		CH'ING (Manchu)

Year of Accession of the Rulers of T'ang

618	Kao Tsu	780	Te Tsung
627	T'ai Tsung	805	Shun Tsung
650	Kao Tsung	806	Hsien Tsung
684	Chung Tsung	821	Mu Tsung
	Jui Tsung	825	Ching Tsung
	Empress Wu	827	Wen Tsung
705	Chung Tsung (restored)	841	Wu Tsung
710	Jui Tsung (restored)	847	Hsüan Tsung (Sywen Tsong)
712	Hsüan Tsung (Ghwen Tsong)	860	I Tsung
		874	Hsi Tsung
756	Su Tsung	889	Chao Tsung
763	Tai Tsung	905	Chao Hsüan Ti

INTRODUCTION

ALTHOUGH we know that high cultures were possible long ago in the dry hot lands of Egypt and Mesopotamia—partly because so many well-preserved museum specimens have been found there—we temperate-zone men have not been disposed to regard the *moist* tropics as conducive to the best flowering of human talent. This prejudice is now being abandoned. The rain forest and monsoon shores have, in fact, produced better things than enervation, laziness, lechery, and dullness of intellect. Indeed a thousand years ago many of the great centers of civilization were situated in the tropics of Asia and America,[1] and we have discovered that we can admire the achievements of the Mayans, the Javanese, the Cambodians, the Singhalese, and many other peoples who flourished in the wet forests many centuries before the European Renaissance. Of course the dark men of the rain-soaked cities were not the only great sources of spiritual and material energy in the Middle Ages. Leaving Europe aside, there was also Islam, in its Persian, Arabian, Syrian, African, and Spanish varieties, in mainly arid lands. Finally, there was China, providing a mixed environment, ranging from beech and spruce forests, sandy deserts, and grassy steppes, through a temperate and subtropical lake country, and beyond that to a loosely held colonial frontier where the tropics begin. This last region is the subject of this book. In particular, I propose to examine its contributions to the knowledge of the medieval Chinese, and also its effects on their senses, sensibilities, and imaginations—or, considered contrariwise, the transformation of this land by the alchemy of the Chinese spirit.

In *The Golden Peaches of Samarkand* I often wrote of the creatures of the southernmost part of the T'ang empire, both organic and crystalline, as "semi-exotics" from the point of view of the Chinese—that is, as not quite so forbiddingly foreign as the fauna and flora of Japan, of Java, or of Jāguda. Now I propose to give closer attention to this ambivalent life zone, so long claimed by the Chinese as their own, but still strange and wonderful in T'ang times. This, then, is a book about the tropics of medieval China represented by the image of the Vermilion Bird, whose identity remains a mystery to the end. It might equally have been represented, as will slowly become apparent, by the charming figure of "The Woman of Viet."

It is undeniable that, in a sense, this study represents my own past—that is, a past particularized and concreted in a way peculiar to myself. Possibly all re-creations of the past are of this sort, but my point is that here my aim is not so much to "conceptualize" the past (to use the abstract term much favored nowadays) but rather to *realize* the past, without sacrificing accuracy, in a vivid, lively, and sensuous fashion. This means attempting to capture the medieval world of the men of T'ang simultaneously as physical environment and as imaginative interpretation. There may be disagreement about what "true" history is, but, while I hope that my story is one among the several possible true ones, I aim primarily at "real" history. In short, if *The Vermilion Bird* turns out to be no stuffed specimen in a museum drawer, but a believable resurrection, having some of the rich vitality now that it had a thousand years ago, I shall be gratified indeed.

I have tried to use contemporary sources exclusively, except in matters of exegesis and interpretation, in order to avoid the anachronisms which could make the characterization of a particular era ridiculous. It is all too easy to suppose that because a custom or a myth existed in Sung times, it must already have existed in T'ang times —to suppose, for instance, that because Ma Yüan was a god of the southern torrents in the eleventh century, he had already been one in the eighth. What is true of the evidence of folklore is equally true of later records of other beliefs, customs, and institutions. I have avoided them wherever possible, because of the danger that they might subtly introduce attitudes, preferences, and selections natural to Sung men but alien to the men of T'ang. Nonetheless I have occasionally consulted Sung (and even Yüan) sources, especially when they tell explicitly of the survival of earlier customs and monuments. I hope that I have done so with sufficient prudence and caution.

Spelling Medieval Chinese

The persistence of the primitive custom of giving words and names from medieval and even ancient China in the much eroded phonetic shapes assumed by their twentieth-century descendants in the Peking dialect commonly styled "Mandarin" is regrettable. There are many reasons for wishing to do away with this convention in a book about T'ang times, and for restoring, as nearly as possible, the actual sounds of Medieval Chinese. Probably the most important are these four: (1) to make the names of medieval persons and places sound approximately as they sounded to the men of those times; this is part of the attempt to recover the sensuous experience of that lost world; (2) to make T'ang transcriptions of foreign words, such as the names of foreign lands and imported ideas and practices, recognizable as Sanskrit or Cham or Old Javanese, or traceable to unexpected sources; (3) to make the many distinctions made between monosyllabic words in the medieval language, but concealed by their reduction to homophones in the simpler phonetic system of modern "Mandarin," apparent (examples below); and (4) to restore the actual rhymes, assonances, onomatopoeias, and other devices relying on sound effects intended by the poet but lost in modern pronunciation. (This last is rather less important here, since I present T'ang poetry in English translation.)

Unfortunately the standard, conservative reconstruction of Medieval Chinese (or "Middle Chinese"; in either case, M.C.) that we owe to the pioneer labors of Bernhard Karlgren (his "Ancient Chinese") is so loaded with diacritics and special symbols that its use outside of technical linguistic studies makes words look awkward or even forbidding. The reader's mind boggles when these hypothetical forms turn up in a text meant to be read continuously and smoothly. A conversion of this system of spelling into a much simpler romanization has long seemed desirable. The late George Kennedy used one in some of his publications, but never promulgated the complete system. Now I have been bold enough to devise one, purely as a matter of convenience, and entirely without any idea of improving on Karlgren's reconstructions or indeed of making any sort of scientific contribution. It employs only one diacritic sign, and will give the illusion, if nothing more, of pronounceable words.[2]

Here are eleven medieval words, all of them now pronounced *hsieh* (Wade-Giles romanization), as they appear in my "modified Karlgren": *ghăi* "apparatus," *ghăăi* "crab," *ghep* "associate," *ghet* "stiff-necked," *hyăp* "ribs," *hyăt* "pause," *sep* "reconcile," *set* "detritus," *sya* "slight," *syet* "diffuse," *zya* "slant." Similarly, underlying Mandarin *ho* are M.C. *gha, ghak, ghăk, ghat, ghap, ghĕk, ghwa, ghwĕt, ha, hak, hăk,* with as many different meanings. And so on. If we put the names of T'ang men in this romanization we sometimes get a kind of false Mandarin, as in the case of Lu Yen-ch'ang—but here the *ch-* may represent a palatal consonant, not a supradental as it would if this were a Wade-Giles spelling of Mandarin. The medieval and modern forms of some names, on the other hand, are completely different. Thus Ngu Myu-lyĕng corresponds to Mandarin Wu Wu-ling. Observe also that our story tells of two men named Li Po (Mandarin). One, however, was the poet Li Băk (M.C.), the other was the engineer and governor Li Bwĕt (M.C.). A poem by Li Hsün (Li Sywin), translated in Chapter XI, looks like this in my transcription:

> ngyo zhi san
> du jwen hĕi
> ywăt nam ywĕn zhu mywang tyung mĕi
> ghăng k'ăk dai dyeu t'en yok mu
> sung ch'win p'u
> dryou t'eng seng seng dei chang yu

The corresponding Mandarin (Wade-Giles) would be:

yü shih san
tu ch'uan hsi
yüeh nan yün shu wang chung wei
hsing k'o tai ch'ao t'ien yü mu
sung ch'un p'u
ch'ou t'ing hsing hsing t'i chang yü

The poem shows a much more diversified sound structure in its original medieval form than it does in Mandarin. One can observe, for instance, that the syllable *yü* in the first, fourth, and last lines of the modernized version conceals original *ngyo* "fisherman," *yok* "desire," and *yu* "rain," while the original rhyme words *hĕi, mĕi,* and *mu, p'u, yu* have disappeared, to be replaced by the false rhymes *hsi, wei,* and *mu, p'u, yü.* The monotony of the Mandarinized reading would surely have annoyed the poet. Much more drastic examples could easily be found.

In this book I give the M.C. forms (i.e., "Middle/Medieval Chinese," corresponding to Karlgren's "Ancient Chinese") in parenthesis after the standard Wade-Giles Mandarin wherever it appears that an approximation to the true phonetic value might be useful to the reader, particularly to a philologically minded reader. For instance, I give only Meng Chiao for the Chinese poet, but I have Mo Hsün (Mak Zyĕm) for the aboriginal princeling presumed to be related to the modern Mak tribesmen who speak a Kam-Sui language. Similarly I give *chin chü* (*kyĕm kywit*) for the golden kumquat (*Fortunella*), and so for other everyday words. I have avoided giving the M.C. form where it does not differ significantly from the Mandarin. Beyond this, I have added the M.C. form to distinguish names and titles which are not distinguishable in Mandarin romanization; for instance, the eighth-century ruler Hsüan Tsung (Ghwen Tsong) must not be confused with the ninth-century monarch Hsüan Tsung (Sywen Tsong), nor the medieval county Ch'in-chou (Gyĕn-chou) with nearby Ch'in-chou (K'yĕm-chou).

Chiang-Nan

Immediately south of the watershed of the Yellow River, the original homeland of the Chinese, lay another great river valley, complicated by a multitude of lakes and artificial waterways, all of whose waters eventually drained off into the Pacific Ocean by way of the mouth of the Yangtze. South of this great river was a temperate and subtropical zone, transitional between the old familiar north and the true tropics which are the subject of this book. This was the great province of Chiang-nan (Kaung-nam) "South of the Chiang," that is, south of the Yangtze River. I shall use the name in this book in the broadest sense, though sometimes I shall refer to its subdivisions, generally using the names of such modern provinces as Hunan, Kiangsi, and Fukien.

Introduction

Nam-Viet

Beyond the fertile lands of Chiang-nan and across a semicircle of low mountains lay a T'ang province about the size of California, a large part of it below the Tropic of Cancer. This southernmost province included what are today the provinces of Kwangtung and Kwangsi, and much of northern Vietnam, in particular the delta of the Red River. The whole region was known by more than one name, but I shall call it by its oldest Chinese name, using a familiar Vietnamese pronunciation: "Nam-Viet" (Mand. Nan-Yüeh; M.C. Nam-Ywăt).[3] This name occurred already in several books of the late Chou period, *Chuang tzu* for instance, as a name for the most southerly of the aboriginal Viet peoples known to the ancient Chinese. When Chao T'o founded his famous kingdom in the last lands to be conquered by the Ch'in armies in the third century B.C. he gave it this respectable name.[4] It was still alive in T'ang times, used more or less informally, but never given official dignity in the administrative geography of that nation. It was especially suitable to literature: thus we find the parrot styled "Bird of Nam-Viet" in an eighth-century poem.[5] As for the name "Viet" itself, it has been suggested that since it is cognate to *viet* (Mand. *yüeh,* M.C. *ywăt*) "a kind of axe," that the ancient Viet peoples were in fact "the people of the stone axe." [6]

Lingnan and Annam

I shall adopt the stereotype of dividing Nam-Viet into two major parts, an eastern called Lingnan (Lyeng-nam) "South of the Mountain Passes," and a southwestern called Annam (Mand. An-nan) "The Secured South," inconsistently employing the forms most widely applied to them today. Lingnan was and is a familiar name for the present provinces of Kwangtung and Kwangsi, but formerly it was sometimes extended to include Annam, in which case it was synonymous with Nam-Viet. I shall prefer to follow the usage of the T'ang minister Lu Chih who, reporting to his sovereign about overseas commerce in Nam-Viet, wrote: "This is all the more true of Lingnan and Annam, for neither is outside your royal soil." [7]

Lingnan was subdivided into four "administrations" (*kuan*), named Kuang, Kuei, Jung, and Yung. Of these, Kuang was the most important, since Chinese control was most firmly established there, especially in the great port of Canton, the administrative seat of Kuang-chou (county) and Kuang-kuan (administration) alike. But it was customary to speak of the "Five Administrations" of Nam-Viet. The fifth was Annam, roughly equivalent to modern Tongking and some little portion of the coast below it, with its chief city, the administrative seat of Chiao-chou (County) and of all Annam, near the site of modern Hanoi. The arrangement was like this:

5

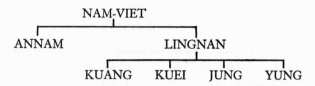

The powerful rulers of the southern Administrations all held the title of "Legate" (*shih*), qualified by a two-word phrase intended to describe the officer's responsibilities. The title "Measuring and Ruling Legate" (*Chieh tu shih*) was ordinarily reserved for the viceroy of Nam-Viet, resident at Canton. This important title, with its implications of complete power to bring order to a disturbed region, incorporated the ancient phrase *chieh tu,* "measure and rule," used in Han times of the operations of planets and of ultimate metaphysical forces, and then extended to the well-regulated order which an imperial commissioner was expected to bring to troubled provinces, so that they might conform once more to the eternal measure and rule of Heaven and its earthly deputy, the Son of Heaven.

The "administrators" (as I shall usually call them) of the unsettled "administrations" of Kuei, Jung, and Yung, with their large aboriginal populations were in fact usually titled "Ranging and Annexing Legates" (*Ching lüeh shih*), which incorporates another classical phrase. Sometimes we read of an "Observing and Inspecting Legate" (*Kuan ch'a shih*) or a "Guarding and Defending Legate" (*Fang yü shih*). Sometimes one officer held several such titles concurrently. Much of the time the chief officer of the fifth and southernmost administration Annam was called "Metropolitan Protector" (*Tu tu*); I shall usually refer to him simply as the "Protector" of Annam.

Each of the Five Administrations was subdivided into lesser administrative districts called *chou*, literally "islands," because of the old tale of the raising of the several regions of China from the primordial waters by the hero Yü, so that their borders were drained by the chief rivers "Under Heaven." I shall give these "Isles" the paraphrastic name "Counties"—compare "Isle of Ely" as a county name in England—since they correspond roughly to the counties of England and the United States in size and function. Sometimes I shall write Kuang-chou (for instance), sometimes Kuang County, sometimes simply Kuang. The counties of T'ang Nam-Viet are listed in Glossary C.[8] Where context is insufficient to show which form is meant I shall give the M.C. equivalents of T'ang county names homophonous in Mandarin: Po (Băk) and Po (Pa); Yen (Ngăm), Yen (Ngyăm), and Yen (Yen). There are two cases of homophony in M.C. (if tone is neglected) which I shall distinguish thus: I (Ngiĕ[a]) and I (Ngiĕ[b]); Kang[a] and Kang[b].[9]

I use the modern name Canton for the administrative seat of Kuang-chou (Kuang County), chief city of Lingnan, and the modern name Hanoi for the administrative seat of Chiao-chou (Chiao County), chief city of Annam (mostly modern Tongking).

Introduction

The governors of these counties were styled "Inciting Notaries" (*tz'u shih*), that is, they were agents of the Son of Heaven whose duty it was to stimulate his subjects to true moral ends.

The county, whose center was a walled city, was further subdivided into "townships" (*hsien*), a word whose etymology is "dependent; subordinate."

Man and Hua

The native inhabitants of these southern provinces were collectively styled "Man"—not the English word "man," but a Chinese expression denoting something like "southern heathen," with cognate words in the semantic range of "winding; bent; snaking; serpentine." I shall have something to say about the reptilian attributes of the Man peoples.

Opposing the Man were the intruding Chinese—the men who today distinguish themselves as "Han." In this book I shall call them by the name they used for themselves in medieval times: Hua (Ghwă)-men or Hsia (Ghă)-men, these being *ablaut* forms of the same old ethnic name. They called the ancient center of their unique civilization in the Yellow River watershed "Central Hua" or "Central Hsia," to contrast it with the less fortunate lands beyond. In medieval times, even a true Chinese might be despised by chauvinistic northerners if he had not been born in Central Hsia.

Sometimes I shall call the Chinese by their national name "men of T'ang," as they had earlier been "men of Sui" and later were "men of Sung." In all cases they were also civilized Hua-men.

Transcendent

Readers will observe, perhaps with dismay, the frequent occurrence in this book of some English words which are either uncommon in everyday speech or are used in an apparently unusual way. These are the equivalents of certain Chinese words of great importance in medieval thought and language. "Transcendent" is one of the most noteworthy of them. This represents the word *hsien,* which others have commonly rendered "(Taoist) immortal." The word actually connotes "having the ability to spring up out of the mire of the material world into the realm of spirit, symbolized by unearthly journeys to sky castles and island paradises," with linguistic cognates meaning "soaring, flying, flapping up." In Han times it had ordinarily been used as a verb to characterize the activity of the "Feathered Men," who were Taoist adepts and initiates, transformed men shown pictorially with angelic wings. I shall normally translate the word by "transcendent" (an equivalence which I did not invent, I am sorry to say), though in a few places I have used "sylph" to suggest the dainty, refined inhabitants of the upper air.

7

Introduction

Numinous

"Numinous" is the quality of things regularly represented by the Chinese word *ling*. It is a spiritual force or energy emanating from or potential in any object full of mana, even such a dull thing as a stone. It radiated abundantly from imperial tombs, from powerful drugs, from magical animals, and from haunted trees. The souls of dead men were also called *ling* "numen; holy spirit." Occasionally I have rendered *ling* by "holy."

Creole

We are accustomed to the French creoles in Louisiana, that is persons of French descent born among the savages of the New World, and the Spanish creoles of the Indies, native to Cuba but not aborigines. I use "creole" in the sense of "persons of Chinese ancestry born among the aborigines of Nam-Viet."

Very old are we men;
Our dreams are tales
Told in dim Eden
By Eve's nightingales.

Walter de la Mare, *All That's Past*

1 Nam-Viet: Foreground and Background

MODERN PEOPLES

IF WE LOOK today at the lands once subject to the ancient warlords Chao T'o and Ma Yüan and to the literate magistrates of T'ang—that is, at Kwangtung, Kwangsi, and northernmost Vietnam—we see an irregular mosaic of races, languages, and cultures. Indeed the whole of the Indochinese peninsula exhibits this bewildering pattern. It is a linguistic and cultural Balkans, in which relatively recent arrivals are intermingled with very ancient groups. The Burmese, the Siamese, and the Vietnamese, for instance, have displaced Mons, Khmers, and Chams in late medieval and early modern times. The Chinese themselves are relative late-comers. Imbedded in the modern nations of this hot region are a multitude of ethnic enclaves, some of them peopled by descendants of the original inhabitants, others the posterity of early immigrants.[1] The whole picture reminds us strongly of California before the invasions of the Spanish and the Yankees. Then it was a *cul-de-sac* of American peoples, spattered with Penutian and Uto-Aztecan tribes, Algonkin and Athabascan villages, and many other kinds of men, speaking the most diverse tongues, and practicing the most varied customs—maize-growing, salmon-fishing, acorn-gathering, and what not.

9

We may plausibly assume that some of the simpler cultures of our region are also the oldest. The illiterate mountaineers high up between Vietnam and Laos, collectively called Moi by the Vietnamese, some of them speaking Mon-Khmer languages, some of them linguistically related to the Chams, probably represent a very archaic substratum.[2] Analogous to these non-Hinduized natives of the upland forests, the lowly relatives of the Cambodians and Chams, are the Muong, turbaned aristocrats around Hoa-Binh in Tongking, whose canoes are guarded by cocks. They are the non-sinicized natives of the Red River basin, the hardly modified remnants of the ancestral Vietnamese.[3] The savage Li (or Loi) people of the highlands of Hainan Island, practicing dry agriculture and honoring cattle, drinking through tubes and divining with eggs, seem to be another very ancient group.[4] Their language shows Thai features, but it may be only distantly related to the true Thai languages. Perhaps it is basically Malayo-Polynesian, with added monosyllabicity and tonality —a member of a transitional group between Indonesian and Thai, which includes also Kelao from south central China and two tongues of the Tongking border. Benedict has styled the group "Kadai."[5] Then there are the Tan "boat people" of the southwestern coast and the shores of the great river estuaries—ear-ringed and braceleted fishers and divers who venerate snakes.[6] Although they now speak Chinese, it has been suggested that they are a remnant of the ancient Viet people of the southern coasts.[7]

Thai is a very important and widespread linguistic group in Indochina. It includes the Siamese and Laotians, the Shan of Burma, the Ahom of Assam, as well as many peoples in Tongking (Thô, Black Thai, White Thai, Nung),[8] and in Lingnan, where their typical representatives are called Ch'uang.[9] These are now, and seem always to have been, civilized rice farmers in flooded valleys and foothills,[10] counting cows and water buffaloes as visible symbols of wealth, decorating their textiles by batik and ikat, and living in pile houses.[11] Despite this far-flung distribution, which is very old, the name Thai (or Tai, or Dai) does not appear in history before the end of the thirteenth century.[12]

Except for its Vietnamese portion, the Chinese are nowadays the dominant linguistic and ethnic group in former Nam-Viet—Cantonese in the south, Hakka in the north, and Hoklo in the east and on Hainan.[13] We shall soon see that this was not always the case.

Even more recent arrivals than the Chinese in the Far South are the peoples whose languages are collectively called Miao-Yao, after two very old names for non-Chinese aborigines, now used in narrower senses than formerly. The Yao are presumed to be immigrants of the Sung-Yüan period;[14] they are now found on Hainan,[15] and in Tongking, where they are simply called "Man." One Tongkingese Man tribe, the Cao-lan, which appears to have lost its original language and now speaks a Thai dialect,[16] have poems in Chinese—for example, a quatrain whose last verse has been translated "La statue du Buddha ne peut être comparée aux beautés du corps de mon amante."[17] These "pagan nature-worshippers,"[18] skilled in witch-craft,[19] grow tubers in burned-over fields on the mountain sides above the Thai tribes. They are descended from the divine dog P'an-hu.[20]

Closely related to these Yao-Man are the peoples who have inherited the old name of Miao. Like the Yao, they occur sparsely in Lingnan (including Hainan) and on the mountaintops of Tongking, where they are called "Mêo," though they call themselves "Mhông."[21] They are more recent immigrants than the Yao, having come, it is thought, in the Yüan-Ming period, to be squeezed into the highest and least desirable parts of the country.[22] They are primitive agriculturalists, with dog and tiger cults, and most of them live in stilt houses (the Yao dwell on the ground), independent and openly erotic, rejoicing in their little ponies.[23]

In a few villages of Binh Thuan in southern Vietnam, no longer in touch with their former Chinese neighbors, are the remnants of the once rich and powerful Chams, now trifling enclaves among the Vietnamese, whom they contemptuously style *yùòn*—that is, *Yavana* (to use the Sanskrit original), or, ultimately, "Ionians"[24] —a term suggesting subnormal, devilish men. Some of them are Muslims and call themselves "Orang Bani"; their pagan brothers, the Chams "Djat," they style "Kaphir."[25] The Muslim Chams have a tradition that their first king was "Noursavan"—that is to say, the Sassanid Anushirvan the Just. His ministers were Ban Ali, Bubaker, Umar, and Asman—in short, the first four successors of Muhammad in somewhat altered guise. But some of them say that Ovloh (Allah) was their first ruler.[26] The pagan Chams preserve some debased vestiges of their ancient cults, in particular the veneration of the linga of Śiva.[27]

If we look back to the T'ang era, as we shall presently, the picture is still confused, but the pattern is different. Some names, such as Li, Tan, and Nung, are the same, but the referents are not the same. Other names are different: instead of the Ch'uang, the Miao, and the Muong, we find (for instance) the Huang, the Mo (Mak), and the Ning; and the Chams are a great nation opposing the southward push of the Hua-men.

But first let us go even further back to prehistoric and early historic times, when the Chinese were first becoming aware of the non-Hua peoples in the south.

ANCIENT PEOPLES

The civilization we recognize as "Chinese," with its remarkable continuity underlying the most complex historical changes, can be traced back to the Stone Ages in the drainage basin of the Yellow River. Even at that remote period the peoples of the southlands were completely different from the Chinese. This great cultural cleavage persisted throughout the Neolithic Age and the Bronze Age, though both agriculture and bronze-working came to the southerners from the Hua-men of the north during these centuries.

Farmers of the Neolithic Age, it is thought, wandered into the rich subtropical country, bringing their ceramic industry and their art of polishing tough stones to the "Mesolithic" hunters and fishers—some, at least, of negroid race—with their tools of chipped pebbles.[28] Three chief cultural areas have been distinguished in south China after the achievement of this Neolithic revolution. One was in the lake area of the Yangtze basin and later became the historic state of Ch'u, subject to strong pressure from the true Chinese of the north; one was a coastal, sea-going culture, stretching from the Huai area to the region of modern Canton—its characteristic tool was the "stepped adze"; one was a jungle culture, ranging from the limestone hills of Kwangsi westward through the mountains of Szechwan and Yunnan and southward into Vietnam—its chief tool was the "shouldered axe." [29] The second of these, the culture of the southeast coast, was much under the influence of the so-called "Lung-shan" or "black pottery" culture known from archaeological finds further north. It has also been plausibly suggested that this region was the hearth of the migration of the Malayo-Polynesian peoples from the mainland of Asia into Oceania. In this view, the emigrants, presumably of mixed race, reached the islands of Micronesia during Shang times, central Polynesia by Han times, and settled Hawaii a thousand years later, about the time of the foundation of the Sung empire.[30]

The polished-stone technology was gradually eliminated, except for survivals in remote areas, with the spread of the art of bronze-working southward from the world of the Shang charioteers. By Han times this produced an efflorescence of art and a unique civilization in the Nam-Viet region which archaeologists and prehistorians call "Dongsonian." [31] Of the languages of the participants we know nothing.

But we have been using the abstract language of prehistory. Let us look at the south at the dawn of history from the point of view of the Hua-men, as we know it from vestiges of their earliest writings.

Beyond their southern frontiers the Chinese of the classical Chou period—the "Age of Confucius" more or less—discerned a kind of buffer belt of "outer states," not entirely pure in race and culture, and beyond them or partly intermingled with them a confused mass of savages, hardly to be distinguished from wild animals or forest demons. Some of these last were styled Miao—a name revived in late medieval times for the cousins of the Yao, as we have seen, and still current in this usage. Tradition said that a civilizing demigod who appeared in the Yellow River valley at the pale dawn of history had warred against them. But we know nothing of the language, social arrangements, or culture of the ancient Miao.[32] A broader term for the benighted heathen of the south, used from early historical times, was Man.[33] Some scholars assert the ultimate identity of these two ancient ethnic names, and add a host of supposed cognates. Meng, Min, Mao, and others [34]—the vast southland is thickly sprinkled with tribal names and place names beginning with m-, with or without the final nasal.

Some of the graphs with which these ancient names were written contain a reptilian element (Man and Min, two of the commonest, are instances), and in Han times these peoples were said to be the kin of serpents.[35] Another tradition said that the word "Man" first described the reptile-infested land, and was later transferred to its human inhabitants.[36] The men of Chou imagined their unpleasant neighbors as slithering about in the shadows on the edge of their enlightened land:

> How they writhed, the Man in Ching!
> Playing rival to our great domain! [37]

The proto-musicians and creator spirits, Fu Hsi and Nü Kua, a divine brother-sister pair, shown with ophidian torsos in Han art, may have been ancestral serpent totems of the tribes on the southern marches before they were assimilated to the official Han cult—such incestuous progenitors are still a commonplace among the modern Miao-tzu and other southern peoples.[38]

Just as high but "barbaric" cultures, characterized by leisure and urbanity, grew up among the aborigines of the American tropics, so unique and substantial cultural complexes developed among the pagans south of the true Hua-men, the ancestral Chinese. So the Pa and Shu peoples (akin to tigers, although the Chinese gave reptilian signs to their names) in what is now Szechwan, were accepted as civilized men by the Chinese at the end of the fourth century B.C. and gradually absorbed.[39] Even more acceptable were the men of the kingdom of Ch'u in the moist lowlands east of the Szechwanese. Most of them were rice-growing Thai, it seems, ruled by a sinicized nobility in late Chou times, and thoroughly assimilated by the beginning of Han.[40] The nations of the southern coast were different from these marsh- and river-dwellers. In Chou times they were known chiefly in two semi-civilized states, the Wu of the Yangtze delta, who lost their identity very early, and the Yüeh (our Viet) south of them in modern Chekiang, perhaps a partly sinicized Thai people ruling subjects of other and unguessable ethnic character.[41] Customs observed among the Vietnamese of later times, such as cropped hair and tattooed skin, were already noticed among these Yüeh of ancient Chekiang.[42] By the fourth or third century B.C., and especially by the time of the ambitious invasions and partial conquests of the Ch'in and Han empires, smaller tribal or national divisions among these peoples were detected by the Chinese and even projected by them into the past. The Eastern Ou were distinguished in Chekiang and parts of adjacent regions, the Min Yüeh lived below them in Fukien, and the Southern Yüeh (our Nam-Viet!) inhabited modern Kwangtung, while the Western Ou, southwest of them, extended into the delta of the Red River.[43]

One modern investigator has discriminated two ethnic elements among these ancient coastal "tribes" (if such they were)—the tattooed peoples and the dwarfish negritoes.[44] Another has suggested that there was a more northerly Yüeh (Ywăt; Viet) people, originally Thai, and a more southerly Lo (Lak) people, of Mon-Khmer stock, akin to the Cambodians.[45] (This last is a persuasive argument if we admit the hybrid character of the modern Vietnamese language.) But what are we to make of such compound names as Ou-Lo (Ou-Lak; cf. Vietnamese Au-lac)—according to one authority, a merging of Mon-Khmer and Thai peoples before the Chinese conquest[46]—and Lo-Yüeh (Lak-Ywăt, i.e. Lak-Viet), another name associated with what is now northern Vietnam? The elements "Ou" and "Lo" had been used of the aborigines of Chekiang and Fukien in very early times, but we know them better when, after successful Chinese invasions of the central coast, they appear further to the south. In any case, the cultural and linguistic identities of these groupings remain mysteries. All we can say with some faint hope of certainty is that for the Chinese Hua of the Yellow River watershed, Yüeh (Viet) was the more general term for the coastal peoples south of the mouth of the Yangtze, while Ou and Lo (Lak) stood for some of their tribal units. The formation of the Vietnamese people of history began, it seems, late in Chou times, with the gradual retreat of "Viet" peoples southward through lands held by their relatives in what is now Kwangtung, Kwangsi, and northern Vietnam.[47]

The northernmost of these poorly known peoples, those close to the Yangtze estuary, were assimilated to the northern Hua by the Second century B.C.[48] Their more southerly relatives were subject to armed attacks and foreign control for many centuries thereafter—this will be the subject of a later chapter.

Throughout history, the lands south of the Yellow River drainage basin seemed to the Chinese a place of refuge from the marauding nomads of the steppes, and at the same time a paradise of fertility and plenty. So the south gradually became the safe granary of the north, and the emigration of Chinese followed after the importation of their food.[49] Southward migration was all the easier because the nomadic stock-breeding culture beyond the northern frontier was a psychological barrier to the Chinese, whose economy was based on intensive cultivation of the land. Though possibly a change towards a more extensive mode of agriculture in the far north may have been, the necessary social revolution would have been much more drastic than that required by settlement among the rice-growing Thai and their neighbors in the Yangtze valley.[50] The northern frontier, then, remained relatively static, while the southern was dynamic, fluid, and constantly receding.[51] Evidently, however, there were few pioneers sufficiently daring to settle as individuals among the southern barbarians. The Hua-men, rather, moved into the rich valleys of the south in "pools"—dense aggregations of hopeful humanity, supported by troops who killed those natives bold enough to resist, leaving the survivors to be indoctrinated, exploited or enslaved by Chinese agents and their aboriginal collaborators. The infiltration has gone on to the present day. The southernmost provinces of China are not truly Chinese even now. They are "interior colonies" of non-Chinese peoples, exploited and oppressed for more than two thousand years by the Chinese settlers and the agents of their northern government.[52] The most extreme case is Kwangsi Province, recently recognized as the "Kwangsi-Chuang Autonomous Region."

The earliest beginnings of this southward movement are shrouded in obscurity.[53] Chinese savants of every period have thought that the lands of the "Hundred Yüeh" tribes were beyond the boundaries of the southernmost "Chinese" provinces defined by the flood hero Yü, though T'ang scholars were by no means in agreement on this point.[54] One authority of that age tells of the defeat of the Man and the Lo-tzu by the partly sinicized soldiers of Ch'u at the end of the seventh century B.C., presumably driving these savages farther south;[55] another T'ang scholar gives the more daring opinion that the natives of Kuei-lin in northern Kwangsi were subject to the Ch'u nation in late Chou times.[56] To tell the truth, we know little more than they did, and if the armies of ancient Ch'u once wandered through the fiercely hostile mountains and jungles of southern Hunan into the barrier ranges of Nam-Viet, they are now no more than ghostly shadows.

In the third century B.C., soldiers of the new empire of Ch'in moved into Kwei-chow, where they established a province named Ch'ien-chung. From there they marched into the troublesome monsoon regions closer to the coast. Bureaucrats far to the north gave names to the three new provinces seized by their perspiring, insect-bitten troops: Nan-hai "South Sea," mainly in Kwangtung; Kuei-lin "Cinnamon Forest," mainly in Kwangsi; and Hsiang "Elephant," partly in Kwangsi, partly in Kwei-chow.[57] But the men of Ch'in remain almost as shadowy to us as their predecessors of Ch'u, and the outlines of the great provinces they claimed are hazy and imprecise.

Jen Hsiao, a governor of the vast Ch'in colony on the shores of the southern ocean, has bequeathed his name to fame through his nomination of his lieutenant Chao T'o to succeed him as agent of the Hua-men in this uncivilized land. This Chao T'o, though a Chinese northerner, married a woman of Viet. His sympathies seem to have been with the native peoples, though he is credited with the introduction of the Chinese languages and its literature to Nam-Viet, and so must be regarded as a great synthesizer of the Hua and Man cultures.[58] As the Ch'in empire fell apart at the end of the third century B.C., Chao T'o declared himself "Martial King of Nam-Viet," a title which was willy-nilly confirmed by the founder of the new Han nation in 196 B.C.[59] A decade later he conquered the country of Ou-Lo (Ou-Lak) in the delta of the Red River,[60] a legacy, as it transpired, to the Han emperors. He died at the great age of 93 in 137 B.C.[61] His divine biography will have our attention later.

In 111 B.C., the victorious Han, asserting their sway over Nam-Viet, named nine provinces there. Four of these laid new claim to old Ch'in holdings (Nan-hai, Ts'ang-wu, Yü-lin, Ho-p'u), three asserted suzerainty over new lands subdued by Chao T'o along with some Cham territory further south (Chiao-chih, Chiu-chen,

Jih-nan), and two registered the first Chinese occupation of the island of Hainan (Tan-erh, Chu-yai).[62] These garrisoned territories seem to have been little disturbed by the immigration of settlers with their strange ways during the earlier Han period. But in the first century of the Christian era, after the definitive conquest of those lands by the septuagenarian hero Ma Yüan, the soldiers were followed by colonists and their magistrates, bringing all the paraphernalia of official culture with them. Parts of Nam-Viet took on the superficial but pleasing aspect of a respectable Chinese province.[63]

These "gains" were never in fact consolidated. Throughout the civil wars and political divisions of the Han-T'ang interval, the poor savages were plundered and harassed, and, at the same time, lured and rewarded by the agents of the several Chinese factions, in Hunan and in Szechwan as much as in Nam-Viet. Ejected from their ancestral homes, they sometimes sought new lands in the interstices of "settled" Chinese regions, even in what we now call Central China. It is astonishing to learn that between A.D. 404 and 561, there were more than forty aboriginal insurrections in the Hupei-Shensi-Honan-Anhwei belt, north of the Yangtze.[64] But the processes of extermination and assimilation went on inexorably. There were some exceptions: the Lao peoples of Szechwan and the lake region were repeatedly attacked by the Chinese "for their own profit" during the first half of the sixth century of our era, but when the foreign (proto-Mongolian?) dynasty of Northern Chou established its authority over them, they were "thereafter treated just the same as Hua-men." [65] This suggests that the foreign origin of this dynasty inclined its rulers to greater compassion toward its new non-Chinese subjects than that shown by the purely Chinese state of Liang which had preceded them. Evidently the natives of Nam-Viet were not so fortunate, since the Northern Chou never extended its power that far to the south.

ANCIENT CHAMS AND KHMERS

Across the southern border of Nam-Viet were arrayed the warriors of the great Cham empire. The Hinduization of the Malayo-Polynesian-speaking Chams had taken place after the first century of our era from the direction of Cambodia: beyond the red brick sanctuaries of the Chams stood the pink sandstone chapels of the Khmers.[66] The Chinese texts present those remoter southerners as black, wavy-haired barbarians of the mountains and jungles—they were *kuei* "ghosts," or "demons." They were also the K'un-lun or Kurung people, akin to the savage mountaineers whom the Vietnamese later called Mêo or Moi. They were the Kāmrūn of the Arab sailors, and also styled "Krom" and "Komr." [67] But these earliest Khmers (or perhaps their predecessors) had created the first Hindu kingdom of the Indies, the nation of Bnam (i.e., *phnom* "mountain") on the Gulf of Siam. Their sovereigns, the Śailarāja

"Kings of the Mountain," were descended from the marriage of a Cambodian princess with a Brahman from India. The event on which this tradition of ethnic mixture is based presumably took place in the first century A.D.[68] In the second century, one of the great Cambodian kings extended his empire on the west to Suvaṇṇabhūmi the "Land of Gold," dimly seen by the Chinese as "Frontier of Gold" (possibly the same as Suvarṇakuḍya "Wall of Gold"), presumed to be in lower Burma,[69] and on the east to Nha-trang in the land of the Chams. Here he erected a stele to commemorate the vastness of his sway, giving his name in Sanskrit as Śrī Māra.[70] This is the oldest Sanskrit inscription in Southeast Asia.[71] Soon after, the Chams learned how to write in the Indian fashion, and so their history begins.[72] The survival of the ancient royal title of the Khmers *kurung* or *krung* (transcribed *ku-lung* "Old Dragon" by the Chinese),[73] as in the honorific *klaung* in the Cham titles of gods and kings (such as Pō Klaung Garai), hints at the importance of the Cambodian contribution to the beginnings of the Cham kingdom.[74]

The Chinese historians tell of a kingdom, which they call "Forest City" (Lin-i, M.C. Lyĕm-iĕp), in this region in the last decade of the second century. Its capital was near modern Huê. The Chinese entered into direct relations with this new nation soon afterwards.[75] Presumably it was already Indianized in some degree. We have Sanskrit inscriptions and records of the Buddhist religion from the fourth century, and, most interesting of all, a text in the Cham language of the same century from the great Mi-sỏn sanctuary at the modern village of Tra-kiêu. This is the oldest document in any Indonesian language.[76] These inscriptions, and the sanctuary itself, which was dedicated to Śiva Bhadreśvara, were the pious work of King Bhadravarman, ruler of Amarāvatī, whose capital was nearby.[77] From this time on, Indian civilization was firmly established south of Col des Nuages, while Chinese culture remained dominant north of there.[78]

The fifth century was an era of conflict between these two zones of influence, marked by border raids, large-scale invasions, looting and devastation. From one punitive attack on the Cham capital the Chinese brought back 100,000 lbs. of fine gold.[79] Even a king of the Chams was captured and decapitated by the Chinese in 446.[80] These wars settled little except the exclusion of the Chams from the Tongking delta, which they had attempted to take earlier in the century. South of there, the border shifted back and forth.[81] Just before the establishment of the T'ang in China, the Chams suffered an enormous indignity. In 605 the Sui emperor, greedy for the riches of Forest City, sent Liu Fang in command of a fleet and army against the Cham capital. The Chinese archers defeated the Cham elephant corps, drove the king from his throne, and returned northward with rich booty and countless captives. The Chinese court could gloat over the golden tablets of the deceased kings of Champa, a company of Cambodian musicians, and many bundles of precious Buddhist books.[82]

APOLLONIUS: *"We go to the South, beyond the mountains and the mighty waters, to seek in perfumes the secret source of love. . . . The stars palpitate like eyes; the cascades sing like the melody of lyres; strange intoxication is exhaled by blossoming flowers; thy mind shall grow vaster in that air; and thy heart shall change even as thy face."*

Gustave Flaubert, *The Temptation of St. Anthony,*
translated by Lafcadio Hearn

2 Hua People

RECONQUEST

THE DISINTEGRATION of centralized rule in China between the third and sixth centuries had allowed the aborigines of the southern provinces a measure of independence, and even the possibility of expansion. The reestablishment of universal Chinese authority under the states of Sui and T'ang met strong resistance from these hopeful defenders of their ancient homelands. Accordingly, as the armies of T'ang swept through the central provinces early in the seventh century and the adherents of Sui gave way, there were repeated "insurrections" of the Lao peoples, especially in Szechwan and adjoining parts of Kweichow and Yunnan.[1] But gradually the indigenes submitted to the new power, sometimes without a fight when they took the men of T'ang to be their natural allies against the oppressive Sui. Such was the case of a chieftain of the Western Ts'uan, whose family had been enslaved for rebellion by the Yang dynasts of Sui—he found it easy to accept the overlordship of the Li family of T'ang, and sent tribute in September of 620.[2] After this, the T'ang soldiery was able to bring about the submission of peoples never before subject to the Chinese. Among them were the Hsieh (Zya) men of Kweichow, who sent tribute in January and February of 630.[3] The Western Chao nearby submitted formally on January 20, 648,[4] and after them came a number of Yunnanese tribes, culminating in the surrender of 23,000 households of the K'un-ming Man on February 21, 672.[5]

The natives of the southeast had been as troublesome to the Chinese in Sui times as had those of the southwest. The most serious of their uprisings had been led by the Li (Vietnamese Ly) clan in Tongking in the second half of the sixth century. It was Liu Fang, the famous Sui general, the ravager of Champa, who restored Chinese authority there in 603.[6] After the collapse of Sui, however, the transition to T'ang control was relatively peaceful, since the Sui mandarins kept a firm grip on their colonial charges until they bowed to the inevitable—indeed the fall of Nam-Viet before T'ang was chiefly a matter of the transfer of power by the only slightly reluctant officers of Sui. Thus Ch'iu Ho, Sui governor in Tongking, transferred his allegiance in 621,[7] and control of the western roads from Canton to Hanoi was surrendered by the Sui "officer" Ning Ch'ang-chen (by his name, a converted aborigine) to the T'ang representative Li Ching on May 23, 622.[8] Indeed, 622 was the year of final victory for T'ang: a native rebel named Teng Wen-chin, powerful in Kuang-chou, together with Ning Hsüan, the Sui agent in Ho-p'u, presumably another aborigine of the powerful Ning clan, and Li Chün, the Sui agent in Jih-nan on the Cham frontier, all recognized the overlordship of T'ang in June of that year.[9] In a few cases, however, the Sui commanders held out, to their own loss— they were destroyed by local chiefs and their adherents.[10] Finally Feng Ang, a man of mixed blood and the last great Sui official in Nam-Viet, surrendered to Li Ching on August 29, bringing with him the control of a number of wild mainland counties, but above all the rule of Hainan Island.[11] With this, effective control of all of Nam-Viet passed into the hands of the new dynasty.

A new administration was established in Tongking in 622, under which the province was known simply as Chiao-chou, a title it retained until 679, in which year it was elevated to the status of Protectorate of Annam—that is, of the "Secured South."[12] During this period, Hanoi (the seat of the government in Chiao-chou) controlled a large area, extending from the coastal plain of northern Annam (Ai, Huan, Yen and Fu-lu) through the Tongking delta (Chiao, Feng, and Ch'ang) and the adjacent uplands (Lu), and along the coast of (modern) Kwangtung, including the Leichow peninsula.[13]

The administrative situation in Nam-Viet remained somewhat fluid during the seventh century. A new system emerged during its last decades and was firmly established by the early years of the eighth century. This was a division of the whole region into five administrative areas, governed by the four "Legates" of Kuang, Kuei, Jung and Yung, and the Protector of Annam. The Legate resident in Canton (Kuang) was paramount.[14] These are the "Five Administrations" or

"Five Offices" (*fu*) of Nam-Viet, familiar in T'ang literature, and corresponding ideally to the quinquipartite arrangement of the mountain passes into Nam-Viet, the *Wu ling*.[15] Of the five, by far the greatest in wealth and prestige, especially during the wonderful years of the first half of the eighth century, was Canton, the great central arsenal for the pacification of the Lao tribes.[16] This metropolis was placed in the large, relatively well-disciplined administration of Kuang, largely safe for the Chinese, and east of the smaller more dangerous administrations of Kuei (in the northwest) and Jung, Yung, and Annam (in the west and southwest).[17]

After the disorders of the Huang Ch'ao rebellion late in the ninth century, the hold of the T'ang authorities on this and other regions gradually loosened—though it is to be noted that when the monarch Hsi Tsung returned to his capital in 885, Lingnan (along with three northwestern provinces) was one of the few regions still to accept his authority.[18] By the end of the century it was the only one to do so.[19] Even as late as 900 Lingnan was ruled by the prince Li Chih-jou, a great-grandson of Jui Tsung. His successor, Hsü Yen-jo, was the last of the T'ang legates there.[20] The wolves were already biting off pieces of the southland: a lieutenant of Li K'o-yung administered Jung-chou in 897;[21] a Hunanese army, sent by Ma Yin, seized the northern counties of Kuei, I, Yen, Liu, and Hsiang (all under Kuei Administration) in 900,[22] and in 902 they captured Shao and besieged Ch'ao in the east;[23] in 905 Chu Ch'üan-yü, the brother of the great rebel Chu Ch'üan-chung and a coarse, worthless fellow, was Legate in Annam.[24] In the year 913 the lands of Nam-Viet were partitioned among five great warlords: Ch'ü Hao ruled Annam; Liu Shih-cheng ruled Kuei; Yeh Kuang-lüeh ruled Yung; P'ang Chü-chao ruled Jung; and Liu Yen ruled Kuang.[25] The last-named of these, Liu Yen, was able to overthrow all of these rivals except Ch'ü Hao, and in 917 he declared himself theocrat (*ti*) of Great Viet—a name he changed to Han in the following year.[26] So Lingnan became an independent nation for the first time in more than a thousand years. As for Annam, it was ravaged by the battles of rival chieftains for more than twenty years after this, until one of them, Wu Ch'üan, emerged victorious and declared himself King of Great Co-Viet in 939.[27] The history of an independent Vietnam begins in that year.

Now it is time to look at the hot southlands themselves, as their new masters saw them.

ROADS AND CITIES

The prospect of the long and arduous trip into Nam-Viet must have evoked ambiguous feelings in the northerner. His feelings of excitement and apprehension would be enhanced at the farewell party normally given by his friends just before his departure. At these gay affairs, often held at a wine shop in the suburb, looking off in the direction the traveler was about to take, it was the usual thing to relate facts and fancies of every kind about his route and destination, and to write poems on the themes of the physical and moral perils to be encountered there. These effusions might, depending upon the whim of their composers, either fill the departing guest with pleasant anticipation for the warmer, greener lands of the south, or else send him off with sinking heart and trembling hands, his mind beset with fear of savage tribesmen and horrible diseases. Such was the effect on his guest, we may imagine, of a farewell poem written by Chang Chi (ca. 765–ca. 830), "Seeing off a Traveler Moving to the South." [28]

> Away, away—far-ranging traveler!
> Amid miasmas waste your blighted body!
> Blue hills and roads without limits;
> White heads—of men who do not return.
>
> Countries by the Sea—they mount elephants in battle,
> Counties of the Man—they use silver in market.
> The family unit split—in several places—
> And who may be seen in spring, South of the Sun?

("South of the Sun" is also the Vietnamese province of Jih-nan; the second verse of the poem refers to the dreaded ravages of malaria.) Little heartened by this sort of thing, the traveler made his way southward through the well-watered valleys south of the great Yangtze, choosing either an easterly route through the Kan basin (in modern Kiangsi), or a westerly route down the Hsiang valley (in modern Hunan), in either case finding the land increasingly green, the weather increasingly warm, and the aborigines increasingly numerous.

Let us now follow him into Nam-Viet, by the several possible routes, looking as we go at the chief Chinese settlements in that land, and regretting that we cannot, for the most part, see them as real cities, with walls, streets, parks, and markets, but now, bound by our meager sources, only as abstract economic entities, salted with some human and historical associations.

The easternmost route may be called the Ch'ien road, since it went southward from O in Hupei, and up the valley of the Kan to Ch'ien-chou, near the Nam-Viet border. From that point it was necessary to go by land over the Great Yü Pass. [29] This was an old road, and, until the eighth century, not an easy one. Then, because of the great development of the profitable overseas trade coming by way of Canton, the great minister Chang Chiu-ling, himself a Nam-Viet creole and a supporter of the southern merchants, was commissioned in December of 716 to see to the building of a new and easier road over that pass. [30] We are fortunate in having Chang's own account of this important engineering work. Of the old road he writes:

Formerly, an abandoned road in the east of the pass,
　Forbidding in the extreme, a hardship for men.
An unswerving course: you clambered aloft
　On the outskirts of several miles of heavy forest,
With flying bridges, clinging to the brink
　Halfway up a thousand fathoms of layered cliffs . . .

And of its importance:

The several nations from beyond the sea
　Use it daily for commercial intercourse:
Opulence of teeth, hides, feathers, furs;
　Profits in fish, salt, clams, cockles." [31]

It was this route which the philosophic Li Ao took when he went out to Nam-Viet
to take up an official post in 809.[32] He left a sketch of his itinerary for posterity.
I summarize it here, omitting his notes on local sight-seeing and other details from
the first part, which tells of his journey towards Nam-Viet:

January 31: left Lo-yang and boarded boat with wife and children.
February 6: departed Lo-yang. Delays because of my own and my wife's illness.
February 11: finally entered Pien Canal, going towards Huai region.
February 12: reached Ho-yin.
February 16: stopped at Pien-chou; I was ill again.
February 18: passed night at Ch'en-liu.
February 20: stopped at Sung-chou.
February 23: reached Yung-ch'eng.
February 25: reached Yung-k'ou.
February 27: stopped at Szu-chou.
March 3: left Pien Canal and entered Huai River system.
March 5: reached Ch'u-chou.
March 10: reached Yang-chou.
March 14: crossed Great Chiang River and reached Jun-chou.
March 21: reached Ch'ang-chou.
March 25: reached Su-chou.
March 28: crossed Sung River.
March 31: reached Hang-chou.
April 5: by water to Fu-ch'un.
April 8: reached Mu-chou.
April 13: reached Ch'ü-chou; delay because of wife's illness; we stayed at a
　Buddhist temple.
May 6: daughter born.
May 28: left Ch'ü-chou.
May 30: ascended pass from Ch'ang Mountain to Jade Mountain.

Seats of Counties Traversed by Li Ao

June 1: reached Hsin-chou.

June 12: reached Hung-chou.

June 23: reached Chi-chou.

July 3: reached Ch'ien-chou.

Hereafter I translate the diary verbatim:

July 12: ascended Great Yü Mountain Pass.

July 13: reached Cheng-ch'ang [a *hsien* attached to Shao-chou, situated on the Cheng River, a tributary of the Chen, just below the pass on the road to the important towns of Shih-hsing and Ch'ü-chiang.] [33]

July 14: ascended Ling-t'un West Pass and saw the Stones of Shao.

July 15: stayed the night at Ling-chiu ("Numinous Vulture") Mountain. [Not far north of Ch'ü-chiang.] [34]

July 16: reached Shao-chou [i.e. the seat of Shao County at Ch'ü-chiang.]

July 17: reached Shih-hsing public house. [Presumably at or near Ch'ü-chiang. Shao-chou was sometimes called Shih-hsing chün; the party had already passed Shih-hsing hsien on about July 14.]

July 19: entered Tung-yin ("Eastern Shade") Mountains; looked at the shoots of the great bamboos, like baby boys and girls. Passed Cheng-yang Ravine.

July 20: stayed the night at Ch'ing-yüan Mountain Ravine [on the Chen River, our North River, between Ch'ü-chiang and Canton.]

July 25: reached Kuang-chou.[35]

At the end of this journal, Li Ao gives a schedule of the distances covered on various stages of his trip, most of which was by water. Essentially his route was from Lo-yang to Yang-chou via the Pien Canal, then southwest through Chekiang into the Kan River system of Kiangsi, then southwards to the Great Yü Pass on the frontier of Lingnan. This rather leisurely journey, consuming almost six months, should be contrasted with Liu Tsung-yüan's trip into exile in 815—it took him a little more than three months to reach Liu-chou in Lingnan from Ch'ang-an.[36]

The entrance to Nam-Viet was a magical stone gateway, the Stones of Shao, for which Shao County was named. These were two great craggy rocks standing opposite each other on the road leading down from the pass. They made a magical and ceremonial portal, one of a series which culminated in the bronze pillars of Ma Yüan at the opposite side of the province. The crags themselves were gray blue, and, in Sung times at least, fragments of Shao stone were taken from the river which flowed between them to make attractive miniature mountains, much desired by collectors.[37]

Shao County, being on the chief land route from the north into Nam-Viet, was exceptionally rich in Chinese traditions, and in ancient relics and literary notices of the Hua-men. The county boasted the remains of a wall said to have been built by Chao T'o to mark the northernmost extent of his kingdom. The wall of the T'ang administrative city in Ch'ü-chiang township had been built by the aboriginal magnate Teng Wen-chin on a new site on the west side of the Chen River.[38] Early in the eighth century the county had a tax-paying population of close to 170,000 persons, most of them, no doubt, concentrated in or near Ch'ü-chiang. The chief products of the county—or at least those most prized by the northern aristocrats— were a fine linen of bamboo fibers, medicinal lime powdered from stalactites, and orchids (more probably desired as drugs than as garden ornaments).[39] The most notable places here were Shih-hsing township above the new road from the Great Yü Pass, and Ch'ü-chiang "Bent River," whose name is identical with that of the famous serpentine water park in the great capital, Ch'ang-an. Ch'ü-chiang was the birthplace of the noble minister Chang Chiu-ling.[40] Its hills and rocks were well-known from the reports of cultivated travelers. There was Silver Mountain in the northeast; there were multicolored arrangements of stones in the north, the home of wild goat antelopes; there was "Glorious Mountain" where a silvery star had fallen early in the seventh century—a favorite place for the recreations of all classes, with a two-storey pavilion for parties, the Shao-yang Lou, whose amenities were celebrated in a poem by Hsü Hun in these words: "With cup of jade and gemmy zither, close to the River of Stars."[41] Then there was Lotus Mountain, west of the administrative seat, boasting a Buddhist temple and a deep grotto with ancient Taoist associations. The Mountain of the Numinous Vulture—so named because it resembled a mountain of the same name in the holy land of India— had a fine Buddhist monastery, said to be the most splendid in Lingnan. Indeed the region was a fairyland of religious establishments, not the least of them a pagoda built early in the ninth century, given fame by the name of the Sixth Patriarch Hui-neng, and noticed in a poem by Liu Tsung-yüan.[42] After a day or two of sightseeing around Ch'ü-chiang, the visitor would proceed by boat down the Chen River to Canton.

The two other gateways to Nam-Viet were both reached by way of Hunan and the Hsiang River valley. The southbound traveler proceeded upriver by way of T'an-chou (or Ch'ang-sha) to Heng-chou. From this point there were two possible routes. One, not of great importance, took him to Ch'en-chou near the Lingnan border, whence he crossed over the Ch'i-t'ien Pass and so down the Chen River.

Much more important was the Kuei-chou road, the westernmost of the three. This went from Heng-chou to Yung-chou (west of Ch'en in southern Hunan), and over a low pass to Kuei-chou in Lingnan.[43]

Kuei was Shao's counterpart in the west, and like Shao was situated in the cool southward sloping hills above the Tropic of Cancer, but with less than half the population of Shao. Still, it was the most considerable of the many small counties of western Lingnan. Its chief products were mats, deer-skin boots, and utensils of silver and copper. Its fine bronze mirrors were particularly admired.[44] But Kuei's greatest advantage was its position on the important route from the lakes and rivers of central China into Nam-Viet, which crossed the mountain pass of the Walled City of Viet, the westernmost of the Five Passes into the tropical south. Here were such natural miracles as glittering limestone grottoes,[45] and such man-made wonders as an ancient wall on the mountain crest, said to have been built by Chao T'o himself to resist the soldiers of Han.[46] Then there was the walled county seat, Lin-kuei, a gem of a city, as witness a poem by Han Yü. The poet alludes to a fine town beyond the source of the great Hsiang River, on the site of a legendary grove of eight cinnamons (*kuei*). In the first quatrain he represents it as a beautiful woman in rich costume—the Cinnamon River girds her, and the surrounding pinnacles are her gemmy headdress. In the second, the city appears as a Taoist paradise ("Sylphdom"), rich in turquoise and gold—under the aspect of kingfisher feathers and oranges:

> A green sheen—the luxuriance of Eight Cinnamons—
> This is that place which lies south of the Hsiang:
> The river makes a blue gauze sash,
> The hills seem cyan jade hairpins.
>
> Doorways there mostly send forth halcyon feathers,
> Households there freely plant out yellow tangerines:
> This far surpasses going off on the ascent to sylphdom—
> So borrow no hitch from a flying simurgh! [47]

Kuei-chou was a haunted and holy place. "Piebald Deer Mountain" nearby was named for a supernatural albino deer which used to frequent an ancient Buddhist temple there.[48] Near the city too was a hill with a shrine to Shun, the primordial potter god. It is mentioned in a poem by Li Shang-yin, and a Sung source notes the presence of an eighth-century inscription on the site.[49] This spot was not far from the supposed graves of Shun's two wives, the goddesses of the River Hsiang, north of the city.[50] Indeed, the whole region between the River Hsiang and the River Kuei, here at the end of civilization, was sacred to these lovely ladies. We shall see them again, along with their august consort, among the great gods of the south.

Li Shang-yin showed the ghostly influences at work in this beautiful region in another poem, which he named "Cinnamon Forest." Its first quatrain describes the physical city; its second, the spiritual city. It ends on a note of alienation: the constant drumming and fluting of the aboriginal shamans are addressed to gods unknown to the Hua-men from the north—they will answer no Chinese prayers.

> Its walls squeezed in—the hills about to press on them;
> Its river spread out—the lands all buoyed up by it.
> East-by-south leads to remote precincts;
> West-by-north possesses a tall tower.

Gods stand guard on its banks with blue sweetgums;
Dragons move out from its chasms of white stone.
In a far-off country, to what can we pray—
Where flutes and drums have not once rested? [51]

The special pride of Kuei-chou was an engineering work, the "Holy Canal," which connected the north-flowing Hsiang with the south-flowing Kuei River.[52] It ran through an attractive landscape, ornamented with the remnants of ancient limestone hills, now called the Hsiang-Kuei Gap.[53] Tradition said that this wonderful waterway was built for the founder of Ch'in in the third century B.C. by a certain Shih Lu, and repaired several hundred years later, by Ma Yüan, the conqueror of Nam-Viet, to facilitate the transportation of provisions to his soldiery. But after that the canal became unusable.[54] Nonetheless, a kind of stream, named Li Water, still trickled through the gap. It was still holy water, even if not useful for commerce or war. Its governing spirit was a dragon, prayed to for rain in mid-T'ang times at a riverside temple. The epigene emissaries or avatars of this deity took the forms of blue snakes, called "dragon colts," which crawled about harmlessly in the vicinity of the shrine, and coiled playfully about the hands and heads of visitors.[55] The canal was redredged twice in T'ang times. In 825, the governor Li Po (Li Bwĕt), after much trouble with inferior materials and the raids of Man tribesmen, made the passage of transport vessels possible once more by employing 53,000 paid workmen to build a great jetty (*hua ti* "shovel dike") of stone and hardwood to divide the stream in two parts and a series of locks (*tou men*) to control the level of the water in the navigable channel.[56] However, after the loss of Annam to the Yunnanese in 863, the old canal was found to be inadequate for supplying the large Chinese armies kept in Lingnan, and special sea-going grain ships were built to carry rations along the coast from Fukien, a journey of something less than a month.[57] In 868–869, a new governor, Yü Meng-wei, rebuilt the system of channel divider and locks to allow "the passage of huge vessels." [58] His report of this restoration, written in 870, is an important historical document.[59] Apparently the canal remained in use through the ninth century, since the army of Huang Ch'ao, decimated by tropical diseases, floated on rafts up from Lingnan into Hunan on the swollen waters of this channel in the late autumn of 879.[60] The remains of the Holy Canal were still admired by tourists in the thirteenth century.[61]

Whether from Shao (Ch'ü-chiang) or Kuei (Lin-kuei), the south-faring traveler, unless destined for a really out-of-the-way and unpleasant place, came ultimately to the only metropolis of Lingnan. This was the city we now call "Canton," the seat of the T'ang administration of Kuang-chou, a county of considerable extent. Sometimes it was the capital of all of Nam-Viet. Though the city was legally divided between the two townships of Nan-hai and P'an-yü, the men of T'ang called the whole of it "Walled-city of Kuang-chou," or simply "Kuang-chou," or often

"Kuang-fu." This latter appellation represented the city as the see of a viceroy,[62] and was widely adopted by seafarers, particularly by the Arabs, in the form Khānfū.[63] Indian merchants, however, knew the city as "China." Their name for the great capital Ch'ang-an was more lofty: Mahācīna "Greater China."[64]

Although set in a distant frontier region, where most settlements were recent, this was an old town. Its beginnings are unknown, but an old tradition told that its original site in Nan-hai township had been marked off by five Taoist transcendents, who came down from the sky riding on multicolored goats and holding beautiful stalks of millet in their hands. Consequently the popular name for the city was "Walled City of the Five Goats"—indeed this was the proper name of the city considered as a physical entity rather than as the seat of an administrative region. The ancient hero Chao T'o built a wall here when he founded his kingdom. A new city wall was constructed by Pu Chih in the third century of our era when he transferred the administration of Nam-Viet from Hanoi to the Canton area.[65] We are told that it was this wall (it had been repaired and extended many times) which was destroyed by fire when Huang Ch'ao pillaged the city in 879.[66]

In the eighth century, Canton had a population of about 200,000.[67] It was a cosmopolitan city with a huge merchant class, chiefly Indochinese, Indonesian, Indian, Singhalese, Persian, and Arab.[68] This rich entrepôt suffered from a diversity of endemic calamities. One of these was fire, which repeatedly swept through the wood, bamboo, and thatch settlements until, in 806, a governor ordered the populace to install tile roofs.[69] Another was piracy: a ferocious raid of Arabs and Persians in 758, possibly from a base on Hainan, ruined the city's trade. But Canton revived early in the ninth century, and remained fairly prosperous until Huang Ch'ao, the peasants' hero, desiring to cut off an important source of revenue for the imperial court, sacked it.[70] The third scourge of the city was a corrupt officialdom which appeared with monotonous regularity but at unpredictable intervals. Despite all of these, the city seems always to have been capable of resurrection.[71] But despite its wealth and importance, it seems that it was not until Liu Yen founded the Viet nation (later styled Han) in 917, that Canton took on something of the appearance of a sophisticated metropolis. With the revival of trade under that monarch, the riches of the Indies poured in again, and he was able to build palaces and government edifices worthy of his new dignity. We are told, for instance, that one of his royal halls was "decorated with silver, with running water beneath it, and images of the sun and moon in crystal and amber on its two towers."[72] Archaeologists would do well to look for relics of the tenth century here.

Always it was a merchant town, where visitors from the north noticed chiefly "the babble of the voices of the Man in the night markets." The words are those of the poet Chang Chi.[73] But the town's riches were not restricted to the gems, incenses, and ivories of the merchant princes. The countryside itself produced much wealth: the distant court exacted annual tribute of silver, rattan matting, bamboo mats, lichees, edible skins of the green turtle, shells of the soft-shell turtle, medicinal python bile, dendrobium orchids, aloeswood, onycha, and kanari copal [74]—that is, household furniture, table delicacies, medicines, and aromatics.

These luxuries were extracted from the aborigines (perhaps partly from Chinese settlers) by agents of the government, who, if not otherwise completely preoccupied with lining their own purses, might distract themselves from ennui, the heat, and fear of native uprisings, by occasional visits to the notable sights of the city, which was, after all, the scene of famous exploits in the heroic past, a quality possessing eternal charm for the Chinese. There were the fragments of an old wall, thought to have been erected by that perennial wall builder King Chao T'o, as well as other ruins connected with his famous reign, such as a terrace or platform not far from the city, called "Terrace of the King of Viet." This structure was mystically identified with other semi-divine rulers of the south and their heavenly powers—notably with another king, the famous Kou Chien, who had ruled over a nation called Viet in Chekiang in Chou times.[75] Chao T'o's platform is frequently mentioned in the poems written by reluctant T'ang sojourners in Canton. It was a good place to visit for a picnic and a nostalgic thrill. One ascended the remains of the terrace and looked off reverently towards the civilized north as Chao T'o is reputed to have done, weeping with well-bred emotion. Of the other sights associated with that king's great name the most notable perhaps was his grave in Nan-hai township. The tomb must have once been a characteristic kingly barrow, but it had been looted almost a millenium before, since an excavation carried out as early as 226 had found it empty—though the tomb of the king's son, dug up at the same time, had yielded such treasures as a jade casket and thirty-six golden seals.[76] There could not have been much for a T'ang visitor to see, though doubtless a thoughtful magistrate had raised a pavilion where one might cool himself while sipping wine—that was the usual thing. Other agreeable sights in or near the city were connected with the names of former governors (such as bits of walls built by them), and of saintly Taoists and Buddhists—for instance, a "Well of Bodhidharma," and the supposed residence of the probably mythical Taoist immortal An ch'i sheng.[77] For the pious there was the respectably "Confucian" Temple to the God of the South Sea in Nan-hai, not to mention many Buddhist establishments. For the practical there was a productive lead mine in Hua-meng township,[78] to say nothing of factories for the cupellation of silver, fisheries, and the docks.

Nowadays we are prone to classify old cities. But it is not easy to find a neat label for Canton. Was it merely a commercial town or was it a true cosmic city, or some kind of hybrid? To put it another way—and to use the language of some social scientists—was it a city of orthogenetic transformation or a city of heterogenetic transformation?

It was in the former type of city, with its rigidly stratified society into which charismatic power streamed down from above through the medium of a god-king, that merchants were normally (though not invariably) outcastes, but their status would seem to have been very different in cities of heterogenetic transformation, particularly in those sub-classified by these authors as "cities of the entrepreneur," where men were concerned primarily with expediential norms and relations between buyer and seller, and where there had developed a consensus appropriate to the technical, rather than the moral, order.[79]

In T'ang times, Ch'ang-an certainly had all the qualities required of a cosmic city of the "orthogenetic transformation," though it had its great markets and its foreign population. It might be urged that its character was corrupted by the intrusion of an educated bourgeoisie, typified by such men as Chang Chiu-ling, into its administration and spiritual life. Canton, for its part, was more than a mere market town. It had been a sacred city of a sort long ago in Chao T'o's golden time—a character it regained in 917 when Liu Yen of Southern Han seized absolute power. Meanwhile it had a wall, and temples to its protector gods, and ruins, and venerated relics of a holy past. Indeed it was (as were all T'ang cities) a secondary source of charismatic energy radiated by the imperial magistrate in his role of surrogate of the divine king in Ch'ang-an, especially when he performed the sacrifices to the God of the South Sea. In short, the town had a dual role and ambiguous character, but its "heterogenetic" features should, perhaps, be regarded as primary in T'ang times.

Most travelers going beyond Canton on regular business, commercial or political, were headed southwestward for Annam. Before tracing their route, let us look at other quarters of Nam-Viet, beginning with the region east of Canton, towards Fukien.

The large county of Hsün, immediately east of Kuang, although profiting from such simple endeavors as the gathering of python bile, shark skins, and onycha from the native animals, along with a few herbaceous drugs, had also developed some industries, and shipped linen, colored rattan-ware, and "mirrored caskets"—we should call them vanity cases—to the well-to-do citizens of northern cities.[80]

Ch'ao, furthest to the east, and closest to the Fukien border, claimed between six and seven thousand Chinese residents in town and country, about half the population of Hsün; it produced bananas, and collected shark skins for sword grips, python bile and sea horses for medicine, onycha for incense, a silvery stone—perhaps muscovite schist—presumably for ornamental purposes, and turtles.[81] This isolated county was also ill-famed for its colony of crocodiles. Its life was chiefly on the salt sea, but it had no important port—modern Swatow was not even a dream.

At the opposite end of the province from the relatively cool northern hills was a long peninsula projecting towards the tropical island of Hainan—our modern atlases show it as Luichow. In T'ang times it was under the jurisdiction of Lei-chou. Despite its hot and humid climate, the region boasted a tax-paying population of more than twenty thousand, and the chief town sent token tribute of silk floss, spotted bamboo, and peafowl to the imperial court.[82] Of the appearance of the walled city we know nothing—it cannot have attracted many visitors. As for the green island of Hainan itself, the most populous of its five counties were Tan and Wan-an, on the northwest and southeast sides of the island: Tan exported gold and copal; Wan-an produced gold and silver, an unrecognized Golden Chersonese.[83] Again, though many political exiles died here, they have left us no description of the hated island.

Communications with Annam (Chiao-chou) were chiefly overland, and were designed chiefly for military conquest and Chinese immigration. Most commerce, it seems, was still in the hands of sea-going foreigners, especially Arabs and Persians. These men played little part in the acculturation of this part of Indochina, in contrast to the southern, more Indianized parts of the peninsula, where sea-borne traders had an important role in modifying its native cultures.[84] Still, Chinese merchants could not have been unknown on these roads. Perhaps most of them were slave traders. Along with soldiers, administrators, and colonists, they journeyed westward from Canton through the richly mineralized but dangerous province of Jung (silver, cinnabar, and mercury).[85] Its administrative town was on the Yü (Iwĕt; the name means "jungly") River, now called simply "West River." The settlement was much troubled by rampant waters until part of the flow was diverted by Szu-ma Lü-jen in 710–711.[86] This hazardous road led to the Vietnamese lands (not yet distinguished as such), and above them to the Tibeto-Burmans of Nan-chao, in deadly rivalry with the T'ang men for the control of the southwest. Many northern visitors must have found it a frightening experience to pass through the Gate of Ghosts,[87] a gap, thirty paces wide, between two crags in Yü-lin ("Jungle Forest") County, analogous to the Stones of Shao on the northern frontier of the province. In T'ang times there was still an ancient stele at this spot, reputed to have been erected by Ma Yüan as he marched southward to subdue the savages at the end of the world. The lands beyond this portal reeked with deadly miasmas. An eighth-century folk-saying about them went:

> The customs barrior at Ghost Gate—
> Ten men go out,
> Nine men return.[88]

The road was first open to the men of T'ang in 622 when the Ning tribes who commanded this coastal passage submitted, and their chiefs Ning Ch'un and Ning Ch'ang-chen accepted T'ang commissions to govern the strategic counties of Lien and Ch'in.[89]

Physically, however, the route from Lingnan into Annam was easy. The passes led through low hills, not at all comparable to the highlands of eastern Lingnan, and not to be mentioned in the same breath with the rugged mountain barriers which inhibited the passage of Chinese farmers into Kweichow on the north.[90]

But some transport was by water. The conqueror Kao P'ien, as Protector of Annam late in the ninth century, enlisted a body of men to dredge a channel through the rocks and shallows along the coast of Po-chou, a county under Jung Administration, immediately east of Lien, and west of the Lei-chou peninsula.[91] This work must have been part of a larger plan to open up a coastal waterway through to the Red River estuary and the capital of Annam, referred to in a report which tells that in the spring of 867 Kao P'ien ordered the elimination of submerged rocks between Canton and Annam,[92] following the example of Ma Yüan who (it was said) built a mole almost to the frontier of Champa, allowing the quiet passage of boats separated from the terrors of the open sea.[93]

The true location of the Chinese capital of Chiao-chou in the Red River valley of Tongking has always been a problem for historians. During the early centuries of our era it seems to have been at the port of Lung-pien. When, after the native disorders led by chiefs of the Li (Vietn. Ly) clan during the sixth century, the Sui general Liu Fang restored Chinese authority in this region in 603, the administrative seat was placed at Sung-p'ing (Vietn. Tông-binh), on the south bank of the river. The Red delta had close to 100,000 inhabitants at this time.[94] The distinguished history of both of these old towns was briefly recognized by T'ang in a temporary toying with administrative geography which established a Sung-chou "county" about Sung-p'ing and a Lung-chou county about Lung-pien in 621—but these ephemeral administrations were abolished a few years later.[95]

The old name Lung-pien means Dragon Twist, and is said to have been given to the place in the dim past because of a *chiao* (*ķău*) dragon which coiled in the river near the newly founded city.[96] The name was well exploited by such T'ang poets as Lu Kuei-meng, who matched Dragon Twist with Tiger Crouch in a couplet describing this savage country. The old town was also sometimes called Dragon's Gulf.[97]

The fortified town which protected the County of Chiao (Ķău—possibly the same as the draconian *ķău?*) was commonly called by the name of its outer wall, the great Lo-ch'eng (La-zheng; Vietn. La-thanh), Enveloping Wall. The history of this citadel, both that of its prototype which surrounded ancient Lung-pien and the more modern one around Sung-p'ing, is obscure. But it appears that the outer wall of the latter town was rebuilt by the Chinese protector Chang Po-i in 767.[98] In the winter of 866/67, Kao P'ien, victorious over the invaders from Nan-chao, built a great new wall, with a circumference of three thousand paces,[99] and ordered a vast project of house-building to make a true metropolis of the ancient fortress-city.[100]

The products of Chiao-chou were bananas, areca nuts, shark skins, python bile, and kingfishers feathers,[101] but Lo-ch'eng and its port also competed with Canton for the great South Seas trade, and sometimes outdid its northern rival in the volume of its foreign commerce. Late in the eighth century, troubled because "in recent days, the argosies and other vessels mostly go to trade in the markets of Annam," the great minister Lu Chih advised the establishment of a special agency whose chief function was to encourage the commercial development of Canton.[102]

For men with business further south, there was a great road which went from the Tongking delta by way of the hardly believable frontier counties of Yen-chou and Huan-chou along the steaming coasts of Champa and Cambodia.[103] We may imagine that it was not as well traveled as the more famous sea lane. Another road, often interrupted, led northward from Chiao-chou through Feng-chou on the upper Red River and the Clear River (Rivière Claire) into Yunnan. This route remained open to the men of T'ang after the destruction of the invading armies of Nan-chao by Kao P'ien in 866.[104]

SOLDIERS

As the inhabitants of Nam-Viet were made passive to Chinese rule, the Hua-men gradually settled among them. It is easy to suppose that their soldiers, in the vanguard of the northerners, would have been among the first to take up permanent residence, unless preceded by unrecorded hunters and travelers. This may in fact have been the case, but we have little evidence of it. Some military colonies were established in Lingnan as early as Han times, but the practice of settling soldiers on the land was not carried out on a large scale there until the last decades of the eighth century. Then colonies of aborigines were also established on the frontiers, lent plows and oxen, and given seed, while being employed in public work projects. Thus agricultural settlements of both the Hua and the Man extended the arts and customs of T'ang into the lands of their old enemies.[105]

The history of soldiers as mutineers in the perilous lands is more intimately documented. This sorry tale had its climax late in the ninth century. A body of eight hundred troops levied in Hsü and Szu (roughly the Huai area, north of modern Nanking), for instance, which had spent six years without relief in Kuei, following active duty in Annam, mutinied in the fall of 868, and looted the countryside.[106] Or again, the T'ang army in Annam turned against its supreme commander in 880, as did the Kuei-chou army two years later,[107] and all the while unhappy soldiers from the northern provinces on garrison duty in Yung Administration were deserting and making their way homewards.[108]

ADMINISTRATORS

With the soldiers, and after them, came the mandarins, to bring the right way of life to the benighted southerners. The Chinese establishment in Nam-Viet was unique, at least as compared with modern imperialist undertakings, in that these hot lands had been nominally Chinese for more than a thousand years. The problems faced by the T'ang administrators were essentially the same as those which had been faced by their remote ancestors of Han. This southern frontier was forever unstable—a wavering, shadowy fringe rather than a clear demarcation. It was a chronic ulceration for which no medicine could be found, differing from the northern frontier of the pastoral nomads in that here there was no "gentlemanly" agreement. In short, the Hua-men did not need to make any concessions to the Thais as they did, for instance, to the Uighurs whose horses they required. Nor were there any southern parallels to the alien dynasties of nomadic origin which had ruled over the northern Chinese from time to time. No southern wall, no fixed series of trading posts, marked the boundary between the Chinese and their jungle neighbors, as they marked the agreed-upon frontier between the Chinese and their northern neighbors and sometimes masters, the lords of the steppe and boreal forest. There was no clear-cut line between civilization and savagery, despite the symbolic gateways and boundary stones, only a stippling of Chinese settlements fading into the immensity of the haunted tropical forests.

But not all southern peoples were alike. The men of Lingnan and Annam were different from the Tibeto-Burman peoples of the western and southwestern highlands. Some of these last remained true foreign nations, often troublesome ones, at this time. The men of T'ang tried to *pacify* the Ning and Huang; they tried to *invade* Nan-chao. The Man tribesmen of Nam-Viet had long been Chinese subjects by right of conquest, and had somehow to be digested. It was not unlike the difference between "our" Texas and "their" Chihuahua for the nineteenth-century American—or, in view of the great time lapse since the Chinese conquest, between "our" Gaul and "their" Germany for the ancient Roman.

A sensitive modern critic, familiar with the experience of the French in their hot colonies, has remarked that there is a "heroic age" of incipient colonialism, with an "epic" literature appropriate to a period of military penetration, full of the exploits and miseries of soldiers, actors in a sinister landscape inhabited by unattractive natives.[109] The natives, for their part, are shown to be brave in battle, but quickly loosing their redeeming virtues after conquest, becoming a miserable and degraded remnant, their valor replaced by false humility. Such too was the scene in western Nam-Viet, even after hundreds of years of nominal subjection. But the Chinese writings which portray this unpleasant scene lack both epic and heroic qualities. They are officially correct histories and biographies, or plain descriptions of geography and natural history, or, in the realm of belles lettres, the brief and often self-pitying quatrains of overheated and resentful mandarins.

It is and was convenient to classify these reluctant administrators as good or as bad. Much depends on what the official records say of them. "Good" means useful in making Chinese culture palatable, or at least acceptable, to the resigned aborigines, while coupling a degree of generosity and fidelity with the necessary sternness. "Bad" means self-seeking—ambitious, self-indulgent or harsh for one's own ends, when these disagreed with moral stereotypes or state policy. Good or bad, avarice was the great agent of corruption. The wealth of the tropics offered the possibility of solace for the dangers, discomforts, and emotional strains of life there.

Such were the difficulties of the terrain "that one inevitably arrives there only after several months," wrote Han Yü, adding that "the Man barbarians are cruel and volatile, and readily show their grievances in rebellion." The famous writer was pleading for recognition of the importance of administrative excellence in such trying surroundings.[110] But most T'ang officials, though fully aware of the problems, were more sensitive to the profits. They found themselves in an incumbency where "the men of Kuang dwell in the land intermingled with the Man—but their duties are slight, while they reap abundant profits in the markets."[111] Distasteful as the barbarians, both indigenous and sea-borne, might be, there were compensations not to be disdained. "This country abounds in treasures and jewels," wrote Ts'en Shen to a friend leaving for a high post in Canton, "—take care that you do not come to despise purity and poverty."[112]

Let us look at a sampling of highly placed T'ang agents, and see how they faced up to the savages and their undeserved treasures. The shallow vignettes which follow are intended to show that although the experiences of T'ang functionaries had a certain uniform character and although their official biographies tended to be bloodless black-and-white-stereotypes, nonetheless some individual, that is to say human, differences can be detected.

Sung Ch'ing-li

While he was a high officer in Lingnan, between 705 and 709, the native tribes of Hainan were ravaging the agricultural settlements and giving great trouble to the Chinese garrisons. T'ang officials were reluctant to accept responsible posts there from fear of malaria and other tropical diseases. Ch'ing-li went to the island in person, persuaded the chiefs to forget their feuds, and established peace. It became possible to reduce the garrison by five thousand men.[113] (Comment: we should like to know how he persuaded them.)

Li Mien

Governor of the whole province, stationed at Canton during 769–771, an efficient administrator, he suppressed the aboriginal leaders Feng Ch'ung-tao and Chu Chishih, who had seized more than ten T'ang counties. He rehabilitated the customs service at the great port, so that where recently only four or five foreign argosies had brought their wealth each year, now more than forty came. On his way home, after his term of duty, he searched the baggage of his retainers and threw a quantity of expensive goods, such as rhinoceros horn, into the river.[114]

35

Hua People

Wang O

This nabob enriched himself while governing Canton between 795 and 800 by plundering hapless foreign merchants, imposing a levy on them far above that required by his superiors. His private lighters, "burdened with horn, ivory, pearls, and shells," filled his coffers in Ch'ang-an higher than those of the public treasury.[115]

Tou Ch'ün

After a great flood had undermined the walls of the administrative seat of Ch'ienchou [in modern Kweichow] in the early fall of 811, this administrator conscripted the wild tribes to repair them. The working conditions were so bad that a general uprising followed, and Tou's efforts to put it down failed. He was degraded, but turned up as chief magistrate in Jung-chou in Nam-Viet in 813–815.[116] (Comment: incompetence could lead to the penalty of reduced status, but not necessarily to removal from the service of the state. It was not the welfare of the native population which concerned the court, only the difficulties and expenses of keeping the peace.)

K'ung K'uei

Ruling Nam-Viet from Canton during 817–819, this man was noted for his rectitude and piety, for which he gained the praise of the exiled Han Yü, himself a man of strict principles. He restored the worship of the God of the South Sea, reduced imposts on foreign goods, abolished the custom of receiving "voluntary" gifts from overseas merchants, and did away with the custom of confiscating the property of deceased merchants when left unclaimed by the heirs for three months.[117]

Li Hsiang-ku

This greedy member of the T'ang royal family was Protector of Annam in 818. Jealous of the prestige of the native magnate Yang Ch'ing, he sent him off to fight against the Huang rebels, but Yang returned secretly and killed him.[118]

Li-Yüan-tsung

"Inciting Notary" in Yung-chou in the summer of 821, subordinate to the Administrator of Jung, he was out of favor with his superior for having restored some recently conquered territory to the Huang barbarians. He took his official seal and some hundred troops and fled to safety in the "Huang grottoes."[119] (Comment: was he a Chinese or an aborigine?)

Lu Chün

An irreproachable legate in Lingnan during 836–840, he refused to enforce laws against the intermarriage of Hua and Lao, protected the property of the natives, and did away with a money tax on them, despite the common feeling against the inter-mingling of the two peoples in towns and farms and the possession of lands and houses by barbarians. A company of several thousand Chinese and Man made a pilgrimage to the great city to ask permission to build a temple and inscribe a monument in his honor, but he stubbornly refused.[120] (Comment: the Chinese settlers seem to have been less "race conscious" than their overlords, revealing their true feelings when a rarely tolerant man came to govern them.)

Ch'en T'ing-szu

This man was a militant protector of T'ang interests in the hot peninsula of Lei-chou between 860 and 873. His secret agents went by boat to ferret out pirate nests on the seacoast as far north as Fukien, and he did not hesitate to raid these noxious dens. His county was secure.[121]

Ts'ai Ching

This man, ruler of western Lingnan for T'ang briefly during 862, was driven out by his own officers because of his cruelty, and after futile attempts to recapture the ad-ministrative town with local conscripts, was sent into exile by the high government. He fled, but was run down and forced to commit suicide.[122]

EXILES

The high commands in Nam-Viet, that is, the offices of Legate at Canton and Hanoi and of the chief administrators in Kuei, Jung, and Yung, were filled by grandees who enjoyed the favor of the court. Such a one was the minister Cheng Ch'üan, who was seen off by Han Yü as he left for the great see of Canton in 823. The writer de-scribed the physical and moral perils of the new post, and admonished the minister to probity in these words:

> In P'an-yü your army depot is thriving—
> I wish to tell of it—hold your cup a while!
> As canopies on the sea, your banners and pennants go out,
> As links with the sky, your lookouts and galleries unclose!
>
> At yamen time, the dragon households gather,
> On the high days, the horse men arrive.
> When the wind is quiet, the frigate birds go away,
> When officials are honest, the mussels and cockles come back.
>
> For wares you will be in touch with the Country of Lions,
> Your music will be performed at the Warrior King's Terrace.
> One affair after another—each utterly strange!
> Do not grudge to condescend your great talents! [123]

37

This poem, full of standard images of Nam-Viet, requires a commentary:

P'an-yü is an old name for Canton; lines 2 and 3 describe the Legate's army, navy, and offices in Canton; the boat-people, akin to dragons, assemble when your office is open for petitions; the horse men (*ma* men) are the hypothetical latter-day descendants of Ma Yüan, the Han conqueror; "frigate birds" is a very tentative identification of *yüan-chü* (*ywăn-kyo*), an ill-omened sea bird mentioned in the Chou classics—they will not appear to condemn the new governor; in Han times, the governor Meng Ch'ang restored the depleted oyster beds near Canton by strict conservation methods; the Country of Lions is Ceylon; the Warrior King is Chao T'o.

Surrounded by such novelties as these, the great mandarins sat cooped up in the walled towns of the southernmost province—high islands in an ocean of sullen aboriginal tribesmen—brooding, many of them at least, on the applicability of Confucian teachings while their captains studied jungle tactics.

But the lesser administrations in the smaller towns were often staffed by exiled metropolitan office holders, often men of rare talent even when not clever politicians —they sometimes had high ethical ideals, and, less often, literary ability. Disgraced politicians were banished to a distance proportional to the degree of the disgrace— the more heinous the crime, the further south they were sent, even to the hot, infected lands of Hainan and Annam, where they were given a minor and unattractive post, with a minimum of the amenities with which they were familiar. This degrading transfer was often accomplished in stages—first a minor post in Hunan, say, then on to Lingnan. The opposite was also true: the unfortunate functionary could be gradually rehabilitated, and proceed northward, post by post, down the temperature gradient to the capital and even to the court. It was in this fashion that Hsüan (Sywen) Tsung brought five magnates banished by his predecessor, the tyrannical Wu Tsung, back to civilization. One of this group was the great Niu Seng-ju, who was transferred in 846 from a minor post is Hsün (Zywin)-chou to another in Hengchou in Hunan.[124] (Seng-ju had been thrice degraded to a post in Hsün—a fact curiously omitted from his official biography, as the Sung scholar Ch'ien I observed.) [125] Even during the last years of dying T'ang, Nam-Viet continued to serve as a place of exile for political offenders. This was because the far south remained loyal to the dynasty long after other provinces had succumbed to warlords hostile to the throne.[126]

Another class of exiles in Nam-Viet were the spoiled favorites of unpopular rulers, most abundant when the royal successors wished to divest themselves of the taint of extravagance and unnecessary luxury at the beginnings of their reigns. Examples are the banishment to Lingnan in January of 827 of the cronies of the assassinated boy-emperor, the self-indulgent Ching Tsung.[127] Another is the musician Li K'o-chi, favorite of the music-loving I Tsung: when his sovereign died in 873, his property was confiscated and he himself was sent to Lingnan.[128]

The ostracized courtier could not always hope to survive his period of exile—or even his southward journey. Death often waited for him on a little-traveled roadside or in a distant town, where the sight of his blood would not provoke an intrigue or a riot. Consider the case of three hundred men, more or less, including royal princes, sent into various parts of Lingnan by the Empress Wu because she suspected them of plotting against her unique regime. She despatched an agent to call them all into Canton in the spring of 693, where they were instructed to commit suicide. When they refused with much noisy shouting, they were herded off to the riverside and their heads chopped off. The responsible agent (it is alleged) forged further evidence of their disloyalty to lay before the empress.[129] Less spectacular examples: Tou Ts'an, exiled in 793, was forced to kill himself ("had death conferred") on the road before reaching his office in Huan-chou in Annam;[130] Hua Huan, an officer of the central administration, was required to kill himself after his arrival in Lei-chou in 806;[131] Yang Chih-ch'eng, accused of manufacturing imperial robes and insignia for himself, was sent to Nam-Viet and butchered on the road on December 24, 834.[132]

The sword and the noose were not really necessary in a great many cases. Other malignant agencies lay in wait for the exiles. The most devastating of these were tropical diseases—malaria above all. The histories record the death of a very large number of banished statesmen soon after their arrival in Nam-Viet. A considerable number of them would have lived if they could have remained at home. But we must postpone the discussion of the diseases of the south until a later and more appropriate chapter.

The families of political exiles—both those which accompanied the disgraced father into the tropics and those which he founded there—suffered severely after his death. "Sons and grandsons, poor and despondent, were unable to return on their own, even though they encountered an amnesty." Some had the good luck of living under a high-minded governor. One such was Lu Chün—we told of him in the preceding section—who helped such unfortunates by defraying the costs of drugs and funeral expenses, and finding wives and husbands for orphaned children.[133]

The specter of banishment was terrifying. Arthur Waley has translated an unpleasant passage about a fearful minister from an early ninth century text:

Even in the days of his early obscurity he was obsessed by the idea that his career would end in banishment, and he had a horror of mentioning the name of any place south of the mountains. Later on it was noticed that when he and his fellow secretaries were looking at maps of China, so soon as they came to a map of the south, Wei shut his eyes and would not look. When he became Prime Minister and took over his new official quarters, he noticed at once that there was a map on the wall. For a week he could not bring himself to examine it. When at last he screwed up his courage and looked, he found it was a map of Yai-chou. And sure enough it was to Yai-chou that he was banished in the end, and at Yai-chou that he died when not much over 40.[134]

Old convention required that the exile bewail his lot at all times, and think only of home—wandering in distant lands was not a pastime to which the Chinese were addicted.[135] Nostalgia was the plague of the whole officialdom of Nam-Viet. When Shen Ch'üan-ch'i was languishing in Huan-chou he greatly missed the "Cold Food" holiday, and longed for the elegant leisure of the bustling capital, where

> Flowers and willows strive to show forth first at dawn,
> And high-railed carts fill the roads to greet them.[136]

To some of these displaced mandarins we owe a spate of good poetry about the new world they had to live in and try to cope with. Some coped well, some ill. Both sorts wrote of their feelings. Most suffered in some degree from the boredom and home-sickness which most colonials know: "L'ennui est, par excellence, la forme élégante de l'inaptitude à recevoir la nouveauté." [137] Typical of the bewildered poets who saw the whole subtropical wilderness of the northern fringe of Nam-Viet as a kind of dolorous hell was Liu Ch'ang-ch'ing:

> The moon goes out from storax woods—the langur's voice is wretched;
> The sky is cold at cassia holm—but cassia flowers are sprouting.
> There is no place herein not fit for dejection—
> Strangers from the Chiang look at each other, their tears like rain.[138]

Among these anxious, alienated writers were some very distinguished personages. The Empress Wu, "Heaven-modeled," degraded her officer Sung Chih-wen to a post in the insignificant township of Shuang. Sung was an admired stylist in verse, praised for his rich language. His name in poetry is usually conjoined with that of Shen Ch'üan-ch'i. But he was not much admired as a man. The official history of T'ang describes him as a rascally self-seeker, "an object of deep derision to public-spirited gentlemen." [139] He went to his new destiny by the usual road (we have already reported Li Ao's description of it) over the Pass of Plums by way of Shao-chou. He has left a series of poems composed on the various stages of this dismal journey—a kind of apprehensive diary in verse. In the one which follows he tells of his descent from the mountains, heading for Ch'ü-chiang, finally to face the well-advertised terrors of Nam-Viet:

> I await the dawn to cross the peaks of Min;
> Riding with spring, I look off to the Platform of Viet.
> Transient clouds fall from the *p'eng*-bird's space-aerie,
> And waning moons open up inside mussels' shells.
>
> Climbing figs sway in the blue air;
> Arenga palms veil the cyan moss.
> Fragrance of liquidambar—encased in much dew;
> Resonance of stones—whirling in thin springs.
>
> Hugging the leaves, the dusky langurs whistle,
> Biting on blossoms, the kingfishers come.
> Though here in the south there is something delectable,
> And that northern town seems daily more hazy—

Yet my glossy black hair will shortly become white,
My loyal-vermilion heart has already turned to ashes.
Then how shall I ever head out on the homeward road
To work the shears on my old garden's weeds? [140]

(Comment: the peaks of Min extend westward from southernmost Fukien; the *p'eng* is an enormous bird mentioned in ancient documents, comparable to the roc; pearls [here miniature moons] were thought to grow inside mussels with the phases of the moon; "climbing figs" are *Ficus pumila* [*p'i-li*]; we shall see the arenga palm or sagwire [*kuang-lang*] later.)

Sung's exile poems reiterate this theme of wronged loyalty and misunderstood submission, as in the next he wrote, which tells of an early departure from Shaochou. After a backward look up the pass he goes forward resolutely towards the "Shore of Pearls" and the "Posts of Bronze," anticipating mists, malaria, molds, damps, and typhoons. Even the weird creatures of the night will be unfamiliar:

Sooner than fend off kobold and troll,
I would rather argue with Otus or Owl!

And another despairing reference to his garden:

Green trees—the road to Ch'in Capital,
Blue clouds—the bridge at Lo Water;
My old garden will long stand under the sun—
My soul is gone—no need to call it back. [141]

Finally, as his boat brings him close to Shuang-chou, the terminus of his hopeless journey, his apprehension increases and his sense of injustice becomes more acute. A new poem, after rehearsing the usual repertory of diseases, apes, dragons, and tattooed savages, protests the poet's gratitude to his distant royal mistress, as he "admires the Capital of Jade from the hazy distance." It ends on a note of sentimentally loyal devotion. [142]

We find these motifs pursued relentlessly—even when his escape from the green hell is conceivable—in a stylized letter written from Kuei-chou, presumably after he had spent some time in Nam-Viet. Here Sung tells of his destiny in these "flaming wilds":

To follow up in gloom the routes of the trolls,
To stay far off in the country of tattooed brows;
   Cyclonic winds shake the trees,
   Ravenous weasels cry through the night;
   Poison plagues traverse the skies,
   Lamenting kites drop through the day;
But—my heart relies on the divine order—
My very being looks for a live return! [143]

Despite his elegantly fervid verses on the sorrows of the south, Sung Chih-wen offers us few new, locally inspired images. He relies rather on such established apparitions as wailing monkeys, intended to express sadness. His eyes and ears were not open to the new life of the near-tropics. Or perhaps he noticed the odd birds and flowers but did not know their names and so they could not enter his sumptuous but conventional poetry. It must be admitted, however, that most exiles from the north suffered from this same purblind insensitivity in some measure. All were prisoners of their ecological lexicons.

As for Sung Chih-wen the man, although his weeping does not endear him to us any more than his overdone patriotism, it must be remembered that this kind of literary self pity was not despised in T'ang times as it is in our own.

Other exiles are better known. Accordingly, less needs to be said of them.

Liu Yü-hsi suffered political misfortune early in his career. His name is usually associated with that of his friend Liu Tsung-yüan, whose downfall he shared. But he was luckier than Liu Tsung-yüan, who died young in his semi-tropical outpost. Yü-hsi was ultimately brought back to the capital, and lived to a ripe age, esteemed for his fine verses. He may have owed his life to his unhappy colleague, since when, in 815, his final place of banishment had been designated as Po-chou (in modern Kweichow), Tsung-yüan is said to have burst into tears, exclaiming, "Po-chou is no place for a human being to live!" and was able to influence the great minister P'ei Tu to procure for Yü-hsi the lighter sentence of a post in Lien (Lyen)-chou.[144] Of particular interest, however, is Yü-hsi's period of residence in an earlier and lesser place of exile, Lang[a]-chou, in southernmost Hupei. Here, in the old kingdom of Ch'u, he wrote new words for the songs of the native shamans, shaping them to the patterns of the classical songs from the same region which we now know as the *Ch'u tz'u*. It is reported that these new verses persisted among the barbarians there, and it has been assumed that their popularity was due to their fitness to the ancient tradition, which was still alive in medieval times.[145] We do not know whether Yü-hsi attempted the same antiquarian literary feats while he was in Nam-Viet—but there, of course, he would have been hard put to find respectably sanctioned antiquarian precedents.

The ill-fated Liu Tsung-yüan is better known, and he turns up frequently in this book. Despite all that has been written about him, it is still difficult to appraise his feelings about the warm lands of his banishment. He seems to have loved the beautiful high landscapes of Yung-chou in southern Hunan, where he spent ten years (805–814), although his full appreciation was apparently inhibited by his feeling of rejection from the civilized world—indeed he wrote of the "imprisoning mountains" during this period.[146] Both elated and apprehensive at his recall to the capital in 815, his ambiguous hopes were dashed and he soon found himself on the southward road again, headed for his final destination in forested Liu-chou.[147] He still hoped for return, as we see in his parting verses to Liu Yü-hsi:

> For twenty years now—together in a myriad affairs—
> Now this morning our roads branch, and suddenly it's east and west!

> If the grace of the Illustrious should permit us to return to our fields,
> In our twilight years we shall surely be gaffers in neighboring huts! [148]

After this sad parting, he had a sadder one. His talented younger brother, who had accompanied him into exile, died. His melancholy increased.[149] But he threw himself into his new official labors, more responsible than those required of him in Hunan. He rebuilt walls, dug wells, planted trees (especially willow trees: *liu* "willow" was both his own and his incumbency's name). Above all, he tried to relieve the sufferings of the natives placed in his charge—his efforts against slavery have been noticed elsewhere.[150] He seems to have had a genuine feeling for them, regarding them as more than mere animals, as they were to many of his colleagues. He wrote sympathetically of their sufferings: "their stout ones pinioned, their old ones killed, they howl and cry," and "curious ulcers spike their bones—their forms are like arrow-shafts." [151] But though he was more adaptable than most Chinese officials, he still suffered. Here he tells of himself in his office in Liu-chou:

> In the dank heat of this south country—drunk as if with wine,
> Sound asleep, leaning on my table—with the north window open.
> Awaking alone at midday—there is no other sound
> Than mountain youths, screened by bamboos, pounding the mortars of tea.[152]

("North window," contrasted with "south country," suggests that he has opened it as a symbolic image of his lost homeland.)

Despite his humane treatment of its people and his appreciation of the beauty of its hills and rivers, Liu Tsung-yüan never completely accepted the land of his death as his home:

> In the wild hills—an autumn day's noon:
> I go up alone—my thoughts of far-off regretted things.
> Why do I look off to my native place?
> The northwest—*that* is Jung-chou.[153]

(The key to this quatrain lies in the last verse. Jung-chou is really southeast of him. There is irony in the ambiguity here: the true savages are the politicians in the northwest, not the so-called barbarians of the southeast. Also, it seems, the old home in the northwest is as remote and difficult of approach as the haunted jungles of the southeast.)

Ambitious young scholars residing in southern Hunan and in Lingnan sought criticism and help from Liu Tsung-yüan. Although he was reluctant to accept the formal role of teacher, he sometimes gave advice, as when he cautioned a young man against the imprecise use of classical particles in his prose.[154] Liu's own best writing was in unadorned prose rather than in poetry—we shall see samplings from it scattered through this book. Accordingly the new southern world provoked no striking imagery in his writing, which is more often discursive and descriptive than metaphorical and imagistic. Even in a poem he presents a southern francolin released from captivity only as the occasion of a decent sentiment on his separation from his friends, not as an emotional sign of a new environment.[155]

(Perhaps an account of literary exiles should not fail to mention Han Yü, the older contemporary of Liu Yü-hsi and Liu Tsung-yüan, who was banished to Ch'ao-chou in 819 for criticizing the Buddhist piety of Hsien Tsung.[156] But his story is well known, and in any case we shall see him again later.)

Most high-placed (in the worldly way) among the ostracized writers was Li Te-yü, the chief minister of the Buddha-hating Wu Tsung in the middle of the ninth century. Upon the accession in 847 of Hsüan (Sywen) Tsung, who gradually restored the monasteries of the realm, he was sent off to Ch'ao-chou in the footsteps of Han Yü, then, in the following year, moved on to endure the greater rigors of Yai-chou. He died there in 849 at the age of 63.[157] His approach to Nam-Viet was characteristically apprehensive: he found the twisted roads bewildering, he feared poisonous fogs and venomous plants, he remarked on such exoticisms as arenga palms, areca palms, and tillage in burned-over fields.[158] Everything was oppressively and forbodingly dark.[159] After reaching his ultimate destination on Hainan, he was still overwhelmed by the black labyrinthine mountain forests which surrounded him:

I go up to the high loft alone, to look off to the Divine King's capital.
To fly like a bird? Still, that is a half-year's journey!
Blue mountains seem to wish to keep a man on here—
A hundred circuits, a thousand turnings—girding the walls of the government town.[160]

He seems to have retained a spark of good humor. In a letter to his talented young friend Tuan Ch'eng-shih, written from Yai-chou, he reports that he is still in good health (though he died soon after) and adds: "Most of the people who live here raise chickens. Time and again they fly into my office building. Now I'm going to be just an old man praying to chickens!"[161] He had in mind the aura of superstition surrounding the barnyard fowl in Nam-Viet, and its importance for divining the future, thinking ironically that even these holy birds could not tell him the hour of his escape.

Looking more closely at the three of these famous five who expressed their feelings most openly in their verses, we see that they all felt bewildered and hurt by what seemed undeserved convictions and harsh sentences. The tropics did not invite any of them—all expected only the worst. But there were differences among them too. Sung Chih-wen, always sure of his own virtue, dreaming only of the metropolis, was hardly able to look at the new lands. Liu Tsung-yüan, though staggered by his misfortunes, was more sensitive, and in love with nature. Accordingly he found much with which to reconcile himself. Li Te-yü was more mature, accepting his lot with gloomy but quiet resignation—the great statesman simply declines and disappears into the tropical night.

CREOLES

But not all literate Chinese in Nam-Viet were of this sort. Some could honestly call
it home. In T'ang times the settlement of Nam-Viet by the Hua people had begun in
earnest. The Chinese populations of the south central lake and river districts, extending from modern Hunan to Chekiang, were growing at an enormous rate, and
spilling over the mountains into Lingnan, especially by way of Hunan and the low
pass at Kuei-chou.[162] Accordingly we begin in T'ang times to distinguish not only
primary settlers but creole magnates, some of them well-to-do, such as Teng Yu, a
native of Shao-chou who rose to be Protector of Annam and a rich man owning a
thousand personal slaves.[163] The cultural level of the new towns was greatly enhanced by the arrival of banished northern literati and of upper-class immigrants
fleeing the horrors of war and pillage which devastated the north in late T'ang times.
Many of these men lived the rest of their lives in Nam-Viet, and their sons and
grandsons grew up as natives, accustomed to the sights and sounds of the far south.[164]

Most distinguished among the Nam-Viet creoles was Chang Chiu-ling, a native of
Ch'ü-chiang in Shao-chou, who, after a successful administrative career in both
capital and provinces (including Kuei-chou), rose to the highest office in the land—
first minister to Hsüan (Ghwen) Tsung.[165] Chang was a foremost example of the
new men in government—administrators of modest "middle class" origins who obtained power through their success in the civil-service examinations, and competed
successfully with the ancient aristocratic families of the north. It was largely due to
the machinations of this established gentry that he ultimately lost his high position,
to be succeeded by one of his enemies, Li Lin-fu. Hsüan Tsung later regretted
Chang's loss; it is reported that when Hsüan Tsung was forced into exile in Szechwan he never thought of Chang Chiu-ling without weeping, and he even sent a
mission to Ch'ü-chiang to make offerings to his manes.[166]

Despite his spectacular rise, Chang remained acutely conscious of his disability as a
southerner. Of another minister, Niu Hsien-k'o, he once said: "Your servant is a
humble, unaffiliated man from 'The Passes and the Sea,' not to be compared with
Hsien-k'o, who was born in Central Hua!"[167] But even lacking the social and political advantages of a northerner, he had one advantage most northerners lacked—the
ability to see the subtropical and tropical frontier as a beautiful place, full of attractions to a man of sensibility.

Unlike the weeping exiles, Chang exulted in the savage but familiar landscape of
Lingnan. Luckily he was a gifted poet. On an official tour south from Kuei-chou, he
wrote of the "delightful hills and rivers" (they are his own words) and the richness
of their life:

45

> Singular crags, winding in front of pinnacles,
> Thriving trees, heaped up among their hollows;
> Apes and birds—voicing instinctive calls,
> Winds and springs—spouting common vapors.[168]

Elsewhere he reproaches the northerners for neglecting the beautiful evergreen "vermilion sourpeel tangerines" of the south—and by implication, the talents of southern men as well:

> You speak only of planting peaches and plums—
> But surely *my* trees won't fail to shade you! [169]

He expressed his sense of desolation when he had to leave the familiar surroundings of Ch'ü-chiang:

> The torrent's flow is clear, and also deep;
> A covering shade of pine and rock overhangs;
> Truly then, a place to be esteemed—
> Why now this unappreciative heart?
>
> It is because I cannot bear partings—
> I am infected even by attachment to brutish things!
> But unless you too are declining at a steady pace
> Can you comprehend this cry of mine? [170]

On a return to visit his old parents "by gift of his glorious lord," he takes a pleasant walk in his old garden, now subtly changed, with his younger brother:

> Forest birds fly to the old hamlets,
> Garden fruits ferment the new autumn.
> Branches are longer on trees of the south court,
> The pool is closer to the flow of the north race.[171]

Lying ill in Ching-chou, far to the north, his life near its end, he dreams of spring in the forest near his native place, where he once planned to build a house: "to return there would be worth a thousand metal coins for every day!" [172] The remains of his studio near Shih-hsing, "shrouded by mountains, blooming with water," were still pointed out in Sung times.[173]

"The south was in his blood," we would say. Yet this opinion has been challenged. The quondam-exile Liu Yü-hsi, writing of the great minister more than half a century later, had this to say of him:

The world says of Chang Chiu-ling that as a minister he stated in words that banished vassals should not be granted good land, and that he had most of them exiled to the uncovered [by vegetation] country of the Five Gorges [of Hunan]. But now I read in his own writings that Chang, going from his duties in the penetralia [of the palace] to become Pastor of Shih-an, had sighs about the plague of malaria, and retiring from his ministry to become Protector of Ching-chou, had thoughts of being held a prisoner—so he committed his symbolism to animals and birds and transferred his phrasing to herbs and

46

trees, in a mood of dark depression, in the same spirit as that of the *Sao*-man (Ch'ü Yüan). So, alas! when he himself was sent to a far-off retreat, once his expectations [of return] were lost, he could not bear it. How much less a Hua-man of gentry stock, required to go off to that ill-favored land! After this my thoughts were gay! [174]

This illuminating document does not dispose us to think well of Liu Yü-hsi's character. In addition to referring to the minister as no proper Hua-man, and seeing his nature-writing merely as conventional protest-writing, he reveals a decidedly mean and ungenerous spirit in taking pleasure in the realization that Chang's weakness was as great as his own. If Chang flinched from a southern exile, we may find good reason in his resentment at exclusion from public affairs and the loss of the pleasures of metropolitan life, to both of which he had become accustomed, and to the prospect of the possible termination of his official career and even of his life. Surely Liu might have forgiven him these weaknesses of his declining years, especially since he might have read more carefully in other passages the plain evidence of Chang's love of his subtropical home.

Whatever their inherent merits, and they were considerable, Chang Chiu-ling's career and writing must be praised for their stimulation of new attitudes toward Nam-Viet, that strange and fearful land. It is a commonplace of poetry that familiar plants and birds suggest home. Alien forms of life, on the other hand, are repulsive and intensify the tenderness of familiar images by contrast. The cry of a magpie or a swallow made the medieval northerner's heart swell with happiness; the call of a langur or chukar made him weep with homesickness. It was the writing of southerners like Chang Chiu-ling which made it possible for later generations to see nature in all of its local manifestations without sentimental or parochial distortion. Perhaps, after all, the vermilion bird of the south might lose its ancient symbolic role and become a happy reality.

My mother bore me in the southern wild,
And I am black, but O! my soul is white.

William Blake, *The Little Black Boy*

3 Man People

LAO AND OTHERS

MOST of the non-Chinese peoples called "Lao" by the Chinese who still lived in southern Shensi and western Szechwan after Han times were by T'ang times converted to Chinese modes of speaking, dressing, and dwelling,[1] though their unassimilated brethren could still be found in more southerly and inaccessible mountains. Among their T'ang-time representatives were the so-called "Lao of Nan-p'ing," who inhabited a large region in southeastern Szechwan.[2] The warlords of this tribe or confederacy (I do not know the proper word) belonged to the Ning clan, a name also famous in Nam-Viet in this period. They lived in pile dwellings called *kan-lan* in Chinese transcription; they wore bamboo ear plugs; their women (not their men) took the initiative in arranging marriage contracts.[3]

It is possible that a group named Ko-lao (*Kat-lau*) or Ch'i-lao (*Ngyĕt-lau*) represented the original Lao, free of Chinese contamination in their Kweichow strongholds, where they came under the influence of the Tibeto-Burman "Black Man," whom we shall observe presently. One authority restores their name as KLAO or TLAO and, with good reason, finds them centuries later in the Coloman or Toloman (i.e., *Klao-man or Tlao-man*) of Marco Polo. Their language shows affinities to Thai, but may not have belonged to that family originally.[4]

As the Lao and their cousins were overwhelmed and enslaved in the Han-T'ang interval, their name was gradually extended by the Chinese to all southern savages as a term of contempt, and by T'ang times the most diverse cultures of Nam-Viet, some quite unlike the original Lao, were styled "Lao" as they had already been loosely called "Man." In Sung times the term "Lao of the Sea" was applied even to the Arabs.[5]

Despite the illusion of uniformity given us by the sweeping extension of the name Lao, the T'ang pioneers who followed the mountain chains southward into the modern provinces of Hunan, Kweichow, and Yunnan actually found very dissimilar tribes resisting their advance. Among them were the Hsieh (Zya) of the East, who planted seeds in burned-over forest clearings and did not know the use of the plow. Very much like them were the Chao (Dyeu) of the West. Both were peoples of eastern Szechwan, western Hunan, and northern Kweichow (that is T'ang Ch'ien-chung), near the Lao of Nan-p'ing. They became tributary to the Chinese in early T'ang times.[6] Possibly they were related to the Yao tribes who appear in Lingnan in Sung times and later.

Beyond them and other tribes were the Ts'uan peoples of Yunnan.[7] These tribes, whose chiefs were styled "Great Ghost Masters,"[8] spoke languages related to those of the Burmans and Tibetans, as did the people of the great Nan-chao nation who lived close by them.[9] The men of T'ang classified the Ts'uan in two large groups, an eastern and a western, and styled them the Black and White Man. They explained these epithets in terms of the costumes of the women of the two groups: those of the eastern Ts'uan wore trailing black dresses, those of the western Ts'uan wore knee-length white smocks.[10] The White Man, some say, were descended from the ancient Ai-lao people, and have modern relatives in the Karen of Burma. They were partly sinicized in T'ang times.[11] The Black Man, whose Meng clan had founded the Nan-chao kingdom, were more conservative.[12] They had already moved into Kweichow in Han times, it seems. The modern Lolo, known to the Hua-men of T'ang as Lu-lu (Lu-luk), may be descendants of a Black Man tribe.[13] During the reign of Hsüan (Ghwen) Tsung in the eighth century, the Chinese tried in vain to enlist the Black Man against Nan-chao, to whom they were related and with whose people they intermarried.[14]

To the west of the Ts'uan, in the highlands of eastern Kweichow, were the Tsang-ko (Tsang-ka), an important group with chieftains of the Hsieh (Zya) clan. They were partly subject to the T'ang, and sometimes sent them tribute.[15]

As for Nam-Viet itself, its aborigines were collectively called "Man" or "Lao" by the Chinese, or sometimes "I," a word which meant little more than "barbarians."[16] Their tribal divisions were seldom clearly distinguished, even by sensitive observers. Evidently they constituted a large part of the whole population there, their numbers increasing proportionately from east to west. Even the people of Hsün (Zywin)-chou, a comparatively civilized (i.e., heavily sinicized) region east of Canton, were described in early Sung times as being "mostly Man and Lao."[17] At the same period, barbarians (I) and Chinese (Hua) lived intermingled in the Tuan-chou area just west of Canton,[18] while at K'ang and Shuang, a little further to the west, all sorts of savages dwelled together.[19] In Jung-chou, says one source, "the barbarians (I) are abundant, the Chinese (Hua) are few," [20]

But let us look at some of the better-known Nam-Viet tribes.

Most prominent among the native peoples were the Huang (Ghwang). They were aggressive leaders among the "Man of the Western Plain" (to be interpreted as "Plateau"?). They were also called "Grotto Barbarians" (as were other tribal groups) because they lived among the steep mountain defiles and limestone caves of Kwangsi or perhaps because their ancestors emerged from caves. The names seem to stand for a kind of anti-Chinese confederacy, sporadically resurrected among the tribes west of Canton.[21] The poet Yüan Chen paired the Huang people with the Persian and Indonesian merchant-princes as typical sights to be expected by a visitor in Lingnan:

> Masters of argosies—treasures stowed at their waists;
> Householders of Huang—dust rising from their stockades.[22]

Their homeland was the Grottoes of Yellow Oranges.[23] Some said that they were the descendants of a soldier named Huang ("Yellow") who had accompanied Ma Yüan to Nam-Viet centuries ago.[24] Probably they spoke a Thai language.[25] Here is Li Ho's vivid picture of them as the scourge of the T'ang, gathering for war against the hated northerners, who seek safety on a raft in mid-stream:

> Tripping with sparrow steps over the sand—the sound *chok! chok!*
> With four-foot horn bows and blue stone arrowheads.
> Black pennants thrice dipped—the bronze drums cry out!
> Making high-pitched langur howls, they shake their arrow quivers!
> Colored linen binds their shins—puttees halfway slanted,
> At the head of the gorge in close-set ranks they light up the kudzu flowers.
> Mountain tarns in evening mists, where the white alligator drones;
> Bamboo snakes and flying scorpions spurt out golden sand.
> Leisurely they goad their "bamboo horses," slowly returning home;
> But the government army is killing itself on rafts by Jung-chou.[26]

(The colorful garments of the tribesmen light up even the wildflowers; I do not know what "bamboo horses" may be.)

The Huang and their allies, the Nung, the Lo (La), the Mo (Mak) and others,[27] ravaged the Chinese colonies in the lowlands in the second half of the eighth and the early part of the ninth centuries.[28] Liu Tsung-yüan, advising the need to put down these obnoxious rebels, wrote of them as flimsily fortified on hillocks, oppressing Chinese emissaries and ravaging Chinese settlements. He added these condescending words:

> Though as mean as foxes and rats,
>   Not deserving a display of our might,
> Yet even tiny things like wasps and tarantulas
>   Can bring destruction on living creatures.[29]

Man People

The noble Ning were peers of the Huang among the Man of the Western Plain: "The Man of the Western Plain dwell in the south of Kuang and Yung and in the west of Jung and Kuei. There are certain Ning clansmen who are their aristocrats; there are also Huang clansmen who dwell in the Yellow Orange Grottoes and are their clients." [30] The Ning clan (or tribe?) also provided the war chiefs of the Lao of Nan-p'ing far to the north of Nam-Viet,[31] just as the Hsieh (Zya) gave captains to the Tsang-ko. At the beginning of T'ang rule, with the subjection of "Ning-Viet" —that is, of the part of Viet controlled by the Ning—the road to Tongking was opened to the Hua victors, and a certain Lao of that tribe, Ning Ch'un (Neng Zhwin), was designated Inciting Notary of Lien (Lyem)-chou on the coast of Kwangtung.[32] Han Yü spoke of this proud people as "the wild Ning." [33] Probably the Ning are not to be distinguished from the Nung who participated with distinction in the incursion against the T'ang settlements in the eighth and ninth centuries.[34] It has been suggested that both "Ning" and "Nung" are ultimately the same as *lung* "dragon." [35] Their modern descendants speak a Thai language,[36] as did, most likely, the majority of the Man of the Western Plains.

At the beginning of the seventh century, a shoeless people whom the Chinese called Mo Yao (Mak Yeu) lived scattered through Hunan. The men were distinguished by their white linen trousers and shirts and the women by their blue linen shirts and variegated linen skirts. It was observed that they used flatirons as wedding gifts.[37] In T'ang times, if not earlier, the Mak people (as I shall call them) were also to be found in regions adjoining southwestern Hunan. A popular literary tale had as its hero a Mak of Lang ᵇ-chou in eastern Szechwan, a kind of aboriginal Androcles, with a grateful elephant in place of a thankful lion.[38] Chieftains of the Mak took part in the general uprisings of the Western Plain barbarians in western Lingnan in the second half of the eighth century: the names of Mo Ch'un (Mak Zhwin) "Prince who Sustains the South" and Mo Hsün (Mak Zyĕm) "Prince of the South Sea" were outstanding among a group of native princes who led the righteous fight against the Hua invaders.[39] The exiled poet Liu Yü-hsi wrote of them in the vicinity of Lien (Lyen)-chou in northern Kwangtung early in the ninth century. Possibly they had infiltrated Lingnan in early T'ang times, or perhaps they had simply not been noticed there earlier. Here then is Liu Yü-hsi's "Song of the Mak Yao," in which the illiterate Mak appear as friends of mermen and consorts of forest goblins ("tree visitors"). We shall have a closer look at both kinds of weird beings later on.

> The Mak Yao once born and grown
> Take names and epithets, but lack tallies and registers;
> In market and trade they mingle with shark-dragon men,
> In wedding and marriage they intermix with "tree visitors."
> By the sites of stars they divine the eyes of springs,
> By sowing in fire they open up the spines of mountains.
> At night they cross gorges of a thousand fathoms,
> The sand mouthers have no power to spurt at them.[40]

51

(The "sand mouthers" are semi-legendary reptiles which spit sand at men's shadows with fatal results. We shall see them later also. Presumably the Mak were immune to their venom.)

Liu Yü-hsi has also described a winter hunt of the Mak tribe in the deciduous forest of the northern uplands, using beaters, hawks, and hounds: [41]

> In sea and sky the lethal vapors thin out;
> An army of the Man—ranks and files shouting.
> The woods are red, the leaves wholly changed;
> The plain is black, the grass newly burned.
> They join in a circle, the profusion of gongs desists;
> Wildfowl rise as great banners shake.
> They spread the nets across the mouth of the track,
> They set the dogs up the waist of the hill.
> Wary hawks—again and again roused to speed;
> Fearful muntjacs—time after time hesitant to jump.

It is evident that the Mak used the primitive fire-field technique to make clearings for their crops, and were skilled hunters. Their culture was different from that of the Thai-speaking, paddy-growing valley dwellers.

There is no reason to doubt that the Mak of the twentieth century, now restricted to a few villages of Kweichow Province, are the remnants of this once widespread people. Most of these have "Mak" as a "surname" and they distinguish themselves clearly from the neighboring Yao (or Miao) peoples, whom they call "Hiu." [42] Their language is now placed in the Kam-Sui ("Grottoes and Water") subgroup of the Kam-Tai family—that is, their speech is not proper Thai, like that of the modern Ch'uang peoples, but distantly related to it.[43]

We have already noticed the modern Tan or Tanka living along the western coast of Kwangtung under the monsoons—"boat people" whose lives are spent on the water. These Tan have been known for centuries as skilled sailors, and their patron god was Fan Li, minister of ancient Viet, whose name is associated with boats, fish-breeding, and trade.[44] The name Tan had already been applied to a southern people in Han times by the *Shuo wen* dictionary; between Han and T'ang, Tan were reported in Szechwan and Hunan; [45] we read of them in southern Szechwan and in Kwangsi in T'ang times: witness Han Yü: "Man of the forests, Tan of the grottoes." [46] In T'ang, the coastal part of the Tan peoples seems to have been styled "dragon people," [47] but it is not certain that the name Tan itself was given to a boat people before Sung times.[48] The Lu-t'ing of T'ang times may also have been kin of the Tan.[49] These men had for their eponymous ancestor a powerful chieftain of the fourth century A.D. When this Lu Hsün was defeated, it was said, the remnant of his host fled into the islands of the sea, where they lived like savages on oysters and other molluscs, whose shells they piled up to make walls.[50] Finally, an early Sung source [51] tells of a people of Lien (Lyem)-chou, gatherers of pearls and "plate aromatic" (onycha) and performers on gourd mouth organs and bronze drums—it calls them the T'o (T'a or Da) of Viet. Their location and livelihood agree with those of the Tan boat people.[52]

The Li (or Lei or Loi) people who now inhabit the interior of Hainan Island were a powerful threat to Chinese supremacy there in medieval times. In T'ang they were also well established on the mainland, along the tropical coast west from Canton, including the Luichow peninsula, where, apparently, they were intermingled with the Tan.[53] We even read of an uprising of Li tribesmen in Tongking in T'ang times, far from their modern home.[54] Some modern scholars see in them the descendants of the ancient Lo (Lak), one of the classical Viet peoples, and their name has also been equated with Lao.[55] They were well differentiated in medieval times—an early Sung source notes four kinds of "Li-Lao" speech, not mutually intelligible, in Yung-chou.[56]

Deep in the mountains between Lingnan and northern Tongking[57] were the Wu-hu, perhaps remnants of the ancient Ou,[58] descendants of the legendary Bamboo King, some of them gatherers of pearls and kingfisher feathers.[59] They appear to have been related to the Vietnamese, but they also resemble the Tan, and have been identified with the Li.[60]

The non-sinicized Vietnamese had no particular name; one source simply calls them the "wild Man." [61] Since antiquity they had been noted for their tattooing and cropped hair; [62] they wore linen ponchos, wielded wooden spears, and shot bone-headed arrows.[63] They also sacrificed men to their agricultural gods.[64] But they shared all of these traits with other peoples of Nam-Viet, and it may well be that they did not yet constitute a distinct linguistic or ethnic entity.

If we try to reconstruct the ethnic map of T'ang Nam-Viet, using language alone, we get a picture almost as confused as the modern linguistic map, with this difference, that although the affinities of the modern languages of that region are, in many cases, uncertain, there is a great deal more uncertainty about the relations of the languages of T'ang, which we know only by name, or in some cases by a few words. A tentative mapping would show the field-burning Mak in the north on the border of Kweichow, speaking a "Kam-Sui" language; the wet-rice-growing Huang, Ning, and others, speaking Thai languages, would appear throughout the west of Lingnan. Beyond these would be the Wu-hu, possibly of Vietnamese speech. Scattered about in remote places, but heavily concentrated on the coast and on Hainan, are the Li, whose tongue now shows features of Thai and of Malayo-Polynesian, and may belong to the hypothetical "Kadai" family. Also on the shore south and west from Canton appear the Tan, whose ancient speech is quite unknown.

Probably the first thing to impress the unlucky Chinese exile or soldier among the aborigines of Nam-Viet was the strange, seemingly inhuman quality of their speech. One observer compared the local tongue to the clucking of a francolin. Here is Liu Yü-hsi's "Song of the Man-tzu": [65]

Man People

The speech of the Man is a *kou-chou* sound,
The dress of the Man is a *pan-lan* linen.
Their odorous raccoons dig out the sand rats;
At seasonal periods they sacrifice to P'an-hu.
Should they meet a stranger riding a horse,
They are flustered, and glance round like startled muntjacs.
With axes at their waists they ascend the high mountains,
Proposing to go where no old road exists.

(*Pan-lan* means "mottled, variegated." I retain the original Chinese word here to show how the poet matched it with the voice of the chukar. "Odorous raccoon [-dog]" is for the more usual "Aromatic raccoon-dog," a name for the civet; this unnamed tribe had, it seems, trained civets as ratters. Their god was the great ancestral dog, P'an-hu.) But no T'ang dialectician comparable to Yang Hsiung of Han was present to note down the specific traits of this stuttering language.[66]

Then there was the bewildering variety of barbarous customs, not associated with any specific tribe. In Jung-chou the natives make linen of banana fiber;[67] the grotto people of Liu-chou have goose-feather garments against the winter season (these must have been similar to the double "coverlets" padded with goose feathers, very warm and soft, used by native notables of Jung)[68] and sew clothes of "mountain wool" (glossed "tree floss," which could be either cotton or kapok);[69] both sexes bathe together in the streams, without shame;[70] the natives of Yung-chou go bare-footed and have mallet-shaped coiffures[71] (these must have been like the four-inch-long knot of hair which projects over the forehead of a modern "Big Knot Loi" of Hainan);[72] the people of Nan-hai generally have thick hair, which they anoint with bear grease, and cut off each year at the time of the rice harvest in the fifth or sixth month, to sell in the markets;[73] the southerners have always tattooed their bodies;[74] they dwell on piles, as if they were birds in tree tops,[75] and these aeries (of a kind widespread among the peoples of Indochina and Oceania)[76] are called *kan-lan* (cf. Cham *kalan*);[77] they are spoken of as cave dwellers (we have already referred several times to the grotto barbarians; it is possible that by T'ang times this was often only an echo of their mythological beginnings, and that in most cases "grotto" had come to mean only "settlement");[78] they eat fish and rice;[79] they drink through their noses;[80] the lowlanders (especially Thai peoples, it seems) plant in water (that is, wet rice fields);[81] uplanders cultivate the ashy soils of burned mountain slopes[82] in a spectacle vividly described by Liu Yü-hsi:

Wherever it may be, they like to burn off the fields,
Round and round, creeping over the mountain's belly.
When they bore the tortoise and get the "rain" trigram,
Up the mountain they go and set fire to the prostrate trees.
Startled muntjacs run, and then stare back;
Flocks of pheasants make *i-auk* sounds.
The red blaze forms sunset clouds far off,

Light coals fly into the city walls.
The wind draws it up to the high peaks,
It licks and laps across the blue forest.
The blue forest, seen afar, dissolves in a flurry,
The red light sinks—then rises again.
A radiant tarn brings forth an old *kău*-dragon;
Exploding bamboos frighten the forest ghosts.
In the color of night we see no mountain,
Just an orphan glow by the Starry Han:
It is like a star, then like the moon,
Each after the other, until at daybreak the wind dies away.
Then first comes a light which beats on the stones,
Then follows a heat which glows up to heaven.
They drop their seeds among the warm ashes;
These, borne by the "essential heat" (*yang*), burst into buds and shoots.
Verdant and vivid, after a single rain,
Spikes of trumpet vine come out like a cloud.
The snake men chant with folded hands;
Neither plowing nor hoeing involve their hearts.
From the first they have found the temper of this land,
Whose every inch holds an excess of "essential cold" [*yin*].[83]

(To "bore the tortoise" is to perform an act of divination with a tortoise's carapace. The Starry Han is the Milky Way. The snake men appear to be shamans or ritual chanters. The doctrine expressed here is that the folk wisdom of the highlanders has led them to compensate for the natural coolness and humidity [*yin*] of the floor of the southern forests by applying natural heat [*yang*], bringing about perfect fertility.)

"Tropical shifting agriculture," or "fire-field agriculture," or "slash-and-burn cultivation" is widespread in tropical countries. It is very ancient, and developed with the art of cultivating roots, rhizomes, tubers, and seeds with a digging stick or hoe. Taro and yams are typical crops, but so also is dry upland rice. "Essentially it involves making a clearing by girdling, felling, or topping the tall forest canopy, slashing the lower layers and burning as much as possible to let light down to the ground, give free space, and fertilize the soil."[84] Anthropologists sometimes use local names for this practice, such as *rây* in Indochina and *milpa* in the American tropics.[85] The T'ang name for it was *she* (*sha*).[86] Peoples who practice *she* cultivation, conjoined with hunting and gathering, are thought to represent an encroachment on the tropical forest, either by migration or by imitation, of a savannah culture, whose true aboriginals, such as the Veddahs of Ceylon and the negrito remnants of Malaya and Indonesia, are a rapidly vanishing remnant.[87]

The natives of the mountainous regions also engage in quarrying and mining, where

> The canopies of pines ring them round with clear assonance,
> The roots of the banyans frame them over in green shadow;

> Men of the grottoes, most of them, hew at stones,
> Women of the Man, half of them, sift for gold.[88]

In parts of Lingnan, at any rate, a market fair called *hsü* (*hyo*) is held each three days (according to another source, each five days):

> His salt encased in glaucous bamboo, a traveler returning to his grotto;
> His rice wrapped in green lotus leaves, a man hastening to the *hyo*.[89]

In Jung-chou they "are practiced at shooting with bow and crossbow";[90] not all hunting is for wild game—a tribe of Ch'in-chou eats men;[91] in Kang ᵃ-chou they weave containers of bamboo and caulk them with the lime of oyster shells;[92] in Jung-chou they enjoy blowing calabash mouth organs and striking bronze drums;[93] the natives are superstitious: "they are fond of shamans and ghosts and give weight to lewd superstitions";[94] they "divine with chickens and divine with eggs";[95] the Lao have a queer social custom: when a woman has born a child, she gets up, but her husband takes to his bed, and eats and drinks like a nursing mother.[96]

When the wife of one of the poor folk in Nan-hai is pregnant, she visits a rich house and, pointing to her belly, offers to sell it. The vulgar speak of this as a "pointing-at-belly sale." Sometimes before her own child "can sustain its dress" [i.e., before it is well out of babyhood], she will make do with the sale of a neighbor's child. When she goes to get it on loan, she breaks a staff so that they will know how short or tall it was then, and when her own child is grown up equal to the staff she immediately repays the loan. So they sell them, male and female, as if they were dung or dirt. Between father and child there is no family feeling.[97]

Nam-Viet was notorious as a supplier of slaves, especially females: "Slave girls of Viet, sleek of buttery flesh," wrote an appreciative Yüan Chen.[98] Most of these unfortunates were aborigines, sold to Chinese and sent to the great cities of the north to tend the wants of the aristocracy. Neighboring Fukien and Kweichow were also sources of human flesh, and in the ninth century Fukien had the additional distinction of being the chief supplier of young eunuchs to the capital.[99] Even Szechwan, long since assimilated to the Middle Kingdom, was a source of native slaves, as Li Te-yü attests, "a majority of the men of Shu sell their girls to become men's concubines."[100]

The chronicle of slavery in medieval China is not a pretty one, despite the efforts of occasional benevolent rulers. The good acts of one did not bind his successor. There were also local magistrates opposed to slavery. Examples from both national and local levels follow. When Li Fu, a scion of the house of T'ang, came to administer Jung in 783, he found that the captured "Western Plain" rebels were being enslaved. He sought out their families, and eventually gave them all their freedom.[101] At about this same time, the sovereign Te Tsung decreed a halt to the traffic in boys and girls in western Nam-Viet.[102] In April of 809 the new ruler Hsien Tsung, acting on the advice of Li Chiang and Po Chü-i, who had pointed out to him the prevalence of selling persons of decent families into slavery in Lingnan, Kweichow and Fukien, decreed the abolition of the slave trade.[103] There is no evidence that these royal acts had any permanent effect. When Liu Tsung-yüan arrived at his humble magistracy in Liu-chou in 815, for instance, he found the custom there of persons pledging themselves as security for loans. If principal and interest were not duly paid, the debtors were enslaved. Liu abolished this hideous usury, partly at his own expense, and his methods became models for other counties in which the practice prevailed.[104] When the good governor K'ung K'uei came to rule over Nan-hai, he received commissions from the magnates of Ch'ang-an to purchase southern slaves, especially women, for them. Not only did he reject these requests, but he forbade the sale of girls in Nam-Viet altogether.[105]

Except for brief and local relief such as this, the non-Chinese peoples of the south were systematically enslaved throughout the T'ang period, whether "willingly" (as for debt) or unwillingly (as prisoners of war). The young women of the Thais and other ethnic communities were the chief sufferers. Not until the flourishing of the romantic *tz'u* style in poetry in the tenth century, especially at the hands of such masters of glamor as Ou-yang Chiung and Li Hsün, did the native girls of Nam-Viet achieve even so ambiguous a status as that of geisha or sing-song girl—to become the early sisters of the sweetly submissive congai of the French colonials of nineteenth-century Annam. We shall see them in this new role presently.

Both conscience and law permitted the enslavement of these subject peoples all the more readily because of two persistent views of them—an older one, that they were not really human, and a younger one, derived from the first, that they were not really civilized. The Man and the Lao and all the rest of them were animalian, and the graphs which represented their names almost invariably showed the recognizable symbol of a wild beast or a reptile. More specifically, the several tribesmen were said to be dragon men, or shark men, or dog men, or tiger men, or whatever—that is, they were semi-men who could convert themselves into animals and shared the attributes and mysterious powers of animals. In consequence, the Hua-men felt free to treat them as animals. Such treatment was given specious justification by the observation of such customs as totemic emblems and hunting taboos. A more "civilized" but accordingly more detestable variant of these notions (which had some basis in aboriginal belief), was the common one that the indigenes *resembled* animals in speech, thoughts, and habits. Even such an intelligent man as Han Yü did not hesitate to write of them as "like langurs or macaques," in short as apelike.[106] For many Chinese, the resemblance must have been embarrassing. To the ordinary immigrant the aboriginal peoples of Nam-Viet presented misshapen, distorted, and bestial copies of himself, and their songs and tales must have seemed grotesque parodies of the holy books inherited from the age of Confucius. Modern studies have revealed the strong affinities between the myths, songs, and rites of the modern non-Chinese peoples of Kwangsi and Tongking and those of the ancient Chinese of the classical Chou period as they are preserved in the canonical books.[107] But the Hua men of T'ang could hardly have interpreted the resemblances as significant of an ancient relationship, since to them the customs of the Man were merely loathsome. They saw only puzzling caricatures, like imperfect images from deteriorated molds. They had long since forgotten that they had once had the same repellent habits, and had purged references to them from their literature. An example is the virile custom of head-hunting, with feasts in honor of the trophies. A Lao of Ch'in-chou "when he got a man's head, straightway gained many wives." [108] We know the custom well from such old and revered Chinese books as the *Tso chuan* and the *Ch'u tz'u*. It survived much longer, along with human sacrifice and cannibalism (also once Hua practices) among the southern peoples.

In any case, the goodmen of the Hua race had a lively vocabulary to characterize these despised clowns, these bad replicas of themselves. When the victorious general Kao P'ien, after his successes in Nam-Viet, was sent to Szechwan in 875 to deal with the Yunnanese incursions, he spoke contemptuously of the "Southern Man" in an official report as "petty rogues, easily stood up to." [109] His mature opinion was not much different from the puerile reaction of the pampered "boys"—stable-hands and falconers—of the emperor Hsi Tsung: in 881 they preceded that unhappy monarch to Ch'eng-tu, fleeing from Ch'ang-an before the peasant armies of Huang Ch'ao; one of them, inspecting a temporary palace there, remarked, "Men say that Hsi-ch'uan is Man—but as I look at it today, it is not so bad after all." The arrogant youth was flogged to death for his impertinence.[110] The fact remained, Szechwan was "Man country"—barbarous! Similarly, Te Tsung reviled his minister Lu Chih, a native of the civilized and only moderately southern town of Su-chou as "old Lao slave!" [111] Lu Chih was no Lao, but as a southerner he could be called a Lao in a moment of passion, as he might be called an ape or a devil. If the snobbery of a northerner of the Yellow River valley could see a boor and a clodhopper (to say the least) in a native of the great lake and river system in the near south, it is easy to imagine his attitude toward the creoles—the Chinese born in Fukien, Lingnan, or Kweichow: they partook of the unpleasant character of the aborigines. This attitude was useful for the diffusion of northern culture. Local Chinese rulers did their best to surround themselves with noted scholars and politicians from the north. This was especially so in the little independent regimes which sprang up after the dissolution of the T'ang empire. Liu Yen, founder of the Han state in Lingnan, for instance, told visitors from the north that "he was ashamed to be the liege of savages and barbarians." [112] Specifically: the natives, of whatever breed, were volatile,[113] miserly,[114] and cruel [115]—"treacherous on the inside, simple on the outside." [116] "They love swords and treat death lightly." [117] But all alike, indigene or creole, lacked real moral standards, and had the avaricious souls of merchants: "South of the Five Mountain Passes men are commingled with the barbarian Lao, knowing nothing of education or public spirit—they take wealth to be manliness." [118] This is the true northern aristocrat's way of ridiculing the upstart southern-born

Chinese bourgeois, who, since late in the century, was privileged to rise to posts of importance through the examination system. But though the yokels were little better than the savages among whom they lived, the abuse they endured was not quite as severe as the humiliation and pain suffered by their aboriginal neighbors.

Yet more enlightened views existed, and on every level of quality. To begin at the greatest eminence: fearful for the safety of T'ai Tsung, who was devoted to hunting, an officer asked that prince to take thought for his subjects: "Heaven has commanded Your Enthroned Eminence to act as father and mother to both Hua and barbarian—how can you treat yourself so lightly?" [119] All men were equal, then, under the divine parent. The sovereign's reply is not recorded. But it is known that his noble father took a humane attitude towards his non-Chinese subjects. "If only our Pastors and Protectors could embrace them with loyalty and good faith," said Kao Tsu, denying the petition of a Szechwanese governor who wished to lead a punitive expedition against the restless Lao tribes, "they would all come of themselves to submit. How may we lightly set buckler and battle axe in motion, fishing and hunting these folk, as if we compared them to birds and beasts? Surely that is not the aim of the Father and Mother of his people!" [120] Occasionally (but rarely, I fear) this admirable attitude was shared by a responsible agent of the Son of Heaven on the frontier. It is told that in 703 P'ei Huai-ku, a well-disposed official in Kweichow, brought about the surrender of a triumphant rebel, the aborigine Ou-yang Ch'ien, and all of his hopeful hordes. Disagreeing with the idea that "the barbarian Lao are faithless," he got in direct touch with that chieftain, saying, "Loyalty and faith allow us to communicate even with divine intelligences—surely, then, with these men of the border!" [121]

Early in the ninth century, when the power of the Huang tribe was broken and the grotto peoples lay at the mercy of the northern conquerors, many men took thought on how best to treat these troublesome neighbors. Among them was Liu Tsung-yüan, who addressed a memorial to the throne on behalf of the minister P'ei Hsing-li, giving direct information on the situation in the Yung Administration, and expressing the prevalent view that ultimately it was only the spiritual forces emanating from the Son of Heaven which subdued the barbarians: "The authority and charisma of Your Enthroned Eminence," he wrote, "mantle the distances, and your spiritual conversions take effect on all sides. Therefore the plots of the faithless and sly expose themselves before their terms, and the gangs of the twisted and perverse are all laid low without slaughter." [122] These holy forces were, in the end, propagated through the institutions believed to have been sanctioned by Confucius and his divine predecessors. So Liu wrote, in an inscription of dedication for the restoration of a Confucian temple in Liu-chou in 815:

The Way of Chung-ni [Confucius] brought kingly transformation to far and near. In antiquity only Liu-chou remained among the southern barbarians, with their clubbed chignons and grass skirts, their assaults and thefts, their fighting and violence. Even the humanity of T'ang and Yü [Yao and Shun] could not soften them, nor the valor of Ch'in and Han overawe them. But now that we of T'ang possess this country, they conform to law and rule for the first time!" [123]

The faith in the inevitability of the acceptance by the aborigines of classical doctrine as expounded in the canonical books of the Hua people remained indomitable in the minds of educated men like Liu Tsung-yüan everywhere. These laws were good laws and eternal laws, as fit for non-Chinese men as for themselves. The T'ang nation could pride itself that it had brought these laws to parts of the world which had never before accepted them. Liu was not alone in claiming new populations converted to the ways of the T'ang. In the very middle of the ninth century, the rich and fog-free lands of Hsün (Zyĕm)-chou on the Yü River, south of Liu-chou, in the heart of the infidels' domain, submitted to the Chinese, and thenceforth "their manners and observances, dress and costume, kerchiefs and sashes, were just like those of the Middle Kingdom." [124] It is to be feared that the young were more ready to accept the conventional and superficial tokens of "high civilization" than the inner spirit—the Chinese style rather than the Chinese soul: "most of the Man youth study to belt themselves with golden hooks." [125] So wrote Lu Kuei-meng, telling a southbound administrator what to expect among his parishioners in Canton.

Missionary activities, both persuasive and compulsive, were most vigorous during the first half of the ninth century. Schools were built, technology was improved, superstition was combated. We may note the example of Yang Yü-ling, who ruled Lingnan from 808 to 810 (the famous philosopher Li Ao was attached to his headquarters), and taught the natives to make tiles for their roofs to lessen the danger of fires, which had repeatedly burned their thatched houses. [126] Then there was Ma Tsung in Annam a few years later, a man of great probity, who reformed the manners of his subjects "through the employment of the arts of the *ju* [Confucian pedagogues]." [127] Wei Tan, in Jung-chou between 801 and 804, taught the folk plowing and weaving, added tea and rice to their products, put an end to their idle habits, and raised school buildings. [128] Han Yü himself is credited with having established the first local schools in Ch'ao-chou, with a program administered by a learned man named Chao Te. [129] Such changes as these required the eradication of customs which might keep the allegiance of the natives tied to the old ways. This is why we see Wei Cheng-kuan, Legate of Lingnan in 849 and 850, assuming the venerable role of the prehistoric culture hero T'ang, who offered his person up to ransom his people from the drought:

It is prevailing custom in the southern quarter to respect ghosts. Cheng-kuan destroyed their lewd shrines and instructed the folk not to make vain supplications. Just then the waters of the sea were spilling over, and men disputed about the elimination of this affliction and the matter of their shrines, taking it that the spirits were dissatisfied. Cheng-kuan mounted the city wall, poured out wine, and took this oath: "If I do not meet the expectations of the spirits, may I, the senior man, be held responsible for this affliction—let it not reach to the lowly folk!" Shortly the waters departed, and so the folk had faith in him.[130]

The proselytizing spirit of these decades had its antecedents in the first years of T'ang. Then there had been such men as Wang I-fang who, banished to the far south soon after the conquest, had undertaken the difficult job of converting the savages under his jurisdiction. He made a selection of chiefs and took them as his pupils:

> He opened up and set forth the canons and texts—
> He carried out and enacted the oblations and rituals—
> With purest song and blowing of flutes,
> Ascending and descending, genuflecting and standing up.[131]

But in some places the revival of the classical spirit did not outlast the first half of the century and the relative peace and mild prosperity which characterized it. The Chinese had the shame of seeing their pupils reject the noblest beliefs of their teachers, retaining only the trappings of their power. So it is told that the great general Wei Kao, subduer of Nan-chao, had brought the young men of the Man peoples to study writing and other humane arts in Ch'eng-tu, thinking thereby to pacify their fierce hearts. This system continued in force for fifty years, and it is reported that many thousands of the alien youth received a Chinese education in Szechwan during that period. But then the program had to be curtailed because of financial difficulties. For this and other reasons, the disgruntled lords of Nan-chao cut off formal tribute relations with China, and, in the winter of 859–860, their new ruler declared himself a divine king on the Chinese model and named his kingdom Ta-li.[132]

INSURRECTIONS

The reconquest of the native peoples of Nam-Viet by the T'ang soldiery and the establishment of a Chinese administration there, a part of the total T'ang achievement in creating an empire on the ruins of the Sui, give a false impression of finality. The triumph of the Hua over the Man was never complete.

Rather than contrive an impressionistic characterization of this cruel and terrible conflict, I am presenting here only a bare chronicle of the struggle of the autochthons to expel the hated aliens. The imaginative synthesis is left to the reader.

622 [9 November–7 December]: Lin Shih-hung (Lyĕm Dri-ghwĕng) rebelled in a remote part of Lingnan and sent his brother to attack Hsün (Zywin)-chou in the east. The enterprise failed and he took refuge in the grottoes of An-ch'eng Mountain, beyond the frontier.[133]

623, 26 May: rebellion of the chieftains P'ang Hsiao-kung (M.C. Baung Hăukyong), Ning Tao-ming (Neng Dau-mywăng), and Feng Hsüan (Byung Hywăn) in the Lien (Lyem)-chou [then temporarily Yüeh (Ywăt)-chou] and Kao-chou region along the coast. They seized an important Chinese town.[134]

——, 4 August: rebellion of Feng Shih-hui (Byung Dri-hwaai) in Kang[a]-chou. It was quickly put down.[135] Both he and P'ang Hsiao-kung had been acting as county magistrates ("Inciting Notaries") for the Chinese.

624, 3 July: the Lao of the Shuang-chou region rose but were soon crushed.[136]

——, 23 October: Chiang Tzu-lu (Kyang Tsi-lu) rebelled in Jih-nan near the Cham frontier. He was defeated by the Chiao-chou government.[137]

624: various chieftains of the aborigines who had held out against the T'ang finally surrendered. "So the southern quarter was settled." But troubles with the Lao tribes of Szechwan continued through the next several decades.[138]

626, 14 June: uprising of Lu Nan (Lu Nam) in Lien-chou (Yüeh-chou); he stabbed the notary Ning Tao-ming. (Ning's earlier rebellion had apparently been forgiven.) [139]

631: revolt of the Lao of Lo-chou and Tou-chou. Feng Ang (Byung Ang), a rich but popular half-breed, former representative of the Sui who had visited the T'ang capital to demonstrate his loyalty, was sent against them and put them down.[140] (Feng Ang was an ancestor of Kao Li-shih, whose name is famous because of his part in the romance of Hsüan Tsung and Yang Kuei-fei a century later. Kao, originally surnamed Feng, was a native of P'ang-chou. He was castrated in Nam-Viet and recommended to the court by a high provincial official. He had some portion of aboriginal blood, since Feng Ang was a descendant of a union between a creole of northern extraction and the daughter of a native chief. The clan was very influential in the coastal counties west of Canton.) [141]

633: Lao outbreaks north of Lingnan were partly repressed by an expedition from Kung-chou.[142]

638: more uprisings along the northern marches of Nam-Viet were put down by expeditions from Kuei and Chiao.[143]

640: the Lao of Lo and Tou rose again. An expedition from Kuang put them down and took more than 7,000 prisoners, male and female.[144]

651/652 [18 December–15 January]: rebellion of Li Pao-ch'eng (Li Bau-zheng) in Tou and I (Ngiĕ[b])-chou; repressed from Kuei.[145]

658: submission of the wild Lao of Lo and Tou, led by the chief To Hu-sang.[146]

663, 10 July: the Man chief Wu Chün-chieh (Ngu Kywĕn-kăi) revolted in Liu-chou. A campaign was mounted against him.[147]

667: Ch'iung-chou in Hainan was taken by the Lao.[148]

687 [14 August–11 September]: the Li people of Lingnan refused to pay increased taxes; their leader was put to death by the Protector of Annam; they rebelled, seized Chiao-chou and killed the Protector. An army from Kuei reduced them.[149]

694 [24 October–22 November]: rebellion of Lao in Lingnan; action against them from Jung and Kuei.[150]

703/704 [13 December–11 January]: Ou-yang Ch'ien of Shih-an (in Kweichow) rebelled with a great horde and took many towns in Lingnan. P'ei Huai-ku, the general sent against him from Kuei-chou, had the good sense to disagree with the accepted view that the aborigines were untrustworthy, and was able to persuade Ou-yang Ch'ien that he would deal fairly with him. The chief surrendered, along with many tribes, and there was peace in Lingnan.[151]

722: great insurrection against Chinese rule in Annam led by Mei Shu-yen (Mai Shuk-yen), self-styled "Black Theocrat" (*hei ti*), with the help of Chams and Khmers.[152] The Chinese general Yang Szu-hsü, a native of Lo-chou, enlisted a great horde of Man youths, led them along the old road to Annam, once used by Ma Yüan, defeated the barbarians with great slaughter, and built a pyramid or tower of their corpses to commemorate the victory.[153] This Yang, though an excellent leader of soldiers, was a harsh, bloody man, much feared by the aborigines. It is reported that he liked to take scalps, and peeled the skin from the faces of his prisoners.[154]

726 [7 February–8 March]: Liang Ta-hai, a Lao of Yung-chou, led a rebellion against the Chinese and seized Pin and Heng (Ghwăng).[155] Yang Szu-hsü spent the period from March of this year to January of 727 in crushing the revolt. He finally took Liang alive, with more than 3,000 of his followers and 20,000 heads.[156]

728, 3 March: the aborigines of Ch'un and Shuang, led by Ch'en Hsing-fan (Dyin Ghăng-bywăm), and of Kuang, led by Feng Lin (Byung Lyin) and Ho Yu-lu (Gha You-lu), rebelled and seized more than forty walled towns. Ch'en declared himself "Theocrat" and "Son of Heaven," with Ho as his army leader and Feng as subordinate "King of Nam-Viet." But the formidable Yang Szu-hsü disposed of this revolt too, and took 60,000 heads. [157]

742: in the forties of the eighth century the leading aboriginal clans were the Huang (Ghwang), the Wei (Wĕi), the Chou (Chou), and the Nung (Nong). Among them the Huang were paramount. They seized many *chou,* and when the Wei and Chou were reluctant to continue in a subordinate position, the Huang attacked them and drove them to the sea.

756: Huang Ch'ien-yao (Ghwang Gyen-yeu) and Chen Ch'ung-yü (Chin Dryung-iwĕt) led an uprising of the Man of the Wu-yang and Chu-lan Grottoes in Lu-chou (Annam).[158] This was the beginning of a series of insurrections coincident with the withdrawal of T'ang troops from Nam-Viet to fight against An Lu-shan and his followers in the north. The result was disastrous for the Chinese colonies in Nam-Viet. Native war chiefs surnamed Liao (Leu), Mo (Mak), Hsiang (Syang), Liang (Lyang), and Lo (La)—presumably the leaders of tribes of these names—declared themselves kings, and leading hordes totaling 200,000 men burned the Hua settlements of western Nam-Viet, carrying the residents off into slavery.[159] From 756 to 771 the administrators of Jung, who controlled the roads to Tongking, were obliged to take up humiliating residence at T'eng or Wu in the north, on the safe edge of the Kuei Administration.[160]

758: some of the Man leaders, with the promise of amnesty, were persuaded to turn against the others, resulting in the capture and decapitation of the greatest ethnic heroes, including Huang Ch'ien-yao, Mo Ch'un (Mak Zhwin), and Mo Hsün (Mak Zyĕm).[161] Soon after, the T'ang administrators were able to establish two new townships (*hsien*) in the "mountain grottoes" of Yung: Szu-lung and Feng-ling.[162]

767 [28 September–27 October]: an insurrection of "mountain Lao" in Kuei-chou drove out the governor, Li Liang.[163] A band of "Javanese" and other Indonesian pirates invaded Tongking; they were repulsed by the Chinese Protector of Annam, Chang Po-i.[164]

771: Li Mien, resident legate at Canton, and Wang Hung, the new Administrator of Jung, suppressed the aboriginal revolutionists in Jung, allowing Wang and his successors to return from their temporary headquarters in the north to the official residency of that province.[165]

773: rebellion of Ko-shu Huang, the Chinese governor of Hsün (Zywin)-chou; he seized Canton and killed the Legate. He and his followers were ruthlessly suppressed three years later by the new legate, Lu Szu-kung, who also exterminated the Li peoples involved in the revolt.[166]

774: the Po Nagar temple, the shrine of the patron deity of Champa near Nha-trang, was burned by lean, black, demoniac seafarers.[167] (Was this related to the raids on Tongking in 767?)

784–789: Tu Yu and Li Fu, successive legates in Canton, put down the Li tribes of northern Hainan, after "three generations of inhospitality in their hazardous bastions." [168]

787: a Cham sanctuary in Pāṇḍuranga was burned by Javanese soldiers.[169]

791: uprisings of the native chieftains Tu Ying-han (Du Yăng-ghan), Feng Hsing (Byung Hyăng), and his son Feng An (Byung An), in Annam. The immediate cause was a doubling of taxes by the Chinese Protector, Kao Cheng-p'ing. The new Protector, Chao Ch'ang, restored order.[170]

794: Huang Shao-ch'ing (Ghwang Sheu-k'yăng), chief of the Ghwang ("Yellow") Grottoes, attacked the Hua men of T'ang in Yung Administration and besieged the walled city of Ch'in (K'yĕm)-chou. While the imperial government vacillated, unable to decide how serious the situation was, the Huang men captured Ch'in (K'yĕm), Heng (Ghwăng), Hsün (Zyĕm), and Kuei (Kwĕi), then besieged Yung-chou town, the seat of the administration. In the end they took thirteen counties. A new commander, Yang Min, was sent to Lingnan, and he subdued the natives with "six or seven battles in one day." [171] But this was not the end.

807, 27 March: the Yung-chou government reported the capture of Huang Ch'eng-ch'ing (Ghwang Zhĕng-k'yăng), leader of the Man of the Western Plain Grottoes.[172]

808 [29 May–27 June]: Huang Shao-ch'ing surrendered. On 9 July he was awarded the post of a T'ang county magistrate ("Inciting Notary"); his younger brother was given a similar post. But they soon turned against the Chinese. Two

Huang groups seized Pin and Luan (in northern Yung, near the Kuei Administration).[173]

816, 23 November: Jung Administration reported raids of the Man of the Yellow Grotto.

——, 26 November: Jung Administration reported the repulsion of the Yellow Grotto Man, and the recovery of Pin-chou and Luan-chou.[174] These actions were part of a campaign undertaken by P'ei Hsing-li (Administrator of Kuei) and Yang Min (Administrator of Jung) with imperial sanction, but against the advice of K'ung K'uei, the prudent legate in Canton. The results of two years' fighting were inconclusive; countless T'ang soldiers died of malaria and other tropical diseases; new uprisings resulted from this "policy" of instant reprisals for the sake of the personal glory of provincial warlords.[175]

817, 19 January: Jung Administration reported that the Yellow Grotto Man had sacked Yen (Ngăm)—in northwestern Jung, on the Yung frontier—and slaughtered its inhabitants.[176]

——: King Harivarman of Champa claimed successful action against Chinese and Cambodians.[177]

819, 8 November: Jung Administration reported that Yang Ch'ing (Yang Ts'yeng; Vietn. Dường Thanh), an Annamese indigene, employed by Li Hsiang-ku, the Chinese Protector, as captain in charge of forces against the Huang-led insurrections in the east, had rebelled. Yang, faced with the farcical opposition of P'ei Hsing-li and Yang Min in the east, and aware of the rapacity and unpopularity of Protector Li in Chiao-chou, fancied the inevitable collapse of T'ang power in Nam-Viet. He led his men back to Chiao, and put the Protector, his family, and his supporters to death.[178]

——, 12 November: Kuei Chung-wu was designated Protector of Annam; Yang Ch'ing was pardoned and given the nominal post of "Inciting Notary" of Ch'iung-chou on the distant island of Hainan.[179]

820 [18 March–16 April]: Kuei Chung-wu arrived in Annam but was refused admission by Yang Ch'ing. Yang, however, met popular opposition for his brutality. Kuei got official disapproval for his procrastination, and P'ei Hsing-li was sent from Kuei-chou to replace him.

——, 15 May: Yang Ch'ing was killed by the Annamese; P'ei died on the road to Annam; Kuei was welcomed by the populace of Chiao-chou, and therefore his appointment was confirmed by the T'ang government.[180]

821, 28 January: Jung Administration reported the defeat of a host of more than ten thousand men under Huang Shao-ch'ing and the destruction of thirty-six stockades.[181] The Administrator of Jung, Yen Kung-su, asked permission of the imperial government to take strong punitive measures against the Huang people. Han Yü, in exile in Ch'ao-chou, sent a memorial to the capital, claiming special insights into the problem, despite the distance of his see from the scene of the troubles, by virtue of his many conversations with experienced and intelligent travelers. He accused the administrators of Jung of self-seeking and incompetence, advancing themselves by means of expensive and glorious actions in retaliation for slight misdemeanors on the part of volatile and ignorant aborigines. As a result, war had become chronic in Jung, to the detriment of Chinese prosperity and prestige there. Self-defense was one thing—harsh reprisals accompanied by greedy expropriation of lands was another. Han recommended the inauguration of a new imperial era to be named "Great Felicitations" (*Ta Ch'ing*), a slogan with overtones of congratulations on or celebration of the happy resolution of difficulties and patient benevolence towards all subjects of the theocrat; also the promulgation of an amnesty for the natives, and the careful selection of prudent and reliable administrators for the frontier regions. His petition was ignored, but the newly acceded monarch Mu Tsung did in fact adopt as his era name "Enduring Felicity" (*Ch'ang Ch'ing*)—perhaps this was intended to show some recognition of the wisdom of Han Yü's policy.[182]

823, 23 May: the Annam Administration reported that the Lao were plundering Lu-chou.[183]

——, 20 August: the Lingnan Administration reported that the Man of the Yellow (Huang) Grottoes were raiding in Yung Administration.[184]

——, 22 August: the Yung Administration reported that the Man of the Huang Grottoes had seized fortifications in Ch'in (K'yĕm)-chou.[185]

——, 19 September: the Yung Administration reported that it had smashed the Man of the Huang Grottoes.[186]

824, 20 February: the Lingnan Administration reported the ravaging of Ch'ing-chou by the Huang Grotto Man and the killing of T'ang officers there.[187]

——, 28 August: the Annam Protectorate reported raids by the Huang Man.[188]

——, 6 December: the Annam Protectorate reported that the Huang Man had joined forces with the Chams, taken Lu-chou and killed Ko Wei, the Inciting Notary.[189]

825/826: the Huang and Nung tribes seized eighteen *chou*.[190]

827–835: systematic reduction of native tribes by T'ang; the "Nung Grottoes" took the leadership among them and sought aid from the Nan-chao nation in Yunnan.[191]

828: revolt of Wang Sheng-chao (Ywang Shĕng-tyeu) in Feng (P'yong)-chou.

——, 10 August: Han Yüeh, Protector of Annam, captured and decapitated him.[192]

——, 8 November: the Jung Administration reported that the army of Annam had mutinied and expelled the Protector Han Yüeh.[193]

843 [25 November–24 December]: Wu Hun, Protector of Annam, compelled his troops to rebuild the city walls; they rebelled, burned the fortifications, and looted the storehouses. Wu Hun fled to Canton. The revolt was put down.[194]

846 [24 September–23 October]: Man raids in Annam; counterattacks by P'ei Yüan-yü the Protector, commanding soldiers from neighboring provinces.[195]

857 [May–July]: Man uprisings in Annam and Lingnan. Mutiny of the Jung-chou army. Sung Yai was given over-all command in Annam and Jung.[196]

858 [19 January–17 Feburary]: Wang Shih, the new Protector of Annam, fortified Chiao-chou city with a palisade and moat. When later the approaching Nan-chao hosts learned of it (we are told) they discreetly withdrew.[197]

——, 25 May: Wang Ling-huan, an army officer of Lingnan, led a revolt.

——, 5 July: Wang's revolt was crushed.

—— [15 July–12 August]: goaded beyond endurance by corrupt and rapacious administrations in Annam, especially that of Li Cho (853–856), who had compelled the indigenes to sell horses and cows for a measure of salt and had killed a native chieftain, the Annamese invited the great Nan-chao nation of Yunnan to invade their country. The first Tibeto-Burman assaults on T'ang territory began this summer.[198]

—— [13 August–10 September]: because of famine and rebellion in Annam, no tribute had been sent to Ch'ang-an and no donatives given to the troops for six years. Wang Shih, having taken vigorous action against the rebels, gave a great feast for his officers and sent "tribute" to the capital. Diplomatic communications between T'ang, Champa, and Cambodia were reopened.[199]

859: the Yunnanese took Po-chou (in Kweichow).[200]

860 [18 October–16 November]: in search of fame, Li Hu, Protector of Annam, went outside his own province and recaptured Po-chou.[201]

861, 17 January: taking advantage of Li Hu's absence, Nan-chao soldiers were welcomed in Tongking by the Annamese, and their joint forces captured the capital of Chiao-chou.[202]

—— [14 February–14 March]: the imperial government ordered the troops of Jung Administration and neighboring regions to take the field and rescue Annam from the Yunnanese invaders.[203]

——, 21 July: Li Hu drove the Yunnanese from the capital of Annam. But because of his earlier failure he was degraded and banished to Hainan. The T'ang government bestowed a handsome title on the father of a native magnate for whose death Li Hu had been responsible.[204]

—— [10 August–8 September]: Nan-chao troops reduced Yung-chou, which was inadequately defended by local militia. Though they departed during September, the responsible T'ang governor was degraded. His successor found only one-tenth of the original population of the towns remaining.[205]

862 [5 March–2 April]: another Yunnanese invasion of Annam; repulsed by a great T'ang army.[206]

—— [25 November–24 December]: 50,000 Nan-chao troops attacked Annam.[207]

862/863 [25 December–22 January]: Chiao-chou city was invested by the Yunnan-ese.[208]

863, 29 January: the Yunnanese, overcoming stout Chinese resistance, took Chiao-chou city on the very day when I Tsung sacrificed to Heaven on the Round Mound and amnestied All under Heaven. Aborigines came from far and wide to submit to the invaders. The T'ang government withdrew its conscript armies into Kwangsi.[209]

—— [22 February–22 March]: the barbarians pressed eastward along both banks of the Yü River towards Yung-chou.[210]

—— [20 June–19 July]: the Protectorate of Annam was abolished, and a "transient Chiao-chou" government was set up at the Stronghold of the Sea Gate (*Hai men chen*) in southwestern Po (Băk)-chou on the coastal road to Annam.[211]

—— [18 August–16 September]: the Protectorate of Annam was reconstituted in exile at Sea Gate, and garrisoned with ten thousand soldiers from Shantung.[212]

864 [11 February–11 March]: Chang Yin, Administrator of Jung, was given command of the exiled "Annamese" government at Sea Gate and instructed to recapture Tongking.[213]

—— [10 April–9 May]: Nan-chao and its allies, 60,000 strong, attacked Yung-chou. The Administrator, K'ang Ch'eng-hsün, claimed a great victory, having inflicted a few casualties on the local natives pressed into service by Nan-chao, and forced the lifting of a siege by burning the barbarian camp—another man's suggestion for which he took the credit. He was despised by his men.[214]

—— [6 August–4 September]: word of K'ang's ineptitude reached the capital, and he was removed. Chang Yin delayed his advance from Sea Gate and was replaced by Kao P'ien, a learned, witty man, who had gained fame by successful campaigns against the Tangut.[215]

865 [29 May–26 June]: a new army of 30,000 crossbowmen, called "South-quelling Army," was created in Hung-chou, far to the north in the valley of the Kan River in Hunan, specifically for the purpose of dealing with the native uprisings in Nam-Viet, and to take the pressure off the troops sent from the Yellow River Valley, who were suffering severely from malaria. Yen Chuan, head of the Kuei Administration, was put in charge of it.[216]

—— [24 September–23 October]: Kao P'ien raided in Tongking, and seized the newly reaped harvest of Feng (P'yong)-chou to feed his troops.[217]

866 [16 July–13 August]: Kao P'ien's successes were concealed from the imperial government by a rival at Sea Gate. The court ordered Kao's removal, but meanwhile he had inflicted a heavy defeat on the Yunnanese, and invested the walled city of Chiao-chou.[218]

—— [11 November–10 December]: the truth about the hero Kao P'ien reached Ch'ang-an; his titles and honors were restored. He crushed the armies from Nan-chao and their local allies, slaughtering them by the thousands. There was peace in Annam for the first time since the summer of 858.[219]

879: The outlaw Ch'en Yen-ch'ien (an aborigine?) captured Liu-chou city.[220]

894: in a single evening, Liu Yin, son of the chief magistrate of Feng (Pyong)-chou, who had just died, exterminated a band of more than a hundred natives who were plotting an insurrection. He was rewarded by the T'ang government with a military command on the Ho River (a tributary of the Yü which passed through Feng). Thus, with the slaughter of aboriginal martyrs, began the fortunes of the Liu family,[221] which, after a few years, founded the rich nation of Han and a unique and brilliant court in Canton.

To sum this up: after the first T'ang settlement of the south early in the seventh century, native resistance was concentrated in the western administrations of Jung and Yung, especially in the coastal counties between Canton and Hanoi. The Feng (Byung) and Ning (Neng) tribes were prominent in this resistance, which always threatened the main line of communications through Nam-Viet. The other administrations (Kuang and Kuei) in the north and east were relatively quiet.

There was comparative tranquility during the first half of the eighth century, except for vigorous revolt in Annam, and a series of insurrections in Lingnan in 722–728. During this period we also detect early signs of foreign interference (Chams and Khmers). Outbreaks became general in Nam-Viet after the mid-century rebellion of An Lu-shan, and there were "Indonesian" raids in Champa and Annam.

The great Huang uprisings began in 794 and continued through most of the first half of the ninth century. The second half saw a major rising in Annam, supported by a large-scale invasion from Nan-chao. It was suppressed by Kao P'ien, a new Hua hero in the mold of Ma Yüan. After 866 there was relative peace.

TURNCOATS

The soldiers who kept the T'ang yoke on the necks of the indigenes were by no means all Hua-men. Many of them were the native neighbors and natural allies of the peoples held in subjection. As Cortés used the Totonac people against the Aztec in Mexico, so did the Chinese employ some of their aboriginal subjects to bring others into subjection. Whether these turncoats served the lords of T'ang out of greed, or fear, or envy, or admiration, or ambition, or vindictiveness, their help tended to achieve the same end—the continuance of Hua domination over the Man. Man clients might even be used against Chinese: when, in March of 892, Wang Ch'ao, the popular young governor of Ch'üan-chou (later Zayton) in southern Fukien, the founder of a dynasty which created the short-lived Min nation there, attacked Fu-chou, the chief city of that province, he got considerable help both the men of the inland "grottoes" and the boats of the coastal Man.[222] But the acceptance of this valuable aid did not make Wang Ch'ao a friend of the Man peoples. In 894 he clinched the hold of the new regime on Fukien province by crushing the hosts of the Huang-lien Grotto, which had had the temerity to lay siege to T'ing-chou, a Chinese town in the western uplands.[223]

But, of course, aboriginal allies were always unreliable. Their ultimate loyalties were divided, and they were relatively undisciplined. For small problems of policing and defense they were adequate; for major campaigns they were useless. So, when the T'ang dominions tottered under all-out assaults, as in the great troubles of the ninth century, everything depended on regular Chinese troops marched down the river valleys from the north.[224]—native levies were quite unimportant.

The illustrious Kao P'ien himself, before he came to Nam-Viet, had employed an aborigine named Lei Man as a petty officer on his staff, but this man later made serious trouble for the Chinese.[225] It seems not to have been unusual for T'ang commanders to employ infidels who could achieve ends difficult for their lordly and noble officers. An instance is Tu Ying-ts'e, a "grotto notable" and lieutenant of P'ei Hsing-li, Protector of Annam early in the ninth century. Tu was able to do the Protector's dirty work, such as the execution of a Cham rebel looking for recruits in Annam and the capture of his family. He disposed of nuisances and got the Protector's indulgence in return. Official irresponsibility was the price of doglike devotion.[226]

Natives were also employed in the civil administration. This followed naturally from the assimilation, genuine or only hoped for, of the local populations to the Chinese way of life. Assimilation depended, irrespective of ethnic origin, on the acceptance of the Chinese language and other basic elements of Chinese culture—the axiom was "act like a Hua man, so be a Hua man." This process seems to have been especially easy when it proved acceptable (as it sometimes did, whether by compulsion or emulation) to the settled rice-growing aborigines of the south—already half-formed Chinese as they may have seemed to the invaders—with their simpler but not completely alien technology and society.[227] But probably the process was harder with the forest-burning, root-grubbing peoples of the uplands such as the Mak, as it is with the Yao today. In any case, when the aboriginal community seemed resigned to T'ang overlordship, a T'ang administration was set up to govern it. Thus when a settlement of Black Man in Liu-chou, presumably immigrants from further west, was "summoned and consoled" in 667, a *hsien* government—that is a local township administration on the Chinese pattern—was immediately established to hasten their conversion to civilized ways.[228]

These new governments were often placed in the hands of "reliable" native magnates, so that the magistrates appointed to represent the Chinese in frontier regions were identical with the hereditary chiefs of tribes. This system had the advantage of making Chinese rule palatable to the conquered people, but it strengthened the power of the chiefs, who tended more and more to assume the character of feudal lords, liegemen of the Son of Heaven—which did not prevent them from sometimes turning against their nominal suzerain.[229]

Such appointments were common from the beginning of T'ang rule: the son of a chief of the Western Ts'uan who had been put to death by the Sui was appointed chief magistrate ("Inciting Notary") of K'un-chou in 620, and his father's body returned for burial, in exchange for his submission to T'ang.[230] The Ning warlords had a long history of acting for the Chinese in this capacity—and were also fierce leaders of rebellions against them. A war chief of that clan had held office under the Ch'en dynasty; a certain Ning Hsüan (Neng Sywen) had governed Ho-p'u for the Sui; Ning Ch'un (Neng Zhwin) was Inciting Notary there in early T'ang times.[231] There were many other such appointments. Occasionally a native might rise to the very highest rank in the provinces: Chao Kuo-chen, Legate of Ch'ieng-chung (modern Kweichow) in 756, was a Tsang-ko barbarian.[232]

In the seventeenth century the selection of aborigines to occupy T'ang offices in their own former territory was put on a regular basis. In 669 the regional commanders in Kweichow, Fukien, and Lingnan were empowered to choose suitable natives for various administrative positions, without going through the Department of Personnel in the capital city.[233] This method of direct recruitment from among the local population was reaffirmed in 675 under the name "Southern Selection." [234]

Most of the counties established in newly pacified territories, having predominantly non-Chinese populations and governed by hereditary native chiefs approved by the conquerors, were styled "Bridle and Halter" counties *(chi mi chou)*, a name taken from the euphemistic vocabulary of conquest of classical antiquity: the Han Son of Heaven was said to "bridle and halter" the subjected barbarians by the force of his social conscience and responsibility.[235] Thus the bestial aliens were bound by the leash of Chinese moral superiority, which they duly recognized in accepting the novel but hybrid administration. From the earliest decades of the seventh century these internal colonies were established on all borders of the realm, northern and southern alike, and the official history of T'ang gives the incredible figure of 856 submissive counties (including those of Turks, Iranians, and the like) at one time.[236] At one indeterminate period of early T'ang, the histories yield a number of 92 Bridle and Halter counties just in western Lingnan and Annam, of which eighteen, ruled from Feng (P'yong)-chou in Annam, had authority over Ts'uan peoples, presumably emigrants from southern Szechwan and Yunnan.[237]

The creation of a native-governed county was sometimes urged by the Chinese governor in order to offset the attractions of assimilation to another powerful nationality, such as Nan-chao or Champa. Such a hopeful administrator was Ma Chih, Protector of Annam, who, in 838, urged the T'ang government to counteract the lures of the "Southern Man" (the Chams?) by elevating Wu-lu *hsien*, whose "dwellers in nests and holes" had been faithful in paying their tax levies, to the status of a *chou*, so giving its chief and people a dignity which they lacked and tending to make them more grateful to the T'ang empire.[238]

The new inspiring counties, and their subdivisions the *hsien*, often incorporated local ethnic names transmuted into Chinese vocables—including such common ones as Lo (La "net"), Lung (Lyong "dragon"), and Lin (Lyĕm "forest"), syllables important in aboriginal folk myth, heroism, and naming generally.[239]

CHAMS

Beyond the rich Red River valley and beyond what Tongkingese coastal settlements the soldiers of T'ang were able to hold for the Son of Heaven lay the strange kingdom of the Chams, known to the Chinese since antiquity as Lin-i (Lyĕm-iĕp). Until the middle of the eighth century, the holy city of this nation was near modern Huê, south of the Bay of Tourane.[240] Then the capital was moved south to Pāṇḍuranga, and after 758 T'ang men spoke of the country as Huan-wang (Ghwăn-ywang).[241] But they also called it Chan-pu-lao (Chem-pyou-lau "Chāmpapura?"), or simply Chan-p'o (Chem-ba "Champa"), or "Walled City of Champa" (Chāmpapura, Chan-ch'eng). This last name becomes prominent in Chinese records after 875, when the dynasty of Indrapura moved the capital to the north again.[242]

The *Book of T'ang* has this to say of it:

> That land is warm in winter, and has much mist and rain. It generates amber ["tiger soul"], *hsing-hsing* beasts [gibbons?], and *chieh-liao* (*ket-leu*) birds [hill mynahs]. They make the second month ["Old Book of T'ang" has "twelfth month"] the head of the year. Rice matures twice in a year. They make beer of areca juice, and mats of coconut leaves. They are ordinarily malignant and aggressive, but resolute in battle and contest. They daub their bodies with musk—daubing twice daily and washing twice. On courtesy visits they join their fingernails and incline their foreheads. They have written characters. They rejoice in the Way of the Buddha, and smelt gold and silver for images, the largest sometimes ten spans round. . . . The king's dress is of *bagtak* or *karpāsa* [cotton goods], draped slanting from his upper arm. For ornaments he has strings of golden beads. He is capped with a gold-flowered hat like a *chang-pu* ["blazoned man," an archaic Chinese ceremonial cap, attributed to the Shang dynasty]. His wife is costumed in a short skirt of "morning-cloud pink" *karpāsa* and hatted with jade-like bead strings. The five thousand men-at-arms of the royal guard ride elephants into battle; rattans make their panoply and bamboos make their bows and arrows. They marshal a thousand elephants and four hundred horses, divided between front and rear. They have set up no penal [code], but if someone is guilty of a crime they have an elephant trample him, though sometimes they escort him to Pu-lao [Pura "City"?] Mountain, with the gift of suicide.[243]

The account of the "Old Book of T'ang" is similar to this, but adds a few things:

> It adjoins Huan-chou. As to the airs of that land, winters are warm and they are unacquainted with mist and rain. At the walled city in which the king resides they have erected trees to make a palisade.

After information on costume, this text notes that the people are black, go bare-footed, and have "fisted" hair [done in a knot like a clenched fist, or merely curly?]; persons of the same surname marry [incestuous sin to the Chinese]; the bodies of the dead are burned in their coffins on funeral pyres—the ashes are put in metal jars and released in the sea. The Chams sent the gift of a "fire orb"—a crystal sphere to concentrate the sun's rays—to T'ai Tsung: it was a lustrous, glittering white, the size of a hen's egg, and could be used to start fires from the rays of the sun.[244]

Archaeology has revealed more about the Chams of that age. The earliest surviving examples of their public architecture are of the ninth century (those of the Khmers are of the eighth century and those of the Javanese of the seventh century).[245] We do know something about Cham art in the eighth century, however, from the beautifully vital sculptures of bearded deities which once adorned a great temple at Mi-son in the capital near modern Huê. This art shows plainly the influence of the style of Gupta India.[246]

In general the warm-red brick tower sanctuaries of Champa, sometimes erected in clusters of two or three along a north-south axis, were much simpler than the enormous sandstone monuments of the Khmers. A little granite was used for such accessories as lintels.[247] All temples open to the east. They are characteristically decorated with pilasters and bulbous ogival moldings above layered doors and false doors. All ornamentation shows a high degree of symmetry. The inner sanctuary had a corbeled ceiling and contained the image of the god, either male or female, beneath which was a *yoni*-basin to catch asperged holy water.[248]

The oldest surviving buildings, the towers of Hoa-lai, belonging to the Pāṇḍuranga realm in the south, show the influence of Dravidian art of the eighth century.[249] This ninth-century architecture has been characterized as noble and classic despite the bizarre floral arabesques which often appear on its pilasters of "burning-red" brick.[250]

During the last quarter of the ninth century, a new style appears. It is represented by the Mahayana Buddhist ruins of Dông-dưởng, the first appearance of this religion in Champa, under the auspices of King Indravarman II.[251] These buildings appear just when the capital had been moved back towards the north. This manner is less classically Indian in appearance, and has an indigenous look—barbaric and tropical.[252]

Then, at about the beginning of the tenth century, a third style appears, this time at Mi-son. It is characterized by a supple and graceful sculpture, such as the justly famous dancing girl of Tra-kiêu, an undoubted nymph and peri.[253] This last development, at a time when the T'ang empire lay in ruins, corresponds to a period of profound Javanese influence on all phases of Cham culture, including both the arts and the science of magic.[254] This was also the period when Sivaite inscriptions in classical Sanskrit, telling of pious gifts and foundations, decrease in number, while monumental texts in the vernacular Cham tongue become more abundant.[255] These texts reveal that in the ninth and tenth centuries, despite the spectacular rise of Buddhism, the bare-footed, ear-ringed kings and queens of Champa, clothed in fine cotton, gold, and fragrant flowers, still worshiped the great image of Śiva, whose moustached face was also the face of the King of the Chams, and paid highest homage in elaborate ceremonies to full-breasted Bhagavati, his consort, known as Po Nagar "Mistress of the Kingdom," on her lotus throne at Nha-trang.[256] It seems that Sivaism remained the aristocratic cult, while Buddhism was the faith of the people.[257]

After the sack of the Cham capital by the soldiers of Sui early in the seventh century, a pseudo-Chinese administration was set up in the conquered land, with three "county" (*chün*) administrations, including the county of Lin-i, that is, of Champa.[258] The Chams quickly regained their independence during the troubles accompanying the collapse of the Sui empire, but prudently sent an embassy in the spring of 623 with gifts for the first ruler of T'ang. These fortunate envoys were entertained by a full-fledged turnout of the nine imperial orchestras.[259]

King Kandharpadharma (Mand. T'ou-li, M.C. Dou-lei)[260] sent another friendly mission in the summer of 630. It presented a trained elephant, fine mail armor, a many-colored sash, "sunrise clouds" pink cotton, a fire orb (mentioned above), a parrot, and a white cockatoo. Along with the Cham ambassadors were representatives of two Indonesian countries—Bali (P'o-li, M.C. Ba-li) and a place called Rākṣasa (Lo-ch'a, M.C. La-tr'ăt).[261] This last nation, whose name is also that of anthropophagous demons, has been identified with both the Nicobars and Ceylon. Its association with Bali here may be casual, but suggests also the possibility that it may have been Timor. In any event, the Chinese court deemed the letter brought by the embassy disrespectful to the majesty of T'ang, and demanded that punitive measures be taken against the Chams. The great T'ai Tsung replied proudly that as conqueror of the Sui emperor and of a great Turkish qaghan, he would gain no merit from such a foolish and unnecessary pretext for war.[262] A nominal, or perhaps only hoped-for, extension of T'ang power southward from Huan-chou led to the establishment of a "bridle and halter county" in Cham territory in 635, but it seems that T'ang had no real control over it.[263] However, goodwill missions from Champa to T'ang continued sporadically until the chaotic years in the middle of the eighth century. The Chams seem to have made inroads on Annam during the next fifty years, since, early in the ninth century, the T'ang Protector there, Chang Chou, with the pretext that the Chams had sent no tribute, led a campaign against the "counterfeit" administrators of Ai and Huan. He won a great victory on 5 October, 809, cut off 30,000 Cham heads, captured fifty-nine king's sons, and took much booty, including war elephants.[264]

There is a mystery about the Chams. Of the remnant of the great people which survives among their ancient enemy in southern Vietnam, about one-third (seven or eight thousand souls in 1891) are Muslims. There is an even larger *émigré* population of Muslim Chams resident in Cambodia.[265] They tell that Lord Allah reigned over their ancestors in the year A.D. 1000. Georges Maspero, the historian of Champa, says of this proud tradition that "il ne semble pas . . . que la religion de Mahomet ait été pratiquée par les Chams avant l'année 1470 qui marque la chute de la royaume de Champa."[266] There is also a small colony of Muslim Chams on the southern coast of Hainan, whose language is more like that of such "proto-Cham" hill tribes as the Radé and Jarai than it is like classical Cham;[267] though they have a tradition that they came to China from the "Western Regions" in T'ang times, and though some say that they reached Hainan in the Sung period, there is no certain knowledge of the time of their arrival.[268]

It seems to me that Aymonier was right when, in 1891, he made the then rash statement that there were Muslim Chams as early as the ninth or tenth century.[269] Indeed there must have been a considerable number of them living among their Sivaite and Buddhist countrymen by the end of the ninth century. This hypothesis, otherwise startling and incredible, would explain the statement in the *History of the Five Dynasties* that the customs of the Chams are "the same as those of the Arabs [lit. Tajik]."[270] It is supported by the Chinese record of the reception of the ambassador of the Cham monarch Indravarman III by the ruler of Chou in 958. The envoy, who brought with him rose water, flasks of Greek fire ("fierce fire oil"), and precious stones, was named (according to the Chinese) P'u Ho-san (Pyu Ha-san)—plainly Abu Hasan, though Maspero did not notice this.[271] King Jaya Indravarman I sent this same man to China again in 961 with a letter on palmyra leaves in an envelope of fragrant wood, and an offering of ivory, camphor, peacocks, and twenty "Tajik [Arab] vases" for the new Sung emperor.[272]

That the influence of Islam was not restricted to the commercial ports where Arab traders congregated is shown by a statement in the *History of Sung*. After noting that among the animals used by the Chams, aside from the water buffalo and the yellow ox (both familiar to the Chinese), there was the "mountain ox" (a banting or a kouprey?) which they did not hitch to the plow but killed as a sacrifice to the ghosts. When about to kill it, their "shamans" invoked it thus: "*A-la-ghwa-gyĕp-băt*" (M.C.), which can be translated (says our source) as "May it soon live in another body!"[273] Despite the pious Buddhist hope for the reincarnation of even a lowly sacrificial victim, claimed as the meaning of this ritual formula, it can hardly be other than butchered Arabic: "Allāh hu akbar!"—"God is great!"

Inscriptions in Kufic script found in southern Vietnam with dates in the second and third decades of the eleventh century show that Muslims, probably merchants and artisans, were well established in Pāṇḍuranga at that time.[274] Probably the infiltration of Islam into Champa was mainly the result of commercial activity:

to the merchants of the ninth century Champa was a rich land, above all the source of heavier-than-water aloeswood even better than that of Cambodia, which they called *čanfi* "of Champa."[275]

It seems likely that if the notables of medieval Champa were Indians or indianized Chams, most usually worshipers of Śiva or Vishnu or other aristocratic Indian gods, and the commons chiefly followers of the compassionate Buddha, there was also an aggressive Muslim bourgeoisie, partly foreign and partly native, already of some size at the end of the ninth century, whose presence was noted by the unbiased Chinese recorders, even if neglected by the courtly Cham scribes.

OTHER FOREIGNERS

Although the aboriginal peoples of Nam-Viet suffered severely under their exploiters, few of them got much profit from their misery. In contrast, seaborne foreigners, though often badly mistreated by the masters of the Chinese realm, hoped for and often gained rich rewards for their pains. These strangers, temporary or permanent, were concentrated in the rich but somewhat makeshift city of Canton, seat of the offices of the T'ang government. Hither came the variegated peoples of the Indies, many of whose ethnic origins can now be hardly distinguished. Yet we can detect among them merchant princes of India and Ceylon with glittering jewels, and hook-nosed seamen of Iran and Arabia with magic incenses— all of them quarreling in their privileged sanctuaries and haggling in their noisy markets.[276] These crowds of ambitious aliens were heavily augmented by unwilling immigrants, destined for the stables and seraglios of the north:

> Argosies laden with slaves from the sea—rings slung from their ears;
> Elephants burdened with girls of the Man—bunting binding their bodies.[277]

But the strangers were not confined to the great port. Some of them found their way into the disease-ridden forests—most, it seems, for religious reasons. Indian monks attached themselves to monasteries in the relatively safe eastern half of Lingnan, above all in the many sacred precincts of Mount Lo-fou in Hsün (Zywin)-chou. Their special knowledge of the well-developed sciences and arts of Buddhist India brought them positions of influence and prestige, at least among the Chinese neophytes who sat at their feet. One of the latter was the monk Huai-ti, a native of Hsün (Zywin)-chou, who became a first-rate Sanskrit scholar through studying with these visitors on the great holy mountain. Lingnan was, it seems, an important center of advanced Indic studies in T'ang times.[278] Epigraphic remains show that even westerners from Turkestan settled in these remote regions. "The stone chamber of Anna of Bukhāra,"[279] with other relics of the mid-seventh century, has recently been discovered near Kuei-lin—she was a spiritual sister of Anna of Kabūdhān,[280] a performer of the whirling dance a century later, and concubine of the emperor Hsüan (Ghwen) Tsung.[281] There is also evidence of the presence of a native of Māimargh, probably a displaced soldier, in Kuei-lin in the eighth century.[282] Perhaps these bewildered refugees were seeking consolation and peace in the remote and quiet jungle temples of Nam-Viet.

All the fabulous wealth of Canton was brought by foreigners in search of profit. It came chiefly in the form of precious substances—gems, woods, drugs, and incenses. Much of the profit departed in the form of silks, porcelains, and slaves:

> The sky-linked waves are quiet—the long whales breathe out,
> The sun-reflecting sails are many—the treasure argosies come.[283]

So wrote Liu Yü-hsi early in the ninth century. His older contemporary, Han Yü, told of the cargoes of these ships: "The commodities of the outer nations arrive daily: pearls and aromatics, rhinoceros and elephant [horn and ivory], tortoise shell and curious objects—these overflow in the Middle Kingdom beyond the possibility of use." [284]

Such riches inevitably brought trouble with them—not only by encouraging venality and corruption among the Chinese, but by causing the exploitation and even the death of the wealth-bringers themselves. A supreme example is the visit of Huang Ch'ao to the city in the autumn of 879. In the early summer, the great revolutionary had demanded of the frightened court in Ch'ang-an the high command in Canton. His request was denied, lest the wealth of overseas commerce fall into his hands. Angered by the offer of a lesser post, he seized the city quickly and put the Legate to death. A medieval Arabic text tells that he massacred 120,000 foreigners there— Muslims, Jews, Magians, and Christians—and cut down the city's mulberry trees.[285] Late in that year the rebel army undertook the systematic looting of the province, but as the men suffered greatly from malaria, their leader was obliged to take them northwards again, by way of Kuei-chou and the Hsiang River.[286]

Great as this disaster was, the plunder taken by Huang Ch'ao could hardly have equaled a small part of the exotic booty garnered over the years by the official representatives of the T'ang government. Since Han times it was accepted tradition that the overlord of Canton enrich himself by gouging the aborigines and mulcting the foreign traders, perhaps as a result of sipping the Spring of Avarice at the Stone Gate north of Canton.[287] "When the traders first arrive in the argosies from the South Sea, after a selection has been made of such superior rarities as elephant [tusks], rhinoceros [horn], and luminous pearls, they must always, by and large, sell these at a reduced price." An outstanding practitioner of this venerable art was Hu Cheng, who held power in Lingnan in 826 and 827. His rapacity gained him a vast estate in Ch'ang-an, staffed by several hundred slaves.[288] His name belongs with those of the rascally governors we have already listed. His antithesis, the noble Wei Cheng-kuan, whom we saw earlier in the role of iconoclast, achieved his unique reputation for honesty twenty three years later chiefly because he made no such exactions.[289]

Official venality could have serious consequences for the prosperity of the city itself. During the second half of the eighth century the exactions were so insupportable that a great part of the commerce coming up from the South Seas was diverted to Lung-pien, the port of Chiao-chou (Hanoi), and trade in Canton came virtually to a standstill, though this situation improved materially during the early decades of the ninth century.[290]

A special form of this disease has been attributed to the rascality of the palace eunuchs. It is reported that, as early as 709, the lady Wu "Modelled on Heaven" and the puppet emperor watched their palace girls play at tug-of-war, and amused themselves at a "palace market"—a kind of frivolous mock market for palace inmates, having antecedents in the scandalous reign of Han Ling Ti, centuries before.[291] The name "palace market" turns up again fifty years later, applied then to the interference of palace eunuchs in commerce, both in Ch'ang-an and in Canton. They compelled the sale of goods on their own terms, as the powerful agents of the Son of Heaven. This plague troubled sensible men (including Han Yü) throughout the second half of the eighth century.[292] Although we hear no more of the direct manipulation of luxury commerce by eunuchs after the beginning of the ninth century, these haughty courtiers continued for a while to control the lucrative appointments to the high posts in Nam-Viet, for which they received substantial bribes. The text which describes this situation, quoting an address to the throne on 25 January 837, goes on to say that even this prerogative had now been taken from them.[293]

In 714 the complaints of the oppressed foreigners and the worries of the fiscal officers brought about the creation of a special imperial commission in Canton, whose business was to bring some order into its disreputable affairs, while seeing to the regular collection of anchorage charges from visiting ships, and assuring the regular transmission of all profits to the imperial treasury, without the intervention of private fingers.[294] The incumbent of this high office—at first often the prize of important eunuchs—had under his watchful eye "The Man barbarians from Liu-ch'iu (then Formosa?), Ho-ling (Kalinga, in Java?), and as far west as Bactria and Samarkand—nations ringing the waters to be numbered in the hundreds." [295]

New relief given to commercial enterprise in the far south during the early decades of the ninth century must be credited to good regimes in the capital, notably the reigns of Hsien Tsung (806–820) and Wen Tsung (827–840), and, corresponding to them, the appointment of sensible and ethical administrators in Canton and Hanoi—such men as Ma Tsung, whose virtue was such, says the panegyric of Liu Tsung-yüan, that it attracted "the great Man barbarians from the midst of the sea, together with argosies floating from west to India." [296]

[The chief's wife] was of good stature, with blacke eies, fat of body, of an excellent countenance, hir haire almost as long as hir selfe, tied up againe in pretie knots, and it seemed she stood not in that aw of hir husband, as the rest, for she spake and discourst, and dranke among the gentlemen and captaines, and was very pleasant, knowing hir owne comelines, and taking great pride therein. I haue seene a Lady in England so like hir, as but for the difference of colour I would haue sworne might haue beene the same.

Sir Walter Raleigh, *The Discoverie of the Large, Rich and Bewtiful Empire of Guiana*, 1596

4 Women

IF I GIVE special attention to the women of Nam-Viet, it is because, like the disgraced politicians and alchemically minded hermits, they had a special part to play in the southern drama.

It has often been said that the role of woman in pre-Han China was much more significant than it has been in our own era.[1] Without making extreme claims about an archaic "matriarchate," it seems reasonable enough to admit that in Shang and early Chou times, the mother, the clan ancestress, the tribal genetrix, had a great role in cult and belief. Above all, the female shaman—medium, dancer, and exorcist—whose body was the actual but temporary repository of the spirits, and whose soul could be sent on frightful or lovely journeys into the hidden worlds of sky and earth, was a common and important figure in the cultural life of north China in the Bronze Age.[2] But in fact female shamans and goddesses never died out in China, despite their exclusion from the official cult during the past two thousand years. The female principle loomed large—even though explained away by accepted "Confucian" exegesis—in the classical literature of China, especially in the songs and chants of the *Shih ching* and the *Ch'u tz'u.* We find it markedly present, perhaps unexpectedly, in the book *Lao tzu,* whose twenty-fifth chapter is a hymn to Tao, conceived (as elsewhere) in feminine terms: "We may take it to be Mother of all under Heaven—I do not know its name, but I style it 'Way-shower' [*Tao*]." One scholar has enthusiastically declared that this entity was a primeval water goddess, the eternal source of man and his culture, probably having originated in the wetlands of the south.[3] Another has even called it the great mother goddess of the Thai peoples, who leads her children in the right path.[4] Indeed it is hard not to see in some of the language of the *Lao tzu* the semblance of the Babylonian ocean mother Tiâmat, source of all creatures. But probably Lao-tzu's Tao was closer to Whitehead's "inscrutable womb of things beyond the ken of rationality"[5] than to the personified cult object advocated by Erkes and Rousselle. At any rate, no trace of the primordial womb of the universal mother can be found in respectable thought of post-Han times, though she may remain in esoteric Taoist writings, concealed behind other figures. In her place, and in place of the dreaming, haunted shamanesses of antiquity, we get, in the Yellow River valley at least, the survival of the anti-woman or amazon—warrior viragos like Hua Mu-lan, and vigorous politicians like Empress Wu.[6] This was an old type too, and, as, a specimen of patriotism, was allowed some semi-official admiration alongside of the meek and self-effacing daughter and wife. The woman openly admired for her special womanly powers is little to be seen—unless perhaps in the antisocial images of hetaira or fox spirit in the short stories of T'ang civil-service candidates.

In the south, however, it was a different story. Evidently matrilineal descent and associated customs, along with shamanesses and goddesses, were once widespread both north and south—indeed, some investigators consider this culture-type characteristic of the whole of Indochina and Indonesia in ancient times.[7] A wave of male supremacy submerged this culture in the north, but it lingered on, in greater or lesser degree, in south China. As early as the Han period, respectable opinion saw something unnatural in the prevalence of the female spirit in Nam-Viet: "The land of Viet abounds in women. Male and female share the same river: the wanton female is dominant."[8] Water goddesses survived in Nam-Viet long after the last girl was drowned in the Yellow River to become the consort of the river god.[9]

In T'ang times, the barbarism of female supremacy beyond the expanding southern frontier must have irritated the austerely male sensibilities of the northern aristocrats and made them itch to abolish it. Early in the seventh century the Chams were ruled by a royal princess—did the knowledge of this alien enormity augment the shame of the old guard in Ch'ang-an and Lo-yang, subjected to the Empress Wu later in that century? But if the story of a tribute-bearing embassy from the "Country of the Female Man," in the middle of the ninth century is true, glamor might almost compensate for impropriety: "They had steep chignons and golden hats—beaded necklaces covered their bodies. Therefore they were called 'Bodhisattva Man' [here Man is the ethnic name]. Accordingly, the gleewomen and players of that time fabricated the 'Song of the Bodhisattva Man.' Literary gentlemen too, now and then, have publicized this air." [10] Though the identity of these jeweled ambassadresses and their relation to a popular song are today somewhat in doubt, the tune undoubtedly existed in late T'ang times, and had an exotic and erotic appeal which more than made up for the outlandish eccentricity of its eponymous theme. The Chinese knew other "Kingdoms of Women" in Indochina and Indonesia,[11] and the modern Chams, Cambodians, and Siamese have their own tales of such unlikely cultures, presumably fed by the same tradition which nourished the Chinese stories.[12]

The venerated figure of the warrior maiden remained as much alive in Nam-Viet as it did in the north, usually to the confusion of the Hua-men, since the aboriginal heroine was no partisan of the conquerors of her own people. Most famous of them, even down to our times, were the sisters Cheng Ts'e (Tyĕng Tryĕk) and Cheng Erh (Tyĕng Nhi), leaders of the Lo (Lak) people. In A.D. 40, indignant at the outrages suffered by their nation at the hands of the Chinese imperialists, they raised a rebellion. The oppressed natives rallied to their banners, and they seized more than sixty walled towns in Annam and southwestern Kwangtung. The intrepid Cheng Ts'e (Vietn. Trung Trac) was hailed as queen in her royal stronghold above the Red River delta.[13] The Han conqueror Ma Yüan, the Wave Subduer, put down the insurgents two years later, captured the heroic sisters, and chopped off their heads.[14]

Another maiden of Nam-Viet, called Chao, had the singular distinction of breasts five feet long. This prodigy rode into battle on the head of an elephant, wearing golden pattens and attended by a bodyguard of young men.[15]

Such traditions of female warriors were still alive in T'ang times, and there were still women who could fill the role. For instance, a warrior maiden of tenth-century Lei-chou, with a band of devoted followers, built a citadel to defend herself against "marauders." [16] Unfortunately we know neither the ethnic identity of this amazon nor that of her marauding enemies.

Not quite in this same tradition, but equally interesting, is our Cinderella, who makes her first appearance in world literature in the ninth century as an aboriginal girl—one of the Man of the Western Plains in Yung-chou.[17] She has a wicked stepmother, a friendly magical fish with red fins and golden eyes (the "fairy godmother"), a cloak of blue halcyon feathers, and golden shoes. She ultimately marries an island king who finds one of the shoes. Arthur Waley thinks this story may have come to the Man tribes of Nam-Viet from the Mon kingdom of Dvaravati, far to the south.[18]

Unhappily, the average woman of Nam-Viet could not figure as a romantic heroine. Rather she could be preyed on like an animal. There were the lustful "women pinioners" who lay in wait on deserted roads with bands of young men carrying white staves—when an attractive woman passed by they bound her and carried her off to be used for a month or two.[19] Ordinarily she was regarded—and well regarded—as a cook:

In the instruction of girls in a household of Lingnan—we need not ask if it is rich or poor—they do not take the needle and floss, and spinning and reeling, to be the right work for them; rather it is personal attendance on kitchen and pantry and zeal for the working of the knife—nothing else. One who excels with vinegar, meat pickle, vegetable pickle, and fish pickle becomes a greatly admired woman. Surely this cannot be a heaven-given temperament in a remote borderland?! But, for this reason, if one of the Li folk, disputing a marriage arrangement, should speak to another thus: "My daughter tailors robes and repairs jackets!" then obviously there would be no union. But if she had cultivated the preparation of water snakes and yellow eels, that single thing would surely win out over any other item.[20]

So we have the heroine and the housewife—but what of the belle, the mistress, the erotic object? We cannot now discover what qualities the warriors of the Ning and the Mak looked for in their sweethearts, unless possibly by analogy with modern times: "Dans les légendes de l'Annam, la jeune fille apparait auréolée d'une grace printanière, mais jamais elle n'a ces désirs, ce charme languissant et sensuel, cette sensibilité frémissante, ces ardeurs passionées dont nos poètes ont paré la femme d'Occident."[21] Like the French in Indochina, the Hua invaders of the early middle ages brought with them a parcel of images into which the ideally beautiful "girl of Viet" could be expected, with some luck, to fit. But it was no native Man sensibility, no true Lao vision, which colored their appreciation of the girls of Nam-Viet. It was a dream of southern loveliness which they had inherited from the remote past —above all, it was a literary tradition and its symbols were entirely verbal.

For the Chinese, the south had always been the land of seductive women and attractive landscapes. An imperishable tradition has the locus of these delights in ancient Viet—that is to say, chiefly in modern Chekiang, south of the mouth of the Yangtze.[22] The chief denizen of this archaic wonderland in the late Chou period was an unlettered country girl—a supreme beauty. Her name was Hsi Shih (Sei Shiĕ). The hoary legend tells that this simple enchantress was educated in the feminine arts by the King of Viet for the purpose of corrupting his rival the King of Wu (Ngu), reigning on the coast just north of him. There are ambiguous tales about the relation between the lovely milkmaid (the transferred rococo epithet seems appropriate) and the famous vizier Fan Li, who escorted her to the court of Wu. It has even been said that she bore him a son on what must have been a very slow northward progress. Whatever the true facts, Hsi Shih has always been the Cleopatra, the Thaïs, and the Queen of Sheba of China. She is every southern beauty—and yet she is unique. Her radiant loveliness was still celebrated in T'ang times. Here is Li Po (Li Băk):

Women

> Hsi Shih, a woman of the streams of Viet—
> Luminous, ravishing, a light on the sea of clouds.[23]

In many nostalgic clichés the southern girl was pictured sitting in a small boat, languidly gathering nenuphars in the warm sun, and blushing at the approach of a stranger. Here is an example from an eighth-century poem:

> Houri of Wu or enchantress of Viet—consorts for a King of Ch'u;
> A playful tussle in the lotus boats—water dampens their dresses.[24]

In the ninth century Han Yü placed the time-honored girl of ancient Viet in tentative juxtaposition to the spectral creatures of southernmost medieval Viet. The beginning of her transference southward appears in this fragment:

> A Viet woman's single laugh—a three-year stay;
> Southward over the transverse pass—into the Continent of Flame
> The high reach of a blue whale, where wave mountains drift;
> The dazzling blaze of a weird troll, where heaped krakens coil.
> Mountain *sao* brawl and bawl—*hsing-hsing* apes roam;
> Poison vapors dissolve the body—yellow grease flows.[25]

(*Sao* are nude prawn-eating pygmies mentioned in an old book; *hsing-hsing* are probably hoolock gibbons.) Many other poets helped to prepare the geographical shift of the classic imagery, especially those poet-politicians who served the imperial government in demeaning exile, some in the subtropical zone south of the Yangtze watershed, some beyond that in the margins of the true tropics—such gifted men as Wei Ying-wu, Po Chü-i, and Liu Yü-hsi, who took pleasure in southern plants and southern geishas, and were attentive to the songs of the south.[26] These poets of the eighth and ninth centuries were the precursors and prophets of a few daring writers of the tenth century, whose fancies were truly tropical, who caught the heat and the violent colors of Nam-Viet even when they employed the conventional figures of the "girl of Viet" and her "lotus boat" in any number of mutations.

Outstanding among these innovators were two poets of tenth-century Szechwan, composers of *tz'u*—poems of irregular meter made to fit popular airs. Their names were Ou-yang Chiung and Li Hsün. Not a great deal is known of their careers. Ou-yang Chiung is almost entirely identified with his native province, and literary men know that he wrote a preface to a famous anthology of *tz'u* (including his own).[27] The story of Li Hsün is more complicated. His ancestors were Persian. His younger brother Li Hsüan sold aromatic drugs for a living in Szechwan.[28] Most important for reconstructing his biography: was he the same person as the Li Hsün who wrote an important treatise on imported drugs called *The Basic Herbal of Overseas Drugs?*[29] The identity of names, the relation between Iranian origin and overseas interests, and the remarkable coincidence of the one's medical studies with the profession of the other's brother, might seem enough to persuade us that poet and pharmacologist were one and the same. There is another connection: despite Li Hsün the poet's brilliant career at the small but splendid court of Shu, a number of his poems show a real feeling for the warmth and color of Nam-Viet—as indeed do some of those of Ou-yang Chiung, who is not known to have visited that region. Even more, they suggest first-hand acquaintance with Lingnan. But Li Hsün the student of sea-borne medicines could hardly have failed to investigate the markets and emporiums of Canton, and interrogated the Persian dealers who were, in any case, his ethnic kinsmen. I find it easy to see one Li Hsün here—hard to see two.

Those poems of Li Hsün and Ou-yang Chiung which express the true tropical flavor are matched to the tune *Nan hsiang tzu,* perhaps translatable as "The Southern Villager." [30] The song, with whatever forgotten words, had been one of those taught at the palace academy for singing girls and upper-class courtesans. [31] The syllabic structure of Ou-yang Chiung's settings is 4/7/7/2/7 or 4/7/7/3/7, while that of Li Hsün's realizations is 3/3/7/7/3/7—that is, five verses for Ou-yang's stanzas, six verses in Li's stanzas. By convention, *tz'u* poems never have individual titles—all poems set to a given air have the traditional name of that air. Sometimes the language of the *tz'u* was appropriate to the name of the tune. [32] This was certainly true of the *Nan hsiang tzu* creations, which are always full of the warm, amorous south. The ear-ringed courtesan in the following *tz'u* by Ou-yang Chiung could hardly be anything but a native girl of Lingnan (I give a word-for-word version to show the syllabic structure):

> Twice/eight//flower/filigree.
> Breast/front/like/snow//face/like/lotus.
> Ear/pendant/gold/ring//pierce/lapis-/lazuli.
> Aurora/dress/tight.
> Laugh/reliant/river/head//beckon/far/visitor. [33]

A free rendering might go like this:

She is sweet sixteen, wearing floral hair-ornaments of gold;
Her bosom is snow-white, her face like a pink lotus.
Golden rings hang from her ears, pierced for lapis-lazuli studs;
Her rose-tinted dress clings tightly.
She laughs confidently by the river bank, and beckons to the stranger come from afar.

Although this stanza could be regarded as a conventional reiteration of the theme of "girl of Viet," there is an eroticism in its wickedly enticing portrayal of her which was taboo to most writers. Here she is in another of Ou-yang Chiung's *tz'u:*

> In a painted shallop, she stops the oars
> Beyond a hedge of hibiscus flowers, at a bamboo-studded bridge.
> Men roving on the water; women on the sand;
> She turns, looks back—
> Laughs, and points to her dwelling inside the banana grove. [34]

Women

The hibiscus hedge and the banana-hidden hut may possibly be in Szechwan, but the spirit is the spirit of Nam-Viet. But there can be no doubt about this *Nan hsiang tzu* by the same author:

> Sleeves gathered up—they are raw shark silk—
> Gathering aromatics in the deep grotto, she invites me with a laugh.
> From the tip of her branch of rattan cane, reed-wine drips;
> She spreads a palm-leaf mat.
> Among the cardamom flowers—the sun runs towards evening.[35]

("Reed-wine" is wine meant to be sipped through a hollow reed; apparently she has a gourd bottle slung at the end of a pole.) This poem is full of the imagery of Nam-Viet: the shark-people's silk (pinna-mussel textiles?); aromatic plants and deep caverns; rattans and fan palms; above all the red flowers of the spicy cardamom. Of all the poems of Ou-yang Chiung in this style, this is the most tropical. He was obviously entranced with the romance of Nam-Viet—did he know it only by repute, perhaps from conversations with Li Hsün?

In still another *Nan hsiang tzu,* Ou-yang Chiung has a grotto, a red-sleeved maiden, a "southern estuary," and a magnolia boat.[36] The magnolia boat (literally "tree-orchid boat"—the "tree orchid" is *Magnolia obovata*) and the painted boat are the characteristic vehicles of these southern courtesans—for courtesans they seem to be. Their claret cheeks are as artificial as the blushes of Greuze's milkmaids.

But now look at a *Nan hsiang tzu* in the peculiar form used by Li Hsün:

> Her cloudy chignon heavy—
> Her kudzu garment light—
> She sees a man—a slight laugh, with much emotion.
> Catching kingfishers? gathering pearls? of what is she capable?
> Is it come on, or go away?
> Can she be the equal of a village-dwelling girl—a weaver at the loom? [37]

(Kudzu is a vine which yields a fiber woven into a fine linen.) Here two facts are clear. First, the woman is a geisha, though perhaps an amateur. Second, the scene is Nam-Viet: the gaudy turquoise kingfisher, whose feathers were indispensable in the jeweler's trade, and the equally popular pearls were both in T'ang times automatically recognizable symbols of Lingnan and Annam, those countries of exotic gems.

These two poets celebrated the beauties of southern flowers and southern women in the rather sentimental manner characteristic of the tenth century *tz'u* genre. They couched their pictures in imagery traditionally associated with ancient Viet—that is, Chekiang—much enriched with the newer and bolder images of Nam-Viet. Their language is a strange mixture, from our perspective, of good "classical" style and what appear to be vernacular constructions. In any case, the hot, bright figures sketched by Li Hsün were probably derived from immediate experience. Many examples will appear further along in this book. We cannot be so sure of those of Ou-yang Chiung.

One problem remains: were the voluptuous charmers of these poems Man aborigines or Hua immigrants? As pearl divers they seem to be the former; with white bosoms, the latter. Probably they are idealized native girls, invested with traits attractive to the Chinese. Their sisters appear in our tropical romances:

The princesses of the coral atolls wore necklaces of the scarlet clianthus, a flower that is a parrot beak or lobster claw. Those are for skins of cinnamon or sandalwood, as are diadems of living fireflies, and frangipani flowers.[38]

Perhaps progress had been made. Renovated metaphors had begun to transform mere mares and tigresses into real women—cyprians perhaps, but entirely lovable.

*I'd seen the tropics first that run—new fruit, new
    smells, new air—
How could I tell—blind-fou wi' sun—the Deil was
    lurkin' there?*

Rudyard Kipling, *McAndrew's Hymn*

5 *Divine Beings*

Taoists

NEWLY ARRIVED Chinese must have been much consoled by the presence of the
partisans and initiates of the great eastern religious-philosophical systems in the supposedly uncultivated south. Prominent among these were the professors of the Tao
—the Way attributed to such semi-legendary mahatmas as Lao Tan and Chuang
Chou, and later defined by historical ascetics, occulists, yogins, and alchemists in
their several arcane and jealously advocated traditions. By proper breathing, thinking, praying, or eating, these adepts hoped for a transformation of their bodies into
a higher and better condition. To adopt the insect imagery (as they often did) they
hoped to progress, by means of these thoughts, airs, and reagents, from the larval (or
merely human) state, by hidden way of active nymph or quiet pupa, to the ultimate
condition of triumphant imago, as winged transcendents or lovely peris—super-
human cicadas or butterflies.

The story begins with the apparition of five transcendents mounted on goats, the
spiritual founders of Canton.[1] But these anonymous and gossamer godlings counted
for little in local memories when compared with the renowned Ko Hung, a Taoist
apologist and refugee in the south during the troubled fourth century. It is said that
he hoped to find in Annam the superior chemicals needed for the experiments described in ancient books which he had inherited, aimed at the perfection of the elixir

of life. His southward progress was halted at Canton by the governor, and so he settled on Mount Lo-fou, the holy hill, where he continued his experiments until his death.[2] So says tradition. He was still a prominent but ghostly figure there in late medieval times, along with his reputed wife, the fairy named Pao Ku, that is "Aunty Pao."[3] During the "Heavenly Treasure" reign of the Taoist monarch Hsüan (Ghwen) Tsung, in the first half of the eighth century, a great temple was founded in his name on Mount Lo-fou.[4]

There was another center of Taoist tradition at Fu-ch'uan in Ho-chou, in northern Lingnan between Shao and Kuei. Here was a building said to have been the house of Heavenly Teacher Chang, now converted into a shrine. Magical fruits grew there, and there was kept a pestle, spoon, and alchemist's cauldron left by the master. This Chang was a lineal descendant of Chang Tao-ling, leader of the great evangelistic movement of the "Yellow Turbans" in Later Han times, and he bore his holy ancestor's title by virtue of inheritance. He is said to have been transfigured at this place in A.D. 353 in a temple called "Cinnabar Sunset clouds."[5]

Many places in Nam-Viet were sanctified by visitations of whole clusters of the immortal saints of Taoism. Remote mountain peaks were most commonly chosen as the scenes of such collective epiphanies. One such was a peak in distant Hsiang-chou, where the transcendents and "their feathered rigs are sometimes seen."[6] Another was a village in Kuei-chou (later named "Hamlet of the Assembled Transcendents") where a host of these divine beings appeared in their winged vehicles in broad daylight—"spread across the indigo void"—as the villagers gazed in wonder.[7] Then there was the assemblage of five hundred flower-headed immortals (though some say they were Bodhisattvas) amusing themselves on a peak of Mount Lo-fou; the spot was consecrated by the erection of a "Terrace of Flower Heads" by pious edict of Hsüan Tsung in 738.[8]

Most eminent among the Taoist adepts of T'ang Nam-Viet—it is hard to say whether they are to be considered as human or divine—was the mysterious Hsüan-yüan Chi. History tells that he enjoyed the fine title of "Mountain Man" at the Taoist court of Wu Tsung. He was driven away in 846 by the reforming Hsüan (Sywen) Tsung, and retired to Mount Lo-fou in his home province of Lingnan.[9] Late in his life Hsüan Tsung, having allowed the partial restoration of the Buddhist church in T'ang, showed some interest in Taoism, and in 857 summoned the Mountain Man of Lo-fou back to the capital to answer questions on the prolongation of life.[10] Hsüan-yüan Chi reached the divine metropolis during the winter of early 858. Here are his words to the sovereign: "If a Kingly One reveres virtue, while fending off desire, he will automatically receive great and lasting felicity. In what other place will he look for long life?"[11] This simple recipe is consistent with another opinion reliably attributed to the Master. He was asked whether governing was difficult, and replied, "If simplified, it is easy." When asked whether Confucianism and Buddhism were ultimately the same or not, he said, "If straightforward, they are the same."[12] A preface to a *Grand Auroral Jade Book,* attributed to his pen, survives.[13] This historical image of the laconic sage is very different from the popular tradition of him. Indeed, his name itself is an omen of his reputation. He was commonly styled Hsüan-yüan Hsien-sheng. The family name Hsüan-yüan was the name of an archaic sky god, sometimes lord of rain and thunder, sometimes garlanded with stars, like the moon— and indeed in an ancient myth the moon itself is called "Mirror of Hsüan-yüan." As for the title Hsien-sheng, it means "first-born," and was used respectfully of nominal elders in wisdom, virtue, or incarnation, and, especially in T'ang times, of gloriously long-lived Taoist initiates. As early as 876, Su O recorded the legend of Hsüan-yüan Chi: the first-born, even after a life of several hundred years, retains a youthful appearance; his hair hangs to the ground, and his eyes dart brilliant light in a darkened room; gathering rare herbs among the crags, he is guarded by poisonous dragons and other fearful creatures; his magic powers are incredible—he can change his form at will, and once made fresh-flowering cardamoms and lichees appear in Ch'ang-an before the Son of Heaven himself.[14] At about the same time, P'i Jih-hsiu composed a poetic fantasy about the ancient of Lo-fou (possibly he was still alive then):

> A confusion of peaks—four hundred and thirty-two;
> One wishes to ask for the "Bespoke Lord"—but in what spot can he be found?
> Red halcyons—several voices echo in gemmy rooms;
> Sandalwood—a single wick deep in a stony loft.
>
> A "hill citizen" is sent to pack in wine from the vintner,
> A "fuel porter" is allowed to look at gold after its conversion.
> Henceforth a court visit to the City will not be deemed too far—
> If the office-seeker first owns the heart of Ko Hung.[15]

An explanatory paraphrase follows:

The first-born is hidden among the many peaks of Lo-fou;
How shall one find him—this great man honored by an imperial summons?
Rare and beautiful kingfishers, winged gems of Nam-Viet, call outside the holy grottoes,[16]
Exotic incense burns in his lonely cell.
Even a wine-bibbing gibbon ["hill citizen"] is innocently permitted to fetch his wine;
Doltish woodcutters are honored by the sight of the golden elixir.
The way to the court is now made easy:
Provided that the candidate is a hermetic alchemist.

In a poem made to match this, Lu Kuei-meng, good friend of P'i Jih-hsiu and a connoisseur of tea, acclaimed the supremacy of Hsüan-yüan Chi in the underground paradises of Lo-fou.[17]

In T'ang times, the hope for eternal life in a world of light and beauty, so oddly akin to the old Christian belief in an enduring life lived in a new and better body in a shining palace in the sky, was still very much alive. It is now virtually extinct, and the memory of its great evangelists and anchorites has decayed—their images have faded even more than those of the monkish competitors, the yellow-robed seekers of Buddhahood.

BUDDHISTS

It would be strange if the first Chinese and foreign Buddhists had not been concentrated in Nam-Viet in early times, since this was an important stage in the propagation of that faith by the sea route beyond the Indies. Indeed, the philosopher Mou Jung, a resident of Annam in Later Han times, makes it clear that Buddhism was flourishing there during his lifetime.[18] It appears that this religion and its attendant philosophical systems were at first better established in the barbarous western part of Nam-Viet (in Wu-chou, for instance)—we may imagine monasteries and missionaries deep in primeval forests, surrounded by demons and headhunters. But by the fourth century Canton was becoming a notable shipping hub; the center of gravity shifted to the east, and more Indian monks were to be seen in the sea-ports than in the mountains.[19] The great exemplar of the sea-borne monks was Bodhidharma, who came to Canton in the sixth century, stopped long enough to point out a place to dig for riches (the wealth turned out to be in water not in gold), and moved on northward to the centers of power—a bird of passage, like so many early notables of Nam-Viet.[20] Yet his influence, and that of the Indian Vinitaruci who came to China soon after him, must have been considerable, since in T'ang times the Ch'an (Zhen; Jap. Zen; from Sanskrit Dhyāna) sect was established in Nam-Viet, with the school which emphasized the Laṅka (Leng-chia, from Laṅkāvatāra) Sutra predominant.[21] Bodhidharma's name is also associated with the chief Buddhist establishment in medieval Canton—a temple in the western market of that city founded in the fourth century by the Indian monk Dharmayaśas. It had originally been styled royal garden (Wang yüan szu), but the men of T'ang called it Dharma Nature (Fa hsing szu)— except for a brief period during the reign of the Empress Wu when it was Great Cloud (Ta yün szu) and a short spell as a Taoist temple under Wu Tsung. In modern times its name has been Shining Filial Piety (Kuang hsiao szu). The sage is said to have stopped off here on his journey north, and an old well called Dharma Well commemorates this visit. It can still be seen on the temple grounds, small, but very deep.[22] Some important Buddhist relics of the T'ang age are also preserved there. There is a pagoda erected late in the seventh century to preserve a holy relic of Hui-neng, the Sixth Patriarch—a bit of his hair. This was restored in the seventeenth century.[23] A roofed pillar inscribed with the text of the *Dharani Sutra*—a relic of tantrism in Nam-Viet—is dated 826.[24] A cast-iron Pagoda of the Thousand Buddhas was erected in the year 967, when the free and independent state of Southern Han reigned here.[25] Finally, there are a number of inscribed marble tablets.

Another important temple was the one styled Light of the Sea (Hai kuang szu) on the coast not far from Canton. It was adjacent to the "Confucian" Temple of the God of the South Sea, which protected the great argosies upon which the wealth of Canton depended. Here weary Buddhist pilgrims might rest and give thanks for their safe arrival before going on to the great metropolitan temples of T'ang.[26]

Recent archaeological exploration has also discovered extensive remains of T'ang Buddhism in the Kuei-chou region, that is, in the northern part of modern Kwangsi. Here, on several peaks and cliffs, are Buddhist images of the seventh and ninth centuries, quite unlike the well-known Buddhist statues of Tun-huang, Yün-kang, and Lung-men in the north. Instead of the austere, uncompromising influence of Gandhara—that is, of the Hellenized Indian style of Bactria—we find simple, good-natured Buddha-figures (Akṣobhya and Vairocana are among them) showing resemblances to the Javanese style of Borobudur, probably under the sea-borne influence of Dravidian India rather than the caravan-carried influence of Aryan India.[27]

Liu Tsung-yüan believed, as many did, that the stubbornly superstitious savages of Nam-Viet might be brought to the light of civilization by the mediation of the Buddhist faith. He tells that when he arrived in Liu-chou in 815 he learned that four Buddhist temples had been built there, three of them north of the river, serving the needs of six hundred households, and one south of it, for three hundred families. This last, the Great Cloud temple (a construction of the reign of Empress Wu like others of that name) had long ago been destroyed by fire, so that the natives of the south part of the town had now reverted to the worship of their old brutish gods. Indignantly, the good governor "chased these gods into the concealing distance and seized their land." Nearby he found a small household of monks, which he greatly expanded, giving this new creation the old name of Temple of the Great Cloud.

I built a great gate, affixing a tablet with that appellation. I erected school rooms to east and west, and a shrine for the worship of the Buddha, where students might reside. I assembled disciples there, and made them an allowance of food. I had them strike lithophones and beat bells, to give dignity to the Way and so to transmit its message. So the men again began to reject their phantoms and to desist from killing, and to press on with devotion towards humanity and love.[28]

Liu planted trees and bamboo groves about the restored monastery, appointed three monks to govern its affairs, and rejoiced in the completion of his pious work in the autumn of 817.

In spite of these evidences of the zealous efforts of both immigrant divines and native administrators to bring the pure faith to the ignorant heathen, so that in a few towns at least its acolytes thrived, the account of an eyewitness observer does not incline us to see Nam-Viet as a truly Buddhist province in T'ang times. "The men of the south," wrote Fang Ch'ien-li, the geographer-administrator, "do not, in the main, believe in Shakya." Not only that, but some of the monks in the few southern monasteries were not too scrupulous about their vows:

Among them are one or two monks who take pleasure in embracing women and eating flesh. They just stay in their houses, incapable of disentangling even the smallest matter of Buddhism. When an autochthon mates his daughter to a monk, they call her "Mistress Teacher." [29]

Nonetheless, Fang does not assert that such unedifying conduct was the rule in Nam-Viet, only that the faith was still little developed. In any case, a number of eminent ecclesiastics honored Nam-Viet Buddhism during the T'ang period. Some were immigrant missionaries, such as Kan-mat-ta-la (the Chinese transcription of his name) who debarked at Canton in 738, bringing an iron statue of the Buddha to Mount Lo-fou,[30] and the thaumaturge Vajra, a native of India, who lived at Ch'ing-yüan north of Canton in the middle of the ninth century—his magic staff and powerful Sanskrit spells could bind demons and monsters, and make the thunder roar.[31] But some eminent Chinese masters, especially of the Zen sect, were also to be found in Nam-Viet during those years,[32] among them (tradition tells) the great court astronomer I-hsing, builder of a monumental armillary sphere, whose name is associated with Yellow Cloud Mountain not far from Canton. The mountain got its name, it is said, after a visit of the scientist-priest, who loved the natural beauty of the place, during which he was illumined by the golden glow of a divine cloud.[33]

When Sung Chih-wen first arrived in Shao-chou, his heart full of bitterness, he made a point of calling on Hui-neng, whose preeminence among the monks of Nam-Viet he recognized.[34] Indeed that man was not only the glory of southern Buddhism, but one of the few great creoles of the T'ang period. His reputation was comparable to that of Chang Chiu-ling, and he was easily the peer of the Taoist patriarch Hsüan-yüan Chi. Hui-neng's secular name was Lu. He was born in Hsin-chou in 638. His father was a northerner, sent into exile there. Of his mother we know nothing—possibly she was an aboriginal woman, since when the young man went to Hupei to hear the Diamond Sutra expounded by the Zen patriarch Hung-jen, that holy man spoke to him in these words: "You are a man of Lingnan. Further, you are a *ko-lao* (*kat-lau*)! In what way are you fit to become a Buddha?" Hui-neng replied. "My *kat-lau* body is not the same as your *Upādhyāya* body—but in what way do they differ or deviate in respect to Buddha nature?" [35] This seems to mean something more that that Hui-neng had the manners and habits of the barbarians among whom he had been brought up. To me it means that he was an aboriginal Lao. But whether he was a Lao on his mother's side or not, even his official hagiography admits his Lao ways: "Although he was soaked and dyed with the airs of the Man and the customs of the Lao, they were not deep in him." [36]

Hui-neng was accepted as Hung-jen's disciple and served him patiently for eight months. A rivalry developed between him and Shen-hsiu, another disciple of Hung-jen. Shen-hsiu maintained the Laṅka doctrines which were not firmly entrenched in T'ang, both north and south. Salvation came by way of hard study, he believed, and the elimination of disturbing thoughts through disciplined meditation. Hui-neng, on the other hand, relying on the *Diamond Sutra,* rejected the notion that some part of the mind was worth cultivating and another part worth discarding—he thought of the mind as indivisible, and pregnant with the Buddha nature, which might suddenly be discovered there without the necessity of elaborate philosophical and religious preparation. The views of Hui-neng ultimately triumphed, and he was officially but posthumously recognized as the Sixth Patriarch in 790.[37] He is regarded as the founder of the "Southern School" of Zen, a sect tending to be subversive of institutionalized religion. His doctrine of immediate enlightenment is expressed in a sermon preserved in the so-called *Altar Sutra,* or *Platform Scripture* as it is sometimes called. This is said to be the only original Chinese sutra honored by inclusion in the Buddhist canon.[38]

Hui-neng died in 713, at the age of 76, in the odor of sanctity—the fragrance is said to have persisted for several days. His monuments were his scripture, propagated by his disciple Fa-hai, and later by Wu-chen,[39] a fine statue of him which still stands at the site of the medieval "Forest of Treasures" monastery (Pao lin szu) by Ts'ao Stream at Ch'ü-chiang in Shao-chou where he had preached,[40] and a funerary inscription telling how he persuaded the aborigines to give up killing both men and animals and to subsist on a vegetable diet, composed by the famous Wang Wei.[41] A century later—on 17 November, 815—Hui-neng was canonized "Dhyāna Master of Great Discernment" (*Ta chien ch'an shih*) by imperial decree. His reliquary at Ts'ao Stream was entitled "Stupa of Holy Illumination." A memorial inscription composed on this occasion by Liu Tsung-yüan summarizes the teachings of the saint:

> His Way—
>   to take the absence of striving to be actuality,
>   to take the void and vacant to be substantiality,
>   to take the broad, large and unruffled to be his final home.
> His doctrine of Man—
>   from the first his nature is good,
>   in the end his nature is good.[42]

GODS

The old Chinese religion, including the approved religion of T'ang, was a conglomeration of state, local, and family cults, in which the worship of nature gods was a significant element. It was, in short, similar to ancient Roman paganism and to Shinto, the native religion in Japan. In the west, the Roman religion was obliterated by Christianity, whose fervent monotheism could not permit the continued existence of a rival pantheon (except where local gods were metamorphosed into "saints"). In Japan, Buddhism, with its complex ethics, metaphysics, and promises of personal salvation, was not so exclusive—the coexistence of the old nature religion was not forbidden. Something like this happened in China too after the advent of Buddhism. But there, in most periods, the ruling classes tended to be xenophobic, and could not long tolerate a religion alien to the indigenous tradition. Therefore, despite its success in medieval China, reaching a climax in T'ang times, Buddhism has not survived into modern times on the highest levels of society. The archaic pre-Buddhist forms of worship remained, however, severely eroded into popular cults and vulgar superstitions, except for the part of them which had been transformed by the aristocracy into a state cult—a purely ceremonious, formal, and impersonal system of behavior and belief—the great gods were worshiped as was needful for the stability of the natural order, but they were infinitely remote from the emotions and imaginations of the elite.

Most of the men of T'ang who came into Nam-Viet held, or had held, some official rank, and therefore accepted, some perhaps only outwardly, the official cult. Many of them also adhered to some form of Buddhism, which yielded satisfactions for inner needs which the state religion failed to supply. In both cases, any simplifying doctrine—though not necessarily a simple one—offered the newcomer some psychic protection against the bewildering or intoxicating complexities of the pagan jungle, whether it was the tradition-steeped political-religious dogmas embodied in the high person of the godlike theocrat, or the hope of nirvana revealed in the placid countenance of the Buddha.

Such seems to have been the case with Han Yü. Though he rejected the alien and dangerous beliefs of the Buddhists,[43] he took a strong interest in the religious life of Nam-Viet, and there can be little doubt that the ancient "Confucian" doctrines (i.e., the official nature and hero cult) helped to support him during his exile among the barbarians.

The great man seems to have puzzled a good deal over the nature of the spiritual world, whose existence he did not deny. He once made a classification of the several kinds of being, as follows:

Entities with form, but without sound—as earth and stone.

Entities without form, but with sound—as wind or thunderclap.

Entities with form and with sound—as men and animals.

Entities without form and without sound—as ghosts and spirits.

Despite their extremely insubstantial condition, spirits could occasionally embody themselves in natural objects or acquire transitory substantiality for the purpose of revealing the rebukes of Heaven to erring men—so a usually silent and bodiless ghost might become visible as a sign of the approach of a well-deserved plague or earthquake.[44]

During his sojourns at various provincial posts, including that on the southern coast, Han Yü wrote many prayers to the nature gods. Among them was his inscription in honor of the God of the South Sea; another was an address to the

Great Lake Spirit at Ch'ao-chou after unseasonable rains had ruined the rice and silkworm crops, in which he offered himself as a scapegoat for the suffering people.[45] This last was one of five prayers to gods important to farmers which he wrote during his stay at Ch'ao-chou. On one occasion he wrote a prayer to accompany an offering of "aromatic fruits," praying "to the spirit of the blue dragon of the Eastern Quarter" for relief from drought in Shao-chou.[46] He has also left a sacrificial ode to the manes of his fever-ridden young friend Liu Tsung-yüan, who had died at his post in Liu-chou in 819, with an offering "to the numen of my departed friend, Liu Tzu-hou." [47]

Here then was a pious Confucian magistrate, behaving with strict propriety on the edges of the tropical jungle and the monsoon-driven ocean. He was also supposed to show honor to the relatively newly recognized city gods—the deities of the walls and moats of the fortified towns in which Chinese culture was preserved against the threats of savagery. The ninth-century poet Li Shang-yin has left us a number of reverent texts addressed to the protector spirits of the citadels of Kwangsi and Kweichow.[48]

Most popular among the officially recognized gods, though nominally ranking far below the deities of the mountains and seas, were the revered spirits of ancient heroes, protectors and expanders of the Chinese realm. The formal recognition by the T'ang court of the godly status of a considerable array of popularly honored soldiers and administrators began early in 731, when regular sacrifices, comparable to those for Confucius himself, were initiated in the metropolitan cities to such heroes as Wu Wang of Chou, Chu-ko Liang the peerless knight of the third century, and even Li Chi, who, in command of the troops of T'ang, had subdued the Koreans on behalf of the first glorious monarch of that nation.[49] This expansion of the official pantheon was closely related to the rise of royal iconography in the eighth century,[50] especially in the times of Hsüan (Ghwen) Tsung, and was climaxed by the casting of images of that sovereign for worship in every county of the realm.[51]

In the mind of the medieval man, deified heroes and divine rulers were hardly to be distinguished from the long-remembered kings of prehistory—most of them euhemerized tribal gods, formerly endowed with totemic and animalian characteristics. One of these was Shun, who was supposed to have traveled in southern Hunan and northern Nam-Viet. He was particularly remembered in Shao-chou, a place named for the music, called *shao*-music, he performed in that region. Traditions of him abounded there, many of them connected with old, strangely shaped stones.[52] Shun's animal was the elephant. The name of the god-king is intimately tied up with the region of Hsiang "Elephant" established by the first Chinese conquerors in Nam-Viet. Hsiang was also called Hsiang-lin "Elephant Forest," a name connected symbolically with Lin-i "Forest City," the old Chinese name for Champa. Shun was, in a sense, the supreme protector of the Hua men in the tropical forests, whose great elephants he tamed and whose contumacious savages he subdued.[53] It was said that

Shun had used elephants to plow his lands in Ts'ang-wu, and that his brother, named "Elephant," had been awarded the fief of Yu-pi "Possessor of Nose."[54] Old legends such as these sometimes disturbed the intellectuals of T'ang, who took them to be history. They must therefore be bad history, they thought. Su O, for instance, took the inconsistencies in these tales seriously and asked how Shun could, as reported, have visited Nam-Viet if he lived to a rarely ripe old age, as also reported? Surely all the poisons which infest that land would have caused his early death![55] Despite his special relation to Shao-chou, Shun's most important temple was west of there, in Kuei-chou. It stood by a crystal tarn at the foot of Mount Yü:

> His elemental numen roams this land,
> In the trees at his shrine the sunlight flashes.[56]

So wrote Sung Chih-wen. The archaic god was prayed to with the flying of flags and beating of drums to bring rain to the farms of that region.[57] Chang Chiu-ling, when he was chief magistrate of Kuei-chou, asked other things of the deity—to help him in carrying out his mission "to constrain and systematize the customs of the borderland."[58] The text of a prayer of thanksgiving to Shun, written at his shrine by the elegant Li Shang-yin, full of pious clichés from classical books, also survives.[59] It had long been supposed that Shun was buried at Chiu-i Mountain in southernmost Hunan, overlooking Kuei-chou. The holy music of Shun could sometimes be heard there, even in T'ang times. The Taoist Shen T'ai-chih, for instance, a kind of spiritual speleologist of the eighth century, exploring the mysterious caverns of the south, was told that there had been a band of five heavenly musicians in a grotto of that mountain. Captured by peasants, they had turned into pigs. Shen traced the pigs to a cave, and found them petrified. Striking them yielded beautifully resonant harmonies, and accordingly the holy man carried them off to present to the emperor Hsüan (Ghwen) Tsung. This story is vouched for by Wang Wei, who wrote a memorial of congratulation to the sovereign on that occasion.[60] In another story Shun is pictured as a great deity in the Taoist style. He appears in the sky, with the sound of heavenly music, the shine of unearthly light, and the odor of divine perfumes, and accompanied by a host of heavenly beings mounted on fabulous beasts. He himself wears a jeweled hat and a cloak of feathers, and is girded with a sword. This magnificent apparition is for the benefit of a female adept engaged in yoga-ascetic practices by the mountain sanctuary. The god delivers a long homily on the frailty and frivolity of secular life and an account of the subterranean geography of Mount Chiu-i, with its hidden mineral palaces guarded by poisonous reptiles and every kind of ferocious animal, and tells of the nine rivers which issue from it, with names like "Water of the Silver Flower" and "Water of Eternal Security." Impressed by her sincerity, Shun gives the maiden his personal instruction with the result that ten years later she ascends to heaven in broad daylight.[61]

Still, despite the special reverence given this antediluvian paragon, some of the captains and kings of the heroic times of Han loomed almost as large among the respectable gods of Nam-Viet. High among them was the King of Viet, the formidable Chao T'o, the peer of the founder of the Han empire. His voice could still be heard through the mouths of mediums: "In shamans at the shrines is the spirit of Chao T'o." [62] Li Shang-yin addressed a grateful ode to this god, like the one he made for Shun.[63] The hero is said to have been buried at Yü Mountain near Canton city.[64] A fine tale of late T'ang times tells of a visit of a young man to his tomb, transformed into a Taoist grotto. Here it is in synopsis:

The time is the end of the eighth century. Ts'ui Wei, a well-to-do youth of Canton spends his inheritance. He helps an old woman. She gives him some potent mugwort, with which he heals a strange man who, ungratefully, decides to sacrifice the young man to a familiar demon. He is rescued by the stranger's daughter, flees into the forest, and falls into a pit where he heals a boil on the lip of a serpent-dragon. The happy dragon carries him deep into the bowels of the rock, where they find a splendid palace. Here he is faced with four riddles: 1. its unnamed prince is absent at a banquet with the god Chu Jung; 2. a lady named T'ien is introduced as his destined bride; 3. he is given "a national treasure, the Solar Igniting Orb"; 4. he is sent home riding on a white goat with the "Emissary of Goat City." All of this is mysterious repayment by the lord of the underground palace for a service done him by our hero's remote ancestor. In Canton, he learns that he has been absent three years! He sells the orb to a foreigner in the Persian Bazaar, who tells him that he has surely been in the tomb of Chao T'o, King of Nam-Viet, since the jewel, a treasure from Arabia, had been buried with him. Later, the young man sees the effigy of the emissary with the figures of five goats at the temple of the god of the city wall and moat—he was, of course, the protector god of Goat City, that is, of Canton. The Lady T'ien is actually brought to him by four ladies-in-waiting. She was the daughter of an ancient king and the concubine of Chao T'o. She had been sacrificed with her four attendants upon the king's death, and entombed with him. The old woman who gave him the mugwort was Pao Ku, wife of the alchemist Ko Hung. So all that had transpired was a pseudo-historical charade. Ts'ui Wei acquired an immortal body from a drink given him by the dragon (another "historical" character), and disappeared from human ken into the fastnesses of Mount Lo-fou.[65]

In the traditions of the Chinese, at any rate, and probably also among the aborigines, no ancient hero could compare with Ma Yüan, the Wave Subduer of Later Han. His is a rich and persistent story. His title of honor, given him as he was about to leave for the conquest of Annam in A.D. 42, was not uniquely his. It had already been bestowed on a certain Lu Po-te, about to lead a fleet on the same errand in 110 B.C., and it was awarded again to other admirals during the following centuries. The title implied more than a mere master of ships and oceans—its bearer was also seen as a conqueror of the barbarians of the Four Seas, sometimes figured as fish, sea serpents, and dragons.[66] Ma Yüan deserved the epithet more than most. He conquered the water everywhere. Whenever he went through a town, "he pierced channels for watering and irrigation, and so profited their folk." [67] Indeed, in later tradition he was a great tunneler and dike builder. Texts of the fourth and fifth centuries have him pushing roadways through mountain barriers and rasing dikes against the incursions of the sea. He became, in short, a typical culture hero like so many of the ancient gods—or (for the Han period) like such other heroes of technology as Li Ping, who played a role similar to his, but as a digger of wells in Szechwan.[68]

Ma Yüan was also associated with monumental bronze castings, and with the construction of monumental gateways. The two themes are conjoined in the story of the bronze columns he built on the southern frontier of Han.[69] It was commonly remembered that there were two pillars, but sometimes there were said to be three, or even five. They might survive transmuted into cliffs or isolated rocks, or as mountains, or even as islands in the sea.[70] Sometimes they existed on a magical island off the Annamese coast, where "soft gold" (an alchemical elixir) could be found.[71] They are all analogues of the Pillars of Hercules, dramatically marking the spiritual frontier between civilization and barbarism, between Hua and Man, between China and Champa, giving protection against monsters—heavenly barriers against creatures of darkness, brought down to earth.[72] It is said that the Sui armies passed by Ma's pillars in Nam-Viet on their way to the pillage of the Cham capital.[73] In T'ang times, they were still believed to exist. Indeed a governor of Ai-chou in southern Annam conceived the profitable notion of melting them down and selling the copper to merchants—although he had not yet found them. Unfortunately the natives regarded the pillars as divine barriers protecting them from death at the hands of "men of the sea." They complained to the Protector of Annam, who ordered the governor to give up his dangerous plan.[74] This anecdote it attributed to the first half of the ninth century. In the same era, the Protector Ma Tsung was honored by the erection of two bronze columns by the aborigines, glorifying him as a new Ma Yüan.[75] But it was said in early Sung times that other pairs had been erected there, not to mention a set raised in Nan-chao.[76] In one account, the original columns of Han survived on the seacoast of Champa, far to the south.[77] But whether further north or further south, on land or on sea, they marked the imagined point of transition between the bright dependable world, and the dark, slippery realm of ghosts and non-men.

A ghostly ship of bronze is also associated with the name of Ma Yüan. Here is one account of it:

Ma Yüan built a bronze boat to cross over the sea. Later he ordered it sunk at an islet. When the sky is bright and the water clear, you may at times see a double-decked ship there, far off. One name for it is "The Ship of the King of Viet." [78]

Usually, however, the bronze boat looms up out of the mist over a lake on dark, rainy days. It has been reported in many places, though it turns up most commonly in the region of Ho-p'u, the home of the ancient pearl fisheries.[79] Traditionally metal boats have always been associated with gods and sorcerers, the only beings capable of floating them. Like stone boats, they are also the vehicles of flood heroes, and may, like the Ark of Noah, be left on the summits of mountains.[80] Other objects of bronze appear in tales of Ma Yüan: he took the bronze drums of aboriginal chieftains as trophies, and his cult also involves him with bronze oxen.[81]

As a part of popular lore and belief, this cult may be almost as old as the actual exploits of the hero. But officially it goes back only to 875. In that year, Ma the Wave Subduer was awarded the title of Numinous and Radiant King, and his worship was authorized for all loyal subjects and magistrates.[82] In T'ang times he had an important temple at the chief city of Kuei-chou.[83] Soon afterwards he became, if he was not already, a god of the waters, particularly of the rapids of Kwangsi rivers,[84] and of the sea off the southernmost coast of Kwangtung, especially around Lei-chou.[85] After T'ang, images of Ma Yüan acquired a bow and arrows as befitted a wave subduer and conqueror of water spirits.[86] In modern times he is also a thunder god, a dragon king, and a subduer of barbarians (who are themselves dragons).[87] He is by no means an exclusively Chinese deity but a representative of Chinese and aborigines alike—both dragon and anti-dragon.

Finally, Ma Yüan was a horse spirit, a divine dragon horse—in short, a kelpie. This naturally followed from his surname, which means "horse." He became, in quite early tradition, the eponymous ancestor of a population occupying the region around his bronze pillars on the southernmost outpost of Chinese power. If these horse people (they may never have existed) were not the hero's descendants, they were, some said, the posterity of a group of his soldiers who remained behind in the tropics.[88] *The Book of T'ang* gives them the name of Hsi-t'u (Sei-du) Barbarians, all surnamed Ma "Horse," and states that their numbers had increased from ten households to three hundred by the end of the Sui.[89]

Other Hua heroes were deified after the fall of imperial Han. An important and early one was Shih Hsieh (Dri Sep; Vietn. Si Nhiêp) who promoted the Han way of life in Annam at the end of the second Christian century, and—so tradition tells—also authorized the propagation of Buddhism there. He was deified in the sixth century, and is still honored by the Vietnamese as King Si.[90]

Even good officials of the modern (T'ang) age were deified soon after their deaths. Liu Tsung-yüan, for instance, was regarded by the natives of Liu-chou as the spirit of the moat there, and Han Yü wrote a memorial inscription for his shrine, in which he says that Liu "did not despise the barbarians." His accompanying prayer begins with the offerings appropriate to the altar of the new god: "The lichees are vermilion—ah, the bananas are yellow." [91] Liu Tsung-yüan had become a truly tropical god.

In contrast to this noble worship of the benefactors of mankind, as it seemed in the eyes of the Chinese, the religion of the natives of Nam-Viet was a running sore and perpetual scandal. The Hua men saw and wrote about those traits in it which were most objectionable to them, including some which they must have recognized as belonging to their own ancestors. But even as tolerant a man as Liu Tsung-yüan could find little good in the customs of the Man:

A man of Viet believes in luck, and is quick to kill—contemptuous of reform and hostile to humane feelings. If his sickness becomes worrisome, he will assemble shaman masters to employ chicken divination. At the beginning he will have a minor victim killed. If this does not do, he will have a medium victim killed. If this still does not do, he will have a major victim killed. If even yet this does not do, he will take leave of kith and kin, and arrange the death business thus: "May the gods not set me aside now!" Then he does not eat, covers his face, and dies. For this reason, their houses quickly deteriorate, and their fields quickly go wild, while their livestock, even if cared for, does not multiply. If you direct them in good manners, these are coarsened; if you bind them with penalties, they run away.[92]

(A minor victim was a chicken or duck, a medium victim was a pig or dog, and a major victim was a cow.) [93]

Liu Tsung-yüan thought that Buddhism would provide the cure. Most magistrates preferred to rely on Confucian pedagogy backed by the force of arms. But little was changed, it seems, in either case. The heathen shrines persisted, and the conquerors believed that the short lives of the natives were the fatal consequence of their superstition:

> There are many blue ghosts in their depraved worship;
> There are few resident men who get white heads.[94]

Here is a more careful description of the Lao gods, who seem not so different from the deified heroes of the Chinese after all:

In the Ou-Yüeh region they are devoted to the service of ghosts; mountain peppers and water shores alike are full of indecent worship. As for the images in these shrines: if it should be virile and resolute, swarthy and imposing one, he is called "Army Leader"; if it is a warm and agreeable, sage and youthful one, he is called "Esquire So-and-so"; if it should be a beldam, reverend and stern, she is called "dame"; if it is a woman of ravishing mien, she is called "maiden." [95]

Little is yet known about these images, but at least, some of the despised aboriginal gods, were carved from magically potent excrescences cut from liquidambar trees.[96]

> The shrine is opened—flying squirrels cry;
> The god descends—Viet shamans speak.

These are the words of Han Yü in a poem "Praying for Rain in Ch'en-chou," [97] and they show the persistence of the old belief in the power of the shamans of Viet. Li Shang-yin put it this way—Hua technology, but Man superstition:

> The houses all hang out Chinese nets—
> The families mostly serve Viet shamans.[98]

These southern god speakers had been viewed with repugnance and fear since the Han dynasty, when their ancient influence began to be systematically undermined. The persecution of the Chinese shamans of the north was initiated on a large scale in 99 B.C., when all of their wayside shrines were abolished. They had enough vitality to survive systematic oppression through the centuries, though greatly diminished in the north by T'ang times. A memorial addressed to the throne in mid-seventh century again asked the suppression of shamans, along with their heterodox demons and fanes "which dazzle and bewilder the people." [99] At about the same time, Ti Jen-chieh, imperial commissioner in Chiang-nan province (ranging from modern Hunan to Chekiang) destroyed 1,700 infidel shrines in that area.[100] Despite this demolition, a century later Li Te-yü was able to find and condemn more than a thousand "depraved temples" in only a portion of this province.[101]

One kind of creature had a special role in the magical and religious activities of the men of Nam-Viet: the common barnyard fowl and its wild relative the Red Jungle Fowl, a kind of wattled pheasant, resplendent in scarlet and green bronze.[102] This wild ancestral bird is still found in the forests of southernmost China and in Indochina.[103] It appears that the bird was first brought into domestication in Southeast Asia, but evidently the purposes for which it was intended were not "practical" by our standards, that is, they had nothing to do with enriching the diet. It is most likely that it was kept primarily for purposes of magic and divination, and also for gaming—but originally these two purposes must have been virtually indistinguishable.[104] The fowl was made at home among men, it seems, long before the Age of Metal. It was already familiar in the great city of Mohenjo Daro in the Indus Valley in the second millenium B.C.[105] It became a sacred bird for both the Persians and the Hellenes. As herald of the sun, it signaled the dispersal of the demons of darkness, and it was a symbol of the resurrection.[106] It is thought that the Chinese were the first to breed varieties particularly for utilitarian purposes. One old variety produced by them is the Buff Cochin China, which is so different from the Jungle Fowl as to suggest a different species.[107] They have bred them for the table and for medicine. They have even produced the elegant and lustrous "silkies" for their fine plumage.[108]

But the Hua men had their own traditions of divination—no chicken could replace the sacred tortoise. Therefore, while they converted the plastic fowl into newer and more useful forms, they left its more "primitive" and spiritual employment as an oracular and sacrificial bird to the non-Chinese of Nam-Viet.[109] In T'ang times the aborigines used the bones of chickens to prognosticate events of the new year.[110] After predicting the future of a newly launched boat from the bones of the divine fowl, they would offer its flesh as a sacrifice to the spirit of the vessel, which they addressed as Lord Meng or Dame Meng.[111] Divination with chicken eggs was also an ancient technique. The native wizards of southern Yung-chou had this method: they would write a spell in ink on the shell, boil the ink, split the egg in half, and interpret the omen in the appearance of the yolk.[112]

Along with chicken divination there was another trait of southern supernaturalism which caught the attention of the Chinese very early and always seemed to have a kind of horrible fascination for them. This was *ku*. *Ku* was evil sorcery, erotic charm, malignant disease—and the artful or natural causes of these things. It was the black magic of Nam-Viet. Usually it has been described as a poison, concentrated from the venoms of insects and reptiles. The *ku*-making ascribed to the Ch'uang women of modern Kwangsi shows many traits identical with those reported in ancient books and is probably not very different from medieval practice:

. . . they go to a mountain stream and spread new clothes and headgear on the ground, with a bowl of water beside them. The women dance and sing naked, inviting a visit from the King of Medecine [sic] (a tutelary spirit). They wait until snakes, lizards, and poisonous insects come to bathe in the bowl. They pour the water out in a shadowy, dark place. Then they gather the fungus [poisonous?] which grows there, which they make into a paste. They put this into goose-feather tubes, and hide them in their hair. The heat of their bodies causes worms to generate, which resemble newly-hatched silk-worms. Thus *ku* is produced. It is often concealed in a warm, dark place in the kitchen.

The newly made *ku* is not yet poisonous. It is used as a love potion, administered in food and drink and called "love-medicine." Gradually the *ku* becomes poisonous. As the poison develops, the woman's body itches until she has poisoned someone. If there is no other opportunity, she will poison even her husband or her sons. But she possesses antidotes.

It is believed that those who produce *ku* themselves become *ku* after death. The ghosts of those who have died from the poison become their servants.[113]

In medieval times it was the common belief that the poison was prepared by putting poisonous creatures in a sealed vessel, where they ate each other until their poisons were concentrated in a single survivor. Such a *ku* creature, according to the T'ang pharmacologist Ch'en Ts'ang-ch'i,

can conceal its form, and seem to be a ghost or spirit, and make misfortune for men. But after all it is only a reptile ghost. If one of them has bitten a person to death, it will sometimes emerge from one of that man's apertures. Watch and wait to catch it and dry it in the warmth of the sun; then, when someone is afflicted by the *ku*, burn it to ashes and give him a dose of it. Being akin to it, the one quite naturally subdues the other.[114]

There was also an ancient belief that the *ku* diseases were induced by some sort of noxious mist or exhalation—just as it was also believed that certain airs and winds could generate worms.[115] We see in this another southern complex: tropical fogs generate both fatal malaria and poisonous animals. Here is a T'ang account of the suffering of the natives of Nam-Viet:

The majority are diseased, and *ku* forms in their bloated bellies. There is a vulgar tradition of making *ku* from a concentration of the hundred kinds of crawling creatures, for the purpose of poisoning men. But probably it is the poisonous crawlers of that hot and humid land which produce it—not just the cruel and baleful nature of the householders beyond the mountain passes.[116]

There were other kinds of atmospheric or meteoric *ku,* to judge from a report made to Tuan Ch'eng-shih, that voracious lore collector, by a Taoist hermit. He was told that he should discard all cracked procelain vessels, since "many thunder *ku,* as well as ghosts and trolls, will hide within them." [117]

Ku-poisoning was also associated with demoniac sexual appetite—an idea traceable back to Chou times.[118] This notion evidently had its origin in stories of ambiguous love potions prepared by the aboriginal women of the south.[119]

If detected in time, there was some hope of cure: "When the chickens fly away of their own accord, for no cause, that family has the *ku.*" [120] Remedies were sometimes homeopathic—one could administer either *ku* ashes, as already described, or else give *ku* derived from particularly venomous creatures to overcome that taken from less lethal creatures. Thus centipede *ku* could be overcome by frog *ku,* serpent *ku* would prevail over frog *ku,* and so on.[121] There were also soberer, though almost as powerful remedies: asafoetida,[122] python bile,[123] civet,[124] and a white substance taken from cock's dung[125] were all used. It is not certain what real maladies these repellent drugs cured, or seemed to cure. Probably they ranged from the psychosomatic to the virus-born. Many oedematous conditions were called *ku,* and it has been plausibly suggested that some cases were caused by intestinal parasites (hence the constant worm motif). Others are attributable to fish poisons and arrow poisons concocted by the forest dwellers.[126]

The Chinese had been familiar with *ku* in very early times, at least from late Chou.[127] The *ku* scandals at the court of Han Wu Ti—dramas of love and death— were notorious. Possibly the belief in *ku* sorcery was once universal in China, but like the shamans and their shrines, was suppressed in the north and survived in the south.[128] But the ancient fear of the uncanny poisons of the south remained among the cities of the Yellow River valley even in T'ang times. During the reign of the Empress Wu the possession of *ku* poison, like the casting of horoscopes, was cause for official suspicion and action:

At that time many tyrannical office holders would order robbers to bury *ku* or to leave prophecies in a man's household by night. Then, after the passage of a month, they would secretly confiscate it.[129]

We know the names and attributes of only a few of the true southern gods. Of these, some were given the homage of the Chinese intruders, others, of whom we know much less, were worshiped only by the autochthons. Many of these deities attended to the prayers of all the races of Nam-Viet—since prudence required that both native and visitor considered all aspects of their own spiritual welfare. If we ignore the imported divinities of Buddhism, the native deities looked very much like the ancient gods of the Chinese—they were the spirits of nature and of vital human activities connected with nature. The official Chinese pantheon allowed, and indeed encouraged, respect and prayer to innumerable gods hidden in the landscape. Most important of these were the gods of the great mountains and rivers—the bones and arteries of the physical world. Indeed, special dignity and reverence was usually required of human visitors to these holy spots, and such a pious emperor as Hsüan (Ghwen) Tsung required that the sacred mountains be regarded as sanctuaries where even animal life was inviolate.[130] Far beneath these great powers and dignities were a myriad spirits whose names could hardly be known even if their separate individualities could be imagined. Such, for instance, were the serpentine and draconian spirits of the sea

> The Hundred Numina of the Sea, secretly, weirdly,
> All emerged at once, in distracting confusion;
> Coiling around and snaking about,
> They came to savor the drink and food.[131]

This is from a description of a ceremonial offering, and shows us the pages, courtiers, and hangers-on, as it were, of the great God of the South Sea approaching the altar. They were nereids, if you please, but it is not always easy to say whether they most resembled the pleasing daughters of Nereus or the greenish marine worms which bear the same name.

Although the great northern rivers had their nymphs, she of the Lo (Lak) being paramount, I have not noticed a comparable naiad in the far south. But there may well have been such a barbaric water maiden, loved by the Man but unknown to the Hua settlers. The indigenes did recognize many divinities of the water.[132] Perhaps, like so many Chinese nature gods, they were embodied in popular heroes and ancient chieftains. Perhaps they too were included in the anonymous hosts mentioned in the official prayers of the Chinese magistrates. But let us look at some identifiable southern gods.

Although, as gods of the fourth class, the Gods of the Four Seas ranked below the high ancestral deities and the great star spirits in T'ang times, they were still very high gods. The God of the South Sea was particularly important since he presided over the Chang-hai, the mysterious southern ocean, inhabited by magicians, monsters, and mythical maidens. This was also the sea which had brought the wealth of the eastern and southern nations to Canton. Appropriately the cult of its god was celebrated at the Bay of Yellow Wood near that city, where ships from as far as Oman, Siraf, and Basra sought safe harbor and rich profits. This wealthy god was also a summer spirit, being the chief deity of the warm south, with fire as his symbol. The temple at which he was offered oxen, vegetables, and wine had been founded in the sixth century, but his greatest fame came in 751, when he was named "Widely Profitable Prince" with loud official acclaim. In 820, a stele lauding his power and the virtues of the governor K'ung Kuei, who had restored his shrine and regularized his worship, in a text written by Han Yü himself, was erected by the temple.[133] This noble spirit was the object of the prayers of all mariners who ventured out on the dark ocean of the Indies. Here are the words of Kao P'ien, written at the temple as he was about to set out over the god's watery domain for the conquest of the Nan-chao armies in Annam:

> The cold green abyss-eight thousand miles—
> Now and in the past we have feared its waves and billows:
> This day the commander of a southbound expedition
> May bring a myriad sail securely over! [134]

This exalted being had another side to his nature—he was thought by some (Han Yü, for instance) to be identical with Chu Jung, the archaic fire, furnace, and forge god of the ancient state of Ch'u.[135] The identification is as artificial as the one which saw the Greek sea goddess Aphrodite in a Roman garden goddess named Venus. But it was also just as natural.

One of the more important gods of Nam-Viet was the thunder god—or, I should say, thunder gods, since there seem to have been a host of them. They were called "thunder lords." The antiquity of their cult is not certain but it was well established in the T'ang period.[136] All T'ang sources agree that it was centered in the county and peninsula of Lei-chou, the "Thunder County," and give the obvious reason:

Some say that there is so much thunder in Lei-chou during the spring and summer that there is no day that lacks it. But during autumn and winter the thunder lords crouch in the earth, and then men catch and eat them. They are shaped like pigs. It is also said that anyone who eats one together with yellow fish will die from a thunderbolt. There are some too who find and bring in "thunder axes" and "thunder ink"—these are used as medicinal stones.[137]

We should expect these loud riders of the sky to have a birdlike appearance, and indeed it has been conjectured that they originally had the forms of owls, but in medieval times they took on other aspects, some horribly manlike, but retaining beak, wings, and talons.[138] Perhaps this latter version appeared first in Sung times, since almost all T'ang sources describe them as hideously bat-winged, rather porcine beings. Here is one account: "In appearance they are like bears or swine, with hairy horns, and fleshy wings of a bluish color." [139] Here is another: "The body was more than two ten-feet long. It was black-colored and piglike, with five- or six-foot horns on its head, fleshy wings of more than a ten-foot, and a leopard's tail. Moreover, it was half-clad in scarlet pantaloons, and its waist was bound with a leopard's skin. Its hands and feet were double-taloned, all golden colored, and they clutched red snakes, which it trampled with its feet, with glaring eyes, as if intending to eat them. Its voice was like thunder." [140] Still another account says simply that they have the heads of pigs and scaly bodies.[141]

We have a ninth-century notice of their cult and folklore:

Each year the common people [*lit.* "the hundred clans"] prepare a thunder cart with linked drums at the shrine of the thunder lords in the west of Lei-chou.

Should someone eat the flesh of fish and swine together, there is instantly a clap of thun-der, from which they always shrink with respect.

Always after great thunder and rain, many jet-black stones are found in the fields. They call them "thunder lords' ink." If you tap them they give a bell-like clang, and they are as bright and lustrous as lacquer. Also, if you go to the site of the thunderclap—sometimes inside the ground or a tree—you will find a wedge like an axe. They call these "thunder-clap wedges." Small children hang them at their belts, and they always ward off fearful and vicious beings. Pregnant women grind them up and take doses of them; as a drug for inducing birth, they never fail to work.[142]

The natives appeased these powerful demon smiters and womb splitters with reverent offerings of meat and wine,[143] and sometimes they dug holes in the hills and concealed oblations, called "thunder hoards," in them[144]—presumably this was during the quiet hibernation of the porcine deities during the winter monsoon.

What with the reverence given to these flying animal gods in some places, and the fear in which they were held generally, it is hard to account for some curious tales of their humiliating capture by careless clods and disrespectful bumpkins, who did not hesitate to eat them.[145] Indeed the creatures seem to have had their softer side, to judge from a tale about a country girl of the Canton region, who was carried off by a "Master of Thunder" to be his wife.[146] But mostly they were grim horrors whose match was hardly to be found among the monsters of the world:

At the end of "Opened Prime" (ca. A.D. 741), there was a fight between thunder lords and a whale at Lei-chou. When its body emerged above the water, several tens of the thun-der lords appeared high and low in the void, loosing fire, and reviling it, and hitting at it. After seven days this stopped. Men who dwelled on the edge of the sea went to look, but could not tell which of the two had prevailed, but they saw that the water of the sea was entirely red.[147]

Here in the south then, the thunder lords were masters of the sky. In their own realm they usurped some of the prerogatives owned by dragons in the north, those ancient masters of the nimbus. It was they, not the northern rain serpents nor the treasure-guarding nagas of the Indianized ocean, who shattered the dark skies and drenched the red soils of Nam-Viet.

Then there were the goddesses—hosts of them, easily absorbed by the Chinese Taoists, as nymphs by a tolerant church, even if not completely differentiated:

On peut penser que les Immortelles célèbres ont été montées en épingle au détriment de la troupe des filles-génies sans individualité et que ces dernières sont les oiseaux blancs depouillés de leur vêtement de plumes.[148]

The unflattering depiction is not inaccurate. Consider the case of Jade Goose Peak on Mount Lo-fou.[149] It was also known as Jade Maiden Peak—"maiden" being a rather weak word to translate *o* (*nga*), an old northwestern dialect word for a woman of fairylike loveliness. The white domestic goose is also *o* (*nga*), hence the confusion of nomenclature. In either case, "jade-white" is an appropriate epithet for both, and beyond that there is the echo of the white swan maidens of familiar legend.

An occasional individual stands out among these hundreds of pallid oreads. One was Lu Mei-niang—but I fear she may be only a legend. Her name, "Black Eyebrow Maiden" referred to her long, threadlike eyebrows. Early in the ninth century, at the age of fourteen, she was sent as a gift from Canton to the imperial court at Ch'ang-an. Among her arts was the ability to embroider the entire *Lotus Sutra*—normally seven scrolls—on a foot of pongee. She tired of metropolitan life, embraced the Tao, and retired to Nam-Viet, where she died, filling a hall with perfume. Later she was often seen roaming over the sea on a purple cloud.[150]

The most completely realized of these tropical peris—in the great perspective of history—was a divine girl later called Ho Hsien-ku, a jeweled being among the tender figures of modern Chinese mythology. Her icon is recognizable today showing a lovely girl who sometimes holds a lotus flower, sometimes a life-giving peach—or she may be shown playing a reed organ, or drinking wine. The many legends about her unique powers and divine gifts are, in the main, of Sung origin, and were well crystallized (with many inconsistencies) by Ming times.[151]

The oldest accounts of Miss Ho's career appear in collections of stories made at about the beginning of the Sung dynasty. An early and persistent version of the manner of her apotheosis relates that she attained an immortal body in the eighth century by ingesting mica on the divine slopes of Mount Lo-fou.[152] In one tale she is a beautiful girl of Canton who weaves shoes for a living. One day, without any preconception of her own divinity, she left her mother and flew to Mount Lo-fou. There she stayed with a band of monks and gathered wild fruits for them. The good fellows realized her exceptional nature when she brought them the fine fruits of a box myrtle from a temple garden on a remote mountain, to which she must have traveled by air. An officer was sent to bring her to Hsüan (Ghwen) Tsung's court, early in that monarch's reign, but her pure soul divined the lustful thoughts of her escort, and she disappeared from human sight on the northward road. This edifying narrative is found in a collection of wonder tales which appears to have been put together early in the tenth century.[153] Another book of about the same age tells that she lived at Tseng-ch'eng, between Canton and Mount Lo-fou, in the time of the Empress Wu. She took a dose of powdered mica and "attained the Tao on Mount Lo-fou." [154] After the tenth century, many other anecdotes gradually accumulated around the etherial figure of the daughter of the Ho family,[155] but her medicinal and life-prolonging fruits or mica have remained with her throughout. In time she has become an "autre gloire féminine du Lo-fou." [156]

One other important divinity remains to be mentioned, this one an ancestral god. The southern neighbors of the Chinese were descended from a marvelous dog named P'an-hu. The story of this totemic divinity is very old, and it is still very much alive. In a reduced form it goes like this: At the beginning of time, a king offered his daughter's hand to anyone who would bring him the head of his enemy, a captain of the western barbarians. A dog of the palace achieved the feat, and the reluctant king was obliged to give his young daughter to the animal, who took her off to a mountain cave in the south. She bore him six boys and six girls, the ancestors of the Man tribes of the southern wilderness. Their descendants proliferated in Hunan and its borderlands in antiquity, and gradually spread into the uplands of Nam-Viet.[157]

In early medieval times, the Man peoples were still defined collectively as "the descendants of P'an-hu," and Liu Yü-hsi, sent to Lingnan in disgrace in 815, wrote of the seasonal ceremonies in honor of P'an-hu.[158]

In our days, P'an-hu is still much remembered among the Miao-Yao peoples of Lingnan and their cousins the Man of Tongking.[159] It is reported of the Yao of Kwangtung that "in the center room of every Yao house, there is a house altar for P'an-ku [sic]." [160] The Vietnamese Man are reluctant to mention the holy name of Bôn Hu, and refrain from eating the flesh of dogs.[161]

P'an-hu's name itself shows that his story has been absorbed into a creation myth. In Chinese it is written with graphs which mean "platter gourd." This gourd is undoubtedly the world calabash, a familiar counterpart of the primordial egg in the Far East. Many legends of the Thai and Miao peoples tell of the great pumpkin-like fruit which was the home of a brother and sister who survived the universal deluge, and whose incestuous union populated the new earth.[162] The dog totem's connection with this cosmic and fecund vegetable is explained in a Chinese legend: In ancient times, a sick old woman of the palace cured herself by extracting a worm from her head. She put it in a gourd, which she covered with a platter. The worm changed into a dog, which was accordingly named "platter gourd." [163] But the "gourd" is the enveloping sky, and the "platter" is the flat earth. They correspond also to the stone room in the southern mountains where the dog and his princess lived and bred their children to become the enemies of the aggressive Chinese. The gourd is the vault of their grotto, the platter its floor. The cavern is also a "grotto heaven," as the Taoists style the divine worlds encapsuled deep in the sacred mountains.[164] The dog myth and the cave-calabash myth must have merged very early. Some dogless versions survive in Chinese lore, while a dog-emphasizing version remains prominent among the Man.

GOBLINS

All travel is perilous. Supernatural enemies threaten the wayfarer as much as physical hazards. Though the dangers, both spiritual and material, increased as one strayed into unknown lands, still one could encounter a specter as easily as a landslide in China, and both are particularly abundant in remote mountains. Accordingly the wilderness surviving in the south was full of spiritual perils. Sung Chih-wen, an excessively nervous exile, was well aware of this. Passing the "Dragon-Eye Shoals" as he descended the Kuei River, he observed:

> By the huge rocks lurk the mountain goblins;
> In the deep bamboos hide the grotto sylphs.
> Birds wander where ravines are hushed and forlorn;
> Apes whistle where high passes are charming and fair.[165]

Men of wisdom prepare themselves properly with periapts and spells for the rigors and terrors of a journey into deep forests and stony wastes. If you are lucky enough to escape the wild beasts in such places, you risk the attack of a tree demon. Indeed carnivorous animals and malignant spirits have much in common, and can be regarded as generically the same. As a tiger, or a tree, or a stone grows old, its spirit acquires new vigor and power, until it can congeal into strange shapings, take on independent life, and join the secret army of forest haunts. The Taoists were particularly well-informed about such beings, and clever at dealing with them. The classic book of Taoist lore, *Pao p'u tzu,* warned that "when any of the Myriad Creatures is aged, its germinal essence can always falsely take on human form to bewilder and mislead the eyes of men." One way of recognizing such ectoplasmic illusions was to carry a mirror into wild places—this revealed their true shapes.[166] Or the venturous traveler, especially if he had access to Taoist secrets, might provide himself with a powerful charm, antagonistic to the "hundred ghosts" and the "myriad ectoplasms." [167] Or again, knowing the secret name of a baleful emanation, you can nullify its power. So, a dragon must be addressed as "master of rain," a fish as "sire of the river," an old tree as "transcendent person," metals and precious stones as "female person," and thus "as you know the name of the creature it is unable to do you harm." [168]

The spectral derivatives of natural objects had preferred forms. The "ectoplasm" or "essential emanation" of a mountain appears as a drum-shaped one-legged being, or perhaps a little childlike, nocturnal eater of crayfish.[169] Old trees may speak like humans; [170] the emanation of an old well takes the form of a beautiful woman playing the flute; [171] the coagulated spirit of an old road or track seems to be a wild man, a savage aborigine—but if you call him by his proper name he will keep you from losing your way.[172] But all this is illusion—tree or gaffer, well or woman, road or infidel—the *ching,* the germinal essence, persists behind the shifting forms.[173]

If the spirit prefers not to reveal itself to your eyes as you pass through the forest, you can borrow the power of birds to make them visible: "If you eat the eyes of a crow, you will be able to see the forest demons, and if you press the liquid from them and pour it into your eyes, you will be able to see ghosts by night." [174] Similarly if you eat owl eyes you can see ghosts in the darkness.[175]

Not that all ghosts and demons were southern. The north, even the far north, had its share. Some were even respectable, as the envoys who brought tribute from the Country of Drifting Ghosts, in islands off the Siberian coast, in the year 640.[176] But there is no doubt that the tropical forests seem to be the particular and natural home of goblins. This may be partly because of the greater richness of perilous life forms in the jungle, ranging from mysterious diseases to poisonous insects.[177] Although the northerners were no strangers to devils and their kind, they did not number them among their more respected deities; rather they preferred (in addition to and even above the great river and mountain spirits) the spirits of the sky, especially the star gods. It is curious that these celestial deities seem little reverenced in the deep south—though sometimes the moon is shown special respect there.[178] Is the reason that the fires of heaven are so often obscured by the forest canopy, the swirling mists and the heavy rain? [179] In any event, once arrived in rain forests, the northerners soon forgot the shining approved star spirits and worried about the lurking heterodox tree spirits. This was as true of the medieval Chinese in Nam-Viet as of the modern French in the same haunted region:

Comment les Européens cuirassés d'indifference et de rationalisme font-ils pour se laisser prendre à ces fables. Quel enchantement les porte donc à croire eux-mêmes aux puissances maléfiques de la forêt? Les fatigues, les privations, la fièvre, l'opium, les exhalaisons lourdes qui montent des décompositions végétales, l'affolement de leurs compagnons indigènes finissent par insinuer dans leur conscience, l'obscur pressentiment du danger. . . . Dans l'humidité chaude des impénétrables fourrés, dans l'air saturé des émanations puissantes de toutes les pourritures tropicales, dans les brouillards du matin étirant leurs bras de fantômes, l'Européen suppose une vie informe animée de desseins perfides. La fièvre des bois cerclant les crânes d'une entreinte de fer, fait surgir alors d'hallucinantes apparitions. L'homme semble dès lors se débattre contre d'invisibles spectres et cette lutte prend un caractère presque surhumain.[180]

Here is a sampling of the rich spectral life of Nam-Viet:

At times, by the margin of the sea, there are ghost markets. They come together in the middle of the night; they scatter when the cock cries. Men who attend them usually find rare things.[181]

The shy dwellers of the coastal forests who took part in these casual and ephemeral exchanges must have seemed ghosts to the Hua men. Not all phantoms were as acceptable as those:

There are often flying heads among the torrents and grottoes of Lingnam, and this is why we have the term "Lao fellows of the Flying Heads." One day before one's head is about to fly, there is a scar on his neck going right around the nape, like a red thread. The wife and children then watch over him and guard him. Now when night comes, that man seems to be ill; his head suddenly grows wings, separates itself from the body and goes away. Then it searches for such food as crustaceans and worms in the mud of river banks. Just before daybreak it flies back. He awakens as from a dream, but now his belly is full.[182]

The crayfish-eating native is hardly to be told from a jungle animal. For the northerner the other side of any aborigine's nature was animalian, and it was easy to imagine him slipping into his alternate form at will. Thus, "now and then the barbarian men are transformed into *ch'u.*" This is said of T'eng-chou.[183] *Ch'u* is a shortened form of *ch'u-meng* (*t'yu-măng*) or *ch'u-man* (*t'yu-man*), which, from old descriptions, seems to have been a carnivorous cat, possibly the so-called "leopard cat" (*Felis bengalensis*) which occurs widely in East Asia. But it is curious that the second syllable of the name has the familiar ring of "the aborigines," "the Man folk."

Werecats and weretigers were common enough in Nam-Viet. To compensate the visitor, perhaps, there were also more recognizably Chinese phantoms, such as the Divinity of the Cauldron Stone who inhabited the waves of the river in K'ang-chou at a place where an antique wonderworker, Childe of the Red Pine, is said to have brewed his elixirs.[184] Presumably this was that alchemists's spirit, adapted to local conditions.

Most feared of the bogies of the south (by the Hua men, at least) was neither ghost nor beast man, but a small anonymous, invertebrate animal. I say anonymous, meaning that it is now hard to put a scientific name to it, if it really existed. There are plenty of popular Chinese names for it: "water crossbow," "sand mouther," "shadow shooter," "shooting artist," "short fox"—I have adopted the name "shooter" for it. There was also an archaic and classical name, Yü (Ywĕk).[185] This last name occurs in the literature of Chou, but it is the Han scholiasts who give the first description of the creature. It begins to emerge as a reptile or insect living in mountain streams or on their shores, spitting water or sand at men, or even at their shadows, with fatal results. A T'ang account of it goes like this:

The "shooting artists" come from mountain forests in the southern quarter—places where the mountain streams are poisonous. They are as large as chicken eggs, and shaped like dung beetles, with a single horn on their heads more than an inch long. On top of the horn are four branches. It is able to fly with the four wings under its black armor.[186]

It is not certain if the venomous *yü* of the ancient "Odes" is the curious beetle of the medieval pharmacologist just quoted. Although an easy first guess might point to the archer fish, *Toxotes jaculator,* a relative of the perches, which shoots down its insect prey from overhanging boughs, that tropical fish seems not to be found as far north as Nam-Viet, and besides the idea that the "shooter" is an insect goes back at least as far as the fourth century.[187] Perhaps it was the snouted, carnivorous, boat-shaped bug *Notonecta,* which both swims and flies.[188] Then there is the offensive conduct of the Bombardier beetles. There are the *Dytiscidae,* carnivorous water beetles with oarlike hindlegs, and the *Gyrinidae* "Whirligig Beetles" which skim about on fresh water. Perhaps no single creature fills the bill. In any case, the prospect of encountering a shooter was a paralyzing thought for most southbound exiles. But there were worse things.

Complaining to the imperial court about the bitterness of his banishment, Han Yü wrote of himself on the hot coast of Lingnan as "dwelling in a land of barbarians and infidels, herded together with trolls." [189] The lament of Sung Chih-wen is even more poignant:

A true-vermeil heart died north of the Chiang,
And my white locks grow south of the passes—
With trolls in a kingdom at the margin of the sky,
Experiencing all sorrows in a citadel above the sea.[190]

The mandarin-poet Yüan Chieh, a successful campaigner against the Man tribes in Jung late in the eighth century, wrote of the monsoon country as troll land itself:

I hear that near the South Sea
Is the very home of the trolls.[191]

These "trolls," as I have called them, are the *ch'ih-mei* (*t'yiĕ-mi*) of the Chinese—perhaps they should be styled "goblins" or "bogles." [192] But the dark, lumbering troll of Scandinavia seems most like the fearful ogre of the wooded mountains of China.[193]

The "trolls" were dark spirits of unusual power. They challenged the regime of the Chinese, the rational rulers of the earth. In antiquity they lurked, like the barbarous Miao tribes, beyond the frontiers of the world of light.[194] In the north, their safety lay in disguise: the benighted peasantry worshiped crypto-foxes, which were actually trolls.[195] But in the south, trolls lived like the Li and the Mak tribes, as outlaws hidden in the high forests—"wood trolls" [196] and "mountain trolls":

Dragon mirrors put the mountain trolls to flight,
As frost and wind break up the barrier of clouds.[197]

Among all the mountain spirits of the far south, the kind one was most likely to meet was the *hsiao* (*syeu*):

On torrent journeys you meet the "water crossbows";
In wilderness taverns you avoid the mountain *hsiao*.[198]

We have just told of the water crossbows, devilish creatures spitting evilly at passers-by in the mountain gorges of Lingnan. The mountain *hsiao* [199] were more human, and their malice had a trace of puckish humor in it. They were oriental oreads of a sort, though no nymphs. Some said that they were a kind of mountain troll, but others asserted that they should be named "flying dragons." There was a blue birdlike species which made its nest in a hole in a tree and decorated it with red and white clay. Some assumed the form of an archer's target.[200] Some people said that they were birds by day but little men with birdlike voices by night, while others thought that these protean bogeys were arsonists,[201] prone to burning houses and huts. They had tiger familiars which protected them from evildoers.[202] I shall call them "imps." Two tales purporting to tell of events in the middle of the eighth century give us some idea of the character of the creatures:

At the end of Heavenly Treasure, a certain Liu Chien was disbursing officer in Lingnan. He chanced to come across a mountain imp on a journey in the mountains there, and called it "grotesque ghost!" The mountain imp was angered and said, "Disbursing Officer Liu! I am walking about for my amusement—what is your concern with me that you should abuse me so?" Then it stood on a branch under a tree and called out, "Streaked lad!" In a little while a tiger came. He commanded it to seize Disbursing Officer Liu. Whipping his horse, Chien made off in great alarm, but was shortly pounced on by the tiger, and made to sit under its feet. The imp laughed at this and said, "Disbursing Officer Liu Chien is greatly alarmed—will he abuse me again or not?" The servants of right and left made the double salute and pleaded for his life. "Let him go," he said calmly, at which the tiger released Chien. Close to perishing from dread and alarm, Chien had to be carried home. After several days of illness he recovered. Whenever Chien met anyone, he told him of this affair.[203]

The same book has the following:

As for the mountain imps—anywhere you may be in Lingnan has them. They are single-legged, reverse-heeled, and their hands and feet are triple-branched. Their dams are fond of applying unguents and powder. They make their nests on great trees out in the open. These have wooden screens, wind canopies, and curtains, and are very well furnished with things to eat. Most of the men of the south who travel in the mountains carry yellow unguent, lead powder [i.e., ceruse], coins, and the like along with them. The males, which they call "mountain lords," always ask for metal and coins. If they come across a female they call her "mountain aunt," and she will always ask for unguent and powder. Whoever gives some can be protected by them. During Heavenly Treasure of T'ang, there was a visitor from the north traveling in the mountains of Lingnan. Most nights, fearful of tigers, he preferred to sojourn up in a tree. Once he chanced to meet a female mountain imp there. Now this man usually had some light luggage with him, so he descended from the tree, gave the double salute, and cried out, "mountain aunt!" From far up in the tree she asked if he had any articles of merchandise, and the man presented her with unguent and powder. Overjoyed, she said to the man, "Lie down and rest without anxiety." So the man spent the night under the tree. In the middle of the night, two tigers wished to come to this place, but the mountain imp descended from the tree, stroked the tigers' heads and said, "I have a visitor, streaked lads! You must go away at once!" So the two tigers departed. With the brightening of day, when he made his excuses for departing, she thanked her visitor most humbly.

What is hard to understand is this: during each year they work the fields along with human beings. When a man goes out to sow in the fields, the excess of plowed land with its sowing and planting all go to the mountain imps. When the cereals ripen, they come and call to the men for their fair share. By nature they are simple and straightforward, and when they share with men they do not take more than they should. Neither do the men take more, because if they did take more they would encounter heaven-sent plagues and diseases.[204]

The *hsiao* of Lingnan, then, were no loutish trolls, no scuttling kobolds, no terrible bogles. We see them perched jauntily on the branches of trees, showing a spirit of dignity and independence, believing themselves the equals of men—they even share human frailties (the females are vain of their complexions). They seem to be compounded of ghosts, gibbons, and pile-dwelling pygmies.[205]

Another typical resident of the mountains of the far south was the "tree visitor" (*mu k'o*). This was a kind of dryad, clawed like a harpy, but—unlike a harpy—a gentle birdlike creature, no befouler of feasts. Indeed, there was a tradition of a true bird, gregarious by habit, called "tree visitor bird." [206] Otherwise our forest haunter was a ghostly anthropoid, but apparently more delicate than the *hsiao* imp—less the boisterous Robin Goodfellow. These bird-footed elves were notably abundant at Jung-shan in Chao-chou,[207] where they assumed small, childlike figures. "In their singing and crying, their shirts and skirts they do not differ from mankind." But they conceal themselves well and their presence is hard to detect, though it was said that their singing and dancing could be heard in the high mountains after a rainstorm.[208] They are skilled at making utensils, which they trade for necessaries with human beings.[209] Like the mountain imps, these little clawed pygmies were part ghost, part ape, and part non-Chinese native, with an admixture of bird, probably because of their tree-dwelling mode of life. Indeed the Mak people of the northern mountains did not disdain to intermarry with them, as we have seen.[210]

All of these wood people, perilous to wayfarers, have their cousins in other parts of the world, from the dreaded nats of the Burmese forests [211] to the fearful wood wives of the old Teutonic woodlands, ancestors of our elves and fairies.[212] There are countless others—shadowy near-people, either the fantastic creations of fear or the partly true images of incomprehension.

I. *"Elephants knew how to show their gratitude to men ..."* (p. 225) [detail of lute plectrum guard. Courtesy of Shosoin, Nara]

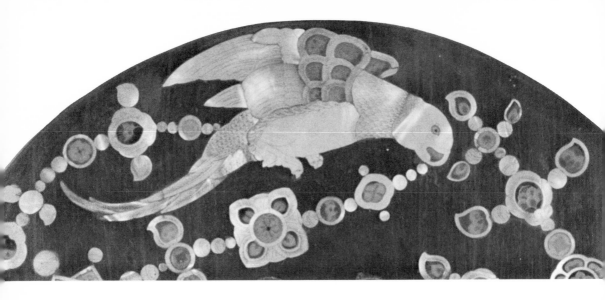

II. "...the newly occupied lands of Nam-Viet provided new and charming varieties of flowerlike parakeets to the parlors of the North" (p. 239) [detail of inlaid lute. Courtesy of Shosoin, Nara]

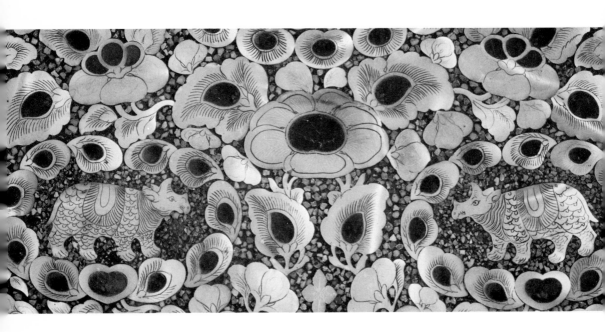

III. "The aborigines of Nam-Viet hunted rhinoceroses with bow and arrow..." (p. 226) [detail of inlaid mirror. Courtesy of Shosoin, Nara]

IV. *"His Way—to take the absence of striving to be actuality..."* (p. 93)
[Image of Hui-neng, in Pao lin szu, Shao-chou. Courtesy of Professor Lo Hsiang-lin]

V."...*the 'Bird of Viet,' as if it were the holy Vermilion Bird itself*..." (p. 237)
[detail of embroidered banner. Courtesy of Shosoin, Nara]

VI. *"...the drum embodied a frog spirit—that is a spirit of water and rain—and its voice was the booming rumble of the bullfrog"* (p. 254) [Laotian bronze drum with frogs. Courtesy of Field Museum of Natural History, Chicago]

VII. *"...the justly famous dancing girl of Tra-kiêu, an undoubted nymph and peri"* (p. 73) [Courtesy of Musée Guimet, Paris]

The world
Goes round in the climates of the mind
And bears its floraisons of imagery.

Wallace Stevens, *The Sail of Ulysses*

6 The World

THE FASHIONER OF CREATURES

FACED WITH the abnormal world of Nam-Viet, the northerner lacked the help of any generally accepted world view, to which he could optimistically assimilate the unpalatable facts of the south. The Hua men of the T'ang period could not call with complacency on such metaphysical principles as "order," "harmony," "unity in diversity," or even "beauty"—all conceptions agreeable to our tradition—to lubricate his difficult adjustment. Indeed we would be hard put to find a medieval Chinese expression which we could reasonably translate with our reasonable (to us) word "nature." [1] In language and thought the problem "what is the world like?" was inextricably entangled with the question "what occasions the world?" Partly immanent creative principles were the rule in medieval thought. For some it was "Heaven," for others "the Way," for still others "the Self-determined."

What then of Heaven? For almost everyone "Heaven" was, in some sense, a source of being and of basic differentiation, especially sexual differentiation:

Heaven gives birth to the myriad creatures, and all of them have masculinity or femininity [*lit.* they are bulls or cows], except for the oyster, which is formed spontaneously by the knotting up of saline water—it is lumpish and immobile.[2]

But Heaven was not quite the same thing to different people. For some it was a glorious but abstract supreme being formally recognized in the state cult, for others it was a vigorously creative ontological principle,[3] for yet others it was only a faded metaphor. Perhaps the archetype of "Heaven," the ancient thunderer T'ien striding the heavens above the loess, was totally forgotten by T'ang times. Probably the common view was the almost agnostic one in which Heaven was much the same as the Way—that is, without specific qualities. Liu Tsung-yüan expressed it thus: "Lacking blue, lacking yellow, lacking red, lacking black, lacking middle, lacking sides—how can we define the pattern of Heaven?"[4] Liu and others found this traditional and noncommittal anti-description unsatisfactory, and toyed with a less orthodox idea of the world, as we shall see shortly

Then there was "the Way." In T'ang times the Tao was still given conventional reverence, being capable, chameleon-like, of taking on any assignable character, even a Buddhist one, but still imprecise enough to remain respectable for upper-class gentlemen. "All things spring from the Way"—who could possibly object to that?"[5] The Way was at least the eternal womb of things and at most the pleroma, the holy uncreated totality. In smug uncritical minds it was the *real* world, if the world were rightly considered.

Closely related to the idea of the great undifferentiated fundamental was the conception of the natural world as *tzu-jan* "natura naturans"—a self-determined entity. This ancient idea had become part of the main stream of respectable "Confucian" belief,[6] though it left no room for the idea of design in nature.[7] Somewhat closer to western notions of an aloof creator were elder gods such as Nü Kua, who built the visible world, and such archaic symbols of creativity as the dragon of the "Canon of Changes."[8] But these figures could only have appealed to old-fashioned people.

There was also a minority body of opinion which was not content with naïve acceptance of the richly varied phenomenal world. Reason seemed to require a metaphysical principle similar to the "God" of A. N. Whitehead, a principle of limitation, concretion, selection, determination, individualization, and realization. Such an agent was already to be found in the ancient book of *Chuang tzu,* where it has the name Fashioner of Creatures (*tsao wu che*).[9] Sometimes it is called Fashioner of Mutations (*tsao hua che*). One T'ang formulation of the metaphysical role of this entity uses the metaphor of a bronzesmith:

> Heaven and Earth are the crucible;
> The Fashioner of Mutations is the artisan.
> *Yin* and *yang* are the charcoal;
> The myriad creatures are the bronze![10]

The creator, then, was an inventor, an artist, or an artisan, akin to the Platonic or Gnostic demiurge—but in no way a savior god or a spirit of justice, mercy, or truth.

This Fashioner is conspicuous in the work of Liu Tsung-yüan, particularly when that writer is speculating about the wonders of the landscape into which he was sent in exile. Liu Tsung-yüan is an almost perfect example of the educated gentleman of the ninth century, neither "Confucian" nor "Taoist," nor merely "Buddhist," but receptive to all exciting ideas about the place of man in nature. Beyond this, his was a sensitive spirit with a gifted pen. No complicated imagist like Li Ho or Wen T'ing-yün, he wrote plainly and precisely, but with grace and style. His prose shows the true poet's sense of the value and depth of each word chosen—though most are very ordinary words. He also wrote thoughtfully. We may observe both of these qualities in an essay he composed while in exile in the highlands of Nam-Viet. It is the well-known "Record of the Little Stone Citadel." [11]

If, after crossing directly northward from the mouth of the West Mountain Road over the Mountain Pass of Yellow Floss-grass, you go down, there will be two roads. One of them goes off to the west; if you follow it, it will get you nowhere. But go east and a little north on the other one, not more than forty ten-feet—where the soil breaks off and the river divides, and piled-up rock extends all along the shore. Above this are the shapes of battlements, beams, and a ridge. From the side protrudes a bastion or redan, and this has a kind of gateway in it. If you peer into it, it is perfectly black. If you throw in a small stone there will be the sound of water, as if in a cavern, and the high-pitched treble of its echo will persist for a good while before it stops. If you circle it, it is possible to ascend and see off a very great distance. Here, without soil or loam, grow excellent trees and fine arrow bamboos, all the more unusual and sturdy for it. Here spread apart and there close set, some bent over and some reaching upwards, they seem to have been disposed in an arrangement by a person of understanding. Ah! I have long wondered if a Fashioner of Creatures exists or not—but with this now, I tend more and more to take it that he does truly exist. But then again, I marvel that instead of making this in the central counties he composed it here among barbarians and savages, and in the course of hundreds, even thousands, of years, there has not been anyone to appraise its artistry. Surely this is to labor uselessly! If we suppose that it is not proper for a divine being to act in this way we must conclude that he does not exist. But some say it is to comfort worthy gentlemen sent here in disgrace; and some say that the holy power of the pneumas here, instead of making men, makes only such objects as this—thus, while men are few southward from Ch'u, there is an abundance of stones. Here are two ideas—I cannot believe either of them! [12]

Perhaps, like Baudelaire, Liu asked himself if there was a hidden meaning here. Perhaps the prodigy symbolized some great truth, or a battle between ancient gods, or a coming cataclysm.

> La Nature est un temple ou de vivants piliers
> Laissent parfois sortir de confuses paroles;
> L'homme passe à travers des forêts de symbols
> Qui l'observent avec des regards familiers. [13]

If he did, the question would have been a natural one—the Chinese saw the messages of Heaven everywhere in nature. But Liu had no firm belief in portents. I imagine that his rhetorical question about the purpose of the Fashioner in placing this bizarre pseudo-artifact in a remote wilderness—surely not for the solace of exiled politicians —expressed his objection to a trivial view of the aims of creation. The creative spirit did not condescend to current taste by making its best creatures easily accessible to city dwellers. The divine plan allowed for a natural stone masterpiece on this far frontier as easily as for a rare flower or a secret waterfall in a similar place.

Other visitors in Nam-Viet were provoked to remember Chuang tzu's Fashioner by the spectacles which greeted them. Sung Chih-wen, morosely crossing the mountain barrier into Nam-Viet, which he regarded as foreign soil, saw the splendid peaks marking the frontier between civilization and heathendom, and commented "we may believe this to be the power of the Fashioner of Mutations"; [14] Wu Wu-ling, awestruck by the strange animal-like figures naturally formed in limestone in the grottoes of Yin-shan at Kuei-chou, wrote, "I do not know if these are indeed metamorphoses and mutations done by the Fashioner of Creatures." [15] For some observers, the wonders of the south needed an explanation beyond mere spontaneity, or the characterless vortex of the Tao. Why these particular phenomena and not others? The traveller into distant places had his eyes and mind opened to the works of the creator as a stay-at-home never did: looking at the mast of his boat outlined against the stars, Ku Fei-hsiung wrote:

> Unless one is a long-wandering traveler
> How will he know the holy power of the Fashioner of Mutations? [16]

But, in fact, probably most visitors to Nam-Viet were content to think of the splendors and terrors of that land—if they had any philosophical thoughts about them at all—either as *tzu-jan* "the Self-determined," spontaneous bubbles on the river of experience, or, in some cases, as symbolic warnings, the concrete signals of the gods.

Beyond these, there were also the specifically Buddhist views of nature and reality —too numerous and subtle to enumerate here, except for the one common opinion: the phenomenal world is illusory, and the real world knowable, perhaps within the human heart, only after the attainment of release from the trammels and filth of the sensible universe. This vision could often be facilitated by retirement into quiet, uninhabited places where the pressure of distracting circumstance was much reduced. But in this view "nature" was not an end sought for its own sake, but only a means to the higher goal of enlightenment.[17] But some medieval Buddhist sects did not reject the world of the senses, and played down the supposed illusory character of human experience. One of these was the Avataṁsaka school, popular in T'ang times, in which the phenomenal and noumenal worlds were accorded equal importance; another was the influential T'ien-t'ai school for which "every color and every fragrance is in the Middle Way"; and there was also the Meditation (Zen) sect, which emphasized life in and love of nature.[18] In short, there was in T'ang Buddhism a tendency towards greater acceptance of this colored, odorous world. It seems possible that the rise of something close to philosophic phenomenalism in T'ang under the auspices of the powerful Buddhist church, coupled with the well-known worldliness of T'ang culture generally, account for the revival of interest in a creator—our "Fashioner"—at this time.

THE PNEUMAS OF EARTH

Below all such grand metaphysical schemes a more homely and immediate agency was much called upon by the medieval Chinese to explain the differences among the many species of creatures which inhabit the earth. This was the conception of pneuma (*ch'i*), in some systems conceived as an infinity of fluid matrices giving forms to creatures according to the prior selection of the Fashioner of Creatures,[19] but more often thought of as energetic emanations of local soil topography—the active principles of what we now call biomes.[20] The results of the activity of these pneumas were faunal, floral, mineral, and even cultural zones. A modern scholar has observed that in China "the Siberian roe deer *Capreolus capreolus pygargus* never runs south of the Tsinling Mountains, and the Indian muntjak *Muntiacus muntjak vaginalis* never runs north of central Yunnan."[21] Observations of this sort were a commonplace in ancient China, and the differences were attributed to *ti ch'i* "land pneuma," or "earth breath." Two millenia ago Chinese books pointed out that the jaunty and loquacious Crested Mynah (*Aethiopsar cristellatus*) could not be found in the Yellow River valley, and that the tangerine of the south gives way to the thorny lime of the north, each being the peculiar product of its own environment.[22] In T'ang times it was observed (by the very observant Tuan Ch'eng-shih) that

> In Shu County [Szechwan] there are neither hares nor pigeons;
> South of the Chiang there are neither wolves nor horses;
> Southward of Chu-t'i [in southern Szechwan], there are neither doves nor magpies.[23]

In 751, a splendid event drew the attention of even the meanest courtier to the action of the exhalations from the earth, and more than that, to the possibility that they could be controlled by the divine emperor. Tangerines planted in the imperial park at Ch'ang-an bore beautiful fruit. The congratulatory essay of the ministers explained the extraordinary phenomenon thus:

> Herbs and trees have their own natures, sustained by the earth breath, which penetrates them from below.
> Therefore these could draw on the rare pomes beyond the Chiang
> To create the gorgeous fruits in the Tabooed Interior.[24]

In other words, the several regions of China were connected by subterranean pipes (as it were) through which the strong mana of the Son of Heaven could draw the pneumas of distant places to produce prodigious vegetables in a climate normally antagonistic to them. Here then was a sort of primitive ecological theory, which did not require a highly developed cosmology or ontology to account for phenomena.

The World

Although the careful observation of natural phenomena was accompanied by some speculation to account for their variety and for local differentiation, the ideas developed in this way were not likely, if the history of scientific thought in the west is any guide, to prove fruitful for the development of physical science and "the control of nature," that is, for an advanced stage of science and technology, each fertilizing the other. They could, however, lead to advances in "natural history," which is now enjoying a renewed reputation in the west as the source of serious studies of the total environment, in all its concreteness. Secondary qualities—color, odor, texture, and the rest—are beginning to count again, as they did in medieval China, and the limited though important role of primary qualities—mass, size, velocity, and the like—is being seen in a corrected perspective.

In the 18th century Buffon in his criticism of Descartes had realized the limitations of abstract thought. Natural history requires description, study of detail, of color, smell, environmental changes, of the influence of man whether his acts are or are not purposive. Modern ecology and conservation also need this kind of examination, for many of their roots lie in the old natural history.[25]

The medieval Chinese were with Buffon. Though the idea, dominant in our own tradition, of a designed earth rooted in mythology and theology, was unimportant in China—the concretions of the Fashioner seem not to be based on an over-all design—the Chinese did have a tradition of the harmonization of creatures to the organisms and airs which surround them, a tradition which owes much to pharmacological and meteorological lore—that is, empirical observations of planets and weather. It is not unlike that favored by the Hippocratic school in the west.[26] But the idea of *man* as an agent of environmental change was as little noticed in the Far East as in the Far West.

Equipped with a rather restricted theoretical apparatus, but endowed with a deep interest in nature, the literate man of medieval China wrote poems and essays expressing his feelings about the natural world. But the nature literature typical of the T'ang period, with which we are so familiar, did not always exist. Although classical sanction had been given to the love of the woods and hills by Confucius [27] and Chuang tzu,[28] it is not until the third century of our era that we first get a kind of simple nature poetry, and then it is connected with the disciplines and formulas of Taoist withdrawal from the troublesome affairs of men and their institutions, and the search for eternal life.[29] "For the blending of cinnabar elixirs," wrote Ko Hung, "one should be amid mountains of repute, in a place without men." [30] And again, "All of the mountains of repute . . . bear the polypores and other herbs with which one can escape the great armaments and the great troubles." [31] The eyes of some men, then, turned to the outdoors world, looking for avenues of escape. But this primitive literary "appreciation" lacks the sophisticated mystical and emotional rapport with nature—perhaps we should write Nature—which begins to appear in the fourth and fifth centuries, pari passu with landscape painting, garden cultivation, a taste for the picturesque, and the search for outstanding examples of scenery.[32] Ancient Taoist ideas were beginning subtly to be modified by Buddhist ideas of a hidden reality, to be realized in meditation or trance, behind the mountains and rivers of this world.[33] The Tao could permit the appearance of reflections of itself in the phenomenal world to the sensitive soul, which could then be led into deeper realms of the spirit.

In the Taoist aesthetics of the sixth century, nature was quite detached from everyday human yearnings and strivings. A set of accepted literary symbols, representing the projection of emotions into that immense outer world, had been developed—"autumn" for "sadness" is an example.[34] But some writers, such as T'ao Ch'ien, had already reached a maturer level of understanding and a more subjective art, in which the human soul was once more fused with the world soul.[35]

But probably the most fruitful and fascinating of the literary modes developed during this age between Han and T'ang was one we might style the "travelogue." This form had vigorous roots in the soul journeys of the ancient Chinese shamans, and the old poetic dream trips of Sung Yü and Szu-ma Hsiang-ju [36]—accounts of wanderings in ideal, paradisiacal worlds which could be either natural or supernatural, most often both, since the real world was a shadow or reflection of the eternal world. The Taoist adept looking for rare mineral drugs in a limestone grotto was also searching for ultimate truth in a mystic underworld. Walking through a beautiful landscape was walking through heaven.[37] The genre was to have great consequences in T'ang, ranging from the extreme of purely descriptive natural history to the opposite pole of transcendent dreams and visions of life beyond the seas, the stars, and the mountains.

For the Buddhists, meanwhile, the utilitarian role of nature in the attainment of "spiritual" ends remained paramount. The vastness of the sky and the quiet of the forest suggested, as they did for the Taoists, withdrawal from the mundane mire. But even more than that, intimations of the emptiness of Nirvana caused a loss of interest in the secondary qualities of color, sound, touch, and taste, a mode of writing and thinking well developed in the verses of Wang Wei, for instance.[38]

With the deepening of the sensibility of the men of the fifth and sixth centuries, then, came new attention to the dazzling, suggestive world outside of familiar cities and farms. This development was particularly noticeable in the kingdoms south of the Yangtze River. But sightseeing literature, whether describing journeys of the soul or trips of the body, was not the only special contribution of this period and region. There was also the florescence of a new kind of poetry, odes on natural species (*yung wu*)—short, vivid, imagistic depictions of flowers, minerals, birds, and the like, quite unlike the older rhapsodic *fu* which exhausted its topic in a flood of rich language.[39]

Such were the foundations of the nature literature of T'ang. However sensitive and precise the best language of that era, it had its models in the Six Dynasties period. Li Po learned from Hsieh T'iao; Tu Fu followed Yü Hsin.[40] Such too was the heritage of the literati of T'ang who stumbled anxiously among the palms and lianes of Nam-Viet.

. . . the bright red dawn, the red as it first falls upon the mountains at the creation or birth of the morning.

Sacheverell Sitwell, *Journey to the Ends of Time*

7 Sky and Air

STARS

THE "NATURE" actually faced by the Chinese exile was an array of specifics, seen, heard, and felt long before a general formulation or brilliant symbol for the whole could be created. The wayfarer found himself literally under new skies, where "stars and planets are spread beyond the compass curve."[1] So wrote a great poet for a southbound friend, meaning that unknown luminaries would be visible beyond the familiar latitudinal lines. Arriving by sea at the port of Annam, the poet Shen Ch'üan-ch'i wrote of "the Three Lights to one side of the sun," referring to three brilliant stars in the southern constellation Scorpio, the red star Antares among them.[2] Canopus also glowed there, floating with our constellation Argo. To the Hua men it was the "Old Man Star," never seen in the north—a beacon to the optimistic searchers for long life in the southern wonderlands:

> Say nothing of malarial pestilence in this place—
> At the edge of the sky you have the Old Man Star in sight![3]

Canopus was one of the glorious sights of the southern sky observed by the members of the expedition sent to Nam-Viet during 723–726 by the Astronomer-Royal Nan-kung Yüeh and his brilliant colleague, the monk I-hsing, to take latitude measurements at eleven stations along a predetermined meridian line:

123

If, beginning in the eighth month, you look off to the south from the midst of the sea, the Old Man Star is remarkably high, and the stars ringed beneath the Old Man Star are resplendent. Large and luminous ones are very numerous—but they are not carried on our charts, and no one can determine their names.[4]

We may imagine the overheated scientists peering at their gnomon shadows in the tropical noon. Their official report gives close reckonings of "the position of the sun north of the sky summit" (i.e., the distance of the observatory south of the Tropic of Cancer), and of the "Height of the Pole" (i.e., the latitude), for both Chiao-chou (Annam) and Indrapura (Champa).[5] What other wonders of the austral skies these learned observers saw is not recorded. Did I-hsing's men discern them on the dark horizon, below the cool fire of Canopus? We inevitably think of the Magellanic Clouds, strange nebulosities in the sky below the equator, known to the medieval Arabs ("two white clouds at the feet of Canopus"),[6] reported by Marco Polo, and remarked on by Abelard.

To most men, however, it was not the new stars of the southern hemisphere which were important for understanding the south. Rather it was a group of constellations in the path of the moon which governed the destiny of Nam-Viet. Astrological prudence was more important than astronomical discovery.

The fate of the southern part of Lingnan—the north was associated astrologically with Hunan—was traditionally tied to two zodiacal asterisms—"Ox Puller," composed of three stars of which the most conspicuous was Altair (α Aquilae), and, more importantly, *"Wu* Girl," composed of four stars centered on ϵ Aquarii, this last being also the girl star alone. So it had been since Han, but the T'ang histories shifted the fateful jurisdiction to two other constellations, "Star Chronicler" governing the east of Nam-Viet, and "Quail Tail"—which had formerly been linked with the destiny of Hunan—governing the west. This was a decided innovation, and the Sung star men accepted the change with some reservations.[7] In any case, in common belief the most significant of the stellar agencies over Nam-Viet was always *Wu* Girl, a dweller in the tenth of the twenty-eight lodges in the celestial zone of the moon, "The Lodge of the Woman." In antiquity this had been appropriately aligned with the first day of summer. It was simultaneously the emblem of the female principle (goddesses and amazons!) and of the hot vapors which infested the rain forests. When Halley's Comet, a dreadful spectacle, swept through *Wu* Girl's constellation in 837, the monarch (Wen Tsung) dismissed forty-eight geishas from his palace.[8]

I have not yet tried to translate the word *wu.* In T'ang usage, and except for poetic metaphor, as we shall see, it was almost entirely restricted to the name of the star and the constellation. The dictionaries, however, say that it meant 1. contumacious, disobedient, and 2. beautiful girl. Assuming that, as is usually the case, these connotations coalesced in one root concept, possible translations would be "hoyden" (a boisterous or carefree girl) or "minx" (a pert or saucy girl). So I shall write here of the "Hoyden Star" or "The Minx" shedding her hot rays on Nam-Viet.

The T'ang poets made a special symbol of her. She was the star goddess par excellence, a sidereal beauty who might be recognized among the jeweled belles of an
earthly court. Especially at a night festival, our "Minx" became "Stella," glittering in
a garden revel, surrounded by lesser lights. Her special epithet was (*pao*) "precious;
treasure; jewel," and she is often paired with the moon nymph Ch'ang-o (Zhang-
nga). Typically, when "sylphine O departs the moon," "precious Wu takes leave of
the stars." [9] The sparkling throng at a popular night fête reflected the spangled sky
above:

> Precious Stella tosses her pearly pendants—
> Constant Luna shines her jade-white disc.[10]

(The alarming Latinisms of my translation—I might have written "Aster" and
"Selene"—conceal *Pao wu* "the gemmy minx," girded with her attendant asteroids,
and *Ch'ang-o,* brighter than her own moon mirror.)

So also when a Chinese princess leaves to marry a Tibetan king:

> Descending from her moon, Rose-gem O goes away—
> Parted from her stars, Jewel-like Wu moves off.[11]

Now, after a long overture, we must openly state the main theme and symbol of
this book, which has appeared and will appear under a multitude of guises. Here it
takes the form of the red planet Mars emerging from the velvet black of the tropical night. To the medieval Chinese it was "the spirit 'Anger of Red Sparks,'" or the
"Dazzling Deluder." His place is in the "Southern Quarter." [12] "Dazzling Deluder"
(*ying huo*) became the common name of Mars, sometimes called "Fire Star," who
represents the Fire-red God (Ch'ih Ti), the great spirit of the south, a kind of Far
Eastern Agni.[13]

"The Fire-red God is embodied in a Vermilion Bird." [14]

Seasons

The northward drift of the sun, inhabited by a red crow (a cousin of the Vermilion
Bird), to its ultimate goal, the Tropic of Cancer, took it about twenty-one miles north
of Canton. The tropics, then, included all of the coast of Nam-Viet west and south of
Ch'ao-chou, including the delta around Canton, the Lei-chou peninsula, and Hainan
Island, the southern part of modern Kwangsi, and all of Annam. In terms of political geography, about half of Kuang was above the tropic, half below; Kuei was entirely north of the tropic, Jung almost entirely south of it; Yung, except for a narrow
northern belt, and Annam were below the tropic. This was the zone, well distinguished by the Chinese, where the shadow of the astronomer's gnomon fell southward in summer, hence the name of the Annamese province of Jih-nan "South of the
Sun," and the familiar phrase "Northward Doors" conventionally used of the peo-

ples of Nam-Viet, whose gates faced the solar warmth coming, unexpectedly, from the north.[15]

Here was the sun's eternal realm, where the expected divisions among the seasons, celebrated in a thousand revered books as the foundation of life and human activity, were virtually obliterated. In particular, the summer heat persisted too long, despite the abundance of mists and clouds:

> Throughout the autumn the skies are still warmer;
> Beside the sea the sun is long shaded.[16]

Accordingly the expected changes did not appear in the foliage: "The land is warm —there are no autumn colors." [17] Indeed everything was topsy-turvy in this strange country:

> To the very end of winter you may be waving your fan;
> At the climax of summer you may be doubling your furs.[18]

Sung Chih-wen, passing through Wu-chou, put it this way:

> The southern country has neither frost nor graupel;
> Year in and out you see the florescence of nature.
> In the blue forest—dark changing of leaves,
> With red stamens—constant opening of flowers.[19]

Even the cycles of growth were not right. Here Tu Shen-yen tells of his place of exile in seventh-century Annam:

> Chiao-chou has a remarkable weather syndrome:
> While cold delays its coming, warmth is once more pressing in.
> In the middle of winter the mountain fruits are ripe,
> In the "corrected" [first] month the wild flowers open.
> Accumulated rain gives birth to gloomy fogs,
> Lightest frost brings down the quaking thunder.
> My old home is more than a myriad miles away;
> The traveler's longing is double what it was before.[20]

And here is Hsü Hun, a gifted poet who held office in Canton, on the same theme of unseasonable growth:

> Before year's end, apricots are already fruiting,
> When winter is out, herbs yield their native scents.[21]

Extremes of cold were unknown there. Chu Ch'ing-yü writes that people who come to the capital from the south say that in winter you can walk on a carpet of red blossoms of the erythrina (Coral Tree) as northerners do upon the snow:

> The Viet passes look southward, where weather and scenery are strange.
> One man after another, coming to the capital city, hands on this saying:
> "One comes and goes, throughout the winter, without treading snow—
> Always walking on top of the thorny erythrina flowers." [22]

Sky and Air

Not only do plants flower and fruit in the winter, but they fructify in astonishing ways: it was reported that the eggplants of Nam-Viet, since they do not wither during the winter, grow into considerable trees, and the vegetables must be harvested with the help of ladders.[23]

If seasons there were in Nam-Viet, they were the seasons of the monsoons, which governed the processes of life and economy throughout the warm shores and seas from South China to East Africa. The northeast monsoon of late autumn and winter, which blew off the mainland of Asia to carry the merchantmen of India and Persia away from Canton was less distinctive and less effective on human sensibilities than the stormy southwest monsoon of summer, which brought the treasure ships to Nam-Viet.[24] The violence of the onset of the summer monsoon upon India is well known in literature. Its arrival in China is different. There it comes gradually and at first inconspicuously.[25] Masses of tropical air from the Bay of Bengal and the Gulf of Tongking begin to invade south China in April, but the heavy increase of rainfall in Lingnan is mostly in May, and in some places only in June. This rainy season lasts through October.[26] The climate of Nam-Viet, accordingly, shows great local variation, according to latitude and altitude equally, and ranging from a "subtropical monsoon climate" in its northern parts to a "tropical monsoon climate" in its southern parts, with correspondingly greater heat and humidity in the southern lowlands, especially along the southwestern coast of Lingnan, the Island of Hainan, and Annam.[27] Though newcomers from the north were astonished at the absence of seasons, they were in fact not yet attuned to the subtler changes of the southern year. The immigrant soon learned the difference between the more temperate climate of Kuei-chou and the north, as contrasted with the hot airs of Annam and the south, and the crude change from the drier land-borne monsoon of winter to the wetter sea-borne monsoon of summer. Later he came to realize that summer meant rain and winter meant drizzle, that seacoasts had frightening thunder and foothills had death-dealing malaria. The four seasons of the north seemed to have been reduced to two, a wetter (April to October) and a drier (November to March). But a count of three was possible, allowing for a muggy-misty transition between the dry and wet monsoons from mid-February to mid-April.[28]

The drenching monotonous rains of the sticky "summer"[29] soon became all too familiar to the tired exiles from the north:

> The road I go—rain drawn out, and out.
> The blue hills—ending only at the brow of the sea.[30]

The incessant wet brought mildew and rot:

In spring and summer, taken altogether, the Five Passes are drenched with rain. As water-soaked days decrease, wading [as it were] through autumn until they end in winter, every single thing is prone to erosion and ruin: thatch (?) and glue, felt blankets and rugs—none will last through the year.[31]

Sky and Air

The oppressive humid climax in the southern part of the Yangtze basin was in June and early July, a little later than it was in Nam-Viet. It was customary to call these early summer rains *mei yü* "apricot rains." "The apricot rain saturates clothing, making it black with rot." [32] But although this precipitation, called up by the Yangtze alligators, coincides roughly with apricot-ripening time, the name reveals a popular etymology. *Mei* "apricot" is a substitute for *mei* "black mold; blight of mildew." [33] But although the phrase, in whatever form, was common in T'ang poetry, it seems always to refer to the rivers and lakes of Chiang-nan, not to Nam-Viet, though summer mildew was even more prevalent in the latter place. Possibly the persistent force of both local (central China) and temporal (June–July) associations prevented its application to Nam-Viet (south China, May–June).

STORMS

The full force of the wet weather was felt along the margin of the sea. "The land of Kang^a-chou borders the great sea. Fair skies are few and rain abundant. Sometimes it encounters extreme winds, and the forest cover is completely uprooted." [34] (Kang^a-chou is a coastal county in the delta just west of Canton). The worst storms were the typhoons (*chü*) which drove in from the South China Sea in the fall of the year. Han Yü knew them well:

> When a typhoon comes up, it is much to be feared—
> Booming and screaming, it tosses hills and heights! [35]

Elsewhere he writes of Ch'ao-chou, his home, in banishment:

> Typhoons for winds, crocodiles for fish—
> Afflictions and misfortunes not to be plumbed!
> South of the county, as you approach its boundary,
> There are swollen seas linked to the sky;
> Poison fogs and malarial miasmas
> Day and evening flare and form! [36]

One of the terrible storms struck the chief city on September 20, 796: "In Kuang-chou the great wind destroyed houses and overturned boats." [37] Such severe typhoons as this would scatter roof tiles "like flying butterflies." [38] Although they might come as often as two or three times a year,[39] "once in thirty to fifty years" [40] there was a premonitory sign. This portent was a kind of nimbus, halo, or multiple rainbow in the high clouds, familiarly called "Mother of Typhoons." [41] Liu Tsung-yüan wrote of this quietly fearful apparition:

> When the rain clears in the mountain's belly, elephant footprints increase;
> When the sun warms the heart of the tarn, *chiao*-dragons' saliva lengthens.
> The crafty "shooters" artfully watch for the shadows of roving men;
> The mother of typhoons whimsically frightens the boats of traveling strangers.[42]

Sky and Air

Some thought that Lei-chou "Thunder County" or "Thunder Isle," the long south-pointing peninsula, got its name from the constant roar of the booming ocean,[43] but others were sure that it was actually from the noise of thunder during the summer monsoon.

RED SKIES

The atmosphere of the realm of the Fire God, and of his messenger and avatar the Vermilion Bird, was itself red.

> . . . full of the breath of sunburnt flowers
> That bloom in a fiercer light than ours . . .
> In every hue of the blood-red sky,
> In every tone of the peacock's cry.[44]

Laurence Hope's image of the fiery sky of tropical India has a soberer counterpart in a description of Hainan by a modern traveler, who tells of the Red Range on that island, near sunset after a lightning storm:

I saw almost immediately that the entire sky over the ridge had magically become an intensive ox-blood red. The shiny translucent jungle surrounding camp reflected this red mist, so that it seemed that the very air I breathed was something tangible, tinted red! On all sides—toward the unseen setting sun westward, toward the north, the south, and the east—the sky's original clouded marble gray had become uniformly, intensely, red. The whole effect was uncanny, and at the time it seemed almost supernatural.[45]

But red was the color of all the skies of Nam-Viet, not just of Hainan. The fiery vapors of that province, the aura of its god, were well known to the T'ang poets. Tu Fu wrote "The Five Passes are all flame hot," [46] and again, "Traveling south to the domain of the sea of flames," [47] and again, "The Five Passes are a land steaming with flame." [48] These verses have multiple references. The "flames" in the air of Nam-Viet are at once the fiery color of the sky, the oppressive heat, and the burning agony of malaria—all of them the work of the Flame-red God.

> Your battle axes and ships ferry over the Swollen Sea;
> Your flags and streamers unfurl against the flaming clouds! [49]

These are farewell words to a military commander leaving for the troubled south. The red sky was not unknown in Kuei-chou either, in the more pleasant highlands, as Hsü Hun tells:

> When malarial rains want to come, the liquidambar trees are black;
> When fiery clouds first rise up, the lichees are red.[50]

129

Sky and Air

MIASMAS

The tropics were infected with corrupting mists and vapors. Nowadays we regard the fogs of the Congo basin (for instance) merely as nuisances, produced by an exceptionally humid climate.[51] But even Europeans of the nineteenth century regarded them as noxious. Here is an account of tropical Africa written in 1881:

From the fact of the intervening valleys not admitting of free perflation, from whatever direction the wind prevails, the products of rapid tropical decomposition, aided as they are by the hygrometric state of the atmosphere, hang over particular spots like clouds, and poison, like so much mephitic gas, those who are exposed to their influence. So well understood is the poisonous character of those emanations that residents close the doors and windows against the land breeze, and usually burn the air in their bedrooms by placing in it a chauffer of lighted charcoal at a safe interval of time before they retire for the night.[52]

These sentences might have been written by a medieval Chinese crouching in a hut in Kuang-chou. His experience was like that of the Europeans in Africa, where, decimated by yellow fever and sleeping sickness, the invaders had to restrict their exploitation to trading and administration.[53] Here are the words of a T'ang administrator:

The mountains and rivers of Ling-piao [i.e., Lingnan] are twisted and jungly; the vapors concentrate and are not easily dispersed or diffused. Therefore there is much mist and fog to cause pestilence.[54]

The exiled poets too were familiar with the venom-laden mists,[55] and their poisonous character was readily attributed to witchcraft. It was reported, for instance, that a certain Feng Ying (Pyong Yeng), an "uncanny outlaw" (read "aboriginal wizard") was able to call up a mist over a distance of several miles.[56]

Even the modern French have been terrorized by the moral miasmas of Nam-Viet, and the mental horrors that were hardly distinguishable from them:

> Tonkin! . . . hideux semeur de fièvres
> Qui brûle notre chair et qui glace nos lèvres.

Commenting on these words of the poet Armand Lafrique,[57] Malleret remarks, "Le soleil ardent, le climat humide et malsain, le spectacle des tombes ont disposé l'écrivain à des pensées morose."[58]

But it was not that there was more disease in the tropics, only more kinds of disease. The ecologist Marston Bates observes:

This reflects the general profusion of tropical nature. . . . The tropics have more kinds of flowers, more kinds of trees, more kinds of birds than the higher latitudes; so also they have more kinds of parasites, which in turn are capable of causing more kinds of disease. This does not necessarily mean a greater amount of sickness.[59]

The men of T'ang knew well that the feared diseases of the south could not be treated properly by traditional methods, which were adapted to a different climate. Therefore their doctors wrote handbooks for the guidance of southern practitioners and southern travelers. Unfortunately, we have now only the titles of these pioneering works in tropical medicine: Li Chi-kao, *Recipes for Travel in the South,* in three scrolls,[60] and an anonymous *Urgent and Necessary Recipes for Lingnan,* in two scrolls.[61]

Of all these hateful scourges, malaria was the most feared by the Hua men. It is still the greatest plague of mankind, and the chief cause of illness and death in the tropics around the globe.[62] "The burning ague" (if *Leviticus* indeed refers to malaria) [63] is caused among men by four species of protozoa having complicated life cycles. In Southeast Asia they are transmitted to humans by the bites of two kinds of mosquitoes, *Anopheles minimus* and *Anopheles maculatus.* These insects breed in quiet upland streams, so that malaria is endemic in tropical foothills.[64] The great deltas around Canton and Hanoi seem to be relatively free of the disease, as is recorded in historical population statistics,[65] but it was and is virulent and mortal on the wooded slopes back of the coastal plains. Accordingly those highlands have not been able to maintain a large population.[66]

The Chinese, finding the disease in the same places where they found constant mists, drizzles, and rain, saw a natural cause-and-effect relationship—for them malaria was a meteorological phenomenon: "malarial rains come from the rainbow." [67] The poet Ch'en T'ao, who wrote that line, also connected the disease with the fearful spirits of Nam-Viet:

> Mountain weirds and water trolls bestride the whirling wind;
> In dreams, incubi gnaw the soul from within the yellow malaria.[68]

In these lines malaria is pictured as a swirling, haunted yellow mist. The pest was also embodied or concentrated in the nocturnal animals of Nam-Viet:

> By the sea in autumn, the Man trees are black;
> At the passes by night, the malarial fowl fly.[69]

Indeed the poisons of malaria were ultimately only a special manifestation of the over-all venomous environment of Nam-Viet, a region which "abounds in malarial plagues, whose mountains have poisonous herbs, sand lice, and pit vipers." [70] However, other explanations were sometimes given—the disease was caused by ghosts, or by disharmony among the elements, or by improper diet.[71] A bizarre view held that small objects from the sky, which gradually became the size of cartwheels, infected the men they hit—these celestial pest bearers were called "mothers of malaria." [72] But certainly the most popular opinion was that the cause was an effluvium, in the form of a morning mist, produced locally by decaying plants and animals.[73]

The T'ang pharmacologists recommended a variety of interesting medicines for malaria: rape;[74] moonseed;[75] jerky of dolphin;[76] skate teeth ground in wine;[77] pangolin armor.[78] An ancient and interesting remedy, or rather a method for forstalling the disease, is connected with the famous name of Ma Yüan. When that warrior was in Nam-Viet he "lightened his body and abridged his desires in order to overcome the malarial vapors." He achieved this desirable condition by eating "Job's tears" (*Coix lachryma-jobi*),[79] a cereal which grows both wild and cultivated in the hills of Southeast Asia, and is much eaten when the rice crop fails.[80] The southern variety produced exceptionally large seeds, and Ma Yüan took a supply back to the north, hoping to grow them there, where they were widely admired "as gems of the southern soil."[81]

Some northerners thought of the whole land south of the Yangtze as the home of malaria, as Tu Fu wrote:

> South of the Chiang is the land of malarial pest,
> Pursuing travelers without wane or gain.[82]

In Sung times, at least, it was realized that some parts of Nam-Viet were exempt, especially the uplands of Kuei-lin, "but everywhere south of there is the home of malaria."[83] But even in T'ang times the toponymy of Nam-Viet reflected conditions, both good and bad: there was a Malaria River in Lien (Lyem)-chou,[84] and a low range of mountains called Malaria Pass:

> In the Island of Flames they net the halcyon birds;
> At the Pass of Malaria we check the Man army.[85]

The malignancy of the Nam-Viet airs was all too familiar to the strategists in the capital, who could read good accounts of the decimation (or worse) of past Chinese armies in the official histories. Accordingly, when it was reported in the fall of 627 that the native magnate Feng Ang had rebelled in Kao-chou, the privy counsellor Wei Cheng urged the prevalence of malaria against military intervention there.[86] The ferocious revolutionist Huang Ch'ao after taking Canton, found that he was losing between 30 and 40 percent of his men to the terrible disease in the autumn of 879. The survivors urged him to leave the rich port, and he allowed himself to be persuaded to turn to the plundering of Hunan and Kiangsi.[87]

Most exiled literati came to this burning land fearful of malaria, and many of them suffered from it. The pestilential mists of Nam-Viet are mentioned everywhere in the literature of that province. Here is a picture of the typical scholar-official:

> The wine which fills my coconut cup may dispel the poisonous fog;
> The wind which follows my banana-leaf fan sends the boat down the Shuang.[88]

Sensitive and susceptible, Liu Tsung-yüan was one of the sufferers. In a letter, apparently written in 814, he said: "Now, left a lonely prisoner, deposed and restricted,

I have repeatedly encountered the malarial pest; morning and evening, wasted and failing, I come closer to death, and can do nothing about it." [89]

But Liu Tsung-yüan died of yet another ailment. In a letter to a friend he said that after nine years residence in the far south he was suffering increasingly from beri-beri.[90] This disease of vitamin deficiency (not of course so described) had been long known as one of the curses on life in Nam-Viet. The old name for the disease was "leg vapors," and vitamin-rich vegetable concoctions had been prescribed for it long before T'ang times [91] ("winds" and "vapors" were pathogenic agents in early Chinese medicine as they were also in European). At the end of the fifth century the wonderful Taoist doctor T'ao Hung-ching had recommended quince; [92] a century later another Taoist, the learned patriarch Sun Szu-miao ordered the use of infusions of gourd; [93] in the eighth century the innovating Ch'en Ts'ang-ch'i prescribed almonds; [94] in the same century a Taoist thought betel nut efficacious against the bloating caused by beri-beri,[95] and in the next century the poetic Li Hsün thought sea algae as good for beri-beri as Meng Shen had believed them to be for male impotence.[96] Sufficient attention had been paid to this disease in the past to admit a small collection of books devoted entirely to the subject to the imperial library of T'ang including a volume of theory and another volume of recipes by Li Hsüan, and a collective study in one scroll by Su Chien, Hsü Yü and others.[97]

Great attention was also given to the relief of the fever and severe gastrointestinal symptoms of Asiatic cholera. It is noteworthy that the pharmacopoeias of T'ang regularly prescribed pungent and heating drugs for cholera, which tradition classified among the "cold" diseases. Along with fresh spring water and water from natural thermae [98] the following were recommended: the pellets rolled up by scarabs; [99] alpinia (so-called wild ginger); [100] peppermint; [101] smartweed; [102] dried ginger; [103] imported pepper; [104] native camphor; [105] and chebulic myrobalans.[106] Ginger was highly favored. There was still hope for a patient near death from cholera if he was given fresh ginger boiled in wine, while ginger was applied externally at the same time.[107] Sometimes bizarre remedies were needed, such as the ashes of the blood-stained clothing of a menstruating adolescent, taken with wine.[108] Equally startling is the advice of Ch'en Ts'ang-ch'i, but doubly interesting in referring to an important item in the history of Far Eastern culture, to wit, toilet paper, called "privy slips." [109] These should be burned under the bed of the cholera patient—such fumigation was equally useful in cases of difficult childbirth.[110]

The fever and delirium of lice-born typhus were as familiar and as baffling as the sufferings of cholera. It had been thought in antiquity that since the disease was most prevalent in the cooler parts of the year it was caused by exposure to severe cold (hardly common in Nam-Viet!), hence the old name "Wounding Cold." A treatise on typhus was written in Han times, and an expanded and edited version of this classical tome, the work of Wang Shu-ho of Chin, was still available and consulted in T'ang times.[111] The best medicine was of course the magical cinnabar pill of the Taoist alchemists (as it was also for cholera),[112] but other substances might prove helpful against headache and other symptoms: ordinary gypsum [113] and its splendent variety satin spar; [114] ginseng; [115] peppermint; [116] bean relish; [117] native grapes; [118] and cowries.[119]

The bubonic plague is also well known to the Far East, but I have found no specific name for it in T'ang literature. No doubt it is concealed under such general terms as "pestilence," and "plague." Probably this was the virulent epidemic disease which filled the streets of the two capitals with corpses in the winter of 682–683.[120] Beyond the cinnabar panacaea,[121] aromatic substances—the stronger the better—were regularly prescribed to repel all "evil vapors" and every kind of devilish emanation, among which these pestilential diseases were classified. A rare and potent example was "Hawkbill Aromatic" imported from overseas. A knowledgeable foreigner stated that burning a pellet of this substance (named for its shape) would protect a whole family from the pestilence, and indeed his claims were born out during a plague which swept Canton eight years later.[122]

Some visitors believed they had found zones free of these horrors, though of course not everyone could choose his place of residence. One might hope for better health in the mountains, for instance, than on the thundering coastal plains, perhaps because the climate there was more like the climate in the northern homeland. Sometimes snow fell in high places! Liu Tsung-yüan discussed the climatic peculiarities of southern Hunan and northern Nam-Viet in terms of the old adage that dogs bark at what is strange:

> I used to hear that south of Yung (Ywǎng) and Shu there was constant rain and little sun. When the sun came out the dogs barked. I took this to be an exaggerated saying until six or seven years ago, two years after I had come south. Luckily we had a great snow which crossed the mountain passes and blanketed a number of counties within Nam-Viet. The dogs of these several counties all ran madly about, pell-mell barking and snapping; finally, after a series of days, the snow was gone, and then they stopped. It was only after this that I came to believe what I had once heard.[123]

But Liu's own life came to a premature end from tropical disease north of the Tropic of Cancer. Liu Yü-hsi, his friend, wrote of Lien (Lyen)-chou in approximately the same latitude: "I seldom suffer from the afflictions of vomiting and diarrhoea—and suddenly I have gloriously candent teeth!" [124] Despite the misfortunes of Liu Tsung-yüan, the relatively cooler counties of Kuei-chou, Lien-chou, and Shao-chou, just below the passes of entry into Nam-Viet, were the preferred places of residence for Chinese compelled to live in these uncivilized and unhealthy lands. Even Sung Chih-wen, who liked none of it, had this to say of Kuei-lin on an autumn day:

> In Kuei-lin weather and scenery are strange;
> Autumn seems like the spring of Lo-yang.
> With evening clearing, river and sky are pleasant—
> Definitely, clearly—it is dejection that kills people! [125]

I watched the water-snakes:
They moved in tracks of shining white,
And when they reared, the elfish light
Fell off in hoary flakes.

Samuel Taylor Coleridge, *The Rime of the Ancient Mariner*

8 Land and Sea

LAND

WHEN a true Chinese—a Hua man—of the Yellow River valley and its vicinity
journeyed southward, he was conscious of striking changes in his physical surroundings. He expected them, since he was familiar with a long tradition of southern
strangeness. He was fully prepared to find himself in surroundings quite different
from the natural and normal ones of the blessed Yellow Earth north of the Ch'in-
ling Mountains. He was going into countries where rain was abundant, where the
growing season was longer, where rice was more important than millet and wheat,
where natural green vegetation covered more hills, where canals, irrigation ditches,
and every kind of waterway began to dominate the landscape, where people traveled
by boat as much as by cart, where water buffaloes replaced donkeys and mules,
where languages were strange, where manners were barbarous, where men were
adventurous,[1] where the whole world was more rich, fertile, and overwhelming.
These and many other contrasts between the old centers of civilization in the north
and the lately developed lands in the valley of the Yangtze and its tributaries had
long been familiar. They were even more accentuated further south. The role
played by the strange warm lands of Ch'u, in Hupei and Hunan, and by Wu and
Yüeh on the eastern coast, in the minds of their ancestors in classical antiquity, was
taken anew by the even stranger and warmer lands of Nam-Viet. The transition

was gradual, however. Northern Nam-Viet was much like southern Chiang-nan, and, in general, northerners preferred these subtropical fringes to the deep south. Then, even beyond Nam-Viet, were the intensely, almost incomprehensibly hot lands of Champa, Cambodia, and Indonesia—as incredibly non-Chinese to the magistrates of T'ang as "Elephant Forest" had been to the soldiers of Ch'in Shih Huang Ti a thousand years before. The imposed pattern of images and reactions was continually shifted southwards.

Let us now look at this new physical world, beginning with its underlying stones—and there were many stones to be seen, stepped on, and climbed over on the way into Nam-Viet.

When the traveler crossed one of the rather low passes across the watershed separating rivers and lakes of Chiang-nan from Nam-Viet, at approximately 25 degrees northern latitude, he looked down, all unknowing, upon the uplifted, crumpled and deeply eroded floor of an ancient inland sea. This intricately furrowed landscape, some of it sandstone—hardened primordial sands, some of it limestone—calcareous remains of billions of tiny sea-creatures, has been deformed by water, weather, and crustal movements to produce sculptured scenery of the most astonishing variety and beauty. One sandstone gorge is a "miniature Grand Canyon"; a deep channel through limestone is adorned by "exquisitely formed cavelike passages showing stalactites, columns, and aprons." [2]

Whichever approach the traveler took from Chiang-nan, the western or the eastern, the destination of most travelers was the rich port of Canton. The city was built in a broad, fertile delta at the junction of the three great rivers of Lingnan—the Ho-yüan flowing from the east, the Chen from the north, and the Yü from the west. Some inselbergs—partially buried fragments of a more primitive landscape—protruded through the sediments to add variety to an otherwise featureless plain. Their counterparts were the numerous rocky islands which lay offshore beyond the reach of the ever-expanding burden of silt.[3] Beyond these was the great sea which carried the merchant argosies of the golden Indies.

A soldier or administrator unlucky enough to have been assigned to one of the three barbarous administrations in the west, Kuei, Jung, and Yung (modern Kwangsi and the western coastal strip of Kwangtung), found himself in some long river valley surrounded by a vast upland area, dissected in the most complex way by the erosional forces of past millenia. Toward the east, this hill country, composed of sandstone and similar insoluble deposits,[4] evoked only mild interest in the exile. On the west and northwest, however, the land rose to a high, broken platform, formed just below the uplifted plateau of mysterious Ch'ien-chung and Yunnan, the lands of the Ts'uan peoples. Here the man sensitive to natural beauty found some compensations for his troubles. Much of this highland was carved out of sea-deposited limestone into spectacular scenery—precipitous spires and fantastic tors rising from the red and yellow plains. This is the famous and exciting karst topography of Kwangsi.[5]

Out over the southern horizon, near the tip of the hot Lei-chou peninsula, was the steep tropical island of Hainan, a true Devil's Island to the unhappy Chinese sent there—a land of monstrous boulders and vertical cliffs clothed in jungle viridian, accessible only to blood-thirsty savages and perhaps to lusty hunters from the pirate colonies of the coast.[6] Looking at it from the north, the peregrine or pioneer saw a green gem dependent from the mainland, as an Indian might look at Ceylon. If we look at it on a map, however, we see that the whole of it—and it is larger than Sicily—lies south of Hanoi, off the coast of Vietnam. It is one of the great tropical islands.[7]

If he were mad enough to avoid the official coastal road, attempting to move through aboriginal territory south- and westward towards Annam, the foolhardy wanderer rode—or perhaps walked—through a country of low hills, much of it decorated by limestone sugar loaves rising from a faulted and twisted base of ancient crystalline rocks, and humanized by rushing streams and shimmering cascades.[8]

Our wayfarer, whether madly adventurous (most unlikely!) or resigned to the intolerable burdens of an administrator, soon found himself, after not too strenuous a trip, in the second of the great delta regions of Nam-Viet—that of the river we call "Red," stained with the rusty silt of distant mountains with which it bloodied the waters of the great gulf beyond.[9] The vast delta of the Song Hoi (the age of the name is unknown) fills a sinking embayment in the coast. This important river, fed by two large tributaries, now called the Clear River (on the left) and the Black River (on the right), pours out of a deep and narrow trench, intimately related to the great gorge of the Yangtze, in the high snowy mountains of Yunnan.[10] Between these hardly imaginable summits and the warm estuary, the river flows through rugged lands penetrated by mysterious marble caverns which terminate the long Annamite cordillera.[11]

Few men of T'ang saw the dangerous border country south of here, and then only the steaming coastal road into Champa. But the sweat-bathed soldiers who tramped along this ultimate and fading extension of the empire saw, on their left, little dune-edged deltas, pleasant anchorages, and enticing offshore islets; on their right rose brief foothills which led quickly into the steep malaria-breeding sierra, built of corroded archaic sediments in the north and long-cooled igneous intrusions in the south.[12]

Over much of the lower part of this strange land, beyond the alluvial deposits of its two great deltas, lay the red and dark-grey soils of the rain forest, rich in iron and aluminum. These were the ancient, infertile lateritic earth, washed free of organic matter (they hardened readily into bricks for the red temples of Indochina). Everywhere too lay the leached ("podzolized") soils of the long-cultivated lowlands.[13]

Land and Sea

SEA

Beyond this land was its complement, the great ocean, as familiar to dwellers in the true tropics as it was strange to the Nam-Viet highlanders. The immediately accessible and familiar part of this expanse of water was called South Sea, and this was also an old name for Canton city. Its god has already been introduced to us. At the beginning of the tenth century Ts'ao Sung tried to suggest its enormous size and the richness of its animal life in these verses, entitled "South Sea": [14]

Toppling over, prancing high, on the frontier of Han—and enriching the many Man:
I stand, looking out: "How could one paint his scene?"
There is no country where it is not like this—thus I am aware of its reach.
Shared, like the sky, without distinction—so I understand its breadth.
The patterned stingray, hidden by mist, sucks in indigo at dawn;
The aging mussel, skipping the waves, spits out vermilion at night.
A myriad forms, a thousand figures—each winning to its own aim—
The long whale, alone by itself, turns its body with difficulty.

Symbolically we may regard this as a distant stretch of "That dolphin torn, that gong-tormented sea" we know from Yeats' "Byzantium," a vast archipelago haunted with strange lights and dangerous sounds. Looked at in the Chinese way, the South Sea was only the nearer part of this great sea extending into infinity beyond the ken of civilized men. The Hua men called this remote and frightening ocean—the true "high seas"—Chang-hai, a name familiar to the Arab seafarers of the Middle Ages, appearing in their geographies as Ṣankhay (earlier Čankhay).[15] In Chinese, *hai* is "sea," and *chang* is an epithet of all full, swelling waters of great extent, even rivers. Chang-hai, then, is the Swollen Sea. Nan-hai—South Sea—regarded as a region of Nam-Viet, then, was bounded on the north by the Five Passes and on the south by the Swollen Sea.[16] This was only one of the China Seas. Besides Swollen Sea and South Sea, there was the famous northeastern sea, called Ts'ang-hai.[17] *Ts'ang* means "cold and blue"—it is that iron blue we once called "watchet." This sea washed the shores of the blessed isles of the Taoist transcendents. Swollen Sea was the southern counterpart of Cold-blue Sea. It was "vague and vast, without boundaries," [18] its currents swirling round the rich Indies and carrying the great merchant ships as far as the Red Sea, or to who knows what strange places. Shen Ch'üan-ch'i, an exile in Huan-chou in Annam, was familiar with it:

The North Dipper hangs at Revered Mount,
The South Wind pulls at Swollen Sea.[19]

(Revered Mount, some said, was in southern Hunan; but it was also reported to be in Nam-Viet.) Tu Fu wrote of north-bound flights of wild geese, which, "seeing the flowers, took leave of the Swollen Sea" [20]—that is, they turned away from the great southern ocean with the appearance of signs of spring.

A feature of the South Sea well known to the residents of its shores was its tides. Ordinary tides were correctly regarded as caused by the sun and the moon: "Now the birth of the tides has its cause in the sun, while their waxing and waning is tied to the moon.[21] But these were the tides of north and south alike. There was also a rare and local tide, unpleasantly familiar to the coast dwellers of Nam-Viet. This was a secondary effect of a typhoon. The great wind, after its unimpeded sweep across the South Sea, sometimes pushed a great mass of water before it, producing a huge supernumerary tide, which destroyed boats, buildings, and farmlands. This disastrous "tide" was called the "heaped tide." [22] Liu Yü-hsi wrote a song about its occurrence in 815, though he knew of it only by report.[23]

Another exciting manifestation of the South Sea was its intermittent display of fireworks. A western student of a hundred years ago may speak of luminescence both to us and for the Chinese:

That the sea, the great extinguisher of fire, should be turned into flame—that the darkness of night should be illuminated by the luminous glow which bathes every ripple, and breaks over every wave—that globes of light should traverse the ocean, or that lightning flashes should coruscate no less in the billows of the sea than in the clouds if the air—are all facts which seize upon the imagination, and enforce attention and consideration.[24]

The light in the sea takes many forms. It may appear as darting sparks, or as a soft, greenish, fairy-like effulgence, or as moonlike patches, or as intermittent flashes, or as a general milkiness of the water.[25] These gaudy apparitions are caused by a great variety of organisms. Prominent among them are small crustaceans (*Entomostraca*), flagellates (*Noctiluca*), and tunicates (*Pyrosoma*).[26] The medieval Chinese called them all *"yin* fire." *Yin* is anything dark, shadowy, or nocturnal, and *yin* fire is fire from hidden places beneath the surface of the earth or sea. The expression is used of the subterranean sources of sulphurous springs and fumaroles, and of other concealed fires, real or metaphysical; but, above all, it refers to marine bioluminescence. Meng Kuan, in his *Study of the Strange Creatures of Lingnan,* has described it as it could be seen off the shores of Nam-Viet:

Fish and molluscs born within the sea show light when placed in a shadowed place. When you first see this, you take it for a strange and fantastic thing, and the men of this land carry this attitude even further. I presume that this is produced by saline water. When water meets *yin* creatures in the sea, waves like burning fire fill the sea. If you strike it with something it will fly out all around like starry fires. But if there should be a moon, it will be seen no more.[27]

Seeing a friend off to Lingnan, Yüan Chen characterized his new home in terms of putrifying flesh, hibernating vipers, jagged clouds, and phosphorescent water:

> When the kites swoop, you know there is malaria;
> When the snakes revive, wait no more for spring.
> With the dawn tide the clouds are spines and spikes;
> On the night sea the fires gleam and glimmer.[28]

This was the fire of the sea god, defining for the northerner his realm of light below the familiar moonglades of the surface.[29]

HILLS AND CAVES

The mountains of Nam-Viet, like those elsewhere, were charged with mana. They were, on the one hand, visible extrusions of the bony framework of the world, and, on the other, batteries charged with the spiritual electricity of Heaven, which flashed close to their summits.[30]

In general, the larger the mountain, the more holy energy was concentrated in it. The greatest of them were the "mountains of name," sought out not only by connoisseurs of landscape for their surpassingly lovely or fantastic views, but also by Taoist and Buddhist hermits as the abodes of supernatural beings. Nam-Viet was mountainous enough, but so much of it was unexplored that the special attributes and values of its hills were largely unknown to the Chinese. Yet the names of a few places admired by the men of T'ang have come down to us. Among them is a low range in Kuang-chou, the Yellow Passes, then respected as "a mountain of name." [31] Maculations like black eyes stared at the passersby from the Mountain of the Cliff of Eyes in Chao-chou, and, near there, Glorious Mountain was famous for its stalactite caves.[32]

One of the most numinous of the mountains of the region was Chiu i shan, Mountain of the Nine Doubts, which stood on the border between Chiang-nan and Nam-Viet. It was sometimes called Ts'ang-wu Mountain, and the great Shun was said to have been buried there. An old explanation of its name attributed it to the bewildering confusion of its peaks, all of which looked alike, so that "travelers had doubts about them." [33] It was thought in Han times that this mountain stood on the frontier between civilized land-men and the sub-men of the water:

South of Nine Doubts, things of the land are few, while things of the water are abundant. Accordingly, the common folk there, who have their hair spread over their backs, tattoo their bodies with representations of scaly animals.[34]

It was cognate, then, to the Shao Stones, the Gate of Ghosts, and the Pillars of Ma Yüan. It is not surprising that in T'ang times Yüan Chieh, in an illustrated description of the mountain, recommended that it replace *Heng shan,* some distance north in Hunan, as the official sacred mountain of the south, while mysterious K'un-lun, far off in Central Asia, should, he thought, be designated sacred mountain of the west.[35]

But the fame of Nine Doubts in Nam-Viet could not compare with the unsurpassed reputation of Mount Lo-fou which, despite all official and semi-official nomenclature, was the holy mountain of the south par excellence—it was the true Olympus of Nam-

Viet. Lo-fou was east of Canton in westernmost Hsün (Zywin)-chou, just below the Tropic of Cancer, between the modern villages of Tseng-ch'eng and Po-lo. The mountain is a long rugged massif, trending from northeast to southwest. Traditionally it had 432 peaks "sweeping up to the sky." [36] Its highest point is close to the western end of its serrated ridge, reaching a little higher than 4,000 feet.[37] The double name of the mountain was explained in this fashion: Long ago two floating hills drifted over the sea to Nam-Viet, where they settled on the hot plains and fused into a single double-peaked mass. The half named Mount Fou "Floating Mountain" was especially rich in maritime lore—in one tale it is a portion of P'eng-lai, the holy Taoist isle, set adrift.[38] There are many other "floating mountains," both real and mythical in China. Some are rocks and sandbanks in shoaling waters, some are boat-shaped crags on the land. Even double mountains are not unknown elsewhere. Canton itself is called P'an-yü after its twinned mountains P'an and Yü. All such are supernatural pairs, male and female—stony conjunctions of the metaphysical forces *yin* and *yang*.[39]

The view from Mount Lo-fou, described by Liu Yü-hsi, was fit for the gods:

> The blackness of the sea—heaven's eaves far-spread;
> The stars and planets come and press close on men.[40]

The same poet recorded the fanciful and persistent tradition of the sun seen at midnight from Mount Lo-fou. The story has been interpreted in many ways—as the early sight of the rising sun from the mountain's summit, as the moon interpreted as the sun of the night, as a Taoist belief in an inverted sun seen in a mystic grotto of the holy mountain.[41] It was very much a Taoist mountain, in fact, and achieved its greatest fame under the Taoist monarch Hsüan (Ghwen) Tsung. He had a great altar constructed on its slopes in 714, and official prayers for rain were offered there.[42] The reasons for its glory appear in many places in this book.

Smaller analogues of the great hills were prominent and isolated rocks. As miniature mountains, less rich in mana than the great eternal mountains, they were more liable to quick Zen-like comprehension, simply because of their spatial limitations. In the ninth century a vogue for them grew up, and bizarre and cavernous specimens were transported at great expense to the gardens of aristocratic arbiters of taste.[43] The best of these were eroded limestone crags. As the T'ang poets in exile discovered, they were abundant in the western half of Nam-Viet. Shen Ch'üan-ch'i wrote of the "odd stones and flying springs" in Tuan-chou.[44] "The weird stones break down, buffeted by the springs," wrote Hsü Hun of the fantastic landscape near there.[45]

There were rocky fantasias of equal merit in the shallow waters of Annam. A twentieth century traveler tells of them:

We then passed among the great rock formations pointing fingerlike to the sky. Thousands of the perpendicular limestone islets rise sheer out of the blue water throughout the Baie d'Along and the Baie Fai Tsi Long to the north. . . . There are bridges with the arches just above the water, numerous narrow, hidden inlets and many grottoes among the rocks. . . . For hours we cruised in the magic fairyland, playing hide and seek among the myriad gray rock towers of a thousand fanciful forms.[46]

Alas! No T'ang writer who might have given a proper account of them did so. Liu Tsung-yüan wrote only of the inland hills. The tropical isles had no poet of their own.

The most fascinating mountains were those permeated by caverns dripping with stalactites, and the chroniclers of local affairs were quick to note them: "Amidst the Man, the malarial waters flow into grottoes."[47] There were several in Chao-chou, and others nearby in Meng-chou.[48] A mountain in Wu-chou, just south of these, glittered with quartz crystals as well as with lime stalactites.[49] The most celebrated of the limestone caverns were in Kuei-chou, only partly because this was a favored part of Nam-Viet, well described by the best litterateurs. Eight or nine grottoes, close to the chief city, in a remoted, darkened region covered with "blue bamboo and green pine," were the constant subjects of laudatory odes by admiring visitors. They gaped at caverns as large as polo fields, in which hundreds of men might stand, decorated by clear springs, rushing streams, and above all by "fantastic stones," hollowed and perforated, in any number of marvelous shapes.[50] Anthropoid, zooid, and teratoid figures, formed from calcite, were the chief attractions of these treasure caves. They showed the fascinated visitor the plain evidence of the instability and interchangeability of beings, as proclaimed by *Chuang tzu,* and also the great antiquity of recognizable forms. The Grotto of White Dragons in Kuei-chou displayed the "discarded bones, like jade," of the prehistoric rain serpents.[51] A brave man, torch in hand, found himself surrounded by albino bats in a grotto in Coiled Dragon Mountain, whose golden sands were also the home of a vermilion-bellied salamander—possibly *Spelerpes longicauda,* the cave salamander. "All of these are the work of divine mutation—they can not be named according to any species." And again, "This is surely the cave-dwelling of gods and transcendent beings."[52]

Secret Mountain (Yin shan), so-called because of its hidden grottoes, was the most exciting of the hollow hills near the capital of Kuei-chou. When Li Po (Li Bwĕt), the canal builder, came there in 762, he explored the stream which emerged from its bottomless recesses and cleared away the tangled vegetation leading "through a forest of stones and a stepped path, like a holy depot built by Heaven."[53] On 18 September, 825, the poet Wu Wu-ling explored the mysteries of these underground tunnels. He regarded them with religious awe as the home of "weird beings" and black waters, the den of all kinds of draconic monsters. He saw halls, pavilions, men and animals of stone, and marveled at the cloud of white bats that swarmed around him. Of course he recommended the caves enthusiastically for sightseeing and picnics.[54]

Liu Tsung-yüan, a zealous amateur of the natural beauties of Liu-chou, wrote a brief guide to the limestone karsts which rise directly out of the plain near the government town, without piedmonts or foothills. In their caves, strange limey shapes figure prominently:

The ancient administrative seat of the county was south of Hsün (Zyĕm) Water, among the mountains and the rocks. Recently it has been shifted to a straight and level place forty *li* north of the Water where, to north, south, east, and west, water is swirling all around. To the north a pair of hills stand sheer and steep on both sides of the road—they are called The Black Stone Hills. There is a branch stream which flows eastward into Hsün Water. Because of this, all of Hsün Water on the north and east lies below a great rampart. This rampart is called Dragon's Rampart. Below it there is an abundance of stones, suitable for palettes.

Across the Water on the south there is a hill without foothills, eight hundred feet broad and fifty feet high, quite uniform from top to bottom. It is called Steam-colander Hill. Everywhere south of this hill there are great mountains, most of singular appearance.

Further south- and westward are the ones called Harnessed Crane Mountains, standing boldly upthrust in a circle. There is a spring in a pit there which, having no outlet, is always full. A lofty mountain south of there, straight and square like a screen, is called Screen Mountain. To the west are the Four Matron Mountains, all standing alone and independent.

Below the shallows of north-flowing Hsün Water, and then west, is the so-called Mountain of the Transcendents' *Go*-game. This mountain can be ascended from the west. There is a cavern at its top, and this cavern has screens, chambers, and eaves. Under these eaves there are figures formed from flowing stone, like lungs and livers, and like eggplants—sometimes heaped up below—and like men, like birds, like utensils and other objects, in great abundance. It is ninety feet from east to west, less than half of that from south to north. If you ascend to the east and go into a smaller cavern, sixteen plus four feet, this suddenly opens out to a very great size, but, having no apertures in it, it is quite black. If you hold candles towards its highest part, you can barely see its roof. Everywhere there is flowing stone in fantastic shapes. Entering a small cavern from inside the chamber south of the screen, and going up twice sixteen feet, it is black at first, but finally there is a great light. This is the upper chamber. Ascending from the upper chamber you will find a cavern. Go out through this to the north and you will be looking down on a great wilderness, and on flying birds—all you will discern of them is their backs. The first person to ascend here obtained a stone game board on the summit, with red veins on a black surface making eighteen pathways, suitable for *go*. This is why it is so named. The mountain abounds in tamarisks,[55] evergreen oaks,[56] tree bamboos,[57] and coltsfoot.[58] As for birds, there are many hawk-cuckoos.

The Mountain of the Stone Fish is entirely stoney, with no large herbs or trees. This mountain is small but high, in the form of an erect fish. Hawk-cuckoos are especially abundant there. To its west is a cavern akin to that at Transcendents' *Go*-game. You enter the cavern from the east and emerge at its northwest.

Numinous Spring is below its eastern toe, and there is a piedmont ringing it. The spring is the size of a wheel hub. It dashes twenty feet to the west with a thunderous roar to a place where there is a vortex among the stones, and there it sinks and is no more to be seen. It abounds in green and blue fish, and in rock bream,[59] and there are many zaccos.[60]

A pair of cliffs at Thunder Mountain are to east and west. There Thunder Water emerges, and where it is impounded between the cliffs it is called Thunder Tarn. It has power to produce clouds and vapors which cause vicissitudes of clouds and rain. If, when a light is visible there, you offer prayers, using trays of fish and trenchers of pork and preparing shaped sacrificial rice and rice wine in a shady place, they will be answered.

In the region south of the Erect Fish are many admirable mountains, deep-extending, but without names. Mount O, in this wilderness, has no piedmont. O Water emerges from it and flows eastward into Hsün Water.[61]

Although Liu Tsung-yüan recognized the supernatural qualities of these beautiful mountains, he is strangely silent about the holy character of their caves. For most medieval men these black and silent fairy grottoes, gushing and spouting with stone, strung with marble icicles, and glittering with cascades of foaming, frozen calcite,[62] were the antechambers of holy worlds and subterranean paradises, accessible, by way of long limestone corridors, to initiates into the arcana of Taoism.[63] The wonderful Lao tzu himself appeared during the good reign of Hsüan (Ghwen) Tsung in such a miniature heaven of stone.[64] Indeed any vaulted grotto was a kind of universe, and epiphanies of divine beings were natural to them. The very word *tung* "grotto" implied *k'ung* "space," *ch'iung* (*k'yung*) "vault," *k'u-lung* (*k'wĕt-lung*) "hole," with ancient cognates in the realm of rainbow-arches and hollow worlds. *K'ung-t'ung* was a name given to a number of Chinese mountains, and in a sense most mountains deserved the name, inasmuch as they were permeated by secret ways leading to the underplaces of the gods. In Nam-Viet these divine passages were particularly accessible: the southland was a kind of vestibule for the fantastic palaces of the earth. There are many examples—let just a few suffice. The "stone chambers" of Tuan-chou were typically the source of uncanny clouds and mists, charged with strange energy, and had two "stone gateways" leading to "the lower metropolis of the transcendents." [65] The "unfathomable" grottoes in Lotus Ridge near Shao-chou were also haunted by abstract powers and glorified presences—such as the phantom of the adept Jung K'ang who had achieved his glorious transfiguration here late in Han times.[66]

Lo-fou was the site of the deepest and most sacred grottoes, such as the one honored by the appearance of the five hundred flower-head beings to which we have already alluded. The sublime mountain had seventy such stone chambers, richly adorned with "divine fowl and jade trees." [67] By far the most wonderful of all these wonderful caverns was the "Vermilion and Luminous Grotto." It lay deep within the floating mountain (*Fou shan*) which had come from the high seas to make up half of Mount Lo-fou, but it was also said to be the portal to another grotto heaven hidden in Mount Fou-ch'iu, west of Canton. This last name means simply "floating hill," and it is clear that the two mountains, east and west of the great town, are mystically one and the same.[68] As a famous paradise in the rocks, Lo-fou was a paramount refuge for holy men, and evil persons approached it at their peril.[69] In Sung times it was said to be presided over by a personage named Chu

Ling-chih, whose splendidly significant Taoist name means "vermilion numinous polypore." [70] The Vermilion and Luminous Grotto also had its own intrepid explorer, the eighth-century Taoist priest Shen T'ai-chih. He allowed himself to be lowered into its deep-plunging entrance portal in a wicker basket. When he was hauled up again, he reported that he had indeed been in an underground world with its own sky, furnished with sun, moon, and an array of stars. [71]

RIVERS AND SPRINGS

Rivers were holy too, and Nam-Viet had its portion of water spirits, entitled to worship and appeasement according to their several degrees. The writers-in-exile there, however, wrote less of the spiritual presences than of the dangers of travel among the cascades and rapids of the mountainous regions, with which they were more familiar. Han Yü, for instance, composed no prayer to the god of the river of Lien (Lyen)-chou, to which place he had been banished in 803, as he did to the God of the South Sea while he was in exile in Ch'ao-chou in 820. On the former occasion he was more concerned with the problem of personal safety than with the appeasement of divinity. But he was new to Nam-Viet at that time:

As to the land—there are hazards of hills and highlands, and the prospect of tigers
    and leopards.
As to the water—there is the cruel urgency of river currents, and rocks traversed by waves.
Procurers of profit, and sword- and bill-men, go up and down in boats; [72]
When they mistake the current's set they are shattered to fragments,
Over and over again there are cases of sinkings and drownings. [73]

In the same year he wrote of the tremendous passage of water through a nearby gorge, named for a divine maiden in antiquity who had disappeared in the stone of its ancient wall. It was The Gorge of the Virtuous Woman.

The river winds through the constriction of the gorge—the spring torrent is imposing.
Thunder and wind contest in battle—both fish and dragon flee.
The plunging flow, with rumble and roar, shoots into the very palace archives of the
    waters.
Through its entire drainage—a hundred *li*—waves are thrown over the clouds
A whirling boat in an array of rocks is rent into a myriad shards—
So the brief measure of human fate, as light as a swan-goose feather. [74]

But in fact the rivers of Nam-Viet were not as meaningful to the Chinese as the rivers of their northern homeland, whose stories were old and rich in familiar lore. Most gods of southern waters were alien spirits, whose qualities had yet to be learned. In T'ang literature we find little of them. Even as important a stream as the Kuei, whose Holy Canal we have already discussed, had not achieved a personification or even a personality (except for the generalized jurisdiction of Ma Yüan, the wave

subduer), even though immigrant poets had noted it well as they were carried southward on its useful waters:

> The post-road runs south along the flow of Kuei Water;
> The sound of langurs is unbroken as far as the Isle of Flames.[75]

The magnificent River Yü (now called West River) is hardly noticed in T'ang history except as an administrative and engineering problem. It had its own hero, Lü
Jen-kao who, in 710–711, built a diversion channel where the river passed by the administrative seat of Yung-chou. Until then, the people had learned to live on only one
bank, because of the destruction and death caused by the bursting floods of summer
and autumn. Now the surplus water was drawn off harmlessly, and thereafter the
huts of the peasants were spread along both shores.[76]

Nam-Viet gushed with a multitude of springs, geysers, and natural fountains. They
are abundantly noted in modern guide books, but only a few had names in the T'ang
baedekers. One of these was Icy Spring, close to the walled city of Wu-chou. The poet
Yüan Chieh made an inscription in its honor, in which he explained that its cool,
sweet water was much favored by the city dwellers during the hot season. Close to it
was Fiery Mountain, smoking through deepset fissures. But:

> Fiery Mountain has no fire—
> Icy Spring has no ice.[77]

Most famous of the springs of Nam-Viet was the Spring of Avarice, at the Stone
Gate on the way to Canton. Its water (as the name implies) had an evil reputation
going back to the earliest times. Many legends are told of it, including an early one in
which the entire army of an invading Han general was drowned at this spot. The
name however suggested the fact that administrators newly arrived in Nam-Viet were
notoriously corrupted, and began lives devoted to plunder and embezzlement—the result either of the change of air after passing over the Great Yü Pass, or else to drinking the tainted water of the Spring of Avarice.[78]

Fiery Mountain, shadowing a deep clear lake on the bank opposite the walled city
of Wu-chou, was a remnant of ancient vulcanism. The nocturnal glow which flared
"like a wild flower" on the mountain at intervals of from three to five days sprang
from dying fires under the ancient soils of Nam-Viet. "Some say that there is a
precious pearl below, whose light shines above like fire," and sweet lichees ripened
early on the warm slopes of Fiery Mountain.[79] But usually the fire from under the
earth was transmitted by way of the water: Nam-Viet was rich in hot springs, a
fact strongly registered in its toponymy. There was, for instance, a county called
Thermae, with a township called Thermal Springs.[80] A western frontier county of
non-Chinese population, which sent tribute of gold, was named Warm Springs.[81]
In Hsün-chou in the east there was a river named Hot Water.[82] Long ago, early in
the fifth century, Wang Shao-chih had described the peculiarities of the hot springs
of Shao-chou. Fortunately, fragments of his little book survive. Here is one:

At the source of Holy Water there is a spring with a bubbling flow, as if it were boiling. At times there are tiny red fish swimming in it, but no one has ever caught one.[83]

Here is another:

At the source of Cloudy Water there is a thermal spring. In its lower flow there are many *chiao*-dragons which do terrible harm. If you should meet one while crossing, laugh and it will surely submerge! [84]

The medicinal value of thermal springs had long been recognized. Baths in them and draughts from them were prescribed by learned pharmacologists. The progressive T'ang herbalist Ch'en Ts'ang-ch'i—although on this subject he made no innovations —attributed the heat of these underground waters to the agency of sulphur:

If there is "fluid yellow" [sulphur] below, it causes a heating of the water, which retains the odor of the fluid yellow. Fluid yellow controls all sorts of lesions, and therefore it does so here also. At a hot spot such as this you may even warm up pork and mutton, or cook a hen's egg.

He recommended baths in the thermae for a variety of rheumatic and dermal ailments:

The several "winds"; cramping and shrinking of sinews and bones; also, coarseness and numbness of flesh and skin, and when hands and feet do not respond; lack of eyebrows and hair; acariasis and herpes. If you go in to bathe for any disease of skin or integument, bone or joint, you are liable to a great emptiness and lassitude after the bath, and should give yourself suppletion and nurture with medicines, food and drink. No man, unless he has a disease, should enter lightly.[85]

But the monster-infested waters of the far south did not yet attract wealthy arthritics. A few familiar thermae in the north, protected by respectable nymphs kin to the Hua race, had to suffice for many years to come.

DESCRIPTION AND APPRECIATION

Since literary Hua men had for several centuries been prepared for the tropics by the intermediate warmth of the Yangtze and Hunan, a liberalized view of the possibilities of natural beauty had been possible for some centuries. During the fourth, fifth, and sixth centuries, visitors to the warm subtropics were assisted by eleven handbooks on the landscape of Ching-chou (Yangtze basin just below the gorges) and eight on the scenery of Hsiang-chou (lake and river country south of there, mostly in Hunan).[86] Nam-Viet was not yet so well studied, and reluctant or torpid visitors in that region had fewer guides to propel them with some sympathy or understanding through a dangerous landscape. We have the titles of a few Nam-Viet travel books written in Han and Chin times; they are now lost, and very little is known of their contents: Lu Chia. *Chronicle of a Journey in Nam-Viet* (Han); [87] P'ei Yüan,

Record of Kuang-chou (Chin);[88] and Huang Kung, *Record of the Two Counties of Chiao and Kuang* (Chin).[89] A precursor of the great local gazetteers of the Canton region, inspired by zeal for eternal life, was the *Record of Lo-fou Mountain,* written in the fourth century by the governor Yüan Hung, the first of a long series of scenic guides to the holy mountain of Nam-Viet.[90]

But if vade mecums for the wayfarer in the remotest south were still uncommon in the first centuries of the Christian era, there were some interesting accounts of the natural history, ethnology, and the manifold wonders of that region—pioneering works, which could help him to appreciate the new forms and behavior of the living beings of that incredible environment, endlessly fascinating to the Chinese. We know something of these lost books from quotations in T'ang and Sung books—and indeed they have been heavily relied on here. The most important of them were Yang Fu, *Study of the Strange Creatures of the Southern Border* (Han);[91] Wan Chen, *Study of the Strange Creatures of the Southern Counties* (Wu);[92] Chi Han, *Descriptions of Herbs and Trees of the Southern Quarter* (Chin);[93] Shen Huai-yüan, *Study of Nam-Viet* (Sung).[94]

Suddenly in T'ang times books about Nam-Viet were no longer rare. Beginning in the early part of the period, there was great activity of an official sort in the fields of cartography and geography, covering all parts of the new empire, and the publication of standard maps and gazetteers, including records of roads, buildings, ancient ruins and local customs—but at this time, most of these covered only the middle South, that is, the Yangtze drainage basin and Chekiang. The greater part of T'ang publication of this kind was in the form of *t'u ching* "standard texts with charts" compiled by local magistrates as part of their regular duties, mostly after the middle of the eighth century. Nam-Viet is not covered by these county geographies, although there must have been reports sent in by the local magistrates, since Nam-Viet is accorded some attention in the comprehensive sets of maps of the nation (*Charts of the Ten Circuits*) issued by the government in 704, 715, and 813,[95] and in the gazetteers called *Studies of the Counties and Countries,*[96] which were abundantly relied on by the great Sung enclycopaedists. The original books are now all lost, including an anonymous one in ten scrolls compiled early in the seventh century, and two later ones, one of them the work of Ts'ao Ta-tsung.[97]

For special studies of T'ang Nam-Viet we must rely on private and less stereotyped studies—a wonderful series of books containing a greater wealth of detailed observation, most of them the work of curious and imaginative administrators temporarily stationed in the south. The most important of these are Liu Hsün's *Register of Strange Things beyond the Ranges,*[98] and Tuan Kung-lu's *Register of North-facing Doors,*[99] both of which report on every aspect of the climate, landscape, natural history, and ethnology of the region, especially when these differed from the usual mode in north China.[100] Mo (Mak) Hsiu-fu (fl. 899), author of the *Record of the Climate and Soil of Cinnamon Forest,* was probably, from his surname, an aborigine of the Mak tribe, then residing in the Kuei-lin ("Cinnamon Forest") region. He must have been thoroughly converted to Hua ways, since his book emphasizes such tourist attractions as scenery associated with famous Chinese, important buildings and shrines, and anecdotes about such great men as Chang Chiu-ling. Among the lamented lost books the most significant would appear to have been Fang Ch'ien-li (fl. 840) *Study of the Strange Creatures of the Southern Quarter,*[101] and his *Miscellaneous Register of One Cast out into the Wilderness,*[102] and Meng Kuan (ninth century), *Study of the Strange Creatures South of the Passes.* [103] From a considerable number of quotations from these important texts which fortunately survive in other books (such as the encyclopaedic *T'ai p'ing kuang chi*) they appear to have been similar in character to the works of Liu Hsün and Tuan Kung-lu.[104] (Despite the loss of his valuable books, Fang Ch'ien-li is no mere cipher to us. He has left us a record of his feelings for his beloved concubine, the Lady Chao, in the prefaces to his poems of official travel, which were intended to console her loneliness.) [105] Among other T'ang books on Nam-Viet (whose contents are virtually unknown to us) are Ta Hsi-t'ung, *Record of a Journey among the Several Foreign Peoples of Hainan;* [106] Chao Ch'ang, *Maps of the Sixty-two Grottoes of Hainan Island;* [107] Chu Chih, *Record of Bnam* [Cambodia]; [108] and an anonymous *Strange Affairs of the South Seas.*[109] There were still others.

While the great administrators were noting down the novelties of the lands and peoples they hoped to control, lesser functionaries with talent for words were beginning to convert the vivid, wet landscape into rhymed verses and smooth-flowing prose. Among them was the poet Yüan Chieh, who loved the wooded mountains of southern Hunan and northern Nam-Viet, and improved and furbished grottoes in the forest there, so that he might enjoy them in a small boat.[110] This new taste, formed in the worn limestone of the far south in the eighth and ninth centuries, was to have a profound effect on the esthetics of the Chinese garden. Liu Yü-hsi was able to comprehend the beauties of these same surroundings. Han Yü wrote ahead to a friend in Shao-chou, asking him to prepare maps and notes to guide him through that region, saying, "The hills and waters of Ch'ü-chiang have long come to my hearing." [111]

Among the exiles (leaving enthusiastic creoles like Chang Chiu-ling out of consideration) it was Liu Tsung-yüan most of all who put these attractive highlands into superb linguistic form. But the form, unlike the other writing I have mentioned, was prose rather than poetry. His limpid "travelogues" of the environment of Yung (Ywǎng)-chou and Liu-chou show the influence of ancient guide-books such as the *Classic of Waters, Annotated,* and in turn had immense influence on future diarists of saunters in the south.[112] Liu Tsung-yüan felt strongly that these low, wild hills were wrongly neglected by connoisseurs of landscape, and hoped very much to change this attitude. He expressed this radical view in an essay on a simple, even austere kiosk he built on a bare mountainside of Yung-chou in Hunan, avoiding all human ostentation which might interfere with the rare and dazzling landscape about him:

This mountain rises in a knotted cluster in the midst of blurred blue. Galloping clouds, running straight up and reaching out ten thousands of miles, coil round this wild retreat. From its head pour great torrents, and all the other hills come to attend its Levee, their contours like stars showing reverence [to the pole star], in deceptive images of watchet blue and halcyon blue, strung in damask design, interlaced in embroideries—indeed it appears that heaven has assembled its choicest blooms in this place.

He concludes with regret that there is no vogue for such a remote and difficult countryside:

Now this pavilion lies out of the way between Min [Fukien] and the Passes, on an excellent frontier—but visitors are rare, or do not write of what they do here, so that the profuse evidence for this is shut up and out of circulation. It is because this leaves a legacy of shame for its forests and gorges that I have described it.[113]

In northern Lingnan Liu Tsung-yüan discovered that the prevalent view that one could see almost all scenery worth seeing in a restricted and familiar part of the empire was mistaken. The mountains of Nam-Viet were unique:

It is altogether the common thing to assume that the places of note for sightseeing saunters in our age are not be observed beyond a single region . . . though you go out to each of the Four Quarters, all are as one, and despite boasting of their strangeness and competition in distinction, none can defer to the other. Only those who travel far and wide through the Subcelestial Realm grasp this. Yet Kuei-chou abounds in numinous mountains, which emerge from the land, craggy and substantial, standing like a forest around the fourfold wilderness.

Liu goes on to compliment the great mandarin P'ei Hsing-li for the elegant villa he built on a rocky islet in the Li River there, with surpassing vistas on all sides. The government's treatment of his pleasure isle was a little more radical than we could approve today. He paid the peasantry to cut down "obnoxious trees" and to cut back "impenetrable herbs," to build a handsome pavilion, and to bring local relics of the past ages to add distinction to the landscape. Still, some things remained unimproved, such as "the ferrying moon, penned by the surrounding gorges." Liu Tsung-yüan wound up his flattering and at the same time sincere essay with a philosophical judgment which admitted that human effort might round off the work of the creator:

Ah! It is now long since the Fashioner of Creatures placed this here—can I take it as groundless to hold that now it has been completed? [114]

With the work of such distinguished men as these we have the beginnings of the appreciation of Nam-Viet in literature, an extension of the long-standing appreciation of Chiang-nan. But this feeling and the art which gave it form were still evoked only by a transition belt in the cooler northern uplands, extending from Kuei-chou in the west to Shao-chou in the east—a zone not altogether different from southernmost Chiang-nan. As yet there was no great writer to celebrate the low, coastal tropics.

It is probable that the fantastic landscape of Kwangsi also appeared first in paint in T'ang times. We are familiar with pictures of its limestone pinnacles swathed in drifting mist made in later ages. It would be hard to prove that their prototypes existed already in early medieval times, but the inference follows reasonably from the fact that there were excellent landscape painters in Nam-Viet in the eighth and ninth centuries. One of these was Ch'en T'an,[115] "Inciting Notary" of Lien (Lyen)-chou and administrator of Yung towards the end of the eighth century. This noble man, described as "unaffected, free, and not of the herd," was required to send his Nam-Viet landscapes to the court as annual tribute.[116] An opinion of the late ninth century says that the stark, rugged isolated peaks favored by the taste that time were not often to be found in the Administrator's compositions. Rather, he painted "tangled and broken" outcrops.[117] Our question is: did he paint the alps of Kwangsi? It is hard to believe that he did not. In any event, he is the first delineator of the Nam-Viet scene known to us. There was also Hsiao Yu, who administered the favored province of Kuei-chou from 827 to 830 and died in office there. His calligraphy was as much admired as his landscape-painting, which was described as "very purposeful and well thought out." He was also remembered by his colleagues as a charming companion on a ramble through the mountain forests he loved.[118] Then there was Yang Yen, one of the great master landscapists of T'ang, a man of "miraculous" talents, who was banished to Yai-chou and forced to commit suicide there.[119] The question is the same for all. Unhappily, the laconic comments of the T'ang critics are of little help in the absence of the actual pictures.

One block, pure green as a pistachio-nut,
There's plenty jasper somewhere in the world.

Robert Browning, *The Bishop Orders his Tomb at St. Praxed's Church*

9 *Minerals*

THE ROCKS and soils of the tropical world are rich in minerals—an example is the copper and uranium of the Congo. But few minerals are restricted to the tropics.[1] The enriched magmas of primordial earth welled up with little regard for latitude. The medieval Chinese found gold in Nam-Viet, but geographically speaking its presence there was as accidental as its abundance in the cold Klondike. Tin deposits happen to be especially abundant in tropical regions, but there once were stannaries in Cornwall. Bauxite, a mixture of aluminum hydroxides, differs from these others in being a peculiar product of the weathering of rocks in tropical and subtropical climates. But the extraction of aluminum from bauxite is a modern discovery.

Nam-Viet itself has good deposits of useful minerals and stones, but those most exploited in modern times (other than the precious metals) such as iron, coal, tungsten, and arsenic,[2] got comparatively little attention from the medieval Chinese. Fancy limestones and marbles are especially abundant there,[3] but the men of T'ang were more interested in their medicinal properties than their technological application, as we shall see. Still the potential wealth of the southern hills must have been an important factor in the T'ang expansion through them. The attention given to precious stones and useful metals there is suggested by the hundreds of toponyms in which their names appear. Though I have found most of them in a Sung gazetteer, many are probably as old as T'ang. Gold Mountain, Silver River, Malachite

Mountain, Lead Mine Ridge, Treasure Mountain, and Magnetite Mountain are only a few of them.[4] Moreover, the relative abundance of metals and other minerals in Nam-Viet appears from the argument of an officer of the central administration against a new law which required the payment of taxes in coin rather than in kind; this enactment, he thought, tended to put value on the currency stored in the treasury rather than on real goods as was proper. The effect of the measure would be especially bad in Lingnan where men were accustomed to use gold, silver, and cinnabar (not to mention ivory) as media of exchange rather than the official coins.[5]

The medieval Chinese found edification and utility in stones as much as in individual mineral species. The composition of many of these is unknown to us, though limestones certainly enjoyed a favored position in their esteem. Those of peculiar shape were most attractive to them—some came from holy caverns, but others could be found scattered about among the trees and bamboo groves. The same Sung gazetteer upon which I drew just now shows Nam-Viet to have been rich in numinous stones, haunted stones and teratoid stones. Their fantastic contours littered the soil of northern Lingnan in particular, and we may be certain that although not all of such Sung names as "coiled dragon stone," "camel stone," and "rainbow stone"[6] had been invented in T'ang times, there were many of similar import then about which we know nothing. These bewildering objects were revered as transformed animals, or relics of a holier past, or the cryptic signs of the gods.

Conspicuous among the numinous stones is a species we have already noticed— the mysterious "thunderclap wedges." They had other names too, such as "thunderclap anvils"[7] and "thunder axes."[8] Some learned men recognized that these were the product of meteoric disturbances. The pharmacologist Ch'en Ts'ang-ch'i observed that the anvils could be found several feet underground at a place struck by lightning. These would be meteorites, which had sometimes been observed to fall with "a noise like thunder."[9] But the same natural philosopher goes on to say: "Their shapes are not uniform: there are some which resemble axe blades or file blades, and some which have two holes."[10] He did not recognize these specimens as tools of the Neolithic age, noting rather that "one opinion is that they come from Lei-chou," the realm of thunder, and stating that they are useful in expelling "demoniac drams and inauspicious things." But the idea that tool-like varieties might have been man-made had occurred to someone, for Ch'en remarks: "Some say that these were made by men to submit to the officers of Heaven. I do not know if this is substantial fact."[11] Our museum men might call them "ceremonial objects," and Ch'en's anonymous informant deserves a certain fame for priority. Most Chinese of this period surely shared the opinions of the old Mediterranean world:

The Greeks and Romans did not identify the actual stone implements of early men. The ones chipped to shape escaped their notice; the ground and polished stone axes they took for thunderbolts fallen from heaven, a superstition found in every part of the world. These thunderbolts were thought to have curative powers. In 1081 the Byzantine emperor Alexius Comnenus presented the German emperor Henry III with one mounted in gold.[12]

Meteorites are very rare indeed. Let us leave them and consider only the artificial thunder axes. Unfortunately the typology and chronology of the stone implements of Nam-Viet is still very poorly known. The so-called Mesolithic chipped pebbles of its western part [13] would probably not have been recognized by any medieval man as artifacts. The chronology of the Neolithic axes, stepped adzes, leaf-shaped arrowheads, and grindstones, many with technological cognates as far away as the Philippines, is extremely vague.[14] But the thunderstones excavated by the farmers of medieval Nam-Viet could have been made in any age, including their own. Stone hoes were still being used in the fields of Annam in Han times while bronze was being smelted elsewhere; [15] slate slabs and grinders were employed in the same time and place, and, for that matter, "it is obvious that the shouldered stone axe was in use in Indo-China as late as in the time of the Sung dynasty." [16] The stone axe head picked up from newly tilled soil by a Hua man of T'ang may have been two thousand years old, or it may have been the tool of an aborigine driven off his land the year before. He would not have recognized it for what it was in either case.

Vaguely akin to these shaped thunderbolts were the famous tools of "blue stone." The term is petrologically ambiguous. It could mean simply "a blue stone," such as that from which were fashioned the gleaming walls of a palace of the gods.[17] But the expression was usually interpreted as "bluestone" (accent on the first syllable), the material used by the natives of Manchuria in Chou and Han times to make their poisoned arrowheads. It has been suggested that this fine stone was a variety of flint.[18] These points were greatly valued by the Chinese.[19] I cannot identify the blue stone used in Wu-chou in T'ang times to make knives and swords, and rings for ladies.[20] It was surely a hard stone—perhaps a chert—capable of taking a high polish.

The limestones of Nam-Viet provided material for a device of extraordinary value, the classical stone chime or lithophone. Gongs of calcareous stone are among the most ancient and revered of Chinese musical instruments, retained for holy and ceremonious occasions long after they had gone out of popular use. Their analogues have been found in such remote places as Venezuela, Ethiopia, and the island of Chios. Possibly the sonorous stones on which Samoan girls pounded their kava were distantly related to the sacred chimes known to Confucius.[21] Indeed the instruments antedate Confucius by a whole millenium—the remains of sets of stones which charmed the gods or kings of Shang have been dug from the soil of north China.[22] The largest examples in the Chinese style survive in the "Confucian" temples of Vietnam,[23] and an ancient set, made to be laid out horizontally like the blocks of a xylophone, with a fine clear tone, has been unearthed in the same country.[24] In T'ang times, excellent stone for the shaping of lithophones was found in the pleasant hills of Le-ch'ang in Shao-chou, where a star "like silver" had fallen early in the seventh century.[25] At Ai-chou, in Annam close to the Cham frontier, an excellent musical stone was found, considered superior even to the favored stone of Hsiang-chou in Chiang-nan.[26]

The limestones of Mount Lo-fou also yielded sacred sounds in northern temples. The musical instruments of a Buddhist monastery in Chekiang, which were believed to go back to the sixth century, were admired by the eighth-century monk Ling-i in these words:

> The water spurts—by chimes of Lo-fou;
> The mountain sings—with bells of Khotan.[27]

Khotan was the major source of jade for the Chinese, and it appears that temple bells were sometimes made of this beautiful stone.

The same holy mountain provided beautiful garden stones in the shape of miniature craggy mountains for avant-garde connoisseurs of the ninth century. Choice specimens came mostly from the lakesides of Chekiang. Although the aesthetic stones of Nam-Viet, still a novel and distant place in T'ang times, did not yet compare with its rocks of holiness and its metals of power,[28] the limestone of sacred Lo-fou had begun to acquire some reputation. The talented young poet Chang Hu, "by nature wary and aloof," fled human involvements in a hut among trees he planted himself. He loved strange stones, and brought the "stone bamboo shoots" of Lo-fou back from Nam-Viet to enrich his solitude. An improvident youth, he died before he was twenty, leaving a pregnant concubine to rejoice in his unusual garden.[29] It is not surprising that the creative and imaginative magnate Li Te-yü introduced a handsome specimen of this novel jagged rock into his famous garden near Lo-yang. Here are the words he inscribed on it:

> A fair scene—I hold a fragrant chrysanthemum.
> A cool sky—I lean on a luxuriant pine.
> The "named mountains"—why must I go to them?
> *This* place has its own cluster of peaks.[30]

Stone employed in the manufacture of palettes for gentlemen's studios, on which they ground their ink and paint, was equally prized. The remote mountains of Tuan-chou, just west of Canton, were quarried early in the ninth century for a glossy purple stone which was greatly admired for this purpose. This Tuan-chou stone increased gradually in popularity to a climax in the thirteenth century. By then it was regarded as best of all. But the "purple stone" of Tuan-chou, most favored in T'ang times, had meanwhile been replaced in the best taste of Sung connoisseurs by orbicular varieties from new quarries close by, fancifully named "grackle eye," "parakeet eye," and the like. All were Triassic limestones, the "eyes" being conspicuous marine fossils.[31] Two important poets of T'ang praised the palettes made of this purple stone of Nam-Viet. Liu Yü-hsi wrote words to go with an inkstone as a gift (perhaps he had brought it back from Nam-Viet with him): "The stone palettes of Tuan-chou are made much of among men." [32] Li Ho, the youthful word magician, made one of them the subject of an entire poem in the most luxuriant language. It begins:

The stone craftsmen of Tuan-chou are as artful as gods—
They tread the sky, whetting their knives, to take slices of purple clouds.[33]

Even this short sample reveals Li Ho's well-known fondness for metonymy and double imagery: the lapidaries are close to the sky in the high quarries, and the limestone resembles purple clouds, but at the same time the divine nature of their art requires that, like spirits, they should actually walk among the clouds. The same poem also reveals that the Sung taste for maculated stone was already being anticipated; Li Ho's material is not of a solid color, but "a blue-flowered purple stone."

The uses of the "silvery stone of stone well," apparently a splendent mica schist, mined in Ch'ao-chou for the delectation of the imperial court, are not known [34]—ink palettes would be a good guess.

Natural lime was honored most of all for its beneficial effects on the human organism, and its most effective form was the stalactite or stalagmite grown slowly in a sacred cave. Its properties were broadly tonic, restorative and aphrodisiac: "It invigorates the primal breath, and augments the business of *yang*." [35] Taken with wine, it was a favorite remedy of the Taoist doctors.[36] Similar virtues were attributed to spring water flowing near a limestone cave, naturally impregnated with calcium: "Many men take the water to employ as a drink, and if used in the fermentation of wine its benefits are great. This water is thick, and if you weigh it will be found to be heavy. If, when you evaporate it, 'salt flowers' form on top, that is the true stalactite [lit. 'nipple; teat'] liquid." [37] The great physician Sun Szu-miao cautioned that the properties of the drug varied considerably according to locality. Varieties which were "clear and white, bright and glossy, as the patterning of gauze, the pinions of birds, or the wings of cicadas" were suitable for medical use. But as for pieces of unknown origin—"Take care not to swallow them, they will kill a man more effectively than any venom or poison." [38] The exiled writers, at least, believed that the stalactites of the northeast were the best. Liu Tsung-yüan says that the material from Lien (Lyen) and Shao is the most famous in the world; [39] his report is substantiated by Liu Yü-hsi, who writes that because of the numinous fluids filtered through the mountains of Lien-chou its medicinal stalactite is the best of all.[40] The marvelous virtues of this calcite were well recognized in the imperial palace, which required several ounces annually as token tribute from both Shao and Lien, and also from Kuang and Ch'un nearer the coast.[41]

Among the mineral species found in T'ang Nam-Viet, the most distinguished in Chinese tradition was cinnabar. This red sulphide of mercury was virtually a sacred stone to the Taoists, for whom its ready conversion into shining quicksilver was a true miracle which, properly understood, could lead to the transmutation of metals and the prolongation of life. It also yielded the pigment vermilion, the color of life and blood and eternity, applied in antiquity to the bodies of the dead, to coffins, to mimics of the gods, in short, to all sorts of holy objects, and, latterly, also to secular pictures. It was also well regarded as a drug for the treatment of serious diseases, and in some opinion it was the true panacea. One pharmacological treatise prescribed it for a sickness endemic to Nam-Viet, the convulsions of cholera:

When the body is cool, though a little warm under the heart, blend two ounces of ground cinnabar with three ounces of wax to make a pellet. Place this in a censer over a fire and fumigate it. Cover it heavily all around so as not to let the smoke leak out, then put it on a fire under the bed, so as to cause a slight warming of the belly. When, after a good while, sweat breaks out, recovery will follow.[42]

In the official *Materia Medica* of T'ang, the "cinnabar of Viet" was recognized as a distinct species:

It may occur as large as a fish, or as small as a chicken's or duck's egg. But although large in form, it is mixed with earth and stone, and is not to be compared with the kind which is fine, and also bright and clean.[43]

Although the most and best cinnabar was produced in the great mines of Shensi and Hunan, we have also noticed that cinnabar was abundant enough in Nam-Viet to pass as currency, and there was even a strong ancient tradition (not supported by the court physicians) of the superiority of the Nam-Viet mineral. Ko Hung had properly sought this native vermilion in the land of the Vermilion Bird—perhaps he found it there. In any case, cinnabar of northern and eastern Nam-Viet was required by the court as annual tribute.[44]

The mineral talc, called steatite or soapstone in its massive, lustrous form, occurred in many parts of the empire. A rather coarse, spotted, bluish variety, for instance, the product of Shantung, was used for making utensils. But the steatite of Shih-an in Kuei-chou had the greater distinction of being recommended for medicinal use: "It is as white as congealed suet, and very soft and sleek." [45] Chen Ch'üan adopted the philosophical principle of similarity in recommending the use of this slippery material as a drug to supply lubrication in aid of difficult childbirth.[46] But the construction of cooking vessels of soapstone was not unknown in Nam-Viet—steatite pots for boiling fish were used on the upper reaches of the Jung River.[47]

The official T'ang pharmacologist, Su Kung, wrote that the "flake bice" brought from Yai-chou on Hainan and by argosy from remotest Indochina, was actually "green bice," that is, the green pigment derived from malachite. Li Shih-chen, in his compendious sixteenth-century pharmacopoeia, stated that Su was mistaken, and that it was in fact the blue bice derived from azurite. I agree with him. But in any case it was a natural copper carbonate. Apparently the deposit of fine banded malachite exploited in Shao-chou under the Sung had not yet been discovered.[48]

Manufactured ceruse or white lead had been used as a pigment and cosmetic since late Chou times, and T'ang fashion decreed its application to women's breasts as well as to their faces.[49] Close to Fu-chou city in northern Lingnan was a seemingly inexhaustible deposit of a white unctuous mineral which had long been chopped out of the ground and marketed by the natives. It was used by the women of Nam-Viet as a cosmetic.[50] This was almost certainly a substance closely related to white lead, the heavy mineral cerussite, native lead carbonate.

Noninflammable textiles made from mineral asbestos were listed by Yüan Chen, along with kapok and sago, among the wonderful wares of Nam-Viet.[51]

Some coal was extracted in K'ang and Ch'un, west of Canton. It was sometimes called "burn stone," but was better known as "stone ink" or "stone carbon." The sense is the same, since ordinary ink was made of carbon black, and this seems to have been its chief use.[52]

A final useful mineral, salt. It was produced from the sea, under government control, along all the coasts of T'ang (inevitably the sodium chloride was mixed with magnesium and calcium salts), and from mines of rock salt. In Nam-Viet there was a considerable native industry on the shore of Ch'ao-chou, where the people evaporated the sea water, "and they came from far and near to obtain their requirements." [53] The identity and uses of a brilliant red salt like "crimson snow," produced in the "salt tract" of En-chou, is a mystery. Sometimes ordinary halite (sodium chloride) is red, but more normally that is the color of polyhalite, a hydrous sulphate of potassium, calcium and magnesium which has been worked in Germany and Austria, and in the western United States.[54]

Bright, hard, and vividly colored, emblematic of immortality and the freshness of paradise,[55] gemstones were the most desirable of minerals. The loveliest of them were never seen by mortals. Medieval poetry is full of allusions, often metaphorical, to exquisite, antique gemstones of vague identity, with which modern jewels could seldom compare. Conspicuous among these was *yao*. This word probably stood for a real mineral in pre-Han times. Since it was then often descriptive of ornamental stone insets in ritual vessels, it may have been turquoise or malachite, or both.[56] A blue-green association was retained after Han, when the specific identity of the mineral had been forgotten, it seems. But the persistence of the word as a handsome epithet of waters and grasses suggests that, for many writers at least, this association had not been entirely forgotten even in T'ang times. On the other hand, it seems sometimes to have been used quite without color relevance, in the general sense of "gemlike beauty." Perhaps our rather obsolete gem name "smaragd" could be used to translate it. Similar to *yao* was *ch'iung,* though its ancient connotation is even more uncertain. I think I detect a certain redness about it; possibly the medieval "carbuncle" suits its image. "Studded with smaragd and carbuncle" would be a suitably archaic way of writing about fairy towers, much more than "inlaid with turquoise and garnet."

Exotic gems, such as the carnelian of Samarkand and the lapis lazuli of Tashkent,[57] stood, for the medieval Chinese, somewhere between native stones and the gems of paradise. Many of the Hua men who came to Canton did so in the hope of finding these treasures in the coffers of the merchant princes of the Indies who assembled there. It is certain that the government, on behalf of the court and the fisc, took an even greater interest. But Nam-Viet itself, in an intermediate position exotically speaking, also produced gems, which accordingly had the slightly commonplace exotic quality assigned to Californian and Alaskan jade in our own culture. But for some the wonder gems of antiquity seemed to go naturally with the wonderland of Nam-Viet. Hence Liu Yü-hsi's description of the rich natural resources of the Lien (Lyen)-chou region:

> Forests rich in cassia and juniper;
> Earths right for pots and ceramics.
> Rocks the equal of *lang-ḳan;*
> Waters pregnant with gold and *pyĕḳ.*[58]

Both *lang-ḳan* and *pyĕḳ* (M.C. for Mand. *pi*) were old mineral names, but lacked the truly archaic glamour of *yao* and *ch'iung,* since both of the former names were still applied to specific stones between Han and T'ang. But *lang-ḳan* was also a gem which, with jade and pearls, and even with *yao* and *pi* (*pyĕḳ*), grew upon the trees of paradise.[59] Sometimes it seems to have been a red bead, perhaps imported beads of Mediterranean coral. One authority thought it was red spinel, the so-called "balas ruby." [60] But in medieval times it was most commonly a coral from the China Seas—sometimes white, turning dull purple on exposure, sometimes blue and green.[61] A T'ang pharmacologist thought that the variety named "tree *lang-ḳan*" was a pale reddish coral, which gradually turns blue.[62] Another wrote of a glassy *lang-ḳan* among the Man peoples of Yunnan.[63] *Pi* (*pyĕḳ*), on the other hand, though a respectably old word, was less brilliant and not exotic at all. In early post-Han times, it had still been the name of a mineral (prase?).[64] By T'ang, it had been reduced to the status of a color word (except in archaic allusions), apparently a blue or green of high saturation and low brilliance—I have sometimes translated it "cyan" or "indigo." Apparently Liu Yü-hsi used it as the name of a Nam-Viet gemstone only artificially and allusively.

Whatever *lang-ḳan* may have been, unambiguous coral (*shan-hu*), presumably a red variety, was a product of Nam-Viet in T'ang times.[65] Indeed the revered many-branched coral trees, twelve or thirteen feet high, which ornamented the garden of the Han palace, had been the gift of Chao T'o, king of Nam-Viet.[66] Coral had another honorable place in the Nam-Viet tradition: there was a well called "Coral Well of Ko Hung" at Mount Lo-fou. It was said that the coral which went into its construction had been the gift of a sea deity to an early alchemist.[67] Independently of the precious *Corallium nobile* imported from the Mediterranean world, then, Nam-Viet had its own fine corals, some of them red. Specimens of lovely red corals of the genus *Corallium* have in fact been found from Japan to the Sulu Sea in modern times.[68]

Otherwise, Wu-chou produced the colorless quartz we style "rock crystal," [69] while Shuang-chou was famous for its perfectly crystallized amethyst, which the T'ang pharmacologists correctly recognized as only a tinted variety of rock crystal.[70]

Probably we shall never know what the "jade" collected at Jade Mountain at

Ch'ü-chiang in Shao-chou was.[71] The most admired kind of true jade was a fine translucent white nephrite,[72] but as far as we know, all of it was imported from Serindian Khotan in medieval times. But the name "jade" was mistakenly applied to some similar stones, such as the much-admired "beautiful jade of Indigo Field," which was actually a siliceous marble, some green, some white.[73] It would be surprising, though not impossible, that a small deposit of real jade was found and soon exhausted in medieval Nam-Viet. Something like a siliceous serpentine seems more probable.

But the most admired of the gems of Nam-Viet were not minerals. Pearls, like coral, are the fruit of a sea animal. Exceptions are the rare coconuts which produce pearls around their impeded embryos: "It is composed of carbonate of calcium, like the pearl of an oyster. These abnormal nuts occur very rarely, so rarely in fact that poreless coconuts bring high prices in the Orient and are found only in the collections of the wealthy Radjas and merchants." [74] The Malays think that these pearls have magical powers.[75] I have found no coco pearls explicitly identified in T'ang literature, though they may well have been among the many dazzling, magical, monster-born pearls brought in from the Indies. For that matter, not all animal-produced pearls come from molluscs. The so-called "luminous moon pearls" or "night-shining pearls," concretions of mana, shining with their own moon-derived light, the playthings of sea dragons or the tears of shark-dragon mermen, the true treasures of the ocean,[76] were in fact the luminescent eyes of sea animals, especially whales. A T'ang description of these leviathans has them

> Drumming the waves to make thunder,
> Spurting out spume to make rain;
> The tribes of the water are afraid,
> And all flee into hiding,

and then: "Its eyes are 'luminous moon pearls.' " [77] Apparently most of these treasured phosphors were imported from the naga-haunted Indian Ocean, but Nam-Viet's eastern country of Hsün (Zywin) also sent "eyeballs of great fish" to the imperial court as annual tribute.[78] Nor are all mollusc-born pearls the offspring of oysters. The fresh-water mussel *Unio* also yields them, as the medieval Chinese well knew. Li Hsün described the pearls of Szechwan as "bright and white, and very fine, but not up to those brought by argosy in color and brilliance." (He adds that pearls must be pierced with diamond drills.) [79] But most of the "true" pearls with which both we and the men of T'ang are familiar are obtained from genus *Pinctada* "the pearl oyster." Li Hsün, however, thought that the "true pearls of the South Sea" were produced by the abalone (*Haliotis*).[80] But although *Haliotis, Nautilus* and a number of other molluscs yield excellent nacre, I am not aware that the abalone is often a mother of pearls.[81]

The looting of the pearl oyster was the source of the livelihood of the coastal dwellers around modern Pakhoi, the classical Ho-p'u, just west of the Lei-chou peninsula. This region had supplied the distant mandarins and their wives with pearls—as well as ivory, tortoise shell and silver—since the second century B.C.[82] The T'ang counties established here were Lien (Lyem)-chou and Po-chou. The latter seems to have been the greater producer.[83] A by-product of this important industry was dried oyster flesh, which was widely sold on skewers in western Nam-Viet as an appetizer to go with flagons of wine.[84] The prosperity of the fisheries depended on the abundance of the oysters (supply) and the fashions in northern cities (demand). Over-harvesting sometimes depleted the oyster beds; sumptuary laws now and then tied up the pearler's boats. A few of these rather erratic changes are registered in the dynastic histories—such as the termination of the pearl tribute on 25 December, 655;[85] another in the summer of 714;[86] the establishment of a government-supervised fishery late in the eighth century;[87] the requirement that the natives submit silver instead of pearls for a period at the end of that century and the beginning of the next;[88] and the abrogation of an undated prohibition of production in 863 in order to restore the livelihood of the natives.[89]

The periodic depletion of this resource was a familiar phenomenon, and had produced, many centuries before, a popular and deified hero whose wise methods of conservation had restored production.[90] A like disaster occurred again in 742 because of faulty management by the responsible officers, and production was not restored until 764.[91] Presumably the establishment of a supervisory office a few years later, under Tai Tsung, was a result of the realization that only strict control of the pearl harvest could maintain it from year to year. In his "Ballad of the Pearl Gatherers" Yüan Chen tells of one of these periods of exhaustion, when the aboriginal divers died in vain, the inappropriate harvest of the sea-god:

> Sea waves—no bottom—and the pearls sunk in the sea;
> And men who gather pearls—doomed to death by gathering.
> Of a myriad men doomed to death—one finds a pearl;
> A bushel measure will buy a slave girl—but where is the man?
> Year after year they gather pearls, but the pearls have fled from men;
> This year the gathering of pearls is left to the god of the sea.
> The sea god gathers pearls until every pearl is dead;
> Dead and gone the shining pearls, empty the waters of the sea.
> Pearls are creatures of the sea, and the sea is subject to the god;
> The god now freely gathers them—but how many more men![92]

Beyond this famous fishery, there was a less well developed bed of oysters at Yai-chou on the northeast coast of Hainan. Still, it was productive enough to supply pearls regularly to the capital.[93] Little note has been taken of the pearling along these southernmost, savage beaches, but Chang Chi, at least, wrote a double quatrain, "Seeing a Visitor from Hainan Off on His Return to His Old Island," which alludes to it:[94]

> Out on the sea—surely the range is far—
> Is a Man household, on a lonely clouded isle.

> In a bamboo boat you came to Cinnamon Estuary;
> In mountain markets you sold your fish-shagreen.
>
> Entering our country, you freely presented jewels;
> Meeting a person, you often gave a pearl.
> Now you go back to the mouth of your vernal grotto,
> To behead an elephant in sacrifice to T'ien-wu.

(T'ien-wu [T'en-ngu] was a sea god remembered only in an ancient Chinese book.[95] The poet has resurrected him to symbolize some anonymous deity to whom the Hainanese stranger would offer an unexpected elephant [on Hainan!] in thanksgiving for his safe return home.)

By T'ang times, Nam-Viet had become an important source of the precious metal needed to decorate the possessions of the well-to-do: gold for granulated and filigreed jewelry; gold dust and leaf for paintings and lacquer; gold to ornament wooden objects, such as expensive zithers; gold to be beaten into thin-walled vases and ewers in the Persian manner;[96] gold to coat holy images in imitation of the golden body of the true Buddha.[97]

Gold was important in literary symbolism and in folklore, and golden imagery cloaked the places of its origin and the persons who had it around them. The Taoist alchemists continued assiduously to seek it in their crucibles: gold was the very essence of incorruptibility and permanence, as they well knew, hoping to transfer these qualities to the human soul.[98] Gold was both yellow and red, and its symbolism was the same—it was the sun substance, fire, blood, the light of consciousness, and the energy of life. But gold had its darker side too, particularly the dangerous "raw gold" whose ore was found among the mountains of Nam-Viet:

The men of the south say that it is the teeth of poisonous snakes fallen among the rocks; others say that it is snake dung stuck on the rocks, or the dung of the *yüan* bird stuck on the rocks. In either case, you smash the poisoned place to get it—this is "raw gold." There is great poison in it which is fatal to men.[99]

Unlike "raw gold," which was apparently discolored auriferous quartz, "yellow gold," presumably the pure shining nuggets from placer deposits, was quite harmless. The medieval belief is not unlike the modern Annamese tradition that gold is a powerful, mana-rich substance, produced from "black bronze," and this in turn from stone—it offers great dangers to the miner, and is useful in sorcery.[100] It seems that these supernatural perils were the portion only of the hard-rock miners, not of the many placer miners.

We do not know what proportions of the gold mined in Nam-Viet came from these two sources. Certainly the alluvial deposits are the more frequently mentioned in T'ang literature. Indeed, ingenious means were devised to obtain this "bran gold" from the rivers. Some washed it out on pieces of felt,[101] while the fortunate natives of one village of Kuang-chou extracted it easily from the faeces of their ducks and geese.[102] Occasionally nuggets could be recovered from the rushing streams by hand; they were tested by biting—true gold is soft and malleable.[103]

The gold deposits were concentrated in the difficult western half of Nam-Viet, but there was some in westernmost Kuang. It occurred on the island of Hainan, in Meng and Jung (Yung) in the Kuei Administration, and in four counties of the Jung (Yong) Administration. But by far the most active producers were deep in the aboriginal counties of the Yung Administration and the Annam Protectorate.[104] There was a special concentration of placer mines along the streams of Yung, where all natives were reputed to make their livings by sifting the sands. The gold from the placers of Ch'eng in that administration was said to be so bright as to be visible in the dark.[105] Of particular importance was a government-operated mine in Jung-chou.[106] The counties of southern Annam were noted for their gold beaters, and sent quantities of gold foil to the artisans of the palace in Ch'ang-an.[107]

In the ninth century, the Arab geographer Ibn Khordādzbeh reported that the fabulous island of Wāqwāq was so rich in gold that its natives wore gold-brocaded tunics, and even made their dog chains and ape collars of the precious metal.[108] Sure to add only further confusion to the vexed question of the identity of this fairy isle off the Chinese coast, I propose, quite irresponsibly, to identify it with the gold-rich island of Hainan.

The magical white luster of silver was the color of the paradise isles.[109] The vulgar world used it for elegant cruets and cruses.[110] Except in Nam-Viet, it was not an ordinary medium of exchange in medieval China, but there it was universally accepted.[111] In this new country, silver was a commonplace, like elephants, to be yawned at as copper and horses were in the old northland.[112] Although widespread in Nam-Viet, "silver is not produced in the same places as gold."[113] Early in the ninth century, the white metal largely replaced the fancy textiles which had been required as "local tribute" in the eighth, possibly because of the opening up of new deposits in the Kuei Administration, where silver production was concentrated in that century.[114] Most, if not all, was produced by cupellation from the glittering cubes of galena, though it was said that the silver brought in from the new localities in Chiang-nan and Nam-Viet was more contaminated with lead than that extracted from an old deposit in Honan.[115]

Copper and its tin-alloyed derivative bronze were old and familiar—so much so that in classical antiquity copper had been called only "metal" in artisans' recipes. But familiarity gave bronze a special charm. The medieval Chinese loved old bronze mirrors, ancient temple bells encrusted with a patina of blue and green salts, and particularly the magical, kingly swords left for centuries in the soil until ready to be claimed by a hero.[116] Even such an everyday substance as this could have the allure of the exotic: the Hua men found in Nam-Viet an indigenous bronze culture, showing remarkable differences from their own, especially in the great bronze drums, the palladia in the houses of the local chiefs. I shall return to them later in this book. The Indochinese bronze civilization seems not to have been of great antiquity, but to have developed out of a Neolithic substratum under the technical influence of Han China. It is often called the Dongsonian Culture, from the type site at Đông-sỏn in Thanh-hoa Province.[117] But although they found many bronze artifacts in Nam-Viet, the Chinese seem not to have found any exploitable copper resources. In T'ang times the great national copper mines were concentrated near the mouth of the Yangtze River, chiefly in modern Kiangsi Province.[118]

Tin, the other ingredient of bronze, was another matter. Alluvial tinstone, or cassiterite, the oxide of the metal, was found in Ho-chou and Kuang-chou in north central Lingnan; there were two smelters on a mountainside in Ho-chou from which the natives made much profit.[119]

Although archaeological finds of iron in ancient Nam-Viet are uncommon as compared with bronze—an iron sword with a bronze guard was found at Đông-sỏn [120]—nonetheless the theme of the pair of ensouled iron swords, male and female, the work of the tribal founder in his roles of wondersmith and destined king, was spread throughout Indochina. A typical example is the story of the adventurer who founded the second dynasty of Champa in the fourth century. He caught two magic carps from which, when they turned to iron, he fashioned swords flashing with supernatural power.[121] Some, though probably not many, of the rich iron deposits of Nam-Viet were explored and worked in T'ang times—we know of mines in Kuang-chou and Ho-chou in the ninth century.[122]

As for the rest, there was a lead mine in northern Kuang-chou,[123] and quicksilver (as always, associated with cinnabar) was to be found in Lien (Lyem)-chou and Jung-chou.[124]

And other some ground perfume out of roots
Gathered by marvellous moons in Asia;
Saffron and aloes and wild cassia,
Coloured all through and smelling of the sun.

A. C. Swinburne, *St. Dorothy*

10 Plants

TROPICAL FORESTS

IT IS NOT quite possible to recover the memory of the appearance of the lowland forests of Nam-Viet in the early Middle Ages, now almost entirely replaced by cultivated fields, except perhaps as we find a specialized variety of it surviving on Hainan. A biome has vanished, and we shall not see the tropical jungle among these fields, savannas, and deciduous woodlands. But I have used the wrong word. Though "jungle" is familiar to us as a name for hot, humid, and mysterious forests in romantic literature, this usage is hardly acceptable to modern ecologists. If it means anything exactly, it refers to the tangled and often impenetrable growth which has taken over abandoned "slash-and-burn" fields, full of weed-eating insects, and the lizards, birds, and rodents which prey on the insects and the vegetation, with the larger predators—snakes and hawks—which live on the lesser animals.[1] This society is not very much like the climax community of the true tropical rain forest, such as still exists in Venezuela, the Congo, and Indonesia—a dim, quiet, seemingly empty cathedral-like realm, with an open floor of quickly decaying leaves, and great buttressed trunks supporting a high canopy, populated by flamelike winged creatures, almost invisible from below.[2]

Jungle carries all the wrong connotations for rain forest: thick vegetation, poison-ous snakes, hordes of biting insects, and all of the other ingredients of green hell. . . . The total effect of the rain forest on intruding man is gloomy rather than hellish.[3]

Nonetheless, I shall obstinately use "jungle" at times in the loose sense of "tropical forest."

There is a deceptive appearance of uniformity in the rain forest. The masses of green conceal a remarkable diversity of life forms. But except for the greenness itself, mass effects, whether of bird species, animal species, or flower species, are uncommon. The great Alfred Russel Wallace observed this in the rain forest of Celebes a century ago:

The reader who is familiar with tropical nature only through the medium of books and botanical gardens, will picture to himself in such a spot many other natural beauties. He will think that I have unaccountably forgotten to mention the brilliant flowers, which, in gorgeous masses of crimson gold or azure, must spangle these verdant precipices, hang over the cascade, and adorn the margin of the mountain stream. But what is the reality? In vain did I gaze over these vast walls of verdure, among the pendent creepers and bushy shrubs, all around the cascade, on the river's bank, or in the deep caverns and gloomy fissures—not a single tree or bush or creeper bore a flower sufficiently conspicuous to form an object in the landscape. In every direction the eye rested on green foliage and mottled rock. There was infinite variety in the color and aspect of the foliage, there was grandeur in the rocky masses and in the exuberant luxuriance of the vegetation, but there was no brilliancy of color. . . . Where, it may be asked, *are* the glorious flowers that we know do exist in the tropics? The fine tropical flowering-plants cultivated in our hot-houses have been culled from the most varied regions, and therefore give a most erroneous idea of their abundance in any one region. Many of them are very rare, others extremely local. . . . During twelve years spent amid the grandest tropical vegetation I have seen nothing comparable to the effect produced on our landscapes by gorse, broom, heather, wild hyacinths, hawthorn, purple orchises, and buttercups.[4]

Indeed, despite an occasional burst of yellow or purple on an isolated tree, the majority of the flowers one encounters in the equatorial forests are inconspicuous blooms of green or white.[5] It is the same with animals as it is with plants. To quote a modern observer:

One day you may come across a band of monkeys; the next day, perhaps, you will find some magnificent orchids and see a pair of macaws. Each kind of thing must be looked for and appreciated separately. Mass effects are exceptional, save for the rather gloomy and oppressive grandeur of the forest itself.[6]

At altitudes above four thousand feet in these same latitudes, the true rain forest gives way to a forest which is also wetted by fog. This is the cool "cloud forest." Here everything drips perpetually, and everything is covered with moss, ferns, and epiphytes—including most of the fancy orchids which ornament our tropical greenhouses.[7] Many of the most vividly colored birds live in these damp, remote highlands—birds of paradise with metallic wires and panaches in New Guinea, hummingbirds with fiery gorgets in Venezuela, and trogons splashed with the richest crimsons and greens in the tropics of both hemispheres.[8]

The pure classical rain forest probably did not exist in medieval Nam-Viet. Placed in the higher latitudes of the tropics, with a marked seasonal variation in rainfall, the primitive woodland must have belonged to the subspecies appropriately called "monsoon forest," with its own fauna and flora, standing somewhere between the typical rain forest and the biomes of subtropical and subtemperate regions.[9] Similarly, the wooden malarial hills of old Nam-Viet could not have been replicas of the cloud forests of the oceanic mountains. They were drier, and inhabited by an admixture of living creatures from milder and more northerly realms. At any rate, a modern student has called even the remnant of the medieval forest which still survives the handsomest and showiest on earth.[10]

It is probable that newcomers of T'ang times, absorbed in other problems, hardly distinguished the different kinds of woodlands through which they passed, though in general they never failed to make two observations: the abundance of evergreen trees ("in the cinnamon forests no leaves fall"),[11] and the number of unfamiliar plants, some introduced to cultivation in native gardens ("flowers from overseas and herbs of the Man are there throughout the winter; wherever you go no household fails to have its garden full of them.") [12]

It may be, however, that the Hua men felt reasonably at home in the higher and cooler forests which were the first to greet them in Nam-Viet. In our own days, only a fragment remains of these ancient woods. Much of them has been burnt off by the fires of the aboriginal *rây* cultivators, and replaced by heavy grass.[13] Strangely, what few efforts have been devoted, until recently, to the reconstitution of the ancient woods by protection and by planting, have been those of the aborigines, not of the Chinese.[14] In consequence, it seems, patches of the old coniferous forests, of a partly xerophytic character, especially junipers, yews, the "Buddhist pine" (*Podocarpus*), a southern pine (*Pinus massoniana*), and the uniquely Far Eastern and misnamed "China Fir" (*Cunninghamia sinensis*) now stand in Nam-Viet's northern hills.[15] Common components of this subtemperate woodland, to judge from its remnants, were chinquapins, tanbark oaks, laurels (spicebush and cinnamon), magnolias, champak (*Michelia*), camellia (*Thea*), and schima.[16] This old forest had little in common, it seems, with the partly deciduous "high monsoon forest" of Southeast Asia—it was much closer to the central Chinese woodlands than to the upland teak woods of Assam and Burma.[17] In the second half of the eighth century, the exiled poet-mandarin Yüan Chieh described this unique transitional landscape in these words:

> Neither fish nor turtles in its waters,
> Neither birds nor beasts in its forests,

At times you hear sounds as of some kind of cicada or fly—but as you listen to them, they are no longer there. Here and there you see great valleys and long rivers, level fields and deep abysses; firs and pines a hundred spans round; dense stands of this or that kind of juniper; blue sedge by white sand; grottoes and caves in vermilion banks; cold springs, flying and flowing; strange bamboos and variegated flowers.[18]

In medieval times, the bamboo-choked slopes and beautiful coniferous ridges of this high woodland descended into and blended with the true monsoon forest, whose outskirts, the beginnings of our romantic jungles, were observed by Liu Tsung-yüan in Liu-chou:

> Wild creepers in a shadowy jungle intertwine to cover the sun;
> Pendent snakes and knotted vipers seem to be grape vines.[19]

Down along the coast below the tropic there must have been farflung broadleaf evergreen forests of the monsoon type. Their closest surviving cognate is probably the monsoon forest of Assam—and indeed the two regions share some of the same plants, such as simal (*Bombax*), "autumn maple tree" (*Bischoffia*), and "silk tree" (*Albizzia*).[20] This long vanished tropical wilderness, unlike the more open, drier and coniferous woodlands of Kuei-chou and Shao-chou, held few attractions for the men of T'ang. Although some hills and streams were holy places, ennobled, after long occupation, by a hundred memorable allusions, the dark, dripping forests were merely repulsive—unless perhaps to the occasional eccentric who lived on wild herbs, rejoicing that other men fled the haunted jungle.[21] As a result, we look in vain in the surviving books of medieval natural history for the names of the typical trees of the monsoon forest of coastal Nam-Viet: what did they call the mallotus or Monkey-face tree? the aglaia or Orchid tree? the desmodium or Tick Trefoil? the dolichandrone or Cat-tail tree? the garcinia or Mountain Bamboo, a relative of the gambodge and mangosteen? Or *Grewia, Desmos,* and *Strychnos,* all of them the true insignia of the lowland savannas and forests. We know only their modern names.

Our knowledge of the medieval names of the plants of the hotter and denser forest of Hainan, bound in lianes and crowned with orchids and begonias, is even smaller, if that is possible.[22] The occasional T'ang poem about that island gives us only the usual clichés, and the names of a few plants notoriously useful to man. So it is in the poem which P'i Jih-hsiu addressed to a friend or colleague in Ch'iung-chou there. Beginning ominously with "A star of virtue, rayed with colors, on the verge of the malarial sky," he notices the "wine tree" which refreshes the wayfarer, a plain meal of sago, and the bright flowers of the cardamom—all of them conventional literary figures, not more specific of barbarous Ch'iung-chou than of comparatively civilized Kuang-chou.[23]

The same is true of Annam, the southernmost part of continental Nam-Viet. The lower Tongkingese forest, like the south Lingnan forests, was intermediate between the subtemperate forests and the true rain forest, with species of truly tropical affinity in the majority. Many genera of its uplands and lowlands (*Aglaia, Mallotus, Cinnamomum, Styrax, Garcinia, Podocarpus, Cunninghamia*) are also found in Lingnan. As, there, so also here, the coastal forest was enriched by palms, lianes, and epiphytes, while the mountain woods were softened by oaks, magnolias, and privets.[24] But here too, though we have the names of the trees in modern Vietnamese, they are mostly absent or unidentifiable in medieval literature.

MAGICAL AND POISONOUS PLANTS

Herbaceous plants got attention chiefly for their utility. Pure botanizing was nonexistent. Aesthetic reactions were not as ours are. To us, the orchids treasured in temperate zone hothouses crystallize the essence of tropical beauty. There is no evidence that the Hua men took a similar view of the orchids of Nam-Viet. Quantities of orchids were shipped respectfully to the imperial court from central Lingnan—that is, from several counties just north and west of Canton [25]—not to be propagated in heated rooms, but to heal the diseases of the noblemen of Ch'ang-an. It was said of the orchids of Shuang-chou: "Their stems are like the forks of golden hairpins; they are indeed of the topmost quality among drugs." [26] These tribute orchids from Nam-Viet, though officially listed under a name usually given to the dendrobium (*shih hu*), were probably another orchid altogether, which resembled both the dendrobium and the "wild ginger" (*Asarum*). Its popular name was "Hairpin Fork" and its scientific name is *Luisia teres*. The alkaloid in its root was used as an antidote to poisons, especially the bites of noxious insects.[27]

The magical, religious, and symbolic uses of plants were hardly to be distinguished from the medical. A holy leaf was a curative leaf, and the medieval pharmacologists, helped by the new listings in the herbals of Ch'en Ts'ang-ch'i and Li Hsün, were quickly learning to exploit the virtues of the strange plants of Nam-Viet. Among these must be counted the substances which were converted into talismans by the aborigines. The name "liquidambar" is applied to two south Chinese trees and the aromatic gum extracted from them. One is the widespread *Liquidambar formosana*, a source of "Chinese storax," and the other is *Altingia excelsa* of the higher mountains of Nam-Viet and Indochina generally, which also yields a "storax" or *rasamala*, as well as a valuable wood.[28] The odorous exudate should have been evidence enough of the supernatural quality of these trees. But there was more than that. The notoriously cunning "shamans of Viet" carved the tumors and excrescences which grew (during violent storms, it was said) on old liquidambars into the shapes of their deities. These "liquidambar men" were very potent and efficacious.[29]

A creeper of Nam-Viet called in English "Indian licorice" or "paternoster pea," and in Latin *Abrus precatorius,* was another medical plant well known to the northerners. We call its poisonous scarlet seeds, which are often used as beads, "prayer beads" or "jequirity seeds" (an Amerindian name).[30] Their Chinese name was "Thinking of you" ("Longing for the other one"), or simply "red beans." [31] This vine was cultivated along fences in Nam-Viet. Some part of the plant, possibly the red berries themselves, were mixed with camphor to give permanence to its odor, and its leaves were thought to heal serious knife wounds.[32] Its most important application is suggested by its Chinese name. It was a love charm, though Wang Wei wrote more delicately of the scarlet seeds as tokens of enduring friendship:

> The red beans which grow in the south country,
> With autumn's coming show forth on old branches;
> I hope, milord, that you will find many to pick—
> With such things, you will think much of me.[33]

Probably the "Thinking of you" drug which was hawked about the streets of Canton during the great holiday on the fifth day of the fifth month was extracted from the same plant: "They sell it to wealthy women as a drug for bewitching men." [34] Akin to it was another creeping plant of Nam-Viet which bore a pale purple flower. Dried and applied to the cheek as a beauty mark it was thought to look exactly like a flying crane: "The men of the south say that it is an herb of bewitchment, and most powerful." [35]

The peepul, the fig under which the Buddha attained the supreme vision, was a holy tree of a different order, found on the cultivated fringes of these native witch woods. Transplanted to China before T'ang times from the Mahābodhi Temple in holy Magadha, it gave the newly converted land a magnificent symbol of the faith.[36] Probably the greatest of them there was a wisdom tree which sprouted in Canton in 502, well before T'ang times, but which is and was most venerated for its association with the good T'ang monk Hui-neng. The *bodhi* tree at the present day *Kuang hsiao szu* is a late eighteenth-century replacement of the original, which ornamented the grounds of Hui-neng's *Fa hsing szu* ("Dharma Nature Temple") in the ninth century.[37] The poet Li Ch'ün-yü saw the sanctuary then and gave it an exotic linguistic setting, with two foreign words, *malli(ka)* "Indian jasmine" and *bodhi* "Buddhist wisdom" in antithetical positions:

> A heavenly fragrance makes the *malli* open,
> The Brahman tree lets its *bodhi* fall.[38]

But, despite its alien charm and potency, this was no true tree of Nam-Viet.

"There are those who see evil in an orchid and not in a buttercup." [39] Strange flowers are puzzling and probably dangerous, homely ones safe and friendly. The supreme instances of foreign botanic evil were concentrated in the hot southland. We have our own legend of the toxic tropic tree—it was most popular in the eighteenth century:

> Fierce in dread silence on the blasted heath
> Fell Upas sits, the Hydra Tree of death.
> Lo; from one root, the envenom'd soil below,
> A thousand vegetative serpents grow.[40]

The solid foundation of the tale of the deadly upas—needless to say, it did not infect the ground and air—can be traced to the *ipoh* poison applied to Malayan darts, an extract of the true upas, *Antiaris toxicaria*.[41] The much-varied story of the malignant and (naturally) gorgeous blossoms of the tropical jungle—like that of the poison maidens whom they resemble—is indestructible, since evidence for its romantic truth can always be found. Here is a sophisticated and languorous version from modern French Indochina:

Autour de moi les bananiers étalent en cercle, au-dessus de leurs feuilles vernissées, les cornets profonds de leurs corolles, pourpres comme le ventre des lézards chanteurs. La conque blanche des arums à l'index rouge, la flûte renversée des daturas d'un vert pâle et mortel, les étamines roses des magnolias blancs, chantent au-dessus de ma tête le concert de leurs couleurs et de leurs odeurs. Aux troncs noueux et sombres des multipliants s'accroche la traîne des strychnos homicides, et eclant ent les lobes stupéfiant des orchidées.[42]

These sentiments would have seemed soundly based to the medieval Chinese traveler as he walked through the disquieting land of Nam-Viet. He believed that his sandals pressed horrid herbs and that his dress brushed venomous vegetables. It is hard to justify that conviction by the study of the medieval *Materia Medica*, in which the great majority of known poisonous plants are northern—noxious species of *Phytolacca, Aconitum, Potentilla, Euphorbia, Arisaema, Pinellia, Parispolyphylla, Pardanthus,* and many others. Indeed, if we inspect the pages of the T'ang pharmacopoeias, it is easier to find the names of antidotes for the poisonous herbs of Nam-Viet than the names of the venomous plants themselves. Occasionally an ambiguous name does appear, such as *yeh-ko* (*ya-kat* "seductive kudzu"? "melting creeper"?): "Among the prevailing customs in Lingnan is this: many make poisonous drugs by having slaves die from eating *yeh-ko,* then burying them in the earth. Fungus grows on apposite parts of the costume. To eat these means instant death. That which grows on the hands, feet or forehead means death the same day." Fungoid growths further away from the corpse act more slowly, taking as much as two or three years.[43] But a homeopathic antidote was available, growing conveniently near the *yeh-ko*.[44] This was the poisonous and purgative root of the White-flowered Liane (*Plumbago zeylanica*), which grows widely in the tropics of the Old World, including the swamps of Nam-Viet.[45] Another local mithridate was *chi-ts'ai* (*kyit-dzai*) a divinely efficacious herb of Hsin-chou which "dissolves all poisons, even the *ku*";[46] the creeper *Ch'en Szu-chi* (apparently named for a local hero) and sometimes called "stone yellow aromatic" or "thousand gold liane," was just as powerful;[47] and tortoiseshell "dissolves the hundred herbal poisons of Lingnan."[48]

Useful Plants

Despite a basic preoccupation with poisons and potions, the immense technological resources of their new lands did not go unnoticed by the Chinese. Tough and handsome woods were needed by their architects, wheelwrights and cabinetmakers. As yet, few of the trees peculiar to Nam-Viet were known to them—in the main they exploited only those families which had already become known in the milder country of Chiang-nan.

The most magnificent of these was the *shan* (*srăm*) (*Cunninghamia*), the grand conifer—miscalled "fir"—of south China, where it has played the cultural role that the pines played in the north:

> Elephants fight by the valley-hugging bamboos;
> Langurs cry in the rain-girded *srăm*.[49]

This tree is not uncommon in medieval poetry about south China, and is particularly prominent in the verses of P'i Jih-hsiu. (The name may sometimes refer to *Cryptomeria,* whose violet-bronze needles do not in fact resemble those of the forest giant *Cunninghamia* very much.) But usually the Hua invaders' sense of beauty did not extend to this alien. If they noticed it at all, it was as a mere shadow and poor replica of the happily twisted pines of the Central States:

> By Kuei Water: plenty of liquidambars and firs [*srăm*],
> South of Ching: enough of mist and rain.
> Still, I wonder, within that indigo color—
> Could those possibly be the crags of Lo-yang? [50]

So went the superscription on a landscape painting which must have shown the befogged limestone cliffs of Kuei-chou (how we wish we might see the picture!)—but the poet could not see the real picture, only a hallucinatory vision of the homely hills of Lo-yang. Moreover, conspicuous as that tree must have been, there is no evidence yet that in T'ang times *Cunninghamia* had anything like the economic importance it has today.

A few southern hardwoods are mentioned in T'ang books because of their use in the manufacture of furniture for rich and noble households. The dusky, aromatic rosewoods (*Dalbergia*) of Hainan and Annam, resembling the prized sanders brought up from the South Seas, were cut up to make fine tables and benches.[51] The wood of several of the spicebushes (*Lindera*), all members of the laurel family, was exploited: the Moonseed (*Lindera strychnifolia*),[52] called in Chinese "Raven-black Drug," was prized for its bitter black roots, which contained a curare-like alkaloid used in the control of cholera.[53] Another species was chopped and sawed by the boat builders of Nam-Viet,[54] but it was regarded as inferior to camphorwood for this purpose.[55] The mottled wood of the "Golden *ching*" which grew in the mountains of Nam-Viet—"colored more lovely than true gold"—was prized by woodworkers, who "value it above aloes and sandal." [56] The name *ching* is used both for *Vitex* ("Yellow *ching*") and *Cercis* ("Purple *ching*," our Redbud). The exotic "Golden *ching*" could well be a *Bauhinia* of Nam-Viet, a close cousin of *Cercis*—perhaps *Bauhinia championi,* whose wood is elegantly patterned.

One tribe of truly tropical trees got due recognition. The graceful beauty of the palms, so obvious to us, giving to the foison of tropical vegetation a characteristic form,[57] seems to have made little impression on the imaginations of the medieval Chinese. They saw palms in abundance, but it is doubtful that they had learned to appreciate their beauty—certainly not in the way a man of the twentieth century can:

To appreciate a palm you must view it as you would a work of art; as if it were a marble statue or a piece of bronze. . . . The grace of their slim, straight trunks of grey or brown, with the leaf scars making ringlike marks around them, like the faint modeling of a statue, comes to have a curious charm for those who live among them. But their glory is in their leaves, those structures so different from the leaves of ordinary trees; so different that even the moonlight when it is reflected from them strikes the eye in bands and not in spots of light. Then too, the whispering of the palm leaves is far different from the sighing of the pine needles or the rustling of the oak and maple leaves. There is a special softness about it.[58]

But although the medieval Hua men neglected entirely their potential symbolic worth as settings for languorous love affairs and gentlemanly poetic musings, they recognized, as easily as did the Li and the Nung, the broad utility and versatility of the palms of Nam-Viet. Indeed, all over the tropical world, in antiquity as in modern times, the fifteen hundred species of palm have been rightly praised as sources of food, fuel, fiber, and shelter.[59] The well-beloved banana, whose broad, frayed leaves whispered outside the studios of many impressionable Chinese scholars, was its precursor on the higher levels of sensibility. The palm itself lurked in the wings of the literary stage. Still, some palms had a modest role in literature because of elevated technological associations. Such a one was the Chinese Fan Palm (*p'u-kuei,* M.C. *bu-gwi; Livistona chinensis*), a native of Nam-Viet, which was familiar even in northern poetry about elegant women and expensive courtesans:

> Roving youths with pellets of storax;
> Singsong girls with fans of *Livistona.*[60]

Another native was the coir palm (*tsung-lü; Trachycarpus excelsa*) which yields an excellent water-resistant cordage.[61]

The famous palmyras, on whose leaves were written the holy sutras of India, had been successfully planted in Ch'ang-an.[62] Indeed one species of palmyra (*pei-to,* M.C. *pai-ta,* cognate to Sanskrit *pattra* "leaf"), which yielded the very best resilient wood for making stone bows, was said to grow even in Annam.[63]

Best regarded among the palms were the food producers, and among these the coconut was preeminent. Textual references to this handsome and useful tree begin in the second century B.C.[64] Its old name was *hsü-yeh* (*syo-ya,* possibly *syo-zya*), but by T'ang times it was called simply *yeh* (*ya*).[65] But the mythology of the coconut was still alien to the Chinese, although they knew by report of Queen

Coconut-leaf, daughter of the Nagas, in ancient Cambodia, and that the Coconut and Areca moieties were distinguished clans among their neighbors the Chams.[66] The association of the fruit with Nam-Viet was reinforced by its popular name "Head of the king of Viet." [67] Most names of this sort refer to Chao T'o, the most famous king of Viet, but in this instance, the old tale told to account for it does not fit his history. It tells that a king of Champa sent an assassin to stab the king of Viet:

He took his head and hung it on a tree. Shortly it changed into a coconut. The king of Forest City, in a fury at it, ordered it split in half to make a drinking vessel. The men of the south imitate this even now. Since the king of Viet was greatly drunk at the time when he was stabbed, its fluid is still like wine.[68]

In T'ang times the inner shells of coconuts were polished to show the natural patterning, or "they painted them with white metal, to make water pitchers of them, precious and rare, worthy of admiration." [69]

Coconut cups, filled with wine, dissolve the poison mists.[70] The "milk" of the coconut was well thought of, since although "it resembles wine, one may drink without intoxication." [71] Li Hsün incorporated this exotic liquid in one of his mildly erotic Nam-Viet poems:

> The mountain fruits are ripe,
> The water flowers are fragrant.
> At house after house, an atmospheric scene with ponds and tanks.
> On a tree-orchid boat, a beaded curtain is rolled up.
> The sound of singing from afar—
> Wine from a coconut pours into a parakeet goblet.[72]

("Tree orchid" is a name for the magnolia, and the boat so named seems to be a courtesan's pleasure boat.)

Other parts of the tree had their own uses. The leaves of the coconut palm made mats for the Chams; [73] they must have been known in Nam-Viet too. Moreover, the flowers yielded an intoxicating beverage—a fermented palm wine, or toddy. Unlike the toddy of the wild date, which comes from the stem bud, and the toddy of the sugar palm and nipa, which is extracted from the peduncle: [74]

> The coconut flower is good for making wine—
> Who is my comrade, to become sloppily drunk? [75]

Despite these rich gifts, for the Chinese the coconut tree provided no soothing, homely images. Disgraced and unhappy, Shen Ch'üan-ch'i, though he found real consolation in the beauty and utility of the palms of Annam, and thought them worth propagating in more northerly latitudes, did not allow them the heart-warming qualities of true natives—no more, at least than he allowed an ancient and well-established exotic, the pomegranate. (In his poem, just below, he calls the pomegranate *t'u-lin* [*du-lyĕm*], apparently an old Iranian name cognate to Sanskrit *dālima,* said to have been introduced by the great Han explorer Chang Ch'ien many centuries before.) [76]

In Jih-nan there are coconut trees,
Aromatic wisps emerging from the prevailing dirt.
Growing thickly, heads as if carved from wood;
Rounded fruit, body like the Areca.
Inside, a chamber of jade, and dew from the Ninth Empyrean!
Prase-colored leaves—spring in the four seasons!
Is it not the equal of the *dālima* fruit,
Whose transferred root came with the Vassal of Han? [77]

The elegant areca palm was called *pin-lang* in China, a word adapted from its native Indonesian name *pinang*.[78] The tree is of Malaysian origin, but has been introduced to southern China and as far west as Socotra and Madagascar.[79] In T'ang times, the betel nut (so-called—properly speaking it is the seed of the palm) was primarily an Annamese product. Tribute from Chiao-chou, Ai-chou, and Feng (P'yong)-chou kept the court supplied. Here is an example of the amounts required: In the first decade of the ninth century, Ai-chou sent five hundred "nuts" annually, along with ten peacock tails, a hundred kingfisher tails, and twenty catties of rhinoceros horn.[80] It has been said that all peoples of south China now chew the betel nut,[81] but although its use was certainly widespread in medieval Lingnan, it is not clear whether many of the Chinese immigrants were then addicted to the astringent fruit. In any case, the attraction lay in its mild stimulant properties (its action on the nervous system is like that of nicotine).[82] The natives were accustomed to take a slice of the nut with sirih—the leaf of the betel pepper, which was also grown extensively in Annam.[83] It was also taken with wine, and as a condiment with dinner.[84] The demand for betel nut in the northern cities was probably the result of its reputed medicinal value: while, like other peppers, the "betel leaf" (sirih) was prescribed for stomach disorders,[85] the palm nut itself was taken to relieve the horrors of beriberi.[86]

A special toddy was made from the sap of the areca by the people of Champa.[87] The Chinese in Nam-Viet must have known it. They also knew that the areca nut counted for much among the peoples of Indochina, especially as a ceremonial gift. The Khmers of Chen-la (Chin-lap), for instance, presented it to guests together with clams and Borneo camphor.[88]

The tall sugar palm called *kuang-lang* (*Arenga saccharifera*) produced both a sago and a jaggery. (The language of palms must be learned: *sago* "palm starch," *jaggery* "palm sugar," *toddy* "palm wine," *gomuti* "palm fiber.") The tree has now been spread through Indonesia and Indochina by human cultivation, and by seeds in the faeces of the civet cat. Its value lies in the starch produced in the stems. This is converted to sugar, which rises in the sap, and can be tapped from the peduncle of the inflorescence. It is probable that this palm provided men with sugar before the sugar cane was exploited.[89] The starchy meal gave the tree its eighteenth- and nineteenth century Anglo-Indian name sagwire—from Portuguese *sagueira*, which is in turn a derivative of *sagu* "sago."[90] This palm flour was commonly eaten with milk, and also made into cakes.[91] But the tree yielded far more than a dietary staple: its handsomely veined purple-black wood was preferred for gaming boards; [92] the pith was prime material for therapeutic cautery; [93] the black coir fibers, properly called gomuti, extracted from the fronds and trunk, made brooms, and cord to lash the planks of ships.[94] To my knowledge, this sugar palm occurs only once in a romantic setting—characteristically shadowing a flirtatious girl of Nam-Viet in a *Nan hsiang tzu* poem by Li Hsün:

> She leaves, basket in hand,
> Homeward from picking water caltrops.
> Wind rises on cyan waves—rain in a fine flurry;
> She follows the bank in her little boat, matched oars urgent.
> Gauze dress damp,
> She gets out, heads for a sagwire—she is standing under the tree.[95]

Many kinds of palm produce sago—and so do the cycads—[96] but the best of these appears to be the sago palm properly speaking, *Metroxylon sagu,* of Indonesia. I do not know that this useful tree is found in Nam-Viet in modern times, but a *sha* tree, whose name is probably a typical Chinese shortening of *sagu* (or a related form), grew there in T'ang times. Possibly the name had been transferred from *Metroxylon* to the "meal tree" *Phoenix hanceana* of Kwangtung (especially Hainan).[97] It produced a light, tasty meal, which was made into cakes, and reported to be superior to the sago of the sagwire (*kuang-lang*).[98]

Another *Phoenix* now grows in southernmost China—*Phoenix dactylifera,* the world-renowned date palm.[99] It was planted within the walls of Canton in the ninth century. These trees bore their palatable fruits once every three years. They were said to resemble Chinese jujubes, though smaller, and were named "Persian jujubes." [100]

Along with the malaria of Nam-Viet, and its "tree visitors," cardamom flowers and sago, P'i Jih-hsiu wrote of "the wine tree, fit to slake the sighs of a banished officer." [101] He was writing of Hainan. But it is not easy to discover the identity of this wine tree. Surely it was a palm—but many palms yielded toddy. One of the famous wine palms is the nipa (*Nipa fruticans*), a tree of low habit which grows in tidal mudflats from the Ganges to Australia.[102] But its northward extension in medieval times, like that of so many plants and animals, is still uncertain. More likely the Hainanese wine palm was *Caryota mitis,* which now grows in Kwangtung, as well as in tropical east Asia generally.[103] From the sap in the flower stalks of this popular plant was collected a "delicious palm sugar called Jaggery, sweeter than barley sugar obtained from malted barley." [104] The word "jaggery" comes from the same root as "sugar," and is used of many palm sugars which will ferment into wine, but especially of *Caryota,* which is par excellence the jaggery palm of our ancestors.[105] If P'i's "wine tree" was not *the* jaggery, it was at least a jaggery producer.

The lianes, along with orchids, arums, gingers, and ferns, are among the most characteristic elements of the tropical flora of Indochina.[106] In Nam-Viet they were almost as useful as the palms, though not so nourishing. Most prominent and typical of these lianes are the rattans, this is, climbing palms of such genera as *Calamus, Daemonorops, Ceratolobus, Calospatha, Plectocomia, Plectocomiopsis* and *Korthalsia,* whose stems are widely employed to make basketry and furniture.[107] Their special position among the palms is rather like that of the bamboos among the grasses.[108] We cannot know whether the rattans of medieval Nam-Viet were as thickly tangled as those seen by Wallace in Celebes, but his description may help us to imagine a lost landscape:

One wonders at first how they can get into such queer shapes; but it is evidently caused by the decay and fall of the trees up which they have first climbed, after which they grow along the ground till they meet with another trunk up which to ascend. A tangled mass of twisted living rattan is therefore a sign that at some former period a large tree has fallen there, though there may be not the slightest vestige of it left. . . . They much improve the appearance of a forest as seen from the coast; for they vary the otherwise monotonous tree tops with feathery crowns of leaves rising clear above them, and each terminated by an erect leafy spike like a lightning-conductor.[109]

Among the true rattans of Nam-Viet was the "purple liane," perhaps the same as the "yellow liane." [110] "Yellow liane" was a recognized article of tribute from Jung (Yung)-chou in the middle of the eighth century.[111] "Purple liane" was a more ambiguous term. To northerners it meant the wisteria, which they planted in their gardens—the word "purple" described its flowers.[112] But the same expression was used of an imported Indonesian incense which they burned in their temple; this was *kayu laka,* a rosewood liane (*Dalbergia parviflora*).[113] But when "purple liane" is matched with "red lichee" in a poem about a Buddhist shrine by P'i Jih-hsiu,[114] we know that he was telling of a Nam-Viet creeper, probably the rattan *Calamus margaritae.*[115] The red-barked *sheng*-liane,[116] whose flexible stems made thongs and pinions,[117] was probably its relative *Calamus latifolius,* which grows from Kwangtung to the Indies.[118] The incense "unicorn gutta"—we would call it "dragon's blood"— extracted from the rattan palm *Calamus* (or *Daemonorops*) *draco* was a regular T'ang import from Indonesia. It now grows in Kwangtung, and was introduced there, it seems, by the tenth century, if not already in T'ang times.[119] Some lianes of Nam-Viet, such as the "thousand gold liane" of Ho-chou,[120] the "water-containing liane" cultivated along roadsides in Annam and Hainan for the cooling liquid wayfarers could find in it [121] (indeed parts of Hainan were devoid both of springs and wells, so that plant juices were necessarily the common beverages of the natives),[122] and the thorny "man-seed liane" of Annam, whose seed or berry looked like a human being [123]—all of these are still unidentified. The liane basketry of Nam-Viet was treasured by the well-to-do of north China. Most prized of all were the many-colored baskets of Hsün (Zywin)-chou [124] and the bright scarlet mats and polychrome cases of Chen-chou and Ch'iung-chou in Hainan, in which the forms of birds and beasts were woven, finer than in silk damasks.[125]

Most useful of all to the peoples of the tropical world is the family of bamboos. Other men have written of it better than I can. Here is Henry Yule, writing of Burma in the mid-nineteenth century:

When I speak of bamboo huts, I mean to say that posts and walls, wall-plates and rafters, floor and thatch and the withes that bind them, are all of bamboo. In fact it might almost be said that among the Indo-Chinese nations the staff of life is a Bamboo. Scaffolding and ladders, landing-jetties, fishing apparatus, irrigation-wheels and scoops, oars, masts and yards, spears and arrows, hats and helmets, bows, bow-string and quiver, oil-cans, water-stoups, dinner-trays, pickles, preserves, and melodious musical instruments, torches, foot-balls, cordage, bellows, mats, paper, these are but a few of the articles that are made from the bamboo.[126]

Wallace, in Indonesia in the same period, wrote:

Almost all tropical countries produce bamboos, and wherever they are found in abundance, the natives apply them to a variety of uses. Their strength, lightness, smoothness, straightness, roundness, and hollowness, the facility and regularity with which they can be split, their many different sizes, the varying length of their joints, the ease with which they can be cut and with which holes can be made through them, their hardness outside, their freedom from any pronounced taste or smell, their great abundance, and the rapidity of their growth and increase, are all qualities which render them useful for a hundred different purposes, to serve which other materials would require much more labor and preparation. The bamboo is one of the most wonderful and most beautiful productions of the tropics, and one of nature's most valuable gifts to uncivilized man.[127]

That the bamboo was a gift of the gods was apparent to the men of Nam-Viet. They had a legend of a boy found in a drifting bamboo stem by a native woman who was washing clothes in a southern river—he became the hero of the aboriginal tribes, and the temples of this totemic "bamboo king" attracted worshipers from throughout Nam-Viet.[128]

The bamboos of China are by no means restricted to the tropical zone. They grow abundantly in its temperate central zone as well. Artifacts wrought skilfully of the many kinds of Chinese bamboo had been used in the bamboo-barren north for a very long time. Virtually every part of Nam-Viet sent bamboo products to the home valley of the Yellow River, in particular, bamboo-matting and bamboo-fiber linens, the latter produced largely in northern Lingnan.[129] An early Sung source pictures the natives of Hsün (Zywin)-chou in these phrases:

> They weave bamboo to make linen;
> The people are mostly Man and Lao;
> The women do the marketing
> While their men sit at home.[130]

A tough, heavy bamboo of Lion Mountain in Kuang-chou, called *p'o-so-mo* (*ba-sa-ma*) was used by the natives there to make their curved bows.[131] The rattan-armored warriors of Champa shot bamboo arrows from bamboo bows;[132] the T'ang warriors themselves used beautifully designed arrows made of the straight bamboos of their southern provinces.[133] Strong staffs could be wrought of the square bamboos of the western marshes of Nam-Viet.[134] Some bamboos made good food—the tender bamboo shoots of Nam-Viet, such as much-planted *Dendrocalamus latiflorus,* are still the delight of the gourmet.[135] A rare and tasty variety noted in the tenth century was the short bamboo of Hainan, called "flat head."[136]

A number of other Nam-Viet bamboos had either a curious physical feature or an encrustation of tradition which brought them to the attention of the diarists. One such was the spiny bamboo,[137] which grew in dense and impenetrable thickets; both aborigines and Chinese settlers planted it around their towns as a defense against raiders.[138] The slender and nicely colored Bamboo of the King of Viet, which grew on rocky places in Yen (Ngyăm)-chou, was cut to make wine sticks (used by topers to keep account of the number of drinks they had had); it was said that the first of the species grew from a wine stick discarded by the king of Viet, probably (as usual) meaning Chao T'o.[139] The slopes of holy Mount Lo-fou were clothed in appropriately striking kinds of bamboo. One was a giant variety, a specialty of the thirteenth peak: one individual of the cluster was said to have grown to be more than twenty feet in circumference, so that an escaped criminal was able to make his getaway in a boat carved from a section of it.[140] Another pride of the sacred mountain was described by Wu Yün in the eighth century in his poetic repertory of the famous bamboos of China: "On Lo-fou their color may be compared to yellow gold."[141] This could well be the yellow-stemmed Golden Bamboo of our modern botanists.[142] The fame of even this splendid plant was less than that of the spotted bamboo which occurred in scattered localities from southern Kiangsi southward to Annam.[143] The purplish maculations on these useful stems were believed to be stains left by the tears of the two consorts of the great Shun, the goddesses of the Hsiang River, as they searched for the god-king's body:[144] "The spotted bamboo was first formed at the Two Consorts' Temple."[145] A dispirited exile could see images of his own tears in these divine stigmata. So did Liu Ch'ang-ch'ing, who also wrote many other bamboo poems:

> In what spot is Ts'ang-wu placed?
> Where spotted bamboos form a natural forest.
> In speck after speck I leave a fallen tear;
> To branch upon branch I confide this heart of mine.[146]

(The bamboo was a favorite subject of many T'ang poets, including Wang Wei, Tu Fu, Liu Tsung-yüan, Han Yü, Yüan Chen, and above all Po Chü-i.) The stems of the spotted bamboo went into the making of all sorts of aristocratic household objects, especially the handles of writing brushes, sometimes decorated with ivory, gold, silver, and sanders.[147] Moreover, the young sprouts were regarded as more delicious than those of any other bamboo.[148]

Among other plants of Nam-Viet which provided useful woods and fibers was the *ko* (*ka*) tree (*Schima confertifolia*), an evergreen hardwood whose tough and durable timber is still of great importance in Kwangtung, as that of other members of this tea-family genus is throughout Southeast Asia. It is also admired for its handsome white flowers.[149] In T'ang times the Persian seafarers of the ports of Nam-Viet preferred this fine wood to provide planking for their ships.[150]

Sandals, handsomely painted in oil colors or gilded and lacquered, were made from the light, soft roots of the *pao* tree (evidently a swamp cypress, *Taxodium*) which grew standing in the rivers of eastern Nam-Viet, especially in Ch'ao and Hsün. These elegant shoes protected noble feet from the mud in the summer rainy season —it is reported that each newly arrived mandarin was presented with a pair.[151]

Some species of *Diospyros*—calamander and ebony—had been imported from the Indies by the Persian merchantmen since the fourth century.[152] An allied species with handsomely marked black wood, called by the Chinese "Raven-patterned Wood," grew in Chiao-chou in T'ang times.[153]

Red brazilwood, or sapan, the heartwood of *Caesalpinia,* furnished an admirable dye for cloth and wood. It was imported from Indochina, and was also a product of Ai-chou in Annam. In early Sung times it could be obtained in Hainan. Perhaps the rich stores of this valuable wood owned by the Hainanese pirate Feng Jo-fang (Byung Nhak-p'yang) who plundered the Swollen Sea in T'ang times, were obtained locally rather than from passing merchant vessels.[154]

A pulverized tropical wood named "yellow detritus" yielded a fine yellow or red dye, and also a remedy for cholera. This was powdered red sanders (*Pterocarpus* sp.), whose handsome, dark timber, used by cabinetmakers for their finest furniture, was known as "purple rosewood." This genus of trees has a wide distribution in Southeast Asia, and is said to occur in Hainan, but in T'ang times "yellow detritus" was chiefly a product of Annam.[155]

Other dye plants were an indigo—not the "true" Indian indigo *Indigofera,* but a *Polygonum* [156]—and a "mountain flower rouge," from an herb of Tuan-chou said to resemble the indigo flower, whose red extract was used both as a cosmetic and as a silk dye.[157]

Lacquer was not especially known as a product of Nam-Viet, but many lacquer trees grew at Tseng-ch'eng in Kuang-chou.[158]

Though the great center of ramie production was the Yangtze basin, fine white ramie cloth was made in Lien (Lyen)-chou and Kuei-chou in Nam-Viet.[159] Most kudzu (*Pueraria*), used for linen, paper, and a popular drug, was also grown in the Yangtze region, but the very finest came from Nam-Viet; Li Ho wrote a characteristically intricate and difficult poem on the subject of a kudzu paper of "devilishly" fine workmanship, made by a hermit of Mount Lo-fou.[160] Finally, cotton was grown and worked in Nam-Viet by the eighth century. The earliest evidence is a verse by the poet Wang Chien which says that the family cotton-weaving industry of Canton was as much a commonplace as the cultivation of red bananas there.[161] In the ninth century the evidence is overwhelming—an example is Po Chü-i's verse about his new cotton cape: "cloth of Kuei, as white as the snow." [162] A rose-dyed cotton fabric was also made in Annam.[163] Sometimes this new and wonderful fiber was confused with kapok, another product of the south, also sometimes called "tree floss," but kapok cannot be woven.[164]

EDIBLE PLANTS

The staple foods of the great civilizations are of tropical origin: rice from the Old World tropics; maize from the New World tropics; wheat, though now cultivated chiefly in temperate lands, probably originated in the high tropics of Abyssinia.[165] The men of the tropical lands live mostly on vegetables—their pigs and chickens are reserved for festival occasions—in contrast to the great stock breeders of the northern grasslands.[166] Indeed the great majority of cultivated food plants, staple or otherwise, come from a few tropical centers: Central America and tropical South America, together with the Asiatic and African tropics, and (just out of the tropics) the ancient Near East.[167] The cereals upon which the "high" cultures depend were probably not the oldest vegetable foods. Roots and tubers may have priority for mankind generally, just as they still retain a basic importance among the simpler cultures today— plants such as cassava (manioc) in America, sweet potatoes in America and Oceania, yams in tropical Asia, and taro in East Asia and Polynesia.[168] If we narrow our focus to southeastern Asia, and ignore the fundamental and universal foods, we can define areas of cultivation with indistinct boundaries: (1) Indonesia-Indochina, with emphasis on coconuts, yams, taro, jackfruit, breadfruit, mangosteens, and durians; (2) South China and Tongking (medieval Nam-Viet), most typically with citrus fruits, bananas, tea, lichees, longans, cabbages, and mulberries—but not lacking yams, taros and coconuts, and to be contrasted with (3) central China and its persimmons, pears, apricots, peaches, millets, and soybeans.[169]

Still, the staple of Nam-Viet was rice. Though this rewarding cereal had been known in north China since Neolithic times, it was a symbol of the south, as millet and wheat stood for the north. The southern rices were dominant, persistent, and prolific. The non-Chinese peoples regularly obtained two rice crops each year, and so did the Tsang-ko enclave in Kweichow and the Chams on the southernmost marches.[170] Presumably the Hua homesteaders were learning from them. A drought-resistant variety, "Champapura rice," introduced into the Yangtze valley from Fukien by imperial decree in 1011, must have been growing in south China by the tenth century at the latest.[171] So sophisticated was the rice culture of the peasants of

Hsin and Shuang in western Kuang Administration that they planted the roe of orphes [172] in their paddy fields. The herbivorous young orphes kept the flooded rice free of weeds, and the edible adults were caught and sold at a profit.[173]

Another ancient and important foodstuff of Indochinese origin and domestication is the starchy rootstock of the aroid plant *Colocasia esculenta,* commonly called "taro," and now planted and eaten as far away as Hawaii. Like rice, this plant needs a great deal of water, testimony to its special relationship to the wet tropical lands. The wild and poorly domesticated varieties are not good to eat, however, being stuffed with irritating acicular crystals.[174] The Chinese had been familiar with the taro since Han times, and it was abundantly cultivated as far north as Chekiang by the fifth century.[175] Nonetheless it is hardly mentioned in literature. It is strange that its great, glossy lotus-like leaves should have escaped the attention of the poets, but tropical foods generally received scant notice from them. The men of T'ang distinguished six races: "blue taro," "purple taro," "true taro," "white taro," *"lien-ch'an (lyen-zhen)* taro"—a name I cannot interpret—and "wild taro." The first five were regarded as only slightly poisonous, but requiring leaching before being cooked with meat to make an excellent soup. The wild taro was avoided as deadly.[176]

These typical aquatic crops of Nam-Viet—rice, taro, water chestnuts and lotuses—had their own unique soil technology, quite different from the traditional agronomy of the north. For instance, "In some areas these rice-paddy soils will not yield well when planted to other crops during winter periods. Many fields under rice in summer therefore lie idle during the winter." [177]

The yam is another cultivated tuber apparently of Indochinese origin. It differs from taro in not requiring quantities of water. Important among a number of species are the "greater yam" (*Dioscorea alata*), developed in cultivation from a wild ancestor in the Nam-Viet area; the "lesser yam," a prickly native of Indochina has been cultivated since very early times; and *Dioscorea hispida,* from which the poisonous alkaloid dioscorine must be leached, is used only as a famine food in tropical Asia.[178] Yams have been grown in central China since antiquity. They are known there as *shu-yü (zho-yo).* The official T'ang pharmacopoeia thought the white variety best, and the blue-black variety inferior. The former also had a place in medicine—it was dried in the sun and powdered for use as a tonic.[179]

Like the taro, the yam passed almost unnoticed in *belles lettres*—though Tu Fu condescends to mention it as a homely food available to travelers.[180] A variety named *kan shu* "sweet yam," mentioned in books of the post-Han period,[181] presents a puzzle. Some modern writers have thought that the name might refer to the sweet potato, whose origin is a little mysterious—it seems to be an American plant, but could it have been introduced to Polynesia in pre-Columbian times? Some have even thought it might have an African origin. But the best opinion is that it did not occur in China before the sixteenth century, coming from the Philippines.[182]

Many of us, if we think of the edible plants of the tropics, dream sweetly of paradisiacal fruits. Alas! the excellent opinion of Wallace, exploring the Moluccas, opposed this vision of a warm Eden:

Most persons in Europe are under the impression that fruits of delicious flavor abound in the tropical forests, and they will no doubt be surprised to learn that the truly wild fruits of this grand and luxurious archipelago, the vegetation of which will vie with that of any part of the world, are in almost every island inferior in abundance and quality to those of Britain.[183]

The devotion of the great scientist to the apples and berries of England is admirable, but he was not loath to speak well of individual tropical fruits, above all the luscious but ill-odored durian. Nonetheless, Wallace's opinion can hardly be maintained in view of the over-all historical picture. Fruit culture is more highly developed in the tropics than it is in the temperate parts of the world. Perhaps a majority of all domesticated fruits come from Indochina and Indonesia—the durian, mangosteen, and many others—and from tropical America—the pineapple, avocado, guava, and papaya.[184]

The delicious fruits of Nam-Viet also incline us to reject Wallace's view, though these were not of uniformly tropical origin. Nam-Viet grew excellent pears, chestnuts, and quinces.[185] Even the asiatic apple was grown in the transitional climate of Shao-chou.[186] This excellent pome, which we hardly think of as exotic or even as exceptional, was steeped in honey and cinnabar, and eaten as an after-dinner dessert with wine. Apparently it was regarded as a powerfully stimulating elixir.[187]

South China's fame as a fruit producer, however, was based chiefly on its many kinds of tasty and juicy citrus fruits, some of which gained worldwide fame in early modern times. The oranges of China were a chief component of the chinoiserie of the European enlightenment, long before the camellia, the rhododendron, and the hibiscus were known to western gardens. The flavor of Canton was distantly savored in the orangeries of the rich English estates of the seventeenth and eighteenth centuries—a notable example being Wren's Orangery at Kensington Palace, commissioned by Queen Anne.

Though the sweet oranges of tropical Asia came to the western world quite late, a few of their relatives had long been known there—the citron in classical antiquity, and the lemon and lime from the time of the crusaders.[188]

As for China itself, the citrus fruits were reported in the earliest literature.[189] Most of them were southern, the thorny lime being an important exception. To the westerner, the "orange" properly speaking, counts for most, though its prestige in China is decidedly below the first class. Its Chinese name is *ch'eng* (*dyăng*). Two species are and were generally recognized. The sour *ch'eng,* widely grown in China, was the ancestor of the Seville orange (or "true orange"), the best kind for making marmalade. It reached the Mediterranean in the ninth or tenth century.[190] The sweet *ch'eng,* or "coolie orange," in many varieties, did not reach Europe until the fourteenth century, but is the source of the Valencia and Navel oranges we know so well.[191]

Rather more esteemed by the Chinese themselves was the great golden citron with its fragrant peel (*chü-yüan,* M.C. *kyo-ywen, Citrus medica*)—the "buffalo lime" (*limau kĕrbau*) of Indonesia and the *turunj* of its Indian homeland, whence it became known to the Greeks after the great venture of Alexander.[192] It and the huge pomelo (*yu,* M.C. *you, Citrus grandis*) of Nam-Viet [193] had both been introduced at an early period.[194] We have a good T'ang description of the citrons of Nam-Viet in Liu Hsün's book:

The fruit is shaped like a melon. Its skin resembles that of an orange, but is the color of gold, so that men make much of it, and they love its fragrant aroma. The elite and nobility close to the royal seat in the capital display them in their households on platters and mats, attracted to them as rare fruits from a distant quarter. The flesh is thick and white, like that of a radish. Female artisans in the south vie at taking its flesh to carve and chase into flowers and birds, which they steep in bee's honey and touch up with rouge. These hold a unique place for their wonderful artistry, not even yielding to the "tree melons" chased by the people of Hsiang.[195]

("Tree melons" are quinces, and the Hsiang region is the Hsiang valley of Hunan.)

For the Chinese of T'ang, the very best of the citrus company were the tangerines, whose many excellent varieties they grouped under two names, *kan* (*kam*) "sweetpeel" (*Citrus nobilis*)—the name is actually identical with *kan* "sweet"—and *chü* (*kywit*) "sourpeel" (*Citrus deliciosa*).[196] Neither species was confined to Nam-Viet —excellent varieties occurred also in Szechwan and Fukien. Among these were the Vermilion, the Milky, the Yellow, the Stone, and the Sand sweetpeels, and the Vermilion, the Milky, the Drooper, the Mountain, and the Yellow Mildling sourpeels.[197] A unique race of Hsin-chou (in Nam-Viet) had the thinnest skin of any sweetpeel tangerines, with the capacity of a pint.[198] Two traits of citrus culture testify to the high level of its development by medieval times: fancy tangerines were wrapped in paper,[199] just as the finest tea was kept in paper bags to retain the flavor,[200] and the markets of Nam-Viet did a roaring business in the nests of yellow citrus ants, which were attached to trees in sweetpeel orchards to control the red scale insects which infested them. The ants were attracted by the honeydew secreted by the insects, and the trees they protected produced the sweetest fruit.[201]

These "mandarin oranges" deservedly attracted the attention of immigrant poets. Liu Tsung-yüan was prominent among them. Not only did he plant two hundred sweetpeels in the northwest corner of the walled city of Liu-chou, as a proud poem tells us,[202] but he wrote a double quatrain in praise of other citrus fruits of the south, in which he compared his own condition to theirs—both poet and plants were assigned by a strange destiny to a life on the torrid soils of Nam-Viet—yet the poet, surrounded by warm and odorous loveliness, still longs for the bitter northland:

> Sourpeel and pomelo hold honorable stuff within,
> And like me accept their fate in this quarter of flames.
> In a dense shade, vermilion radiant in green,

> In the evening of the year some perfume still remains.
> Alien winds cut me off from the clear Han,
> Flying snow blocks me from my old home;
> As I pull down a branch, what is it I sigh for,
> Looking off to the north, to Hsiung and Hsiang? [203]

(Hsiung and Hsiang are classical names of mountains in Hunan, marking the final frontier.) The third verse of this poem is strikingly like the lovely couplet of Andrew Marvell, who, in his "Bermudas," praised the aesthetic discrimination of God in putting the red-yellow sheen of the orange in exactly the right setting:

> He hangs in shades the orange bright
> Like golden lamps in a green night.

A century or so later Goethe restored the image, omitting the deity: "Im dunkeln Laub die Goldorangen glühn." We may guess that Liu Tsung-yüan saw the discrimination of the Fashioner of Creatures here too.

We are not surprised to learn that the most celebrated of the sweetpeel tangerines of Nam-Viet grew on the sacred slopes of Lo-fou. This fairy fruit is said to have been bred first on the grounds of a Buddhist temple there early in Hsüan (Ghwen) Tsung's reign, and thereafter sent regularly to that monarch's court from an imperial orchard established on the mountain.[204] The transmission of the divine tribute was accelerated by Hsüan-yüan Chi, the Taoist thaumaturge. He conjured the Lo-fou tangerines up in the presence of Hsüan Tsung, and the sovereign tasted them with pleasure.[205] Indeed there was a special affinity between the spirit of that humane monarch and the enchanting fruit. In the very year when he was driven to establish a court-in-exile in Szechwan, the Lo-fou tangerines failed to fruit.[206] Another tradition tells that these delicate tangerines withheld themselves during the absence from the capital both of Te Tsung late in the eighth century and of Hsi Tsung a hundred years later.[207]

But the holy sweetpeels were not the only rare fruit of Mount Lo-fou. Equally famous was a winter-ripening citrus called "Golden Sourpeel" (*chin chü*, M.C. *kyĕm-kywit*) or "Mountain Sourpeel" or, sometimes, *lu-chü* (*lu-kywit*). In the first of these names we see our anglicized kumquat, and in the last our loquat (for us, not a citrus at all). *Lu-kywit* was already ambiguous in T'ang times. It was then given sometimes to the Golden Sourpeel and sometimes to the fruit we call loquat (*Eriobotrya*).[208] But in Nam-Viet it seems always to have meant the winter citrus of Mount Lo-fou and its environs, a species of *Fortunella*:[209] "When yellow sweetpeels are still unpicked, the *lu-kywit* is flowering again."[210] The handsome *Fortunella* also grew abundantly in Ch'ao-chou, east of Lo-fou. But a courtly poet of the eighth century made the Golden Sourpeel a very symbol and exemplar of the luxury of the gilded halls of Ch'ang-an.[211] The men of Nam-Viet, who also boasted the quality of their citron peel and parched coconut, liked to eat kumquat rinds steeped in honey, regarding their rich flavor and beautiful amber color as incomparable.[212]

The problem of the banana is more a problem of taxonomy than of cultural history. Bananas were of the greatest importance to the peoples of medieval south Asia, including the Chinese. But it is not easy to make precise statements about what we mean by "banana." Ancient man, it seems, evolved many useful races from more than one wild species of *Musa,* these last occurring both in Africa and Asia.[213] Practical botany, at any rate, requires that we distinguish two important kinds or groups of *Musa*—the banana, known in temperate lands as a sweet yellow table fruit, but not too important in tropical diets, and the plantain, a larger, starchy, green fruit, which is a staple item in the cookery of the eastern tropics. If scientific botany can afford to be sceptical of this simple division among a host of varieties (e.g., "banana" = *Musa sapientum;* "plantain" = *Musa paradisiaca*), even students of China may find it hard to match the popular names with respectable Linnaean equivalents.[214] Here is one scheme: *pa-chiao* (*pă-tseu*) is *Musa basjoo,* planted for decorative purposes; "sweet *chiao*" is *Musa paradisiaca,* edible; and "beautiful person *chiao*" is *Musa coccinea.*[215] This last seems to be the same as the "red *chiao*," which was extravagantly admired in medieval poetry for its beautiful red flowers, an appropriate tree for the domain of the Vermilion Bird. The name *pa-chiao* itself would appear to be a distant cognate of the scientific name *Musa,* which is from Indic *moca,* but from what language directly I do not know. The word *moca* itself was brought to medieval China directly in the travel diary of the T'ang hierarch Hsüan-tsang, in the form *mao-che* (*mou-cha*).[216] But the whole question of the specific applications of names is still vexed. The Malay name *pisang* is widely used—but to what does it refer? Ivor Brown writes with some indignation: "Being a Malayan by birth-place, I was brought up as a child to call a banana a 'peesang.' . . . I was also led to despise the West Indian species which now dominates our home-market. The eastern peesang . . . was smaller and more delicate than the banana of our common acquaintance. That was deemed only fit for horses by knowing people in the East."[217] Some kinds of banana or plantain, at any rate, were eaten in tropical Asia and Indonesia in prehistoric times, but the earliest evidence of its cultivation occurs in the art and literature of ancient India. Probably some form was indigenous in Nam-Viet, but it did not come to the attention of Chinese writers until Later Han times, and a standard text on farming written in the sixth Christian century treated it as a foreign plant.[218] But by this time the banana was already a favorite image in poetry, and by T'ang times it was an important element in the economy of Nam-Viet—not so much as a food but as a source of textiles. All species of banana yield a fiber from their leafstalks, and these have been widely used to manufacture cordage and cloth—we are familiar with the so-called "Manila hemp" or "abaca" of the Philippines.[219] In T'ang times, large quantities of fine "banana linen" were sent to the capital from Nam-Viet. The industry was especially well developed in the relatively "civilized" districts of eastern and central Lingnan, and in Chiao-chou in Annam.[220]

The tall, waving leaves and drooping floral panicles of the banana were also well established as ornaments in gardens both north and south. At Canton one might enjoy the sight of "the milky banana flowers opening in front of the court of litiga-tion." [221] One might also taste its fruit: "The fruit of those produced south of the Passes is large and its flavor is sweet. But those in the north have flowers without fruit." [222] One of the loveliest gardens of the mid-tenth century belonged to the Su family of Canton. A considerable part of it was "a green banana forest," where one of the rulers of the small but vigorous kingdom of Southern Han—probably Liu Ch'ang, the last, a man of luxurious tastes, including a predilection for Persian girls —came to relax with his favorite, the Lady Li, whose curious and probably humor-ously intended title was "Toad Consort." [223] Possibly the image was not as ugly as it sounds to us, but was an allusion to the supposed toad in the moon—we can pic-ture the lady as a pale, smooth-skinned, large-eyed, lunar creature. It was as a garden plant that the banana was most mentioned by the poets, and it was the leaves and inflorescence that caught their imaginations, not the fruit. But, of course, it bore no fruit in northern gardens. The plant is even less noticed in English poetry, but a rare instance is decidedly un-Chinese. I quote Ivor Brown again:

Noticing in a Serenade by Douglas Grant Duff Ainslie the enticing first two lines
> Lady of the lovely thighs
> Curving like banana fruit

I wondered why bananas have been so little present in our poetry. They are as suave in sound as in flesh. Why should peaches and cherry-ripe and apple-of-the-eye have such powerful positions in the vocabulary of affection? Obviously one would not look for a banana-tinted cheek, but for sweetness and richness there is surely a happy image for the love-lyricist in a ripe banana.[224]

The Chinese imagery had no relation to human figures, even beloved ones. (A rare exception is a verse of Po Chü-i, discussed later, where the red banana plant personi-fies a young girl.) It was the *sound* of the huge leaves, even more than their shape and color, which gave a unique atmosphere. The wind rustling them, the rain drip-ping from them, enhanced the slightly melancholy or introspective mood associ-ated with darkness, or storms, or decay, or autumn. Here is a selection of character-istic T'ang verses:

> The rain drips down where the banana is red;
> The frost breaks off where the tangerines are yellow.[225]

Another:

> As bananas are set in motion by the rain,
> So I plant them in front, facing the window.[226]

And especially:

> The wind plays with the red banana, with sound of leaf on leaf.[227]

This line combines the lonely but pleasing sound of the wind in its leaves with the visual beauty of the red-flowering race of banana which was so extravagantly ad-mired. But although this plant had the glamor of the exotic to fire the mind, it could

not warm the soul of a northerner, as Liu Tsung-yüan recognized in a poem entitled "Red Banana":

> Objects from afar are made much of by the world—
> But it is they that hurt the heart of a traveler.[228]

Such too is the banana's ambivalent role in Li Shen's quatrain "Red Banana Flower":

> The red banana flowers' shape—badge of the Quarter of Flames;
> At malarial water torrent's edge—the color extremely deep.
> Deep in the cluster where leaves are fullest—the crimson might be fire,
> Not just to burn my eyes—much more to set my heart aflame! [229]

By the tenth century, however, it was possible for the bold red of the south, then
being fully realized as the Red Bird's domain, to be treated without lingering aver-
sion or despondency. Han Wo's "Rhapsody on the Red Banana" is a typical production of both the age and the author—a richly purple effusion comparing the flower to
the red spot on the crown of the sacred Manchurian crane, to a scarlet cockscomb, and
to much else of that kind.[230] Very typical of that century and of the awakening of
literary romanticism about Nam-Viet is the fully realized red and green symbolism
transferred from the tropical plant to a desirable woman's dress and body found, not
unexpectedly, in a *Nan hsiang tzu* song lyric by Li Hsün, the pharmacologist-poet:

> She tidies her cloudy chignon
> Backed with a rhino-horn comb.
> Banana red glows in her blouse, lappets of green net.
> Below the terrace of the king of Viet, the winds of spring are warm—
> Flowers fill the banks.
> Strolling, enjoying, I will always invite the company of that neighbor girl.[231]

The lichee is regarded as a jewel among fruits in China. (As for the United States,
if we leave out Hawaii where it is long since acclimatized, the recent introduction of
the lichee among the fruits of Florida may ultimately remedy our undeserved neglect
of this small, delicious fruit.) [232] Although excellent lichees were grown in Fukien
and Szechwan in T'ang times, Nam-Viet was its true home—a statement which
would have been loudly disputed by partisans from those other provinces. In Nam-
Viet, the center of production was a coastal region west from Canton, including
Hsin, Kao and P'an, where the fruits matured in the fifth and sixth Chinese months
—about our June and July. The lichees of the subterraneously heated "Fire Mountain" in Wu-chou, north of these places, were ripe a month earlier. Specially bred
fancy varieties included a large, crystal white, seedless fruit, and a yellowish "wax
lichee." [233] The lichees sent by the magistrates to the Great Luminous Palace were
necessarily somewhat less than fresh,[234] since, as Li Hsün reported, "on the first day
the color changes; on the second day the taste changes." [235] But according to tradition the lovely Lady Yang demanded fresh lichees by post horse from Nam-Viet.[236]
One medieval writer at least did not believe the romantic tale:

Yang the Precious Consort was born in Shu [Szechwan] and so was fond of lichees, but those grown in South Sea [Canton] surpassed others by far. Accordingly these were submitted by flying post every year. But because of the heat of summer, they would deteriorate after a single night. Posterity is altogether unaware of this.[237]

Whether altered or not (dried lichees are as tasty as the fresh ones), Hsüan Tsung's well-loved consort adored the fruit, and her taste was honored when a new song presented to the royal pair by the court musicians in the winter palace at the hot springs east of the capital was named "Lichee Fragrance."[238] It is doubtful that northerners generally—outside of the palace, that is—appreciated the rare qualities of the lichee, which they could not, after all, hope to eat fresh. The creole minister Chang Chiu-ling properly regarded this product of his homeland as best among all the fruits, and he tells that he tried in vain to persuade his colleagues of its superiority. He reports that one man among them, who had spent a brief period in Canton in his youth, sighed at the memory of its unsurpassable flavor. These remarks preface Chang's poetic rhapsody on the lichee, in which he praises not only its excellent savor, but also the ruddy color of the fruiting tree, so appropriate to the sultry land which gave it birth—"a fruit imbued with the germ of fiery *li*."[239] (*Li* is the cabalistic sign of the flaming sun in the *Canon of Changes*.) By the end of the ninth century the residents of Canton were making a holiday of the lichee-ripening. They visited the best orchards and gardens, decked out with all sorts of festive hangings, to admire "the new fire among the leaves" and "the cinnabar on the trees."[240] The red of the lichee vied with the red of the banana. This lichee festival had its most sumptuous expression in the tenth century when Liu Ch'ang, the unfortunate last ruler of Southern Han (we have seen him just now in a celebrated banana grove), formally established "The Feast of the Red Cloud" to celebrate the appearance of the scarlet-clothed fruit.[241] The late T'ang poets had already discovered a relationship between the red-shelled lichee and the dangerous red mists of Nam-Viet. Here is Hsü Hun:

> Malarial rain is soon to come—the liquidambar trees are black;
> Clouds of fire begin to rise—the lichees are turning red.[242]

But the picture yielded no erotic image as did the other red flora of the Red Bird's realm. Perhaps I have missed it—it was possible in tenth-century China, and Li Hsün would have been the poet to develop it. I have seen it actualized only in recent times in the words of the West Indian creole Leconte de Lisle:

> A l'ombre des bois-noirs touffus, et du Letchi,
> Aux fruits moins pourprés que ta bouche.[243]

The simile belongs in tenth-century Nam-Viet.

An accidental association gives a special interest to a poem written by Po Chü-i on a lonely carouse in Szechwan, at a wine shop ornamented by mature lichees:

The lichees are newly ripe, the color of a cock's crown;
The burnt wine has just been opened, with an aroma of amber.
I desire to pluck one branch, to tip one goblet,
But there is no visitor in this western tower with whom to share their savor.[244]

The connoisseur of words will observe that the expression "burnt wine" is an exact replica of German *Branntwein* and of Dutch *brandewijn,* the source of our good English "brandy." And indeed, many centuries later, this very term was the ordinary word for brandy or distilled spirits in Chinese. Most scholars, however, have assumed that the art of distillation was introduced only after the Mongol conquest. So, late in the sixteenth century, Li Shih-chen wrote that "burnt wine [or 'burning wine'] is no ancient art," puts its discovery in Yüan times.[245] It has been usual to discount Po's verse (for no good reason, in my opinion, except that it is hard to explain). But there is another poetic reference to "burnt wine" in the verses of another ninth century writer. Yung T'ao wrote, on arriving at the chief city of Szechwan,

Since I reached Ch'eng-tu the burnt wine has matured—
I have no thought that this body will enter Ch'ang-an again.[246]

It appears, then, that the art of distilling spirits was practised in western China by the ninth century, but remained a local and little-known specialty, to be reintroduced a half a millenium later with a new process and under a new name—rice brandy was for a while called "arrack" until the old name triumphed once more.[247] Brandy and lichees must have gone very well together in Szechwan—but Nam-Viet missed the combination.

Two other close cousins of the lichee were eaten in Nam-Viet, though neither enjoyed its prestige. Of the two the better known is the longan or "dragon eye." Like the lichee it was known in Han times, but it has been ignored in literature.[248] A popular name for it was "Slave of the Lichee," since it ripened later than that fruit, and the name meant that it followed behind it, like a slave behind his master.[249] Su Kung, the court pharmacologist, said of the longan: "It resembles the lichee, but the leaves are like the apple's, and the color of the flower is white." [250] The other near-lichee was the pleasantly subacid rambutan, called *shao tzu* in China, a name which suggests the fruit of the God Shun, or of his holy place in Nam-Viet, Shao-chou.[251] It was the least noticed of the three *Nephelia.*

These were the great fruits of Nam-Viet. But what of the supreme tropical fruit, first among the fruits of the Indies, the divine mango, important in the lore, mythology, and ceremony of South Asia? "The mango may well have been the first fruit tree to be cultivated by man; certainly it was among the first." [252] The fresh fruit is admired for its fine flavor; its seeds are widely used in medicine. It is now familiar, especially as preserved in Indian chutneys. Like cotton, the tree grows best in tropical climates with a marked distinction between rainy and dry seasons—that is, in a pronounced monsoon climate, such as prevails in eastern Java.[253] A modern map of its distribution shows its northern limit in central Vietnam, Hainan, and the tip of the Luichow peninsula—that is, southernmost Nam-Viet of T'ang times.[254] But apparently the men of T'ang knew it only as a foreign fruit. It was known to occur in Cambodia;[255] Hsüan-tsang listed it among the trees of India under its Sanskrit name *āmra;* a T'ang Buddhist lexicon gave it only as exotic fruit.[256] Otherwise it does not appear in literature until Sung times, and then only in medical texts. Except for the pious pilgrims, then, the men of T'ang missed the rare flavor of this juicy red and yellow fruit—unless some embittered political refugee, sweating among the savages of Hainan, tasted one but did not trouble to write a letter home about it.

The astringent myrobalans, the *triphalā* "three fruits" of classical India—true vegetable elixirs—were, on the other hand, well known to the men of T'ang. Probably some Indochinese species were passed off as the holiest Indian varieties by unscrupulous merchants, since the taxonomy of the family of myrobalans is notoriously vague and complicated, but the Chinese pharmacists recognized them only under the three old and respected Indian names. The emblic myrobalan, *āmalakī,* grew, they said, in the Canton region, and in Annam, and it was sent as tribute to the court to replenish the emperor's store of rare drugs.[257] Only an Annamese distribution was claimed for the belleric myrobalan, *vibhītakī;* beyond that, we hear nothing of it.[258] The story of the chebulic myrobalan, *harītakī* (now sometimes called in Persian *halīla-i-Kābulī* "Kabul myrobalan"),[259] in Nam-Viet is quite different. It is a tale of fame. The tree had been planted in Canton by the third century, and was observed by an Indian visitor in the fifth century on the grounds of the Buddhist temple which was to become glorious as the *Fa hsing szu* of T'ang times.[260] Forty or fifty trees grew there at one time during that epoch. The monks served distinguished visitors a wholesome broth made from pure well water with five myrobalans to one inch of licorice.[261] But the seafaring monk Chien-chen reported only two of the ancient myrobalans there, bearing fine large fruit in the mid-eighth century.[262] Though they seem to have been re-propagated in Sung times, all had disappeared by the beginning of Ch'ing rule in the seventeenth century. New plantings were made in modern times, and one of these latter-day myrobalan trees, apparently over a hundred years old, still survives on the grounds of the temple, now called the *Kuang hsiao szu.*[263]

> With the winter flowers we pluck the *lu-kywit,*
> With the summer fruit we pick the *yang-mai.*[264]

We recognize the late-fruiting kumquat in the first verse of this couplet. The evergreen *yang-mei* (*yang-mai*) "poplar apricot" of the second verse is a fruit characteristic of the cooler northern uplands of Nam-Viet. We foreigners sometimes call it "strawberry tree" (*Myrica rubra*). According to old tradition this attractive tree grew most abundantly in malarial regions,[265] a view confirmed in a poem written by Chang

Pi in T'ang times: "When the high forest is girded with rain, the poplar apricot is ripe." [266] A variety which yielded a large and sweet *white* fruit grew near the coast, in P'an-chou.[267]

A small race of the true Chinese apricot (sometimes called "plum") [268] grew in Nam-Viet. A kind of dry preserve, called "red apricot" north of the Passes, was prepared by the natives, using salt, cardamom flowers, citron, and hibiscus to give the fruit a lovely crimson color. The people of Lingnan also pickled their larger apricots and carved them into the shapes of little pots and girdle ornaments.[269]

An acid, yellow apricot-like fruit, often cooked in honey or taken with wine by the southerners, had been familiar since early post-Han times. Because of its appearance it was called "muntjac eye" (*chi mu,* M.C. *ki myuk*), which suggests our phrase "doe-eyed," though I doubt that the name of the Chinese fruit was ever applied metaphorically to languishing damsels. An alternate name "ghost eye" (*kuei mu,* M.C. *kwěi myuk*) [270] appears to be a phonetic corruption. I do not know its true identity.

An assortment of other fruits and nuts, not all identifiable, have left traces in medieval literature. A wild "mountain walnut" [271] (the familiar walnut of Europe was an early introduction), or "butternut" as we might call it, grew in Nam-Viet. The tonic pistachio nut, once an import from Iran, grew there in the ninth century.[272] These delicacies can be recognized in T'ang literature, but the identity of the fragrant and delicious *tu-hsien* (*tzu*) (*tu-ghǎm* [*tsi*]) [273] and of the large "swine flesh" nut of Tuan-chou, supposed to taste like pork when roasted, are not known.[274]

A brief spectrum of Nam-Viet vegetables follows. The white flesh of the "Viet melon," a kind of muskmelon,[275] was sometimes eaten raw, sometimes kept in a pickle of wine lees.[276] A thorny shrub bore the "bitter eggplant" ("or sour aubergine") (*Solanum dulcamara*), for which there is also the modern Anglo-Chinese name "bittersweet," [277] though I would prefer to revive the older and more handsome Anglo-Indian word for the aubergine: "brinjaul." [278] The sour brinjaul was believed to control malarial miasmas, and its root was considered a desirable addition to a hot bath.[279] An aquatic, white-flowered relative of our sweet potato, *Ipomoea aquatica* (called in Chinese "*yung* leaf-vegetable") was cultivated in shallow water or marshland; it provided a pickle.[280] Hainan produced a large gourd, styled "gourd of Tan and Yai," and also a tall large-seeded "mustard of Tan and Yai." [281] Meng Kuan once bought some of this last, took it home and forgot it for several days. The seeds developed four legs, a head and tail, and a long mantis-like torso, and walked off—an example of how creatures change their forms after the rainy season.[282] The slightly narcotic roots of the "Sleep Vegetable," grown like lotuses in flooded fields, were pickled, and used medicinally as a hypnotic; nowadays it has gained the English names of "bogbean" and "marsh trefoil." [283] The onion-like quillwort or (as the Chinese called it) "water leek" was another edible aquatic plant grown in ponds.[284] Fresh-water vegetables were important, but the sea provided its food too: various salt-water algae, or "sea wrack" as they called them, were eaten in the far south, and were thought to augment virility, though debilitating to northerners.[285]

Nam-Viet was not noted as a producer of first-rate teas—these were a specialty of Fukien. But the tender leaves of a tree which grew in the central mountains of Ling-nan, called *kua-lu* (*kwǎ-lu*) or *kao-lu* (*kau-lu*) or *kuo-lo* (*kwa-la*) or *wu-lo* (*mywĕt-la*) by the natives, a wild relative of the domestic tea plant, were brewed into a rather bitter and astringent substitute, much valued by the aborigines. This beverage was used as a stimulant to prevent drowsiness.[286] Another tea substitute, particularly favored among the grottoes of the Huang men in Jung-chou, was called "bamboo tea" because of the bamboo-like appearance of the leaves. The drink made from it was thought to be extremely delicious.[287]

Sugarcane had been known as a product of Nam-Viet since Chou-Han times, and "stone honey"—little cakes dried from the extracted juice—had been manufactured in Annam since the third century; by T'ang times the cane was being grown as far north as Szechwan and Chekiang.[288] By then, two varieties were recognized—a red cane called "K'un-lun sugar," a name which suggests a special affinity with Malaysia, and a so-called "reed-sugar" or "bamboo sugar."[289] Refined crystalline sugar, how-ever, was not well known until Sung times; there are indications that it was already manufactured in Szechwan in late T'ang.[290]

AROMATIC PLANTS

In a lyrical mood, Wallace wrote of the plants of the tropics:

> Sweet canes, and wondrous gums, and odorous spice;
> While Flora's choicest treasures crowd the teeming earth.
> Beside each cot the golden Orange stands,
> And broad-leaved Plantain, pride of Tropic lands.[291]

The priority he gave to plants of exceptional flavor and odor agrees with modern and medieval estimates of the most valuable products of the torrid zones. Plants whose wood, seeds, leaves, or flowers yielded desirable odors formed a very important class among the exotics of Nam-Viet. They partook of the godly and beneficial, and at the same time of the deadly and devilish, and in T'ang times were as common in the well-to-do household as in the wealthy temple, the popular druggist's shop, or the courtesan's fragrant parlor.

First among the aromatic herbs and woods of Nam-Viet were the several kinds of cardamom, the south Chinese equivalents of our familiar nutmeg, chiefly because they combined the qualities of divine taste and aroma with the great symbolic color of the land which produced them—red. The seeds of the "black" or "bitter" carda-mom (*Amomum amarum*), of Nam-Viet and Indochina generally, were added to honeyed rice dumplings, and their curative merits ranged from intellectual stimulus to bladder control.[292] The "true" cardamom (*Elettaria cardamomum*)—the usual referent of the word *tou-k'ou* (the imported nutmeg was "fleshy *tou-k'ou*")—provided leaves, husk, and fruit for the enormous drug trade of T'ang. Chiefly it was obtained from Annam: the tribute of Feng (P'yong)-chou at the beginning of the ninth century consisted of 3,300 cardamoms, 100 sets of iridescent kingfisher feathers, and forty catties of prime rhinoceros horn.[293] Another species was the "Chinese" or "herbaceous" cardamom (*Amomum globosum*), also primarily an Annamese product.[294] One variety of this plant had yellowish flowers, like cardamoms generally, but typically its blooms were red,[295] and these provided one of the most characteristic images of their visible environment in Nam-Viet for the poets of the ninth and tenth centuries. For some, such as Li Hsün, it was even more exotically captivating than the red banana flower or the red lichee fruit.[296] Presumably it was the red flowers of the herbaceous cardamom which Li She found so pleasant with an old friend and a beaker of wine in Wu-chou:

> Above the river, by malarial hills, we see each other again;
> Immersed in drink, we look together at cardamom flowers.[297]

But now for Li Hsün and a typical water scene, with a pearl fisher (whom I take to be female, only because the identifiable persons of his poems are always female) returning in the quick shadows of evening. It is almost chinoiserie:

> The homeward road is near—
> She knocks the gunwales, singing.
> There, at the place where she gathers true pearls, was too much water and wind;
> Here, at the little bridge on the winding bank, hills and moon pass by.
>   Deeply bound by mist,
> Cardamom flowers droop: a thousand, a myriad blooms.[298]

And the same poet again, expectant of a rosy assignation:

> Red cardamoms—
> Purple roses—
> I pray at the maiden's house—will she meet me by the King of Viet's Terrace?
> For one round of a village song, palms clapped in unison,
>   Worth an appreciative stroll.
> Then a round of wine from a conch cup, over the flowing water.[299]

Earlier in this volume I was tentative about the association of Li Hsün, usually known as a poet of Szechwan, with Nam-Viet. The pearls and cardamoms and, above all, the atmospheric embellishments, should by now, I think, make it certain that Li Hsün the poet is beyond doubt Li Hsün the pharmacologist of the South Seas.

But that is not the end of "red cardamoms." Botanically close to the cardamoms was another ginger-like plant, *Alpinia officinarum,* which bore red-centered white flowers, and whose rhizome, known in the commercial jargon of the China Seas as "galangal," was then called "Kao-liang ginger." It grew in western Lingnan and in Hainan, and provided a much sought after drug. The plant also produced reddish seed capsules, enclosing pungent aromatic seeds which we call "galangal cardamom." In T'ang times these were called "red cardamom," and were used to counteract the effects of excessive drinking.[300] A close relative, the pink-flowered "mountain ginger" (*Alpinia japonica*) had an inedible root, but the leaves were eaten by the men of Lingnan.[301] They also ate the so-called "ginger of Lien (Lyem)", which is not related to true ginger.[302] The "cardamoms" and "red cardamoms" so common in the verses of such taste-, color-, and sound-sensitive writers as Han Wo, Tu Mu, and Wu Jung, may not always have been the flowers of the herbaceous cardamom, but sometimes the red-spotted blossoms of Alpinia, and even its brown-red capsule.[303]

It was said that when the cinnamon trees in the mountains about Kuei-chou blossomed, the whole forest was fragrant.[304] Long ago, Chao T'o, King of Nam-Viet, had sent the Han monarch a vessel of cassia preserve or pickle [305] made from bark gathered in this far-reaching forest. In the fifth century the most fragrant bark was brought up from Kuei-lin under the name of "Turtle Shell Aromatic." [306] But by the eighth century, although there were cinnamons everywhere south of Kuei-lin as far as the sea, one had to go southwards a short distance to Liu-chou and Hsiang-chou to see really dense stands,[307] and by early Sung times there were no cinnamons at all in Cinnamon Forest, the ancient name of the Kuei-chou region. By then, one had to travel far to the southwest, to Iᵃ-chou and Pin-chou, to find old groves of these handsome trees.[308] It appears that Chinese cinnamon hunters and aboriginal fire-cultivators together had already removed a good part of the primeval forest in this northern and comparatively well-settled province.

The word I have been rendering as "cinnamon" is *kuei,* a name which was given to other trees besides *Cinnamomum cassia,* whose bark is the "cassia" of commerce. Not only were other species of *Cinnamomum* subsumed under the name, but also some trees which are not members of the laurel family.[309] Western Nam-Viet sent considerable quantities of "cassia heart" northward as annual tribute (it was much desired as a remedy for internal pains caused by "cold winds") along with some "cassia seeds"—that is, the dried immature fruit. "Cassia heart" was a name for the best Chinese cinnamon, the inner bark sliced from young branches.[310] Much of this was exacted from the natives in the "bridle and halter counties," one of them significantly named *Ku-kuei,* Old Cinnamon, west of Kuei-chou proper.[311] A distinctive species, the Indian Cinnamon, also grew in Nam-Viet, but its bark was bitter. Nonetheless the pharmacologists said that its warming and curative properties were identical with those of the common kinds of cinnamon.[312] The poets took note of the *kuei* chiefly for its rich aroma, though the image of the *kuei* was not particularly restricted to the far south, since it was already being planted in northern gardens. It also had an ancient association with the moon—indeed it was fancied that the tree could be seen growing on that satellite,[313] so that it was natural for a sophisticated man of medieval China to admire any *kuei* by moonlight. But it is doubtful that the original moon-*kuei* was the cinnamon—more likely it was the fragrant-flowered *Osmanthus,* a genus whose odor is one of the delights of the Far East. *Osmanthus fragrans* is an autumn flowerer, and associated with the moon, which fits Li's ode and the old moon legend as well. But the usual *Osmanthus* has white or yellowish blossoms, and the so-called Red *Osmanthus* is said to be a sport which appeared only in Ming times.[314]

How shall we identify the Red *Kuei* which Li Te-yü brought from a rivulent near holy Mount T'ien-t'ai in Chekiang in the ninth century to augment the artificial woodlands of his splended estate near Lo-yang?[315] He was evidently proud of this novelty, and wrote a poem in its honor, to which he prefaced the remark that its flower was red with a white center:

> I desired to find a creature beyond our grime—
> This tree indeed is from the Turquoise Forest!
> Behind—plain white conjoined with an excess of ornament,
> Like cinnabar seen through to its very heart.
> Lovely form without trace of blemish;
> Odorous soul committed to shrouded depths.
> My wish is to have the color of sylphine blooms
> In bitter frost light up a deep blue pool.[316]

The imagery of this poem is Taoist, suffused with the pure colors of paradise. Perhaps a paraphrase or commentary will bring this out:

I wanted a tree of ideal color and form for my park;
This one is surely worthy of the jewelled groves of heaven.
The flowers are white, richly laced with red;
As if carved from a vermilion elixir whose core is absolutely pure.
Though endowed with a divine or fairy perfection,
The blossoms must be looked for (like esoteric wisdom) in the surrounding darkness of heavy foliage.
I shall plant this paragon where its scarlet flowers—the color of life and regeneration—
Will reflect the solar warmth in the cold water when summer is already gone.

It cannot be said for certain what this heavenly tree was. The name Red *Kuei* is given in our own time to a variety of the *Osmanthus,* and it seems to me that Li's Eden tree was indeed a race of this genus, bred or mutated in the T'ien-t'ai region, the rising garden center of China in the ninth century.

That is not quite the end of the story. The name Red *Kuei* is given, in modern times at least, to an *Artocarpus,* a cousin of the jackfruit. It is also akin to the prized breadfruit of Oceania.[317] This was an old introduction into Nam-Viet, and splendid specimens stood by the temple of the God of the South Sea near Canton in T'ang times.[318] This native relative of these famous species is now planted around the city of Canton, and grows wild on the island of Hainan.[319] But I have no certain evidence that any Red *Kuei* of T'ang times was an *Artocarpus*. One of the laurel cinnamons is a possibility, and an *Osmanthus* most probable.

Next to camphor, the most prized aromatic substance in the highly scented ceremonial halls of the T'ang empire, both secular and religious, to say nothing of its use for the encouragement of erotic feelings and activities, was aloeswood, which our ancestors called "garroo," or, if it was the best quality, "calambac."[320] Regular supplies of the black, scented, resin-impregnated, diseased heartwood of trees of the *Aquilaria* genus, held holy by the Chams, and (because of its great weight) called "Sinking Aromatic" by the Chinese, were required of the magistrates of Canton and of Huan-chou in Annam by the emperors of T'ang,[321] and they in turn exacted it of the native foresters. There is something of a puzzle in the Canton quota. The true aloes (*Aquilaria agallocha*) is an Indochinese tree, absent from Lingnan. It is said to occur on Hainan, but the problem of specific identification is always present.[322] But there are many T'ang reports of "sinking aromatic" in Lingnan. For instance, the trees which yield it were reported to be abundant in the region of Kuang-chou early in the ninth century,[323] and long before that when T'ai Tsung asked Feng Ang, the great chieftain of Kao-chou on the coast, "Is my minister's house near to or far from the Sinking Aromatic?" that magnate replied, "These aromatic trees are produced both to left and right of my house, though the living ones lack the aroma— only when they are decayed do they begin to be aromatic."[324] This certainly sounds like *agallocha*. But there is another species of aloeswood which occurs in Lingnan— *Aquilaria sinensis*. This is probably the *chan* (*dran*), an aromatic tree of T'ang Lo-chou, whose bark was made into a speckled ashy white paper, and also the *mi* (*myit*) aromatic of Chiao-chou, which had exactly the same properties.[325]

If I mention the so-called "Chinese olive" here, it is not primarily because of its fruit, which ripens in the late fall on a tree named *kan-lan* (*kam-lam*), although its flavor was much admired by the southerners, who said also that it was superior to cloves for sweetening the breath. They also cooked *kan-lan* "olives" in a kind of broth which alleviated the effects of too much alcohol. An exceptionally tasty and expensive variety was the "silver mine *kan-lan*," so named because it grew near an old silver mine at Kao-liang.[326] The *kan-lan* tree is our "kanari," hence its specific name *Canarium*.[327] Its chief product was an elemi or brea, composed of oleoresins, called "kanari sugar" in Chinese because of its granular texture. This was turned into an excellent varnish for caulking the hulls of sea-going ships.[328] But despite its double significance to southerners, the *kan-lan* was hardly noticed in T'ang belles lettres, although I find the fruit in a single verse of Po Chü-i. None of this justifies its inclusion here among the *aromatic* plants of Nam-Viet. It is put here only to be close to its cousin *Canarium copaliferum*, whose sugary elemi smelled of lemon and turpentine, and was loved by aborigines and Chinese alike as a major ingredient in incenses for holy rites. The Hua men gave the name of *"chan (chem)* sugar" to this wonderful copal. Apparently this word is cognate to modern Vietnamese *trâm* "kanari."[329] The tree grew in many parts of Nam-Viet, but chiefly in Tan-chou on Hainan.[330] (An undistinguished relative of the useful "olives" was called *"Mu-wei [Muk-wĕi]* Seed." It was harder than the *kan-lan* fruit, but could be eaten if the husk were removed.[331])

A miscellany of the most prized of the scented plants of Nam-Viet must include the clove (named, from its shape, both "chicken-tongue aromatic" and "nail aromatic"), which was produced in Annam. It was used to sweeten the breath, and admixed in many magical and medicinal potions and fumes.[332] Something which passed for saffron, and was much valued in medicine and fancy cuisine, gave a golden yellow image to the late T'ang poets. It was said to grow in Nam-Viet, though true saffron was imported.[333] Possibly it was a transplanted turmeric or zedoary. The best "white lemon grass," better known to us as citronella, was imported by argosy from the Indies, but it was also grown in Annam, and was recommended by Taoist adepts as an ideal ingredient in elegant baths to perfume the carnal form.[334]

BEAUTIFUL PLANTS

The south was full of odorous woods, leaves, and roots, but T'ang literature makes little of the fragrant flowers of Nam-Viet. Those which were noticed were naturalized exotic plants brought from the shores of the Indian Ocean, not native forest flowers. Both the Persian and Indian jasmines had been grown there since long before T'ang times, presumably introduced by Persian seafarers.[335] The scent of the white blooms of *yāsaman* (*Jasminum grandiflorum*), originally of Rome and Iran, which was compared to the delicious odor of *trâm* elemi, suggesting the love of beautiful women, filled the air everywhere in Lingnan.[336] The intense Indian *mallikā* (*Jasminum sambac*) [337] was, if possible, even more admired. The poet P'i Jih-hsiu wrote of a banquet among the moonlit *mo-li* (*mat-li*) flowers, with bronze drums beating in the distance.[338] The prestige of the Indian jasmine in the tenth century is suggested by an anecdote about the ruler of the independent Southern Han kingdom, who boasted to a northern envoy that the *mallikā* was "the strength of the little south," but later, himself a captive in Lo-yang, felt obliged to admit that the peonies there were "the triumph of the great north." [339] Today the Indian jasmine is familiar as the *pikake* of Hawaii.

The name most likely to conjure up the odors of the scented Indies for a westerner is "frangipani"—which sounds like a word from some Oceanic dialect, but is in fact the name of the sixteenth-century Marquis Muzio Frangipani. The plant is also sometimes called "red jasmine," though it was no true jasmine. It provided a perfume and a fragrant almond-cream dessert much admired in former centuries. Although now widely planted in warm climates, the frangipani is a native of tropical America, and its scientific name *Plumeria rubra* has given an everyday word to the Hawaiians, for whom the plumeria is a common flower. It is also widespread in Indochina and Indonesia in our times; there it is given the name *chĕmpaka*.[340] This last word is more properly applied to an Oriental exotic for which Shelley found an appropriate place in his "Indian Serenade":

> The wandering airs they faint
> On the dark, the silent stream—
> And the Champak odours fail
> Like sweet thoughts in a dream.

The frangipani then, so dear to our occidental hearts, has been confused not only with the jasmine, but with the classical champak of India, *Michelia champaca*, whose fragrant, magnolia-like blossoms were worn in the hair, rubbed on the body, and offered at holy shrines.[341] This exotic was known to the Chinese of T'ang, and treated occasionally in poetry as an Indian plant, under the transcribed name of *chan-po* (*chem-bĕk*).[342] But the appearance of this loan word in a couplet of the ninth century poet Li Ch'ün-yü, suggesting a fine southern smell, in somewhat anomalous:

> I prefer to borrow the image of the banana,
> Perfectly to achieve the odor of champak.[343]

This might seem incomprehensible, except for the fact that there is a native south Chinese *Michelia*:[344] "The flowers are brownish yellow edged with light carmine, and exhale a strong banana fragrance."[345] It would appear then that the late T'ang poets, who, at first glance, seem not to have recognized the native *Michelia*, actually discovered it in Nam-Viet, and properly gave it the imported name of *champak*. On the other hand, when a tenth century epicurean compared the scent of "champak" to that of sandal (as osmanthus to camphor, and magnolia to musk),[346] he may well have been writing about the true Indian champak. (The frangipani/jasmine/champak confusion was further compounded in T'ang China by the belief that the gardenia was a kind of native champak—the gardenia itself was an ancient plant in China.[347] Needless, perhaps, to say, the frangipani was unknown in medieval Nam-Viet; it appears here anachronistically to intensify the related image of the champak.)

Among the Nam-Viet plants celebrated for their color it is no surprise to find that the red ones were most esteemed. Among these the most spectacular was the "Thorny *T'ung*"—a species of *Erythrina* whose Chinese name allies it superficially with the Phoenix tree (*wu t'ung; Firmiana simplex*), the Tung-oil tree (*yu t'ung; Aleurites fordii*), and the lovely flowering paulownia (*hua t'ung; Paulownia fortunei*).[348] A common name for many of the *Erythrinas*, which are native to the tropics of both hemispheres, and whose loads of red flowers shade both the cacao plantations of Trinidad and the roads of Lingnan, is "coral tree," though in America it is most often called "immortelle." It was probably introduced to south China before T'ang, but by late T'ang times its thick foliage and showy flowers were familiar along roadsides from Nam-Viet northward to Fukien.[349] The coral trees of the latter province have the greater modern fame for purely linguistic reasons. Marco Polo's name for the Fukienese port of Ch'üan-chou was Zayton, a form evidently based on a dialectical variant of the popular name of that city, Walled City of the *Tz'u t'ung* (*ts'iĕ dung*), that is, City of the Thorny *T'ung,* or immortelle. The town was already famous for its brilliant stands of these trees, which had been introduced from Nam-Viet, in the mid-ninth century. The ninth-century poet Ch'en T'ao praised them there, and added that "the men of Viet plant Thorny *T'ung* flowers in abundance," and found an appropriate if archaic symbolism in styling them "trees from within the Palace of the Red God-king"—that is, of the God of the South—and proper perches for the bird of the south, which he called the Cinnabar Phoenix.[350] A century later we find the gorgeous immortelle in a new setting, and just where we should expect it—in a *Nan hsiang tzu* by Li Hsün:

> At the place where I see her,
> A clear sky at evening,
> Under Thorny *T'ung* flowers, in front of the Terrace of Viet:
> She turns her dark pupils to me, fixed deeply with meaning,
> Drops a pair of kingfisher ornaments—
> Then mounts her elephant, turns her back on me, goes ahead over the water.[351]

Although no pronouns of the first or any other person appear in this and other poems in this form by Li Hsün, I have used the first rather than the third in my translations, since the apparition of the dark-eyed native girl under luxuriant foliage is evidently a favorite dream image of the poet. In this particular poem his language rises to the level of pure fantasy, climaxed by the almost frightening appearance of the elephant in the last line. Here the exoticism is so rich (immortelle, Viet Terrace, kingfisher feathers, elephant steed) as to seem almost artificial, excluding the possibility that the poem recreates a real liaison.

Among the showy red flowers of China one of the most familiar to us is the camellia—an exotic which symbolizes the gardens of mid-nineteenth century Europe just as the orange represents the eighteenth. For Sacheverell Sitwell it has a special affinity with the forties of that century, and its paler varieties seem to him to belong with Chopin. Of the dappled and striped varieties he wrote: "One wonders where, and by whom these Second Empire Camellias were raised. They are far removed from the atmosphere of Chopin, with the music of whom it is very easy to associate the more pallid and waxy Camellias. These striped flowers have their analogy more with the music of Gounod." [352] A hundred years later the elaborately bred family of pink and white camellias, mostly derived from the familiar *japonica* species, was made almost old-fashioned by the introduction from the monastery gardens of Yunnan of a completely new species, *Camellia reticulata*—a tree-sized shrub whose lustrous red flowers are as much as nine inches in diameter.[353] Two points must be made about the camellia before discussing its place in medieval Nam-Viet: first, most taxonomists no longer admit its generic separation from the tea plant, and prefer *Thea japonica* to *Camellia japonica;* and second, although the camellia is more a southern than a northern plant, it would be wrong to call it a tropical plant, since it ranges far into central and western China. There are races which flourish in tropical China however, and these would be the kinds observed by the wide-eyed and wondering expatriate from Ch'ang-an as he trudged through the wooded hills of Nam-Viet: there were *Thea hongkongensis* (which occurs in Annam as well as in Hong Kong) with rose-colored flowers, the white-blossomed *Thea paucipunctata* of Hainan, and many others.[354]

Like so many garden flowers of south Chinese origin which have become familiar to us, the camellia was virtually unknown to the Chinese themselves before the ninth century. Even then it was not familiar enough to gain the attention of the poets. But Tuan Ch'eng-shih, who observed everything, did not miss it: he called it (as the Chinese still do) "Mountain Tea," observed its scarlet color, compared it to the pomegranate flower, noted that it bloomed in the twelfth Chinese month (chiefly our January), and recorded its presence both in Kuei-chou and in Szechwan. (The plants of anciently assimilated Szechwan prepared the northerner for the novelties of Nam-Viet. The two regions shared not only camellias, but also sweetpeel tangerines and lichees, and many other subtropical treasures).[355] Tuan's patron, the grandee Li Te-yü, was apparently the first person—or at least the first person of consequence—to introduce the camellia to cultivation. Although most of the new trees he brought northward for his magnificent estate—osmanthus, golden larch, nandin, ormosia, and many others—[356] were native to the coastal regions near the mouth of the Yangtze, especially to Mount T'ien-t'ai, one of his prized novelties was "the Mountain Tea of P'an-yü," which is to say, Cantonese camellias.[357] But the earliest record of the camellia in poetry I have been able to find is in a quatrain by the greatly gifted poet-monk Kuan-hsiu, who survived the ruin of T'ang to become an ornament of the independent Szechwanese dynasty of the tenth century. He saw many of them in a paradisiacal plantation, their color suggesting the crimson textile dye then called "gibbon's blood."[358] Except for him, the camellia remains unnoticed in the literary arts until Sung times.[359]

If any flower has captured the modern western imagination as the tropical bloom par excellence, it is the hibiscus, a close relative of the hollyhock and other mallows. Perhaps we owe something to both Hawaii and Hollywood for this. But our familiar kinds of hibiscus are not natives of the Sandwich Islands. This is not to say that the genus is foreign to America, though few of us recognize the okra pods which go into the thick soup called "gumbo" in the southern United States as the fruit of *Hibiscus esculentus*—nor is that the only American hibiscus. But the gaudy shrubs admired in so many of the tropical and subtropical gardens of the world are chiefly of Chinese origin. Four species of hibiscus are well-known plants of Nam-Viet: the pink or white "cotton rose" (*Hibiscus mutabilis*);[360] the "rose of Sharon" (*Hibiscus syriacus*) with a similar range of color, sometimes called simply "althaea," though this is properly a name of the hollyhock—[361] it is thought that this hollyhock-like flower is the *chin* (*kyĕn*) of the ancient Classics; the red "China rose" (*Hibiscus rosa-sinensis*);[362] and finally, the yellow or "sunset hibiscus" (*Hibiscus tiliaceus*), which is indeed the familiar streamside *hau* of Hawaii.[363] All these fine flowering shrubs occur in Nam-Viet; the first three (the rosy ones) also grow somewhat further north, but the yellow hibiscus is a purely tropical plant, whose range extends only this far north.[364] None of them are particularly prominent in T'ang literature, though the China rose gets a little attention, and that, like other southern flowers, almost entirely in the ninth century. But it was Li Shang-yin who really loved the *rosa-sinensis,* which he introduced into many of his luscious stanzas, among them two entirely devoted to "The Vermilion Hibiscus Flower." They are characteristically hard to translate intelligibly, being loaded with complex historical allusions to red hues and flame colors, such as the Han palace destroyed by fire and restored on the advice of Viet shamans, and a peak in Chekiang called Red City-wall.[365] Liu Hsün compared the vermilion hibiscus of Nam-Viet to the great mallow of Szechwan, and reported that the village girls gathered and sold them—several dozen for a single coin.[366] By the ninth century, at least, this red hibiscus was regularly planted in temperate northern gardens—it appears in one poem in company with the phoenix tree,[367] and in another spread along a fence, matched with a green poplar.[368] The last-mentioned verses are enlivened by the bellow of an alligator, from which we may set the poem in the lake district of central China. But much of the charm of this scarlet southerner lay in its mythological associations, which inspired or were inspired by its local name in Nam-Viet—*fo-sang* (*bywĕt-sang*) or *fu-sang* (*byu-sang*). This word had been familiar for centuries as the name of the sun tree and the barely imaginable fairy-land below the eastern horizon where it spread its immense boughs. Beyond the great Eastern Sea was a sweet and saltless Indigo Sea (so went the old legend), and in it lay the land of the *fu-sang.* Its fruit, eaten by the Taoist elect, suffused their bodies with a lovely golden radiance, and gave them the power to soar in the empyrean like hawks.[369] The second syllable of the world tree's name was written with the graph for *sang* "mulberry," and so it was thought that it had some resemblance to the Chinese mulberry, and indeed the indefatigable Tuan Ch'eng-shih records the fused name *sang chin* "mulberry hibiscus" (instead of *fo-sang* or *chu chin*) for a double-blossomed variety, and explains this by the supposed resemblance of its foliage to that of the mulberry tree.[370] It might at first seem curious that a flowering shrub adorned with the red flowers of the south should be identified with a mythical tree in the unattainable East—until we remember that the primordial *fu-sang* tree was the birth- and death place of the flaming sun, in which the red essence of the south was congealed. This theme was not neglected by the poets.

Indeed it was extravagantly developed in a florid rhapsody (*fu*) by Chu Yeh.[371] *rosa-sinensis* is familiar in the warmer gardens of the world today.

The other showy red plants of the south get shorter shrift in literature. The manglietia, for instance, is a small genus, but it is distributed from Celebes to China, and is one of the typical elements of the flora of Indochina.[372] The Chinese name for this tree, which produces fragrant pink flowers, is "tree lotus" (*mu lien*). Tuan Ch'eng-shih compared its leaves to those of the magnolia and its flowers to the lotus and gave Szechwan as its habitat.[373] Po Chü-i admired it among the precipitous gorges leading into that province, and sent a poetic description of it to a friend at court, comparing its blooms both to the pink lotus and to the deep crimson peony.[374] The more varied and abundant manglietias of Nam-Viet passed unnoticed. Similarly, the showy red flower clusters of the Chinese *Ixora,* which is also found in the woodlands of Indonesia, are ignored by the T'ang poets, though it was listed among the plants of Nam-Viet in the T'ang *Materia Medica.*[375] Another fine red show was provided by a large tree of the gardens of Canton, the so-called Circassian bean or red-sandalwood tree (*Adenanthera pavonina*)[376] which the Hua men called "overseas red bean," comparing its berries to the native jequirity seeds. It would seem that this was an introduction from further south, and since Li Hsün remarks that it had only recently been planted in Szechwan, we can readily imagine that he—or possibly his brother—is to be credited for the diffusion of the red-beaded tree in western China.[377]

It is a disappointment that the shade-loving begonia, the jewel of the wet forests of south China, was (it seems) completely unknown to the T'ang poets. Its name would have crowned the symbolic company of the red flowers of Nam-Viet.[378]

But now it is necessary to leave the dominant reds of the Nam-Viet flora and look at some less brilliant exotics which the Hua men recognized there. The "Persian lilac" (*Melia azedarach*)—which also enjoys such fine names as "China tree" and "pride of India"—is cultivated throughout south Asia, including south China, for its fine scent and especially for its grateful shade. In China it was called simply *lien* tree. In an ancient classic, its fruit was the unique diet of a divine bird,[379] but both the naturalists and poets of T'ang ignored it, as they did the other melias of Nam-Viet. The government pharmacologists, however, noticed that the trees were bisexual, and that the roots of the male were very poisonous.[380] The odorous white magnolia-like "night-closing flower" (it opens at dawn, but sheds its fragrance at night) is now cultivated in tropical China, and its blossoms are used to flavor tea and to ornament the hair arrangements of its women. In a poem on his feelings on a summer night, the poet Tou Shu-hsiang wrote, "Night-closing flowers open— their aroma fills the courtyard."[381] The name seems to refer to *Talauma pumila,* sometimes called *Magnolia coco.*[382]

The yellow "gold-coin flower," one of the rayed *Compositae,* which was also known by the Indian name of *viśesa,* was an adapted foreign plant. It was said to be a sixth century introduction to Canton, where the girls sold them threaded on multicolored gossamer threads,[383] but its chrysanthemum-like habit does not agree with the proper image of a tropical flower. We would call it "elecampane." [384] P'i Jih-hsiu imagined its golden discs as coins minted by the great Fashioner:

> *Yin* and *yang* were the charcoal, earth was the furnace;
> Smelting brought forth these golden coins, without the use of a mold.[385]

Still, though climatically ambiguous, a golden flower fits the spirit of the golden south tolerably well.

Then there were the easily recognized exotics. The *Nymphaea*, which we style "water lily"—often confused both in popular and formal iconography with the sacred lotus of India—was well known to the men of T'ang, especially in its cerulean form from the vale of Kashmir, the true *nīla-utpala*, our "nenuphar." [386] But the natives of Nam-Viet had their own shy *Nymphaea*, no import. It was basically white, but with some color varieties. They named it "sleeping lotus" because it retired each night below the surface of the tropical ponds.[387] The fragrant white henna flowers, the "camphire" of the Bible, whose ancestors stained the hands of Egyptian ladies, were grown in Nam-Viet in the ninth century, where they were called "finger-nail flowers." Although Tuan Kung-lu professed not to understand the meaning of this name, it is clear that it referred to the use of their juice to stain the fingernails of fashionable women.[388] Several kinds of oleander, native or introduced, grow between Portugal and Japan, some finely flowered, some nicely fragrant, some poisonous. One of these, probably the sweet-scented, bamboo-leaved oleander of Persia, was cultivated in Kuei-chou in T'ang times under the name *chü-na-wei* (*kyu-na-ywei*).[389]

Other popular flowering plants are even harder to identify now. The "yellow ring" creeper, a native of Nam-Viet much planted in gardens, remains a problem despite a modern identification with the wisteria (a rare color then!); [390] and another white-flowered twiner attained the ultimate in medieval anonymity with the name of "nameless flower." [391] But there were hundreds of other truly nameless flowers there.

Some plants are hallmarks of the tropics, even though they lack conspicuous flowers. Their luxuriantly branching habit represents precisely the seemingly abnormal pressure of the life force in the eternally hot and humid lands. One of these unavoidable symbols was the banyan. Even if we do not recognize in its multiplicity of stems and far-extended shade one of the great figs of Indian and Chinese tradition, we may recall it from *Paradise Lost,* where Milton, apparently seeing Eden close to the Indian Ocean, has Adam and Eve cover their surprising genitals with banyan leaves:

> There soon they chose
> The fig-tree—not that kind for fruit renowned,
> But such as, at this day, to Indians known,

> In Malabar or Decan spreads her arms
> Branching so broad and long that in the ground
> The bending twigs take root, and daughters grow
> About the mother tree, a pillared shade
> High overarched, and echoing walks between.[392]

Three species of banyan flourish in modern Lingnan and northern Vietnam,[393] but it is impossible to tell which were the races that were widely planted in the chief cities of Nam-Viet, in T'ang or in pre-T'ang times.[394] To the traditionally oriented mentality, the banyan, of whatever kind, posed a real problem. Trees of "connected venation"—that is, double-trunked trees sharing the same sap—were still regarded in T'ang times as omens of good fortune for the state. Alas—to the men of Nam-Viet the multiple-stemmed banyan was a commonplace sight, and to report its occurrence (as the statutes required) to the court augurs was recognized as quite unnecessary.[395] But despite its long history as a publicly encouraged tree in Nam-Viet, the exiled poets did not deem it worthy of serious attention. Only Liu Tsung-yüan (always to be considered an exception) took the occasion of the defoliation of the banyans of Liu-chou city in an unseasonable March storm to suggest his own misery and bewilderment.[396]

The relative neglect of a magnificent and useful tree, characteristic of many new lands, is in fact great attention if we compare it with the absolute indifference of the T'ang men to one of the most typical of all tropical plants all round the world—the mangrove.[397] In its peculiar watery way the mangrove—its very name belongs with mango and mangosteen in a tropical Asian alliterative series—resembles the banyan, with its multiple-arched buttressing roots thick in the salty coastal swamps. It also recalls our own swamp cypress. But though the bark of the tentacled mangrove has for centuries provided an excellent material for the tanners of Southeast Asia, and it has been said that this "cutch" (as the commercial product is called) gave a fine henna color to the conquering sails of Cheng Ho in the fifteenth century,[398] the men of T'ang ignored it. Evidently the hot swamped shores held no attraction for them. Most astonishing, even collectors of southern *curiosa* like Tuan Kung-lu fail to mention this true index of the tropical coastal biome.

Where beyond the extreme sea wall, and between
the remote sea gates,
Waste water washes, and tall ships founder, and
deep death waits;
Where, mighty with deepening sides, clad about
with the seas as with wings.
And impelled of invisible tides, and fulfilled of
unspeakable things,
White-eyed and poisonous-finned, shark-toothed
and serpentine-curled,
Rolls, under the whitening wind of the future, the
wave of the world.

A.C. Swinburne, *Hymn to Proserpine*

11 Animals

INVERTEBRATES

Our zoological view of Nam-Viet, because of the special interests of medieval observers, the relative abundance of animal species, and the chance survival of texts, will necessarily be incomplete. All kinds of creatures will appear intermingled, without systematic separation into faunal zones or biomes. Goat antelopes will hobnob with gibbons, as if modern ecology did not exist. We shall start off low on the evolutionary ladder, with a hodge-podge of spineless animals.

> In a wilderness of gorges, poisonous birds come pecking after the boat;
> By the blackness of caverns, vindictive snakes come flying from the trees.[1]

So wrote Chang Pin on the fortunate return of a friend from the perilous confines of Annam. Envenomed wildfowl and winged serpents were part of the expected furniture of the monsoon forest. Even more zoologically plausible poems which tell of the animal life of Nam-Viet are turbulent with wild elephants, thunder-breeding dragons, monster sea turtles blowing up waves, and prodigious clams glowing in their subaqueous lairs.[2] Indeed even sober prose accounts tend to emphasize reptiles and slimy invertebrates—all of the hideous and demoniac crawlers of the sodden soils and heated seas of Nam-Viet.[3] Although mammals and birds are more precisely delineated in the T'ang texts, we still get the impression of a land overrun with anonymous lizards and their loathsome like. A little information is given about some specific insects and molluscs, while there is almost total silence about the simpler phyla.

We begin with a marine coelenterate, a jellyfish of Nam-Viet which the men of T'ang called *tse* (*trăk*), or sometimes "sea mirror," or, most often, "water mother." This was a medusa, probably an *Aurelia,* of such tenuous substance that it was regarded as "basically a creature formed by the congealing of dark (*yin*) water." [4] The human inhabitants of the tropical coast did not disdain to eat these humid animals, properly cooked and flavored with *alpinia* ("wild ginger"), cardamoms, cassia, and fagara.[5] Their repute among the Hua men, however, was chiefly based on the observation that little shrimps swam along under their soft canopies, acting (it was thought) as eyes to warn of danger.[6] This remarkable symbiosis provided a useful and hardly avoidable moral—a large but insensitive organism might profit from the help of lesser but more alert creatures. This was the theme of an elaborate *fu* written by Yang T'ao to the sententious rhyme scheme "having/mutual/need/so/later/assist/one." [7]

Moving up the evolutionary scale to the successful molluscs, we must begin with the most magnificent before attending to the more believable. The mysterious *ch'en* (*zhin*), akin to the treasure-hoarding sea dragons, but usually imagined as a gaping, pearl-producing, monster bivalve, was perhaps realized in the form of one of the giant clams of the tropical seas—*Chama* or *Tridacna.* A well-known creature of fantasy, it may have haunted the dreams of the pearl dealers, whose daily preoc-cupation was with the smaller relatives, particularly the pearl oysters of the offshore beds just west of the Lei-chou peninsula. The oysters' pearls were much appreciated in the north, but one writer complained that the delicate flesh of their close cousins, much appreciated by the people of Nam-Viet, was ignored by the men of the north. The southerners boiled them, removed the shells, and ate them with pleasure.[8] They were particularly enjoyed when taken with a cup of wine,[9] and (contrariwise) the Lu-t'ing people of the water margin brought them impaled on skewers to exchange for wine in the public markets.[10] This kind of edible oyster was called *mou-li*—the first syllable of its name written with the character for "bull; male animal." But Tuan Ch'eng-shih was careful to point out that the *mou* vocable's masculinity was purely adventitious, and that the oyster was in fact a concretion, without benefit of sex, from saline water.[11] He remarks that this is a unique instance, apparently not being aware of the spontaneous generation of the jellyfish claimed by a contemporary. Despite uncertainty about the distinction between the pearl-growing oyster and the esculent oyster, common speech distinguished clearly between these salt-water creatures on the one hand and the nacreous fresh-water mussels of Nam-Viet, which sometimes also produced pearls. These last were named *pang,* and were members of the family *Unionidae.*[12]

The fame of the cowrie (*Cypraea* sp.) was ancient in the Far East. As in other parts of the world, its handsome shell had been employed for currency in prehistoric times, especially in regions remote from the sea.[13] Li Hsün reports that even in T'ang times the common cowrie (*pei-tzu*) was still the usual medium of exchange in Yunnan.[14] A variety of particular importance in Nam-Viet was the "purple cowrie."[15] Su Kung, the pharmacologist, describes it like this: "The purple cowrie comes from within the southeastern sea. Though its shape is like that of the *pei-tzu* [common cowrie], it is two or three inches long. All are bone white with purple maculations. The southern heathen collect them, and they are used in commodity exchange."[16] If we can rely on a line of Lu Kuei-meng's poetry, these superior cowries were accepted or even required for payment of taxes on merchandise by the Nam-Viet magistrates: "All taxes on treasures must be paid up with purple cowries."[17] Centuries before, the mighty Chao T'o had not disdained to send fifty purple cowries (with a pair of white jade rings and a thousand iridescent kingfishers) as a royal gift to the Han court.[18] Indeed purple cowries were symbols of royal and even of divine glory. When Keng Wei wrote of a New Year's Day levee in the great capital, he imagined the splendor of the Chinese court in terms of its underwater counterpart, the palace of the Sire of the Ho, the ancient god of the Yellow River:

> Purple cowries are wrought for his high pylons,
> Yellow Dragons are raised on his great standards.[19]

(There was an old tradition that the Sire's ceremonial gate in the silty depths of his river was made of these shells—presumably brought from salty tributary princes in the South China Sea. The Yellow Dragon was also a creature of the Yellow River and its lord.)[20]

Among other shelled molluscs of the South China Sea was the gastropod whose operculum supplied onycha to mix with musk and aloeswood in the incenses of the great northern temples, and also to lend a pleasing fragrance to the wax of a lady's lip rouge.[21] Then there were the lovely vermilion "Parrot Snails," spotted with blue-green, with glittering nacreous interiors, which were converted to elegant wine goblets.[22] This name evidently corresponds to our pearly nautilus,[23] a beautifully housed cephalopod of the southern oceans.

Another cephalopod—but without shell—well known in Nam-Viet was the squid, called Raven-black Brigand.[24] The name suggests the flaccid animal's predatory habits, and his private supply of black ink: "The men of the sea say this of it: a bag for counting slips dropped into the sea by the king of Ch'in on an eastward journey was transformed into this fish. Therefore its shape still resembles it, and the ink is still in its belly." [25] The coastal dwellers of Ling-nan were discriminating enough to appreciate the delicate flavor of the squid—they caught them, fried them, and ate them with ginger and vinegar, rightly regarding this as an exceptionally tasty dish. Squid were also preserved by salting and drying. [26] The squid's chitinous "bone" or "gladius" (which we put in the cages of canaries) was also "carved to make playthings," whose forms can scarcely be imagined now. [27]

Accompanying the large-eyed cephalopods in the warm Nam-Viet waters were the arthropods. The most interesting of these was the primitive trilobite-like King Crab or Horseshoe Crab, which was no crab at all—indeed some taxonomists have thought it more closely allied to the spiders. [28] The Chinese name for it was *hou (ghou)*. Here we shall adopt its scientific name "xiphosura," which describes its long stiletto-like tail. Liu Hsün described this shallow water worm- and mollusc-eater very plainly: "Its shell is hyaline clear, as sleek as a blue porcelain bowl. Kettle-backed —its eyes are on its back. Its mouth is placed below its belly, which is a blue-black color. On each side of the belly there are six feet. It has a tail, more than a foot long, and three-edged like a palm stem." [29] The same writer tells us that the spinelike tail of the xiphosura contains a yellow pearl, larger and more buoyant in the male. The tail itself was used by the southerners as a wish-fulfilling wand. [30] Curious tales of the inseparability of the male and female animals were current—some said that the female carried the male on her back, others that the female lacked eyes, and was always led about by the male. In any case, if you caught one, the other fell easy prey. [31] I have no personal experience of the quality of the flesh of the xiphosura as I do of the squid, but the men of Nam-Viet prized it in a sauce or pickle. [32]

Among the crustaceans, Chinese visitors to Nam-Viet noticed particularly a kind of giant crab, which they called *chiu-mou (tsyou-mou)*:

The largest of the *chiu-mou* are more than a foot long. The pair of chelae are very strong. In the eighth month it is capable of fighting with a tiger. [33]

And, adds one authority, "Oftentimes it grips men and kills them." [34] Despite the tall tales of the ferocious nature of this creature, it seems actually to be one of the several kinds of sea crab, such as the genus *Neptunus,* which have paddles instead of claws on their hindmost feet. Some of them are quite large, though far from being man eaters or tiger killers. [35] Apparently they were edible. [36]

The Red Crab, taken on the coasts of Hainan, had a multitude of other names, ranging from Sword Presser to Tide Summoner—and the name *chiu-mou* has also been applied to him. [37] Apparently there are local dialectical variants. The shell of this crab was naturally adorned with twelve spots of rouge. It and the red-and-yellow-striped shell of the Tiger Crab made attractive wine cups. [38] The rich yellow fat of the Red Crab and of the "Yellow Fat Crab," mixed with the "five flavors" (sweet, sour, salt, bitter, pungent) was reputed to be a delicious dish. [39]

The men of Nam-Viet were also fond of small shrimp, which they served up alive with green vegetables and rich sauces; [40] a large red decapod (perhaps a lobster?) of the coastal counties had its shell transformed into cups and other vessels, some having lips decorated with "white metal." [41]

Perhaps it is surprising that we read so little in medieval literature about the insect life of Nam-Viet, since more kinds of insect and more individual insects live in the tropics than in any other region of the world. But then, even in our own times only about 10 per cent of the existing species have been scientifically described. Most are inconspicuous creatures hidden under bark or soil. [42] The more flamboyant or annoying varieties, however, command immediate attention, and did so in the T'ang tropics as much as in our own. When a gigantic "centipede" (admittedly not an insect in the narrow sense) was washed ashore near Canton in 745—a single "claw" yielded 120 catties of meat— [43] that was no more than could be expected of the wildly extravagant arthropods of the lands below the sun. But the catawumpuses and gallinippers [44] whose repulsive shapes haunted the dark forests between Canton and Hanoi have not left their individual footprints on the pages of the T'ang naturalists. They appear for the most part only collectively and anonymously in such conventional (but nonetheless frightening) phrases as "poisonous insects."

To get individual attention, it was necessary that a tropical insect show its worth to the Chinese nation. The lac insect of Annam and Cambodia was one such admirable animal. It supplied a desirable dye for the famous polychrome silks of China, and a cosmetic rouge for its handsome women. [45] It was in consequence given prominent recognition in the records of T'ang. Edibility, of course, was a high recommendation for lasting fame. Accordingly, we hear of a blue, cicada-like (but unidentifiable) insect of the Canton area, whose tart flavor was considered delicious, [46] and a sauce made of ant eggs and salt was a rare delicacy available only to the personal friends of, or official visitors to, a chieftain of the aborigines. [47] Usefulness in medicine or in magic was a supreme recommendation, and here the family of bees and wasps was easily the most remarkable. The black-headed, red-winged, earth-nesting, spider-eating wasp of Lingnan [48] was known to the pharmacologists, as was the black one-legged bee (so-called) which perched queerly on the roots of trees. This last was roasted, ground, mixed with oil, and applied externally to all sorts of boils and tumors. [49] A dangerous species was a black wasp, an avatar of a poisonous mushroom, which severed men's heartstrings with its sawlike snout. [50] A desirable species was the bee or wasp which could hardly be distinguished from the leaf of the brea-yielding *kan-lan* tree. It could be used as a love medicine. [51] Probably none of these equivocal hymenoptera was as much admired as the honest bees of Annam, makers of the yellow wax which was sun-bleached and used to staunch the bleeding of parturient Chinese women, and to darken the hair of their graying husbands. [52]

But gorgeous color was the most desired attribute of southern insects, and many possessed it. The chrysochlorous beetle called *tamamushi* in Japan lent its iridescent

wing cases to the ornamentation both of expensive furniture and of female bodies
—though the continuous demand for it seems to disprove the tale that "as soon as
the insect dies, the golden color is extinguished, like the light of a firefly." [53] This
winged emerald was also worn on the costume as a love charm. [54] But although its
metallic hues shine on the epidermis of many kinds of tropical insects, especially the
butterflies, they are conspicuously rare on the insects of temperate lands. The rainbow wings of the rain-forest butterflies are replaced by dull-earth colored moths in
our deciduous woodlands. Indeed the gorgeous butterflies of the tropical forests usually provide more colors than do the flowers. Wallace's classic study of the Indonesian
rain forest gives the best picture of them:

We meet with the most intense metallic blues, the purest satiny greens, the most gorgeous
crimsons, not in small spots but in large masses, relieved by a black border or background.
In others we have contrasted bands of blue and orange, or of crimson and green, or of
silky yellow relieved by velvety black. In not a few the wings are powdered over with
scales and spangles of metallic green, deepening occasionally into blue or golden or deep
red spots. Others again have spots and markings as of molten silver or gold, while several
have changeable hues, like shot-silk or richly-coloured opal. [55]

The most spectacular are the *Morpho* butterflies of tropical America, and even beyond them the *Ornithoptera,* the bird-wing butterflies of Indonesia and New
Guinea. [56] But though Nam-Viet had its splendid butterflies too, it does not appear
that these true jewels of the high forest canopy were noticed by the Chinese intruders.
Among the famous poets, Li Shang-yin was the most attracted by the *Lepidoptera,*
but his are not tropical butterflies; and the beautifully colored fairy butterflies of the
grottoes of Lo-fou—originally transformed from the discarded clothing of the alchemist Ko Hung—do not appear before Sung times. [57] The flimsy aerial beings provide
the perfect allegory of the awakened Taoist adept: "The ascetic butterfly emerges
from the greediest of early stages," and, "There are whole species of these creatures
who have no mouths and no stomachs and therefore, understandably, do not eat or
drink. Brief life must be the portion of such unnourishable 'flowers of the air.' " [58]
They are even more rarified beings than the Taoist transcendents, who at least nourished themselves on air and dew. They are the true progeny of Chuang Chou, dream
creatures and angels, akin to the brightly colored birds of the divine south. Therefore the holy butterflies of Lo-fou belong psychologically in Nam-Viet. Someone may
yet discover them there in T'ang times. Certainly the metamorphic powers of the
butterfly were well-known. In particular, they were specimens and examples of animals who could become plants, or the other way round. Tuan Kung-lu saw what appeared to be a many-colored tree by a river in Nam-Viet, but when a servant brought
him a branch he found it covered with butterflies of every size and color, some "as
large as bats," some "with golden eyes," and some "with lilac eyes." That ardent
student of southern natural history decided that the leaves of the tree had turned into
butterflies, and in his account of the miracle, he cites other lore about butterfly-

bearing plants, and finally opines: "In every case, the Fashioner of Mutations caused it to be so—surely this is no empty talk!"[59] Although I cannot give it its correct name, one of a number of so-called "Butterfly trees" in China may have been the casual home of the wonderful creatures seen by Tuan Kung-lu.[60] Wallace saw a similar insect in Sumatra, the leaf-butterfly *Kallima paralekta,* protectively colored "a rich purple, variously tinged with ash color, and across the fore wings there is a broad bar of deep orange," conspicuous when the insect is on the wing, but not to be distinguished from a dry leaf when it is resting on a tree.[61]

The ancient art of raising the domestic silkworm was adapted to a southern caterpillar, which was fed its favorite leaves in the cosmetic boxes of the women of Nam-Viet. After pupation, it was transmuted into an orange-colored butterfly, which a hopeful lady could wear on her person, calling it "bewitching butterfly"—another love charm.[62]

Fish and Frogs

As for vertebrate animals, since they are on the whole larger and more conspicuous than the invertebrates, impinging more directly on the senses and activities of men, they are more adequately represented in literature. This is as true of T'ang Nam-Viet as it is of any other place and period. Among them, however, the fishes, adapted to a life in an environment alien to the human species, get comparatively less attention than the land dwellers—reptiles, mammals, and birds. This despite an ancient and intimate relation between the Chinese and the fresh-water fishes. The cultivation of carp in the Far East goes back well before the beginning of the Christian era, and fish-farming in rice fields, lily ponds, and in every sort of waterway in south China is now remarkably efficient and productive.[63] Such homegrown fish as the carp and the orphe—to say nothing of molluscs and crustaceans encouraged in the same waters —provided an important diet supplement. Salting was the usual method of preservation,[64] though the spicy, fermented fish pastes and sauces of Indochina were also introduced to the northerners who ventured into the far south. I cannot speak from personal experience, but it does not appear that the fermented fish preparation of south China, called *cha* (*tră*)—the T'ang pharmacologist Ch'en Ts'ang-ch'i warned that it was likely to produce sores on the body—was as strong-smelling a preparation as the *nùớc mắm* of modern Vietnam, whose odor is reputed to have a close resemblance to that of tiger's urine.[65]

In our days of great public aquaria and of home fish tanks provided with heated water and other amenities, most of us are familiar with the flamboyant colors and often astonishing shapes of tropical fish. The warm waters of the world, fresh and salt alike, including the waters of the South China Sea and the Gulf of Tongking, are rich in fish kinds. The shallow coastal waters of Nam-Viet support a great population, though, in general, greater abundance of individuals is characteristic of northern waters, greater variety of species of southern waters.[66] Whether any of these handsome southerners were bred for pure pleasure I cannot say. The Paradise Fish (*Macropodus*), a beautifully colored relative of the popular gouramis of our household tanks, is said to have been bred in China "for centuries," especially for its attractive mating display, and because of the lovely nest of foam it builds for its young.[67] Its modern Chinese name means "fighting fish," but I have not found it in the T'ang records.

It is not surprising that most of the Nam-Viet fish noticed in T'ang times had something odd or fantastic about them—this was the climate of the times. The most astonishing of these monsters was a giant sea loach—the smallest more than a thousand feet long—which was occasionally sighted by trading vessels on the Annamese coast. But Liu Hsün denies with confidence that they swallow ships.[68]

Like us, the medieval Chinese found it only natural that the warm seas should breed such a wonder as a flying fish. Before T'ang times flashing "cicada-winged" bodies (I use the Chinese image) were reported off the coast of Champa, flying up "to reach the clouds" and plunging into the depths of the seas.[69] Ch'en Ts'ang-ch'i wrote of them as skimming the seas south of Hainan in companies. The natives, he says, regarded them as harbingers of typhoons. He also tells that they were caught, burned to ashes, and taken with wine by pregnant women to facilitate birth, apparently on the magical principle that their easy passage from water to the world of air could contribute to the similar transition of the foetus.[70] The little sea horses (the Chinese called them both "sea horses" and "water horses") caught in the coastal waters of Ch'ao and Hsün, were used in precisely the same way. Ch'en Ts'ang-ch'i regarded them as a species of shrimp.[71]

Another wonderful creature of the southern seas was the Fish Tiger:

Its head is like a tiger's, and the skin of its back is like a hedgehog's, with spines which strike a man like the bite of a serpent. There are also cases of its changing itself into a tiger.[72]

This was the self-inflating Balloon fish or Porcupine fish (*Diodon holacanthus*), of worldwide distribution in tropical seas. The true identity of the medieval "sword fish" is less certain. Tuan Ch'eng-shih writes that "a sea fish becomes a sword-fish in a thousand years. One name for it is 'lute fish,' as its shape resembles a lute and it is fond of singing." [73] The ancient lute had a pear-shaped body narrowing gradually towards the pegged neck. The description matches that of the true swordfish (*Xiphias gladius*) of tropical waters better than some of the fish given this name in modern source books.[74]

Some smaller fish of Nam-Viet, however, had a good reputation, but only as food. There was the flat silvery pomfret (*ch'ang*), delicious and fattening when served broiled.[75] The tiny *yü* (*ywĕt*) of En-chou, which I cannot identify, was relished, when dried and preserved in salt, for its exceptionally fine flavor.[76] Smallest of all were the inexhaustible little fish, not more than an inch long, which thronged an icy Annamese mountain stream of Tibetan origin; they were boiled in abundance to make a kind of stew.[77]

REPTILES

Among the reptiles, turtles and tortoises have the most respectable reputation in China, largely due to a venerable tradition of divination by the application of heated rods to their shells. The gods gave their opinions in the form of cracks in the shell, thus, after a fashion, sanctifying the whole family of chelonians. A superior kind of tortoise for divination was collected in Ch'ao-chou in Nam-Viet in T'ang times.[78] There were other sorts of magical and numinous testudinates there. The giant sea turtle which supported, in some tales, the isles of the immortals on its massive back was probably an inflated recollection of the giant leatherback (*Dermochelys coriacea*), which is widespread in tropical seas and has been reported off the coast of south China.[79] A flowing spring in Kuang-chou was blessed by the presence of a giant soft-shell turtle (*Pelochelys bibroni*) girded with a bronze ring: "When there was any defilement of this water, it will bring salubrious rains."[80] The self-purifying turtle is only the old rain dragon in a different form. The seas off Canton also produced a large "osprey turtle," but it seems to have been merely strange, "like an osprey" (whatever that may mean), not especially numinous.[81] A "red softshell" of the fresh water of Lo-chou and Pien-chou, just north of the Lei-chou peninsula, had a malignant nature: "Should any bird or beast without exception, even water cattle [carabaos], enter the water it is dragged down into a deep tarn, where its blood is sucked and it dies. Some say it is a *kău*-dragon that pulls them down, but I do not know why this should be so."[82] A "vermilion softshell" of Nam-Viet, with a blood-red belly, was less fierce. It caught nothing larger than sea horses. The reptile was itself caught by men and worn as a talisman against sword wounds, and by women to gain beauty.[83] This leads us to medicinal turtles. The powdered shell of an otherwise unidentified "numinous turtle," presumably used as a royal drug, was sent as tribute from Ch'ao-chou, while Kuang-chou sent the shells of a softshelled turtle, but for what purpose we do not know. Presumably they too were for the stores of the court pharmacy.[84] We are better informed about a reptile named *mao* (*myou*):

Snake-headed and softshell-bodied, it goes into the water, and climbs up trees and shrubs. It lives in Lingnan. The men of the south call it *mao*. Its fat is most profitable, but stored in vessels of copper or ceramic it will seep out. If you fill the shell of a hen's egg with it, it will not leak. It controls swellings and poisons.[85]

This might be the softshelled turtle *Amyda steindachneri,* a native of Nam-Viet with a long, peculiar snout, whose flesh is highly prized.[86]

Fresh-water-dwelling softshell turtles of one kind or another were an old story to the Hua men—the northerners had relished their succulent flesh since the earliest times. But the large, important chelonians of tropical seas—the hawksbill, the logger-head, and the green turtle—had only been indeterminate figures of uncertain report in the classical era. By the T'ang period however these too were being exploited for their many advantages to man. Chief among them was the hawksbill, the source of the handsomely mottled commercial "tortoiseshell." The chief centers of supply were Annam and Hainan, but only that from Chen-chou on the southern, windward coast of Hainan was thought to be as fine as that imported by foreign argosy.[87] Foreign or domestic, the shell had a multitude of uses, most importantly in ladies' hair ornaments, for rich inlays in wooden furniture, and to make plectrums for lutes.[88] Another virtue of the substance was its power over poisons, for it was said to be the equal of the far-famed bezoar. It was especially efficacious if taken from the live reptile, in which case it had the power to dissolve every poison of Nam-Viet.[89] It is told that the coast-dwelling Lu-t'ing aborigines presented a live hawksbill to a prince of the royal T'ang house who was acting as governor in Lingnan in the last decade of the ninth century. The Li scion kept the beast alive in a pond, and, after cutting two pieces from its carapace to be attached to his arms as antivenins, returned it to the Lu-t'ing, who released it in the sea.[90] The word *tai-mei* "hawksbill; tortoise-shell" appears quite frequently in late T'ang poetry, but only as a richly maculated translucent substance, as in Wen T'ing-yün's romantic reconstruction of the bed curtains of the Lady Yang at her hot springs palace (tortoiseshell hooks for lotus-patterned curtains),[91] or else transferred to other dappled things, such as garden flowers;[92] it is hardly to be found, except in prose, as the name of the admirable turtle itself.

The hawksbill's cousin, the great loggerhead, known as *tzu-hsi* (*tsiĕ-ghwei*) in Chinese, was large enough to carry a man on its back. It provided combs and cups for the men of Canton, though its shell was not as highly regarded as that of the hawksbill. It was captured chiefly along the coasts of Ch'ao and Hsün—that is, north-east of the city.[93]

With the decline in popularity of tortoise-shell ornaments in our own age, the green turtle, called "the world's most valuable reptile,"[94] is now supreme among the sea turtles. The famous delicately flavored, easily digested soup made from the greenish, gelatinous essence called "calipee," which is obtained from its plastron, was as much appreciated in eighth- and ninth-century China as in eighteenth- and nine-teenth-century England, although perhaps not obtainable in the same quantities.[95] In this the medieval Chinese differed from the modern peoples of Indochina, who eat the green turtle's eggs but not its flesh.[96] The T'ang men, or their aboriginal employees, caught the reptiles in the seas off Nam-Viet, under the following perilous conditions:

The men must first make a sacrifice, and state the number to be taken. They emerge voluntarily and then are taken. But if they have no faith in them, wind and waves will capsize the boat.[97]

Once more we see a water reptile as an avatar of the protean dragon.

Looking to the terrestrial reptiles, other than snakes, we find only one much noticed in T'ang Nam-Viet. Its name was *ko-chieh* (*kap-kǎi*). The various reports of its appearance and habits agree only moderately well—they may tell of different varieties. One says that it was an earthy yellow color, with a froglike head, and lived in trees and walls.[98] Another tells that it was pale green with ochre spots "like old brocade," a dweller in holes in ancient trees.[99] Still another has it that it emerges from the water at night to stay in banyan trees.[100] At any rate, it was split, dried, and sold in the drug market for lung ailments.[101] Its identity is a puzzle. It ought to be a species of the "Toad-headed Lizard" (*Phrynocephalus*), but this is a resident of arid regions of north China and Mongolia.[102] There was also a bright-eyed chameleonlike fence-lizard in Nam-Viet, sometimes red sometimes yellow, which was reputed to be poisonous.[103]

As for the legless relatives of the lizards, they were well represented, even though not always conspicuous. Fang Ch'ien-li was a careful observer of nature, yet he made the rather startling statement: "The several counties southwest of Hsin-chou produce absolutely no snakes, mosquitoes, or flies. Though I was ten years a derelict in the southern quarter, I never once laid eyes on a snake." His explanation of their rarity was that they were all eaten by the aborigines.[104] But there were strange serpents in Nam-Viet. One of the oddest was the "two-headed snake" of Shao-chou and the north, said to be a transformed earthworm.[105] This is no fairytale creature. *Calamaria septentrionalis,* a resident of bamboo thickets in Nam-Viet, has markings on its tail which mimic its head, and when in danger it is the tail which moves aggressively.[106] The same hill region was the home of the deadly "indigo snake," whose tail was an antidote to the poison of its head.[107] Bright tropical colors also characterized a peacock-like gold-and-blue snake and a blood-red snake, both of Lei-chou.[108] A snake called Requiter of Wrongs followed any man who trod on it, and if he killed it, he found himself surrounded by a hundred of its kin.[109]

A kind of bezoar, a heavy globule called "snake yellow," was extracted from the bellies of some Nam-Viet serpent, and was well thought of as a remedy for infants' convulsions and for difficulties in childbirth.[110] But this snake drug counted for little when compared with the sovereign medicine made of the bile of the python. The gall bladders of the black-tailed pythons of Nam-Viet not only cured bloody diarrhoea and other disabling hemorrhages, for which purposes they were sent in great quantities to Ch'ang-an, but they also protected the residents of Nam-Viet from malarial miasmas.[111] (It is not certain that the pig's bile and tiger's bile regularly substituted for the genuine article had a comparable effect.) [112] The usual practice was to stab the great reptiles to death with bamboo skewers, or to stake them down alive and snip out their gall bladders.[113] In the southernmost counties of Lo and Lei, professional python farmers got a steady supply of the precious bile from their serpentine livestock.[114]

In medieval times the crocodilians constituted a significant part of the fauna of China, a role they have lost in modern times, chiefly as a result of centuries of persecution. The alligator (*t'o,* M.C. *da*), emerging in the spring like a rain-bringing dragon from its muddy lair in the Yangtze and lake region was familiar to the Chinese of antiquity. It is rare there in our times.[115] It was a classical reptile, mentioned in the ancient literature of the Hua men. The man-eating, saw-toothed crocodile (*e,* M.C. *ngak*) which infested the coastal shallows and estuaries of Nam-Viet in T'ang times, on the other hand, was free of old cultural associations. Its fame was chiefly due to the writing of a single man. But its fate in China has been even worse than that of the alligator—now it is never seen in its old haunts at all.[116] Folklore made the bear the only mortal enemy of the crocodile,[117] but the true bane of the species was man. The ostracized Han Yü was the great prototype of the human exterminators. Passing through Shuang-chou in 819 en route to his bitter post in Ch'ao-chou, he already anticipated the terrors of that place, among which was the reptile on which he ultimately declared war. He set down in verse the warning of a local official:

> There is a county, from the first named "Tide" (Ch'ao),
> Whose evil torrents are rife with pestilence and poison;
> Thunder and lightning boom and rumble unceasingly.
> The crocodile fish is larger than a ship—
> Its fangs and eyes bring terror and death to us.[118]

Arriving finally on the coast, he addressed his famous mandate to these malevolent lizards.[119] In it he tells how the great kings of antiquity had banished monsters beyond the realms of men, but that with the degeneration of the Chinese sovereigns in later times, these creeping basilisks had pressed closer in from the Four Seas. But now the glorious and virtuous T'ang nation has extended its rule over the southern Man peoples, there could be neither peace nor coexistence between the animals of darkness and the representative of the Son of Heaven. He therefore commands the whole tribe to depart his jurisdiction. Should they fail to do so, he will have them exterminated with poisoned arrows.[120]

DRAGONS AND THEIR KIN

Spiritually akin to the crocodile, and perhaps originally the same reptile, was a mysterious creature capable of many forms called the *chiao* (*k̯au*). Most often it was regarded as a kind of *lung*—a "dragon" as we say. But sometimes it was manlike, and sometimes it was merely a fish. All of its realizations were interchangeable. We shall look at each of these avatars in turn.

It is not easy to give a name to the *k̯au* (I shall continue to use the medieval form of its name). The word "dragon" has already been appropriated to render the broader term *lung*. "Kraken" is good since it suggests a powerful oceanic monster —but we have quite recently decided to allot it to the giant squid. We might name the *k̯au* a "basilisk" or a "wyvern" or a "cockatrice." Or perhaps we should call it by the name of its close kin, the double-headed crocodile-jawed Indian *makara,* which, in ninth-century Java at least, took on some of the attributes of the rain-bringing *lung* of China.[121] But all of these possibilities suffer from some defect of character, just as does the now accepted equation of *lung* and "dragon." Still, "dragon" shall remain my generic term to include, as well as the *k̯au,* many others such as the water monster called *ch'ih* (*t'yi*) which beat the water of the river at Yung-chou city, overturning boats and killing men, thus presaging the death of the town's chief magistrate, a royal prince, as we know on the authority of Liu Tsung-yüan.[122] Indeed "dragon" serves as a convenient general cover for every sort of water monster, and in fact all such creatures were regarded as transformed *lung* in the Far East. Ho Lü-kuang, the chief administrator of Lingnan in the mid-eighth century, was a native of Yai-chou in Hainan. He owned a house by the sea, and once said that he had seen three great wonders near his home: first, a monster fish caught between two rocky sea mounts—its voice was like thunder, the spume sprayed from its mouth seemed a muddy rain, and the sky was darkened by the vapor it spouted; second, things like gigantic toads on a large island, whose breath at night was brighter than moonlight; third, a serpent hundreds of *li* long on a sea isle, which drank the water of the ocean until suddenly one day it and its island were swallowed up by some unidentifiable Thing.[123] The protagonists in sailors' yarns such as these, some of them familiar to Arabian and Persian mariners,[124] although they resembled whales, snakes and, crocodiles, were all "dragons." Indeed the dragon (we understand the Chinese word *lung*) was capable of infinite formal variety. It could take the shape of a slender bamboo named *lung-tsung* and, so disguised, fecundate the ancestress of the Lao peoples.[125] At the opposite pole from this phallic semblance, it could show itself, in the old Hua tradition, as a beautiful rainbow maiden, or an argus-like guardian of paradise.[126] In the south, where it was as much a rain spirit as it was in the north, controlling the prosperity of the rice fields and fertility of the Man women, its cult took and still takes the form of a dragon-boat ceremony. Its twentieth-century remnant is chiefly a race between carvel-built boats propelled by two files of paddle-bearing men, and steered by a long sweep over the stern.[127] In antiquity it was a more serious affair, involving a human sacrifice, a trace of which seems to survive in the legend of the drowned Ch'ü Yüan.[128] The Chinese form of the cult is probably only a local variety of one once widespread in Southeast Asia and Oceania, expressing itself in such extremes as the crocodile-headed dugouts of Borneo and the gilded royal barge of Siam.[129] Analogues, if not relations, are well-known to us in the dragon ships of the Viking sea rovers. I do not know its form in T'ang times, but I can record an old myth, related to this boat ceremony, which was still current in tenth-century Nam-Viet. Long ago a woman of K'ang-chou found a huge egg in a river. She took it home, and from it came a strange little creature, a foot long. It grew to a length of five feet, was a good fisher, and loved to sport in the water. It left when the woman accidentally cut off its tail, but returned a year later, shining brightly, and they became friends again. The great monarch of Ch'in ordered her to bring the dragon child to court, but when they started off, the creature pulled the boat back, and in the end the pair could never be persuaded to leave Nam-Viet. When its protector died, the dragon built a mound of sand over her tomb: "Men called it the 'Dragon with the Digging Tail.' The making of boats like dragons with digging tails by the men of the south goes back to this." [130] Another version of this tale was current in the ninth century. In this, the little dragon was one of a brood of five, hatched from eggs taken home by a widow of Yüeh-ch'eng township, who wove cloth for a living. She became famous for her miraculous powers, and was rightly styled "Mother of Dragons." [131] She is, of course, a goddess, a protector of the Yü River, and a true dragon lady. Her cult is much alive in the twentieth century.[132]

But let us look more closely at the *kău* species of *lung,* a form best known in the south. Centuries before, the polymath Kuo P'u had attempted, not too successfully, to distinguish the *kău* from others of the tribe of divine serpents:

> Neither snake nor dragon,
> Scaly, many-colored, shining, refulgent,
> It prances and jumps on wave and billow.[133]

Though they disported themselves on the surface of the raging sea, the lairs of the *kău* were submarine grottoes, as the T'ang poets knew: "Rumbling thunder churns and smashes the caverns of the *kău* dragons." [134] These strange creatures constantly raise their heads above their watery domains in the poetry of Tu Fu.[135]

Like that of all dragons, the *kău's* shape was not always the same. Moreover it underwent ontogenetic changes, about which men held different theories. Long ago it had been thought that after a life of five hundred years a water viper [136] became a *kău;* after another thousand years this was in turn transformed into a full-fledged *lung.*[137] A T'ang writer reports, however, that a *fish* which achieved three hundred and sixty years became a *kău*-dragon, with the ability to fly out of the water.[138] In any case the *kău* was a numinous being, the peer of the holiest animals of China:

> At Cinnabar Hill the phoenixes are hiding;
> In water temples the *kău* dragons gather.[139]

Perhaps this parallel would have seemed presumptuous to a northerner, but it was evidently natural to its author, a tenth-century resident of Lingnan. In the southern tradition the *k̆au* was a fearful creature, ready, like the aborigine poised in the jungle, to attempt the restoration of chaos by disturbing the civilized order established by the true *lung,* the spirit-emblem of the kings of China.[140] From the point of view of the Chinese it embodied the maleficent and destructive aspects of water, as opposed to its beneficent aspects represented by the *lung.*[141] The *k̆au's* descendants survive in our own time as the terrible *thuông-luông* of modern Vietnam and the black, red-crested water serpent of the Tay, the *tu-ngùôc,* which eat humans, and take the daughters of men down to watery mansions to bear their children.[142]

From the earliest times, the coastal peoples of Nam-Viet had tattooed their bodies with representations of these masters of the sea, as a T'ang writer says, "in order to avoid suffering from the *k̆au*-dragons." [143] This was a good practical undertaking for divers and fisherfolk, but it is said that the kings of Annam engraved dragon figures in their skins as late as the fourteenth century to show their descent from and kinship to the serpentine sea kings.[144] These draconian defenders of the peoples of Nam-Viet had insidious ways of taking revenge on the Hua invaders. It is told that a eunuch, returning from a mission there in the eighth century, was taken ill with a severe fever after drinking from a wayside stream. A wise palace physician recognized from his antic behavior that he was the victim of a *k̆au*-dragon, and gave him a potion of niter and realgar. The unhappy man vomited up a scaly young *k̆au* several inches long.[145]

We have it on the word of Yüan Chen that "when a *k̆au* is old, it is transformed into a weird woman or girl." [146] The Chinese phrase suggests a witchwife, either young or old. The temptation should be avoided to see in such a creature a Mediterranean nereid, a sea nymph out of Shakespeare,[147] or an undine, whether the inhuman elemental agent of Paracelsus, or the exquisite fairy of De la Motte Fouqué's romance. She was a kind of oriental mermaid, sharing the qualities of shark or crocodile and the attributes of a Nam-Viet indigene. Moreover, there were *k̆au* men as well as *k̆au* women. Here is the classical statement about them:

In the midst of the South Sea are the houses of the *k̆au* people who dwell in the water like fish, but have not given up weaving at the loom. Their eyes have the power to weep, but what they bring forth is pearls.[148]

Probably the product of the looms of the sea people was even more famous than their nacreous tears. A romantic inventory of the rich furnishings of Yang Kuo-chung's mansion tells that among the most treasured of them were a screen on which the figures of women of antiquity were inlaid in tortoise shell and horn and ornamented with pearls and lapis lazuli, and a curtain made of "*k̆au* silk" [149] of the filmiest texture which was warming in the depths of winter and cooling in the summer heat.[150] This was the gift of an aboriginal chieftain of Nam-Viet. I suspect that the fabric from the looms of the *k̆au* maidens of the South China Sea was in fact the famous *pinikon,* the cinnamon-golden cloth woven from the byssus of the mussel

Pinna squamosa, an inhabitant of the warm waters of the Indian Ocean and Persian Gulf. To the well-known myths of the water sheep and the water silkworm,[151] which attempted to explain this mysterious textile, we must add the legend of the dragon weavers.

In recent centuries the Tan boat-people, for such plausible reasons as their life on and in the water and their snake and dragon myths, have been called "dragon house-holders."[152] This usage goes back at least to Yüan times.[153] It is also said that the Tan women and children are otters. This tradition seems to be as old as Sung.[154] I have not found either story in T'ang literature. Apparently the fact that the shore- and boat-people of T'ang Nam-Viet were the kinsmen of dragons and cronies of *kău* mermaids had not yet been registered in popular nomenclature, despite its classical precedents.

Finally, there was the lowly *kău* fish, apparently a simple and undeveloped form of the *kău* dragon, as far beneath the latter in dignity as the dragon was below the *kău* sea witches. It was the prey of ordinary men, and its skin was turned into useful objects. An early Sung description of this humble creature follows:

The *kău* fish has the aspect of a round fan. Its mouth is square and is in its belly. There is a sting in its tail which is very poisonous and hurtful to men. Its skin can be made into sword grips.[155]

A simpler but comparable picture is given in a T'ang source: "The *kău* comes from the South Sea; in figure it resembles a softshelled turtle, but it lacks feet and has a tail."[156] In short, it has a round or oval shape and a conspicuous tail. There can be no doubt of the identity of this fish—it is a sting ray. (Occasionally it is some other elasmobranch, such as a shark.) Rays were taken along the coast of T'ang China from Chekiang to Tongking, and up the great West River—then the Yü River—and their skins sent to Ch'ang-an,[157] where they made excellent abrasives and the rough, unslipping covers on the hilts of swords.[158]

MAMMALS

The mammalian population of the tropical forest is not so gaudy as other forms of animal life there, and certainly not to be compared with the birds and insects. If we think of the mammals at all, we imagine lurking predators, such as tigers, forgetting that there are tigers in Siberia; or apes and monkeys—but macaques leave their footprints even in the snow of Japan. A real difference between north and south is a more generalized one: with the exception of the squirrels, most mammals of the deciduous woodlands are ground-living, while in the hot forests most are arboreal.[159] But there are important exceptions there too. If we narrow our focus to China, we see in the north such animals as bears, wolves, lynxes, hares, roedeer, and many such special forms such as the Birch Mouse. Some occur both north and south, with varietal differences; among them are the goat antelopes—the gorals and serows. As for Nam-Viet, some zoologists distinguish three types of fauna mingled there: a "South Chinese" group extending from the Yangtze valley to the highlands of Nam-Viet, marked by the presence of the Harlequin and Horseshoe Bat, Bamboo Rat, Snub-nose Langur, Crab-eating Mongoose, and Goat-antelope; a "subtropical" group, concentrated in lowland Nam-Viet, especially along the coast and in Annam, with the Tube-nosed Bat, the Giant Flying Squirrel, and tree shrews, muntjaks, and marmoset mice; and a "Malayan" group in lowland Indochina generally with intrusions in Nam-Viet, including pangolins, gibbons, civets, mongooses, elephants, sambars, rhinoceroses, and many other true tropical mammals.[160]

A historical view of the southern components of this mixed fauna distinguishes an "Oriental" group, of vast extent, including macaques, palm civets, pigs, squirrels, buffalo, and deer, spreading in prehistoric times out through Southeast Asia to the then connected islands as far as New Guinea; then another wave of migrants—leaf monkeys, cats, weasels, bears, zebus, elephants, and rhinoceroses following them, but stopped by a new water barrier eastward of Bali.[161] All of these wandering mammalian tribes found their way into Nam-Viet, and, in the warmer ages of the remote past, some went even further north. The "Oriental" faunal area, extending from India eastward, was the scene of a remarkable and successful activity in animal domestication, as if the peoples of the Indies were obsessed with the search for new animals which could be adapted to their needs and pleasures. Hence came the useful pig and zebu, the hard-working water buffalo and elephant, and many domestic ducks, geese, chickens, pheasants, and peacocks. Other animals were and are tamed for loving pets, or entertainers or household flunkeys—all kinds of apes and monkeys, performing cobras and Himalayan bears, and sharp-toothed mongooses.[162] The bringing of these and other animals into the human family is apparently a necessary step on the way to complete domestication and control of the life cycle. We shall see some of these friends of man presently.

So shy were many of these southern mammals, or so nocturnal, or so hard to see in the treetops, that many of them were missed by the Chinese newcomers of T'ang altogether—or have at least gone unrecorded. Indeed the medieval records which comment particularly on the general character of the animal life of Nam-Viet usually remark on what is absent rather than what is present. Foxes and rabbits are not to be found in Nam-Viet, they say.[163] Or rather, as one observer noticed, the small rabbits of Lingnan have hair which is useless for the manufacture of the writing brushes, without which a northern literatus felt de-souled.[164] This was a serious matter, much commented on. Brushes had to be made from the hair of deer, or of the raccoon-dogs of Nam-Viet, or above all of the hair of the "blue goat"— apparently the south China goral.[165] If this were not depressing enough, in many

Nam-Viet counties scholars had to use pens made of chicken feathers, and in former times even of duck and pheasant plumes. It was admitted however that these odd "brushes" could trace even the finest characters.[166]

But before considering the T'ang men's narrow view of the wild mammals of Nam-Viet, let us look briefly at their chief domestic animals (here including birds). The ancient and universal breeds were dogs, swine, and fowl. Peculiar to the warm climates were the carabao, the zebu, the elephant, and the original jungle fowl, not to mention the "semi-domestic" peafowl, raised as decoys, and the popular mongoose.

Most important were the cattle. Unfortunately no general agreement has yet been reached about their classification, even for the single genus *Bos*. One modern authority finds four basic kinds, to say nothing of various mixtures: a descendant of the now extinct aurochs (*Bos primigenius*), the long-horned black ox of the Palaeolithic cave-paintings of Lascaux; a smaller short-horned descendant of *Bos longifrons,* known from Neolithic times; a different black descendant of the latter in the north; finally, the zebu (*Bos indicus*) in the south.[167] The men of T'ang themselves took a rather simpler view: "The men of the south have 'water oxen' for oxen; the men of the north have yellow oxen and raven-black oxen as their oxen." [168] Which is to say, the carabao or water buffalo is characteristic of the south, the yellow cow and black cow are typical of the north. This is a fair generalization, but the yellow cow was also known in the south, and may even have had a southern origin, with some zebu blood; on Hainan island it was even saddled and bridled like a horse.[169] But this traditional classification shows few correspondences to the modern "scientific" statement.

The carabao (*Bubalus bubalis*) was domesticated either in south China or in Indo-china; it is noteworthy that three species of wild *Bubalus* have been discovered from the Pleistocene of China.[170] If the Far East was indeed its home, it must have been adapted to life with man at a very early date, since its figure appears far away on Akkadian seals of the third millenium B.C.[171] The carabao varies greatly in size, ranging from the huge beasts of India to the tiny buffalo of the Chinese rice fields.[172] It does not seem to have been usual to eat the flesh of this useful beast in Nam-Viet, but it is reported that in T'ang times, the natives of southern Jung Administration enjoyed it, both roasted and baked in a wrapper. They capped the meal with a relish or dessert composed of salt, milk, ginger, and cassia, mixed with the partly digested herbs from the carabao's stomach.[173]

The long-faced, humped zebu is probably of Indian origin, and was well established in the earliest civilizations of India and Mesopotamia.[174] Its history in China is obscure, but it was certainly known in the southern provinces before medieval times, and probably before the beginning of the Christian era. One T'ang source ascribes it particularly to Lei-chou, adding that it could "travel three hundred *li* in a day"—in short a very hardy beast.[175] The usual T'ang name for the zebu seems to have been *feng* (*pyong*). This word is curiously registered in an early Sung dictionary as "a *wild* ox." [176] From this it would appear that *feng* was simply a collective term for humped cattle. The "wild" *feng* would most likely be the white-rumped and white-stockinged banting (*Bibos banteng*),[177] which also has a mound on its shoulders, and ranges from Indonesia to Tongking and Burma. It has been domesticated in Java and Bali, and to some degree in Indochina.[178] It must have roamed the forests of Nam-Viet in T'ang times. Its heavy-set, thick-horned, blue-eyed upland relative, the gaur (*Bibos gaurus*), has been much less susceptible to domestication, though the semi-domestic cowlike gayal (*Bos frontalis*) of northeast India and Burma seems to derive from it somehow.[179] More than three decades ago, Carl Whiting Bishop suggested that the animal called *szu* (*zi*), well known in the records of ancient China, was no rhinoceros but a gaur, more widely distributed towards the north in early historic times, like the elephant and rhinoceros, than it is now.[180] After the disappearance of this enigmatic animal from its northern haunts, it seems, the Chinese confused it with the rhinoceros, apparently because of the prominence of its horns—those of the *szu* were important in antiquity as wine beakers. I am in agreement with Bishop, while thinking that some of these ancient *szu* and medieval *feng* may not have been gaur but banting.[181]

In T'ang Nam-Viet then, there were domestic carabao, yellow oxen, and possibly zebu, and wild gaurs or bantings, these last not then recognized as the horned beasts canonized in the Confucian classics.

A cultural note: the slaughter of cattle in Nam-Viet was the job of *female* butchers:

She always binds the ox to a large tree, takes knife in hand, and accuses it of a number of crimes: "I led you in season to plowing, but you would not go ahead; I rode you in season to cross the water, but then you would not move. Why should you escape death now?" She lifts its neck with a bamboo stick, brandishes her knife and decapitates it.[182]

The elephant, a kind of bewildered survival from the Age of Mammals into the Age of Man, has an old history in China. But its story there has almost been forgotten, since the great creature is no longer to be found in its former Chinese haunts. It has gone the way of the elephants of ancient Syria and the north African elephants which proved so useful to Hannibal.[183] It is probable that elephants were still common in the Yellow River valley in the second millenium B.C., and were tamed by the men of Shang. If so, the art disappeared as the behemoth's favorite habitat receded southward, and in historical times we read almost exclusively of wild elephants, excepting always the docile ones, sent from Champa as tribute, which marched in imperial corteges from Han times to the Ch'ing dynasty.[184] Herds of wild elephants trampled the cultivated fields of Honan and Hupeh in the fifth Christian century, and were not a rarity in Huai-nan in the sixth.[185] In T'ang times, they still roamed the woodlands of Nam-Viet, and were even abundant in the northeastern counties of Ch'ao and Hsün.[186] One T'ang source tells of a race of black elephants with small pink tusks in Hsün and Lei.[187] Perhaps this describes the true Chinese race itself, whose furious representatives had been subdued by the agents of the kings of Shang. In any case, the peoples of Nam-Viet caught and killed them with poisoned arrows in T'ang times, and roasted their trunks to make delicacies for tropical feasts.[188] The tusks, or some of them, were sent to northern artisans for conversion into chopsticks, hairpins, combs, plectrums, footrules, note tablets, and for inlays in fancy cabinet work, the ivory being dyed in a variety of colors.[189] The naturally pink ivory of the local elephants was well favored, indeed regarded as equal to the ivory imported from overseas, but the bulk of the regular tribute ivory for the use of the court came from Huan-chou in Annam.[190] I know nothing of its natural color.

Not all elephants were killed for food or profit. If the Chinese had forgotten the art of taming them, the Man peoples of Nam-Viet had not. Their children taught obedience to young elephants;[191] their colorfully clad women rode about on the adults;[192] they even trained them to perform for parties, as the Chinese envoys to a prince of the Man learned at an elaborate reception in front of his high pavilion. Dancing elephants were led in by actors:

> Golden halters webbed their heads,
> Brocade draperies hung from their bodies.
> With obedient knees they pranced and stepped,
> Moving their heads and waving their tails.[193]

The Chinese were learning elephant legends too. They heard of the gigantic serpent —a magnified python, no doubt—which swallowed elephants whole, and turned their flesh and bones to water. The skin of an elephant, they were told, should be taken on ocean voyages for protection against the fearful *ḳău* dragons.[194] Elephants knew how to show their gratitude to men who protected them from their terrible enemies: we have the medieval tale of a hunter who shot a huge black beast, saving the life of an elephant, which rewarded him with an abundance of ivory.[195] Elephants were wise, and could distinguish truth from falsehood: it was said that an ancient Cambodian king, who also reared tigers and crocodiles, employed them to observe litigants and eat "the crooked ones."[196] This old Indochinese tradition had a T'ang descendant, the Chinese story of an elephant which roamed the hills of Annam, allowing honest folk to pass in safety, but tossing false witnesses into the air with its trunk, to catch and break them on its tusks.[197]

Elephants are rather rare in T'ang poetry. I notice a short poem called "Elephant" by Li Ch'iao, who was something of a specialist in tropical subjects. He merely recapitulates the traditional history of the great animal in China—not failing to mention the classical torch-bearing elephants of Ch'u.[198] Otherwise I have seen only a few unexceptional courtly *fu* in honor of gift elephants from Champa, and here and there it turns up as a conventional monster of Nam-Viet, always matched with some reptilian horror:

In the belly of the mountains the rain has cleared—but fills the tracks of elephants;
In the heart of the tarns the sun is warm—drawing out the spittle of dragons.[199]

Or:

Startled by fire, the elephants of the mountains emerge;
Struck by thunder, the giant turtles of the ocean dive.[200]

Or:

In a little shop, the serpent soup is black;
On an empty hill, the elephant dung decays.[201]

All of these quotations are from poems of the introverted and politically weak ninth and tenth centuries, a period in which a fanciful giant of the wilderness was more interesting than a submissive pachyderm sent as token of vassalage, the latter being the more common image of the elephant in the imperialistic seventh and eighth centuries.

Another thick-skinned wanderer from the Pliocene (as it seems) was the Chinese rhinoceros, which can no longer be seen in China. Widely spread there in antiquity, in T'ang times it was found only in parts of Nam-Viet, especially the fastnesses of Jung Administration (Tang and Yü-lin), and in the remote woodlands of western and southern Hunan; it was apparently still common in Annam.[202] The animal carried two horns, on its brow and nose, and Liu Hsün gives as its proper name "gaur rhinoceros" (*szu hsi*), presumably because its horns resembled those of that classical wild ox. He also tells of a single-horned rhinoceros, the Westerner's Cap Rhinoceros (*hu mao hsi*), doubtless so called because its horn looked like a Phrygian cap, but not as a resident of the T'ang empire.[203]

Three species of rhinoceros now live in east Asia and Indonesia. The Asian or "Sumatran" Rhinoceros (*Rhinoceros* or *Didermocerus sumatrensis*) is the smallest and hairiest of our rhinos, and has two horns, of which the posterior is very small, almost invisible on females. Once spread from Bengal to Borneo and Sumatra, it is now very rare—chiefly because of the great demand for its horn for carving and medicine in China. The medieval Chinese rhinoceros, *szu hsi,* must have been a race of this species. There are also two one-horned species, one being the Greater One-horned or "Indian" Rhinoceros (*Rhinoceros unicornis*), the largest Asian rhino, with a large thick horn; once common in north India and Indochina it is now on the verge of extinction. The other is the Lesser One-horned or "Javan" Rhinoceros (*Rhinoceros sondaicus*), a smaller species with a shorter horn; once a native of Indochina and Java, now only a few survive on the western tip of Java.[204] One of these two will have been the "westerner's cap rhinoceros" described by Liu Hsün.

The aborigines of Nam-Viet hunted rhinoceroses with bow and arrow [205] and delivered their skins and horns to the local Chinese magistrates, who forwarded this booty to the cities of the north. Though some old-fashioned rhinoceros-hide armor was still being made,[206] the real demand was for the wonderful horn. Its uses were similar to those of ivory. It was carved into elegantly designed cups, boxes, bracelets, paperweights, knife hilts, chopsticks, note tablets, belt plaques, wish-fulfilling wands, and women's head ornaments.[207] The various kinds of horn available were evaluated on the basis of their natural patterning.[208] In particular, the image of a bird or animal in the venation of the horn greatly enhanced its value. The artisans of Canton were wonderfully skilled at fusing various kinds of horn together in handsome naturalistic designs. They joined mottled pieces to white pieces by the use of chemical reagents and iron clamps, just as they welded the shell of the hawksbill turtle to that of the loggerhead.[209] Even the Arabs knew of their work. The geographer Ibn Khordādzbeh, writing in the ninth century, spoke it in his account of the rhinoceroses of Kāmarūpa, adjacent to China, a land also rich in gold:

On y trouve le rhinocéros, animal qui porte sur le front une corne, longue d'une coudée et épaisse de deux palmes. Quand on la fend, on trouve dans l'intérieur, et se détachant un blanc sur un fond noir comme le jais, l'image d'un homme, d'un quadrupède, d'un poisson, d'un paon ou de quelque autre oiseau. Les Chinois en fabriquent des ceintures dont le prix varie de trois cents dīnār jusqu'à trois et quatre mille dīnār.[210]

But even beyond this, rhinoceros horn was held in esteem as an antidote to poison. It would heal the wound caused by a poisoned arrow in an instant. Some thought that this miraculous power was the result of the diet of the rhinoceros—poisonous thorns and brambles.[211] Indeed this horn had many other amazing properties, for those who understood them, and T'ang books are full of allusions to such wonders as a magical piece of horn which shone by night,[212] and a specimen owned by Wen Tsung, which cooled a lecture hall instantly when that monarch felt overheated.[213] Among other strange rhinoceros lore, we observe a species which could walk unwetted in the sea,[214] and the mystical rapport between the pachyderm and the poison bird of the tropics:

Among the mountains and rivers of the south, places which have poison birds (*chen,* M.C. *dyĕm*) will surely have the rhino ox; places which have sand fleas and water shooters will surely have *chu-yü* (*chok-ngyok*).[215]

These associations may not be imaginary. We shall later identify the "poison bird" as the Serpent Eagle of Southeast Asia; its habitat may well have been the same as that of the rhinoceros. The *chu-yü* is a wading bird whose identity is not easy to ascertain. It is said to have a long neck, red eyes, and dark purple plumage. This description agrees well with the appearance of the Black Bittern (*Dupetor flavicollis*) of south Asia, including south China, a nocturnal eater of frogs and other (supposedly) poisonous animals.[216]

The word "rhinoceros" has no important role in Chinese literature, except commonly by metonymy for its own horn, as in the phrase "elephant and rhinoceros," meaning "ivory and horn." But there is no poetry devoted to the disappearing native rhinoceros itself—or rather, I have seen only a couplet by the tenth century poet-monk Kuan-hsiu, in which he remarks that:

> Malaria mingles with the rain of Chiao-chou;
> Rhinoceroses rub against the stele of Ma Yüan.[217]

Even this is not very imaginative. Otherwise we have only poetic references to foreign rhinos, especially those sent as tribute to the Chinese sovereign. Po Chü-i, for instance, found a moral in the animal sent to the Son of Heaven in 796 by a barbarian nation seeking submission to an illuminated prince:

> The birthplace of the tame rhinoceros is in the heat of the southern quarter;
> Where there is not white dew in autumn, nor snow in winter.

The unhappy beast died of the cold in the imperial park the following year.[218] The allusion is clear. The huge animal shared the fate of the strange sea bird of *Chuang tzu*—no creature can survive out of its proper environment.

Among the catlike animals of China, the tiger is by far the most remarkable for size and ferocity, and for its importance in folk belief, ritual, and custom, northern as well as southern.[219] Chinese literature from the earliest times is full of tiger stories—man-eating tigers, weretigers, symbolic tigers, anti-tiger spells, tiger hunts—tigers in China are like mice in a cheese factory. We have seen them already as the cronies of the sprightly imps of the southern mountains. They were also the companions of the holy saints who dwelt in the tiger-protected mountains—for tigers ruled the mountains of China as dragons lorded it over its lakes and sea.[220] On certain days which were their special days, a tiger might appear to you on mountain roads in the semblance of a man. A wise traveler who encountered a person calling himself "forester's bailiff" would know the reality underlying the mask, and so take magical measures to protect himself.[221] Tiger-familiars and weretigers, however, were not peculiar to the Chinese; they were found all over Asia.[222]

Not all holy hermits made peace with the guardians of the mountains. Some, regarding them as evil pagan creatures, took action against them. The story of an Indian monk who lived in the hills of Shao-chou at the beginning of the fifth century was current in T'ang and Sung times. It told that tigers were so numerous there that one hill was formerly called "Market place of Tigers"—but they disappeared after the hermit took up residence there.[223] And there was various other tiger lore. Let a few examples stand for the mass:

The moon has a nimbus when tigers copulate. The sylph man Cheng Szu-yüan always rode a tiger. As for the tiger's night vision, one eye emits light and one eye looks at things. Hunters watch for this, and so shoot them. The light falls and goes into the ground, becoming a white stone, which will control the "frights" of little children.[224]

The tiger is fairly familiar in T'ang poetry, though never as a very friendly creature. Nor is he particularly associated with the south—he is a hazard everywhere:

> South mountain, north mountain—trees dark and dreary;
> Fierce tigers, under white sun, walk round the woods.[225]

("Under white sun" connotes also "in broad daylight.") Probably tigers were commoner in T'ang Nam-Viet than further north. Li Shang-yin shows them quite indifferent to the works of the intruding agents of the Son of Heaven and walking the post road there with impunity:

> When it is still early spring in Kuei-lin,
> Here in Chao-chou the sun stands due west.
> Tigers fight right in the government road,
> Monkeys howl up in the post office loft.
>
> Ropes rot in the wells of golden sand,
> Pines dry as ladders in stalactite caves.
> A voice from home can startle you terribly;
> But you can still get sloppy drunk—like mud![226]

Next to the tiger stood the leopard. Its literary appearances are chiefly symbolic of valor and craft in battle,[227] and, according to the medical texts, its flesh imparts heroism to the human will, strengthens the kidneys, and dispels all sorts of obnoxious spirits.[228] The familiar pan-Asiatic leopard (*Felis pardus*) was not regarded as an especially southern animal, though there was a separate southern race. Nor was it distinguished from the other leopard-like cats of Nam-Viet, such as the Clouded Leopard (or Tortoise-shell Tiger, or Mint Leopard—*Felis nebulosa*) with its leaflike blotches, or the melancholy Golden Cat (*Felis temminckii*), or the little Tiger Cat (*Felis bengalensis*). As far as I can tell, these unexampled rovers of the Nam-Viet forests went unnoticed by literate visitors to that land.[229]

The shy, nocturnal civet got little more attention. This tawny, short-legged long-tailed animal (*Viverra zibetha*) ranges all the way from Africa to the Indies, including most of south China below the Yangtze River. Although a ground dweller, it eats some fruit, but in Nam-Viet it lives chiefly on snakes, crabs, and insects. A near relative, the Lesser Civet (*Viverricula* sp.), was and is common in Nam-Viet, in some places even commoner.[230] The T'ang name for these civets was "Perfume *li*" (*hsün li*), where *li* stands for the foxy "raccoon-dog" (*Nyctereutes*), which the civet somewhat resembles. It was also named "Numinous Cat" (*ling mao*). I have already suggested, on the basis of a poem of Liu Yü-hsi, that the aborigines of Nam-Viet may have trained the little animal as a hunter and rat catcher, chasing lesser animals into their burrows. Its skill at digging is alluded to in a poem of Kuan-hsiu (its literary career is otherwise undistinguished):

> By lotus roots in the pond, an odorous *li* is digging;
> The spirits of the mountains move about under the white sun.[231]

East and west, the civet is most admired for the yellowish musky secretion of glands near its genitals, now used as a foundation for perfumes,[232] but in T'ang times chiefly valued as a drug. It was dried and taken with wine for the same afflictions for which Chinese musk was efficacious—evil odors, *ku* poisons, flying corpses, demon possession, incubi, and nightmares.[233]

Very much like the civet is the dark, obscurely spotted Palm Civet or Toddy Cat (*Paradoxurus hermaphroditus*) and the Lesser Palm Civet (*Paradoxurus minor*). These are tree dwellers, with retractile claws, and a more strictly tropical distribution than the common civet.[234] Much like them is the Masked Civet (*Paguma larvata*), also omnivorous, nocturnal, tree-climbing, but unspotted, and masked by a black and white facial pattern.[235] None of these ghostly palm climbers—called "wind racoon-dogs" (*feng li*) in T'ang—got any literary attention. But the pharmacologist Ch'en Ts'ang-ch'i recorded that they lived from Yung-chou southwards, where "they wait for the wind to blow them to other trees." He noted that they ate fruit, and could be tamed in order to obtain their rare milklike urine for medicinal purposes.[236] Beyond that, the modern Chams, their glory long since gone, believe that the souls of dead children enter the bodies of Palm Civets.[237] I have found no comparable medieval belief—indeed no kind of reputation at all, beyond the medical one.

There is little to tell of the mongoose, although two species, the Rufous-faced Mongoose (*Herpestes rubrifrons*) and the badger-like Crab-eating Mongoose (*Herpestes urva*) are both common in Nam-Viet.[238] Under the name of *meng-kuei,* the mongooses of southern Annam had been known as better than cats as rat catchers.[239] In T'ang times, Tuan Ch'eng-shih recorded another and unique name for the ichneumon, *wu-yüan,* along with the remarkable statement that domestic cats are also called *meng-kuei.*[240]

The toothless, termite-eating pangolin (*ling-li*), burrowing the hills of south China,[241] also attracted remarkably little attention. It appeared briefly but gloriously as a strange southern creature in the *Rhapsody on the Metropolis of Wu,* at the beginning of the fourth century,[242] but the T'ang poets ignored its oddness. Characteristically, a T'ang pharmacologist did not fail to mention its name: its ashes were helpfully applied to serious lesions, and would control malaria and other pestilences bred in the mountain mists.[243]

In ancient times, the *Book of Han* had said that the deer of Viet were the *chu* and the *ching.*[244] These southern ruminants appear to have been the sambar and the muntjac respectively.

The big, dark-brown, long-tailed sambar ranges the mountains of Southeast Asia from Yunnan to Indonesia.[245] It must be the large southern deer called *chu* by Szu-ma Hsiang-ju and later writers. Unfortunately the only part of the noble animal much noticed in literature was its tail, which made an admirable chowry for punctuating the remarks of learned lecturers.[246]

China has several kinds of midget deer, whose names are unhappily much confused both in literary and vernacular usage. The old name *ching* refers to one or more of them. By the descriptions, the tusked and hornless little Musk Deer

(*Moschus*) and Water Deer (*Hydropotes*) seem ruled out. Of the remaining possibilities, the range of the Tufted Deer (*Elaphodus*) barely reaches northern Nam-Viet. This leaves the well-horned muntjac, of which there are two species there.[247] These smart and dainty little animals were much sought after, not for their tails, but for their skin, which was made into a fashionable kind of boot, usually dyed red: [248]

> A visitor of Viet comes from the south, boasting his muntjac of Kuei,
>   Made by artful sewing, by superior artisans with useful ideas.[249]

No matter how much feared and fled from or valuable and sought for in the tropical forest, the mammals there were on the whole elusive and inconspicuous. The exceptions were the primates, nonhuman as well as human. Moreover, despite the presence of monkeys in Gibraltar and Japan, the primates (including ancestral man) are chiefly tropical, and are mostly inhabitants of the rain forest—and *all* of great apes live in the tropics of Africa and Asia.[250] In medieval Nam-Viet the largest representatives of the group were the long-armed, tailless, arboreal gibbons. Today two kinds of gibbon haunt the fringes of that region: the hoolock howls from the western borders of Kwangsi and Yunnan, and the Black Gibbon swings through the other forests of Hainan and Annam.[251] Their ranges in T'ang times must have been wider, but are now hard to determine precisely. The garrulous and bibulous *hsing-hsing,* familiar in medieval lore, may have been either or both of these spectral creatures.[252] Alleged to have the power of speech (apparently because of the rather indistinct boundary between ape and aborigine in many minds), it often appears as a kind of sylvan wiseacre, as in the tale where it appears as interpreter for a white elephant in Hsün (Zywin)-chou, enlisting the aid of a hunter's poisonous arrows against a monster serpent.[253] In poetry however, the *hsing-hsing* appears chiefly as a disembodied cry— the ominous wail of a tropical phantom, natural in the baleful miasmas of the south, as even Li Po recognized: "A gibbon cries in the mist, ah!—a ghost whistles in the rain." [254] Even Li Hsün, the tenth-century innovator, whose tropical images were not always stereotypes, preserved this unnerving figure, so unlike the jolly figure of popular tales:

> The fishers' market disperses,
>   Ferrying boats are scarce—
> South of Viet the clouded trees are barely within view;
> A journeying stranger awaits the tide—the sky is close to sunset.
>   A farewell by the spring estuary—
> We listen anxiously as a gibbon howls in the malarial rain.[255]

The legend of the *fei-fei* (*pĕi-pĕi*) is hardly distinguishable from that of the *hsing-hsing.* Perhaps *fei-fei* was the name of a separate gibbon species, or, more likely, the two were dialect words for the same kind of anthropoid. The name *fei-fei* itself reminds us of the English wahwah—meaning "gibbon." In any case, the word was less alive than was the word *hsing-hsing.* It was more suggestive of a name seen on an old tattered scroll than the name of a living animal:

By drinking its blood it will be possible for you to see ghosts. Its strength is such that it will carry a thousand catties on its back. Whenever it laughs its upper lip covers its forehead. In outward form it is like a *mi-hou* [macaque]. It can make the speech of men, but with a birdlike sound, and it has knowledge of life and death. Its blood will serve to dye scarlet, and its hair will do to make wigs. In old story it has reversed heels; hunters say that it has no knees, and always leans on something to sleep.[256]

Other old traditions said that the *fei-fei* had a manlike face and red hair. The description fits the orangutan, which seems impossible! They also said that it was cannibalistic.[257] Evidently we have here a mixture of vague reports of various tropical apes mixed with stories of just as unattractive southern tribesmen. The *fei-fei* has nothing like the place of the *hsing-hsing* in literature.

Among the smaller primates, the typical southern monkey was the long-tailed, slender, arboreal, leaf-eating langur, one of a tribe once classified under the general term *Pithecus,* but now usually subclassified among the *Colobidae* as either a Capped Leaf Monkey (*Trachypithecus*), a Snub-nose Monkey (*Rhinopithecus*), an Indian Holy Monkey or Hanuman or Purple-faced Monkey (*Semnopithecus*), a Mitred Leaf Monkey (*Presbytis*), or a Douc Langur (*Pygathrix*). Probably the common langur (*yüan*) of Nam-Viet was the black and white monkey we now call Tonkin Langur (*Trachypithecus francoisi*). Most men of the northern provinces knew them not, though they were familiar with the heavy-bodied macaque. (There is also a rock-dwelling, scarlet-faced macaque in Lingnan.) [258]

Color varieties observed by medieval travelers are not always easy to identify. In 869, Tuan Kung-lu found the "scarlet langur" to be common in the hills near the Lei-chou peninsula, and he even caught and tamed one of these beautiful creatures, thickly cloaked in "yellowish scarlet." [259] This orange-furred pet might have been one of the Golden Monkeys (*Rhinopithecus*), though these are typically found in the high mountains of western China.[260]

Li Po himself had written of "white langurs" springing lightly "like flying snow" by Autumn Estuary.[261] I cannot tell if he was referring to the tame and affectionate white langur of the far south, celebrated by Li Te-yü. That magnate noticed also that the snowy monkey was wont to show a haughty attitude towards mere macaques, which stood in fear of it.[262] Perhaps it was in fact the Silvery Langur (*Trachypithecus obscurus argenteus*), nowadays found in Annam and Laos.[263]

Then there was the chance of meeting a ghost langur. A certain Wang Chi lived in a wild and rocky place where he was visited one night by a skinny foreigner (an Indian or Iranian) with white eyebrows and temple locks, who styled himself "mountain lord." The hermit conversed with this stranger, whose manner made him suspect that he was a goblin. He shone a mirror on him to reveal his true shape, at which the "westerner" turned into a langur and fell dead.[264]

Langurs flit like shaggy little specters through countless T'ang poems. Free, they symbolized the abnormal surroundings of the traveler or exile in the south—Szech-

wan and Hunan as well as Nam-Viet; captive in cages, their pitiful demeanor re-
minded the Chinese wanderer of his unmerited exclusion from civilized affairs.
Above all it was their cries which haunted the imaginations of the medieval writer.
For him they seldom simply cried out—most frequently they howled; they often
whistled; and sometimes they roared, shouted, or wailed. Indeed they were disembodied sounds—shrieking roadside phantoms—and were therefore frequently
coupled with birds in T'ang verses, and these unnatural mates call sadly together.
Here is a langur poem written by Liu Tsung-yüan in the "yellow gorges" of Yung-
chou in southern Hunan:

> By the gorge road—it twists a thousand *li*—
> Mourning langurs cry—anywhere at all.
> A lonely vassal, my tears now all used up,
> Empty—I make a bowel-rending sound.[265]

An Annamese monkey called *kuo-jan* (*kwa-nhen*), whose nostrils pointed to
heaven, was shot with poisoned arrows. Its black and white fur was transformed
into warm, silky capes and blankets, and its flesh, dried and prepared with spices,
was eaten to alleviate the fevers of malaria.[266] This was certainly one of the Snub-
nose Monkeys, some species of which are blotched in black and white.[267] Like
other langurs, this snub-nose was afflicted by a tendency to sadness:

Should anyone injure one of their kind, the assembled tribe wails in sorrow, nor will
they go away even if you kill them. Here is a case of man's heart inside the forms
of birds and beasts.[268]

In poetry, the *kuo-jan,* like other langurs, was paired with southern wildfowl. Here
it is in a ninth century poem about Lingnan:

> Bush warblers converse with hill mynahs;
> Langurs howl with snub-noses.[269]

The English word douc registers the native Indochinese name of yet another langur
(*Pygathrix*), races of which, noted for their variegated fur—gray, black, white, and
red—are found in Hainan and Annam. The same word found its way into Chinese
as *tu* (*duk*), and in T'ang times Ch'en Ts'ang-ch'i recommended that sufferers from
the piles find relief by sitting on pieces of its luxuriant pelt.[270]

Of the mammals of the sea, the only one specifically associated with Nam-Viet was
the long-snouted White Dolphin (*Sotalia chinensis*), which cavorts along the coasts
and estuaries of south China, a distant relative of the white dolphins of the Amazon.[271] This black-eyed, pink-finned plunger, ignobly named "Sea Pig," [272] was
hardly noticed by T'ang writers, and then only by a pharmacologist, who described
it leaping and spouting in large companies, and prescribed its dried flesh as a remedy
against "flying corpses, *ku* poisons, and malarial fevers." [273]

Further yet beyond the normal habitat of mammals were the furry winged creatures which skimmed the skies of the southland. Among all the mammals, the bats, especially the flying foxes or fruit bats, are best developed in the tropics, next only to the primates.[274] They stand, therefore, between men and apes on the one hand and birds on the other. Appropriately the Chinese called them "transcendent rats," or (perhaps) "sylphine rats" (*hsien shu*) in T'ang times,[275] registering their unique power among the epigene mammals to rise above the dust natural to them and soar in the kingdom of the air.

Fittingly, the most famous of all southern bats were the gay-winged red bats of Shuang-chou.[276] Male and female, in inseparable pairs, they darted among the flowers and the great rustling leaves of the red banana. Because of their mutual devotion, they were caught and pinned to girl's costumes as love charms, as potent for allure as the "elephant-nosed insect" which lurked in longan trees, the yellow pearl of the xiphosura, the mysterious *p'ang-chiang* (*baung-kaung*) which cried loudly from the kanari trees, and the submarine *no* (*nak*, from naga?) dragon.[277] Whether a true bat or a ruddy flying squirrel[278] of Nam-Viet, this red night flier was closely akin to the Vermilion Bird, the crystallization of the spirit of the new Chinese tropics. Still, these peri-mice were closer to men than to birds—not so angelic, not so unearthly.

BIRDS

The tropics are the zone of birds. About 85 per cent of all avian species are entirely tropical, and many others winter in the tropics, undertaking long migratory flight to breed in cooler and less competitive climates.[279] Subjectively, some groups of birds seem more proper to the tropics than others equally deserving. The gaudy parrots belong there, we think, despite the parrots of the temperate antipodes and the late Carolina parakeet, but we are surprised to learn that the pigeons, especially the glittering tribe of fruit pigeons, are just as much at home there. Still, there are many bird kinds which do not live in our temperate lands at all, and are indelibly labeled "exotic." Such are the trogons and barbets which inhabit the tropics of both Old and New Worlds. Then, restricted to the Americas, the very paradise and nursery of birds, there are the jacamars, the motmots, the toucans, the hummingbirds, the puff birds, and the todies; confined to the "Oriental" tropics are the bee-eaters, the hornbills, the rollers, the pittas, and the pheasants. Finally, restricted to the Far Eastern tropics are the hill tits, the green bulbuls, the gapers,[280] and others.

Our first thought about these tropical birds is that they are brightly colored. Walter Raleigh, writing of Guiana, expressed exactly what we expect:

We saw birds of all colours, some carnation, some crimson, orange tawny, purple, green, watched, and of all other sorts both simple and mixt, as it was unto us a great good passing of the time to beholde them.[281]

There is some justification for this expectation. The tropics do indeed produce color-ful birds, many with iridescent metallic feathers. Some regions even have their typi-cal colors, as Wallace observed: parrots of two quite distinct families in the Moluccas and New Guinea are bright red, while Australasia has both black parrots and black pigeons—and parrots and pigeons alike are black and crimson in Madagascar.[282] But this is not the whole story. There are brilliantly tinted birds, such as the Mandarin Duck and the Wood-duck, in northern lands, and temperate China and Mongolia can boast the lovely shimmering plumage of the gold and silver pheasants.[283] Conversely, in open, brightly lit parts of the tropics, where the land shows mostly sand, or bare rock, or dried grass, the birds are dun, tan, and rust-colored.[284] Nonetheless the shadowy tropical forests are rich in handsomely colored birds, but in that dense and gloomy environment they are not easily discerned.

The equatorial forest is popularly pictured as a place of bright and varied colours, with extravagant flowers, an abundance of fruits, and huge trees hung with creepers where lurk many venomous but beautiful snakes with gemlike eyes, and a multitude of birds as bright as the flowers; paradise indeed, though haunted by a peril. Those details are right, but the picture is wrong . . . the toucans and macaws of the Madeira forest, though common, are not often seen, and when they are seen they are likely to be but obscure atoms drifting high in a white light.[285]

It is only the patient, contemplative observer who will discover the jewel-like birds and flowers of the rain forest.[286]

In T'ang times, a sensitive and observant visitor from the north could not have overlooked such wonders in the monsoon forest of Nam-Viet. It was a spangled world of bright birds, totally unlike the northern crow land, hawk land, sparrow land. To borrow the style of the *fu,* it was a world of

> Fierce lustrous drongos,
> Fluttering scarlet minivets,
> Skulking polychrome pittas,
> Darting iridescent bee-eaters—
>
> Fire-breasted flowerpeckers,
> Fork-tailed sunbirds—
>
> Verditer flycatchers,
> Paradise flycatchers—
>
> Babblers and bulbuls,
> Trogons and tragopans.

To say nothing of drongo shrikes, tailor birds, fantail warblers, babbling thrushes, white-eyes, Java sparrows, weavers, and barbets [287]—a world to seduce the imagination to feverish dreams. We know that some of the Hua men looked high enough to see it, but they did not describe it, partly because they had no names for these strange glowing creatures. The Chinese traditions of birds, best represented by the augurs and the pharmacists, and to some extent by the poets, allowed real personalities only to the birds typical of the old Chinese heartland—the valley of the Yellow River— neglecting, with a few conspicuous exceptions, all shore- and sea-birds, all shy forest birds, and the highly colored birds of the nonclassical south.[288] On the whole, exiles in Nam-Viet noticed only what was absent, not what was present: "The flight of northern birds does not reach this far." So wrote a northerner languishing in P'an- chou on the hot coast of Lingnan.[289] Or if an ostracized poet mentioned the birds in the trees around him at all, he saw only stereotypes and formal symbols of the south, as Shen Ch'üan-ch'i did in his hermitage near Huan-chou:

> I should like to accompany the music of parrots,
> I yearn to stay by the side of the chukar.[290]

Parakeet and francolin had been known to the Chinese in classical times, and were part of the standard repertory of southern images, familiar to all T'ang writers. But nothing is said about sunbirds and minivets. It was not even necessary to see an actual Annamese parrot or a living chukar to write these verses. Most Chinese writers of this period were hardly different from our medieval Latinists, who, though they often wrote of birds, never looked at nature, but drew on a conventional fund of bird meta- phors and bird allegories which their readers would recognize instantly. In painting, the story is the same: parrots and peafowl were shown in medieval Chinese paint- ings, but they were pets and royal gifts, not wild inhabitants of the woods of Nam- Viet. The famous bird painter Chiang Chiao, much honored by Hsüan (Ghwen) Tsung, was exiled to Ch'in-chou in 722, but if he passed the weary hours there paint- ing hornbills and drongos, there is no record of the fact.[291]

Most splendid and regal of the birds of Nam-Viet was the peacock—a phoenix visible. Though some kind of peafowl, homeland unknown, had been displayed in northern parks in much earlier times, it is not until the third century A.D. that there is clear evidence of the graceful presence of peacocks certainly caught in Nam- Viet in aristocratic gardens.[292] This was not the Indian peacock familiar in our West- ern zoos, but the so-called "Burmese" or "Javan" Peacock (*Pavo muticus*), glittering in a coat of bronze and metallic green. Today this lovely bird is found in only one part of China, the remote Burmese frontier of Yunnan, and it is a rarity even there.[293] In T'ang times it was very different: peafowl were abundant in the forests of Lo- chou and Lei-chou, where they were captured live for shipment to the capital. They were also abundant in Annam; the Protectorate sent quantities of the tails of the cock bird as annual tribute to Ch'ang-an.[294] The natives of Nam-Viet tethered the chicks in the woods as decoys for netting their wild kin.[295] They also kept them in their villages, that they might the more easily harvest the spangled golden-halcyon feath- ers for the manufacture of fans.[296] In a late T'ang quatrain, set to a popular tune, Sun Kuang-hsien contrasts the gold filigree of the Javan peacock's plumage to the jewel-blue of the kingfisher's feathers; both fairy birds are fit prey for the sylphine maidens of Nam-Viet (the great fowl is, as commonly, called *"k'ung* bird"):

In the train of the *k'ung*-bird's tail, golden threads are long—
It flies up in dread of man, into the scent of lilacs.[297]
Girls of Viet, on a sandy headland, vie at catching halcyons—
Now call to each other, going off homewards, their backs to the declining sunlight.[298]

The ocellated tail plumes of the peacock, made into fans, should properly be called "morchals." [299] These were as important in court ceremonies as the Reeves' pheasant fans had been in classical antiquity. They also made handsome curtains and dazzling dusters—"splendent to view—truly from divine fowl!" [300] Peacocks had other practical uses: they were ignominiously stewed by the aborigines (their flavor was said to resemble that of duck), and the blood and head served as antidotes to powerful poisons.[301]

The lore and mythology of peacocks seems to have been mostly of southern, partly of Indian origin. The common tale of a peafowl copulating with a serpent [302] is probably only a Chinese transformation of an Indic image of some divine sunbird victorious over a dark chthonic spirit.[303] The other familiar attributes of the peacock are as familiar in the west as in the east—in particular, their vanity (T'ang men said they would peck enviously at the rich garments of young men and women),[304] and their stately dance (which gave us the name of the "pavane" of the Late Renaissance).

The peacock was an important avian symbol of Nam-Viet. It appears frequently in T'ang literature as the "Bird of Viet," as if it were the holy Vermilion Bird itself, and indeed it sometimes filled that symbolic niche, alternating it seems with the Argus Pheasant and other dazzling southern birds—though neither of those two is red.[305] Originally the Bird of Viet may have been a generalized gallinaceous bird, sharing the attributes of the jungle fowl, the peacock, and many kinds of pheasants. By T'ang times, at any rate, it was always the Javan Peacock. In the body of a poem titled *"K'ung*-bird," Li Ying calls it also "Bird of Viet"; "its entire body," he writes, "is golden-halcyon—not to be won with paint!" [306] For the alienated poets, however, the Bird of Viet was not the Vermilion Bird—the peacock of Nam-Viet rarely represented the sacred principle of the south and the mystical power of the sun for them. Rather it stood for the emotional and physical qualities of the hot, alien land, to be contrasted with homely, happy things. In the words of Li Te-yü:

I cannot bear the tearing in my bowels, thinking of my home place;
When, among the red hibiscus flowers, the Bird of Viet screams.[307]

The harsh cry of the peacock appears constantly as a metaphor of nostalgia: "The Bird of Viet startles your dream of home." [308] Sometimes added to this contemporary theme of the Bird of Viet, as to the figures of the Maiden of Viet and the flowers of Viet, were often complicated allusions to some event or myth of the ancient state of Viet of Chou times.

Kingfishers are not restricted to the tropics, though they are well represented there, and the most colorful kinds seem to belong there. The family is well represented in China, including the small blue and orange Common Kingfisher (*Alcedo atthis bengalensis*), an abundant resident of every part of that country; the shrill-voiced Pied Kingfisher (*Ceryle varia,* or *Ceryle rudis*), in its black and white motley, a fisher of lowland fresh waters; and its upland cousin the Spotted Kingfisher (*Ceryle lugubris*). There are a number of others. Among them the most beautiful, the most sought after, and the most persecuted was the so-called White-breasted Kingfisher (*Halcyon smyrnensis*), whose common name does not reveal that its head and belly are maroon, and that its back shines with iridescent cobalt and glinting turquoise. This southern crab-eating species, called in T'ang literature *fei-ts'ui,* deserves the classical name of "halcyon," which I have regularly applied to it.[309] Sacheverell Sitwell has said of these big-headed little fairies that they "must appear to us to be the ghosts of genius," and, more appropriately to our present theme, "Nothing surpasses the burnished fire of their blue wings and shoulders. They are the epitome of burning summer weather."[310] In China they were as much a source of jewelry as was lapis lazuli- or sapphire-studded limestone. *Ts'ui,* the shortened form of its Chinese name, occurs abundantly in literature, not only in such reduced doublets as *k'ung ts'ui* "peacocks and halcyons"—a pairing of metallic greens and blues—and, as a color image in "halcyon-blue eye shadow" suitably parallel to the red skirts of beautiful women (to say nothing of "halcyon willows" and "halcyon stones"), but above all in phrases reflecting the social fact of the popularity of "enameled" jewelry of the true kingfisher blue. Such clichés of romantic verse as the "halcyon aigrettes" (*ts'ui ch'ai*) of the costly costumes of court beauties are common. Dresses shimmering with kingfisher feathers, fit for the gods, are virtually as old as written records in China. "Halcyon cloaks and leopard shoes" were worn in mid-Chou times,[311] and the lovely blue plumage must surely be counted among the "feathers" listed among the rich wares of the south, along with ivory, cinnabar, and rhinoceros hides, in the semi-legendary *Tribute of Yü.* Even as late as T'ang times, a kingfisher-feather cape could still be the fantastic garment of a favorite courtier.[312] In these latter days this important resource was exploited chiefly along the coast of Lingnan, west from Canton, and above all in Annam.[313] The vigor of the commerce in halcyon feathers is attested in many poems. Early in the ninth century Hsü Hun wrote of their sale in the markets—to which he applied the southern dialectical name of *hsü* (*hyo*)—of Hsinchou.[314] His near contemporary Han Yü remarked that while the yellow orange was the characteristic household product in Nam-Viet, the commodity typically offered for sale by the same family which grew that fruit was blue halcyon feathers.[315] The following couplet by Chou Yao suggests that the much desired feathers were also imported, possibly from Champa:

> In mountain villages, elephants trample sagwire leaves;
> Beyond the seas, men gather halcyon plumage.[316]

The dominant images of angelic cloaks and twinkling hair ornaments fashioned from the plumage of the fierce little southern fishers were rarely forgotten by the T'ang poets. An exception, in which the bird appears only as itself, is this quatrain by Ch'ien Ch'i:

> Finding its object between the lotus leaves,
> Down in a twinkling from a tall tree,
> Tearing the wavelets, taking the submerged fish,
> A single spot of halcyon light goes off.[317]

Parrots have been popular since antiquity in the east as much as in the west, both as household pets and as exemplary symbols much pointed at by wiseacres. The ancient Greeks and Romans apparently knew only the Ringneck Parakeet,[318] and these pretty green-necked birds were also familiar to the medieval English as "popinjays" or "papingoes." That clever talker, the African Gray Parrot, a friend of seafarers in modern times, does not appear until the sixteenth century. Soon both birds were put in the shade by the big splashes of primary colors in the plumage of the American macaws.[319]

In classical times the Chinese had parrots in the western hills of their own northland. This race was ultimately exterminated, presumably by hunters and collectors, so that its identity is now uncertain. Possibly it was a variety of the green and violet Derbyan Parakeet, still found in Szechwan, although parrots from westernmost Shensi were sometimes described as yellow.[320] I cannot be sure if these golden parakeets were typical of that vanished tribe or were rare sports. At any rate, by Han times or soon after, they were partly displaced in the public fancy by more gaudy tropical parrots from Indochina and the islands of the Pacific, including such occasional novelties as crimson lories and pure-white cockatoos.[321] At the same time, the newly occupied lands of Nam-Viet provided new and charming varieties of flowerlike parakeets to the parlors of the north. In the twentieth century three species are found there. These are the Rose-ringed Parakeet (*Psittacula krameri*), bright green and blue, with a black throat and rosy collar; the common Red-breasted Parakeet (*Psittacula alexandri*), in various shades of green, with a plum-gray head and wine-red breast; and the Blossom-headed Parakeet (*Psittacula cyanocephala*), clad mostly in green, with splashes of crimson in its wings, pink cheeks, lilac nape, and a black collar.[322] Even the Indian Lorikeet (*Loriculus vernalis*), mostly green but red-billed and flaunting a bright red rump, is found in the Canton region.[323] The naturalists of T'ang who tell of beautifully colored parrots flocking in the fruit trees of the coastal counties west of Canton, do not distinguish among these species. One report, rather more specific than others, describes parrots with turquoise collars and vermilion beaks which could speak and sing like men. They were smaller than the classical northern parrots,[324] but they cannot be identified with certainty now.

As in the western world, the dainty parakeets of the eastern tropics were admired genuinely for their chromatic garb, and sententiously for their wisdom, proved by their ability to learn the Chinese language—an outstanding example being a parrot kept in a ninth-century Buddhist monastery which recited the *Diamond Sutra* every day upon hearing the morning bell.[325] But the learned birds had their repellent aspect too—the men of Nam-Viet were usually afraid to touch them for fear of contracting the mortal disease which has been called psittacosis in our own times, or most recently ornithosis, since it is by no means restricted to parrots.[326] These and other attributes—the pity inspired by the sight of intelligent birds in cages, and abundant allusions to Indian and Buddhist tales—appear in T'ang poetry, and even their green plumage and red beaks are occasionally mentioned. But in all this writing of parrots the Nam-Viet parakeets are almost never shown in their native forests. I have noticed only one ambiguous verse: "The wild bird with human speech reflects the red banana." [327] These words tell of a parakeet or lorikeet of Nam-Viet whose plumage shows the borrowed color of the red banana flower. But the word "parrot" does not occur in the poem.

For the average T'ang poet the bird of the south, par excellence, was a francolin which he called *che-ku*. This white-throated partridge is well-known in south Asia, and its Chinese name reflects an Indic name like *chakor* or *chikūr,* related to Sanskrit *cakora.* The old Anglo-Indian form is *chikore,* and the bird (or a very close relative) is known in North America, where it has been successfully introduced as a game bird called "chukar." [328] I shall call the Chinese *che-ku* a chukar. In T'ang times the chukar was found abundantly in the Yangtze basin, and was even more common in Nam-Viet.[329] Nowadays this Chinese partridge or francolin (it is *Francolinus pintadeanus*), a buff-colored scuttler in the grasslands, occurs from Fukien southeastwards to Kwangsi, and there are occasional reports of its presence as far north as Chekiang.[330] Taken unsentimentally, the chukar was a tasty fowl. In the words of Liu Tsung-yüan, its white flesh was "sweet and plump," [331] and superior to both chicken and pheasant.[332] Moreover, this delicate meat, taken in a suitable quantity of wine, was praised as a cure for mushroom poisoning and for the many pestilences of Nam-Viet, effective even when the patient was on the point of death.[333] On the symbolic or mystical level, however, the chukar was a solar bird which feared both frost and dew.[334] A follower of the solar warmth (*yang*), the chukar was sometimes called "Pheasant (or Partridge?) of Viet," and in flight always soared toward the south.[335] Even its melancholy cry proclaimed its preference: it said, "Just south, not north!" [336] In India, however, the francolin is a drinker of moonbeams,[337] and a trace of this lunar association may have found its way into medieval China: Tuan Ch'eng-shih reports that the chukar's activity is related to the cycle of lunar months—it makes only one flight in the first month, remaining otherwise in its nest, but flies out twelve times in the last month of the year, and so on.[338]

For the T'ang poets, however, the chukar was less a cosmic symbol than a token of human feeling. A modern writer says, "Its weird resounding cry once heard can never be forgotten, and is one of the most characteristic sounds of the Chinese country-side." [339] The displaced men who heard its sad voice felt that it spoke for them, and wept for their lost homes:

> In spotted bamboo branches by Hsiang River,
> Chukars fly on brocade wings.[340]

This couplet appears to be an innocent description of the Hunan landscape, but the poem is in fact devoted to the sorrows of parting, and the handsome chukar represents a noble but anguished spirit. The conqueror of Annam, Kao P'ien, found in the bird a ready image for his own sense of an overly prolonged tour of military duty. He addressed a quatrain to an officer lucky enough to have been recalled to the imperial capital:

> Clouds and water blurred in the blue distance—sun close to cropping;
> In the deep places, in the wild mists, a chukar is despondent.
> I know that you go, lord, a myriad miles to the Levee of Heaven:
> Speak for me there—five autumns now have I made war in the south! [341]

Since the fourth century, reports of magnificent jungle fowl, whose incredibly large, hollow, yellow bills were turned into wine beakers by the natives, issued from Nam-Viet, to the astonishment of the northern Hua men, who were accustomed to birds of more reasonable dimensions.[342] Their name was *meng-t'ung* (*mung-dung*), but they were also styled "King of Viet birds." That is, they were the golden-crowned kings of the southern avifauna, comparable to Chao T'o, unique king of the Viet peoples. Fa-chen, a Buddhist monk who visited Mount Lo-fou in the middle of the fifth century, wrote of these noble birds which have long since vanished from that part of the southland. He said that their bills, considered as goblets, "are more precious than patterned snails," that is, better for cups than richly maculated sea snails. He went on to describe their eating habits:

> They do not tread the ground;
> They do not drink of river or lake;
> They do not gulp the Hundred Herbs;
> They do not nip at reptiles or fish;
> They only sup of leaves of trees.

Their dung resembles *kunduruka* [frankincense] aromatic, and whenever the men of the mountain come across it, they use it for incense; moreover it cures all sorts of ulcers.[343]

The holy priest's tale is more vivid than precise. The creature he describes is omnivorous: though it prefers to eat fruit, it does not reject small reptiles and mammals, and will even favor a large insect.[344]

The bird in question was the noisy black and white Homrai Hornbill (*Dichoceros bicornis*), one of a group with hollow or honey-combed bills and casques, including the Pied Hornbill, the White-headed Hornbill, and others, but not at all the same bird as the Helmeted Hornbill (*Rhinoplax vigil*) from more southerly lands, whose solid ivory casque was carved into finely intricate designs by Chinese artisans of Ming and Ch'ing times.[345] All belonged to a considerable tribe, closely related to the kingfishers, motmots, and hoopoes, which is restricted to the Indochinese and Indonesian tropics. Several of the natural historians of T'ang noticed the hornbill, but their descriptions did not ordinarily go beyond those of their predecessors of five hundred years earlier.[346] Like them, they all took special note of the conversion of the beautiful hollow casques into drinking vessels. But one adds, "They are bent-necked and long-legged; on the head is a yellow cap like a goblet, which they use to store water. They exchange food and drink with the community of birds and chicks."[347] Another writer, after praising the beauty of the enormous black and yellow bills, "as if painted by a human," states that the hornbills come from Tongking and further south.[348] Evidently they were rare in Kwangtung, or had disappeared from that province since the fifth century, unless indeed Fa-chen wrote of what he had heard rather than what he had seen.

There was a kind of boat named *meng-t'ung* (*mung-dung*) like the hornbills, or in T'ang times, often *meng-ch'ung* (*mung-ch'ong*).[349] This was a long narrow war vessel, a cutter equipped with a ram. Indeed the second of its names was written with characters meaning "covered ram" (representing a popular etymology?), and a contemporary source tells us that the boat was entirely covered with cowhide, except for oar holes, and ports for crossbows and pikes to repel enemy attacks. But its specialty was speed, not combat.[350] These vessels had become famous in their first and most glorious appearance in history, when Chou Yü used them successfully against the forces of Ts'ao Ts'ao at Red Wall in A.D. 208.[351] The fierce little destroyers were still employed with excellent effect against pirates in the lake region of central China in the ninth century,[352] but it is doubtful that their name was connected with that of the superb hornbill by the men of T'ang, unless by the philologically minded. But naming boats after birds was an old story in China. Although the rams of Chou Yü may once have been "hornbill boats," it is more likely that the great-beaked forest birds were "ram-cutter birds," the great bill having suggested the hull of the boat and the ornamental casque the deck house. In any case, they were huge, ghostly cruisers of the shadowed jungles, akin to those geese of the south which "apparaissent comme des bateaux-fantômes circulent dans les milieux de marins de la région de Canton."[353] The hornbill is obviously what all birds are fundamentally. Saint-John Perse has made the general observation: "L'étudiant, ou l'enfant trop curieux, qui avait une fois disséqué un oiseau, gardait longtemps mémoire de sa conformation nautique . . ." and so on, with revealing details in enriched language.[354] Sacheverell Sitwell, in contrast, regards all hornbills as masked actors, which "wherever found, dwell in fantasy, in a world apart. They are cast for roles of wisdom, and as much human meaning may be imputed to them as to the marionettes or puppets of the shadow theatre." [355] But the T'ang poets seem not to have noticed these spectral, boat-billed harlequins.

The mountainous part of the Far East is the homeland of the splendid family of pheasants, and many dazzling kinds occur in China proper, especially in the highlands of Szechwan and Yunnan. They are the bird emblems of the Tibetan foothills, as the rhododendrons are the characteristic flowers of that zone of rarified air and deep snow. A few handsome species were known to the lowland dwellers of classical China, and attained an important position in their material culture, their folklore, and their literature. I cannot comment with confidence on the view that the great bird spirit of Chinese mythology, to which we have given the barely appropriate name of "phoenix," is an idealized form of the Argus Pheasant—an Indochinese rather than a Chinese bird. More likely its form in art (like the image of the Bird of Viet) is a composite of many pheasants with the peacock, birds thought to be suitable models for representations of the archaic bird symbol. [356] Otherwise five kinds of native pheasant had names well established in the ancient language, corresponding to their significant role in a primitive culture in which feathers played a great part—magical, ceremonial, and aesthetic:

chih (dyi): Ring-necked Pheasant (*Phasianus colchicus*), also generally "pheasant,"
ti (dek): Reeves' Pheasant (*Syrmaticus reevesii*),
hui (hwĕi): Pucras or Koklass Pheasant (*Pucrasia macrolopha*), [357]
ch'ang (ch'ang): Golden Pheasant (*Chrysolophus pictus*),
hsien (ghăn): Silver Pheasant (*Gennaeus nycthemerus*, or *Lophura nycthemera*).

Nam-Viet itself was not particularly rich in pheasant kind, though the adaptable Ring-necked Pheasant occurred there, as almost everywhere, and one could see such residents of the northern highlands as Darwin's Pucras Pheasant and Cabot's Tragopan. [358] But the pheasant with a special affinity to Nam-Viet was the Silver Pheasant, although it also occurred beyond the limits of that province. [359] The white-mantled Silver Pheasant, with its metallic blue head and scarlet face and legs, is actually one of the Fireback Pheasants. It is apparently to this genus that the Chinese name *hsien* applies. The proud white bird itself is always called "white *hsien*"— that is, "white fireback," or "white lophura." [360] Although not a well-established symbol of the south (the color was wrong for one thing), the Silver Pheasant could pose as a transient symbol of Nam-Viet, as it does in a poem by Chang Chi, in which the writer confidently predicts that the arrival of a respectable governor, appointed by the Son of Heaven, would be welcomed by voluntary displays of the most handsome members of the local flora and fauna:

> White firebacks will fly around the official barge in welcome;
> Red hibiscus will open nearby the banquet at the visitor's pavilion. [361]

Hearing of these beautiful fowl, Hsüan (Ghwen) Tsung, an avid bird collector, ordered a specimen brought to Ch'ang-an to take its place among the many handsome and numinous fowl in his palace gardens. In the fall of 751, Hsiao Ying-shih found himself returning to the capital from the Yangtze region in company with this caged royal bird. He was much moved by its lonely and pathetic cries, and wrote an ode in praise of it. He described its appearance accurately, from black-spotted candent plumage to vermilion feet, and plainly took it to be a distinguished creature, a free spirit not readily taken or tamed, and seldom seen by mere men. He saw the emblems of ancient ceremonial robes traced in its feathers, and compared its red cheeks to "the matchless countenance of a bewitching courtesan." Like a Taoist transcendent,

> Its roving is always by the border of the sea;
> Its roosting is always up among the clouds.[362]

But the fairy bird was still little known to the men of T'ang. It rarely appears in poetry. I noticed it only in two sets of verses. One was written by Sung Chih-wen to tell of a friend's gift of a zither of precious paulownia wood and a Silver Pheasant. He gave the bird its freedom.[363] The other is the work of Li Po. In it (and in its preface) he tells of the pair of Silver Pheasants owned by a friend, so tame that they would eat out of his hand. Li Po desired them for himself, and offered a pair of white jade rings (the color being appropriate) in exchange, comparing the birds' plumage to white silk:

> They roost by night in the quiet of the cold moon,
> They pace at dawn in a pen of fallen flowers.[364]

It is a poem of white and silver—Li Po's favorite color images—displayed in the whiteness of jade, moon, damask, and pheasant, and also in an evergreen nandin tree with its showy panicles of white blooms.[365] This was a true moon bird—the polar opposite to the Vermilion Bird of the lands of the sun, a kind of anti-symbol identified with its rival.

The characteristic bird of the cultivated lowlands of central and south China was no bird of beauty, but a sociable black creature with yellow bill and legs. The physical shortcomings of the Crested Mynah (*chü-yü*, M.C. *gyu-yok*, *Aethiopsar* [*Acridotheres*] *cristellatus*) were more than made up for by its cheerful, gregarious habits, and its adaptability to life in a cage and among human beings.[366]

Its talented cousin, the best of all speaking birds, was the Chinese Hill Mynah (*Eulabes* sp.),[367] proud in its black plumage shot with purple and green, its orange bill and its yellow wattles. It was called *chieh-liao* (*ket-leu*) or (*Ch'in*) *chi-liao* ([*Dzyin*] *kyit-leu*) in T'ang times.[368] It was accurately described by Liu Hsün,[369] and strange red and white mutants gained the attention of Tuan Kung-lu.[370] But its infrequent occurrences in poetry (Li Po, Yüan Chen, Chang Chi, Po Chü-i) do not show it as the jaunty field farer of the southlands, but always as a parrot-like stereotype—a talkative, wise-seeming bird.

A night flier of Nam-Viet, a skillful catcher of gnats and gadflies, was called *hsiu-liu* (*hyou-lyou*), or sometimes "Roving Woman Who Moves by Night," a goblin bird which preyed on babies.[371] It was identical with the female ghost bird called *ku-huo* (*ku-ghwak*), a stealer of men's souls, which could shed its suit of feathers at will. Some said that these nocturnal hunters were the souls of women dead in childbirth, and that they retained the breasts of women in their new shapes.[372] Similar to them were the Ghost Carts—or perhaps this was a generic name.[373] The batlike habits, the insectivorous diet, and the silent mothlike flight of this bird make it certain that the Ghost Cart, under whatever name, was a south Chinese nightjar.[374] But sometimes the name *hsiu-liu* was applied to the owlets, or pygmy owls (*Glaucidium* sp.) of south China, which have crepuscular habits like the nighthawks and nightjars, and mix insects with small birds in their diet—in this differing from the usually rodent-eating owls.[375] Their ghostly character has been recognized outside of China, as in modern Trinidad, where the pygmy owl is named "jumbie bird"—that is, spook bird. The confusion of owlet and nightjar is natural. But for men born in the south, owls were not the ill-omened, evil-voiced birds they were in the north—here they were hardly distinguished from the happy magpies, and were caught and sold in the markets as efficient rat catchers.[376]

Another raptor traditionally associated with the south was a great serpent-eating bird which was said to frequent the tops of areca palms. Its flesh was believed to be poisonous, doubtless because of its diet.[377] Its name *chen* (*dyĕm*) also means "poison; venomous." Accordingly it had an evil reputation, and on the rare occasions when it ventured into the inhospitable north, it was burned as a menace in the public market place.[378] Diet and habitat make the black-crested Chinese Serpent Eagle (*Spilornis* = *Haematornis cheela*) a reasonable identification of the monster. This eagle hovers over the hills from Hainan to Burma, looking for the reptiles on which it feeds. But its bill is slaty blue, not the red reported by one T'ang observer.[379]

"The Humming Birds and the Birds of Paradise are the two most beautiful families in nature, being only rivalled by the Trogons." [380] Twenty species of trogon occur in all parts of the world—tropical America, South Asia, and Africa. When not eating fruit or hawking after insects, they sit quietly in the branches of forest trees, making soft, sad calls.[381] "Green and crimson are the predominant colours in the quetzal and trogon, and they come from nature's dye-pot, fast colours which do not run in the rain showers." [382] The gorgeous, carmine-breasted quetzal is the most famous of the trogons. Its emerald feathers were woven into Montezuma's robe, playing a role in medieval America analogous to that of the halcyon's feathers in medieval China,[383] as Mexican jadeite paralleled Chinese nephrite as a ritual mineral. China has its "Red-headed Trogon" (*Harpactes erythrocephalus*). This quiet bird, with olive back and crimson breast, lives in the deep forests of Fukien and Nam-Viet.[384] I have often wondered whether the beautiful creature could be identified in medieval literature—surely no observer could forget it. But I have found no trace of it except in a reference to a long-vanished painting. This was an old picture in the possession of Hsüan (Ghwen) Tsung which showed the auspicious bird known as "Joy of the Season" with "cinnabar head, red breast, vermilion cap, and green wings." A courtier tried to persuade the monarch that a many-colored parrot recently sent from the South Seas was the original of this painted bird.[385] I think he was mistaken: the description fits the Red-headed Trogon much better,[386] and I am convinced that the good-omened "Joy of the Season" had been studied and delineated some time before the eighth century, and its identity and source afterwards forgotten. It was a true Vermilion Bird, still unrecognized.

Among the many other wild birds of Nam-Viet, only a few have been noticed by T'ang writers, and then only casually, as the white egret whose plumes were needed for military insignia,[387] and the repulsive, ominous Adjutant Stork, which scavenged the lake margins of the South.[388] There are a few which are mentioned but cannot be identified with certainty. Examples are a green magpie-like bird whose elongated tail feathers resemble Chinese arrows—bare except for the tips. This may well have been the glittering Racket-tailed Tree-pie or Bronzed Pie (*Crypsirina temia*).[389] Or again, there was the pretty little duck called *"han-p'eng (ghan-běng)* bird," said never to have been seen in the north.[390] Perhaps this was the Cotton Teal or Pygmy Goose (*Nettapus coromandelianus*), whose motley of white and dark green-glossed brown is seen from India to Fukien.[391] The sinister chicken-sized dark bird called "Mother of Gnats," because of the gnats which were said to fly from its mouth when it cried, stalked the ponds of Nam-Viet looking for fish.[392] Perhaps it was some kind of rail or crake. But the Hua men seem to have been unprepared for the most characteristic tropical birds. The Paradise Flycatcher (*Terpsichore incei*), a kind of miniature magpie, whose little maroon body, metallic green-black head, long tail, and prominent crest—a summer migrant from Malaysia through Nam-Viet and even much further north—[393] would hardly have escaped the notice of sojourners in the south. But the first mention of it seems to be—not unexpectedly—in an eleventh-century pharmacopoeia;[394] in poetry it seems to be unknown before the Yüan period; Li Shih-chen knew it well in the sixteenth century;[395] it is shown plainly in early modern paintings and embroideries;[396] but the men of T'ang knew it not.

The sunbirds (*Nectariniidae*), tiny iridescent sippers of nectar and eaters of insects, are the Old World equivalents of the American hummingbirds. They live in the tropics of Asia and Africa. Sitwell describes them best:

The Sun Birds, which range over India, China, the East Indies, and have one race in South America, can be compared only to the Humming Birds. They even much resemble those in their iridescent and golden plumage with its metallic reflections, in their long sickle bills, and in the peculiar darting and hovering that is characteristic of their flight. The Malachite Sun Bird is a coppery green "self" as though cut out from the heart of the Siberian copper mine; while a Sun Bird from Ceylon has a throat of amethyst reflecting lilac and purple, a yellow belly, brown-purple wings, and a little bright-green cap.

Among them is

Dabry's Scarlet-chested Sun Bird from Burma and China, with red-purple cap and golden rays or reflections, red chest and back, yellow belly, and blue tail.[397]

This last, a jeweled ornament against the rhododendrons of south and west China, is one of the six species of *Aethopyga* to occur there.[398] Any of them might qualify as the true, hoped-for fairy spirit, the Vermilion Bird of Nam-Viet. But all passed undetected. So also did the tiny Flowerpeckers (*Dicaeidae*) that dashed brightly after insects in the tree tops of the Nam-Viet forests. Prominent among them was the Flower-breasted Flowerpecker (*Dicaeum ignipectum*)—metallic green, with black face and crimson breast.[399] It was unknown to the eager naturalist-administrators of T'ang. The torrid zones also have pigeons embellished with rich metallic colors, hardly expected by those of us who know only the inhabitants of temperate city parks. Hainan in particular is rich in such splendid kinds as *Sphenurus, Treron,* and *Ducula.*[400] But trogons, sunbirds, flowerpeckers and fruit pigeons alike, the true spirits of the tropical forests, were to the men of T'ang as mysterious as were the seemingly invisible begonias and mangroves, however abundant. Here they serve only as latter-day symbols of the unknown world beyond the bamboo fences which insulated the "civilized" intruders from its unique beauties.

Be not afeard; the isle is full of noises,
Sounds and sweet airs, that give delight and hurt
  not.
Sometimes a thousand twangling instruments
Will hum about mine ears, and sometimes voices
That, if I then had waked after long sleep,
Will make me sleep again: and then, in dreaming,
The clouds methought would open and show
  riches
Ready to drop upon me, that, when I waked,
I cried to dream again.

William Shakespeare, *The Tempest*

12 The Vermilion Bird

Southern Odors

THE PRECEDING catalogue of the notable landscape forms and living creatures of medieval Nam-Viet has followed, conceivably, the sequence of the days of creation and the disembarkation from the ark—sky and sea, rocks and rivers, beasts and birds, each by each, but without any unifying vision. Now, but briefly, I propose to cut across these simple categories and ask which among the odors, tastes, sounds, and colors of the daedal southern world, regardless of the objects to which they were attached, impressed the senses, and through them stimulated the imaginations or troubled the minds of the T'ang men in Nam-Viet.

I shall begin with the smell of the south. The association of odorous woods, gums, and flowers with the warm woods of Nam-Viet was respectably old, and made it possible for an ancient book to speak of a mountain there as covered with "many aromatic forests." [1] It is this composite image which is referred to by the

T'ang poet Tu Mu in his phrase the "aroma of Viet." [2] The contrast between the fragrant south and the more austere north appears in a set of verses by Li Ch'iao which tell of the triumphant return of Chinese troops from a campaign against the barbarians of Jung. They wear the traditional costume of the steppes—strange garb in the tropics:

> A bow sings—a blue-gray falcon drops;
> A sword moves—a white langur wails.
> Fragrant trees make our Tibetan pipes drone;
> Gloomy bamboo thickets induce the Airs of Ch'u. [3]

But when the poets of T'ang tell of a particular fragrance in the humid air, it is rarely that of rosewood, camphor, or cloves. Most frequently it is the scent of one of the many kinds of flowering orange:

> The aroma of kumquat blossoms sweeps over the anglers' mole—
> That delightful person still dances in her dress of Viet gauze! [4]

Even Sung Chih-wen could admit a melancholy delight in this rich southern perfume:

> The mountain passes of Viet—compounded a thousandfold;
> The mountain streams of Man—slanting ten miles down.
> Bamboos entangle the faggot boy's track,
> Duckweed wraps round the fisherman's house.
>
> The forest is darkened by interlaced liquidambar leaves,
> The gardens are fragrant from a cover of tangerine blossoms.
> But who is my neighbor here beyond the wastes?
> To console my loneliness clouds and sunsets must suffice. [5]

It might have been thought that the pleasant scents of Nam-Viet, so near to the sweet-smelling gardens and temples of Indianized lands, would have inspired comparisons with the Perfumed Land of the Buddha. ("Comme vous êtes loin, paradis parfumé." [6]) But it was not so; here was no Eden, but a fearful wilderness, whose evils were only partly offset by the awareness of orange blossoms in the heavy air.

SOUTHERN FLAVORS

As for the tastes of Nam-Viet, opinion was divided. One T'ang official, presumably bred on wheat and millet, thought the fine white rice cakes of that province a rare and precious delicacy. [7] Indeed the little dumplings of T'ang Nam-Viet still survive, probably in altered forms: Tuan Kung-lu lists *man-t'ou* (*man-dou*) cakes and *hun-t'un* (*ghwěn-dwěn*) cakes among the many viands peculiar to the Canton region. Their names survive today in the gift cakelets of modern Japan called *manjū,* and the Cantonese ravioli called *wonton*.[8] But the flavor of baked rice was not completely alien to the northern stomach. King crabs, oysters and frogs were something else again.[9]

I marvel why frogs and snails are with some people, and in some countries, in great account, and judged wholesome food, whereas indeed they have in them nothing else but a cold, gross, slimy and excremental juice.[10]

This seventeenth-century European opinion was shared by many T'ang Chinese. The only amphibian of Nam-Viet which got the attention of the Hua immigrant was the edible frog, and that because the notion of eating it was detestable to him.[11] The great Han Yü himself was very conscious of the place of frogs in the Nam-Viet diet. He takes pains in more than one place to point out that a different name for frog (*ha-ma* [*ghă-mă*], *wa* [*wă*], *ko* [*kăp*]) did not change the ugly reality. For example, in a poem addressed to Liu Tsung-yüan in 819 on this subject he writes:

> The *ghă-mă* may dwell in water,
> But where the water is unique it changes its figure and form;
> We may be compelled to call it *wă* or *kap*,
> But in reality there is nothing to contrast in them.[12]

In this long rhymed self-analysis, rich in historical allusions, the famous critic admits his conservatism:

> At first I could not get them down my gullet;
> Lately, though, I can manage just a little.
> I have always feared infection by the Man infidels.

He confesses however that his young friend Liu is more adaptable, and in doing in Rome as the Romans do—at least in the matter of frog-eating—has the example of Confucius himself. We have a little information on southern methods of frog cookery, rather painful for the frog. After alluding to the extreme popularity of frogs at banquets in Nam-Viet, one source goes on to say:

First put water in a cauldron, drop in small taros, and bring it to a boil. Wait until the hot water is bubbling as if with fish eyes, then put in the frogs. One by one they will clutch a taro, and there be cooked. For this reason they call this "Soup with Embraced Taro."

A similar preparation required bamboo shoots in place of taro, and the guests found the "staring eyes and gaping mouths" of the scalded frogs, each mounted on his little bamboo rocket, most amusing.[13] Perhaps I should say nothing of such reputed delicacies as "honey peepers," a euphemism for newborn rats, red and wriggling, stuffed with honey and laid out on the banquet tables. As they crawled about cheeping plaintively, they were picked up with chopsticks and eaten alive.[14] And what did the simple northerners make of sauerkraut of water buffalo cud (properly spiced and salted, of course),[15] or of a delicate sauce of ants' eggs? [16] Their feelings, no doubt, approximated those of their modern descendants faced with such a delicacy as *Lethocerus,* the giant water bug of Siam, steamed and excavated like a lobster: "The meat is said to have a strong flavor, reminiscent of Gorgonzola cheese. It is used, dried and pulverized, to add zest to curries, or combined with shrimps, lime juice, garlic and pepper, to make a popular sauce called 'namphla.' " [17]

Even the beverages of Nam-Viet were odd. Tea was a southern drink, now becoming popular in the north, but it was produced in Kiangsi and Fukien, above the tropics. Such great tropical drinks as coffee (Abyssinian) and chocolate (American) were unknown there.[18] But some strange wines were fermented in Nam-Viet, other than the palm toddies I have already mentioned:

In Hsin-chou there are many excellent wines. In that southern quarter they do not use yeast or malt. They grind rice into powder, and make a paste with the juice from the leaves of a number of herbs, including the Foreign Creeping Herb (*Gelsemium elegans*)[19] the size of an egg. This is placed in garden daisies (*Chrysanthemum coronarium*) and kept covered in the shade. After the passage of a month it is finished. They use this, conjoined with glutinous rice, to make wine. Accordingly, after you have drunk to excess, even when sober again your head will burn miserably—this is because the herbs contain poison.[20]

An even more interesting wine was fermented with pomegranate flowers at Yai-chou on Hainan: "Its flavor and aroma are excellent, and it has the power to make men drunk." [21] Indeed this statement, and the following one taken from a poem of Ch'en T'ao, indicate that by the tenth century some native brews were winning favor with the Chinese, although Ch'en T'ao was a Lingnan creole, and may have been biased in their favor:

> The wines of Viet—how could they not be sweet? [22]

Contrast the nostalgia of Shen Ch'üan-ch'i in Huan-chou three centuries earlier:

> In what year will a writ of amnesty come,
> That I may drink once more the wine of Lo-yang? [23]

This acceptance or tolerance of southern edibles was most evident among Chinese who had spent much time in southern provinces. So the poet Hsü T'ang could write to a friend in what is now Kweichow province, "On milord's banquet mat there are the flavors of Viet aplenty." [24] Han Yü made a mighty effort to accustom himself to these strange dishes, even though, as he admits, some made him flush and sweat.[25] Yüan Chen was less charitable. At a farewell party for a southbound friend, he gave him, as was customary, a parting gift of words, in particular good advice about the foods of Nam-Viet. Beware of *ku*-poison, he said. Wild mushrooms are plentiful, but you should only eat those already nibbled by insects, since they are not poisonous. Similarly, one should prefer the kinds of fruit which are pecked at by birds. Worst is sea food: "As to creatures of the sea, most are rich and rancid—taste them and you want to retch and defecate." They should only be eaten after salting.[26] The northerners were on the whole not yet ready to accept the viands of Nam-Viet, rich and heavy with fruits, spices, and the flesh of obnoxious sea creatures.

SOUTHERN SOUNDS

"The principal sensation one gets in the tropical forest is the mystery of the unknown voices. Many of these remain forever mysteries unless one stays long and seeks diligently."[27] So wrote the American bird painter Louis Agassiz Fuertes, who despite his intimate knowledge of the creatures of the rain forest, could not help feeling the ghostly quality of their furtive calls.[28]

Not all tropical sounds were made by spirits and living beings. The tropical jungles and beaches sounded with the motions of air and water. The Chinese have always been sensitive to such music. The tinkle or roar of moving water, and the mystery of the shifting forms of water, are particularly evident in the old "rhapsodies" (*fu*) of Sung Yü and Szu-ma Hsiang-ju.[29] The T'ang travelers and exiles in Nam-Viet were well prepared by these classical precedents to listen for inspiring gurgles and swishes. On the other hand, the sounds were not unique to the south, and they heard in them something familiar, even if strange and exciting, rather than something alien and repellent. So too, the rustle of wind in leaves was a homely but disquieting theme to the Hua men. Even the special character of the play of the air in the palm fronds and banana leaves, so different from the sound of northern winds in pines and willow, was already known to them, since those handsome plants were grown in temperate gardens, even if they did not fruit there. The incessant drip of water from the rain-forest canopy is peculiar to the humid tropics. The T'ang poets in Hainan and Annam seem to have missed it.

Prefigured by the calls of the chukars and langurs, which could be heard in central as well as in south China (to the T'ang men they were livelier images of the south than the more restricted and typical animals of Nam-Viet), it was the noises of the fauna rather than the inanimate voices of running water and rushing wind that caught the attention of the strangers. They listened, above all, to the apes and birds, those elves and sprites of the leafy wilderness, as in this couplet from Meng Chiao's "Chant of Lien-chou":

A grieving langur cries where flowers die;
A hawk-cuckoo rends the stranger's heart.[30]

The dolorous cries of the southern monkeys have already been commented on. The birds shall concern us briefly here. It has often been said that just as the flowers of the tropical forest are sparsely distributed and undistinguished in color, so the birds of the wet woods, even if brightly colored, are undistinguished singers. But despite the harsh cries and annoying chatter of many tropical wildfowl, there are drab and retiring birds there which, like the colorless thrushes and wrens of cooler climates, often have beautifully resonant songs.[31] Alas! the T'ang men did not hear these avian bells and gongs—the bewildering and unclassifiable variety of new bird calls was registered only in vague collective words. As Wang Chien had written in the mid-eighth century that "South of our skies is an abundance of bird sounds," [32] so many decades later Chang Chi could find neither foul croak nor haunting melody to characterize Nam-Viet—only "sounds" or "voices":

> In coconut leaves—the damp of malarial clouds;
> In cinnamon thickets—the sounds of the birds of the Man.[33]

The voices of the Man and Lao themselves were little different from those of birds—strange, indeterminate, bewildering. When Han Yü found that the government office at Lien-chou was not properly staffed, and that official business was carried on by a dozen families of native bailiffs living among the bamboo thickets on the edge of the river, he remarked, "All have the speech of birds with the faces of heathen," adding that he was quite unable to communicate with them except by scratching characters on the ground.[34] The animalian chatter of Man voices also filled the marketplaces of Nam-Viet [35] and were even to be heard in the ranks of the soldiers.[36] Liu Tsung-yüan, however, although he used the old cliché "shrike-tongued" to describe the voices of the Man, soon found himself accustomed to them:

What particularly distinguishes the sound of voices in Ch'u and Viet is its shrike-tongued, noisy clamor. But I listen to them placidly and without astonishment now. Indeed I am now one of a kind with them, as the instinctive babble of the little lads who live in my household fills my ears day and night. But when *they* hear the speech of a man from the north, they shriek and cry, and run off to hide.[37]

No doubt most of this annoying gibberish was phrased in one of the Thai languages, though some of it was probably in a divergent creole form of Chinese. Some T'ang men, such as Chang Chi, could detect no tune in the songs of Nam-Viet, but then that writer was noted for his classical rectitude in all matters, having gone so far as to reproach the great Han Yü himself for taking pleasure in idle games.[38] To him "tuneless" woud have meant "unorthodox." Others, such as Sung Chih-wen, were hopeful that the classic fame of the songs of the south would prove justified by modern experience there. But in the end his feeling of alienation would not allow him to accept the supposed descendants of the ancient masterpieces:

> The oar boys join in heathen songs,
> The faggot girls come home to chants of Viet.
> I had long expected that these would be beautiful—
> Despondent on the frontier, I have only automatic rejection.[39]

There were other barbarian sounds. From their bamboo bastions the Chinese invaders heard the forest resound with the booming of bronze drums and the shrill shaking of reed organs. These instruments were somewhat familiar, if not exactly homely, in that they had analogues in Hua civilization going back to a time when it was not so sharply differentiated from the culture of the Man.

The heavy bronze drums were the palladia of noble aboriginal families. Great drinking parties celebrated their casting, and they were sounded to mark the onset of attacks arising from a blood feud between clans.[40] Their sonorous voices were reputed to be "not inferior to that of the crying alligator."[41] Accordingly the Chinese valued them as trophies of victory over the infidel. A famous example, taken from the tomb of a chieftain, was placed in the temple of the God of the South Sea early in the ninth century—it can still be seen there.[42] These emblems of dignity and power were richly decorated with the figures of flowering plants, fish, and crawling animals. Most characteristic were frogs, for the drum embodied a frog spirit—that is a spirit of water and rain—and its voice was the booming rumble of the bullfrog. The drum could even take the form of a living frog. A T'ang story tells of a person who pursued a crying frog, which leaped into a hole. Excavation discovered the grave of a Man chieftain containing a bronze drum with a rich green patina, covered with batrachian figures.[43] In a broader sense, the drums were coagulations of energy and fertility—they brought wealth and power, and they were ensouled with the soul of the Man people, who were themselves incarnate sea dragons and had power over water.[44]

Modern archaeologists have found ancient bronze drums throughout Southeast Asia, from the Malay peninsula to Yunnan.[45] The oldest represent the work of the people encountered in Nam-Viet by the earliest Chinese invaders, and typify the so-called Dongsonian culture. They were presumably first made in Nam-Viet in Han times or possibly earlier, and subsequently copied throughout Indochina;[46] it has been plausibly suggested that the peoples of the south learned the art of making ceramic drums from their northern neighbors, and that when bronze metallurgy was introduced later from the same Chinese source, the Lao and their kin began to fashion similar drums of metal.[47] Accordingly, the soldiers of Han found them in the villages they conquered, and like bronze boats and pillars, bronze drums have come to be associated with the valiant name of Ma Yüan.[48]

(Nowadays we think of bronze gongs, especially in sets of chimes, rather than bronze drums in connection with Indochina. But the T'ang sources do not mention them. As far as the south is concerned, I find them earliest in southern Kweichow or northern Kwangtung in 984: the Sung sovereign was persuaded to lift a prohibition on bronze casting in order that the natives might have the bronze drums and gongs they needed for their religious ceremonies.[49] Possibly the gong was a northern instrument, adapted to the bronze culture of Nam-Viet in late T'ang times.[50])

To the Chinese in Nam-Viet the reed organs wailing in the jungle night must have seemed like the distant horns of a primitive tropical elfland. Not being altogether alien—since a kind of reed organ was played in respectable northern orchestras—they were acceptable and only pleasantly strange. The reed organ (Chinese *sheng*) is basically a set of canes inserted in a gourd which acts as a windchest. Holes in the lower part of the canes are provided with free-beating tongues. A mouthpiece is added to the gourd. Nowadays the Chinese play pentatonic tunes on the *sheng*, with a parallel set of notes sounded a fourth or fifth below. Something more like the ancient Chinese music seems to be preserved in Japan, where there is a more complex harmony, consisting mainly of the notes of the pentatonic scale sounded simultaneously.[51] Many odd varieties also occur among the simpler peoples of Southeast Asia; one such is the reed organ of the Hei Miao, equipped with fourteen-foot bamboo pipes set with brass reeds.[52] By the sixth century the *sheng* was known in Persia, as *muštaq sini* (Chinese *muštaq*). In the eighteenth century Johann Wilde found a *sheng* in St. Petersburg; from its example, free reeds were introduced to European pipe organs, stimulating a varied progeny of harmonicas, accordions, harmoniums, and the like in the nineteenth century.[53]

The Hua men found the natives of Nam-Viet blowing *sheng* with evident pleasure,[54] and were astonished to learn that these seemingly archetypal instruments were equipped with thirteen reeds (to sound the twelve semitones and the octave) with a fine clear sound, and conformable to the classical modes of China.[55] One writer, however, regarded the sound of the Nam-Viet gourd organs as inferior to the Chinese; but he observed that in the metropolitan north lacquered-wood sound boxes had replaced the calabashes, though the old materials were still employed to some extent in the Yangtze valley.[56] The T'ang men learned of even stranger varieties however—the largest pipes of the Burmese *sheng,* with which they became acquainted in the ninth century, were more than eight feet long.[57]

Like the bronze drum, the reed organ was a divine instrument, but its divinity was more impersonal, remote, and dignified. This was because of its antiquity in Chinese culture, and its association with a still respected technic deity, the culture heroine Nü Kua, or "Woman Kua." She was no goddess of the Man, but was worshipped in remote times in northeastern China, though perhaps she was ultimately of southern origin. By T'ang times her cult had almost vanished, and she was known mostly only to literary people through old books. She was a snake goddess with power over the wind, and the inventor of musical instruments which speak with the wind's voice—in particular, the pipe and reeds of the calabash organ. In ancient times her image showed her as a kindly Lamia, with a human head topping a serpent's body.[58] But in Han times at least, "vulgar paintings of the image of Nü Kua gave her the figure of a woman." [59] It is curious that her name *Kua* (it also occurs in the forms *Wa* [*Ăăi* or *Wă*], or Hsi [*Hĕi*]) is plainly cognate to *wa* "frog," *wa* "puddle," and *kua* "snail." If etymology points where it seems to point, the lady was an archaic spirit of rain pools, and of the moist, slimy animals which live near them. She was once, then, similar to the rain-bringing frog spirits of Nepal, which were also *naga* serpents, and to the ancestral frog of the Bahnars in Indochina.[60] What could have been her relation to the frog spirits of the bronze drums of the Man?

Nü Kua ("Woman Frog"?) had a larger, cosmic aspect. Not only were there legends of her elevating the primordial sky and of patching the shattered heavens, but she was also said to be creator of the world, "the transformer of the Myriad Creatures." [61] Moreover she was specifically the maker of man,[62] as Li Po remembered:

> Nü Kua played with the yellow soil—
> Lumped it to make ignorant and lowly man.[63]

Occasionally tokens of the presence of this primeval serpentine spirit appeared in T'ang times. When her reputed grave was washed under the Yellow River after a wild rainstorm in 754, a tall, strange woman appeared in the camp of the future monarch Su Tsung. Her arms were scaly, and she carried a pair of carp. Later the prince realized her identity because of a simultaneous apparition by the site of her tomb.[64] On June 29 of 758 the tomb suddenly reappeared from the water, adorned with two willows. The court ordered official paintings to be made of this gracious scene.[65]

Surely the Hua men of T'ang thought of Nü Kua when they heard her pipes among the cinnamon trees. But what spirit spoke to the Lao and Man in those pipings is now a mystery.

SOUTHERN COLORS

Brightly colored things were wonderful, magical things in medieval China. Each basic color was full of cosmic import, and the five of them (yellow, black, red, blue, white) displayed together in nature was a sign of great and blissful fortune. Hence the more than ordinary esteem placed on polychrome parakeets imported from Indonesia, and the feeling of hidden forces in gaudy sunset skies. The totemic dog P'an-hu also showed his holy quality to the human eye—his fur was patterned in the Five Colors, and accordingly his progeny, the manifold Man tribes, were "weavers and spinners of the bark of trees, which they dye with herbs and fruits, taking pleasure in pentachromatic dress and costume." [66] But this pretty legend does not tell us the true colors of Nam-Viet, which no Chinese ever thought of as endowed with the whole mystical spectrum.

Men's choice of colors for practical or mystical purposes, or above all for the subtly prismatic illumination of their imaginations, is not freely made, but determined by cultural traditions, and among these most often by linguistic and literary traditions.[67] Men rejoice or despair in tune with a named selection from among the infinite gradations of the rainbow. Hence the poetic popularity of the ancient Five in China, and after them, their culturally determined variants, such as vermilion, an alternate of primary red, but tinged with the lore of alchemy and the craft of painting, and dark reds and purples, the colors of magic power, unearthly radiations, and Taoist specters.[68] But in ancient times these color names were, in the main, used symbolically (so autumn was white, sad, and deadly), and it was not, it seems, until the fifth century of our era, more or less, that men—or writers at least—began to appreciate all the various colors of nature and, above all, to intensify them, to see their environment as a glowing, paradisiacal painting, a garden world to be enjoyed, not just a dark, undifferentiated hermitage for the melancholy ascetic.[69] They could then search their dusty dictionaries and precious anthologies for the right words for these wonderful hues and their emotional overtones.

If we ask, what are the colors of the south, a minimum of reflection might give first place to white. To the Cambodians and the Annamese, white shows forth the uncontaminated invisible world—a holy dancing girl is white of both skirt and skin, and white are the sacred elephant, the sacred parasol, and the sacred lotus.[70] But white symbolized the spirit world for the Chinese too; it was the angelic color of the moon, of moon-bred jade, of numinous albino animals, and above all of the pinnacled islands of paradise.[71] The holiness of white, then, was universal, non-local, nondistinctive. Even forgetting symbolic usage and looking at the phenomenal world, as reflected in literature, white is the color of such familiar northern birds as the crane, the egret, the goose, and the gull.

"Yellow" is the common epithet of refulgent orioles and tasty tangerines, lovers of the warm lands, but no T'ang man thought of yellow as a southern color, except remotely and secondarily, as it was also in the West, the color of the sun and of the gold of the Indies:

> Tum cynaeis eripit ab undis
> Insula, quae prisci signatur nominis usu
> Aurea, quod fulvo sol hic magis orbe rubescat.[72]

Little of this golden imagery got into conventional language in China. Yellow had its own nobility, however, as the first words of Chang Chieh's ode to that color show:

> Sorrowful indeed is the exhalation of autumn,
> As the year fades and comes to an end,
> And chrysanthemum flowers are right for snipping.[73]

But, above all, yellow was the natural hue of the arid northern lands, the true home of the Hua men. It was the color of their great, surly river, of the yellow loess which carpeted their fields, and the yellow camels which trod it. It was tawny, tan, and dun, it was the color of the chert, of the steppes, of the dust-hidden sun. It was isabelline yellow, sand yellow, filemot yellow, and dung yellow. It was the old, conservative, dependable color of the mother country. It was absolutely antipathetic to Nam-Viet.

But the dark green of forest trees—and, drained of sunny yellow by heavy shade, mists or distance, their blue green and indigo—was a true southern color. Despite the glory of tropical flowers, the jungle was a dense mass of somber foliage.[74] The expression "green shade" is very common in medieval poetry, and should be particularly apt for the darkened woodlands of Nam-Viet. But the green of that phrase has a hint of yellow in it, and poets sensitive to the character of the world under the tropical tree canopy had to find darker images, greens impregnated with cobalt and ultramarine, as Hu Ts'eng did for a poem telling his impressions as he descended through Shao-chou by boat:

> Wild figs and more than enough rain—the hills turn to kohl;
> Reeds and rushes, and the mist all gone—the isles like indigo.[75]

Or, better yet, the hot sodden lands were a pattern of green and red. In T'ang poetry the contrast appears most often in the gleam of rocks, blue green in some lights, red orange in others. The good mandarin Li Po (Bwĕt) found the south a red dreamland or a rubious paradise, but he tempered the rosy vision with a cooler and darker color. The wild lands of Hunan were within the realm of the Flaming God; beyond that was the divine country of the Primordial Smith, the timbered slopes of the passes into Nam-Viet:

> Blue peaks and cyan cliffs, where cloudy auroras perch;
> Vermilion banks and purple gullies, where gods and sylphs are housed.[76]

Or again, we have the words of Tu Shen-yen, describing the Mountain of Confused Stones in the Canton region:

> In the hot sunshine of morning, they flush with cinnabar and purple;
> In the pale moonglow of night, they gleam with azure and halcyon.[77]

This pairing of reds and blues was honorably ancient before it was found to be exemplified in the limestone hills which plunged towards Canton. Not only were blue hills and red cliffs an old story, but indigo brows and pink cheeks had just as long a pedigree, and the art of the painter was said to be skill with "vermilion and azure," in the literal senses of those nouns. The transference of the old dyad to the vegetable mantle of Nam-Viet was easy, but often subdued and civilized into recognizable metaphors, as by Po Chü-i, for whom the "green cinnamon" could personify a handsome youth and the "red banana" his lovely paramour.[78]

The expected colors of Nam-Viet were the scarlet of its birds and flowers displayed against the deep blue-green backdrop of its thick evergreen vegetation. Surely the Vermilion Bird ruled the forest! Even if in reality the sight of a red bird or maroon flower against the green black of the monsoon forest was a rare and isolated event, the minds of the educated men of T'ang were prepared for the vision, which should have sparked their imaginations, like a rare flash of spirit against the vast darkness of the universe. Red was the true color of the south, and had been since the earliest times:

The Great Earth altar of the Son of Heaven is an altar made of earth in five colors. When his Illustrious Son is enfeoffed as a King, he receives earth from the Earth altar of the Son of Heaven, in accordance with the color of the quarter in which he is enfeoffed . . . if the southern quarter, he receives red.[79]

So went a ritual formulation of the Han period, more than half a millenium earlier. Red was one of the cosmic colors, but beyond that it was peculiarly the color of the "South Facer," the Son of Heaven himself. The ceremonial entrance way to his holy palace was always the south gate. In the case of the "old" palace of early T'ang this was named "Gate of the Vermilion Sparrow." That which led to the newer "Palace of Great Illumination" was called "Gate of the Cinnabar Phoenix." The guest honored by admission to the palace city advanced through this holy gate, then proceeded northward through a series of sacred basilicas, beginning with a great audience hall where the Son of Heaven assumed the south-facing position, the attitude of majesty and sovereign might, while his assembled vassals faced north, the direction of subjection.[80]

Moreover, it was reasonable that red should have been the color of the south. Not only was it the universal symbol of fire and the burning and life-giving sun, of hot, life-sustaining blood, and of life itself,[81] but it was, more than yellow, the ideal color of gold and of the lands of gold, the wealth-giving Indies, Suvaṇṇabhūmi (even to us, Indochina remains a land of fiery rubies). In the Chinese tradition these were the Isles of Flame, presided over by the Vermilion Bird. Men's feet pressed closer to the sources of life there, where red fire mountains spurted up out of the subterranean darkness, as from a rupture in a cosmic artery.[82] Nonetheless, the scarlet energy could show itself sometimes in the dark north sky—a portent of great significance, and all the more exciting in that the volcanoes of Java were, after all, known to the Chinese only by report. An auroral display of July 24, 708, was reported in these words: "There was a red vapor on the edge of the sky, brightening the land with light; after three days it stopped. A red vapor is a portent of blood." [83]

Naturally, not all literary reds were consciously southern. The poetry of P'i Jih-hsiu is full of the hot part of the spectrum. In one quatrain he has red candles with coral tears,[84] in another wild roses tinted with "Gibbon's Blood," [85] and a single couplet glows with "crimson trees," "purple deer," "cinnabar sands," and "red fish." [86] Allusions to the south here are subtle, distant, faint.

But in some literature the reds are directly, plainly, and immediately southern, as when Han Wo wrote of a lovely girl clad in the gay red of excitement and allure: "Her tight dress and short sleeves are Man-floss red." [87] (This "Man" is the ethnic name.) This seductive costume had been tailored of the Indochinese cotton called

"Sunrise Clouds of Morning," a fine auroral pink, thought suitable for the costumes of the queens of Champa when ornamented with pearls and golden chains.[88] The holy color could easily be seen in the skies and soils of Nam-Viet. Earlier in this book we noted the red mists overhead and the red laterite underfoot. There were red rocks, such as the fiery ridge near Canton which a Cambodian tried to buy, believing it to be full of gold: the governor refused to sell such a sacred hill, a protector of the south-land.[89] Above all, its red fruits and flowers expressed the genius of Nam-Viet, as in this vignette by Ou-yang Chiung:

> A road goes off to the south—
> In the dark of sagwire leaves, knotgrass flowers redden;
> By men's houses on both banks, after a slight rain,
>   They gather red beans.
> By the bottom of the tree, fine and fragile, her pale hands take them up.[90]

Wu Wu-ling, a lover of the southern landscape, wrote of a lovely spot in the Kuei-chou region, full of caverns and rushing water, where Li tribesmen had their huts all along the stream: "The flowers there are red and purple through the four seasons—seen from afar, lush and dense, they might be coral and carbuncles." He even expressed doubt that the grottoed sacred mountains K'un-lun and K'ung-t'ung, reputed to be covered with jewel-like blossoms, could offer views to surpass this picturesque vista.[91]

The red azalea offered the men of T'ang a perfect floral symbol of the south, and may now do the same for us. This is all the more surprising in that rhododendrons and azaleas are not especially tropical plants, and are at their best in alpine regions, as where we may see (in Sitwell's words) "Tibetan lamaseries among the rhododendrons and snows." [92] In China the most glamorous kinds were in Yunnan, then the kingdom of Nan-chao. Nonetheless six or seven species of azalea occurred in the hills of Nam-Viet.[93] The best known of these were the yellow azalea *Rhododendron molle* of the open hillsides of eastern China, and the red azalea *Rhododendron Simsii*, well known also in the Yangtze valley. Neither of these was familiar either to gardeners or poets before the ninth century. Then Po Chü-i, the first great azalea fancier, made the red azalea—known as "Mountain Pomegranate" or "Hawk-cuckoo Flower"—popular. In literature, the rose-red Chinese azalea came to be an image of fire, blood, and enchanting women.[94] Not every writer found the azaleas of Nam-Viet entrancing, however. Han Yü thought them interesting only in mass effects, and even then not to be compared with the flowering trees of his northern homeland.[95] This sour, conservative opinion was far from being shared by Meng Kuan, who evidently had some of the same feeling for azaleas that we have for such tropical exotics as the hibiscus, the bougainvillea, and the poinciana:

Most of the flowers in the south are pink or red, and indeed these are the colors of that quarter. The azaleas excel them all. At times they occur north of the Passes, but not in the luxuriant abundance of the south. Here they grow among all the mountain valleys. When they open in the second month, they shine as brilliantly as fire, and are not spent in more than a month.[96]

But Meng Kuan was exceptional. Few men found beauty in the southern reds. The red paradise and its red souls realized as birds had receded still further beyond the southern horizon.

The sensations of the south were not unprecedented, since the invaders sensed what they expected to sense and failed to notice what their symbols had not prepared them for. Or if truly novel sensations did not entirely escape them, they were rejected wholly or in part by preconditioned imaginations. The south had an unpleasant flavor on the whole, except for some delicious fruits and exhilarating beverages. It had a heady aroma, but it was not a refined and classical one. The sounds were either mere jabber and twitter or else disturbing and terrifying. Although more intense and rather differently distributed than at home, and the reds not so completely realized as might have been expected, the colors of Nam-Viet were not really alien.

THE VERMILION BIRD

Such is the history of the medieval domain of the Vermilion Bird. The bird itself, as creature and as symbol, deserves a few words.

The red bird for which the sacred gates of Ch'ang-an were named was a primitive image, an auspicious sign of divine blessings on the man or country to whom it appeared. The Chinese dynastic histories are full of solemn reports of red sparrows, red swallows, red crows, and other birds pigmented with the color of the ancient gods. Usually these notices are accompanied by official glosses interpreting the happy auguries.[97] The Vermilion Bird, in whatever particular shape, was a divine messenger carrying red-inked messages to human paragons—holy men and rulers of exceptional merit and power.[98] Indeed its mere visible presence was itself a message. It was the true firebird, infused with the spark of divine solar energy: "The vermilion sparrow is the germ of fire," said an ancient Taoist tract.[99] It follows that it was also a sunbird, often showing itself in the form of a "red crow":

> Fiery glowing—the red crow;
>   It is the germ of the sun;
> Vermilion feathers on cinnabar body;
>   It is born in exceptional epochs.[100]

One of these flew down in 776 to confirm the good reign of Tai Tsung.

The angelic creature in red plumage was also the ghost of the tropical firelands, as Liu Yü-hsi remarked. Looking at holy Heng Mountain, the residence of the First Smith, the poet imagined "its summit swept by the pinions of the Vermilion Bird." [101] Indeed this bird was preeminent among the five directional birds. The dark swallow of the north, the white egret of the west, the blue-gray hawk of the east, and the yellow oriole of the center all seem artificial afterthoughts, lacking the liveliness of the ancient austral bird.[102]

Since red tropical birds purporting to be the genuine divine articles, were sometimes submitted to the imperial court by southern chiefs and princes, and since ruddy fowl occasionally appeared unexpectedly at the gates of the capital city as the messengers (it was thought) of Heaven itself, we may legitimately ask what actual birds, northern or southern, were allowed this divine significance. A red bird perched on the ridgepole of a palace hall in Ch'ang-an would presumably have been a native northern species, such as a rosefinch or crossbill, wandering from the forests of Inner Mongolia.[103] None of these northern birds could have been very large or spectacular, but then legend did not require that they should be. Of birds seen in or sent from the far south, candidates often proposed for the supreme role, with greater or less propriety, are the wild jungle fowl, the peacock, and even the chukar partridge. The fireback pheasants would have been just as suitable. However, these larger wild fowl suffered from a degree of chromatic inadequacy. But some of the smaller birds of Nam-Viet display a fine uniform scarlet. Such are the Fork-tailed Sunbird (*Aethopyga christinae*), the Fire-breasted Flowerpecker (*Dicaeum ignipectum*), and the Great Scarlet Minivet (*Pericrocotus speciosus*), fantastic foragers among the flowering trees and shrubs of tropical glades and gardens.[104]

But no particular kind of bird observed in medieval Nam-Viet received the divine accolade from the Hua men. The Chinese trogon and the little sunbirds both went unnoticed; the Chinese parrots remained merely curiosities; the pheasants and their kind were practical suppliers of fine feathers to the milleners and armorers of the court. Occasional individuals were cast in the sacred role, but no species retained it permanently. The classical red bird of happy augury remained a pure, unearthly emblem, not realized in any specific flier of the troubled airways between the Passes and the South Sea.

A parrot or trogon, displaying in its red and green plumage both the exotic flowers of the tropics and the green forest background, makes an ideal Vermilion Bird for us moderns. It is even possible to imagine it escaped from China, or reborn outside of China, incarnate perhaps in the cherry-red lory of the Moluccas, or the splendid emerald quetzal of Guatemala. A beautiful exemplar would be the Vermilion Flycatcher which flutters over the Colorado Desert of California, Arizona, and the hot, arid lands of Mexico and South America:

Darting like a flame up into the flood of sunlight, he reaches a point about a hundred feet from the earth, and then, with scarlet crest spread out like a hussar's hood and head thrown back, he floats lightly down on trembling wings.[105]

In fact a hybrid form of the Vermilion Bird may be seen in a painting by the American artist Morris Graves, much of whose work is populated by Chinese creatures and artifacts. His "Bird of the Spirit" shows a blue-eyed, three-legged bird of uncertain identity, probably the three-legged red crow of the sun, embedded in a red, crystalline jelly or ectoplasm.[106] So the multiplicity of possible realizations of the Vermilion Bird could lead to a fanciful but universal symbol in our own century.

Lacking a specific fleshy crystallization, we may still ask what was the role of this ancient symbol in T'ang times? Did it exemplify a new idea or only the old one? Specifically, did it embody hopes about the possibility of new experiences and an enriched way of life in Nam-Viet? Was the Vermilion Bird simply an image of escape—did its flashing wings suggest merely the power to flee from dangerous involvements? Or did the men of T'ang see in its enameled body a more perfect version of their own mortal bodies, and a symbol of their very selves and souls, free to roam the unexplored gardens of the air?

To ask such questions is not just to ask what came into the minds of the men of T'ang when they pondered the vision of the Vermilion Bird. Perhaps few of them did. Rather it is to ask what was the total character of the T'ang experience in Nam-Viet. It is to enquire about the domain of the Vermilion Bird in the imaginations and aspirations of the medieval Hua men who came down from the temperate zone, and its place in their literature. Although there is no evidence that the intruders tried to cultivate familiar homely flowers in their new steaming courtyards, or that they could smile at caged larks and buntings in their bamboo studios—perhaps such heart-warming mementos were unavailable to most of them—in their poetry they lamented the absence of such distant commonplaces. Only a few, perforce, came to consider the merits of the birds and flowers native to Nam-Viet. Most were more conscious of what they had left behind than of what they might discover.

The poetry of the north was full of severity and harshness; it shivered with bitter frost, desert winds, and ambiguous images of moon and snow on the steppes. This true Chinese world was stern, sober, and correct. But there was also the old legacy of appreciation of the mild, warm, and colorful world of the Yangtze basin.[107] This, however, gave only partial preparation for the deeper south. For the man banished to Nam-Viet the alienation from things he knew was almost total. Gazing wide-eyed at such wonders as a great yellow-casqued hornbill floating under the high forest canopy, or at flying fishes darting brightly away from his boat, he was as far as possible from the world of the pious founders of his Way of Life—the loess and the birches, the tented nomads and camel caravans which surrounded his symmetrical cities and tidy farms. The mountains and the sea cut him off from his family, his friends, his ordinary occupations, and, above all, from all of the figures and images hallowed by venerable tradition and reinforced by innumerable treasured documents. The constant themes of the medieval texts are fear, irritability, riches, corruption, intoxication, mystery, magic, and hallucinations, revealed in such stereotyped images as mist-born diseases, wild savages, imported treasures, and demoniac haunters of the woods. Vivid impression and bright colors mark the writings of some visitors, but most could think of the new country only in clichés.

The *colonial* mentality was active among many of the mandarins who were faced with the savages and the grottoes. These were practical men, realistic, conscious of superiority, even as they jotted careful notes on natural history. There was something to interest those few administrators who were also connoisseurs of picturesque mountain scenery, and something for the adventurous gardener and the collector of curiosa.

Native sons like Chang Chiu-ling, who loved their homelands as a matter of course, were neither numerous not influential.

The *exotic* mentality might have been found only among sensitive guilt-ridden souls who yearned for an alien perfection, not provided by the glorious norms of T'ang. There were few of them in this early medieval world. We know them well among our own contemporaries who have tasted strange fruits on the edges of the rain forests:

> Faire escale parfois dans quelque port d'Asie;
> Y retrouver l'Eden, oublier le retour;
> Goûter d'étranges fruits ou quelque étrange amour,
> Voir des lotus géants dont l'âme s'extasie! [108]

Rousseau, Loti and Conrad could hardly have existed in Nam-Viet before the fall of T'ang. The magistrates, soldiers, and exiled politicians there were more the counterparts of the Spanish in Tenochtitlan than of the French in Tongking.[109]

The idea of a paradise below the sun, populated by mysterious and alluring houris wearing hibiscus flowers over their ears—a kind of Tahiti or Hawaii where the ennui or horror of everyday life could be forgotten—eluded the men of T'ang until the very end. The attempt to superimpose on the conventional *mise-en-scène* of toxic herbs, slithering reptiles, pseudo-human apes and anthropoid goblins, red skies and black forests, magic, uncertainty, and suspicion, the poetic imagery of the old beloved south of pre-T'ang literature, with its apple-cheeked maids of Viet languidly blushing in lotus ponds, of pleasure boats and mist goddesses, was only partly successful. It was not until the T'ang empire was crumbling, late in the ninth and early in the tenth century, that a new synthesis between the traditional rose-tinted romanticism derived from the *Ch'u tz'u* and the aesthetic naturalism of such men as Liu Tsung-yüan and Chang Chiu-ling became possible. The change came when the northerners found it possible to see advantages in the isolation of Nam-Viet, already tested by their uncles and cousins. Suddenly, instead of a purgatory, or a very hell, it became a blessed sanctuary. Then the province began to acquire a new and unconventional romantic aura, displayed for us in the haunting poems of Li Hsün and Ou-yang Chiung. Only then were the old images transformed and given new life: the Vermilion Bird became incarnate in the red-sleeved girls of Nam-Viet.

But local, exotic atmosphere is a transitory stage between the old colonial-imperial approach and the final stage of the enrichment of literature generally. The experience of new places, new men, and new words can, in time, produce fresh images of universal validity.[110] Although the tropical Eden was only tentatively and partly realized, a steady stream of new metaphors and mental pictures flowed northward to enrich the language and the thoughts of the Chinese. The dusty, conservative land-lubbers were steadily being transformed into men ready for any kind of world and every rare experience.

The Vermilion Bird, a fictive icon imposed continually upon the new south (wherever it might be) could never exist completely. The oriental firebird, a qualified vision for Liu Tsung-yüan, nesting peacefully in the heart of Chang Chiu-ling, and realized narrowly but brilliantly in the neoromantic verses of Li Hsün, could be actualized broadly and abstractly only in the language and literature of post-T'ang times.

NOTES

Introduction (Pages 1–8)

[1] Bates (1952), 79–80.

[2] I have followed E. G. Pulleyblank, "The Consonantal System of Old Chinese," *Asia Major*, 9/1 (1962), 58–144; 9/2 (1963), 206–265, in making a few modifications and eliminating what appear to be unnecessary distinctions. For instance I owe the spelling -au- for Karlgren's -å- to Pulleyblank. Beyond this, I have adapted the regular Vietnamese digraph tr- to the spelling of the whole series of Middle Chinese supradental affricates and spirants, to yield dr-, sr-, and the like. I have

avoided raising technical phonological problems: my ty- represents Karlgren's ţ-, without regard to the possibility that the sound in question may have been a supradental or cerebral stop rather than a palatal stop. Neither have I attempted to work out a consistent phonemic spelling, after the manner of Samuel E. Martin, *The Phonemes of Ancient Chinese* (Supplement to Vol. 16 of *Journal of the American Oriental Society*, 1953). I leave this undertaking to my betters. Here is a table of correspondences:

Initials

Schafer	Karlgren	Schafer	Karlgren
h-	χ-	nh-	ńź-
gh-	γ-	sh-	ś-
k-	k-	j-	dź-
k'-	k'-	y-	(j)i̯-
g-	g'-	t-	t-
ng-	ng-	t'-	t'-
ch-	tś-	d-	d'-
ch'-	tś'-	n-	n-
zh-	ź-	ts-	ts-

Schafer	Karlgren		Schafer	Karlgren
ts'-	ts'-			
dz-	dz'-			**FINALS (I)**
s-	s̥-			
z-	z̥-		Add to medials:	
ty-	t̂-		-m	-p
t'y-	t̂'-		-n	-t
dy-	d̂-		-ng	-k
ny-	n̂-			
tr-	tṣ-			**FINALS (II)**
tr'-	tṣ'-			
dr-	dẓ'-		-a	-â
sr-	ṣ-		-ă	-a
zr-	ẓ-		-aai	-ǎi
p-	p-		-ăi	-ai
p'-	p'-		-ăăi	-āi
b-	b'-		-au	-âu
m-	m-		-ău	-au
			-ei	-iei
	MEDIALS		-ĕi	-(j)ɛi
			-eu	-ieu
-a-	-â-		-i	-(j)i
-ă-	-a-, -ɐ-		-iĕ	-(j)iɛ
-au-	-å-		-ou	-əu
-e-	-ie-		-u	-uo
-ĕ-	-ə-		-wa	-uâ
-o-	-uo-		-wă	-ʷa
-u-	-u-		-wai	-uâi
-wa-	-uâ- (-wâ-)		-waai	-uǎi
-wă-	-ʷa-, -ʷɐ-		-wăi	-ʷai
-we-	-iʷe-		-wăăi	-ʷāi
-wĕ-	-uə-		-wei	-iʷei
-ya-	-(j)i̯a-		-wĕi	-(j)ʷɛi
-yă-	-(j)i̯ɐ-		-wi	-(j)ʷi
-ye-	-(j)i̯ä-		-wiĕ	-(j)ʷiɛ
-yĕ-	-(j)i̯ə-		-ya	-i̯a
-yi-	-(j)i̯ĕ-		-yăi	-i̯ɐi
-yo-	-i̯ʷo		-yei	-(j)i̯äi
-yu-	-i̯u-		-yeu	-(j)i̯äu
-ywa-	-(j)i̯ʷa-		-yo	-(j)i̯ʷo
-ywă-	-(j)i̯ʷɐ-		-you	-(j)i̯əu, -i̯əu
-ywe-	-(j)i̯ʷä-		-yu	-(j)i̯u
-ywĕ-	-(j)i̯uə-		-ywa	-i̯ʷa
-ywi-	-(j)i̯uĕ-, -(j)i̯ʷĕ-		-ywăi	-(j)i̯ʷɐi
			-ywei	-(j)i̯ʷäi

In addition there are a couple of special rules: drop -w- after a labial initial (writing *pan*, not *pwan*) and -y- after a palatal initial (writing *chin*, not *chyin*). Where Karlgren has a glottal stop before initial (j)i̯-, write i- instead of y-, thus distinguishing (for instance) *iwen* and *ywen*.

³ With a contemporary reference, "Nam-Viet" is also used nowadays for southern Viet-Nam. See the usage in Lafont (1964), 157.

⁴ Aurousseau (1923), 259; Lo (1960), 7.

⁵ Chang Hu, "Ying-wu," ChTS, *han* 8, *ts'e* 5, ch. 1, 4b.

⁶ Possibly the eponymous axe was a perforated round axe like those known archaeologically from the Neolithic of Kwangsi but unknown in north China, with related forms in many parts of Oceania, such as the *nbonet* of New Caledonia and the widespread ceremonial "club" called *patu*. See Ling (1960b), 24–25. Ling believes that the Chinese *ju-i* "scepter" is a late descendant. Other authorities think that the *yüeh* was a stepped adze. See Serruys (1962), 279, n. 35

⁷ TCTC, 234, 4b. Another name for the whole Nam-Viet region in post-Han times was Chiao-Kuang, suggesting its dual nature rather than its unity.

⁸ I follow TLT, 3, 24a–24b, giving the system for the mid-eighth century, with some modifications depending on such other texts as YHC, 34, 1003; 37, 1037; 38, 1071; 38, 1081–1082. This hybrid and "average" list, which attempts to simplify a fluid and constantly changing picture, is also shown on my map, which derives ultimately from the map in Hsü (1939). But see n.17 to Chapter II for important changes.

⁹ It will be necessary to distinguish the modern province of Kweichow from the T'ang counties Kuei-chou (Kwĕi-chou) and Kuei-chou (Kwei-chou).

CHAPTER 1 (Pages 9–18)

¹ I owe some of the phrases in this section to Benedict (1947), 379.

² Brodrick (1942), 110; Benedict (1947), 380.

³ Brodrick, 1942, 77 and 115. The Muong speak an archaic form of Vietnamese, preserving initial consonant clusters such as pr-, kr-, and bl-. Benedict (1947), 380. The affiliation of Vietnamese itself is disputed. Some regard it as fundamentally related to Thai (Sebeok [1943], 352, following H. Maspero); others as basically Mon-Khmer (Benedict [1947], 380; Forrest [1948], 91). Benedict's view that it is hybrid Mon-Khmer/Thai, rich in Mon-Khmer roots with strong Thai influence including tones and monosyllabicity, is persuasive.

⁴ These selected traits are part of a long list in Eberhard (1942), 221–229 and in Wiens (1954), 54. Unfortunately most of the listed characteristics of this people, as for others of south China, are not distinctive. Such traits as tattooing, pile houses, bronze drums, and many others occur among many of the Eberhard/Wiens culture types, and we are hard put to find truly distinctive features.

⁵ Stübel and Meriggi, (1937), 297; Duyvendak (1939), 407; Benedict (1941), 129; Benedict (1942), 576, 580, 582; Benedict (1947), 384; Forrest (1948), 97. See also Fuson (1929), 10–11.

⁶ Fuson (1929), 10–11; Eberhard (1942), 326–330; Wiens (1954), 54.

⁷ V. K. Ting regarded them as an offshoot of the Yao, adapted to a life in boats. Wiens (1954), 39.

⁸ Brodrick (1942), 110–113, 169; Benedict (1947), 381; Briggs (1949), 61.

⁹ Li (1948), 2–3. They are now found also on Hainan, as the Be or Ong-Be. Benedict (1941), 129. Li's system puts them in one branch of the Kam-Tai family, the other being the Kam-Sui with the Mak (see below) as a prominent member. Benedict regards Thai as basically related to Indonesian, but heavily infiltrated with Chinese borrowings, including monosyllabicity and tone, fea-

tures which it passed on to Vietnamese. Benedict (1947), 382.

[10] Hsü (1939), 78–87; Brodrick (1942), 110–113; Benedict (1947), 381; Wiens (1954), 39.

[11] Eberhard (1942), 176–196; Wiens (1954), 53. The pile houses are not distinctive. Many peoples of Indochina and Indonesia have them; among them are the Thô, the Man Côc, the Muong, and the Moi. See Nguyen (1934), 20–39.

[12] Briggs (1949), 65.

[13] Fuson (1929), 10; Benedict (1941), 129.

[14] Brodrick (1942), 110–113; Benedict (1947), 379; Wiens (1954), 96, 106–107. But some think the Yao were aboriginal in south coastal China; see Hsü (1941), 42; Wiens (1954), 96. Ku Yen-wu thought they spread south from Hunan. Hsü (1941), 42. Hsü Sung-shih found evidence in Yao folksongs to show that they moved into Lingnan during the Huang Ch'ao disorders of the ninth century, and caused trouble for the Chinese in Sung times. See Wiens (1954), 106–107. The Miao-Yao language family, now quite well established, is regarded by Chinese scholars as a stock of the Sino-Tibetan family. Forrest (1948), 91, however, think it close to Mon-Khmer. Sebeok (1943), 353 rightly points out the tentative and controversial nature of all of these groupings of Southeast Asian languages.

[15] Benedict (1941), 129.

[16] They do not all speak "Miao-Yao" languages. Of five Man tribes studied in Tongking by Bonifacy, one spoke an old kind of Chinese, one spoke a Thai language, and three spoke "true" Man (i.e., Miao-Yao) dialects. But all of their songs and poems were in Chinese. See Bonifacy (1903), 85–89.

[17] Bonifacy (1925), 71–77.

[18] Fuson (1929), 10–11.

[19] Brodrick (1942), 110–113.

[20] Brodrick (1942), 110–113; Eberhard (1942), 196–221; Wiens (1954), 39, 51–52.

[21] Fuson (1929), 10–11; Forrest (1948), 89; Wiens (1954), 87–88.

[22] Wiens (1954), 87–88, 96.

[23] Brodrick (1942), 250–274; Eberhard (1942), 250–274; Wiens (1954), 51.

[24] Aymonier and Cabaton (1906), 401.

[25] Aymonier (1891), 206. There are also Muslim Chams living in Cambodia.

[26] Aymonier (1890), 153, 183–184. *The Book of Anushirvan,* a cosmological work, is sacred to the Chams. It is translated in Durand (1907), 321–339.

[27] Finot (1901), 13.

[28] Chang (1959), 124. "(1) The Mesolithic South China is separated from the North by the absence of a micro-blade tradition and by the physical anthropology of inhabitants (Oceanic Negroid in contrast to Mongoloid); (2) Although the Neolithic Cultures in South China are historically related to those in the North, they exhibit quite distinct features as the result of adaptation to a widely distinct ecological zone and of diverse historic experience; and (3) The ending of the South China Neolithic stage is the result of Sinicization at various periods of time." Chang (1959a), 76.

[29] Chang (1959a), 76–84.

[30] Chang (1959a), 97–98.

[31] Chang (1959a), 84.

[32] For a summary of legendary and traditional beliefs about archaic Chinese relations with the southern "barbarians" see Lin (1941), 270 ff. Ruey states that in late Chou times the Miao people occupied a broad region extending through the Yangtze basin from Szechwan to Kiangsi. Ruey (1962), 181.

[33] From Sung times "Miao" appears to have been used in the same general and contemptuous way that "Man" had been used before. Wiens (1954), 68. Ruey believes that though the name Miao disappears between Han and T'ang, the people remained as the dominant group in

western Hunan and eastern Kweichow, hidden under the collective name "Man." Ruey (1962), 180, 184.

[34] See Hsü (1939), 27–28, for a considerable list. He notes, for instance, that the tribal name Min-p'u is an alternate of Man-p'u; that a modern Miao tribe of Kweichow calls itself Mun; that Mount Min in Szechwan is also called Mount Meng, and so on. Wiens (1954), 77 proposes the affinity of Man and Mon (of Mon-Khmer).

[35] Ruey (1938), 193, citing *Shuo wen*.

[36] Ruey (1941), passim. There were also "dog characters" for some barbarians, such as the Lao. These became very abundant in Sung and Yüan times.

[37] *Shih ching,* T'ung kung, Ts'ai ch'i. Legge's translation hardly captures the squirming image: "Foolish were the savage tribes of King, Presuming to oppose our great region."

[38] Ruey (1938), 182.

[39] Li (1928), 241. Ruey distinguishes these from the more primitive Lao of the same region.

[40] Wiens (1954), 81.

[41] Wiens (1954), 124. Ruey (1957), 128–129 criticizes Eberhard on the ground that he distinguishes Lao, Yao, Thai, and Yüeh (Viet) in southernmost China in the third millenium B.C., though the Chinese sources of the earliest period have only "Viet."

[42] *Chuang tzu,* Shao-yao yu.

[43] Aurousseau (1923), 234; Li (1928), 245.

[44] Li (1928), 246.

[45] Coedès (1962), 45. Madrolle (1937), 311–312 writes of Moi ("Indonesian") and Muong elements in early Vietnamese language and culture.

[46] Coedès (1962), 45.

[47] See Aurousseau (1923), 260–261.

[48] Li (1928), 246.

[49] Wiens (1954), 170–171, 178.

[50] Lattimore (1962), 91.

[51] Lattimore (1955), 115–117; Lattimore (1962), 104.

[52] Spencer (1940), 163–164; Lattimore (1962), 90.

[53] For the early history of the Chinese expansion southward, see Maybon (1919), 238–244; Aurousseau (1923), passim; Maspero (1924), passim; Wiens (1954), 130–141; Coedès (1962), 43–53. Maspero provides a good check on some rash affirmations by Aurousseau.

[54] YTCS, passim. E.g., Ch'in (K'yĕm)-chou is described as beyond the ancient known world (119, 1a, quoting YHC). YTCS, 89, 1b notes that TS puts all of Lingnan beyond the archaic province of Liang-chou.

[55] TT, 187, 997a.

[56] KLFTC, p. 1.

[57] TT, 187, 997a. I follow Maspero (1924), 389, in rejecting the notion that Hsiang was in Tongking. He points out that in A.D. 76 its territory was divided between Tsang-ko and Yü-lin; that is to say, it lay northeast of Nan-hai, not southeast of it.

[58] Wiens (1954), 134; Coedès (1962), 49.

[59] HS, 95, 0603d.

[60] Wiens (1954), 135.

[61] Wiens (1954), 136.

[62] HS, 6, 0306a; CTS, 41, 24a; YTCS, 89, 2a.

[63] Coedès (1962), 46–47. This is the era of the Han brick tombs in Tongking. For a complete account of Ma Yüan's expedition, see Maspero (1918), 11–28.

[64] Wiens (1954), 85. For Hunan during this period see Wiens (1954), 86; for Lingnan see Wiens (1954), 141.

[65] TT, 187, 997a.

[66] I owe the term "chapels" in this context to Sitwell (1962), 75.

[67] Stein (1947), 217–218; 229–230. Stein suggests the possible affinity of Chin-lin "Frontier of Gold" with these names. He draws attention also to the similarity of the

name of the modern Khmu people (p. 246).

⁶⁸ Coedès (1962), 61. Perhaps this earliest nation in Cambodia was ethnically Mon rather than Khmer.

⁶⁹ Coedès (1962), 62. Suvaṇṇabhūmi is Pali; Suvarṇakudya occurs in Sanskrit texts.

⁷⁰ Coedès (1962), 61–62.

⁷¹ Aymonier (1891), 189.

⁷² For the early history of Champa see Coedès (1962), 66–70.

⁷³ Allied to *K'un-lun* et al.

⁷⁴ Ferrand (1919), 313–314.

⁷⁵ Coedès (1948), 77; Coedès (1962), 66. The name "Champa" does not appear in epigraphy until early in the seventh century. Coedès (1948), 79.

⁷⁶ Coedès (1948), 78, 85; Coedès (1962), 66.

⁷⁷ Coedès (1962), 67–68. The names of early Cham kings in Chinese histories do not agree with the Sanskrit titles in the inscriptions. Stein explained this by saying that the kings of Lin-i known to the Chinese were not the same as the Sanskrit-named kings further south (Amarāvatī was in Quang-nam province) whose land was later conquered by Lin-i. See Coedès (1948), 85.

⁷⁸ Coedès (1962), 67.

⁷⁹ Coedès (1948), 99.

⁸⁰ In A.D. 413. Aymonier (1891), 190.

⁸¹ Aymonier (1891), 190; Coedès (1948), 99.

⁸² Aymonier (1891), 190–191; Coedès (1948), 121.

CHAPTER 2 (Pages 18–47)

¹ TCTC, 188, 5a, and elsewhere. This source records many examples of resistance to T'ang dominion in the Wu Te (618–626) reign, and some in later eras.

² TCTC, 188, 9a.

³ Envoys of the Eastern and Southern Hsieh came to the T'ang court on January 29 of that year; chiefs of the Tsang-ko, also surnamed Hsieh, sent tribute on February 16. TCTC, 193, 7a. Cf. TC, 197 3158a.

⁴ TCTC, 198, 16a–16b.

⁵ TCTC, 202, 2a. Cf. TCTC, 199, 13a; TCTC, 200, 3a, for other peoples of Yunnan.

⁶ Coedès (1962), 51.

⁷ TS, 90, 7b; Bui (1963), 30.

⁸ TCTC, 190, 4a–4b.

⁹ TCTC, 190, 5a.

¹⁰ See events of 620 in TCTC, 188, 15a.

¹¹ TCTC, 190, 6a.

¹² TS, 43a, 9b; TPHYC, 170, 2b; Coedès (1962), 51; Bui (1963), 31.

¹³ Maspero (1910), 550.

¹⁴ See Introduction.

¹⁵ YTCS, 89, 3b–4a.

¹⁶ YHC, 34, 1004; Han Yü, quoted in YTCS, 89, 8a.

¹⁷ Among the many changes made in this administrative system a few of the more important follow: Annam was called Chen-nan between the years 757 and 768 (TPHYC, 170, 2b–3a; Bui [1963], 32); the Yung Administration was abolished in 820 and its territory incorporated in that of Jung, but it was reestablished in 822 (TCTC, 241, 10b; 242, 13a; TPHYC, 166, 3b); the traditional fivefold division was abolished in June of 862, and replaced by two great Tao "Routes," an eastern, governed by a "Measuring and Ruling Legate" from Canton, and a western, governed by a Legate from Yung (TCTC, 250, 10a–10b; YTCS, 106, 4a–4b); after the recovery of Annam from the Nan-chao invaders the Protectorate was renamed "Sea-Quieting Army" (*Ching hai chün*) in 866 and ruled by a Legate (TCTC, 250, L9a).

¹⁸ TCTC, 256, 6a.

¹⁹ Schafer (1954), 351.

²⁰ TCTC, 262, 3a.

²¹ TCTC, 261, 4b.

²² TCTC, 262, 4b.

[23] TCTC, 263, 12a.

[24] TCTC, 265, 4b–5a.

[25] Schafer (1954), 351.

[26] Schafer (1954), 352–353.

[27] Bui (1963), 33–34.

[28] Chang Chi, "Sung nan ch'ien k'o," ChTS, han 6, ts'e 6, ch. 3, 2a.

[29] For the names of these roads I follow Aoyama (1963), 8. For details of the five great mountain passes into Lingnan see Aurousseau (1923), 142–152.

[30] See, for instance, Schafer (1963), 17.

[31] Chang Chiu-ling, "K'ai Ta yü ling lu chi," CTW, 291, 1a–2a.

[32] His itinerary took him directly to Canton in 809. But CTS, 160, 8b, says that he became chief magistrate of Kuei-chou in 810. Presumably he paid his respects to his superior in the chief city first.

[33] YHC, 34, 1020.

[34] YHC, 34, 1019.

[35] Li Ao, "Lai nan lu," CTW, 638, 9b–11b.

[36] Wu (1962), 229.

[37] Schafer (1961), 66. These rocks are also referred to by Yüan Chen in his "Sung Ts'ui shih yü chih Ling-nan," ChTS, han 6, ts'e 9, ch. 11, 4a.

[38] YTCS, 90, 11a. Traces of Chao T'o's wall were still visible in Sung times.

[39] TS, 43a, 1b.

[40] TS, 43a, 1b. The site of Chang's house was still venerated here in Sung times. See YTCS, 90, 11b.

[41] YTCS, 90, 7a–7b, chiefly quoting from YHC.

[42] YTCS, 90, 8a–10b.

[43] Aoyama (1963), 8.

[44] TS, 43a, 6b; YHC, 37, 1038.

[45] YTCS, 103, 12b.

[46] YTCS, 103, 13a, quoting YHC.

[47] Han Yü, "Sung Kuei-chou Yen Ta-fu t'ung yung nan tzu," ChTS, han 5, ts'e 12, ch. 9, 3a.

[48] YTCS, 103, 11a.

[49] YTCS, 103, 13b. It is not certain if this is the same stele on Shun Mountain referred to in this source on p. 8a.

[50] YTCS, 103, 14a.

[51] Li Shang-yin, "Kuei-lin," YCSSHC, 2, 3b–4a.

[52] There were other notable engineering achievements here, such as the "Wave-turning Dyke," built in 798 to break the force of the Kuei. TS, 43a, 6b; YTCS, 103, 9a and 12b, quoting T'ang sources.

[53] Spencer (1954), 32. For the history of the canal and a description of its present condition, with a map, see Lapicque (1911), 425–428.

[54] TS, 118, 14b.

[55] KLFTC, 4.

[56] TS, 43a, 6b; TS, 118, 14b; TPHYC, 162, 8b; Roy (1963), 42.

[57] TCTC, 250, 14a.

[58] TS, 43a, 6b.

[59] Yü Meng-wei, "Kuei-chou ch'ung hsiu Ling ch'ü chi," CTW, 104, 10a–12b.

[60] TCTC, 253, 14a.

[61] YTCS, 103, 8b.

[62] CTS, 41, 24a says it was short for *Kuang-chou tu-tu-fu*, established in 624.

[63] Pelliot (1959), 275.

[64] Nakamura (1917), 247.

[65] HNYC, cited in TPHYC, 157, 8b; YHC, cited in YTCS, 89, 9b. The date of the *Hsü Nan Yüeh chih* is unknown; presumably it is late T'ang or tenth century.

[66] HNYC, cited in TPHYC, 157, 8b.

[67] Balazs (1932), 23, 56. Balazs cites the testimony of Abu Zayd for 878, the supposed year of Huang Ch'ao's raid, to the effect that there were 120,000 foreign merchants living in the city. Probably these aliens were not included in the official census. TS, 43a, 1a, gives the registered population of the whole county (including thirteen townships) as 221,-500.

[68] Nakamura (1917), 487–488.

[69] Balazs (1932), 55.

[70] Nakamura (1917), 558; Wang (1958), 82–84.

[71] Nakamura (1917), 560.

[72] Schafer (1954), 352.

[73] Chang Chi, "Sung Cheng shang shu

ch'u chen Nan-hai," ChTS, han 6, ts'e, ch. 3, 20b.

[74] TS, 43a, 1a.

[75] This mound was confused with another, sometimes called Ch'ao Han t'ai, west of the city, from which Chao T'o offered (it is said) distant homage to the ruler of Han in the north. But no doubt there were a number of such structures connected by tradition with his famous name. See KCC (quoted in TPHYC, 157, 6b). YTCS, 89, 16b, places the Terrace of the King of Viet on the grounds of the Sung Buddhist temple Wu hsing szu.

[76] YTCS, 89, 17a–17b.

[77] For these and other relics, see YTCS, 89, 15b–17b, which frequently quotes YHC. In Sung times both of these sites were on the grounds of Buddhist temples.

[78] TS, 43a, 1a.

[79] Wheatley (1963), 178.

[80] TS, 43a, 1b.

[81] TS, 43a, 2a.

[82] TS, 43a, 3b.

[83] TS, 43a, 4a.

[84] Coedès (1962), 52.

[85] TS, 43a, 8a.

[86] TS, 43a, 4a–4b.

[87] TS, 43a, 8a; TPHYC, 167, 4a.

[88] STC, in TPYL, 172, 9b; CKC, in YTCS, 121, 6a.

[89] TS, 222c, 16b; TCTC, 190, 4a–4b.

[90] Spencer (1954), 32; Wiens (1954), 11.

[91] TS, 43a, 8b. This work was done during the reign period 860–873.

[92] TCTC, 250, 19b; T'ung (1937), 12.

[93] NYC, b, 3a.

[94] Maspero (1910), 552–554; Coedès (1962), 51. TS, 43a, 9b, gives 99, 652 taxable persons.

[95] TS, 43a, 9b.

[96] T'ung (1937), 11.

[97] Lu Kuei-meng, "Feng ho Kung Mei Wu chung yen huai chi Nan-hai erh t'ung nien," ChTS, han 9, ts'e 10, ch. 9, 7b.

[98] T'ung (1937), 12. T'ung tells of it as the wall of Lung-pien, apparently an anachronism. See Maspero (1910), 556–559 for a history of T'ang wall-building in this region.

[99] T'ung (1937), 12 gives a circumference of 19,805 feet.

[100] TCTC, 250, 19b.

[101] TS, 43a, 9b.

[102] Lu Chih, "Lung Ling-nan ch'ing yü An-nan chih shih p'o chung shih chuang," CTW, 473, 14a–14b.

[103] YHC, 38, 189.

[104] Pelliot (1904), 141.

[105] Wiens (1954), 142, 195; Twitchett (1959), 190.

[106] TCTC, 251, 1a–1b.

[107] TCTC, 253, 17a; TCTC, 255, 3b.

[108] TCTC, 253, 17a.

[109] Malleret (1934), 61–64.

[110] Han Yü, Preface to "Sung Cheng shang shu," HCLCC, 21, 10b.

[111] TS, 170, 5a; cf. CTS, 151, 5b.

[112] Ts'en Ts'an, "Sung Yang Yüan wei Nan-hai," ChTS, han 3, ts'e 8, ch. 3, 7b.

[113] TS, 130, 4a–4b.

[114] TS, 131, 3b; CTS, 131, 2a; Nakamura (1917), 356–357.

[115] TS, 170, 4b–5a; CTS, 151, 5b; Nakamura (1917), 360.

[116] TCTC, 238, 14b; TS, 175, 1b; CTS, 155, 5b.

[117] Nakamura (1917), 364–365; Schafer (1962b), 204–208. Other officials who attempted to deal fairly with the Cantonese merchants early in the ninth century were Hsü Shen and Li Ao. See Nakamura (1917), 360.

[118] TS, 80, 11a; CTS, 131, 5b.

[119] TCTC, 242, 13a.

[120] TS, 182, 6a.

[121] KTTC, p. 4126a. I have not found the original T'ang source for this interesting passage.

[122] TCTC, 250, 11b.

[123] Han Yü, "Sung Cheng shang shu fu Nan-hai," HCLCC, 10, 8b–9a.

[124] TCTC, 248, 12b.

[125] NPHS, a, 7.

[126] TCTC, chs. 264–265.

[127] TCTC, 243, 15b.

[128] TCTC, 252, 8b.

[129] TCTC, 205, 8a–8b.

[130] TCTC, 234, 9b.

[131] TCTC, 237, 6b.

[132] TCTC, 245, 3a.

[133] CTS, 177, 9a.

[134] Waley (1963), 167–168.

[135] Liu (1962), 55.

[136] Shen Ch'üan-ch'i, "Ch'u ta Huan-chou," ChTS, han 2, ts'e 5, ch. 2, 8a.

[137] Malleret (1934), 128.

[138] Liu Ch'ang-ch'ing, "Ju kuei chu tz'u sha niu shih hsüeh," ChTS, han 3, ts'e 1, ch. 5, 17a.

[139] TS, 202, 2b; CTS, 190b, 9b. Sung was banished a second time by Jui Tsung, this time to Ch'in-chou.

[140] Sung Chih-wen, "Tsao fa Shih-hsing chiang k'ou chih Hsü shih ts'un tso," ChTS, han 1, ts'e 10, ch. 3, 5b.

[141] Sung Chih-wen, "Tsao fa Shao-chou," ChTS, han 1, ts'e 10, ch. 3, 8a.

[142] Sung Chih-wen, "Ju Shuang-chou chiang," ChTS, han 1, ts'e 10, ch. 3, 4b.

[143] Sung Chih-wen, "Tsai Kuei-chou yü hsiu shih hsüeh shih Wu Ching shu," CTW, 240, 14a.

[144] TCTC, 239, 8b; Han Yü, "Liu Tzu-hou mu chih ming," HCLCC, 32, 6b; Wu (1962), 226.

[145] CTS, 160, 9a–9b; Hsü (1939), 295; Miyakawa (1960), 40.

[146] Wu (1962), 221.

[147] Wu (1962), 225.

[148] Liu Tsung-yüan, "Ch'ung pieh Meng-te," LHSC, 42, 18b.

[149] Wu (1962), 230.

[150] Wu (1962), 236–237.

[151] Liu Tsung-yüan, "Chi Wei Hsing," LHSC, 42, 9a.

[152] Liu Tsung-yüan, "Hsia chou ou tso," LHSC, 43, 9b.

[153] Liu Tsung-yüan, "Teng Liu-chou O-shan," LHSC, 42, 14a.

[154] Wu (1962), 247. Wu is little interested in Liu's obvious sensitivity to nature; he regrets, in a rather formal Marx-ist way, his relative indifference to social and economic conditions.

[155] Liu Tsung-yüan, "Fang che-ku tz'u," LHSC, 43, 16b.

[156] TS, 176, 1a–6a.

[157] TS, 180, 9a–9b.

[158] Li Te-yü, "Che Ling-nan tao chung tso," LWKC, pieh chi, 4, 204.

[159] Ibid., and "Tao wu ch'i yeh po Lu tao," LWKC, pieh chi, 4, 204–205.

[160] Li Te-yü, "Teng Yai-chou ch'eng tso," LWKC, pieh chi, 4, 205.

[161] PMSY, 8, 67.

[162] Li (1928), 236. This route was determined by a study of the growth of town populations. After descending to Canton, immigration continued mainly westward along the coast toward Annam, and to a certain extent north from Lien (Lyem)-chou into modern Kwangsi. See Li (1928), 251–252.

[163] CYCT, 1, 5b.

[164] WTS, 65, 4468d.

[165] TS, 126, 7a–10a; CTS, 99, 6a–8b. His predecessor in the ministry, Chang Yüeh, had noticed the young man while he was in temporary exile in Canton and advanced his career in the central government.

[166] CSYC (in TTTS, 4), 18a.

[167] TCTC, 214, 10a.

[168] Chang Chiu-ling, "Hsün an tzu Li shui nan hsing," ChTS, han 1, ts'e 9, ch.

[169] Chang Chiu-ling, "Kan yü, shih erh shou," (No. 7), ChTS, han 1, ts'e 9, ch. 1, 10a–10b.

[170] Chang Chiu-ling, "Ch'u fa Ch'ü-chiang ch'i chung," ChTS, han 1, ts'e 9, ch. 2, 9b.

[171] Chang Chiu-ling, "Yü ti yu chia yüan," ChTS, han 1, ts'e 9, ch. 3, 11a–11b.

[172] Chang Chiu-ling, "Shih-an nan shan hsia . . . yu huai tz'u ti," ChTS, han 1, ts'e 9, ch. 1, 7b; and cf. "Pieh hsiang jen nan huan," ChTS, han 1, ts'e 9, ch. 3, 7a, written to a fellow townsman returning to the south.

[173] YTCS, 93, 6a.

[174] Liu Yü-hsi, "Tiao Chang Ch'ü-chiang," LMTWC, 2, 5b; ChTS, han 6, ts'e 2, ch. 1, 2b.

CHAPTER 3 (Pages 48–78)

[1] Ruey (1957), 749. See TT, 187, 999a–999c for the early history of the Lao, and an account of their customs. Tai (1948), 55 notes the earliest occurrence of the name "Lao" in Chang Hua, *Po wu chih* (third century), as among the peoples southwest of Ching-chou. From this century they became very prominent in history, especially as a plague to the peasantry of that region (CS, 121, 1390a); WS is the first dynastic history to have a special section dedicated to them (WS, 101, one of the restored chapters). Cf. Pelliot (1904), 136–137.

[2] To Chih-chou in the east, Yü-chou in the south, Fu-chou in the west. See TS, 222c, 16a; CTS, 197, 4b, and cf. TT, 187, 999a.

[3] TS, 222c, 16a–16b.

[4] Ruey (1948), 345–350. Their dwindling modern representatives are T'u-lao (=Toloman). For their culture see, with care, Eberhard (1942), 229–237; Wiens (1954), 52–53 and 95. Ling (1938), 73–76 and especially 81 relates them to the White Man; Hsü (1939), 100, says that they are ultimately the same as the Tsang-ko. Benedict (1942), 576, and Benedict (1947), 384 puts their language in his novel Kadai family, in which case it was not Thai but a cousin of both Thai and Indonesian. Forrest (1948), 96–97 also regards their language as only partly Thai.

[5] Ruey (1957), 765. Ruey has attempted to sort out the many cultural traits attributed to the Lao, but because of the loose application of the name, can find few which distinguish particular groups of non-Chinese aborigines. Eberhard (1942), heavily relied on by Wiens, though more certain of the allocation of particular traits to particular peoples, must be used with caution, because of the great chronological range of the sources.

[6] CTS, 197, 3a; TS, 222c, 13a; TT, 187, 999a; TC, 197, 3158a.

[7] Ling (1938), 62–64, believes that the Ts'uan were a "Chinese" clan of the Ch'u area in Han times which migrated to Yunnan and intermarried with the Tibeto-Burmans there. By T'ang times "Ts'uan" was taken to be an ethnic designation, and they were regarded as a Man group.

[8] TS, 222c, 10b.

[9] Ling (1938), 73–76, 81; Hsü (1947), 4, 6.

[10] TS, 222c, 11b. Ibid., 10a has a precise description of their location. Pelliot (1959), 181 states the identity of the Black Man and the Qara-Jang (Black Jang) of Marco Polo.

[11] Ling (1938), 62–64. See TT, 187, 1002c, for a contemporary account of them, and Eberhard (1942), 306–326 and Wiens (1954), 53–54 for an attempt to reconstruct their culture.

[12] Ling, loc. cit.

[13] Wiens (1954), 95; Pelliot (1904), 137; and especially Pelliot (1959), 173–176, on the doubtful racial composition of Nan-chao. See Eberhard (1942), 97–129 and Wiens (1954), 50 for a reconstruction of their culture, which was apparently under strong Tibetan influence.

[14] TS, 222c, 11a.

[15] TS, 222c, 22b; CTS, 197, 4a.

[16] Ruey (1957) presents a minute analysis of the old sources in an attempt to distinguish the traits of the different kinds of Lao, with little success. Very few points of distinction between Li, Wu-hu (for which see below) and other natives can be proved; in common Li and Wu-hu have "nest dwellings" (pile houses), bamboo bows and poison arrows, bronze arrowheads, and fondness for killing (p. 164). But a long list of characteristics is attributable to the Lao generally. These

include, in addition to others listed elsewhere, catching and eating insects and reptiles; hunting tigers, leopards, and monkeys; domestic oxen, horses, dogs, and goats; nose drinking; "mallet coiffures" (women); bearskin hats with gold and silver ornaments (chiefs); single- and double-edged swords; youthful vigor prized above age; gongs, drums, and flutes; seven-month gestation; murder compensated in goods; female initiative in marriage. See pp. 752–753 for a complete list.

[17] TPHYC, 159, 11b.

[18] TPHYC, 159, 7b.

[19] TPHYC, 164, 3a.

[20] STC, b, 23b.

[21] TS, 222c, 18a. Devéria (1886), 109 states that they moved into the Cao-bang region of Tongking in the mid-ninth century, Hsü (1939), 93 and 176 regards them as the ancient Viet people (as distinguished from the Yao), and places them particularly in the grottoes of Lo and Tou (i.e., Lo-chou and Tou-chou). He thinks that the elements Lo (La) and Ku in medieval toponymy identify their former presence. Probably these linguistic units represent particular groups, distinct from the Huang and Nung, among the Man of the Western Plain. Thus a certain Lo Ch'eng (La Zheng) was a leader in the Western Plain rebellion. G. B. Downer found, in field studies, that *tung* "grotto" now refers to upland, rice-growing plateaus in several languages of South China (Cantonese, Yao, Yunnanese, Mandarin).

[22] Yüan Chen, "Ho Lo-t'ien sung k'o yu Ling-nan, erh shih yün," ChTS, han 6, ts'e 9, ch. 12, 5b.

[23] TS, 222c, 18a.

[24] Stein (1947), 30.

[25] TPHYC, 166, 11b, puts them among the wet-rice growers, therefore presumably Thai.

[26] Li Ho, "Huang chuia tung," ChTS, han 6, ts'e 7, ch. 2, 4a.

[27] Surnames of leaders, probably representing tribal names, include Wei (Wĕi), Chou (Chou), Chen (Chin), Wu (Myu), Liao (Leu), Hsiang (Syang), Liang (Lyang). TS, 222c, 18a.

[28] TS, 222c, 18a.

[29] Liu Tsung-yüan, "Wei P'ei chung ch'eng ch'i t'ao Huang tsei chuang," LHSC, 39, 8b.

[30] TS, 222c, 18a.

[31] TS, 222c, 16a–16b.

[32] TS, 222c, 16b; TCTC, 190, 4a–4b.

[33] HCLCC, 1, 26b.

[34] TS, 222c, 18a–19b; Devéria (1886), 109. Are these the ancestors of the Thai-speaking Nung of northern Tongking?

[35] Madrolle (1937), 320; Tai (1948), 69. N- and l- are interchangeable in many south Chinese dialects, but we do not know to what extent the Chinese word for "dragon," or a recognizable cognate, was in use among the Man of T'ang times.

[36] Benedict (1947), 381.

[37] SS, 31, 2441b.

[38] KIC (in TPKC, 441), 3a–4a.

[39] TS, 222c, 18a.

[40] Liu Yü-hsi, "Mo yao ko," LMTWC, 8, 6a.

[41] Liu Yü-hsi, "Lien-chou la jih kuan Mo yao lieh shan hsi," LMTWC, 5, 2a.

[42] Li (1948), 2, 38. Li found them concentrated in Lai-po *hsien* in Kweichow.

[43] Kām (written with the Chinese character for *tung* "grotto") is the Mak word for a cave or grotto. The proposed Kam-Sui branch of Kam-tai includes Kam, Sui, T'en and Mak. Li (1948), 2–3.

[44] Stein (1947), 308; Schafer (1957), 90 (notes 97, 98). Lo Hsiang-lin regards the Tan as the ancient Viet people, and cognate to the Thai and Shan. See Lo (1934), 17, 40–41.

[45] Lo (1934), 14; Ch'en (1946), 47.

[46] Han Yü, "Ch'ing ho chün kung Fang kung mu chieh ming," CLHSC, 27, 6a.

[47] Han Yü, "Sung Cheng shang shu fu Nan-hai," CLHSC, 10, 7b.

[48] Lo (1934), 26.

[49] Ch'en (1946), 25 denies the relationship.

[50] LPLI, a, 5; Schafer (1957), 77, 90.

[51] TPHYC, 169, 2b.

[52] However their name suggests that of the Tai-speaking Tho of northern Tongking.

[53] Counties of Kao, Lei, Ch'in (K'yĕm) and Lien (Lyem). Lo (1955), 185, based on Sung information. Their culture is described for early Sung times in TPHYC, 169, 9b and 13a–13b. Their tattoos showed their rank; they murdered travellers and kept their teeth on necklaces as trophies.

[54] TCTC, 204, 2a.

[55] Tai (1948), 58; Lo (1955), 185; Ruey (1957), 764. Cf. Madrolle (1937), 329. Lo equates Li with Lei ("thunder"), and suspects an ancestral M'lai or B'lai, i.e., "Malay." But Forrest (1947), 97 gives an archaic K'lai.

[56] TPHYC, 166, 5a.

[57] Especially in Lan-ning *chün* (TT, 188, 1005a) and Sung-time Ning-chou. This was in western Kwangsi. CKC, quoted in TPHYC, 162, 9a.

[58] Tai (1948), 58; Ruey (1957), 763–764.

[59] CKC, quoted in TPHYC, 162, 9a.

[60] Little is known of the medieval Vietnamese peoples and their divisions, though Hsiung (Ghyung) seems to have been an ancient tribal name in Tongking. See PYTC, 2a; Tai (1948), 58.

[61] TS, 222c, 16a.

[62] Aurousseau (1923), 238.

[63] FYC, quoted in TPYL, 172, 10b. There was a *Fang yü chih* in 130 chapters written by Hsü K'ai of the tenth century, but it is now lost.

[64] Ling (1960), 429.

[65] Liu Yü-hsi, "Man tzu ko," LMTWC, 8, 16b.

[66] YTCS, 118, 3b, on the basis of local gazetteers of the Sung period, notes that in Lei-chou, for instance, there are three languages: "official speech" (*ḳuan yü*), understood by all government officers; "visitor speech" (*ḳ'o yü*), everyday language, presumably of the Chinese residents; "Li speech" (*li yü*), the language of the aborigines, not fully comprehensible. These would seem to represent the Chinese of the capital, the Chinese of Lingnan (proto-Cantonese?), and the Li (Loi) languages respectively. But no details are given.

[67] STC, b, 23a.

[68] LPLI, a, 5; PHL, 2, 1b–2a.

[69] Liu Tsung-yüan, "Liu-chou tung meng," LHSC, 42, 14b–15a.

[70] TT, 188, 1005a, attributes this to the ancient inhabitants of Nam-Viet; TPHYC, 166, 11b, attributes it to the Sung-time people of Kuei (Kwĕi)-chou.

[71] YCTC (T'ang or early Sung), quoted in TPYL, 172, 8a.

[72] Clark (1938), 398; ill. p. 395.

[73] NHIS, in TPKC, 483, 2a–2b. The author is unknown.

[74] TT, 188, 1005a. Tattooing, in Li Chi's opinion, is an index of the Thai peoples of China, along with the related Vietnamese. Liu (1936), 198 calls it typical of the Li people. The Li women of modern Hainan are more elaborately tattooed than the men. Stübel and Meriggi (1937), 34, 105.

[75] Chang Chi, "Sung nan k'o," ChTS, han 6, ts'e 6, ch. 3, 6a.

[76] Bishop (1938), 413. Bishop believes that they were once used by the Chinese and Japanese too. He sees in some elongated two-storey buildings with projecting second-floor galleries, found in the Yangtze region, simply pile-dwellings with the lower storey enclosed. The *nagaya* "long house" of Japan is similar. Ibid., 414–415.

[77] Coedès (1948), 86.

[78] Waley (1963), 152. The father of the Cinderella story in YYTT translated by Waley, is called "cave owner" or "grotto master," evidently a local chieftain.

[79] SAC, in TPYL, 172, 5b, referring to the Kuei (Kwei)-chou region.

[80] STC, b, 23b.

[81] SAC, in TPYL, 172, 5b, for Kuei (Kwei); TPHYC, 166, 11b, for Kuei (Kwĕi).

[82] SAC, in TPYL, 172, 5b.

[83] Liu Yü-hsi, "She t'ien hsing," LMTWC, 9, 4b–5a.

[84] Spencer (1954), 85.

[85] *Caingin* in the Philippines, *ladang* in the Indies, *tam rai* in Thailand, *taung ya* in Burma, and so on. Pelzer (1945), 16; Spencer (1954), 85. Other names are Anglo-Indian *jhoom* and *coomry,* not to mention Swedish *svedjande,* and the *sartage* of the Ardennes. Yule and Burnell (1886), 351.

[86] *She* is defined in KY (hsia p'ing, ma yün) thus: "Burn the jungle and seed the field." See Eberhard (1942), 74–76 for burnt-field agriculture among the Yao and other tribes in China. For detailed description of both shifting and sedentary cultivation (wet and dry), see Pelzer (1945), 16–78. In modern China (eastern Kwangtung and western Fukien), mountain-dwelling Yao people are called She. Hsü (1939), 143 regards them as the "Mountain Viet" of antiquity.

[87] Renner (1927), 60–61.

[88] Hsü Hun, "Sui mu tzu Kuang chiang chih Hsin-hsing wang fu chung t'i Hsia shan szu, szu shou," (No. 3), ChTS, han 8, ts'e 8, ch. 10, 5a.

[89] Liu Tsung-yüan, "Liu-chou tung meng," LHSC, 42, 14b–15a. See also STC, b, 23b, which gives the five-day interval. NPHS, h, 79, gives the three-day interval. NPHS puts these markets "south from Tuan-chou," i.e., in southern Kwangtung. LPLI, a, 4, notes a trading center of the aborigines at the mouth of "Stone Torrent" in Yung-chou, known therefore as "The Lao Market."

[90] STC, b, 23b.

[91] TPHYC, 167, 15a. For early Sung.

[92] CKC, in TPYL, 172, 2b.

[93] STC, b, 23b.

[94] SAC, in TPYL, 172, 5b.

[95] YCTC, quoted in TPHYC, 172, 8a. Chang (1962), 638 notes quotations from this book in Sung sources; the name of the author has been lost.

[96] NCHW, quoted in TPKC, 483, 4a.

[97] NHIS, quoted in TPKC, 483, 2b.

[98] Schafer (1963), 44.

[99] TCTC, 250, 16b.

[100] TS, 180, 4a; Schafer (1963), 45.

[101] TS, 78, 10b.

[102] Schafer (1963), 45, from CTW, 50, 6b–7a.

[103] TCTC, 237, 17a.

[104] Han Yü, "Liu Tzu-hou mu chih ming," HCLCC, 32, 6a; TS, 168, 10b; CTS, 160, 11b.

[105] CTS, 154, 2b. Cf. Schafer (1963), 45.

[106] Han Yü, "Chiang lin t'u chung chi han lin san hsüeh shih," HCLCC, 1, 26b.

[107] See especially Maspero (1950), 139–194; the contributions of Marcel Granet must not be forgotten, especially in the area of courtship and marriage.

[108] TPHYC, 167, 15a, quoted in Ling (1960), 429. This is for early Sung, but was undoubtedly also true of T'ang.

[109] TCTC, 252, 12b.

[110] TCTC, 254, 7a.

[111] Ruey (1948), 346.

[112] Schafer (1954), 354.

[113] TT, 184, 984b.

[114] YCTC, cited in TPYL, 172, 8a.

[115] STC, b, 23b.

[116] YCTC, in TPYL, 172, 8a; TT, 184, 984b.

[117] SAC, in TPYL, 172, 5b.

[118] TT, 184, 984b.

[119] TCTC, 193, 17b.

[120] TCTC, 192, 3b–4a. Reported for 7 January 627.

[121] TS, 197, 6a–6b; TCTC, 207, 11a–11b.

[122] Liu Tsung-yüan, "Wei P'ei Chung-ch'eng tsou Yung-kuan Huang chia tsei shih i chuang," LHSC, 39, 1b.

[123] Liu Tsung-yüan, "Liu-chou Wen hsüan wang hsin hsiu miao pei," LHSC, 5, 2b.

124 YTCS, 110, 3a, quoting an old local gazetteer. In Sung times this region had the additional virtue of being free of savages—assimilated or converted?

125 Lu Kuei-meng, "Ho sung Li ming fu chih jen Nan-hai," FLHSWS, 9, 26b–27a.

126 TS, 163, 14b.

127 TS, 163, 15a.

128 TS, 197. 8a.

129 So Su Tung-p'o tells us. See Han Yü, "Ch'ao chou ch'ing chih hsiang hsiao tieh," HCLCC, wai chi, 5, 3b–4a.

130 TS, 158, 3b.

131 TS, 112, 1a–1b.

132 TCTC, 249, 19a–19b. Usually the name of the nation is written with *li* "structure; texture" in its second syllable; here it has *li* "propriety."

133 TCTC, 190, 8a.

134 TCTC, 190, 12b.

135 TCTC, 190, 12b.

136 TCTC, 191, 1a.

137 TCTC, 191, 5b.

138 TS, 222c, 16b.

139 TCTC, 191, 10a.

140 TCTC, 193, 19b.

141 TS, 110, 1a; 207, 2a–4a; CTS, 184, 3a–4b.

142 TS, 222c, 17a.

143 TS, 222c, 17a; TCTC, 195, 7b.

144 TS, 222c, 17a.

145 TCTC, 199, 12a.

146 TS, 222c, 17a.

147 TCTC, 201, 3a.

148 TCTC, 201, 13a.

149 TCTC, 204, 2a; Bui (1963), 31.

150 TCTC, 205, 11b.

151 TCTC, 207, 11a–11b; CTS, 197, 6a–6b.

152 The sources disagree about his name. Shu-yen is from TCTC, 212, 10b–11a; TS, 207, 1b–2a, calls him Mei Shu-man; CTS, 184, 2a–3a, has Mei Hsüan-ch'eng. Coedès (1962), 79 and Bui (1963), 32 (from Vietnamese sources?) give Mei Shu-luan, *luan* being merely a graphic variant of *man*.

153 TCTC, 212, 10b–11a; TS, 207, 1b–2a; CTS, 184, 2a–3a.

154 TCTC, 213, 7b–8a.

155 TCTC, 213, 1a–1b.

156 TCTC, 213, 3a.

157 TCTC, 213, 7a–8a; TS, 207, 2a.

158 TS, 222c, 18a.

159 TS, 222c, 18a.

160 CTS, 157, 1a.

161 TS, 222c, 18a.

162 TS, 43a, 4a–4b.

163 TS, 222c, 17a; TCTC, 224, 7b.

164 Coedès (1962), 79; Bui (1963), 32, relying on Vietnamese annals.

165 CTS, 157, 1a; TCTC, 224, 16b. The leaders of the newest rebellions had been Liang Ch'ung-ch'ien, Chang Hou, and Hsia Yung.

166 TS, 138, 5b; TT, 188, 1007a.

167 Coedès (1962), 79, from a Sanskrit inscription.

168 TS, 166, 3b; TCTC, 233, 14a; Li Fu, "Shou fu Ch'iung-chou piao," CTW, 620, 4a–4b.

169 Aymonier (1891), 191; Coedès (1962), 79.

170 TS, 170, 8a; TCTC, 233, 16a; Coedès (1962), 79; Bui (1963), 32.

171 TS, 222c, 18b; TCTC, 234, 15b–16a.

172 TS, 222c, 18b; TCTC, 237, 8b.

173 TS, 222c, 18b; TCTC, 237, 14a.

174 TCTC, 239, 16b–17a has Man-chou for Luan-chou; I follow TS, 222c, 18b.

175 TS, 163, 2a–2b; 222c, 18b.

176 TCTC, 239, 18b.

177 Aymonier (1891), 191.

178 TCTC, 241, 8a–8b.

179 Ibid.

180 TCTC, 241, 10b; cf. Bui (1963), 32.

181 TCTC, 241, 14b.

182 Han Yü, "Huang chia tsei shih i chuang," HCLCC, 40, 4a–4b; TS, 222c, 19a; TCTC, 241, 14b–15a.

183 TCTC, 243, 1b.

184 TCTC, 243, 2b.

185 TCTC, 243, 2b; TS, 222c, 19b.

186 TCTC, 243, 3b.

[187] TCTC, 243, 4a.

[188] TCTC, 243, 8a–8b.

[189] TCTC, 243, 8a–8b.

[190] TS, 222c, 19b.

[191] TS, 222c, 19b.

[192] TCTC, 243, 19b.

[193] TCTC, 243, 19b.

[194] TCTC, 247, 13a.

[195] TCTC, 248, 13a. Bui (1963), 33 mistakenly treats these as Yunnanese invasions.

[196] TCTC, 249, 11b–12a.

[197] TCTC, 249, 13b.

[198] TCTC, 249, 15a–15b. Some texts mistakenly take these as Cham incursions.

[199] TCTC, 249, 16a.

[200] TCTC, 250, 7a.

[201] TCTC, 250, 7a–7b.

[202] TCTC, 250, 7a–7b. Cf. Bui (1963), 33.

[203] TCTC, 250, 7b.

[204] TCTC, 250, 8b.

[205] TCTC, 250, 8b–9a.

[206] TCTC, 250, 9b. Cf. Bui (1963), 33. The T'ang commander at this time was Ts'ai Hsi.

[207] TCTC, 250, 12a–13a.

[208] TCTC, 250, 12a–13a.

[209] TCTC, 250, 12b–13a. Cf. Bui (1963), 33.

[210] TCTC, 250, 13a.

[211] TCTC, 250, 13b.

[212] TCTC, 250, 13b.

[213] TCTC, 250, 15a.

[214] TCTC, 250, 15b.

[215] TCTC, 250, 16a; Cf. Bui (1963), 33.

[216] TCTC, 250, 16b–17a.

[217] TCTC, 250, 17a; Cf. Bui (1963), 33.

[218] TCTC, 250, 18b.

[219] TCTC, 250, 19a–19b. Cf. Bui (1963), 33.

[220] TCTC, 253, 15b.

[221] TCTC, 259, 19b.

[222] TCTC, 259, 2b.

[223] TCTC, 259, 19a–19b.

[224] Wang (1963), 11.

[225] TCTC, 254, 15a.

[226] TS, 129, 2a.

[227] I owe this idea to Lattimore (1962), 170.

[228] YHC, 37, 1047.

[229] Lattimore (1955), 115.

[230] TCTC, 188, 9a.

[231] TS, 222c, 16a–16b.

[232] TCTC, 218, 1a–1b.

[233] TCTC, 201, 17b.

[234] TS, 45, 6a–6b; cf. Rotours (1932), 47, 283–284.

[235] SC, 117, 0257c.

[236] TS, 43b, 1a. Cf. CTS, 197, 4a; TT, 187, 997a; Pelliot (1904), 140–141.

[237] The official figures are Kuei (7); Yung (26); Annam (41); Feng (18). For a period late in the eighth century at least, both Huan and Feng, on the outskirts of Annam, were designated "protectorates" (*tu-tu-fu*) to govern these new subjects. TS, 43b, 13b; 222c, 16a; Wiens (1954), 210.

[238] It became Lu-chou. TS, 184, 1a; CTS, 176, 8b.

[239] TS, 43b, 14a–14b.

[240] Coedès (1962), 79.

[241] TS, 222c, 1a.

[242] Coedès (1962), 79.

[243] TS, 222c, 1a–1b; CTS, 197, 1a.

[244] CTS, 197, 1a. For fire orbs in T'ang see Schafer (1963), 237–239.

[245] Stern (1942), 8.

[246] Coedès (1962), 79.

[247] Aymonier (1891), 196.

[248] Parmentier (1901), 246–251; Stern (1942), 9.

[249] Coedès (1962), 79.

[250] Stern (1942), 9.

[251] Coedès (1962), 79–80.

[252] Stern (1942), 9–10; Coedès (1962), 80.

[253] Stern (1942), 11.

[254] Stern (1942), 109–110.

[255] Aymonier (1891), 203.

[256] Finot (1901), 14–15. This image of Bhagavatî (Umâ) is still venerated by the Vietnamese.

257 Aymonier (1891), 203–204.

258 TCTC, 190, 12a; TPHYC, 171, 14b–15a; Stein (1947), 124.

259 TCTC, 190, 12a; TS, 222c, 1b.

260 See Maspero (1928), 87; Coedès (1948), 122.

261 For the equivalence, see Soothill and Hodous (1937), 471–473.

262 TCTC, 193, 12a–12b; TS, 222c, 1b. TCTC gives the Turkish ruler's name as Hsieh-li (Ghet-li) Qaghan. This seems to be a form related to Turkish *küli/ külüg/kül* "famed, renowned," a frequent element in Turkish royal titles, for which information I am indebted to my colleague J. E. Bosson.

263 TPHYC, 171, 14b–15a; Stein (1947), 124–125.

264 TS, 222c, 1b; TCTC, 238, 2b.

265 Aymonier (1891), 206.

266 Maspero (1928), 14.

267 Benedict (1941), 129–130, 134.

268 Benedict (1941), 129.

269 Aymonier (1891), 206.

270 WTS, 74, 4480d.

271 WTS, 12, 4405a; 74, 4480d; Maspero (1928), 119.

272 SuS, 489, 5714c.

273 SuS, 489, 5714b.

274 Maspero (1928), 13.

275 Ibn Khordādzbeh and Sulaymān, quoted in Ferrand (1914), 30, 40.

276 Schafer (1963), 15–16.

277 Tu Hsün-ho, "Tseng yu jen pa chü fu Chiao-chih p'i ming, "ChTS, han 10, ts'e 8, ch. 2, 8b.

278 Lo (1960), 13.

279 An Yeh-na (An Ya-na).

280 Ts'ao Yeh-na (Dzau Ya-na).

281 Lo (1962), 74. For the dance, see Schafer (1963), 56.

282 Lo (1962), 76.

283 Liu Yü-hsi, "Tsai ch'ou Ma fu jen," LMTWC, wai chi, 5, 8a.

284 Han Yü, Preface to "Sung Cheng shang shu," HCLCC, 11a.

285 TCTC, 253, 13a–14a; the Arabic source puts the capture of Canton in 878, a year early. Reinaud (1845), 64.

286 TCTC, 253, 14a.

287 Nakamura (1917), 248–249.

288 CTS, 163, 2b.

289 TS, 158, 3b.

290 Nakamura (1917), 361–364; Schafer (1963), 16, 208. Piratical raids also had something to do with this; see above, under "Roads and Cities."

291 TS, 4, 14a.

292 TS, 176, 1a; Nakamura (1917), 351–352, 355–356; 362; Schafer (1963), 16.

293 TCTC, 245, 18a.

294 Nakamura (1917), 353; Wada (1960), passim.

295 Liu Tsung-yüan, "Ling-nan Chieh tu shih hsiang chün t'ang chi," LHSC, 26, 6a.

296 Liu Tsung-yüan, "Ts'ao ch'i ti liu tsu szu i Ta-chien Ch'an-shih pei," LHSC, 6, 1a–2b.

CHAPTER 4 (Pages 79–86)

1 Said most vociferously by Eduard Erkes and Erwin Rousselle.

2 See Erkes (1935), passim, for a rather strong summary of this point of view. Erkes thought (p. 172) that a change to "patriarchal" customs was underway at an accelerating rate already in late Shang times. Important scholarly studies of women in archaic myth, ritual, and literature have been made in China by Wen I-to, T'ao Hsi-sheng, and others.

3 Erkes (1935), 173.

4 Rousselle (1941), 142–143.

5 Whitehead (1949), ch. 1, p. 5.

6 Rousselle (1941), 131.

7 Bishop (1938), 411: "Goddesses and 'priestesses' (the latter often nothing more than female shamans or exorcists) play a conspicuous role in religious belief and observance. There are traces of a former matriarchate with female rulers, and of a custom of brother-and-sister marriage, at least among ruling families."

[8] HS, 27c, a, 0415b.

[9] Stein (1942), 66 ff.

[10] NPHS, e, 48. Cf. Schafer (1963) 286, n. 205. Pelliot notes that "P'u-sa-man" was used as a song title already by Li Po in the eighth century. Pelliot (1963), 721–723.

[11] Pelliot (1963) 721.

[12] Pelliot (1963), 723.

[13] TCTC, 43, 9b; TT, 184, 978a. Cf. Brodrick (1942), 88.

[14] TCTC, 43, 11b.

[15] NYC, 3a. Cf. TPHYC, 171, 5b. Her dates are not known, but she would appear to have lived in early post-Han times.

[16] YTCS, 118, 6a.

[17] YYTT, hsü 1, 172–173.

[18] Waley (1963), 154.

[19] NHIS, in TPKC, 483, 2a.

[20] THTL, in TPKC, 483, 5a–5b.

[21] Malleret (1934), 222.

[22] See for instance Liu (1962), 57.

[23] Li Po, "Sung Chu Pa chih hung tu fu te wan sha shih," LTPWC, 15, 3b. Li Po provides other examples of this theme in a series of *Yüeh nü tz'u*.

[24] Wang Ch'ang-ling, "Ts'ai lien ch'ü," ChTS, han 2, ts'e 10, ch. 4, 3a.

[25] Han Yü, "Liu sheng shih," HCLCC, 4, 1a.

[26] Baxter (1953), 143. Compare also the "P'u-sa-man" song of Wei Chuang, translated in Liu (1962), 56. Wei Chuang was a refugee south of the Yangtze during Huang Ch'ao's rebellion. He expressed the hope that he might end his days in that beautiful country.

[27] HCC.

[28] MTKH, 2, 10b.

[29] HYPT. An abundance of quotations from his writings on materia medica survive in PTKM.

[30] Seventeen by Li Hsün in this style are among fifty-four of his *tz'u* preserved in ChTS, han 12, ts'e 10, but only ten appear in our edition of HCC, 10, 6a–7a. All presumably derive from the old collection of his poems *Ch'iung yao chi*. There are also three *shih* under his name in ChTS, han 11, ts'e 6. Eight *Nan hsiang tzu* by Ou-yang Chiung are in the same volume of ChTS (also in HCC, 6, 1b–2a); there are also four (two paired stanzas) by Feng Yen-chi. Ou-yang Chiung is reputed to be the originator of the originator of the single stanza form, Feng Yen-chi of the double stanza form.

[31] CFC (in TTTS, 8), 87a. It has been claimed by Hu Shih that some of the song titles listed in this eighth-century catalogue are later interpolations—*P'u-sa-man* is an example. See Baxter (1953), 119, n. 41. But despite the tale of the origin of that song in the ninth-century visit of jeweled ladies, it might have had earlier beginnings.

[32] Baxter (1953), 130.

[33] Ou-yang Chiung, "Nan hsiang tzu," ChTS, han 12, ts'e 10, ch. 8, 13a.

[34] Ou-yang Chiung, "Nan hsiang tzu," ChTS, han 12, ts'e 10, ch. 8, 13a.

[35] Ou-yang Chiung, "Nan hsiang tzu," ChTS, han 12, ts'e 10, ch. 8, 13a.

[36] Ou-yang Chiung, "Nan hsiang tzu," ChTS, han 12, ts'e 10, ch. 8, 13a.

[37] Li Hsün, "Nan hsiang tzu," ChTS, han 12, ts'e 10, ch. 8, 2a–2b.

[38] Sitwell (1959), 286.

CHAPTER 5 (Pages 87–114)

[1] PYTC, 1a. Cf. above, under "Roads and Cities."

[2] CS, 72, 1272a.

[3] YTCS, 89, 22a.

[4] Soymié (1956), 22.

[5] KLFTC, 7; YTCS, 213, 10a.

[6] KLFTC, 8.

[7] KLFTC, 6.

[8] PKLT, 5, 28a; Soymié (1956), 20.

[9] TCTC, 248, 12a.

[10] CTW, 928, 10a; TCTC, 249, 13a.

[11] TCTC, 249, 14a.

[12] TKSP (TTTS, 2), 67a.

[13] CTW, 928, 10a.

[14] TYTP (TTTS, 2), 59b–61a.

[15] P'i Jih-hsiu, "Chi t'i Lo-fou Hsüan-yüan hsien sheng so chü," ChTS, han 9, ts'e 9, ch. 7, 12a–12b.

[16] *Hung ts'ui* "red halcyon" is the name of a mountain bird says PKLT, 5, 28a. This could well be *Halcyon coromanda* (= *Callialcyon lilacina*) the Eastern Ruddy Kingfisher, a red bird of the high forests of the Himalayas, not common in south China and Southeast Asia. See Caldwell (1931), 219.

[17] Lu Kuei-meng, "Ho chi t'i Lo-fou Hsüan-yüan hsien sheng so chü," FLHSWC, 9, 27a and ChTS, han 9, ts'e 10, ch. 9, 6b.

[18] Lo (1960), 8–9.

[19] Lo (1960), 11.

[20] YTCS, 89, 22a–22b.

[21] Lo (1960), 19.

[22] Lo (1960), 3, 11, 17, 29–30.

[23] Lo (1960), 3; illustrated in Pl. 9.

[24] Lo (1960), 3; illustrated in Pl. 14.

[25] Lo (1960), 3; illustrated in Pl. 16.

[26] Lo (1960), 177–178. The shrine is mentioned in the romantic wonder tale of Ts'ui Wei, preserved in TPKC, 34.

[27] Lo (1960), 2, 22–24.

[28] Liu Tsung-yüan, "Liu-chou fu Ta yün szu chi," LHSC, 28, 4b–5a.

[29] THTL, in TPKC, 483, 4a–4b. I emend *shih lang* to read *shih niang*.

[30] Soymié (1956), 5. Soymié (p. 6) also tells of a translator of scriptures, Huai-ti, who moved from the court to Lo-fou in 713 and founded a monastery there. He does not mention his ethnic origin.

[31] TPKC, 96, 5b–7a.

[32] YTCS, 90, 14a, gives examples for Shao-chou; 97, 7b, for Hsin-chou; and also for some other places.

[33] YTCS, 89, 22a–22b; Schafer (1957), 79. It must be confessed that this statement is based on late Sung and Yüan sources.

[34] Sung Chih-wen, "Tzu Heng-yang

chih Shao-chou yeh Neng ch'an shih," ChTS, han 1, ts'e 10, ch. 1, 5a.

[35] Ruey (1948), 346; Chan (1963), 30–31.

[36] SKSC, 754c. This biography has been blamed for incorporating much legendary material. Chan (1963), 11. See also Lo (1960), 20–21.

[37] Chan (1963), 7–18.

[38] Chan (1963), 20. It was included in the Ming (1440) canon; but an earlier version of it was found at Tun-huang by Aurel Stein. The sermon was recorded by his disciples, and is thought to be genuine; there are other later and less reliable parts, including an autobiography. Cf. Lo (1960), 3.

[39] Chan (1963), 148–149.

[40] Lo (1960), 85 and Pl. 4.

[41] Wang Wei, "Neng ch'ang shih pei," WYCCC, 25, 1a–3b.

[42] Liu Tsung-yüan, "Ts'ao ch'i ti liu tsu szu shih Ta chien ch'an shih pei," LHSC, 6, 1a–2b.

[43] His attack on a Buddhist relic is "Lun fo ku piao," HCLCC, 39, 3b–6a.

[44] Han Yü, "Yüan kuei," HCLCC, 9b–10a.

[45] Han Yü, "Ch'ao-chou chi wen," HCLCC, 22, 12a.

[46] Han Yü, "Ch'ü-chiang chi lung wen," HCLCC, 23, 5a.

[47] Han Yü, "Chi Liu Tzu-hou wen," HCLCC, 23, 1b–2a.

[48] Li Shang-yin, in FNWC, 5, 3a–4b.

[49] TCTC, 213, 13b.

[50] Schafer (1963b), 158–159.

[51] It is said that P'an-chou in coastal Kwangtung had the unique distinction of two such images; an extra one was ordered there by that great eunuch Kao Li-shih, whose birthplace it was. TPHYC, 161, 11b.

[52] YTCS, 90, 5a–6b.

[53] Erkes (1939), 309–313.

[54] Eberhard (1942a), 266, 269; Stein (1947), 186, 292. Eberhard thinks that

Shun's cult originated in eastern China and was transferred later to the far south, where he was a god of rice agriculture.

[55] SSYI, 1–2.

[56] Sung Chih-wen, "Kuei-chou Huang t'ang Shun tz'u," ChTS, han 1, ts'e 10, ch. 3, 5a.

[57] KLFTC, 1.

[58] Chang Chiu-ling, "Chi Shun miao wen," CTW, 293; 10a–10b.

[59] FNWC, 5, 4b–5b.

[60] Wang Wei, "Ho ku yüeh piao," CTW, 324, 2b–4a.

[61] Tu Kuang-t'ing, "Wang Miao-hsiang," CHL, quoted in TPKC, 61, 1a–3b.

[62] Yüan Chen, "Ho Lo-t'ien sung k'o yu Ling-nan, erh shih yün," ChTS, han 6, ts'e 9, ch. 12, 6a.

[63] Li Shang-yin, "Sai Yüeh wang shen wen," FNWC, 5, 5b–6a.

[64] TT, 184, 978b.

[65] "Ts'ui Wei," CC, in TPKC, 34, 2a–6b.

[66] Kaltenmark (1948), 1–2.

[67] HHS, 54, 0747c.

[68] Stein (1947), 147.

[69] Stein (1947), 147, 185.

[70] Stein (1947), 169.

[71] Stein (1947), 157.

[72] Stein (1947), 169, 197; Kaltenmark (1948), 48, 57.

[73] Stein (1947), 161.

[74] LPLI, a, 3–4.

[75] TS, 163, 15a.

[76] YTCS, 119, 5b.

[77] TS, 222c, 1a.

[78] CKC, quoted in YTCS, 121, 4a.

[79] Stein (1947), 153–155. Stein points out that most of this lore—building and submerged bronze boats—has also been attributed to Li Ping in Szechwan. There were also bronze oxen: Kaltenmark reconstructs an ox god cult among the coastal peoples of Nam-Viet, exemplified in bronze ox images and actual water buffaloes, a restrainer of water demons.

See Kaltenmark (1948), 36–39. I do not yet have precise evidence for this cult in T'ang times.

[80] Kaltenmark (1948), 31–32; Yamada (1957), 307, points out a passage in LPLI which states that bronze boats sail each year beyond Annam to engage in trade. He takes the term "bronze ships" (*t'ung ch'uan*) to be a mistake for *"t'ung* ships," a phrase attested for fast transport and cargo vessels built of wooden planks, especially of camphorwood. See Ch'en Ts'ang-ch'i in PTKM, 34, 29a, who tells of the use of camphorwood in Chekiang for this purpose; see CHC, 25, 20a, and CTS, 19a, 5a, the first of which tells of their construction, the second of their use.

[81] Kaltenmark (1948), 22–43.

[82] TPHYC, 162, 6b; Kaltenmark (1948), 3.

[83] KLFTC, 2; TPHYC, 162, 6b.

[84] Kaltenmark (1948), 6–13.

[85] Kaltenmark (1948), 13–20.

[86] His legend is much like that of Ch'ien Liu (852–932), ruler of the Wu–Yüeh kingdom in Chekiang, who built a dike in 910 to protect the harbor of Hang-chou against the famous tidal bore, and had bowmen shoot magic arrows at the waves, as representatives of the sea gods. Later Ch'ien Liu himself became a sea god. Kaltenmark (1948), 45–46, based on E. Chavannes.

[87] Kaltenmark (1948), 6–7, 20, 80.

[88] Stein (1947), 163–165; Kaltenmark (1948), 69–77.

[89] TS, 222c, 1a.

[90] SKC, 49 (Wu, 4), 1041d; Coedès (1962), 49–50.

[91] Han Yü "Liu-chou lo ch'ih miao pei," HCLCC, 31, 5a–7a.

[92] Liu Tsung-yüan, "Liu-chou fu Ta yün szu chi," LHSC, 28, 4b–5a.

[93] CYCT, 5, 3b.

[94] Liu Yü-hsi, "Nan chung shu lai," LMTWC, wai chi, 8, 13b.

[95] Lu Kuei-meng, "Yeh miao pei,"

FLHSWC, 18, 38a; and quoted in PKLT, 68, 21b.

[96] LPLI, quoted in TPKC, 407, 3a.

[97] Han Yü, "Ch'en-chou ch'i yü," ChTS, han 5, ts'e 10, ch. 8, 2a.

[98] Li Shang-yin, "I su," ChTS, han 8, ts'e 8, ts'e 9, ch. 1, 3a.

[99] Ch'en Tzu-ang, in TS, 107, 6b.

[100] TS, 115, 1b.

[101] TS, 180, 1b.

[102] *Gallus gallus bankiva* or *Gallus bankiva*.

[103] There are other closely related species in south India, Ceylon, and Indonesia. See La Touche (1934), 224; Burkill (1935), 1030–1035; Cheng (1955), 99–100; Zeuner (1963), 443.

[104] Bates (1952), 60–61; Bates (1963), 276–277. Bates observes that the use of the fowl purely for play is characteristic of the "civilized" Christian and Muslim cultures of south Asia; only the pagan peoples retain the religious uses.

[105] Zeuner (1963), 443.

[106] Peters (1913), 378; Bates (1963), 276–277

[107] Peters (1913), 374.

[108] Burkill (1935), 1030–1035.

[109] For chicken oracles in Chinese tradition see Eberhard (1942a), 449–454; for egg oracles see *ibid.*, pp. 445–448.

[110] Liu Tsung-yüan, "Liu-chou tung meng," LHSC, 42, 14b–15a.

[111] PHL, 2, 6a–7b.

[112] PHL, 2, 4b–6a.

[113] Feng and Shryock (1935), 11–12.

[114] Ch'en Ts'ang-ch'i, in PTKM, 43, 21a.

[115] Feng and Shryock (1935), 3, 5.

[116] LPLI, a, 1.

[117] YYTT, 11, 88.

[118] For 541 B.C. Feng and Shryock (1935), 2, from *Tso chuan.*

[119] In addition to the modern description of erotic *ku,* quoted above, see Eberhard (1942a), 137–141.

[120] YYTT, 16, 126.

[121] Ch'en Ts'ang-ch'i, in PTKM, 43, 21a.

[122] TPT, in PTKM, 34, 31b.

[123] Ch'en Ts'ang-ch'i, in PTKM, 43, 24a.

[124] Ch'en Ts'ang-ch'i, in PTKM, 51a, 31a.

[125] Ch'en Ts'ang-ch'i, in PTKM, 48, 5a.

[126] Li (1960), 272.

[127] Eberhard (1942a), 137–141 assigns the earliest reference to the *I ching.*

[128] See Feng and Shryock (1935), 30.

[129] YYTT, 3, 31–32.

[130] Schafer (1962), 279–280.

[131] Schafer (1962b), 211. The passage is taken from Han Yü's stele in honor of the God of the South Sea.

[132] Liu Tsung-yüan, "Liu-chou tung meng," LHSC, 42, 14b–15a.

[133] CTS, 8, 18a; Schafer (1962b), 204–208, 219.

[134] Kao P'ien, "Nan hai shen tz'u," ChTS, han 9, ts'e 7, 1b.

[135] Schafer (1962b), 205; see also Eberhard (1942a), 45–49.

[136] Eberhard (1942a), 254–255.

[137] TKSP, c, 18a.

[138] Maspero (1963), 274. A painting reproduced here as fig. 14 ("after Li Lung-mien, 11th cent.") shows "two thunders," with beaks, talons, and bat wings, but carrying bows and arrows; later traditions make them animal-like with red hair, sometimes ape-headed (Eberhard [1942a], 254); a modern illustration shows one with a chaplet of drums and a mallet to beat the thunder from them.

[139] CC, in TPKC, 394, 1b.

[140] LIC, in TPKC, 393, 8a.

[141] THTL, c, 18a.

[142] LPLI, in TPKC, 394, 4b.

[143] THTL, in TPHYC, 169, 5a.

[144] PYTC, 1a.

[145] YTCS, 118, 4b, quoting TKSP. Another tale tells of a native of Lei-chou who chopped one of the thunder spirits

in two, and thereafter was afflicted by "fire of heaven," that is, lightning. See THTL, in LNTS, 1, 17a.

146 CSL, in TPKC, 395, 6b.

147 KIC, in TPKC, 464, 2a–2b.

148 Soymié (1956), 112.

149 Soymié (1956), 16.

150 TYTP, in TPKC, 66, 6b–7a.

151 Private communication from Richard Yang, dated 15 August 1963, makes her cult quite late. Professor Yang writes: "The only reliable 'official' record is perhaps the *Ling-ling hsien chih*. This is not available to me, but it contains one of the two dominant traditions, namely that the fairy girl was a native of Hunan. I believe, however, that the tradition of her birth near Canton is older.

152 Soymié (1956), 16, 21. The event is supposed to have occurred in 710–711. Tradition reports several apparitions of her on the holy mountain later in this century.

153 "Ho Erh-niang," KIC, recorded in TPKC, 62, 7a. Some authorities date the collection in T'ang, some in Sung. In any event it precedes the compilation of TPKC in 978.

154 HNYC, quoted in TPHYC, 157, 7b–8a. Cf. the similar account in YTCS, 89, 22a. I cannot place HNYC, but it must have been written before the Sung *T'ai p'ing hsing kuo* era, and is probably T'ang. Both of these stories, then, existed in written form by about the middle of the tenth century. Presumably their oral prototypes were somewhat earlier.

155 K'ung Ch'uan in PKLT, 5, 28a, tells of one of her divine accomplishments: "She would take a single stone, and put it in place on the top of a small stone loft-building; looked at afar, it resembled a painting." K'ung's additions to Po Chü-i's encyclopaedia, made in the twelfth century, relied heavily on late T'ang sources.

156 So Soymié (1956), 16.

157 A multitude of sources tell this tale. A kind of generalized T'ang version is in TT, 187, 997a; cf. SSC, 14, 91, which has some differences of detail. A translation of an older version (from HHS, 116) can be found in Laufer (1917), 419–420. For summary studies of the tradition, see Liu (1932), passim; Lin (1941), 333–334; Liu (1941), passim; Eberhard (1942a), 18–26. Liu thinks the myth spread from two centers, one in north Asia, one in south Asia. He claims to have found Thai cognates for two words for the princess' headdress and costume given in HHS.

158 ChS, 49, 2338c; LMTWC, 8, 16b. The entire poem is translated above.

159 Laufer (1917), 421. Although in antiquity the dog god appears as the forefather of *all* the Man, nowadays it is assumed that he is the ancestor of only the Miao-Yao-speaking tribes, whose history begins only in late medieval times. There is an important unresolved problem here.

160 Bonifacy (1903), 85–89.

161 Stübel and Meriggi (1938), 372.

162 Stübel and Meriggi (1938), 371–373; Stein (1942), 50.

163 SSC, 14, 91.

164 Stein (1942), 50.

165 Sung Chih-wen, "Hsia Kuei chiang lung mu t'an," ChTS, han 1, ts'e 10, ch. 3, 4b. "Mountain goblins" translates *shan kuai. Kuai* connotes "weird, eerie, uncanny, fantastic," here "an uncanny, fantastic being."

166 PPT, 17 (Teng she), 2a.

167 PPT, 17 (Teng she), 13b. "Ectoplasms" here renders *ching,* which I translated "germinal essence" just above. These dangerous spirits of old stones and stumps were particularly common on the "lesser" mountains; hence alchemists, searching for the holy solitude in which to perform their experiments, preferred the "great" mountains, inhabited by great and noble spirits. See Obi (1962), 280.

168 PPT, 17 (Teng she), 7b–8a.

[169] HsCC, quoted in TPYL, 886, 4b–5a; PTT, quoted in TPYL, 886, 6b; PPT, 17 (Teng she), 7a. PTT is listed in the Sui bibliography and must therefore belong to the period from the third to the sixth century.

[170] PPT, 17 (Teng she), 7a.

[171] PTT, in TPYL, 886, 6a.

[172] PTT, in TPYL, 886, 5b.

[173] Yamada (1963), 66.

[174] See Schafer (1963d), item 10, quoting Ch'en Ts'ang-ch'i, from PTKM, 49, 11a.

[175] Ch'en Ts'ang-ch'i, in PTKM, 49, 12b.

[176] TCTC, 195, 14a.

[177] Renner (1927), 95, thinks that a multitude of demons is a particular trait of the culture of the hunters and gatherers in the tropical forests, but I have seen no statistics comparing their numbers with those of the boreal forests.

[178] Renner (1927), 97.

[179] The suggestion is mine, not Renner's. Renner (pp. 98–99) makes another equation: forest agriculturalists are more interested in the soul, ancestor worship, and the great river spirits. Possibly it is so.

[180] Malleret (1934), 84.

[181] PYTC, 1a. See Pelliot (1963), 622–624 for a general account of the "dumb trade" in Asia.

[182] YYTT, 4, 38; Cf. TS, 222c, 16a.

[183] CKC, in TPYL, 172, 4a.

[184] YTCS, 101, 3a and 5a, quoting CKC as reported in TPHYC. Ch'ih sung tzu is mentioned in HS, 40, 1459c as a Taoist hermit or immortal. He is also a rain deity of prehistoric antiquity.

[185] SHC, 15, 70a. HS, 27c, a, 0415b; SSC, 12, 85; MSS, 6, 63.

[186] Ch'en Ts'ang-ch'i, in PTKM, 42, 20b.

[187] PPT, in TPYL, 950, 7b. Cf. MSKY, b, 135.

[188] This may be the unidentified insect illustrated in *Kokuyaku honzō kōmoku*

(Tokyo, 1930), X, 321. Cf. PTKM, 42.

[189] Han Yü, "Ch'ao-chou tz'u shih hsieh shang piao," HCLCC, 39, 7a.

[190] Sung Chih-wen, "Fa T'eng-chou," ChTS, ts'e 19, ch. 3, 5b–6a.

[191] Yüan Chieh, "Sung Meng chiao shu huan Nan-hai," ChTS, han 4, ts'e 6, ch. 2, 9b. "South Sea" in the poem is both the South China Sea and the Canton region, known since antiquity as "South Sea." For Yüan Chieh's biography see TS, 143, 4b.

[192] *Ch'ih-mei* is often shortened to *mei* when qualified by a monosyllable, hence *shan mei* "mountain troll," and *mu mei* "tree troll."

[193] Soymié (1956), 109 n. 2, equates "mountain trolls," "mountain imps," and "wild men" (i.e., savages of the forest) as hairy black fauns of the mountains, all closely akin to the "Hairy Men" and "Tree Visitors." But though the usual terrified northerner might lump all these goblins together, it is certain that the local oldtimers knew how to distinguish them.

[194] *Tso chuan,* Wen kung, 8.

[195] CYCT, in TPKC, 447, 5b.

[196] Yüan Chieh, "Sung mu mei," ChTS, han 4, ts'e 6, ch. 1, 12b–13b.

[197] Ch'ien Ch'i (fl. 766), "Sung Li Fu-jen fu Kuang-chou," ChTS, han 4, ts'e 5, ch. 1, 4a.

[198] Chang Ku, "Chi ch'ien k'o," ChTS, han 8, ts'e 5, ch. 1, 9a.

[199] Among T'ang phonetic (dialectical?) variants are *hsiao* (*seu*), *sao* (M.C. *sau*) and *hsiao* (M.C. *syeu*). YYTT, 15, 119.

[200] SSC, 12, 84–85; YYTT, 15, 119. This source gives other curious and suggestive names for the creature. A respected modern dictionary, *Tz'u hai,* transfers the name "mountain *hsiao*" to the African mandrill!

[201] SSC, 12, 84–85.

[202] SSC, 12, 84–85; YYTT, 15, 119.

[203] KIC, in TPKC, 428, 2a.

[204] KIC, in TPKC, 428, 1b.

[205] For other accounts of the *hsiao*-imps

in other times and places, see Eberhard (1942a), 30–32.

[206] *I wu chih,* perhaps the *Nan fang i wu chih* of Fang Ch'ien-li, quoted in TPYL, 927, 4a.

[207] YHC, 37, 1044, has Ying shan.

[208] NKC, p. 2a.

[209] HWC, in TPKC, 482, 6a, quoting Kuo Chung-ch'an, *Hsiang-chou chi.*

[210] See Liu Yü-hsi's poem translated above in Chapter III, and Eberhard (1942a), 29–30.

[211] Hastings (1962), III, 23.

[212] Hastings (1962), V, 685.

CHAPTER 6 (Pages 115–122)

[1] Needham believes that the Chinese saw "order in Nature," but campaigns stoutly against the idea that they saw this order as a law dictated by a "rational personal being," or a creator *ex nihilo.* Needham and Wang (1956), 581.

[2] Ch'en Ts'ang-ch'i, in PTKM, 46, 36a.

[3] The word *ch'ien* had for centuries stood for the energetic, creative aspect of "Heaven." See Wilhelm (1957), 462, 475.

[4] Liu Tsung-yüan, "T'ien tse," LHSC, 14, 6a. Cf. the paraphrase of this passage in Needham and Wang (1956), 561.

[5] See Needham and Wang (1956), 37–38, for a comparison with the *logos* of Heracleitus—a kind of "naturalist pantheism, which emphasises the unity and spontaneity of the operations of Nature." But sinological literature is full of facile remarks about the Tao. They add up to very little of philosophical importance.

[6] In some modern opinion this is the *only* Chinese view of nature; see for instance Liu (1962), 49. See Needham and Wang (1956), 51 for the use of the term in *Chuang tzu* and *Huai-nan tzu.*

[7] LH, ch. 14.

[8] Wilhelm (1957), 468–469.

[9] Some of this section is a paraphrase and abridgement of Schafer (1964a), which see for more elaborate treatment of the Fashioner.

[10] PKLT, 90, 23b.

[11] Liu Tsung-yüan, "Hsiao shih ch'eng shan chi," LHSC, 29, 5b–6a.

[12] Translations appear also in Giles (1923), 141–142, and Margouliès (1926), 229–230. Giles converts the Fashioner into a rather Christian deity, and makes it appear that Liu finally doubted his existence. I take a different view.

[13] Charles Baudelaire, "Correspondences," *Les Fleurs du Mal.*

[14] Sung Chih-wen, "Tsao fa Ta yü ling," ChTS, han 1, ts'e 10, ch. 1, 6b–7a. The frontier is called "boundary between Hua and I (savage)."

[15] Wu Wu-ling, "Hsi k'ai Yin shan chi," CTW, 718, 13a.

[16] Ku Fei-hsiung (fl. 836), "Hsia yeh Han chu kuei chou chi shih," ChTS, han 8, ts'e 4, 5a.

[17] For the necessity of retirement into deserted places as a condition of this release, see Mather (1958), 73–74.

[18] Chan (1957), 310–311.

[19] Schafer (1964a).

[20] Contrast Schafer (1962), 293, which presents the view that Earth (not Heaven!) is the source of all beings, and that water "is the blood and pneuma of the earth, flowing throughout as if through sinews or veins."

[21] Spencer (1954), 91.

[22] Yeh (1958), 51, based on *Chou li;* Schafer (1963d), 210.

[23] YYTT, 16, 126.

[24] YYTT, 18, 146; "Ho kung nei kan tzu chieh shih piao," CTW, 962, 15b–16b.

[25] Glacken (1962), 4.

[26] Glacken (1962), 1.

[27] *Lun yü,* "Yung yeh."

[28] *Chuang tzu,* "Chih pei yu." Giles translates the passage thus: "Mountain forests and loamy fields swell my heart with joy."

[29] Frodsham (1960), 73–78, 102. A good idea of its character, says Frodsham,

can be gained from verses of the fifth-century poet Chiang Yen, imitative of earlier Taoist poetry.

[30] PPT, 4, 6b.

[31] PPT, 4, 19a–19b.

[32] Obi (1962), 274.

[33] Frodsham (1960), 98.

[34] Obi (1962), 47–48, 50–51, 344.

[35] Obi (1962), 232.

[36] Obi (1962), 66 ff.

[37] Obi (1962), 141, 275–277.

[38] See especially Mather (1958), 67–68.

[39] Obi (1962), 289.

[40] Obi (1962), 602–604.

CHAPTER 7 (Pages 123–134)

[1] Yüan Chen, "Ho Lo-t'ien sung k'o yu Ling-nan, erh shih yün," ChTS, han 6, ts'e 9, ch. 12, 5b.

[2] Shen Ch'üan-ch'i, "Tu an hai ju Lung-pien," ChTS, han 2, ts'e 5, ch. 3, 10a.

[3] Chang Chi, "Sung Cheng Shang-shu fu Kuang-chou," ChTS, han 6, ts'e 6, ch. 4, 9b.

[4] CTS, 35, 6a; cf. TS, 31, 5b; Cf. Needham, Wang and Robinson (1962), 45–46.

[5] TS, 31, 6b. It has been suggested, however, that the readings for the capital of Champa, and perhaps for Annam as well, were not made on the spot, but by extrapolation. Indeed my colleague Paul Wheatley, in a private communication dated 5 October 1964 makes an even severer indictment. He thinks that the measurements given by I-hsing for the southern stations were actually copied from a record said to have been made by a Chinese expedition in the fourth century. This view contrasts strongly with Needham's opinion that the T'ang men made a pioneering achievement in field observation. See Beer et al. (1961), 26–27, for support of Needham's position. The

T'ang histories say, at any rate, that readings were taken at Chiao-chou.

[6] As reported about the beginning of the eleventh century; Muslim navigators steered by them. See terminal note by Louis Massignon (not paginated) in Pelliot (1963).

[7] YTCS, 89, 1b.

[8] CTS, 176, 20a.

[9] Wang Po, "Hsin-chou Ch'i-hsien Tou-shuai-szu Fou-t'u pei," CTW, 184, 2b.

[10] Li Shang-yin, "Ch'i hsi ou t'i," ChTS, han 8, ts'e 9, ch. 2, 34a.

[11] Hsüeh Chi, "Feng ho sung Chin ch'eng kung chu shih Hsi-po ying chih," ChTS, han 2, ts'e 5, 5b.

[12] CCW, "Wen yao chü," in YHSS, ts'e 43, 3b.

[13] Cf. *Wen tzu,* in TPYL, 78, 6a: "The Fire-red God makes the calamities of fire."

[14] CCW, "Ho ch'eng t'u," in YHSS, ts'e 44, 1b.

[15] Stein (1947), 173; and cf. pp. 124–126. Hence the title of Tuan Kung-lu's book on Nam-Viet, *Pei hu lu (Register of the Northward Doors).*

[16] Ch'ang Kun, "Feng nan chung shih chi ling wai ku jen," ChTS, han 4, ts'e 9, 2b.

[17] Li Shang-yin, "Kuei-lin lu chung tso," ChTS, han 8, ts'e 9, ch. 1, 19b.

[18] Han Yü, "Chiang-ling t'u chung chi Han-lin san hsüeh shih," HCLCC, 1, 26b.

[19] Sung Chih-wen, "Ching Wu-chou," ChTS, han 1, ts'e 10, ch. 2, 7a.

[20] Tu Shen-yen, "Lü yü An-nan," ChTS, han 2, ts'e 1, 3b.

[21] Hsü Hun, "Sui mu tzu Kuang Chiang. . . . t'i hsia shan szu, szu shou," ChTS, han 8, ts'e 8, ch. 10, 5a.

[22] Chu Ch'ing-yü, "Ling-nan lu," ChTS, han 8, ts'e 6, ch.1, 2b. For discussion of the *Erythrina* "coral tree" see below.

[23] LPLI, b, 9.

[24] Schafer (1963), 11–12.

[25] T'u and Hwang (1945), 9; Spencer (1954), 46.

[26] T'u and Hwang (1945), 14, 19.

[27] Fuson (1928), 241; McCune (1947), 339.

[28] Cressey (1934), 353; McCune (1947), 341.

[29] Spencer (1954), 49.

[30] Chang Chi, "Sung nan k'o," ChTS, han 6, ts'e 7, ch. 3, 6a.

[31] LNIWC, in TPYL, 416, 5b.

[32] Ch'en Ts'ang-ch'i, in PTKM, 5, 21b.

[33] T'u and Hwang (1945), 19–20; Schafer (1962b), 63.

[34] CKC, in TPYL, 172, 2b.

[35] Han Yü, "Chiang-ling t'u chung chi Han-lin san hsüeh shih," HCLCC, 1, 26b.

[36] Han Yü, "Ch'ao-chou tz'u shih hsien shang piao," CLHSC, 39, 5a.

[37] TS, 35, 2a–2b.

[38] LPLI, a, 1.

[39] LPLI, a, 1.

[40] TKSP, c, 18a.

[41] LPLI, a, 1; TKSP, c, 18a.

[42] Liu Tsung-yüan, "Ling-nan chiang hsing," LHSC, 42, 14b.

[43] THTL, in TPHYC, 169, 5a.

[44] Laurence Hope, "The Teak Forest," *India's Love Lyrics.*

[45] Clark (1938), 399–400.

[46] Tu Fu, "Chi Yang Wu Kuei-chou . . . chih jen," CCTS, 349–350.

[47] Tu Fu, "Feng sung Wei Liu chang yu shao fu chih chiao Kuang," CCTS, 233.

[48] Tu Fu, "Chi Li Shih-erh Po, erh shih yün," CCTS, 339.

[49] Ch'üan Te-yü, "Sung An-nan P'ei tu huo," ChTS, han 5, ts'e 8, ch. 4, 5b.

[50] Hsü Hun, "Sung Tu hsiu ts'ai kuei Kuei-lin," ChTS, han 8, ts'e 8, ch. 9, 9b.

[51] See Renner (1927), 40–42 on these tropical mists.

[52] Charles A. Gordon, *Life on the Gold Coast,* quoted in Evans (1949), 17–18.

[53] Bates (1952), 24. In America and Australia, on the other hand, with their chiefly temperate climates, the white men brought diseases which finished off the natives.

[54] LPLI, a, 1.

[55] See for instance Wang Chien, "The South," translated in Waley (1961).

[56] YYTT, 5, 44.

[57] A. Lafrique, "Soirée triste," in *Rimes tonkinoises.*

[58] Malleret (1934), 132.

[59] Bates (1952), 135–136. Preventative medicine has been more developed in temperate latitudes; malaria was once common in New England and in Scandinavia, and the bubonic plage was well-known in Europe.

[60] Li Chi-kao, *Nan hsing fang,* in the T'ang bibliography, TS, 59, 20b.

[61] TS, 59, 20a.

[62] Bates (1952), 144. Dengue fever, related to malaria, is also epidemic in this part of the world. Spencer (1954), 109–111. The medieval Chinese seem not to have distinguished the two.

[63] *Leviticus,* XXVI, 16.

[64] McCune (1947), 343; Bates (1952), 144.

[65] Wiens (1954), 180.

[66] Spencer (1954), 108.

[67] Ch'en T'ao (fl. 841), "P'an-yü tao chung tso," ChTS, han 11, ts'e 4, ch. 1, 4a.

[68] Ch'en T'ao, "Tseng pieh li," ChTS, han 11, ts'e 4, ch. 1, 12b.

[69] Hsiang Szu (fl. 836), "Sung Ou-yang Kun kuei Min chung," ChTS, han 9, ts'e 1, 1a.

[70] TS, 222c, 16a. The text refers to the "Nan-p'ing Lao," probably including Nam-Viet in part. Among the "pit vipers" are the American rattlesnakes; there were a number in south China belonging to the genera *Agkistrodon* and *Trimeresurus.*

[71] Hoeppli (1954), 91–92.

[72] LPLI, a, 1.

[73] Hoeppli (1954), 92.

[74] Hsiao Ping, in PTKM, 26, 29a.

[75] Ch'en Ts'ang-ch'i, in PTKM, 34, 29a.

76 Ch'en Ts'ang-ch'i, in PTKM, 44, 31a.
77 Ch'en Ts'ang-ch'i, in PTKM, 44, 31b. The skate is here styled Sea Sparrow-hawk.
78 Chen Ch'üan, in PTKM, 43, 22a.
79 HHS, 54, 0748a.
80 Burkill (1935), 629–631.
81 HHS, 54, 0748a. This is presumably the variety which now preserves the hero's name: *Coix lachryma-jobi* var. *Ma-yuen*. See Sato (1959), 339. The modern Hainanese distill a fine coffee-colored "whisky" from Job's tears. See McClure (1934), 592.
82 Tu Fu, "Meng Li Po," CCTS, 79.
83 KHYHC, 28b.
84 TT, 184, 983b.
85 Ma Tai (fl. 853), "Sung tsung shu fu Nan-Hai mu," ChTS, han 9, ts'e 2, ch. 1, 1b.
86 TCTC, 192, 10a.
87 TCTC, 253, 14a; YTCS, 89, 4b.
88 Lu Kuei-meng, "Ho chi Ch'iung-chou Yang she jen," FLHSCW, 9, 27b.
89 Liu Tsung-yüan, "Yü shih kuan Han Yü . . . i shih shu," LHSC, 31, 2b.
90 Liu Tsung-yüan, "Ta Wei chung wei lun shih tao shu," CTW, 575, 13a.
91 Liu and Needham (1951), 14–15.
92 MIPL, in PTKM, 30, 6a; so also did Ch'en Ts'ang-ch'i.
93 Lu and Needham (1951), 15.
94 Ch'en Ts'ang-ch'i, in PTKM, 29, 1b.
95 WTPY, in PTKM, 31, 14b.
96 Li Hsün and Meng Shen, in PTKM, 19, 4a.
97 TS, 59, 20b.
98 Ch'en Ts'ang-ch'i, in PTKM, 5, 24a.
99 Ch'en Ts'ang-ch'i, in PTKM, 7, 27b.
100 WTPY, in PTKM, 14, 36a.
101 TPT, in PTKM, 14, 43a.
102 Chen Ch'üan, in PTKM, 16, 22a.
103 Chen Ch'üan in PTKM, 26, 31a.
104 Li Hsün, in PTKM, 32, 17b.
105 Ch'en Ts'ang-ch'i, in PTKM, 34, 29a.
106 Su Kung, in PTKM, 35b, 39a.
107 WTPY, in PTKM, 26, 31b.
108 CCF, in PTKM, 52, 40a.
109 *Tz'u ch'ou.*
110 Ch'en Ts'ang-ch'i, in PTKM, 37, 55b.
111 TS, 59, 19a.
112 WTPY, in PTKM, 9, 38a.
113 Chen Ch'üan, in PTKM, 9, 41a.
114 Chen Ch'üan, in PTKM, 11, 7b.
115 Chen Ch'üan, in PTKM, 12a, 15a.
116 TPT, 14, 43a.
117 Ch'en Ts'ang-ch'i, in PTKM, 25, 20b.
118 Su Kung, in PTKM, 33, 21a.
119 Chen Ch'üan, in PTKM, 46, 38b.
120 TS, 36, 12b.
121 As in WTPY, in PTKM, 9, 38a.
122 CIL, b, 60a.
123 Liu Tsung-yüan, "Ta Wei chung wei lun shih tao shu," CTW, 575, 13a.
124 Liu Yü-hsi, "Lien-chou tz'u shih t'ing pi chi," LMTWC, 27, 2b.
125 Sung Chih-wen, "Shih-an ch'iu jih," ChTS, han 1, ts'e 10, ch. 3, 5a.

CHAPTER 8 (Pages 135–151)

1 Cressey (1934), 15.
2 Fuson (1928), 243, referring to the canyon of the Taan Ha in the first instance, and the gorges of the Lien River in the second. The same author (p. 249) reports of the northern border region that "one worldwide traveler was heard to state that he had seen no more beautiful scenery in all his traveling."
3 Spencer (1954), 34.
4 Spencer (1954), 32.
5 Cressey (1934), 349; Spencer (1954), 32–34; Wiens (1954), 11–12, 15–16.
6 Clark (1938), 406.
7 It is not certain if the name Hainan "South of the Sea" was applied specifically to this island before Sung times. See Pelliot (1959), 243. Szu-ma Kuang uses it when writing about T'ang times (e.g., TCTC, 201, 13a: "the Lao of Hainan"), but it is not certain if the name occurs in the source upon which he draws.

[8] Brodrick (1942), 110; Spencer (1954), 25; Wiens (1954), 11.

[9] Brodrick (1942), 41.

[10] Brodrick (1942), 110; Spencer (1954), 26.

[11] Brodrick (1943), 54, 110; McCune (1947), 337; Spencer (1954), 25.

[12] McCune (1947), 336, 338; Spencer (1954), 25.

[13] Brodrick (1942), 267; McCune (1947), 342; Spencer (1954), 77; McNeil (1964), 97–98.

[14] Ts'ao Sung, "Nan hai," ChTS, han 11, ts'e 2, ch. 2, 6b.

[15] Ferrand (1914), 7.

[16] CTS, 41, 24a.

[17] Cf. CHC, 6, 6a: "Besides 'South Sea' and 'Great Sea' there is 'Swollen Sea.'"

[18] CTS, 41, 26a.

[19] Shen Ch'üan-ch'i, "Tu an hai ju Lung-pien," ChTS, han 2, ts'e 5, ch. 3, 10a.

[20] Tu Fu, "Kuei yen," CCTS, 544.

[21] Lu Chao (ninth century), "Hai ch'ao fu," CTW, 768, 2a.

[22] LPLI, a, 1.

[23] Liu Yü-hsi, "T'a ch'ao ko," LMTWC, 9, 6b–7a. Cf. YTCS, 89, 10b.

[24] Collingwood (1868), 391.

[25] Collingwood (1868), 393.

[26] Collingwood (1868), 394–401.

[27] LNIWC, in TPKC, 466, 3b–4a.

[28] Yüan Chen, "Ho Lo-t'ien sung k'o yu Ling-nan, erh shih yün," ChTS, han 6, ts'e 9, ch. 12, 6a.

[29] Much of the conventional imagery of the sea, including the phenomenon of phosphorescence, is derived from the famous "Rhapsody on the Sea," written long ago in Chin times—the "Hai fu" of Mu Hua (Mu Hsüan-hsü). See for instance, Ku K'uang, "Sung tsung hsiung shih Hsin-lo," ChTS, han 4, ts'e 9, ch. 3, 6b.

[30] See Soymié (1956), 1–2.

[31] In Pao-an *hsien*. See TLT, 3, 25a.

[32] TT, 184, 980a.

[33] SCC, 38, 5a.

[34] HNT, 1, 7a.

[35] Yüan Chieh, "Chiu i shan t'u chi," CTW, 382, 5a.

[36] YHC, 34, 1011.

[37] Soymié (1956), 2.

[38] YHC, 34, 1011.

[39] Soymié (1956), 51–52, 63, 68–71.

[40] Liu Yü-hsi, "Hsieh Lo-fou shih," LMTWC, 1, 9b.

[41] Soymié (1956), 97–98, 103.

[42] Soymié (1956), 112.

[43] Schafer (1961), 6–7.

[44] Shen Ch'üan-ch'i, "Hsia shan fu hsü," CTW, 235, 9b.

[45] Hsü Hun, "Sui mu tzu Kuang chiang . . . hsia chih, szu shou," ChTS, han 8, ts'e 8, ch. 10, 5a.

[46] Moore (1931), 199.

[47] Chang Chi or Tu Mu, "Man chou," ChTS, han 6, ts'e 6, ch. 5, 3b.

[48] YHC, 37, 1044, 1053.

[49] YTCS, 108, 4a, quoting NYC.

[50] KLFTC, p. 2.

[51] Li Po (Bwět), Preface to "Nan ch'i [po lung tung]," ChTS, han 7, ts'e 10, 4a.

[52] PHL, 1, 17a–20a. For the "salamander" (*t'a* [*t'ap*], see KY, ch. 5, rhyme 28).

[53] TPHYC, 162, 4b–5a.

[54] Wu Wu-ling, "Hsin k'ai Yin shan chi," CTW, 718, 12b–15a.

[55] *Tamarix chinensis.*

[56] *Quercus myrsinaefolia.*

[57] *"Yün-tang* bamboo," probably *Dendrocalamus latiflorus.*

[58] *Ligularia tussilaginea.*

[59] *Plectorhynchus pictus.*

[60] Cyrprinoid fish related to the dace.

[61] Liu Tsung-yüan, "Liu-chou shan shui chin chih k'o yu che chi," LHSC, 29, 6b–7a.

[62] Cf. Schafer (1963a), 102.

[63] Stein (1942), 42–45; Soymié (1956), 88–96.

[64] PKLT, 6, 10a.

[65] STC, in TPYL, 172, 3b.

[66] YTCS, 90, 8b, quoting CKC.

[67] PKLT, 5, 27a.

[68] YTCS, 99, 4b, 13a.

[69] YTCS, 99, 3b, quoting a source of unknown date.

[70] Soymié (1956), 25. I do not know how old his tradition was.

[71] PKLT, 5, 28a; Soymié (1956), 93–94.

[72] Different editions of the text give different words here; my rendering is rather arbitrary.

[73] Han Yü, "Sung Ch'ü Ts'e, hsü," HCLCC, 21, 1a.

[74] Han Yü, "Chen nü hsia," HCLCC, 3, 5b.

[75] Liu Ch'ang-ch'ing, "Chiang lou sung T'ai-k'ang Kuo chu po fu Ling-nan," ChTS, han 3, ts'e 1, ch. 5, 12b.

[76] TS, 43a, 4b; TPHYC, 166, 3b.

[77] Yüan Chieh, "Ping ch'üan ming," CTW, 382, 13a–13b.

[78] YTCS, 89, 10b.

[79] LPLI, a, 1.

[80] TT, 184, 983c.

[81] TS, 43b, 13b.

[82] YTCS, 91, 5a, quoting YTKC.

[83] ShHC, in CHC, 7, 7b.

[84] ShHC, in TPYL, 930, 5b.

[85] Ch'en Ts'ang-ch'i, in PTKM, 5, 23b.

[86] Obi (1962), 414–415.

[87] *Nan Yüeh hsing chi.*

[88] *Kuang chou chi.*

[89] *Chiao Kuang erh chou chi.*

[90] Obi (1962), 390.

[91] *Nan i i wu chi.*

[92] *Nan chou i wu chih.*

[93] *Nan fang ts'ao mu chuan.*

[94] *Nan Yüeh chih.* Wang Fan, *Springs and Autumns of Chiao and Kuang* (*Chiao Kuang ch'un ch'iu*), of the Chin period, would appear to be a historical work.

[95] Aoyama (1963), 457.

[96] *Chün kuo chih.*

[97] TS, 58, 18a; SuS, 204, 4994a; Chang (1962), 85–86.

[98] *Ling piao lu i.*

[99] *Pei hu lu.*

[100] Tuan Kung-lu frequently cites the authority of Ch'en Ts'ang-ch'i the pharmacologist, who must also be counted among the important contributors to our knowledge of T'ang Nam-Viet.

[101] *Nan fang i wu chih.*

[102] *T'ou huang tsa lu.*

[103] *Ling nan i wu chih.*

[104] Both *Nan fang i wu chih* and *Ling nan i wu chih* are listed in the T'ang bibliography (TS, 58, 18b) as books of one scroll each.

[105] Fang Ch'ien-li, "Yu ling chiao shih, hsü," CTW, 760, 20b–21a; Preface to "Chi ch'ien Chao shih," ChTS, han 8, ts'e 6, 5a.

[106] *Hai nan chu fan hsing chi.* See TS, 58, 18b.

[107] Aoyama (1963), 526. This gazetteer was submitted to the throne in the summer of 807, after the submission of the tribes of Hainan. I cite the title as given by Aoyama in Japanese. The original may have been slightly different.

[108] TS, 58, 18b.

[109] SuS, 204, 4994a, listed among the T'ang geographies.

[110] YTCS, 92, 7a.

[111] Han Yü, "Chiang chih Shao-chou . . . t'u ching," HCLCC, 10, 10b.

[112] Obi (1962), 453. One critic, Wu (1962), 248–249, thinks that the Liu-chou essays are more purely descriptive, less emotional than those written in Yung-chou.

[113] Liu Tsung-yüan, "Yung-chou Ma t'ui shan mao t'ing chi," LHSC, 27, 2b–3b.

[114] Liu Tsung-yüan, "Kuei-chou Tzu chia chou t'ing chi," LHSC, 27, 1b–2b.

[115] The characters given for his name in my glossary are from LTMHC, 10, 7a. TCMHL, 11a, has a different character for T'an (Dam).

[116] TCMHL, 11a.

[117] LTMHC, 10, 7a–7b.

[118] TS, 169, 9a; LTMHC, 10, 10a.

[119] TCMHL, 7b–8a.

CHAPTER 9 (Pages 152–164)

[1] See Bates (1952), 236.
[2] Fuson (1928), 243.
[3] Ibid.
[4] YTCS, 98, 5b (for En-chou), and YTCS, 103, 8a (for Kuei-chou).
[5] Schafer (1963), 9; TCTC, 242, 3b. The date of the memorial was 821; its author was Yang Yü-ling.
[6] YTCS, 90, 8b, for Shao-chou.
[7] My "anvil" is actually a fulling block.
[8] Li Hsien-yung (fl. 878), "Shih pan ko," ChTS, han 10, ts'e 2, ch. 1, 3a.
[9] Ch'en Ts'ang-ch'i, in PTKM, 10, 6a; for many T'ang records of meteors and meteorites see Chang (1921), 324–325.
[10] Ch'en Ts'ang-ch'i, in PTKM, 10, 6a.
[11] Ch'en Ts'ang-ch'i, in PTKM, 10, 6a.
[12] Grigson and Gibbs-Smith (1957), 376.
[13] Chang (1959), 104. The "Mesolithic" culture of south China survived long after the Neolithic was well established in the north. See Cheng (1964), 182.
[14] Maglioni (1952), 3–5; *K'aoku t'ung hsün* (1956), 5; Mo (1957), 9–10.
[15] Janse (1947), xvii.
[16] Janse (1947), 54–57.
[17] SIC, p. 9a.
[18] Chang (1921), 145.
[19] HHS, 115, 0896c; Schafer (1961), 78–79.
[20] CKC, quoted in TPYL, 172, 4a; YTCS, 109, 2b.
[21] Sachs (1940), 168–169.
[22] Harich-Schneider (1955), 91.
[23] Sachs (1940), 168.
[24] Harich-Schneider (1955), 91.
[25] YTCS, 90, 7b, quoting CYC.
[26] YHC, 38, 1086.
[27] Ling-i, "Ching lin ching she," ChTS, han 12, ts'e 1, ch. 1, 2a.
[28] In early Sung times, however, small specimens of a grayish stone which weathered into strange blue peaks, gathered from a river bed in Shao-chou, were much admired. See Schafer (1961), 66.
[29] Lu Kuei-meng, "Ho kuo Chang Ku ch'u shih Tan-yang ku chü, hsü," ChTS, han 9, ts'e 10, ch. 10, 6a–6b.
[30] Li Te-yü, "T'i Lo-fou shih," ChTS, han 7, ts'e 10, 9b.
[31] Hung (1940), 14; Schafer (1961), 82–83.
[32] Liu Yü-hsi, "Tseng Tuan-chou tzu shih yen," LMTWC, 4, 4b.
[33] Li Ho, "Yang sheng ch'ing hua tzu shih yen ko," ChTS, han 6, ts'e 7, ch. 3, 9a.
[34] Schafer and Wallacker (1958), 228.
[35] Chen Ch'üan, in PTKM, 9, 44a.
[36] See for instance WTPY, in PTKM, 9, 43b.
[37] Ch'en Ts'ang-ch'i, in PTKM, 5, 23b.
[38] Sun Szu-miao, in PTKM, 9, 43b.
[39] Liu Tsung-yüan, "Ling-ling chün fu ju hsüeh chi," LHSC, 28, 1a. Cf. Liu Tsung-yüan, "Yü Ts'ui Lien-chou lun shih jung ju shu," LHSC, 32, 2b–4a.
[40] Liu Yü-hsi, "Lien-chou tz'u shih t'ing pi chi," LMTWC, 27, 2b.
[41] YHC, 34, 1004, 1019; Schafer and Wallacker (1958), 57–58, 228. The stalactites of Chao-chou were famous. YTCS, 107, 6b, quoting YHC.
[42] WTPY, in PTKM, 9, 38a.
[43] Su Kung, in PTKM, 9, 37b.
[44] Schafer and Wallacker (1958), 227, and map 13.
[45] Su Kung and Ch'en Ts'ang-ch'i in PTKM, 9, 42a.
[46] Chen Ch'üan, in PTKM, 9, 42a.
[47] YTCS, 104, 6a, quoting "Chiu T'ang (ti li?) chih."
[48] PTKM, 10, 3a; Schafer (1961), 81; Schafer (1963), 213.
[49] Schafer (1956a), 430–436.
[50] LPLI, a, 3.
[51] Schafer (1963), 200.
[52] CKC, for 806–820, quoted in TPHYC, 158, 10a; LPLI, quoted and

[53] YHC, 34, 1013; cf. Schafer (1963), 216–217.

[54] PHL, 2, 10b–11b.

[55] For a development of this theme, see Schafer (1963a), 100.

[56] Schafer (1963a), 96.

[57] Schafer (1963), 228, 230.

[58] Liu Yü-hsi, "Lien-chou tz'u shih t'ing pi chi," LMTWC, 27, 2b.

[59] HNT, 4a, 2a–2b.

[60] Chang (1921), 24–25, 30. *Lang-kan* is mentioned in the *Yü kung, Erh ya,* and *Shan hai ching.*

[61] Schafer (1961), 94–95.

[62] Ch'en Ts'ang-ch'i, in PTKM, 8, 35b.

[63] Su Kung, in PTKM, 8, 35b.

[64] TPYL, 809, 2a, quoting a book called *Chin T'ai k'ang ti chi,* gives it as a product of Yunnan. *Kuang ya* quoted in the same place states that some *pi* is blue and some is green, and that it is produced in Yüeh and in Yunnan.

[65] Su Kung and Su Sung, in PTKM, 8, 35b.

[66] Su Sung, in PTKM, 8, 35b.

[67] Schafer (1957), 74.

[68] Wheatley (1959), 79.

[69] YHC, 37, 1040; Schafer and Wallacker (1958), 57–58, 229.

[70] LPLI, a, 3.

[71] YHC, 34, 1019.

[72] Schafer (1963a), 96.

[73] Schafer (1963), 223–227.

[74] Fairchild (1944), 124–125.

[75] Burkill (1935), 613–614.

[76] Kaltenmark (1948), 58–66; Schafer (1952), 160; Schafer (1963a), 95.

[77] CHKCC, p. 38.

[78] YHC, 34, 1010.

[79] Li Hsün, in PTKM, 46, 37a; Burkill (1935), 1733.

[80] Li Hsün, in PTKM, 46, 37a.

[81] Burkill (1935), 1730.

[82] Schafer (1952), 155.

[83] TS, 43a, 8a–8b. At least only Po-chou is listed as sending them as tribute.

[84] LPLI, a, 2.

[85] TS, 3, 3a.

[86] Schafer (1952), 161.

[87] STSK, ts'e 62 (ch. 42), 1b. This Ming source states that during the reign of Tai Tsung "The sea isles of Jung-chou also produced pearls; an office was established to take charge of this." Jung-chou does not touch the sea; I suppose that Jung-kuan is meant. This may refer to the first T'ang creation of the "Pearl Administration" at Ho-P'u. I have not found the contemporary source on which this statement is based. But there had been a "Pearl Administration" here in the third century; see Schafer (1952), 157.

[88] TT, 6, 37c; Schafer (1963), 244.

[89] TS, 9, 2a; Schafer (1963), 244.

[90] Schafer (1952), 157.

[91] Ning Ling-hsien, "Ho-p'u chu huan chuang," CTW, 438, 5a.

[92] Yüan Chen, "Ts'ai chu hsing," ChTS, han 6, ts'e 10, ch. 23, 3b.

[93] Schafer and Wallacker (1958), 57–58, 228.

[94] Chang Chi, "Sung Hai-nan k'o kuei chiu tao," ChTS, han 6, ts'e 6, ch. 3, 8b.

[95] SHC.

[96] Schafer (1963), 251–252.

[97] Schafer (1963a), 92.

[98] Schafer (1963a), 91–92.

[99] Ch'en Ts'ang-ch'i, in PTKM, 8, 31a.

[100] Przyluski (1914), 16.

[101] Ch'en Ts'ang-ch'i, in PTKM, 8, 31a.

[102] LPLI, a, 2.

[103] Ch'en Ts'ang-ch'i, in PTKM, 8, 31a.

[104] Schafer and Wallacker (1958), 228, 230, 238, map 11; YHC, 37, 1049, 1053; 38, 1079, 1083, 1086, 1090, 1091.

[105] LPLI, a, 2.

[106] Schafer and Wallacker (1958), 238. TS, 7, 1b, reports the reopening of this mine (we are not told how long it was closed) on 18 August 779, soon after the accession of Te Tsung.

[107] Schafer and Wallacker (1958), 230; YHC, 38, 1086, 1090.

[108] In Ferrand (1914), 30–31.

[109] Schafer (1963a), 92–93.

[110] Schafer (1963), 255–256.

[111] Han Yü, "Ch'ien chung wu ch'ing chuang," CTW, 549, 7b.

[112] Schafer (1963), 80.

[113] Su Kung, in PTKM, 8, 31a.

[114] Schafer and Wallacker (1958), 227, map 12. YHC, 34, 1016–1017, 1038–1079. Compare K'ai yüan tribute with Yüan ho tribute.

[115] Su Kung, in PTKM, 8, 31a.

[116] Schafer (1963a), 91–92.

[117] Goloubew (1932), 137; Janse (1947), xviii; Chang (1959a), 87–88.

[118] Schafer and Wallacker (1958), 238, map 13.

[119] YHC, 34, 1006; 37, 1042.

[120] Janse (1947), 48.

[121] CS, 97, 1337b; Stein (1947), 285–290.

[122] YHC, 34, 1006; YHC, 37, 1043. These mines were in Huai-chi *hsien* and Kuei-ling *hsien*. The second of these had been exploited since Sui times.

[123] YHC, 34, 1006. In Hua-meng *hsien*.

[124] Schafer and Wallacker (1958), 57–58, 229, map 13.

CHAPTER 10 (Pages 165–205)

[1] Bates (1963), 121, 284.

[2] Bates (1952), 196–197; Bates (1963), 120–121.

[3] Bates (1963), 120–121.

[4] Wallace (1869), 244–245. Cf. Malleret (1934), 137, where this theme reappears.

[5] Wallace (1878), 60–61.

[6] Bates (1952), 179.

[7] Bates (1952), 184–185; Bates (1963), 120, 236.

[8] Bates (1963), 236. Much of this, I fear, is only paraphrase of Bates, with some adjectival embellishment.

[9] Bates (1963), 120.

[10] Fenzel (1929), 78.

[11] Liu Ch'ang-ch'ing, "Sung P'ei erh shih Tuan kung shih Ling-nan," ChTS, han 2, ts'e 5, ch. 1, 18b.

[12] Chang Chi, "Sung Hou p'an kuan fu Kuang-chou ts'ung chün," ChTS, han 6, ts'e 6, ch. 4, 6b. Cf. Nakamura (1917), 567.

[13] Wiens (1954), 11–12.

[14] Fenzel (1929), 78.

[15] Fenzel (1929), 56.

[16] Fenzel (1930), 98.

[17] See Renner (1927), 27, for a characterization of this forest species.

[18] Yüan Chieh, "Chiu i shan t'u chi," CTW, 382, 4b.

[19] Liu Tsung-yüan, "Chi Wei Hsing," ChTS, han 6, ts'e 1, ch. 2, 7b.

[20] Fenzel (1930), 110–111.

[21] Cf. Obi (1962), 268–269, on the bitterness of the life of the old Chinese hermit.

[22] For an impression of the Hainan forest, see Clark (1938), 399, 406; McClure (1934), 583–585 gives a short but vivid list of the conspicuous wild plants encountered there.

[23] P'i Jih-hsiu, "Chi Ch'iung-chou Yang she jen," ChTS, han 9, ts'e 9, ch. 7, 2a.

[24] Gourou (194), 366–367.

[25] YHC, 34, 1004, 1019; 37, 1042; Schafer and Wallacker (1958), 221, map 5. They were tribute from Kuang, Ho, Shao, Shuang, Feng, Ch'un and Ch'in.

[26] NPHS, e, 42.

[27] Ch'en Ts'ang-ch'i, in PTKM, 13, 31b; Stuart (1911), 249.

[28] Burkill (1935), 116–121; Ch'en (1957), 398–400.

[29] LPLI, b, 11.

[30] Stuart (1911), 1–2; Burkill (1935), 4–9; Read (1936), 110. "Jequirity" is from the Tupi-Guarani language.

[31] The expression "thinking of you" (*hsiang szu*) is also applied to two trees, the so-called Circassian Bean or Red Sandalwood (*Adenanthera pavonina*) and the "Chinese Hackberry" (*Celtis sinensis*). See Sauer (1947), 41, 49.

[32] PHL, 3, 16b–17a.

[33] Wang Wei, "Hsiang szu," ChTS, han 2, ts'e 8, ch. 4, 9b.

[34] THTL, in TPKC, 483, 5a. An abbreviated version of the same text is given in LNTS, 36, 14a.

[35] PHL, 3, 12b–14a.

[36] YYTT, 18, 149; Schafer (1963), 122–123.

[37] Lo (1960), 147, 154, 156–157.

[38] Li Ch'ün-yü (fl. 847), "Fa hsing szu liu tsu chieh t'an," ChTS, han 9, ts'e 3, ch. 2, 7b.

[39] Sitwell (1959), 216.

[40] Erasmus Darwin, "Loves of the Plants," *The Botanic Garden.*

[41] Grigson and Gibbs-Smith (1957), 43. The legend is richly documented in Yule and Burnell (1886), 726–732, 865–866.

[42] Albert de Pouvourville, "La vierge verte," quoted in Malleret (1934), 137.

[43] CYCT, 1, 2a.

[44] Ibid.

[45] Su Kung, in PTKM, 18, 49a; Burkill (1935), 1775–1776; Read (1936), 50.

[46] THTL, in TPKC, 408, 4b–5a.

[47] Ch'en Ts'ang-ch'i, in PTKM, 18, 46b.

[48] Ch'en Ts'ang-ch'i, in PTKM, 45, 34a.

[49] Yüan Chen, "Sung Ts'ui shih yü chih Ling-nan, erh shih yün," ChTS, han 6, ts'e 9, ch. 11, 4b.

[50] Huang-fu Jan (714–767), "T'i hua chang, erh shou," ChTS, han 4, ts'e 7, ch. 1, 7a.

[51] Ch'en Ts'ang-ch'i, in PTKM, 35, 41b; Schafer (1963), 136. For instance, the Hainan rosewood *Dalbergia benthami* (*hua li*) whose "heavy, dark red, aromatic heartwood . . . is highly esteemed for making furniture and carved work." McClure (1934), 586. See this same source for other Hainanese hardwoods.

[52] A synonym of *Cocculus laurifolius.* See Burkill (1935), 594; Read (1936), 163; Chia (1946), 765; Ch'en (1957), 357.

[53] Ch'en Ts'ang-ch'i and Li Hsün, in PTKM, 34, 29a.

[54] Su Kung and Ch'en Ts'ang-ch'i, in PTKM, 34, 29a. The Chinese name is *tiao chang.* There are several species of

Lindera in both central and south China, e.g., *Lindera umbellata* (Ch'en [1957], 355) and *Lindera sericea* Silky Spicebush (Read [1936], 157).

[55] Ch'en Ts'ang-ch'i, in PTKM, 34, 29a. In medieval times the wood of the Chinese camphor (*chang*) (*Cinnamomum camphora*) seems to have been more highly prized than the aromatic "dextrocamphor" extracted from it, which was in turn regarded as inferior to the "dragonbrain" camphor (laevo-borneol) imported from the Indies. See Schafer (1963), 166–167.

[56] TYSIL, in TPYL, 959, 3b; used in Stein (1947), 161–162. Stein misinterprets *chung hsia* "Central Hsia" (i.e., north China) in this passage as "en été."

[57] I owe this observation to Bates (1952), 180–181, and thank Ivor Brown for restoring "foison" to our vocabulary.

[58] Fairchild (1944), 163–164.

[59] Bates (1952), 180–181.

[60] Li Tuan, "Ch'un yu yüeh," ChTS, han 5, ts'e 3, ch. 1, 3b; cf. Po Chü-i, "Li ch'iu hsi yu huai Meng-te," ChTS, han 7, ts'e 6, ch. 29, 4a. For a survey of the important Chinese palms see Ch'en (1957), 88–100.

[61] Ch'en Ts'ang-ch'i, in PTKM, 35, 41b. Ch'en lists many of the palms of Lingnan, some recognizable, such as the sagwire, betel, and coconut; some not readily identifiable, as "winter leaf," "*hu-san*," and "*to-lo* (*ta-la*)."

[62] It was grown from imported seeds in the great *Hsing shan szu.* Chang Ch'iao, "Hsing shan szu pei-to shu," ChTS, han 10, ts'e 1, ch. 2, 1a. Cf. Schafer (1963), 270–271.

[63] YYTT, 18, 150.

[64] SC and HS, from Szu-ma Hsiang-ju. See Han (1946), 36.

[65] Han (1946), 36–37.

[66] Stein (1947), 259.

[67] YYTT, 16, 126.

[68] NFTMC, c, 2a–2b.

[69] LPLI, b, 12.

[70] Lu Kuei-meng, "Ho chi Ch'iung-chou

Yang she jen," FLHSCW, 9, 27b. Cf. the matching poem by P'i Jih-hsiu below, note 101. Perhaps Lu refers to palm wine rather than to coconut milk.

[71] Li Hsün, in PTKM, 31, 14b.

[72] Li Hsün, "Nan Hsiang tzu," ChTS, han 12, ts'e 10, ch. 8, 2b.

[73] TS, 222c, 1a.

[74] Li Shih-chen, PTKM, 31, 15a; Burkill (1935), 610–611.

[75] Yin Yao-fan (fl. 827), "Tsui tseng Liu shih erh," ChTS, han 8, ts'e 2, 3b.

[76] Laufer (1919), 282–283. Actually the pomegranate seems to have been introduced to China about two centuries *after* Chang Ch'ien.

[77] Shen Ch'üan-ch'i, "T'i yeh tzu shu," ChTS, han 2, ts'e 5, ch. 2, 9a.

[78] *Areca catechu.* Burkill (1935), 223. I do not know if the "mountain *pinang,*" a similar plant of the interior of Hainan, has been exploited in the same way. See Ch'en (1957), 99.

[79] Burkill (1935), 223–230.

[80] Su Kung, in PTKM, 31, 14a; YHC, 38, 1083, 1085, 1088; Schafer and Wallacker (1958), 217.

[81] Eberhard (1942a), 291–292.

[82] Burkill (1935), 223–230.

[83] Su Kung, in PTKM, 14, 37a.

[84] Schafer (1963), 151.

[85] Ibid.

[86] Li Hsün, in PTKM, 31, 14b.

[87] TS, 222c, 1a.

[88] TS, 222c, 3a. For a possible etymology of Chen-la (Chin-lap), suggested by Pelliot, see Schafer (1963), 5.

[89] Burkill (1935), 230–236.

[90] Yule and Burnell (1886), 590. The word "sagwire" was also applied to a toddy. I have not yet seen evidence of a wine made from this palm in T'ang times.

[91] YYTT, hsü 10, 249; PHL, 2, 9b; LPLI, b, 11, Ch'en Ts'ang-ch'i, in PTKM, 31, 15a. Cf. Schafer (1963), 133. Burkill says that this sago produces bowel complaints.

[92] PHL, 2, 9b–10b; LPLI, b, 11.

[93] PHL, 2, 9b–10b.

[94] PHL, 2, 9b–10b; LPLI, b, 11; Yule and Burnell (1886), 590; Burkill (1935), 230–236.

[95] Li Hsün, "Nan hsiang tzu," ChTS, han 12, ts'e 10, ch. 8, 2a.

[96] Fairchild (1944), 194.

[97] Ch'en (1957), 100.

[98] Ch'en Ts'ang-ch'i and Li Hsün, in PTKM, 31, 15b.

[99] Ch'en (1957), 99. Besides its fruit, the date palm yielded a favorite rope fiber for the ancient Egyptians. See Grigson and Gibbs-Smith (1957), 333. I do not know if the Chinese used it.

[100] LPLI, b, 11; Schafer (1963), 121–122.

[101] P'i Jih-hsiu, "Chi Ch'iung-chou Yang she jen," ChTS, han 9, ts'e 9, ch. 7, 2a. For exotic wines in T'ang China see Schafer (1963), 142.

[102] Burkill (1935), 1557–1561.

[103] Ch'en (1957), 100.

[104] Fairchild (1944), 174.

[105] Yule and Burnell (1886), 340–341. "Jaggery" is related to Sanskrit *śarkarā* "grit, gravel."

[106] Wallace (1869), 148.

[107] Burkill (1935), 1869.

[108] Bates (1952), 182. Important lianes of south China, some of which have fragrant flowers, belong to the genus *Desmos,* e.g., *shan chih chia* "mountain finger nail" (*Desmos hainanensis*)—the name relates it to henna—of Kwangtung and Hainan. I have not found it in the T'ang records. See Burkill (1935), 796; Ch'en (1957), 314–315.

[109] Wallace (1869), 276.

[110] The identity of the two is asserted by Ch'en (1957), 96.

[111] YHC, 37, 1049.

[112] Ch'en Ts'ang-ch'i, in PTKM, 18b, 51b.

[113] Schafer (1957a), 134.

[114] P'i Jih-hsiu, "Ch'u hsia yu leng-chia ching she," ChTS, han 9, ts'e 9, ch. 2, 12a.

[115] Ch'en (1957), 96, NFTMC, b, 5b, gives an incense-bearing "purple liane" as a product of Nam-Viet. Possibly it was

this, but I do not know if *Calamus margaritae* has aromatic properties.

[116] *Sheng t'eng.*

[117] Ch'en Ts'ang-ch'i, in PTKM, 18b, 51b.

[118] Ch'en (1957), 96.

[119] Schafer (1957a), 133–134; Ch'en (1957), 97.

[120] YHC, 37, 1042.

[121] Li Hsün and Ch'en Ts'ang-ch'i, in PTKM, 18b, 51a. The plant was first described in CCC (LNIS), 1, 4b.

[122] YYTT, 4, 36.

[123] YYTT, hsü 9, 246.

[124] YHC, 34, 1010; Schafer and Wallacker (1958), 57–58, 230, map 16.

[125] PHL, 3, 6b–7a, 10a–10b.

[126] Henry Yule, *Mission to Ava* (1858), quoted in Yule and Burnell (1886), 41.

[127] Wallace (1869), 87.

[128] CKC, in TPHYC, 162, 9a.

[129] YHC, 34, 1004, 1019, 1042; Schafer and Wallacker (1958), 217, 220, 229, 234, map 15.

[130] TPHYC, quoted in YTCS, 91, 3b.

[131] YHC, 34, 1007.

[132] TS, 222c, 1a–1b.

[133] Schafer (1963), 264.

[134] In Ch'eng-chou and Yung-chou. PHL, 3, 10b–11a. Perhaps this was *Chimonobambusa quadrangularis.* See Chia (1946), 1184; Ch'en (1957), 83.

[135] Chia (1948), 1187; Ch'en (1957), 86–87.

[136] CIL, 2, 29b.

[137] *Bambusa stenostachys,* nowadays planted around houses as a windbreak. Ch'en (1957), 85–86.

[138] LPLI, b, 10; YYTT, 18, 145.

[139] NFTMC, c, 6a–6b; PHL, 3, 14a–14b.

[140] LPLI, b, 10; SP, p. 13a. *Dendrocalamus giganteus* of south Asia may occur in Kwangtung (Ch'en [1957], 87), but its stems are only 5–7 inches through.

[141] Wu Yün, "Chu fu," CTW, 925, 9a.

[142] *Arundinaria murielae.* Chia (1946), 1183.

[143] *Phyllostachys puberula,* which has a cultivated variety *boryana.* Schafer and Wallacker (1958), 220. A widely distributed species, *Bambusa vulgaris,* is also called "spotted bamboo." It is thought that its variety *striata* "a garden race with striped and spotted stems" may be of Chinese origin. Burkill (1935), 300. I do not know if the two are related in any way. I wonder if the "spotted linen" sent as tribute from Chen and Fu (Schafer and Wallacker [1958], 236) could be a cloth made of the fibers of this attractive kind of bamboo.

[144] PHL, 2, 19b–20a; Eberhard (1942a), 12.

[145] Yüan Chen, "Feng ho Tou Jung-chou," ChTS, han 6, ts'e 9, ch. 18, 6b.

[146] Liu Ch'ang-ch'ing, "Pan chu yen," ChTS, han 3, ts'e 1, ch. 2, 11b.

[147] Schafer (1963), 134.

[148] PHL, 2, 19b–20a.

[149] Burkill (1935), 1973–1974; Ch'en (1957), 820.

[150] Li Hsün, in PTKM, 35, 42a. For the Persians in Canton see Schafer (1963), 10, 15, and elsewhere.

[151] LPLI, b, 11; PHL, 3, 9b. The word *pao* is nowadays used of a drought-tolerant oaks; another tree altogether.

[152] Schafer (1963), 138; see Yule and Burnell (1886), 110 for calamander.

[153] SSYI, b, 28. Also noticed in NFTMC, quoted in TPYL, 960, 6b.

[154] Su Kung, in PTKM, 35, 41a; TPHYC, 169, 10a; Schafer (1963), 211.

[155] Ch'en Ts'ang-ch'i, in PTKM, 37, 55b; YHC, 38, 1083, 1086, 1090; Ch'en (1957), 539; Schafer and Wallacker (1958), 57–58, 223.

[156] Su Kung, in PTKM, 16, 21a.

[157] PHL, 3, 11a–12a.

[158] YHC, 34, 1007.

[159] YHC, 38, 1075; Schafer and Wallacker (1958), 57–58, 238, map 19.

[160] Li Ho, "Lo-fou shan fu yü ko p'ien," ChTS, han 6, ts'e 7, ch. 2, 5a.

[161] Quoted in Schafer (1963), 206.

[162] Po Chü-i, "Hsin chih pu ch'iu," ChTS, han 7, ts'e 1, ch. 1, 18a. Cf. Schafer (1963), 205.

[163] Schafer (1963), 206. See especially the best of all studies of the history of cotton in the Far East in Pelliot (1959), 425–531, a monograph of great elegance and erudition.

[164] Schafer (1963), 200.

[165] Bates (1952), 58.

[166] Bates (1952), 155–156.

[167] Bates (1952), 58.

[168] Bates (1952), 55, 156, 162.

[169] Spencer (1954), 83–84.

[170] CTS, 197, 1b, 4a–4b.

[171] Schafer (1954a), 70.

[172] *Huan* (*Ctenopharyngodon idellus*), a much cultivated and eaten cyprinid, sometimes called the "grass carp." It resembles the European ide.

[173] LPLI, a, 3; Ch'en Ts'ang-ch'i, in PTKM, 44, 27a, observes them also in the lake district of central China.

[174] Burkill (1935), 638–642.

[175] T'ao Hung-ching, in PTKM, 27, 37b.

[176] Su Kung, in PTKM, 27, 37b.

[177] Spencer (1954), 77–78.

[178] Burkill (1935), 814, 818–819.

[179] Su Kung, in PTKM, 27, 37b.

[180] Tu Fu, "Fa Ch'in-chou," CCTS, 90.

[181] NFTMC, a, 3a. (It also appears in *Ch'i min yao shu*).

[182] These remarks are based on an unpublished study of the sweet potato and yam made some years ago by B. E. Wallacker.

[183] Wallace (1869), 374.

[184] Bates (1952), 166–167, 169.

[185] PHL, 2, 13a–14a.

[186] *Malus asiatica*. Chinese *lin-ch'in*. PHL, 2, 13b.

[187] CIL, a, 39a.

[188] Bates (1952), 166–167.

[189] *Yü kung, Chou li,* et al. See Yeh (1958), 2.

[190] *Citrus aurantium*. Burkill (1935), 566–567.

[191] *Citrus sinensis*. Burkill (1935), 574–575.

[192] Burkill (1935), 571–572; Ch'en (1957), 570.

[193] Ch'en Ts'ang-ch'i, in PTKM, 30, 9b.

[194] The citron is described in NFTMC, c, 4b (later in *Ch'i min yao shu*).

[195] LPLI, b, 12. See Ch'en Ts'ang-ch'i, in PTKM, 30, 10a for a shorter description.

[196] Burkill (1935), 573–574; Ch'en (1957), 579, 582.

[197] Ch'en Ts'ang-ch'i, in PTKM, 30, 9b. Yellow Mildling, is intended to suggest a small fruit with little flavor, and is a translation of *huang tan tzu*. See Schafer and Wallacker (1958), 222, map 2.

[198] PHL, 3, 2a.

[199] Of Szechwanese sweetpeels sent to the court. TTHY, quoted in TPYL, 966, 2a.

[200] ChC, (in TTTS, 10), 35a.

[201] LPLI, c, 24; YYTT, 18, 146; Flanders, Gressit, and Fisher (1958), 75.

[202] Liu Tsung-yüan, "Liu-chou ch'eng hsi pei yü chung kan shu," LHSC, 42, 18a.

[203] Liu Tsung-yüan, "Nan chung jung chü yu," ChTS, han 6, ts'e 1, ch. 4, 3b.

[204] TKSP, c, 19b; YHC, 34, 1010; Soymié (1956), 5.

[205] TYTP, as reported in Soymié (1956), 6.

[206] CTS, quoted in TPYL, 966, 1b; YYTT, 18, 146; TKSP, c, 19b.

[207] HNYC, quoted in TPHYC, 157, 4b. I can not identify the author of this book. It must have been written in the tenth century, give or take a few years.

[208] Shinoda (1963), 356–357, thinks that in T'ang poetry the word usually means our loquat (*Eriobotrya*); I am not quite convinced.

[209] Yeh (1958), 71–72. A number of *Fortunella* species occur in the coastal provinces from Anhwei southwards. *F.*

hindsii and *F. polyandra* occur in Nam-Viet. See Ch'en (1957), 566–567.

[210] Yu Shao (eighth century), "Sung Fang pieh kuan hsün Nan-hai, hsü," CTW, 427, 19b.

[211] Wang Chien, "Kung tz'u," ChTS, han 5, ts'e 5, ch. 6, 5a.

[212] PHL, 3, 3a–3b.

[213] Note the astonishment of Fairchild, accustomed to our domesticated seedless bananas, when he encountered the wild banana of Halmahera: "It was quite unlike any banana I had ever seen before, for its copper-colored fruits split open as they mature, and their thick skins curl back from the point, displaying something quite as striking as a large yellow flower would be: a mass of brilliant yellow flesh packed with black seeds."

[214] Burkill (1935), 1507–1518; Bates (1952), 168; Wheatley (1959), 107. Burkill thinks one species, *Musa nana,* is a cultigen original to the Nam-Viet region.

[215] Ch'en (1957), 101–102.

[216] Reynolds (1951), 23–24.

[217] Brown (1961), 43.

[218] Reynolds and Fang (1940), 167; Reynolds (1951), 405, 12. The Han reference is Yang Fu, *Nan i i wu chih;* the later one is *Ch'i min yao shu.*

[219] Burkill (1935), 1508, 1516.

[220] See K'ai yüan tribute as reported in YHC, 34, 1004, 1013, 1016, 1017; 37, 1042; 38, 1075, 1083; Schafer and Wallacker (1958), 217.

[221] P'i Jih-hsiu, "Sung Li ming fu chih jen Hai-nan," ChTS, han 9, ts'e 9, ch. 7, 3a.

[222] Su Kung, in PTKM, 15, 10b.

[223] CIL, a, 27a.

[224] Brown (1953), 18–19.

[225] Ts'en Ts'an, "Hsün-yang ch'i lang chung tse chi shih," ChTS, han 3, ts'e 8, ch. 3, 17b.

[226] Tu Mu, "Pa-chiao," ChTS, han 8, ts'e 7, ch. 5, 18b.

[227] Tu Hsün-ho, "Min chung ch'iu szu," ChTS, han 10, ts'e 8, ch. 3, 2b.

[228] Liu Tsung-yüan, "Hung chiao," LHSC, 43, 13a–13b.

[229] Li Shen, "Hung chiao hua," ChTS, han 8, ts'e 1, ch. 4, 4b.

[230] Han Wo, "Hung pa-chiao fu," CTW, 829, 16b–17a.

[231] Li Hsün, "Nan hsiang tzu," ChTS, han 12, ts'e 10, ch. 8, 2a.

[232] The scientific name of the lichee is *Litchi* (or *Nephelium*) *chinensis.* For a fanciful Chinese etymology of this word, see FNC, in TPKC, 406, 2b. "An almost forgotten Chinese fruit, the lychee, a bright red, rough skinned, plum like delicacy, is being promoted by Florida growers for use in salads and desserts. About a third of the 1958 crop of 45,000 pounds was sold to New Yorkers. Growers have set their sights for 1959 on a crop of 100,000 pounds." *The Sacramento Bee,* 12 January, 1959.

[233] LPLI, b, 12; PHL, 3, 1a–2a.

[234] YHC, 34, 1004; Schafer and Wallacker (1958), 220.

[235] Li Hsün, in PTKM, 31, 12b.

[236] Schafer (1963), 119.

[237] CSYC (in TTTS, 4), 18a.

[238] TS, 22, 2b.

[239] Chang Chiu-ling, "Li-chih fu," CTW, 283, 2a–3b.

[240] Ts'ao Sung, "Nan-hai p'ei Cheng szu k'ung yu li yüan," ChTS, han 11, ts'e 2, ch. 2, 9b.

[241] CIL, a, 40b.

[242] Hsü Hun, "Sung Tu hsiu ts'ai kuei Kuei-lin," ChTS, han 8, ts'e 8, ch. 9, 9b.

[243] Leconte de Lisle, "Le Manchy," *Poèmes Barbares.*

[244] Po Chü-i, "Li-chih lou tui chiu," ChTS, han 7, ts'e 4, ch. 18, 11a.

[245] PTKM, 25, 25a.

[246] Yung T'ao, "Tao Shu hou chi t'u chung ching li," ChTS, han 8, ts'e 6, 4b.

[247] The Po Chü-i quotation is well-known, even if unexplained. Mr. John Jameson discovered the Yung T'ao quotation for me.

248 The nomenclature is variable— *Nephelium longana* or *Euphoria longana.*

249 NFTMC, c, 3b.

250 Su Kung, in PTKM, 31, 13a.

251 *Nephelium lappaceum.* The pulasan of Indonesia (*N. mutabile*) is much like it. See Ch'eng Ts'ang-ch'i, in PTKM, 31, 16a; Burkill (1935), 1543–1548.

252 *Mangifera indica.* Bates (1952), 166.

253 Burkill (1935), 1402–1406.

254 Spencer (1954), 84.

255 SS, 82, 2534a.

256 TTHYC, 2 [10a; this edition is not actually paginated]; ICCYI, 8. Hsüan-tsang gives the Indic names of three trees in Chinese transcription, all very similar. *An-mo-lo* (*Am-mět-la*), *An-mi-lo* (*Am-miě-la*), and *A-mo-lo* (*A-mat-la*). The first of these appears to be the mango, but in other Chinese sources the transcription *an-lo* (*am-la*) is more usual; see PTKM, 30, 7a, for instance. The second is said to correspond to transcribe *āmla,* the Indian tamarisk, and the third to correspond to *āmala[ki],* the emblic myrobalan. See Demiéville (1929), 30; Soothill and Hodous (1937), 387.

257 Su Kung, in PTKM, 31, 13b; YHC, 34, 1004; Schafer (1963), 145–146.

258 Su Kung, in PTKM, 31, 13b.

259 Yule and Burnell (1886), 465.

260 Lo (1960), 17, 147. Apparently they grew naturally in Annam. See Su Kung, in PTKM, 35, 39a.

261 LNIWC, quoted in Lo (1960), 148–149; NPHS, g, 71.

262 Lo (1960), 151–152; Schafer (1963), 145–146.

263 Lo (1960), 151, plates 32 and 33.

264 Sung Chih-wen, "Teng Yüeh wang T'ai," ChTS, han 1, ts'e 10, ch. 3, 5a.

265 Ch'en Ts'ang-ch'i, quoting *Po wu chih,* in PTKM, 30, 10b.

266 Chang Pi, "Wan tz'u Hsiang-yüan hsien," ChTS, han 11, ts'e 4, 2a.

267 PHL, 3, 5a. This must be *Myrica rubra* v. *alba.* See Ch'en (1957), 133. A Hainan variety (*M. adenophora*) (Ch'en

[1957], 134), seems not to have been noticed in T'ang literature.

268 Li (1959), 48. *Prunus mume* "botanically is classified with the apricots rather than the plums."

269 PHL, 3, 6a–6b.

270 NFTMC, quoted in TPYL, 974, 3b; Ch'en Ts'ang-ch'i, in PTKM, 31, 15b.

271 Stuart (1911), 224, gives *Juglans sieboldiana;* Read (1936), 200, gives *J. mandshurica.* The Chinese name for walnut is literally "foreign peach."

272 Schafer (1963), 147.

273 Ch'en Ts'ang-ch'i, in PTKM, 31, 16a. Read (1936), 88, identifies it as the cashew nut (*Anacardium occidentale*), an American plant!

274 YHC, 34, 1016.

275 Read (1936), 15; *Cucumis melo* var. *conomon.*

276 Ch'en Ts'ang-ch'i, in PTKM, 28, 40b.

277 Read (1936), 29.

278 Yule and Burnell (1886), 86–87.

279 Ch'en Ts'ang-ch'i, in PTKM, 28, 39b.

280 NFTMC, a, 7b; PHL, 2, 18b–19b; Ch'en Ts'ang-ch'i, in PTKM, 27, 34a.

281 YYTT, 10, 251.

282 LNIWC, in TPKC, 416, 5b.

283 PHL, 2, 17b–18a. Stuart (1911), 263, identifies it as *Menyanthes trifoliata.*

284 PHL, 2, 18a–18b; YYTT, 19, 160. Identified as *Isoëtes japonica* in Chia (1946), 1242.

285 Meng Shen, quoted in CHCCLPT, 9, 12b.

286 ChC, (in TTTS, 10), 35a; Ch'en Ts'ang-ch'i, in PTKM, 32, 20a; identified as *Thea sinensis* var. *macrophylla,* or *Thea macrophylla.* See Read (1936), 77; Chia (1946), 422.

287 ChC, in TPHYC, 167, 3b. This might be the "coral" plant, or "bamboo-joint tea," of Ch'en (1957), 109.

288 Schafer (1963), 152–153.

289 Meng Shen, in PTKM, 33, 21a.

290 Schafer (1963), 154.

[291] A. R. Wallace, "The Tropics," in *Tropical Nature and Other Essays* (London, 1878), p. v.

[292] Ch'en Ts'ang-ch'i, in PTKM, 14, 37a; Schafer (1963), 184. The Chinese name was *i chih tzu*, Wisdom-augmenting Seeds.

[293] Su Kung and Li Hsün, in PTKM, 14, 36a; YHC, 38, 1088; Schafer and Wallacker (1958), 218; Schafer (1963), 184–185.

[294] YHC, 38, 1083.

[295] Su Kung, in PTKM, 14, 36a.

[296] See above where Hsüan-yüan Chi produced cardamoms and lichees magically for Hsüan Tsung, presumably to represent the handsome plants of his homeland.

[297] Li She, "Yü Wu-chou Liu chung ch'eng," ChTS, han 7, ts'e 10, 14a.

[298] Li Hsün, "Nan hsiang tzu," ChTS, han 12, ts'e 10, ch. 8, 1b.

[299] Li Hsün, "Nan Hsiang tzu," ChTS, han 12, ts'e 10, ch. 8, 2b.

[300] Su Kung and Li Hsün, in PTKM, 14, 35b; Stuart (1911), 32; Chia (1946), 1015; Schafer and Wallacker (1958), 219.

[301] NFTMC, a, 2b; Chen Ch'üan, in PTKM, 14, 35b; YHC, 34, 1004; Stuart (1911), 31; Read (1936), 207.

[302] Ch'en Ts'ang-ch'i, in PTKM, 14, 35b. Stuart (1911), 226, describes it as a scitamineous plant with a root similar to *Kaempferia galanga*.

[303] Cf. Schafer (1963), 185.

[304] *Ti li chi* (otherwise unidentified), quoted in TPYL, 957, 6a. The reference is actually to Kuei-yang *chün*. that is, to Ch'en-chou in southernmost Hunan, adjacent to medieval Kuei-lin. NFTMC, b, 2a–2b notes that cinnamon trees in Lingnan tend to form pure, unmixed stands.

[305] HS, 95, 0604b.

[306] ShIC, quoted in TPKC, 408, 4b.

[307] Ch'en Ts'ang-ch'i, in PTKM, 34, 26a. Su Kung speaks earlier, in PTKM, 34, 25b–26a, of cassia from Kuei, Jung (Yung), Shao, and Chiao.

[308] KHYHC, quoted in YTCS, 103, 9a–9b.

[309] The taxonomy of these trees is complicated. The best usage seems to be as follows: *chang, Cinnamomum camphora; jou kuei, Cinnamomum cassia; T'ien-chu kuei, Cinnamomum pedunculatum; yüeh kuei, Osmanthus fragrans;* but historically there have been many inconsistencies in the use of these and other *kuei*-terms. See for instance Ch'en (1957), 332 ff.

[310] Ch'en Ts'ang-ch'i, in PTKM, 34, 26a; YHC, 37, 1049; Schafer and Wallacker (1958), 218.

[311] TS, 43b, 13b.

[312] Li Hsün and Ch'en Ts'ang-ch'i, in PTKM, 34, 27a. The "Orchid Cassia" (*lan kuei*), tribute of Shao-chou (YHC, 34, 1019), remains unidentified.

[313] YYTT, 1, 6, based on HNT, as quoted in TPYL, 957, 5a.

[314] Li (1959), 151–153.

[315] Li Te-yü, "P'ing ch'üan shan chü ts'ao mu chi," (TTTS, 7), 48a.

[316] Li Te-yü, "Hung kuei shu," ChTS, han 7, ts'e 10, 19a–19b.

[317] *Artocarpus communis.*

[318] It is *Artocarpus integra*. Schafer (1962b), 220.

[319] *Artocarpus hypargyraea*. Perhaps this is the same as the "red *kuei*," *Artocarpus lingnanensis* of Sauer (1947), 50.

[320] See Schafer (1963), 163–165. *Calambac* is related to Malay *kĕlĕmbak;* I would suppose that the Chinese versions of this word (probably post-T'ang) *chianan* (*gya-nam*) and *chia-lan* (*gya-lam*) are of Cham origin. See Yule and Burnell (1886), 110, for the Anglo-Indian permutations.

[321] YHC, 34, 1004; 38, 1086; Schafer and Wallacker (1958), 221.

[322] Ch'en (1957), 871–872; Wheatley (1959), 69–72. Aside from *Aquilaria*, a similar substance is taken from *Gonystylus bancanus.*

[323] YHC, 34, 1008.

[324] KSTI, in TPKC, 414, 2a.

[325] PHL, 3, 7b–9a, describes the *chan* in just the same language used of the *mi* in NFTMC, b, 4b–9a. Ch'en Ts'ang-ch'i, in PTKM, 34, 28a, says that the *mi* aromatic tree of Annam yields the precious substance after it has been cut down and left to rot for five years. *Aquilaria sinensis* occurs on Hainan, where it is now artificially bled for its resin, which coagulates to make the desired incense. McClure (1934), 588; Wheatley (1959), 69–72. I have not yet found T'ang evidence of this occurrence or practice. Ch'en (1957), 871–872 reports *A. sinensis* chiefly from the mountains around Tung-kuan, east of Canton.

[326] PHL, 3, 3b–4b.

[327] Two species grow in Lingnan, especially in Hainan: *Canarium album* and *Canarium pimela*.

[328] Schafer (1963), 165.

[329] Schafer (1963), 166.

[330] Su Kung, in PTKM, 34, 31a; STC, b, 23b; Schafer and Wallacker (1958), 222, 230.

[331] Ch'en Ts'ang-ch'i, in PTKM, 31, 13b. His account is based primarily on the older KCC. Read (1936), 99, thinks this may be *Canarium pimela*, the "black olive."

[332] Su Kung, in PTKM, 34, 28a; Schafer (1963), 171–172. "Nail aromatic" also means "lilac" in T'ang times, especially in poetry—again, from the shape of the florets.

[333] Su Kung, in PTKM, 14, 38a.

[334] Ch'en Ts'ang-ch'i, in PTKM, 14, 40a. Well-known species in India and Indochina are *Cymbopogon citratus, C. martini,* and *C. nardus.* See Burkill (1935), 724–728. I cannot tell if there was another species native to Annam, or if one of these foreign ones had been introduced here.

[335] Schafer (1948), 61. See also Li (1959), 126–130; Schafer (1963), **173**.

[336] YYTT, 18, 153; cf. NFTMC, a, 2b.

[337] Cf. Malay *mĕlati;* Burkill (1935), 1265–1266.

[338] P'i Jih-hsiu, "Wu chung yen huai chi Nan-hai erh t'ung nien," ChTS, han 9, ts'e 9, ch. 7, 4a.

[339] CIL, a, 32a.

[340] Burkill (1935), 1776–1778.

[341] Yule and Burnell (1886), 167–168, give the Anglo-Indian form "chumpuk." See also Burkill (1935), 1464–1466; Li (1959), 148–149. The modern Chinese name is *po lan hua* White Orchid Flower, probably meant to suggest white magnolia. See Ch'en (1957), 299, for Chinese names of other species of *Michelia*.

[342] So in a poem of P'i Jih-hsiu. See Schafer (1963), 129.

[343] Li Ch'ün-yü, "Hsiang chung pieh ch'eng wei tu li," ChTS, han 9, ts'e 3, ch. 1, 10b.

[344] *Michelia fuscata* or *M. figo,* sometimes called Banana Shrub. Its modern Chinese name *han hsiao hua* does not appear in T'ang literature.

[345] Li (1959), 149.

[346] Schafer (1963), 157.

[347] YYTT, 18, 147.

[348] The name of the Chinese species, which also occurs in south Asia, is sometimes given as *Erythrina indica* and sometimes as *E. variegata*. Perhaps there are actually more than one there. See Burkill (1935), 945–949.

[349] LNIWC, in TPKC, 406, 3a–3b; Wang Ku (fl. 898), "Tz'u t'ung hua," ChTS, han 10, ts'e 8, 3a. Li Hsün gives it the alternate name of *hai t'ung "t'ung* from overseas." See PTKM, 35, 35b.

[350] See Ch'en T'ao (fl. 841), "Ch'üan-chou tz'u t'ung hua yung chien ch'eng Chao shih chün, liu shou," ChTS, han 11, ts'e 4, ch. 2, 14a. The relation between the name Zayton and the *Erythrina* seems to have been first suggested by Kuwabara Jitsuzō; but see especially Pelliot (1959), 583–597. Pelliot was still uncertain of the identification.

351 Li Hsün, "Nan hsiang tzu," ChTS, han 12, ts'e 10, ch. 8, 2a.

352 Sitwell (1948).

353 The first specimen arrived in the United States about 1948.

354 For these and others see Ch'en (1957), 810–815, and for Chinese camellias generally see also Li (1959), 79–85.

355 YYTT, 10, 250; hsü 9, 245.

356 Schafer (1964), 108.

357 Li Te-yü, "P'ing ch'üan ts'ao mu chi," (in TTTS, 7), 48b.

358 Kuan-hsiu, "Shan ch'a hua," ChTS, han 12, ts'e 3, ch. 2, 6a.

359 Huang T'ing-chien has a *fu* and Mei Yao-ch'en a *shih* on the camellia.

360 *Mu fu-jung* "tree lotus." See Burkill (1935), 1167–1172; Ch'en (1957), 764–766; Li (1959), 137–144, for all of these species. *Hibiscus mutabilis* is sometimes called *pud-tān* in Siamese and *botan* in Malay. Burkill (1935), 1167. These names suggest the medieval Chinese *mu-tan* (*mou-tan*), yielding Sino-Japanese *botan*, which means "(tree) peony." Is it possible that the Chinese name for the peony, otherwise still unexplained, is a transference from an Indochinese name for the hibiscus?

361 Chinese *mu chin* "tree hibiscus." This plant spread westward to Europe by Way of Syria, hence its name.

362 Chinese *chu chin* "vermilion hibiscus," or *fo-sang*.

363 Chinese *huang chin*.

364 The specific difference between *Hibiscus manihot* and *H. tiliaceus*, both of which have been equated with Chinese "yellow hibiscus" is not clear to me.

365 Li Shang-yin, "Chu chin hua," ChTS, han 8, ts'e 9, ch. 3, 31b.

366 LPLI, b, 13.

367 Liu Wei (fl. 844), "Ch'iu jih shou ch'en ching fou hsiu ts'ai," ChTS, han 9, ts'e 3, 2a.

368 Yü Fu (fl. 841), "Huai hsiang," ChTS, han 8, ts'e 10, 3b.

369 ShCC, 9b–10a.

370 YYTT, hsü 9, 247.

371 Chu Yeh, "Fu-sang fu," CTW, 901, 2b–3b.

372 Burkill (1935), 1407–1408. *Manglietia fordiana* occurs through south China generally; *M. tenuipes* and *M. aromatica* grow in Kwangsi. Ch'en (1957), 297–298; Li (1959), 147–148.

373 YYTT, hsü 9, 245.

374 CTS, 166, 15a; Po Chü-i, "Huan mu lien hua t'u chi Yüan lang chung," ChTS, han 7, ts'e 4, ch. 18, 4a.

375 Su Kung, in PTKM, 36, 51b. The Chinese name is *mai tzu mu*. Stuart (1911), 221, gives *Ixora stricta*; Ch'en (1957), 1133, gives *Ixora chinensis*.

376 Ch'en (1957), 503–504. Chia (1946), 582, gives *Erythrina crista-galli* for the identity of *hai hung tou*, but the former is a native of Peru!

377 Li Hsün, in PTKM, 35, 43a.

378 The modern name is *ch'iu hai t'ang*. Although Li (1959), 173–174, says that it has long been cultivated in China and adds that it "is a flower of romance in China. An ancient legend says . . ." etc., it does not appear in literature before Sung times, and was probably not introduced to cultivation until Sung or Yüan.

379 *Chuang tzu.*

380 Burkill (1935), 1441–1445; Ch'en (1957), 598; Su Kung, in PTKM, 35a, 36a. Ch'en lists a *Melia dubia* of Lingnan.

381 Tou Shu-hsiang (fl. 769), "Hsia yeh su piao hsiung hua chiu," ChTS, han 4, ts'e 10, 2a.

382 Burkill (1935), 1393; Ch'en (1957), 295. The same name (*yeh ho hua*) is given to a species of *Albizzia*, a mimosa. See Ch'en (1957), 497; Li (1959), 154–155. I have relied on Ch'en's primary identification.

383 PHL, 13, 16a. Cf. YYTT, 19, 161. Apparently there was a native north Chinese relative with which the exotic was confused.

384 *Inula* sp.

385 P'i Jih-hsiu, "Chin ch'ien hua," ChTS, han 9, ts'e 9, ch. 8, 8a.

386 Schafer (1963), 131–132.

387 PHL, 3, 17b; YYTT, 19, 159; Stuart (1911), 288. It is *Nymphaea tetragona,* the "pygmy water lily."

388 *Lawsonia inermis.* PHL, 3, 16a–16b; Burkill (1935), 1323–1325; Sauer (1947), 22; Li (1959), 194–195. Li observes that the same Chinese name was given, at least from the thirteenth century, to *Impatiens balsamina,* an introduction from India used for the same purpose.

389 YYTT, hsü 9, 245; Burkill (1935), 1550; Ch'en (1957), 1072.

390 Su Kung, in PTKM, 18, 44a; Stuart (1911), 492; Ch'en (1957), 546.

391 PHL, 3, 15a–16a.

392 *Paradise Lost,* IX.

393 *Ficus retusa,* the "true banyan"; *F. wightiana,* "the "bird banyan"; and *F. altissima,* the "large leaf banyan" of Hainan. See Ch'en (1957), 235–236.

394 LPLI, b, 10; NFTMC, b, 1b.

395 LPLI, b, 10. For a Taoist interpretation of the cool-shadowing banyan, see Schafer (1953), passim. For the position of trees of connected venation in the official auspices of T'ang, see Schafer (1963d), 201.

396 Liu Tsung-yüan, "Liu-chou erh yüeh jung yeh chin lo ou t'i," ChTS, han 6, ts'e 1, ch. 3, 2b.

397 The name is given to quite unrelated genera of similar habit and habitat, but chiefly to *Rhizopora.*

398 Fairchild (1944), 93.

CHAPTER 11 (Pages 206–247)

1 Chang Pin, "Hsi yu jen Jih-nan hui," ChTS, han 10, ts'e 10, 11b.

2 Yüan Chen, "Sung Ling-nan Ts'ui shih yü," ChTS, han 6, ts'e 9, ch. 17, 9a.

3 For instance, LPLI, c, enumerates many southern fishes, reptiles, crustaceans, molluscs and other phyla.

4 LPLI, c, 22.

5 PHL, 1, 22a–22b; LPLI, c, 22.

6 LPLI, c, 22; Ch'en Ts'ang-ch'i, in PTKM, 44, 31a.

7 Yang T'ao, "Shui mu mu hsia fu," CTW, 950, 20a–21a.

8 Meng Shen in CHCCLPT, 20, 8a. This edible oyster is distinguished in the Sung pharmacopoeias from the pearl oyster, which it closely resembles, but some sources indicate that the flesh of the pearl oyster was itself esteemed.

9 Schafer (1963), 140.

10 LPLI, c, 21.

11 YYTT, 17, 140.

12 Especially *Anodonta chinensis.*

13 For the Far Eastern history of the cowrie, see Pelliot (1959), 531–563.

14 Li Hsün, in PTKM, 46, 38b.

15 Apparently *Cypraea macula.* See Tu (1933), 1283.

16 Su Kung, in PTKM, 46, 38b.

17 Lu Kuei-meng, "Ho sung Li ming fu chih jen Nan-Hai," FLHSWC, 9, 26b–27a.

18 HS, 95, 0604b.

19 Keng Wei (fl. 773), "Yüan jih tsao ch'ao," ChTS, han 4, ts'e 10, ch. 2, 4a.

20 A yellow dragon was actually seen at Hsia-k'ou in the Yangtze basin—hardly its right place—in A.D. 229, and so the southern prince Sun Ch'üan adopted "Yellow Dragon" as the name of his reign, and had its image, displayed on a great standard, carried before his army in battle. SKC (Wu chih), 17, 1066a.

21 Onycha from *Eburna japonica* was a product of the coastal strip south of Hangchow as far as Annam. YHC, 34, 1004, 1010, 1013; 38, 1089; Schafer (1963), lacker (1958), 232, map 8; Schafer (1963), 175.

22 LPLI, c, 20.

23 Tu (1933), 2630.

24 *Wu tsei.* There are several genera of cuttlefish, of which *Sepia* is the best known. Read (1939), 44, gives *Sepiella japonica* for *wu tsei.*

25 Ch'en Ts'ang-ch'i, in PTKM, 44, 31a.

26 LPLI, c, 18.

27 YYTT, hsü, 8, 239.

28 It is now generally regarded as constituting a distinct family, the *Xiphosuridae,* composed of a few genera, including *Tachypleus* of the South China Sea. The old comprehensive genus *Limulus* has now, it seems, been abandoned.

29 LPLI, c, 17.

30 YYTT, 17, 139.

31 LPLI, c, 17; YYTT, 17, 139; Ch'en Ts'ang-ch'i, in PTKM, 45, 35b. Tuan Ch'eng-shih adds an incomprehensible story about a seven- or eight-inch high ridge on its back, called a *"ghou* (M.C.) sail." There seems to be some confusion here with the "sail" of some such jellyfish as the Portuguese Man-of-war.

32 LPLI, c, 17; YYTT, 17, 139.

33 YYTT, 17, 139.

34 LPLI, c, 21.

35 Tu (1933), 1960.

36 YHTC, 5, 4b. I am still uncertain about the authenticity of this source. Looked at internally it seems to be genuine T'ang material, but the history of the text is obscure, even suspicious.

37 PHL, 1, 12b.

38 PHL, 1, 12b–13b; LPLI, c, 20; Tu (1933), 818–819. Tu identifies a Far Eastern "red crab" as *Crapsus heimatocheira.*

39 LPLI, c, 20.

40 LPLI, c, 19.

41 PHL, 2, 2a–3a.

42 Bates (1952), 186; Bates (1963), 132.

43 NPHS, e, 50.

44 "Catawumpuses" is from Mary H. Kingsley, in West Africa in 1897–1899, quoted in Evans (1949), 102; "gallinippers" is from Anthony Trollope, in the West Indies in 1859–1860, quoted in Evans (1949), 117.

45 Schafer and Wallacker (1958), 232; Schafer (1963), 210.

46 *Ch'ing fu.* Ch'en Ts'ang-ch'i, in PTKM, 40, 10a.

47 LPLI, c, 24; THTL, in TPKC, 479, 1a.

48 Ch'en Ts'ang-ch'i, in PTKM, 39, 6b. Identified as *Vespa simillima* in Tu (1933), 1630.

49 Ch'en Ts'ang-ch'i, in PTKM, 39, 6b. Tu (1933), 2018, identifies it as *Sirex japonicus.*

50 YYTT, 17, 142.

51 THTL, in TPKC, 478, 7a.

52 YHC, 38, 3091; Schafer and Wallacker (1958), 233; Schafer (1963), 193.

53 PHL, 1, 16b. Cf. Schafer (1963), 115–116. It seems to have been a species *Chrysochroa.*

54 Ch'en Ts'ang-ch'i, in PTKM, 41, 16b.

55 Wallace (1878), 73–74. See especially pages 96–98 for the iridescent colors of other tropical insects, especially the beetles.

56 Bates (1952), 186–187; Bates (1963), 132, 186.

57 Soymié (1956), 34.

58 Brown (1961), 44–45.

59 PHL, 1, 14a–15a.

60 The Bat-leaved Bean (*Lourea vespertillionis*), the Winged Nut (*Pterocarya stenoptera*), and *Viburnum Hanceanum* all have this name in Chinese, and I suspect they deserve it for their winged seeds rather than for their butterfly-colored leaves. See Sauer (1947), 47, 58, 67.

61 Wallace (1869), 140–143.

62 PHL, 3, 12b–13a; LPLI, b, 9. PHL compares these to a little bird, whose skin was worn for the same erotic ends, apparently since Han times. Cf. YYTT, 16, 130.

63 Spencer (1954), 102.

64 Spencer (1954), 104.

65 See Shih (1958), 89, for the preparation of *cha,* and elsewhere in the same source for other old pickles and sauces; see Brodrick (1942), 22, for the description of Vietnamese fish paste; and see Ch'en Ts'ang-ch'i, in PTKM, 45, 32b, for the medicinal data.

66 Spencer (1954), 98.

[67] Zeuner (1963), 482–483. See Nichols (1943), 241–242, for the species of *Macropodus* found in south China.

[68] LPLI, c, 19.

[69] LiIC, in *Shou fu*, han 61 (ts'e 124), apparently the same as the *Lin-i kuo chi* of the Sui and T'ang catalogues.

[70] Ch'en Ts'ang-ch'i, in PTKM, 45, 31b–32a. YYTT, 17, 138, also reports a flying fish, about a foot long, in the fresh waters of Lang shan. There are a great many kinds of winged fish, with enlarged pectoral fins, ranging from the "sea moths" (*Pegasidae*), a fantastic family found from Africa to Hawaii, to the gliding "butterfly fish" (*Pantodon*) of the fresh waters of Africa. See Herald (1962) for these and other winged and "flying" fishes.

[71] Ch'en Ts'ang-ch'i, in PTKM, 44, 32a; YHC, 34, 1010, 1013; Schafer and Wallacker (1958), 226.

[72] Ch'en Ts'ang-ch'i, in PTKM, 45, 32a.

[73] YYTT, hsü 8, 243.

[74] Tu (1933), 1898, gives *Lepidopus tenuis,* which has no sword, and does not otherwise match Tuan's description.

[75] Ch'en Ts'ang-ch'i, in PTKM, 44, 28a. For identity (*Stromateoides argenteus*) see Read (1939), 35. It is also called "white butter fish."

[76] PHL, 2, 9a–9b. CHKCC, c, 39, remarks the presence of a fish of the same name in Chekiang.

[77] CYCT, 4, 6b.

[78] At Hai-yang *hsien*. YHC, 34, 1013.

[79] Pope (1935), 21; Soymié (1956), 55–56; Schafer (1962a), 73 n. 5.

[80] YHC, 34, 1007.

[81] Ch'en Ts'ang-ch'i, in PTKM, 45, 34a.

[82] CYCT, in TPKC, 467, 4a.

[83] Ch'en Ts'ang-ch'i, in PTKM, 45, 35a.

[84] YHC, 34, 1013; Schafer and Wallacker (1958), 226.

[85] YYTT, 17, 143.

[86] Pope (1935), 63–64, Pl. IV.

[87] YHC, 38, 1089; Schafer and Wallacker (1958), 226; YYTT, hsü 8, 240.

[88] Schafer (1963), 245.

[89] PHL, 1, 2a; Ch'en Ts'ang-ch'i, in PTKM, 45, 34a.

[90] LPLI, a, 3.

[91] Wen T'ing-yün, "Kuo Hua ch'ing kung," ChTS, han 9, ts'e 5, ch. 6, 6a.

[92] Schafer (1963), 245.

[93] LPLI, c, 23, calls it a "mountain turtle," but there is no land tortoise large enough to support a man in this region. Liu Hsün must have heard of females coming ashore to lay their eggs. Ch'en Ts'ang-ch'i, in PTKM, 45, 34a, correctly says that "they breed on the shore of the sea . . . they are not land turtles." Cf. Schafer (1962a), 74.

[94] Parsons (1962), 1.

[95] See YHC, 34, 1004; 38, 1089; Schafer and Wallacker (1958), 225; Schafer (1962a), 74; Parsons (1962), passim. The Chinese name for the reptile was *kou pi* (kou-pek) or *hsi-pi* (*ghei-pyek*). This name, but especially in its modern form *kou-pi,* has an interesting resemblance to "calipee," which, however, is thought to have a West Indian origin.

[96] Parsons (1962), 1.

[97] YYTT, 17, 139.

[98] LPLI, c, 21.

[99] PHL, 1, 11b–12a.

[100] Li Hsün, in PTKM, 43, 23a.

[101] LPLI, c, 21; Li Hsün, in PTKM, 43, 23a.

[102] So Read (1934), 326, and Shirai (1934), X, 380. But Pope (1935), 469–471 reports this creature only from the northern deserts.

[103] THTL, in TPKC, 478, 6b.

[104] *Ibid.*

[105] LNIWC, in TPKC, 456, 4a; cf. PHL, 1, 10–11b.

[106] Read (1934), 347; Pope (1935), 306–308, Plate XII.

[107] Ch'en Ts'ang-ch'i, in PTKM, 43, 25b. Possibly it was the poisonous green *Trimeresurus stejnegeri.*

[108] PHL, 1, 10b–11a.

[109] CHCT, 5, 6a.

[110] Su Kung, in PTKM, 10, 6a.

[111] Tribute of the whole coastal region, and of a large extension into Kwangsi. YHC, 34, 1004, 1010, 1013; 37, 1042; 38, 1083, 1088, 1091; Chen Ch'üan, in PTKM, 43, 24a; Schafer and Wallacker (1958), 226, map 9; Schafer (1963), 192.

[112] Meng Shen, in PTKM, 43, 24a.

[113] PHL, 1, 9a; LPLI, c, 22–23.

[114] NPHS, e, 42.

[115] See especially LPLI, c, 10; Schafer (1962b), 199–201

[116] See especially HWC, quoted in TPKC, 464, 5a–5b, which makes them particularly abundant along the coast west of Canton. See also YTCS, 121, 4b; Schafer (1962b), 201–203. YTCS, 89, 10a, tells of a "crocodile lake" east of Canton, in which the reptiles had formerly lived —but they were gone by late Sung times. Apparently the destruction of the animals and their habitat in eastern Kwangtung was already well under way.

[117] HWC, in TPKC, 464, 5a–5b.

[118] Han Yü, "Shuang Li," HCLCC, 6, 5b–6a.

[119] Translated in Giles (1923), 128–130; Margouliès (1926), 217–219.

[120] Han Yü, "E yü wen," HCLCC, 36, 5b–7a.

[121] Coral-Rémusat (1936), passim.

[122] Liu Tsung-yüan, "Yung-chou tz'u shih Li kung chih," LHSC, 10, 3b.

[123] KIC, in TPKC, 464, 1b–2a.

[124] For example, the story of enormous serpents in the mountains of az-Zābag (Djāwaga) which devour men, buffaloes and sometimes elephants, reported by Ibn Khordādzbeh (9 cent.), in Ferrand (1914), 26, and many other analogues.

[125] Soymié (1956), 41–42. Cf. Eberhard (1942a), 422.

[126] Schafer (1963a), 90–91.

[127] Bishop (1938), 416.

[128] Bishop (1938), 417; Eberhard (1942a), 423; Wen (1961), 79. In general see Wen (1961), especially pages 70–71,

80, 83. The cult has spread northward to the Yangtze basin.

[129] Bishop (1938), 417–419.

[130] NYC, in TPHYC, 164, 4a–4b.

[131] LPLI, a, 7.

[132] Ng (1936), 18–20.

[133] Kuo P'u, "Chiao tsan," in CSKW, 123, 4a.

[134] Szu-k'ung T'u (837–908), "K'uang t'i, shih pa shou," ChTS, han 10, ts'e 1, ch. 3, 1b.

[135] E.g. in Tu Fu, "Yung huai, erh shou," CCTS, p. 240.

[136] There are several poisonous snakes of the family *Hydrophiidae* in the South China Sea, e.g., *Thalassophina viperina,* which is found from Kwangtung to the Persian Gulf. See Pope (1935), 356.

[137] ShIC, a, 6a.

[138] YYTT, 16, 126. Tuan Ch'eng-shih also says that a fish weighing 2,000 catties is a *chiao.*

[139] Ch'en T'ao, "P'an-yü tao chung tso," ChTS, han 11, ts'e 4, ch. 1, 4a.

[140] Kaltenmark (1948), 36.

[141] Kaltenmark (1948), 2.

[142] Bonifacy (1914), 19–22; Bonifacy (1918), 25.

[143] YYTT, 8, 62. Cf. Liu (1936), 221; Eberhard (1942a), 414–416; Ch'en (1946), 13; Kaltenmark (1948), 2. The Li of Hainan tattoo themselves today, though not with obvious dragon figures. They give as one explanation of the custom that it wards off evil spirits; the practice is especially prevalent among women—it is thought that it enhances their beauty and makes them marriageable.

[144] Hastings (1962), I, 538.

[145] MHTL, in TPYL, 930, 7a.

[146] Yüan Chen, "Sung Ling-nan Ts'ui shih yü," ChTS, han 6, ts'e 9, ch. 17, 7a.

[147] *Tempest,* I, ii.

[148] ShIC, b, 20a.

[149] *Chiao hsiao. Hsiao* ordinarily connotes "raw silk." I take this *chiao (kău)* to be a substitute for *kău* (dragon or fish).

[150] TYTP (in TTTS, 2), 32b.

[151] Schafer (1963), 203. Cf. Wheatley (1959), 121–122.

[152] Ch'en (1946), 13–15; Kaltenmark (1948), 2.

[153] See Schafer (1957), 77.

[154] Ch'en (1946), 14–15.

[155] TPHYC, 165, 5b. Various sources use the graph *kău* "dragon" and *kău* "fish" as free alternates.

[156] Su Kung, in PTKM, 44, 31a.

[157] YHC, 34, 1010, 1013; 38, 1083; Schafer and Wallacker (1958), 57–58, 225, map 6.

[158] Schafer (1963), 109. YHTC, 4, 29 (TSCC), or 4, 5a (SPTK), if we can rely on it, mentions drum heads of *kău*-skin. Even in modern times the Chinese have imported ray skins from Malaysia. Burkill (1935), 1020.

[159] Bates (1963), 183.

[160] Tate (1947), 24–27.

[161] Spencer (1954), 92.

[162] Spencer (1954), 93.

[163] LPLI, a, 4.

[164] PHL, 2, 3a–4b. There are indeed few hares and squirrels in Nam-Viet, except for the endemic Hainan Hare. See Allen (1938), 571.

[165] LPLI, a, 4; PHL, 2, 3a–4b. A letter to me from the late A. de Carle Sowerby dated June 14, 1954, gives *ch'ing yang* as the name of the North China goral, and adds "I believe the same name is used for the South China form." For a description of the animal, see Tate (1947), 325. It lives in the high mountains, and has a distinctive pale-orange throat patch.

[166] LPLI, a, 4; PHL, 2, 3a–4b.

[167] Zeuner (1963), 236.

[168] Ch'en Ts'ang-ch'i, in PTKM, 50, 19a. For general remarks on southern breeds of cattle and their uses, see also Burkill (1935), 495–498.

[169] Schafer (1963), 73.

[170] Zeuner (1963), 248.

[171] Zeuner (1963), 249.

[172] Zeuner (1963), 248. Zeuner (1963),

245 gives the anoa or dwarf buffalo of Celebes as a distinct species, *Bubalus depressicornis*. See also Burkill (1935), 379–382. The African buffalo is quite distinct: it is *Syncerus caffer*.

[173] LPLI, a, 5.

[174] Zeuner (1963), 237–240.

[175] YHC, quoted in YTCS, 118, 4b. The quotation goes on to say that this is the *po-* or *pao-ox* mentioned in the *Erh ya*.

[176] KY, under the rhyme *chung*.

[177] Or *Bibos sondaicus*. *Bibos* interbreed freely with *Bos* and are regarded as a subgenus of *Bos* in some systems.

[178] Burkill (1935), 354; Tate (1947), 319–320; Spencer (1954), 93; Zeuner (1963), 253.

[179] Burkill (1935), 354; Tate (1947), 318–319; Spencer (1954), 93; Zeuner (1963), 245, 253.

[180] Bishop (1933), passim.

[181] Still another humped ox, the kouprey (it is uncertain whether it is a *Bos* or a *Bibos*) of Cambodia, was apparently unknown in China. It was not discovered until the 1930's! See Tate (1947), 321–322; Zeuner (1963), 202–203.

[182] NHIS, in TPKC, 483, 2b. I do not have the date of this book, but SuS, 204, 4994a, lists it among the T'ang geographies.

[183] See Zeuner (1963), 276.

[184] The state of Ch'u routed the troops of Wu in 506 B.C. using infuriated elephants with torches tied to their tails. Armored, saber-wielding elephants were employed by Liang against Western Wei in A.D. 554. Southern Han placed a batallion of elephants in the field against invaders in 948 and in 971. Schafer (1957b), 289–291.

[185] Schafer (1957b), 289.

[186] LPLI, b, 6.

[187] PHL, 2, 8a.

[188] LPLI, b, 6; PHL, 2, 8a–8b; KIC, in TPKC, 441, 4a.

[189] Schafer (1963), 240.

[190] PHL, 2, 8a–8b; YHC, 38, 1086; Schafer and Wallacker (1958), 224.

[191] Hsiang Szu (fl. 836), "Man chia," ChTS, han 9, ts'e 1, 2a.

[192] Schafer (1963), 80, quoting Tu Hsün-ch'üeh (ninth century).

[193] LPLI, a, 6.

[194] WCL, in TPKC, 459, 2b.

[195] KIC, in TPKC, 441, 4a–5a.

[196] ShIC, in TPYL, 892, 3a.

[197] CYCT, in TPKC, 441, 6b–7a.

[198] Li Ch'iao, "Hsiang," ChTS, han 2, ts'e 1, ch. 4, 8b.

[199] Liu Tsung-yüan, "Ling-nan chiang hsing," ChTS, han 6, ts'e 1, ch. 3, 1b.

[200] Chang Pin, "Sung jen kuei nan chung," ChTS, han 10, ts'e 10, 6a.

[201] Kuan-hsiu, "Sung jen chih ling wai," ChTS, han 12, ts'e 3, ch. 7, 3a.

[202] YHC, 38, 1083, 1085–1088; TPHYC, 165, 6b; YTCS, 121, 4b; Schafer and Wallacker (1958), 57–58; Schafer (1963), 58. The Tang and Yü-lin locations are given in Sung sources; presumably these were the last refuges in Lingnan.

[203] LPLI, b, 15. The text is a bit confused. He also mentions another two-horned species. But there is only one species of two-horned rhinoceros in the Far East. Possibly he regarded the Chinese as distinct from the "Sumatran." The Sung source TPHYC, 165, 6b, says this about the animal's habits: "It eats brambles and thorny plants. In the winter months, it digs into the earth and conceals itself, with nose protruding, to escape inauspicious things."

[204] Tate (1947), 352–354; Talbot 1960), 13, 31, 48.

[205] Li Hsün, in PTKM, 51, 26b.

[206] Schafer (1963), 260.

[207] PHL, 1, 1a–2a; Schafer (1963), 241–242.

[208] LPLI, b, 15, describes this in some detail.

[209] PHL, 1, 1b.

[210] As translated in Ferrand (1914), 29.

[211] PHL, 1, 1a. Cf. Schafer (1963), 241–242.

[212] TYTP (in TTTS, 2), 49a.

[213] PKLT, 97, 10a.

[214] LPLI, b, 15.

[215] TKSP, b, 9b.

[216] See Caldwell (1931), 309; Delacour (1931), 75. But it is possible that we have to do with an ibis.

[217] Kuan-hsiu, "Sung chien kuan nan ch'ien," ChTS, han 12, ts'e 3, ch. 4, 1a.

[218] Po Chü-i, "Hsün hsi," ChTS, han 7, ts'e 1, ch. 3, 9a.

[219] The South China Tiger is a subspecies of *Felis tigris*. See Allen (1938), 480–486; Tate (1947), 193–194.

[220] See Soymié (1956), 111. On p. 8 he cites the example of the monk Hui-yüeh of the Sui dynasty.

[221] PPT, "Teng she," (ch. 17), 7b.

[222] Hastings (1962), VIII, 210.

[223] YTCS, 90, 7a, quoting the "Old Canon"—i.e., an earlier gazetteer.

[224] YYTT, 16, 132.

[225] Chang Chi, "Meng hu hsing," ChTS, han 6, ts'e 6, ch. 1, 2b.

[226] Li Shang-yin, "Chao-chou," ChTS, han 8, ts'e 9, ch. 2, 27b.

[227] Schafer (1963), 87–88.

[228] Meng Shen and Sun Szu-miao, in PTKM, 51a, 26a.

[229] Allen (1938), 459–477; Tate (1947), 189–194.

[230] Allen (1938), 424–429; Tate (1947), 174–176.

[231] Kuan-hsiu, "Wen Wu-hsiang tao jen shun shin, wu shou," ChTS, han 12, ts'e 3, ch. 5, 1b.

[232] Burkill (1935), 2249.

[233] YYTT, 16, 134; Ch'en Ts'ang-ch'i, in PTKM, 51, 31a.

[234] Yule and Burnell (1886), 707; Allen (1938), 430–433; Tate (1947), 176–178.

[235] Allen (1938), 433–440; Tate (1947), 178–179.

[236] Ch'en Ts'ang-ch'i, in PTKM, 51, 32a. YYTT, 15, 119–120, says this urine was used to cure "wind" diseases.

[237] Brodrick (1942), 265.

[238] Allen (1938), 441–445; Tate (1947), 184–185. See Zeuner (1963), 404, for the

history of the mongoose in the west.

239 Kuo P'u, commentary on *Erh ya,* ch. 18.

240 YYTT, hsü 8, 242.

241 Allen (1938), 516–521; Tate (1947), 113. The Scaly Anteater is not a very large animal, but the Giant Pangolin of Africa is six feet long.

242 Tso Szu, "Wu tu fu," in *Wen hsüan.*

243 Chen Ch'üan, in PTKM, 43, 22a.

244 HS, 28b, 0429d.

245 Allen (1938), 1169; Tate (1947), 339–340.

246 Schafer (1956), 268–269. When used with reference to Hainan, *chu* may refer to the thamin or Panolia Deer (*Cervus eldi = C. platyceros*). Tate (1947), 344, gives a description. There is also a southern variety of the common Chinese sika. Allen (1938), 1188–1190; Tate (1947), 341.

247 *Muntiacus muntjak* and *M. reevesi.* Allen (1938), 1143, 1148, 1154; Tate (1947), 328–335. *Elaphodus* has only incipient horns, and has been described as looking like a rudimentary muntjac. The males of both animals are tusked, though not so prominently as the Musk Deer and Water Deer.

248 Tribute of Kuei-chou. Schafer and Wallacker (1958), 233; Schafer (1963), 106.

249 Li Ch'ün-yü, "Hsüeh shih yü ch'u ch'i hsüeh," ChTS, han 9, ts'e 3, ch. 2, 12b.

250 Bates (1952), 193.

251 They are *Hylobates hoolock* and *H. concolor* respectively. Allen (1938), 306–311; Tate (1947), 138–141.

252 Schafer (1963), 209.

253 CC, in TPKC, 441, 6a–6b.

254 Li Po, "Yüan pieh li," LTPWC, 3, 1a.

255 Li Hsün, "Nan hsiang tzu," ChTS, han 12, ts'e 10, ch. 8, 2a.

256 YYTT, 16, 135.

257 Ch'en Ts'ang-ch'i, in PTKM, 51b, 36b. The accusation of cannibalism comes from *Erh Ya.*

258 Allen (1938), 294; Tate (1947), 123, 126–131.

259 PHL, 1, 7b–9a.

260 Tate (1947), 129–130.

261 Li Po, "Ch'iu p'u ko, shih ch'i shou," No. 5, in ChTS, han 3, ts'e 4, ch. 7, 1a.

262 Li Te-yü, "Po yüan fu," CTW, 696, 21a. Li takes pains to distinguish between *yüan* "langur" and *hou* "macacque" (if I am right in so identifying the words), which were confused by the old writer Fu Hsüan of Chin, who mocked at all monkeys—an attitude which pained Li Te-yü.

263 Tate (1947), 126.

264 TIWL, quoted in PKLT, 97, 24b.

265 Liu Tsung-yüan, "Ju Huang ch'i wen yüan," ChTS, han 6, ts'e 1, ch. 3, 13a.

266 Ch'en Ts'ang-ch'i, in PTKM, 51b, 36a–36b, and quotations from NFTMC and *Nan chou i wu chih.*

267 E.g., *Presbyticus* (= *Rhinopithecus?*) *avunculus* of Tongking (Tate [1947], 131), or *Rhinopithecus brelechi* of Kweichow (Allen [1938], 304–305).

268 TKSP (in TTTS, 4), 66a.

269 Yin Yao-fan, "Tsui tseng, shih erh," ChTS, han 8, ts'e 2, 3a.

270 Ch'en Ts'ang-ch'i, in PTKM, 51b, 36a; Tate (1947), 128–129.

271 Allen (1938), 499–500; Tate (1947), 200.

272 *Hai t'un.* The Chinese River Dolphin (*Lipotes vexillifer*) of the Yangtze and Lake Tung-t'ing was called River Pig (*chiang t'un*). Ch'en Ts'ang-ch'i, in PTKM, 44, 31a; Allen (1938), 499–500; Tate (1947), 200.

273 Ch'en Ts'ang-ch'i, in PTKM, 44, 31a.

274 Wallace (1898), 118–119. For the kinds of south Chinese fruit bats see Tate (1947), 71–75.

275 CHKCC, p. 35; Su Kung, in PTKM, 48, 8b.

276 Also noted in Annam.

277 PHL, 1, 15a–16b; LPLI, b, 15; YYTT, 8, 242; NPHS, g, 66. Some of

the Horseshoe bats (*Rhinolophus*) have red phases, but I do not know if they frequent banana trees. The fruit bat *Cynopterus brachyotis* eats bananas and other fruits in Kwangtung and Annam, but I do not know its color. See Allen (1938), 153–155; Tate (1947), 106.

[278] *Petaurista* sp. See Allen (1938), 731; Tate (1947), 241; Schafer (1963d), 212.

[279] Bates (1952), 191; Bates (1963), 195.

[280] Wallace (1898), 99, 319–320.

[281] Sir Walter Raleigh, *The Discoverie of the Large, Rich and Bewtiful Empire of Guiana* (1595), quoted in Evans (1949), 132.

[282] Wallace (1898), 264.

[283] Wallace (1898), 163.

[284] Wallace (1898), 163.

[285] H. M. Tomlinson, *The Sea and the Jungle*, Ch. 6.

[286] Wallace (1898), 99, 165; Bates (1952), 191.

[287] Vaughan and Jones (1913), passim.

[288] Schafer (1963d), 198.

[289] Li Ming-yüan, "Yüan che wei P'anchou szu ma," quoted from TSCS, in YTCS, 117, 9b.

[290] Shen Ch'üan-ch'i, "Ts'ung Huanchou . . . tseng Su shih chün," ChTS, han 2, ts'e 5, ch. 3, 8a.

[291] LTMHC, 9, 12a–12b.

[292] Schafer (1963), 96–97. Erkes (1951), 70 reports peacocks on Shang bronzes.

[293] La Touche (1934), 223; Cheng (1955), 109.

[294] TS, 43b, 14a; YHC, 38, 1083, 1085, 1090–1091; Schafer and Wallacker (1958), 225; Schafer (1963), 97.

[295] PHL, 1, 2b. The text of Fang Ch'ien-li, *Nan fang i wu chih,* which tells of methods of capture is translated in Schafer (1963), 97.

[296] LPLI, b, 15, for Annam.

[297] *Ting hsiang,* normally "lilac" in T'ang poetry, not "clove" as later. For an explanation of the term, see Schafer (1963), 171.

[298] Sun Kuang-hsien, "Pa p'o man," (a *tz'u* form), ChTS, han 12, ts'e 10, ch. 9, 11b. Another fine peacock poem is P'i Jih-hsiu, "Ping k'ung ch'üeh," ChTS, han 9, ts'e 9, ch. 6, 8a.

[299] An Anglo-Indian word of the seventeenth century. See Yule and Burnell (1886), 449.

[300] PHL, 1, 2b–3a; Schafer (1963), 111–112.

[301] CW, in TPKC, 461, 1a.

[302] E.g., CW, in TPKC, 461, 2b.

[303] Erkes (1951), 67, 72.

[304] CW, in TPKC, 461, 1a.

[305] A rubbing taken from an early Han tile shows the Bird of the South (Wu [1963], 49, Pl. I) with three large ocellated tail feathers. It is more like a peacock than an Argus Pheasant, however. In any case, the Argus is not brilliantly colored, but mostly brown, with some ruddiness. See Austin (1961), 96.

[306] Li Ying, "K'ung ch'üeh," ChTS, han 9, ts'e 7, 8a.

[307] Li Te-yü, "Che Ling-nan tao chung tso," LWKC, pieh chi, 4, 204.

[308] Li Chung, "Sung jen nan yu," ChTS, han 11, ts'e 5, ch. 3, 3b.

[309] Vaughan and Jones (1913), 181–184; La Touche (1934), 72–81; Cheng (1955), 209–216. Another crab-eating *Halcyon* is *H. pileatus* Black-headed Kingfisher, which frequents the coasts from India to Korea and is, like *smyrnensis,* hunted for its attractive feathers.

[310] Sitwell (1947), 203–205.

[311] *Tso chuan,* Chao 12 (530 B.C.)

[312] CIC (in TTTS, 17), 18a–18b.

[313] TT, 184, 978c; YHC, 38, 1083–1092; Schafer and Wallacker (1958), 225 and map 7; Schafer (1963), 110.

[314] Hsü Hun, "Sui mu tzu Kuang chiang . . . , szu shou," ChTS, han 8, ts'e 8, ch. 10, 5b.

[315] Han Yü, "Sung Kuei-chou Yen ta fu," CLHSC, 10, 13a–13b.

[316] Chou Yu, "Sung Yang Huan chiao shu kuei Kuang-nan," ChTS, han 10, ts'e 1, 2b. The matching of sagwire and king-

fisher occurs earlier in Chang Chiu-ling, "Sung Kuang-chou Chou p'an kuan," ChTS, han 1, ts'e 9, ch. 2, 7a.

[317] Ch'ien Ch'i, "Hsien yü ts'ui niao," ChTS, han 4, ts'e 5, ch. 4, 18b.

[318] Scott (1961), 177.

[319] Scott (1961), 178–179. The macaw is "inexplicably named after the Portuguese colony of Macao on the coast of China." Scott notes the mystery of a painting of the mid-seventeenth century at Woburn that shows a Sulphur-crested Cockatoo—though Australia, its home, was not officially discovered until 1770!

[320] As in CSh, 17, 5894d.

[321] See Schafer (1963), 99–102.

[322] La Touche (1934), 61–63. For the modern distribution of these parakeets, see Cheng (1955), 173–174.

[323] Cheng (1955), 174–175. Delacour and Jabouille (1931), 161, mentions it for Laos and Annam.

[324] PHL, 1, 5a–6b; Schafer (1959), 275. Parrots were sent as tribute from Lo-chou and Chiao-chou. YHC, 38, 1083; Schafer and Wallacker (1958), 57–58, 225.

[325] YTCS, 95, 7b–8a.

[326] PHL, 1, 5a–6b.

[327] Lu Kuei-meng, "Hu Wu chung yen huai chi Nan-hai erh t'ung nien," FLHSWC, 9, 28b.

[328] Yule and Burnell (1886), 148–149; Pelliot (1959), 231–232. Pelliot remained surprisingly uncertain that Chinese che-ku was indeed cognate to cakora.

[329] LPLI, b, 15.

[330] La Touche (1934), 260–261; Smythies (1953), Plate XXII; Cheng (1955), 82.

[331] Liu Tsung-yüan, "Fang che-ku tz'u," ChTS, han 6, ts'e 1, ch. 4, 7a.

[332] LPLI, b, 15.

[333] PHL, 1, 4b; TPT, in PTKM, 48, 7a.

[334] CHKCC, p. 32.

[335] CCh, 7a. Similar passages are in YYTT, 16, 125–126; hsü 8, 244.

[336] KC, quoted in PHL, 1, 5a.

[337] Pelliot (1959), 231–232.

[338] YYTT, hsü 8, 242; repeated in NPHS, e, 48.

[339] Vaughan and Jones (1913), 353.

[340] Li I, "Shan che-ku tz'u," ChTS, han 5, ts'e 3, ch. 2, 8a. Cf. Li She, "Che-ku tz'u, erh shou," ChTS, han 7, ts'e 10, 2a.

[341] Kao P'ien, "An-nan sung ts'ao pieh ch'ih kuei ch'ao," ChTS, han 9, ts'e 7, 6a.

[342] CCC, in TPYL, 928, 2a.

[343] TLSS, in TPYL, 928, 1b. Soymié (1956), 132, gives the correct title of this book as *Hsü Lo-shan shu;* it was supplementary to an earlier account of the mountain.

[344] Delacour and Jabouille (1931), 328.

[345] Delacour and Jabouille (1931), 327–328; Burkill (1935), 1194–1196; Cammann (1950), 19–22. Cf. PTKM, 47, 1b.

[346] YYTT, 16, 129.

[347] LPLI, b, 13. The last sentence is obscure.

[348] NFIWC, in TPYL, 928, 2a. The text has *ts'ao wu chih* in the title; the emendation to *i wu chih* is obvious.

[349] The former is registered in KY. Though the T'ang histories prefer the second form, it goes back to Han times. It has been suggested that these binoms were formed by dimidiation of ancient *$*mld'ung$* and *$*mt'lung$* respectively. See Serruys (1962), 255.

[350] TT, 160, 848c–849a.

[351] SKC, 54 (Wu chih, 9), 1049d.

[352] By Ts'ui Yen. TS, 163, 6b; CTS, 155, 4a.

[353] Soymié, (1956), 61.

[354] Saint-John Perse, *Oiseaux.*

[355] Sitwell (1947), 182.

[356] Sitwell (1947), 191, writes that Reinhardt's Argus Pheasant was "proved" by Marquess Hachisuka, a phasianist, to be the Chinese "phoenix." I do not know the history of the interesting identification.

[357] CCh, p. 3, describes the *hui* as a pheasant of many colors. This fits the Pucras, which is found all over China.

[358] La Touche (1934), 228–232, 240–243, 247–249. For the distribution of

Darwin's Pucras, see Cheng (1955), 101.

[359] Cheng (1955), 97–99. Its range is from Chekiang southward, and west to Yunnan.

[360] See La Touche (1934), 243–244; Schafer (1963), 111.

[361] Chang Chi, "Sung Cheng shang shu fu Kuang-chou," ChTS, han 6, ts'e 6, ch. 4, 9b.

[362] Hsiao Ying-shih (717–768), "Po hsien fu," CTW, 322, 8a–9b.

[363] Sung Chih-wen, "Fang po hsien p'ien," ChTS, han 1, ts'e 10, ch. 1, 11a.

[364] Li Po, "Tseng Huang-shan Hu kung ch'iu po hsien," ChTS, han 3, ts'e 5, ch. 11, 7a.

[365] For *Nandina domestica,* see Schafer (1964), 108.

[366] Su Kung, in PTKM, 49, 10a; Vaughan and Jones (1913), 174; La Touche (1930), 291–292; Schafer (1963d), 210. The so-called Chinese Grackle or Black-necked Mynah (*Gracupica nigricollis*), has habits and attributes similar to both the Crested Mynah and the Hill Mynah, but I cannot identify it in medieval literature. I suspect it was subsumed under the names of the other two birds.

[367] Different authorities give different specific names—*sinensis, javanus,* and *intermedius.* A Hainan form may be a distinct species. In any case, the bird is closely related to the talented Indian Hill Mynah. Instead of *Eulabes,* some give *Gracula.*

[368] David and Oustalet (1878), 365–366; Delacour and Jabouille (1931), 254–255; La Touche (1930), 280–281.

[369] LPLI, b, 13. He found it especially in Lien-chou and Po-chou on the coast. TS, 222c, 1a, makes it a bird of Champa.

[370] PHL, 1, 6b–7b.

[371] LPLI, b, 14; Schafer (1963d), 221.

[372] Ch'en Ts'ang-ch'i, in PTKM, 49, 12b.

[373] LPLI, b, 14; Ch'en Ts'ang-ch'i, in PTKM, 49, 13a; Eberhard (1942a), 155–157.

[374] The Japanese Nightjar (*Caprimulgus*

indicus) migrates all along the Chinese coast; Swinhoe's Nightjar (*C. monticolus = C. affinis*) is a resident of Nam-Viet. La Touche (1934), 97–100.

[375] Delacour and Jabouille (1931), 137–141; La Touche (1934), 126–129; Schafer (1963d), 221, n. 255.

[376] LPLI, b, 14.

[377] Sun Szu-miao, in PTKM, 31, 14b; Su Kung, in PTKM, 49, 12b.

[378] CS, 33, 1177c, gives an incident for the third century; CCHS, quoted in TPYL, 927, 8a–8b, gives one for the fourth.

[379] Su Kung, in PTKM, 49, 12b. For *Spilornis,* see La Touche (1934), 164–165; Cheng (1955), 63–64. Its modern Chinese name is *she tiao* "snake eagle."

[380] Sitwell (1947), 174.

[381] Austin (1961), 172–173.

[382] Sitwell (1959), 143.

[383] See Sitwell (1947), 175.

[384] La Touche (1934), 87–88; Cheng (1955), 208–209. The bird was first identified in Fukien in 1898; other subspecies were found further south, including one in Annam. The modern Chinese name is *yao chüan* (cf. *tu-chüan* Hawk cuckoo).

[385] CTS, quoted in TPYL, 924, 4a–4b. YYTT, 16, 128, mentions the incident without listing the colors. See Schafer (1959), 278. There I agreed with the courtier's opinion; I do so no longer.

[386] See the illustration of the Redheaded Trogon in Smythies (1953), Pl. 18.

[387] Schafer (1963), 111. There are several white species of egret there, not to mention such related birds as the gray Reef Heron, the orange and white Cattle Egret, the Indian Little Green Heron and others. See La Touche (1934), 445–451.

[388] Schafer (1963d), 219.

[389] LPLI, b, 13; Delacour and Jabouille (1931), 289–290; Smythies (1953), Pl. 1.

[390] LPLI, b, 14.

[391] La Touche (1934), 476–478; Caldwell (1931), 376.

[392] PHL, 2, 1a–1b; LPLI, b, 13–14;

Ch'en Ts'ang-ch'i, in PTKM, 47, 3b.

[393] La Touche (1930), 177–179; Caldwell (1931), 193–194.

[394] CYPT, in PTKM, 49, 10b. Its name is *lien ch'üeh.* See Read (1932), No. 298.

[395] PTKM, 49, 10b.

[396] Sowerby (1940), 22.

[397] Sitwell (1947), 211–212.

[398] David and Oustalet (1878), 80, and Atlas, Pl. 11; Vaughan and Jones (1913), 71; La Touche (1930), 461–463; Delacour and Jabouille (1931), 132–161, Pl. 56–58.

[399] Vaughan and Jones (1913), 72–74; La Touche (1930), 467–468.

[400] Cheng (1955), 161–164.

CHAPTER 12 (Pages 248–265)

[1] NYC, 6, 2a.

[2] Tu Mu, "Chung ch'eng Yeh Shen-t'ao . . . ch'üan," ChTS, han 8, ts'e 7, ch. 5, 2b.

[3] Li Ch'iao, "Chün shih k'ai hsüan tzu Yung-chou shun liu chou chung," ChTS, han 2, ts'e 1, ch. 5, 5a.

[4] Hsü Hun, "Pieh piao hsiung chün ts'ui," ChTS, han 8, ts'e 8, ch. 7, 9a.

[5] Sung Chih-wen, "Kuo Man tung," ChTS, han 1, ts'e 10, ch. 2, 7a.

[6] Charles Baudelaire, "Maesta et Errabunda," *Les Fleurs du Mal.*

[7] PHL, 2, 11b–13a.

[8] PHL, 2, 15b.

[9] Listed by Han Yü, "Ch'u nan shih i Yüan shih pa hsieh lü," HCLCC, 6, 8a–9a.

[10] Tobias Venner, *Via recta* (1620).

[11] YHTC, 6, 44, mentions Kuei-chou as a center of frog-eating. I have noticed the doubtful reputation of this text in Chapter XI, n. 36.

[12] Han Yü, "Ta Liu Liu-chou shih chia-ma," HCLCC, 6, 9a–10a. Cf. Han Yü, "Ch'u nan shih i Yüan shih pa hsieh lü," HCLCC, 6, 8a–9a, written in the same year. There he observes, *"ḳap* is in fact *ghǎ-mǎ;* the same reality with a superfluously different name."

[13] NCHW, in TPKC, 483, 5b.

[14] CYCT, 2, 5a.

[15] PHL, 2, 14b; LPLI, a, 5; PYTC, 1b.

[16] PHL, 2, 14a.

[17] Bates (1952), 188.

[18] Bates (1952), 171–173.

[19] The so-called Yellow Jessamine, which contains a poisonous alkaloid. Read (1936), No. 174.

[20] THTL, in TPKC, 233, 3b–4a. This source has other interesting information on southern wines.

[21] CKC, quoted in TPYL, 172, 13b.

[22] Ch'en T'ao, "Chiang kuei chung ling tseng Nan-hai Li shang shu," ChTS, han 11, ts'e 4, ch. 1, 7a–7b.

[23] Shen Ch'üan-ch'i, "Ch'u ta Huan-chou," ChTS, han 2, ts'e 5, ch. 1, 5b.

[24] Hsü T'ang, "Chi Ch'ien-nan Li shang shu," ChTS, han 9, ts'e 8, ch. 1, 3a.

[25] Han Yü, "Ch'u nan shih i Yüan shih pa hsieh lü," HCLCC, 6, 8a–9a.

[26] Yüan Chen, "Sung Ts'ui shih yü chih Ling-nan, erh shih yün, hsü," ChTS, han 6, ts'e 9, ch. 11, 4a.

[27] Fuertes (1914), 342.

[28] Fuertes (1914), 1–2.

[29] See Obi (1962), for examples.

[30] Meng Chiao, "Lien-chou yin," ChTS, han 6, ts'e 5, ch. 6, 3b.

[31] Fuertes (1914), 168. Of one group of birds Fuertes writes: "Perhaps no songs heard in the tropics are so characteristic, or make such a strong impression on the mind and desire of a naturalist, as these romantic and mysterious Wren songs." Fuertes (1913), 343. But the wren family is centered in America.

[32] Wang Chien, "Nan chung," ChTS, han 5, ts'e 5, ch. 3, 1a. I have reproduced Waley's translation of the whole poem in Schafer (1963), 244.

[33] Chang Chi, "Sung Man k'o," ChTS, han 6, ts'e 6, ch. 3, 4b.

[34] Han Yü, "Sung Ch'ü Ts'e, hsü," HCLCC, 21, 1a.

[35] Chang Chi, "Sung Cheng shang shu ch'u chen Nan-hai," ChTS, han 9, ts'e 8, ch. 1, 5b.

[36] Hsü T'ang, "Chi Mu-chou Lu lang chung," ChTS, han 9, ts'e 8, ch. 1, 5b.

[37] From a letter written by Liu Tsung-yüan in Yung-chou, in TS, 168, 6a.

[38] Chang Chi, "Sung Yen ta fu chih Kuei-chou," ChTS, han 6, ts'e 6, ch. 3, 13a; biography of Chang Chi in TS, 176, 6b–7b.

[39] Sung Chih-wen, "Ts'ao ju Ch'ing-yüan hsia," ChTS, han 1, ts'e 10, ch. 3, 8a–8b. For another reference to the Songs of the Man, see Schafer (1963), 80.

[40] TT, 184, 984b.

[41] LPLI, a, 4.

[42] Schafer (1962b), 220.

[43] LPLI, a, 4.

[44] Kaltenmark (1948), 23–27. Cf. Hsü (1939), 235–246 for other magico-religious uses of the drums. Gray (1949), 8, writes of them as associated with the death cult, and believes that the ship represented on some of them is a ship of the dead. It is not to be denied that they were buried with their great owners.

[45] Karlgren (1942), 25; Gray (1949), 8–9. Some drums show the forms of magical deerlike animals and bird-headed dancing men. See Karlgren (1942), 15–17. Karlgren found stylistic affinities with his "Huai" art of Central China, in the use of voluted decorations for instance. See Karlgren (1942), 12–13. G. B. Downer tells me that he found bronze drums associated only with Mon-Khmer speakers, such as the Khmu and Lamet, in Laos. Possibly this means that the Mon-Khmer family was once more widely spread than it is now.

[46] Goloubew (1932), 137–138, 149; Karlgren (1942), 4–5, 7–8. Karlgren prefers to date the Đông-sơn culture three or four centuries earlier than Goloubew, in late Chou times. Cf. Brodrick (1942), 76–78.

[47] Eberhard (1942a), 395.

[48] Kaltenmark (1948), 22–36.

[49] SuS, 493, 5724a–5724b.

[50] Sachs (1950), 240 claims to trace them back to the sixth century, and suggests that they are modifications of the "shamanic frame drum." Gong chimes are shown in an eleventh century relief at Angkor. See Sachs (1940), 241–242.

[51] Sachs (1940), 182–183.

[52] Sachs (1940), 183.

[53] Sachs (1940), 184.

[54] STC, b, 23b (and quoted in TPHYC, 167, 3b).

[55] LPLI, a, 5. The calabashes used for these instruments were called *p'ao,* and are identifiable as the bottle gourd *Lagenaria leucantha,* probably originally an African native, introduced to the Far East about the first century A.D. See Wheatley (1959), 52–53.

[56] TT, 144, 753c.

[57] TS, 222c, 9a.

[58] See, for instance, quotations from *Ti wang shih chi* and *Shih pen* in TPYL, 78, 4b; CHKCC, p. 31; Maspero (1924), 53, 74–75, 84. Ruey (1938) suggests her southern origin.

[59] LH, "Shun ku."

[60] Hastings (1962), I, 516.

[61] *Shuo wen,* ch. 12. Cf. Schafer (1964a).

[62] Ruey (1938), 180.

[63] Li Po, "Shang yün yüeh," LTPWC, 3, 9a.

[64] YYTT, 1, 3.

[65] CTS, 37, 4a.

[66] SSC, 14, 91.

[67] Skard (1946), 174.

[68] See Schafer, (1963a), 88.

[69] I owe this idea to Obi (1962), 301, 327.

[70] Malleret (1934), 224.

[71] For more, see Schafer (1963a), 89–90.

[72] Avienus, *Description of the World* (ca. A.D. 370), quoted in Wheatley (1961), 133, with this translation "Then there emerges from the azure waves an island which by ancient usage is known as 'the Golden,' because there the yellow orb of the sun glows with a ruddier light." This is a paraphrase of the second century narrative of Dionysius Periegetes about

the fabulous orient realm of Chryse the Golden.

[73] Chang Chieh, "Huang fu," CTW, 405, 2a–2b.

[74] See Bates (1952), 179–180.

[75] Hu Tseng, "Tzu ling hsia fa i tao Ch'ing-yüan hsia tso," ChTS, han 10, ts'e 2, 2b.

[76] Li Po, "Szu k'ung Hou An-tu miao chi," CTW, 712, 12b–14b.

[77] Tu Shen-yen, "Nan-hai luan shih shan tso," ChTS, han 2, ts'e 1, 1b.

[78] Po Chü-i, "Tung t'ing hsien wang," ChTS, han 7, ch. 18, 4a.

[79] TuT, b, 23.

[80] Schafer (1963c), 140.

[81] It was also a symbol of forces which protected life against the powers of darkness; hence "Red everywhere is inimical to witchcraft of all kinds, and is constantly used, from Donegal to Japan, both alone and as a strengthener of other amulets against the evil eye." Hastings (1962), V, 613.

[82] I owe the conception of the volcano as a fiery jet of life to Sacheverell Sitwell (1959), 323.

[83] TS, 34, 10a.

[84] P'i Jih-hsiu, "Ch'un hsi chiu hsing," ChTS, han 9, ts'e 9, ch. 8, 2b–3a.

[85] P'i Jih-hsiu, "Ch'ung t'i ch'iang-wei," ChTS, han 9, ts'e 9, ch. 8, 2b.

[86] P'i Jih-hsiu, "Nan-yang Jun-ch'ing chiang kuei Lei-p'ing yin erh yu tseng," ChTS, han 9, ts'e 9, ch. 7, 6b.

[87] Han Wo, "Hou Wei shih Hsiang-chou ta . . . pu chih," ChTS, han 10, ts'e 7, ch. 4, 9b.

[88] YHC, 38, 1091; Schafer and Wallacker (1958), 236; Schafer (1963), 206–207.

[89] Schafer (1957), 79.

[90] Ou-yang Chiung, "Nan hsiang tzu," ChTS, han 12, ts'e 10, ch. 8, 13a.

[91] Wu Wu-ling, "Yang-shuo hsien t'ing pi t'i ming," CTW, 718, 15a–15b.

[92] Sitwell (1959), xx.

[93] For a list, see Sauer (1947), 60.

[94] Schafer (1964), 113.

[95] Han Yü, "Hsing hua," CLHSC, 3, 9a–9b.

[96] LNIWC, in TPKC, 409, 7a.

[97] Schafer (1963d), 201.

[98] Schafer (1963d), 199.

[99] TTC, a, 9.

[100] A third century ode translated, slightly differently, in Schafer (1963d), 213.

[101] Liu Yü-hsi, "Wang Heng shan," ChTS, han 6, ts'e 2, ch. 2, 4a.

[102] See Schafer (1963d), 198.

[103] Schafer (1963d), 200.

[104] Schafer (1963d), 198.

[105] Fuertes (1914), 98.

[106] In the Whitney Museum of American Art, New York.

[107] See Obi (1962), 585–586.

[108] Alfred Droin, "D'escale en escale," quoted in Malleret (1934), 125.

[109] For "colonial" vs. "exotic" literature," see Malleret (1934), 47.

[110] See Malleret (1934), 353.

BIBLIOGRAPHY

Primary Sources

Parenthetical abbreviations stand for books listed under "Collectanea and Encyclopedias" in the bibliography. They represent the edition used in footnote documentation unless otherwise stated in the note. Chou classics are not listed here.

CC	P'ei Hsing 裴鉶, *Ch'uan ch'i* 傳奇
CCC	Liu Hsin-ch'i 劉欣期, *Chiao chou chi* 交州記 (LNIS)
CCF	Sun Szu-miao 孫思邈, *Ch'ien chin fang* 千金方
CCh	Shih K'uang 師曠, *Ch'in ching* 禽經 (POHH)
CCHS	*Chin chung hsing shu* 晉中興書
CCTS	Tu Fu 杜甫, *Chiu chia chi chu Tu shih* 九家集注杜詩 (*Concordance*, 1940)
CCW	*Ch'un ch'iu wei* 春秋緯
CFC	Ts'ui Ling-ch'in 崔令欽, *Chiao fang chi* 教坊記
ChC	Lu Yü 陸羽, *Ch'a ching* 茶經
CHCLPT	*Ch'ung hsiu Cheng ho cheng lei pen ts'ao* 重修政和證類本草 (SPTK)
CHKCC	Ma Kao 馬縞, *Chung hua ku chin chu* 中華古今注 (TSCC)
CHL	[*Yung-ch'eng*] *chi hsien lu* 墉城集仙錄
ChS	*Chou shu* 周書 (KM)
CIC	Hsüeh Yung-jo 薛用弱, *Chi i chi* 集異記
CIL	T'ao Ku 陶穀, *Ch'ing i lu* 清異錄 (HYHTS)
CKC	*Chün kuo chih* 郡國志
CLHSC	Han Yü 韓愈, *Chu wen kung chiao Ch'ang-li hsien sheng chi* 朱文公校昌黎先生集 (SPTK)
CS	*Chin shu* 晉書 (KM)

321

CSh	*Chin shih* 金史 (KM)
CSL	Hsü Hsüan 徐鉉, *Chi shen lu* 稽神錄
CSYC	Liu Ch'eng 柳珵, *Ch'ang shih yen chih* 常侍言旨
CTS	*Chiu T'ang shu* 舊唐書 (SPPY)
CW	Niu Su 牛肅, *Chi wen* 紀聞
CYC	*Chiu yü chih* 九域志
CYCT	Chang Cho 張鷟, *Ch'ao yeh ch'ien tsai* 朝野僉載 (PYTPC)
CYPT	Chang Yü-hsi 掌禹錫, *Chia yu pen ts'ao* 嘉祐本草
FLHSWC	Lu Kuei-meng 陸龜蒙, *Fu li hsien sheng wen chi* 甫里先生文集 (SPTK)
FNC	Chu-chih 竺芝, *Fu-nan chi* 扶南記
FNWC	Li Shang-yin 李商隱, *Fan nan wen chi chien chu* 樊南文集箋註
FYC	*Fang yü chih* 方輿志
HCC	Chao Ch'ung-tso 趙崇祚, *Hua chien chi* 花間集 (1900)
HCLCC	Han Yü 韓愈, *Han Ch'ang li ch'üan chi* 韓昌黎全集 (SPPY)
HHS	*Hou Han shu* 後漢書 (KM)
HNT	Liu An 劉安, *Huai nan tzu* 淮南子 (SPTK)
HNYC	*Hsü Nan Yüeh chih* 續南越志
HS	*Han shu* 漢書 (KM)
HsCC	Kuo P'u 郭璞, *Hsüan chung chi* 玄中記
HWC	Cheng Ch'ang 鄭常, *Hsia wen chi* 洽聞記
HYPT	Li Hsün 李珣, *Hai yao pen ts'ao* 海藥本草
ICCYI	Hui-lin 慧琳, *I ch'ieh ching yin i* 一切經音義 (TSDZK, v. 54)
KC	Kuo I-kung 郭義恭, *Kuang chih* 廣志
KCC	*Kuang chou chi* 廣州記
KHYHC	Fan Ch'eng-ta 范成大, *Kuei hai yü heng chih* 桂海虞衡志 (PSNIC)
KIC	Tai Chün-fu 戴君孚, *Kuang i chi* 廣異記
KLFTC	Mo Hsiu-fu 莫休符, *Kuei lin feng t'u chi* 桂林風土記 (TSCC)
KSTI	Liu Su 劉餗, *Kuo shih tsuan i* 國史纂異
KY	Lu Fa-yen 陸法言, *Kuang yün* 廣韻 陳彭年 (rev. by Ch'en P'eng-nien)
LH	Wang Ch'ung 王充, *Lun heng* 論衡
LHSC	Liu Tsung-yüan 柳宗元, *Tseng kuang chu shih yin pien T'ang Liu hsien sheng chi* 增廣註釋音辯唐柳先生集 (SPTK)
LIC	Tu Kuang-t'ing 杜光庭, *Lu i chi* 錄異記
LiIC	*Lin-i chi* 林邑記
LMTWC	Liu Yü-hsi 劉禹錫, *Liu Meng-te wen chi* 劉夢得文集 (SPTK)
LNIWC	Meng Kuan 孟琯, *Ling-nan i wu chih* 嶺南異物志
LPLI	Liu Hsün 劉恂, *Ling piao lu i* 嶺表錄異 (TSCC)
LTMHC	Chang Yen-yüan 張彥遠, *Li tai ming hua chi* 歷代名畫記 (1600)
LTPWC	Li Po 李白, *Li T'ai-po wen chi* 李太白文集 (Hiraoka, 1958)
LWKC	Li Te-yü 李德裕, *Li Wei kung hui ch'ang i p'in chi* 李衛公會昌一品集 (TSCC)
MHTL	Cheng Ch'u-hui 鄭處誨, *Ming huang tsa lu* 明皇雜錄

Bibliography

MIPL	T'ao Hung-ching 陶弘景, *Ming i pieh lu* 名醫別錄
MSKY	Mao Chin 毛晉, *Mao shih ts'ao mu niao shou ch'ung yü su kuang yao* 毛詩草木鳥獸蟲魚疏廣要 (TSCC)
MSS	Lu Chi 陸璣, *Mao shih ts'ao mu niao shou ch'ung yü su* 毛詩草木鳥獸蟲魚疏 (TSCC)
MTKH	Huang Hsiu-fu 黄休復, *Mao t'ing k'o hua* 茅亭客話 (CTPS)
NCHW	Yü-ch'ih Shu 尉遲樞, *Nan Ch'u hsin wen* 南楚新聞
NFIWC	Fang Ch'ien-li 房千里, *Nan fang i wu chih.* 南方異物志
NHIS	*Nan hai i shih* 南海異事
NKC	Teng Te-ming 鄧德明, *Nan K'ang chi* 南康記 (SF)
NPHS	Ch'ien I 錢易, *Nan pu hsin shu* 南部新書 (TSCC)
NYC	Shen Huai-yüan 沈懷遠, *Nan Yüeh chih* 南越志 (WCHS)
PHL	Tuan Kung-lu 段公路, *Pei hu lu* 北戶錄 (HPHSIS)
PMSY	Sun Kuang-hsien 孫光憲, *Pei meng so yen* 北夢瑣言 (TSCC)
PPT	Ko Hung 葛洪, *Pao p'u tzu* 抱朴子
PTKM	Li Shih-chen 李時珍, *Pen ts'ao kang mu* 本草綱目 (*Hung pao chai* ed.)
PTT	*Po tse t'u* 白澤圖
PYTC	Cheng Hsiung 鄭熊, *P'an-yü tsa chi* 畨禺雜記 (SF)
SAC	*Shih-an chi* 始安記
SC	*Shih chi* 史記, (KM)
SCC	Li Tao-yüan 酈道元, *Shui ching chu* 水經注 (SPTK)
SHC	*Shan hai ching* 山海經 (SPTK)
ShCC	*Shih chou chi* 十洲記 (LWPS)
ShHC	Wang Shao-chih 王韶之, *Shih-hsing chi* 始興記 (TSCC)
ShIC	Jen Fang 任昉, *Shu i chi* 述異記 (HWTS)
SIC	*Shen i ching* 神異經 (HWTS)
SKC	*San kuo chih* 三國志 (KM)
SKSC	T'ung-hui 通慧, *Sung kao seng chuan* 宋高僧傳 (TSDZK, v. 50)
SP	Tsan-ning 贊寧, *Sun p'u* 筍譜 (PCHH)
SS	*Sui shu* 隋書 (KM)
SSC	Kan Pao 干寶, *Sou shen chi* 搜神記 (TSCC)
SSYI	Su O 蘇鶚, *Su shih yen i* 蘇氏演義 (TSCC)
STC	Liang Tsai-yen 梁載言, *Shih tao chih* 十道志 (HTTLSC)
STSK	P'eng Ta-i 彭大翼, *Shan t'ang szu k'ao* 山堂肆考
SuS	*Sung shih* 宋史 (KM)
TC	Cheng Ch'iao 鄭樵, *T'ung chih* 通志 (Shanghai, 1935)
TCMHL	Chu Ching-hsüan 朱景玄, *T'ang ch'ao ming hua lu* 唐朝名畫錄 (MSTS)
TCTC	Szu-ma Kuang 司馬光, *Tzu chih t'ung chien* 資治通鑑 (Tokyo, 1892)
THTL	Fang Ch'ien li 房千里, *T'ou huang tsa lu* 投荒雜錄
TIWL	*T'ang i wen lu* 唐異聞錄
TKSP	Li Chao 李肇, *T'ang kuo shih pu* 唐國史補 (HCTY)
TLSS	Chu Fa-chen 竺法真, *Teng Lo-shan shu* 登羅山疏
TLT	*T'ang liu tien* 唐六典 (Kyoto, 1935)
TPHYC	*T'ai p'ing huan yü chi* 太平寰宇記 (1803 ed.)
TPT	Su Kung 蘇恭, *T'ang pen ts'ao chu* 唐本草注

TS   *T'ang shu* 唐書 (SPPY)

TSCS   *T'ang shih chi shih* 唐詩紀事

TT   Tu Yu 杜佑, *T'ung tien* 通典 (Shanghai, 1935)

TTC   *Ts'an t'ung ch'i* 參同契 (TSCC)

TTHY   Liu Su 劉肅, *Ta T'ang hsin yü* 大唐新語

TTHYC   Hsüan-tsang 玄奘, *Ta T'ang hsi yü chi* 大唐西域記 (SPTK)

TuT   Ts'ai Yung 蔡邕, *Tu tuan* 獨斷 (TSCC)

TYSIL   Tu Pao 杜寶, *Ta yeh shih i lu* 大業拾遺錄

TYTP   Su O 蘇鶚, *Tu yang tsa pien* 杜陽雜編

WCL   Yü T'i 于逖, *Wen ch'i lu* 聞奇錄

WS   *Wei shu* 魏書 (KM)

WTPY   Wang Tao 王燾, *Wai t'ai pi yao* 外臺祕要

WTS   *Wu tai shih* 五代史 (KM)

WYCCC   Wang Wei 王維, *Wang Yu-ch'eng chi chu* 王右丞集注 (SPPY)

YCSSHC   Li Shang-yin 李商隱, *Yü-ch'i sheng shih hsiang chu* 玉谿生 詩詳注

YCTC   *Yung-chou t'u ching* 邕州圖經

YHC   Li Chi-fu 李吉甫, *Yüan ho chün hsien (t'u) chih* 元和郡 縣(圖)志

YHTC   Feng Chih 馮贄, *Yün hsien tsa chi* 雲仙雜記 (SPTK, 'TSCC)

YTCS   Wang Hsiang-chih 王象之 *Yü ti chi sheng* 輿地紀勝 (1849)

YTKC   *Yü ti kuang chi* 輿地廣記

COLLECTANEA AND ENCYCLOPEDIAS

CHC   *Ch'u hsüeh chi* 初學記

ChTS   *Ch'üan T'ang shih* 全唐詩

CSKW   *Ch'üan Shang ku San tai Ch'in Han San kuo Liu ch'ao wen* 全上古三 代秦漢三國六朝文

CTPS   *Chin tai pi shu* 津逮祕書

CTW   *Ch'üan T'ang wen* 全唐文

HCTY   *Hsüeh chin t'ao yüan* 學津討源

HPHSIS   *Hu-pei hsien sheng i shu* 湖北先生遺書

HTTLSC   *Han T'ang ti li shu ch'ao* 漢唐地理鈔

HWTS   *Han Wei ts'ung shu* 漢魏叢書

HYHTS   *Hsi yin hsüan ts'ung shu* 惜陰軒叢書

KM   *K'ai ming* edition 開明

KTTC   *Kuang-tung t'ung chih* 廣東通志   (1934 ed.)

LNIS   *Ling-nan i shu* 嶺南遺書

LNTS   *Ling-nan ts'ung shu* 嶺南叢述

LWPS   *Lung wei pi shu* 龍威祕書

MSTS   *Mei shu ts'ung shu* 美術叢書

PCHH   *Po ch'uan hsüeh hai* 百川學海

PKLT   *Po K'ung liu tieh* 白孔六帖

PSNIC   *Pi shu nien i chung* 祕書廿一種

PYTPC   *Pao yen t'ang pi chi* 寶顏堂祕笈

SF   *Shuo fu* 說郛 (1647 ed.)

SPPY   *Szu pu pei yao* 四部備要

Bibliography

TSDZK   *Taishō Daizōkyō* 大正大藏經
SPTK   *Szu pu ts'ung k'an* 四部叢刊
TPKC   *T'ai p'ing kuang chi* 太平廣記
TPYL   *T'ai p'ing yü lan* 太平御覽
TSCC   *Ts'ung shu chi ch'eng* 叢書集成
TTTS   *T'ang tai ts'ung shu* 唐代叢書 (1864 ed.)
WCHS   *Wu ch'ao hsiao shuo* 五朝小説
YHSS   *Yü han shan fang chi i shu* 玉函山房輯遺書

Secondary Sources

ALLEN, G. M.

1938   *The Mammals of China and Mongolia* (Natural History of Central Asia, Vol. XI, Pt. 1; New York, 1938 and 1940).

AOYAMA SADAO

1963   *Tō-Sō jidai no kōtsū to chishi chizu no kenkyū* (Tokyo, 1963).

AUROUSSEAU, L.

1923   "La première conquête chinoise des pays Annamites," *Bulletin de l'Ecole Française d'Extrême-Orient*, Vol. 23 (1923), 137–266.

AUSTIN, JR., OLIVER J.

1961   *Birds of the World: A Survey of the Twenty-seven Orders and One Hundred and Fifty-five Families* (New York, 1961).

AYMONIER, ETIENNE

1890   "Légendes historiques des Chams," *Excursions et Reconnaissances*, Vol. 14 (1890), 145–206.

1891   "Les Tchames et leurs religions," *Revue de l'histoire des religions*, Vol. 24 (1891), 187–237, 261–315.

AYMONIER, ETIENNE, and ANTOINE CABATON

1906   *Dictionnaire Čam-Français* (Publications de l'Ecole Française d'Extrême-Orient, Vol. 7, Paris, 1906).

BALAZS, STEFAN

1931   "Beiträge zur Wirtschaftsgeschichte der T'ang-Zeit," *Mitteilungen des Seminars für orientalische Sprachen*, Vol. 34 (1931), 1–92

1932   "Beiträge zur Wirtschaftsgeschichte der T'ang-Zeit," *Mitteilungen des Seminars für orientalische Sprachen*, Vol. 35 (1932), 1–73.

BATES, MARSTON

1952   *Where Winter Never Comes: A Study of Man and Nature in the Tropics* (New York, 1952).

1963   *Animal Worlds* (New York, 1963).

BAXTER, GLEN W.

1953   "Metrical origins of the 'Tz'u," *Harvard Journal of Asiatic Studies*, Vol. 16 (1953), 108–145.

BEER, A., Ho PING-YÜ, LU GWEI-DJEN, J. NEEDHAM, E. G. PULLEYBLANK, and G. I. THOMPSON

1961   "An Eighth-Century Meridian Line: I-HSING's Chain of Gnomons and the Pre-history of the Metric System," *Vistas in Astronomy*, Vol. 4 (1961), 3–28.

BENEDICT, P. K.

1941 "A Cham Colony on the Island of Hainan," *Harvard Journal of Asiatic Studies,* Vol. 6 (1941), 129–134.

1942 "Thai, Kadai, and Indonesian: A New Alignment in Southeastern Asia," *American Anthropologist,* Vol. 44 (1942), 576–601.

1947 "Languages and Literatures of Indochina," *Far Eastern Quarterly,* Vol. 6 (1947), 379–389.

BISHOP, CARL WHITING

1933 "Rhinoceros and Wild Ox in Ancient China," *China Journal,* Vol. 18 (1933), 322–330.

1938 "Long-Houses and Dragon-Boats," *Antiquity,* Vol. 12 (1938), 411–424.

BONIFACY, A. L. M.

1903 "Etude sur les chants et la poésie populaire des Máns du Tonkin," *Premier congrés international des Etudes d'Extrême-Orient, Hanoi (1903). Compte rendu analytique des séances* (Hanoi, 1903), 85–89.

1914 "Nouvelles Recherches sur les génies thériomorphes au Tonkin, (troisième série)," *Bulletin de l'Ecole Française d'Extrême-Orient,* Vol. 18 (1918), 1–50.

1925 "Une mission chez les Mán, d'Octobre 1901 à la fin de Janvier 1902," *Etudes Asiatiques publiées à l'occasion du vingt-cinquième anniversaire de l'Ecole Française d'Extrême-Orient,* Vol. 1 (1925), 49–102.

BRIGGS, L. P.

1949 "The Appearance and Historical Usage of the Terms Tai, Thai, Siamese, and Lao," *Journal of the American Oriental Society,* Vol. 69 (1949), 60–73.

BRODRICK, A. H.

1942 *Little China: The Annamese Lands* (London, New York, Toronto, 1942)

BROWN, IVOR

1953 *A Word in Edgeways* (London, 1953)

1961 *Words in Season* (London, 1961)

1963 *A Word in your Ear, and Just another Word* (Dutton paperback, New York, 1963).

BUI QUANG TUNG

1963 "Tables synoptiques de chronologie vietnamienne," *Bulletin de l'Ecole Française d'Extrême-Orient,* Vol. 51 (1963), 1–78.

BURKHILL, I. H.

1935 *A Dictionary of the Economic Products of the Malay Peninsula* (London, 1935).

CALDWELL, H. R., and J. C. CALDWELL

1931 *South China Birds* (Shanghai, [1931?]).

CAMMANN, SCHUYLER

1950 "The Story of Hornbill Ivory," *University Museum Bulletin,* Vol. 15 No. 4 (Philadelphia, December, 1950), 19–47.

CHAN, WING-TSIT

1957 "Neo-Confucianism and Chinese Scientific Thought," *Philosophy East and West,* Vol. 6 (1957), 309–332.

1963 *The Platform Scripture: translated with an introduction and notes* (New York, 1963).

CHANG HUNG-CHAO

1921 *Shih ya* (*Ti-chih chuan-pao,* Ser. B, No. 2; Peking, 1921).

CHANG KUO-KAN

1962   *Chung-kuo ku fang-chih k'ao* (Shanghai, 1962).

CHANG KWANG-CHIH

1959   "Chinese Prehistory in Pacific Perspective," *Harvard Journal of Oriental Studies,* Vol. 22 (1959), 100–149.

1959a "A Working Hypothesis for the Early Cultural History of South China," *Bulletin of the Institute of Ethnology, Academia Sinica,* Vol. 7 (Spring, 1959), 75–103.

CH'EN HSÜ-CHING

1946   *Tan-min ti yen-chiu* (Shanghai, 1946).

CH'EN JUNG

1957   *Chung-kuo shu-mu fen-lei-hsüeh* (Shanghai, 1957).

CHENG TSO-HSIN

1955   *Chung-kuo niao-lei fen-pu mu-lu.* Vol. 1: *Fei-ch'üeh-hsing mu* (Peking, 1955).

CHÊNG TÊ-K'UN

1964   "New Light on Ancient China," *Antiquity,* Vol. 38 (1964), 179–186.

CHIA TSU-CHANG, and CHIA TSU-SHAN

1946   *Chung-kuo chih-wu t'u-chien* (2nd ed., Shanghai, 1946)

CLARK, LEONARD

1938   "Among the Big Knot Lois of Hainan; Wild Tribesmen with Topknots Roam the Little-known Interior of This Big and Strategically Important Island in the China Sea," *National Geographic Magazine,* September, 1938, 391–418.

COEDÈS, G.

1948   *Les états hindouisés d'Indochine et d'Indonésie* (Paris, 1948).

1962   *Les peuples de la péninsule indochinoise: Histoire—civilisations* (Paris, 1962).

COLLINGWOOD, CUTHBERT

1868   *Rambles of a Naturalist on the Shore and Waters of the China Sea: being Observations in Natural History during a Voyage to China, Formosa, Borneo, Singapore, Etc., made in Her Majesty's Vessells in 1866 and 1867* (London, 1868).

Concordance

1940   "A Concordance to the Poems of Tu Fu," *Harvard-Yenching Institute Sinological Index Series,* Vol. II, Suppl. 14 (Cambridge, 1940).

CORAL-RÉMUSAT, GILBERTE DE

1936   "Animaux fantastiques de l'Indochine, de l'Insulinde et de la Chine," *Bulletin de l'Ecole Française d'Extrême-Orient,* Vol. 36 (1936), 427–435.

CRESSEY, GEORGE B.

1934   *China's Geographic Foundations; A Survey of the Land and its People* (New York and London, 1934)

DAVID, A., and E. OUSTALET

1878   *Les Oiseaux de la Chine* (Paris, 1878)

DEMIÉVILLE, P.

1929   *Hôbôgirin* (Tokyo, 1929)

DEVÉRIA, G.

1886   La frontière sino-annamite (Paris, 1886).

DURAND, E.-M.

1907   "Notes sur les Chams," *Bulletin de l'Ecole Française d'Extrême-Orient,* Vol. 7 (1907), 313–355.

Bibliography

DUYVENDAK, J. J. L.
1939 "Review of H. Stübel, *Die Li-Stämme der Insel Hainan,*" *T'oung Pao,* Vol. 35 (1939), 404–407.

EBERHARD, W.
1942 *Kultur und Siedlung der Randvolker Chinas* (Supplement to *T'oung Pao,* Vol. 36, 1942)
1942a *Lokalkulturen im alten China,* Teil 2: *Die Lokalkulturen des Südens und Ostens* (*Monumenta Serica* Monograph III; Peking, 1942).

ERKES, EDUARD
1935 "Das Primat des Weibes im alten China," *Sinica,* Vol. 10 (1935), 166–176.
1939 "Zur Sage von Shun," *T'oung Pao,* Vol. 34 (1939), 295–333.
1951 "Der Pfau in Religion und Folklore," *Jahrbuch des Museums für Völkerkunde zu Leipzig,* Vol. 10 (1926/1951), 67–73.

EVANS, HAROLD
1949 *Men in the Tropics; A Colonial Anthology* (London, Edinburgh, Glasgow, 1949).

FAIRCHILD, DAVID
1944 *Garden Islands of the Great East: Collecting Seeds from the Philippines and Netherlands India in the Junk "Chêng Ho"* (New York, 1944).

FENG, H. Y., and J. K. SHRYOCK
1935 "The Black Magic in China known as *ku,*" *Journal of the American Oriental Society,* Vol. 55 (1935), 1–30.

FENZEL, G.
1929 "On the Natural Conditions Affecting the Introduction of Forestry as a Branch of Rural Economy in the Province of Kwangtung, Especially in North Kwangtung," *Lingnan Science Journal,* Vol. 7 (1929), 37–102.
1930 "Problems of Reforestation in Kwangtung with Respect to the Climate," *Lingnan Science Journal,* Vol. 9 (1930), 97–113.

FERRAND, GABRIEL
1914 *Relations de voyages et textes géographiques arabes, persans et turks relatifs a l'Extrême-Orient du VIIIe au XVIIe siècles* (Paris, 1913–1914).
1919 "Le K'ouen-louen et les anciennes navigations interocéaniques dans les mers du sud," *Journal Asiatique,* Vol. 11, No. 13 (1919), 239–333, 431–492; Vol. 11, No. 14 (1919), 5–68, 201–241.

FINOT, L.
1901 "La religion des Chams d'après les monuments," *Bulletin de l'Ecole Française d'Extrême-Orient,* Vol. 1 (1901), 12–33.

FLANDERS, S. E., J. L. GRESSITT, and T. W. FISHER
1958 "Casca chinensis, an internal parasite of California red scale," *Hilgardia,* Vol. 28 No. 5 (Berkeley, November, 1958), 65–91.

FORREST, R. A. D.
1948 *The Chinese Language* (London, 1948).

FRODSHAM, J. D.
1960 "The Origin of Chinese Nature Poetry," *Asia Major,* n.s., Vol. 8 (1960), 68–104.

FUERTES, LOUIS AGASSIZ
1913 "Impressions of the Voices of Tropical Birds," *Bird-Lore,* Vol. 15 (1913), 341–344.
1914 "Impressions of the Voices of Tropical Birds," *Bird-Lore,* Vol. 16 (1914), 1–4, 96–101, 161–169, 342–349, 421–428.

Bibliography

FUSON, CHESTER G.
  1928 "The Geography of Kwangtung," *Lingnan Science Journal,* Vol. 6 (1928), 241–256.
  1929 "The Peoples of Kwangtung: Their Origin, Migrations, and Present Distribution," *Lingnan Science Journal,* Vol. 7 (1929), 5–22.
GILES, HERBERT A.
  1923 *Gems of Chinese Literature,* Vol. I: *Prose* (2nd ed., Shanghai, 1923).
GLACKEN, CLARENCE J.
  1962 *Three Great Traditions concerning Man and the Earth: Studies in the History of Geographic Ideas from Antiquity Through the Eighteenth Century* (dittoed; Berkeley, 1962).
GOLOUBEW, V.
  1932 "Sur l'origine et la diffusions des tambours métalliques," *Praehistorica Asiae Orientalis,* I (Premier Congres des Préhistoriens d'Extrême-Orient; Hanoi, 1932), 137–150.
GOUROU, PIERRE
  1940 *L'utilisation du sol en Indochine française* (Paris, 1940).
GRAY, BASIL
  1949 "China or Dong-son," *Oriental Art,* Vol. 2 (1949), 99–104.
GRIGSON, GEOFFREY, and C. H. GIBBS-SMITH
  1957 *Things: A Volume of Objects devised by Man's Genius which are the Measure of his Civilization* (New York, 1957).
HAN WAI TUN
  1946 "Yeh yü," *Nan-yang hsüeh-pao,* Vol. 3 (1946), 36–46.
HARICH-SCHNEIDER, ETA
  1955 "The Earliest Sources of Chinese Music and Their Survival in Japan," *Monumenta Nipponica,* Vol. 11 (1955), 85–103.
HASTINGS, JAMES
  1962 *Encyclopaedia of Religion and Ethics* (New York, 1962).
HERALD, E. S.
  1962 *Living Fishes of the World* (New York, 1962).
HIRAOKA TAKEO
  1958 *Rihaku no sakuhin* (Kyoto, 1958).
HO KO-EN
  1960 "Tan-tsu chih yen-chiu," *Journal of Oriental Studies,* Vol. 5 (1960), 1–40.
HOEPPLI, R.
  1954 "Malaria in Chinese Medicine," *Sinologica,* Vol. 4 (1954), 91–101.
HOU K'UAN-CHAO
  1957 *Kuang-chou chih-wu chien-so-piao* (Shanghai, 1957).
HSÜ SUNG-SHIH
  1939 *Yüeh-chiang liu-yü jen-min shih* (Shanghai, 1939).
HSÜ YÜN-CH'IAO
  1947 "Nan-chao fei t'ai-tsu ku kuo k'ao," *Nan-yang hsüeh-pao,* Vol. 4, No. 2 (1947), 1–8.
K'ao-ku t'ung-hsün
  1956 "Kuang-tung Ch'ao-yang hsin-shih-ch'i shih-tai i-chih, tiao-ch'a chien-pao," *K'ao-ku t'ung-hsün,* Vol. 10 (1956), 4–11.

HUNG, WILLIAM
  1940 "The Inkslab in Chinese Literary Tradition," *Yenching University Occasional Papers*, No. 3 (May 7, 1940).
JANSE, OLOV R. T.
  1947 *Archaeological Research in Indo-China*, I (Harvard-Yenching Institute Monograph Series, Vol. VII; Cambridge, 1947).
KALTENMARK, M.
  1948 "Le dompteur des flots," *Han-Hiue*, Vol. 3 (1948), 1–112.
KARLGREN, B.
  1942 "The date of the early Dong-so'n culture," *Bulletin of the Museum of Far Eastern Antiquities*, Vol. 14 (1942), 1–28.
LAFONT, P.-B.
  1964 "Contribution a l'étude des structures sociales des Cham du Viêt-Nam," *Bulletin de l'Ecole Française d'Extrême-Orient*, Vol. 52 (1964), 157–171.
LAPICQUE, P. A.
  1911 "Note sur le canal de hing-ngan (Kouang-si)," *Bulletin de l'Ecole Française d'Extrême-Orient*, Vol. 11 (1911), 425–428.
LA TOUCHE, J. D. D.
  1930 *A Handbook of the Birds of Eastern China (Chihli, Shantung, Kiangsu, Anhwei, Kiangsi, Chekiang, Fohkien, and Kwangtung Provinces)*. Vol. I (London, 1925–1930).
  1934 *A Handbook of the Birds of Eastern China*. Vol. II (London, 1931–1934).
LATTIMORE, OWEN
  1955 "The Frontier in History," *Relazioni, X. Congresso Internazionale di Scienze Storiche; Roma 4–11 Settembre, 1955*, Vol. I (Firenze, 1955), 105–138.
  1962 *Studies in Frontier History; Collected Papers, 1928–1958* (London, 1962).
LAUFER, BERTHOLD
  1917 "Totemic Traces among the Indo-Chinese," *Journal of American Folklore*, Vol. 30 (1917), 415–426.
  1919 *Sino-Iranica: Chinese Contributions to the History of Civilization in Ancient Iran, with Special Reference to the History of Cultivated Plants and Products* (Field Museum of Natural History, Publication 201, Anthropological Series, Vol. 15, No. 3; Chicago, 1919).
LI CHI
  1928 *The Formation of the Chinese People: An Anthropological Inquiry* (Cambridge, 1928).
LI FANG-KUEI
  1948 "Mo-hua chi-lüeh," *Kuo-li chung-yang yen-chiu-yüan, Li-shih yü-yen yen-chiu-so chi-k'an*, Vol. 19 (1948), 1–80.
LI, H. L.
  1959 *The Garden Flowers of China* (New York, 1959).
LI HUI
  1960 "Shuo tu-ku yü wu-shu," *Kuo-li chung-yang yen-chiu-yüan, Min-tsu-hsüeh yen-chiu-so chi-k'an*, Vol. 9 (1960), 271–282.
LIN YUEH-HUA
  1941 "The Miao-Man peoples of Kweichow," *Harvard Journal of Asiatic Studies*, Vol. 5, Nos. 3–4 (January, 1941), 261–344.
LING SHUN-SHENG

1938   "T'ang-tai Yün-nan ti W-Man yü Po-Man k'ao," *Jen-lei-hsüeh chi-k'an*, Vol. 1
        (1938), 57–82.
1960   "Kuo-shang li-hun yü kuo-shou chi-hsiao," *Kuo-li chung-yang yen-chiu-yüan,
        Min-tsu-hsüeh yen-chiu-so chi-k'an*, Vol. 9 (1960), 411–449.
1960a "Chung-kuo ku-tai chi-chung yü-shih ping-ch'i chi ch'i tsai T'ai-p'ing-yang-ch'ü
        ti lei-yüan," *Kuo-li chung-yang yen-chiu-yüan, Min-tsu-hsüeh yen-chiu-so chi-k'an*,
        Vol. 10 (1960), 15–26.

LIU, CHUNGSHEE H.
1932   "The Dog-ancestor Story of the Aboriginal Tribes of Southern China," *Journal
        of the Royal Anthropological Institute of Great Britain and Ireland*, Vol. 62
        (1932), 361–368.
1941   "On the Dog-Ancestor Myth in Asia," *Studia Serica*, Vol. 1 (1941), 277–314.

LIU HSIEN
1936   "Nan-hai li-jen wen-shen chih yen-chiu," *Kuo-li chung-yang yen-chiu-yüan,
        Min-tsu-hsüeh yen-chiu-so chi-k'an*, Vol. 1 (1936), 197–228.

LIU, JAMES J. Y.
1962   *The Art of Chinese Poetry* (Chicago, 1962).

LO HSIANG-LIN
1934   "T'ang-tai tan-tsu k'ao, shang p'ien," *Kuo-li Chung-shan ta-hsüeh wen-shih-
        hsüeh yen-chiu-so yüeh-k'an*, Vol. 2, Nos. 3–4 (1934), 13–56.
1955   *Po Yüeh yüan-liu yü wen-hua* (Taipei, 1955).
1960   *T'ang-tai Kuang-chou Kuang-hsiao-szu yü Chung-Yin chiao-t'ung chih kuan-hsi*
        (Hongkong, 1960).
1962   "T'ang-tai Kuei-lin Hsi-yü jen Mo-yai t'i k'o k'ao," *Proceedings*, International
        Association of Historians of Asia, Second Biennial Conference (Taipei, 1962),
        73–79.

LU GWEI-DJEN, and JOSEPH NEEDHAM
1951   "A Contribution to the History of Chinese Dietetics," *Isis*, Vol. 42 (April,
        1951), 13–20.

McCLURE, F. A.
1934   "The Lingnan University Sixth and Seventh Hainan Island Expeditions,"
        Lingnan Science Journal, Vol. 13 (1934), 577–601.

McCUNE, SHANNON
1947   "The Diversity of Indochina's Physical Geography," *Far Eastern Quarterly*,
        Vol. 6 (1947), 335–344.

McNEIL, MARY
1964   "Lateritic Soils," *Scientific American*, November, 1964, 97–102.

MADROLLE, C.
1937   "Le Tonkin ancien; Lei-leou et les districts chinois de l'epoque des Han. La
        Population Yue-chang," *Bulletin de l'Ecole Française d'Extrême-Orient*, Vol. 37
        (1937), 263–332.

MAGLIONI, RAPHAEL
1952   "Archaeology in South China," *Journal of East Asiatic Studies*, Vol. 2 (Uni-
        versity of Manila, 1952), 1–20.

MALLERET, LOUIS
1934   *L'Exotisme Indochinois dans la Littérature Française depuis 1860* (Paris, 1934).

MARGOULIÈS, GEORGES
1926   *Le kou-wen chinois; recueil de textes avec introduction et notes* (Paris, 1926).

MASPERO, GEORGES

1928 *Le Royaume de Champa* (Paris and Brussels, 1928).

MASPERO, HENRI

1910 "Le Protectorat Général d'Annam sous les T'ang. Essai de Géographie His-
torique," *Bulletin de l'Ecole Française d'Extrême-Orient,* Vol. 10 (1910), 539–
584, 665–682.

1916 "Etudes d'histoire d'Annam," *Bulletin de l'Ecole Française d'Extrême-Orient,*
Vol. 16, No. 1 (1916), 1–55.

1918 "Etudes d'histoire d'Annam," *Bulletin de l'Ecole Française d'Extrême-Orient,*
Vol. 18, No. 3 (1918), 1–36.

1924 "Legendes mythologiques dans le Chou King," *Journal Asiatique,* Vol. 214
(1924), 1–100.

1924a "Review of L. Aurousseau, La première conquête des pays annamites (IIIᵉ
siècle avant notre ère)," *T'oung Pao,* Vol. 23 (1924), 373–393.

1950 "La société et la religion des Chinois anciens et celles des Tai modernes," *Les
Religions Chinoises (Melanges Posthumes sur les religions et l'histoire de la
Chine,* I; Paris, 1950), 139–194.

1963 "The Mythology of Modern China," *Asiatic Mythology; A Detailed Description
and Explanation of the Mythologies of All the Great Nations of Asia* (2nd
English ed., New York, 1963), 252–384.

MATHER, RICHARD

1958 "The Landscape Buddhism of the Fifth-Century Poet Hsieh Ling-yün," *Journal
of Asian Studies,* Vol. 18 (1958), 67–79.

MAYBON, C. B.

1919 "La domination chinoise en Annam (111 av. J.C.—939 ap. J.C.)," *The New
China Review,* Vol. 1 (1919), 237–248, 340–355.

MIYAKAWA HISAYUKI

1960 "The Confucianization of South China," *The Confucian Persuasion* (Stanford,
1960).

MO CHIH

1957 "Kwang-tung Pao-an-hsien hsin-shih-ch'i shih-tai i-chih tiao-ch'a chien-pao,"
K'ao-ku t'ung-hsün, Vol. 18, No. 6 (1957), 8–15.

MOORE, W. ROBERT

1931 "Along the Old Mandarin Road of Indo-China," *National Geographic Magazine*
(August, 1931), 157–199.

NAKAMURA KUSHIRŌ

1917 "Tō-jidai no Kanton," *Shigaku zasshi,* Vol. 28 (1917), 242–258, 348–368, 487–
495, 552–576.

NEEDHAM, JOSEPH, and WANG LING

1956 *Science and Civilisation in China,* Vol. 2 (Cambridge, 1956).

NEEDHAM, JOSEPH, WANG LING and K. G. ROBINSON

1962 *Science and Civilisation in China,* Vol. 4, Pt. 1 (Cambridge, 1962).

NG YONG-SANG

1936 "Lung Mu, the Dragon Mother: The Story of West River's Own Guardian
Angel," *China Journal,* Vol. 25 (1936), 18–20.

NGUYEN VAN HUYEN

1934 "Introduction a l'étude de l'habitation sur pilotis dans l'Asie du sud-est," *Austro-
Asiatica; documents et travaux publiés sous la direction de Jean Przyluski,* Vol.
IV (Paris, 1934).

NICHOLS, JOHN T.

1943 *The Fresh-Water Fishes of China* (Natural History of Central Asia, Vol. IX; New York, 1943).

OBI KŌICHI

1962 *Chūgoku bungaku ni arawareta shizen to shizenkan—chūsei bungaku o chūshin to shite* (Tokyo, 1962).

PARMENTIER, HENRI

1901 "Caractères généraux de l'architecture chame," *Bulletin de l'Ecole Française d'Extrême-Orient,* Vol. 1 (1901), 245–258.

PARSONS, JAMES J.

1962 *The Green Turtle and MAN* (Gainesville, Florida, 1962).

PELLIOT, PAUL

1904 "Deux itinéraires de Chine en Inde a la fin du viiiᵉ siècle," *Bulletin de l'Ecole Française d'Extrême-Orient,* Vol. 4 (1904), 131–413.

1959 *Notes on Marco Polo,* Vol. I (Paris, 1959).

1963 *Notes on Marco Polo,* Vol. II (Paris, 1963).

PELZER, K. J.

1945 *Pioneer Settlement in the Asiatic Tropics; Studies in Land Utilization and Agricultural Colonization in Southeastern Asia* (New York, 1945).

PETERS, JOHN P.

1913 "The Cock," *Journal of the American Oriental Society,* Vol. 33 (1913), 363–396.

POPE, CLIFFORD H.

1935 *The Reptiles of China; Turtles, Crocodilians, Snakes, Lizards* (Natural History of Central Asia, Vol. X; New York, 1935).

PRZYLUSKI, JEAN

1914 "L'or, son origine et ses pouvoirs magiques. Etude de folklore Annamite," *Bulletin de l'Ecole Française d'Extrême-Orient,* Vol. 14, No. 5 (1914), 1–17.

READ, B. E.

1932 *Chinese Materia Medica; Avian Drugs* (Peiping, 1932)

1934 "Chinese Materia Medica; VII. Dragons and Snakes," *Peking Natural History Bulletin,* Vol. 8 (1934), 297–362.

1936 *Chinese Medicinal Plants from the Pen Ts'ao Kang Mu A.D. 1596* (3rd. ed., Peking, 1936).

1939 *Common Food Fishes of Shanghai* (Shanghai, 1939).

REINAUD, J. T.

1845 *Relations des voyages faits par les Arabes et les Persans dans l'Inde et la Chine dans le ixᵉ s. de l'ère chrètienne* (Paris, 1845).

RENNER, JR., G. T.

1927 *Primitive Religion in the Tropical Forests; A Study in Social Geography* (New York, Columbia University, doctoral dissertation, 1927).

REYNOLDS, P. K.

1951 *Earliest Evidence of Banana Culture* (Supplement to *Journal of the American Oriental Society,* No. 12, December, 1951).

REYNOLDS, P. K., and C. Y. FANG

1940 "The Banana in Chinese Literature," *Harvard Journal of Asiatic Studies,* Vol. 5 (1940), 165–181.

ROTOURS, R. DES

1932 *Le traité des examens; traduit de la nouvelle histoire des T'ang (chap. xliv, xlv)* (Paris, 1932).

333

Bibliography

ROUSSELLE, ERWIN
   1941   "Die Frau in Gesellschaft und Mythos der Chinesen," *Sinica*, Vol. 16 (1941), 130–151.

ROY, G. W.
   1963   "The Importance of Sui and T'ang Canal Systems with Regard to Transportation and Communication," *Phi Theta Papers* (Publication of the Honor Society in Oriental Languages of the University of California, Berkeley), Vol. 8 (1963), 35–49.

RUEY YIH-FU [JUI I-FU]
   1938   "Miao-tsu ti hung-shui ku-shih yü Fu-hsi Nü-kua ti ch'uan-shuo," *Jen-lei-hsüeh chi-k'an*, Vol. 1 (1938), 155–194.
   1941   "Hsi-nan shao-shu min-tsu ch'ung-shou p'ien-p'ang ming-ming k'ao-lüeh," *Jen-lei-hsüeh chi-k'an*, Vol 2 (1941), 113–190.
   1948   "Lao wei ch'i-lao shih-cheng," *Kuo-li chung-yang yen-chiu-yüan, Li-shih yü-yen yen-chiu-so chi-k'an*, Vol. 20, Pt. 1 (1948), 343–356.
   1957   "Lao-jen k'ao," *Kuo-li chung-yang yen-chiu-yüan, Li-shih yü-yen yen-chiu-so chi-k'an*, Vol. 28 (1957), 727–771.
   1962   "The Miao: their Origin and Southward Migration," *Proceedings*, International Association of Historians of Asia, Second Biennial Conference (Taipei, 1962), 179–190.

SACHS, CURT
   1940   *The History of Musical Instruments* (New York, 1940).

SATŌ JUNPEI
   1959   *Kanyaku no genshokubutsu* (Tokyo, 1959).

SAUER, G. F.
   1947   *A list of Plants Growing in the Lingnan University Campus and Vicinity* (Canton, 1947).

SCHAFER, EDWARD H.
   1948   "Notes on a Chinese Word for Jasmine," *Journal of the American Oriental Society*, Vol. 68 (1948), 60–65.
   1952   "The Pearl Fisheries of Ho-p'u," *Journal of the American Oriental Society*, Vol. 72 (1952), 155–168.
   1953   "Li Kang: A Rhapsody on the Banyan Tree," *Oriens*, Vol. 6 (1953), 344–353.
   1954   "The History of the Empire of Southern Han according to Chapter 65 of the *Wu Tai Shih* of Ou-yang Hsiu," *Silver Jubilee Volume of the Zinbun-Kagaku-Kenkyusyo* (Kyoto, 1954).
   1954a *The Empire of Min* (Rutland and Tokyo, 1954).
   1956   "Cultural History of the Elaphure," *Sinologica*, Vol. 4 (1956), 250–274.
   1956a "The Early History of Lead Pigments and Cosmetics in China," *T'oung Pao*, Vol. 44 (1956), 413–438.
   1957   "A Fourteenth Century Gazetteer of Canton," *Oriente Poliano* (Rome, 1957), 67–93.
   1957a "Rosewood, Dragon's Blood, and Lac," *Journal of the American Oriental Society*, Vol. 77 (1957), 129–136.
   1957b "War Elephants in Ancient and Medieval China," *Oriens*, Vol. 10 (1957), 289–291.
   1959   "Parrots in Medieval China," *Studia Serica Bernhard Karlgren Dedicata* (Copenhagen, 1959), 271–282.

1961   *The Stone Catalogue of Cloudy Forest; A Commentary and Synopsis* (Berkeley and Los Angeles, 1961).

1962   "The Conservation of Nature under the T'ang Dynasty," *Journal of the Economic and Social History of the Orient*, Vol. 5 (1962), 279–308.

1962a "Eating Turtles in Ancient China," *Journal of the American Oriental Society*, Vol. 82 (1962), 73–74.

1962b "Notes on T'ang Culture," *Monumenta Serica*, Vol. 21 (1962), 194–221.

1963   *The Golden Peaches of Samarkand: A Study of T'ang Exotics* (Berkeley and Los Angeles, 1963).

1963a "Mineral Imagery in the Paradise Poems of Kuan-hsiu," *Asia Major*, Vol. 10 (1963), 73–102.

1963b "The T'ang imperial icon," *Sinologica*, Vol. 7 (1963), 156–160.

1963c "The last Years of Ch'ang-an," *Oriens Extremus*, Vol. 10 (1963), 133–179.

1963d "The Auspices of T'ang," *Journal of the American Oriental Society*, Vol. 83 (1963), 197–225.

1964   "Li Te-yü and the Azalea," *Asiatische Studien*, Vol. 18/19 (1965), 105–114.

1964a "The Idea of Created Nature in T'ang Literature," *Philosophy East and West*, Vol. 15 (1965), 153–160.

SCHAFER, EDWARD H., and B. E. WALLACKER

1958   "Local Tribute Products of the T'ang Dynasty," *Journal of Oriental Studies*, Vol. 4 (1957–1958), 213–248.

SCOTT, AMORET and CHRISTOPHER

1961   "The Social History of the Parrot," *The Saturday Book*, Vol. 21 (London, 1961), 177–192.

SEBEOK, T. A.

1943   "The Languages of Southeastern Asia," *Far Eastern Quality*, Vol. 2 (1943), 349–356.

SERRUYS, P. L.-M.

1962   "Five Word Studies on *Fangyen* (second part)," *Monumenta Serica*, Vol. 21 (1962), 222–319.

SHIH SHENG-HAN

1958   *A Preliminary Survey of the Book Ch'i Min Yao Shu; An agricultural encyclopaedia of the 6th century* (Peking, 1958).

SHINODA OSAMU

1963   "Tō-shi shokubutsu shaku," *Chūgoku chūsei kagaku gijutsu no kenkyū* (Tokyo, 1963), 343–362.

SHIRAI KŌTARŌ

1934   *Kokuyaku honsō kōmoku* (Tokyo, 1929–1934).

SITWELL, SACHEVERELL

1947   *The Hunters and the Hunted* (London, 1947).

1948   *Old Fashioned Flowers* (2nd ed., London, 1948).

1959   *Journey to the Ends of Time*, Vol. I "Lost in the Dark Wood" (London, 1959).

1962   *The Red Chapels of Banteai Srei; And Temples in Cambodia, India, Siam and Nepal* (London, 1962).

SKARD, SIGMUND

1946   "The Use of Color in Literature: A Survey of Research," *Proceedings of the American Philosophical Society*, Vol. 90 (1946), 163–249.

SMYTHIES, B. E.
1953   *The Birds of Burma* (2nd ed., London, 1953).

SOOTHILL, W. E., and L. HODOUS
1937   *A Dictionary of Chinese Buddhist Terms: With Sanskrit and English Equivalents and a Sanskrit-Pali Index* (London, 1937).

SOWERBY, ARTHUR DE CARLE
1940   *Nature in Chinese Art* (New York, 1940).

SOYMIÉ, MICHEL
1954   "Le Lo-feou chan; étude de géographie religieuse," *Bulletin de l'Ecole Française d'Extrême-Orient,* Vol. 48 (1954), 1–139.

SPENCER, J. E.
1940   "Kueichow; an Internal Chinese Colony," *Pacific Affairs,* Vol. 13 (1940), 162–172.
1954   *Asia East by South; A Cultural Geography* (New York, London, 1954).

STEIN, R.
1942   "Jardins en miniature d'Extrême-Orient," *Bulletin de l'Ecole Française d'Extrême-Orient,* Vol. 42 (1942), 1–104.
1947   *Le Lin-yi; sa localisation, sa contribution à la formation du Champa et ses liens avec la Chine* (*Han-hiue,* Bulletin du Centre d'Etudes Sinologiques de Pekin, II; Pekin, 1947).

STERN, PHILIPPE
1942   *L'art du Champa (ancien Annam) et son évolution* (Paris, 1942).

STUART, G. A.
1911   *Chinese Materia Medica; Vegetable Kingdom* (Shanghai, 1911).

STÜBEL, HANS
1938   "The Yao of the Province of Kwangtung," *Monumenta Serica,* Vol. 3 (1938), 345–384.

STÜBEL, HANS, and P. MERIGGI
1937   *Die Li-Stämme der Insel Hainan: Ein Beitrag zur Volkskunde Südchinas* (Berlin, 1937)

TAI I-HSÜAN
1948   "Lao-tsu yen-chiu," *Kuo-li chung-yang yen-chiu-yüan, Min-tsu-hsüeh yen-chiu-so chi-k'an,* Vol. 6 (1948), 55–91.

TALBOT, L. M.
1960   *A Look at Threatened Species; A Report on some Animals of the Middle East and Southern Asia Which are Threatened with Extermination* (London, 1960).

TATE, G. H. H.
1947   *Mammals of Eastern Asia* (New York, 1947).

TU YA-CH'ÜAN
1933   *Tung-wu-hsüeh ta-tz'u-tien* (2nd ed., Shanghai, 1933).

T'U, CHANG-WANG, and SZE-SUNG HWANG
1945   "The Advance and Retreat of the Summer Monsoon in China," *Bulletin of the American Meteorological Society,* Vol. 26 (1945), 9–22.

T'UNG CHEN-TSAO
1937   "Yüeh-nan T'ang-tai ku-ch'eng k'ao," *Yü kung,* Vol. 6, No. 11 (1937), 11–15.

TWITCHETT, DENIS
1959   "Lands under State Cultivation under the T'ang," *Journal of the Economic and Social History of the Orient,* Vol. 2 (1959), 162–203.

VAUGHAN, R. E., and K. H. JONES
  1913 "The Birds of Hong Kong, Macao, and the West River or Si Kiang in South-East China, with special reference to their Nidification and Seasonal Movements, *Ibis,* ser. 10, Vol. 1 (1913), 17–76, 163–201, 351–384.

WADA HISANORI
  1960 "Tōdai ni okeru shihakushi no sōchi," *Wada Hakushi koki kinen tōyōshi ronsō* (Tokyo, 1960), 1051–1062.

WALEY, ARTHUR
  1961 *Chinese Poems* (London, 1961).
  1963 *The Secret History of the Mongols and other pieces* (London, 1963).

WALLACE, A. R.
  1869 *The Malay Archipelago: The Land of the Orang-utan, and the Bird of Paradise: A Narrative of Travel, with Studies of Man and Nature* (New York, 1869).
  1878 *Tropical Nature and Other Essays* (London, 1878).

WANG GUNGWU
  1958 "The Nanhai Trade: A Study of the Early History of Chinese Trade in the South China Sea," *Journal of the Malayan Branch of the Royal Asiatic Society,* Vol. 31, No. 2 (June, 1958), 1–135.
  1963 *The Structure of Power in North China during the Five Dynasties* (Kuala Lumpur, 1963).

WEN CH'UNG-I
  1961 "Chiu-ko chung ti shui-shen yü huan-nan ti lung-chou sai-shen," *Kuo-li chung-yang yen-chiu-yüan, Min-tsu-hsüeh yen-chiu-so chi-k'an,* Vol. 11 (1961), 51–119.

WHEATLEY, PAUL
  1959 "Geographical Notes on some Commodities involved in Sung Maritime Trade," *Journal of the Malayan Branch of the Royal Asiatic Society,* Vol. 32, No. 2 (June, 1959), 1–140.
  1961 *The Golden Khersonese: Studies in the Historical Geography of the Malay Peninsula before A.D. 1500* (Kuala Lumpur, 1961).
  1963 "What the Greatness of a City is said to be," *Pacific Viewpoint,* Vol. 4, No. 2 (September, 1963), 163–168.

WHITEHEAD, A. N.
  1949 *Science and the Modern World* (Mentor Book, 2nd printing, New York, 1949).

WIENS, H. J.
  1954 *China's March Toward the Tropics* (Hamden, 1954).

WILHELM, HELLMUT
  1957 "Das schöpferische Prinzip im Buch der Wandlungen," *Eranos-Jahrbuch 1956,* Vol. 25 (Zürich, 1957), 455–475.

WU WEN-CHIH
  1962 *Liu Tsung-yüan p'ing-ch'uan* (Peking, 1962).

WU, NELSON I.
  1963 *Chinese and Indian Architecture: The City of Man, the Mountain of God, and the Realm of the Immortals* (New York, 1963).

YAMADA KEIJI
  1963 "Chūsei no shizenkan," Yabuuti, ed., *Chūgoku chūsei kagaku gijutsu no kenkyū* (Tokyo, 1963), 55–110.

YEH CHING-YÜAN

1958   *Kan chü* (Shang pien: *Chung-kuo nung-hsüeh i-ch'an hsüan chi,* A, 14; Shanghai, 1958).

YULE, HENRY, and A. C. BURNELL

1886   *Hobson-Jobson: being a Glossary of Anglo-Indian Colloquial Words and Phrases, and of Kindred Terms; Etymological, Historical, Geographical, and Discursive* (London, 1886).

ZACH, ERWIN VON

1952   *Han Yü's Poetische Werke* (Harvard-Yenching Institute Studies, VII; Cambridge, 1952).

ZEUNER, FREDERICK E.

1963   *A History of Domesticated Animals* (London, 1963).

GLOSSARY A

Names and Titles

An-ch'eng	安成	Chao Ch'ang	趙昌
An ch'i sheng	安期生	Chao Kuo-chen	趙國珍
An Yeh-na (An Ya-na)	安野那	Chao Te	趙德
Chan-ch'eng	占城	Chao T'o	趙佗
Chan-p'o (Chem-ba)	占婆	Chao Han t'ai	朝漢臺
Chan-pu-lao (Chem-pyou-lau)	占不勞	Chen [river]	溱
Chang Chi	張籍	Chen (Chin) [tribe]	真
Chang Chieh	張階	Chen Ch'ung-yü (Chin Dryung-iwĕt)	
Chang Chiu-ling	張九齡		真崇鬱
Chang Chou	張舟	Chen Ch'üan	甄權
Chang-hai	漲海	Chen-la (Chin-lap)	真臘
Chang Hou	張侯	Chen-nan	鎮南
Chang Hu	張祜	Ch'en Hsing-fan (Dyin Hăng-bywăm)	
Chang Pi	張泌		陳行範
Chang Pin	張蠙	Ch'en-liu	陳留
Chang Po-i	張伯儀	Ch'en Szu-chi	陳思發
Chang Tao-ling	張道陵	Ch'en T'an	陳雲
Chang Yin	張茵	Ch'en T'ao	陳陶
Chang Yüeh	張說	Ch'en Ts'ang-ch'i	陳藏器
Ch'ang	常	Ch'en T'ing-szu	陳聽思
Ch'ang Ch'ing	長慶	Ch'en Tzu-ang	陳子昂
Ch'ang-o (Zhang-nga)	嫦娥	Ch'en Yen-ch'ien	陳彥謙
Chao	趙	Cheng-ch'ang	湞昌

Most forms in parentheses are in Middle Chinese, others are appropriately marked or self-evident

339

Cheng Ch'üan	鄭權	Fa-hai	法海
Cheng Erh (Tyĕng Nhi)	徵貳	Fa hsing szu	法性寺
Cheng Szu-yüan	鄭思遠	Fan Li	范蠡
Cheng Ts'e (Tyĕng Tryĕk; Vietn. Trung Trac)	徵側	Fang Ch'ien-li	房千里
		Fang yü shih	防禦使
Cheng-yang	潯陽	Feng An (Byung An)	馮安
Chi Han	嵇含	Feng Ang (Byung Ang)	馮盎
Ch'i-lao (Ngyĕt-lau)	仡獠	Feng Ch'ung-tao	馮崇道
Ch'i-t'ien	騎田	Feng Hsing (Byung Hyăng)	馮興
Chiang Chiao	姜皎	Feng Hsüan (Byung Hywăn)	馮暄
Chiang Tzu-lu	姜子路	Feng Jo-fang (Byung Nhak-p'ywang)	
Chiang Yen	江淹		馮若芳
Chiao-chih	交趾	Feng Lin (Byung Lyin)	馮璘
Chieh tu shih	節度使	Feng-ling	封陵
Chien-chen	鑑真	Feng Yen-chi	馮延己
Ch'ien Ch'i	錢起	Feng Ying (Pyong Yeng)	封盈
Ch'ien-chung	黔中	Fou-ch'iu	浮丘
Ch'ien I	錢易	Fu-ch'uan	富川
Ch'ien Liu	錢鏐	Fu-ch'un	富春
Ch'ih sung tzu	赤松子	Fu Hsi	伏羲
Ch'ih Ti	赤帝	Fu Hsüan	傅玄
Ching	荊	Fu-nan (Byu-nam; Bnam)	扶南
Ching hai chün	靜海軍	Hai kuang szu	海光寺
Ching lüeh shih	經略使	Hai men chen	海門真
Ch'ing-yüan	清遠	Hainan	海南
Chiu-chen	九真	Hai-yang	海陽
Chiu-i	九疑	Han Wo	韓偓
Ch'iu Ho	丘和	Han Yü	韓愈
Ch'iung yao chi	瓊瑤集	Han Yüeh	韓約
Chou (Chou)	周	Heng shan	衡山
Chou Yao	周繇	Ho [river]	賀
Chou Yü	周瑜	Ho Hsien-ku	何仙姑
Chu Chi-shih	朱濟思	Ho Lü-kuang	何履光
Chu Chih	竺芝	Ho-p'u	合浦
Chu Ch'ing-yü	朱慶餘	Ho-yin	河陰
Chu Ch'üan-chung	朱全忠	Ho Yu-lu (Gha You-lu)	何遊魯
Chu Ch'üan-yü	朱全昱	Ho-yüan	河源
Chu Jung	祝融	Hsi Shih (Sei Shiĕ)	西施
Chu-lan	朱蘭	Hsi-t'u (Sei-du)	西屠
Chu Ling-Chih	朱靈芝	Hsia (Ghă)	夏
Chu-t'i	朱提	Hsia-k'ou	夏口
Chu-yai	朱崖	Hsia Yung	夏永
Chu Yeh	朱鄴	Hsiang [province]	象
Ch'u	楚	Hsiang [river]	湘
Ch'uang	幢,橦	Hsiang (Syang) [tribe]	相
Ch'ü-chiang	曲江	Hsiang chou chi	湘州記
Ch'ü Hao	曲顥	Hsiang-lin	象林
Fa-chen	法真	Hsiao Ping	蕭炳

Hsiao Ying-shih	蕭穎士	Ko-shu Huang	歌舒晃
Hsiao Yu	蕭祐	Ko Wei	萬維
Hsieh (Zya)	謝	Kou Chien	勾踐
Hsieh-li (Ghet-li)	頡利	Ku Fei-hsiung	顧非熊
Hsieh T'iao	謝朓	Ku-lung (= Kurung)	古龍
Hsiung (Ghyung) [tribe]	雄	Kuan ch'a shih	觀察使
Hsü Hun	許渾	Kuang hsiao szu	光孝寺
Hsü K'ai	徐鍇	Kuei Chung-wu	桂仲武
Hsü Shen	徐申	Kuei-lin	桂林
Hsü T'ang	許棠	Kuei-ling	桂嶺
Hsü Yen-jo	徐彥若	K'un-lun (= Kurung)	崑崙
Hsü Yü	徐王	K'un-ming	昆明
Hsüan-tsang	玄奘	K'ung K'uei	孔戣
Hsüan-yüan Chi	軒轅集	Kuo Chung-ch'an	郭仲產
Hu Cheng	胡証	Kuo P'u	郭璞
Hu Ts'eng	胡曾	Lai-po	荔波
Hua (Ghwǎ)	華	Lang-ning	朗寧
Hua Huan	滑渙	Lang shan	朗山
Hua-meng	化蒙	Le-ch'ang	樂昌
Huai-chi	懷集	Lei Man	雷滿
Ḥuai-ti	懷廸	Leng-chia (Skt. Laṅka)	楞伽
Huan-wang (Ghwǎn-ywang)	環王	Li (= Loi)	俚黎
Huang (Ghwang)	黃	Li (Vietn. Ly)	李
Huang Ch'ao	黃巢	Li [river]	灕
Huang Ch'eng-ch'ing	黃承慶	Li Ao	李翱
Huang Ch'ien-yao	黃乾曜	Li Chi-kao	李繼皋
Huang Kung	黃恭	Li Chiang	李絳
Huang-lien	黃連	Li Ch'iao	李嶠
Huang Shao-ch'ing (Ghwang Sheu-k'yǎng)	黃少卿	Li Chih-jou	李知柔
Huang T'ing-chien	黃庭堅	Li Ching	李靖
Hui-neng	慧能	Li Cho	李涿
Hui-yüeh	惠越	Li Chün	李畯
Hung-jen	弘忍	Li Ch'ün-yü	李羣玉
I-hsing	一行	Li Fu	李復
Jen Hsiao	任囂	Li Ho	李賀
Jih-nan	日南	Li Hsiang-ku	李象古
Jung K'ang	容康	Li Hsüan	李玹
Jung shan	榮山	Li Hsüan	李暄
Kan [river]	贛	Li Hsün	李珣
K'ang Ch'eng-hsün	康承訓	Li Hu	李鄠
Kao Cheng-p'ing	高正平	Li K'o-chi	李可及
Kao Li-shih	高力士	Li K'o-yung	李克用
Kao-liang	高梁	Li Liang	李良
Kao P'ien	高駢	Li Lin-fu	李林甫
Keng Wei	耿湋	Li Mien	李勉
Ko Hung	葛洪	Li Pao-ch'eng (Li Pau-zheng)	李寶誠
Ko-lao (Kat-lau)	葛獠,獦獠	Li Ping	李冰
		Li Po (Li Bǎk)	李白

Li Po (Li Bwĕt)	李渤	Lu-t'ing	盧亭
Li Shang-yin	李商隱	Lung-pien	龍編
Li She	李涉	Lü Jen-kao	呂仁高
Li Shen	李紳	Ma Chih	馬植
Li Shíh-chen	李時珍	Ma Tsung	馬惣
Li Te-yü	李德裕	Ma Yin	馬殷
Li Ying	李郢	Ma Yüan	馬援
Li Yüan-tsung	李元宗	Man	蠻
Liang (Lyang) [tribe]	梁	Mao	毛
Liang Ch'ung-ch'ien	梁崇牽	Mei Hsüan-ch'eng	梅玄成
Liang Ta-hai	梁大海	Mei Yao-ch'en	梅堯臣
Liao (Leu) [tribe]	廖	Mei Shu-luan	梅叔鸞
Lin-i (Lyĕm-iĕp)	林邑	Mei Shu-man	梅叔蠻
Lin-kuei	臨桂	Mei Shu-yen (Mai Shuk-yen)	梅叔馬
Lin Shih-hung (Lyĕm Dri-ghwĕng)		Meng	詺蒙
	林士弘	Meng Ch'ang	孟嘗
		Meng Chiao	孟郊
Ling-chiu	靈鷲	Meng Kuan	孟琯
Ling-i	靈一	Meng Shen	孟詵
Ling-t'un	靈屯	Miao	苗
Liu Ch'ang	劉鋹	Min	閩
Liu Ch'ang-ch'ing	劉長卿	Mo (Mak)	莫
Liu Fang	劉方	Mo Ch'un (Mak Zhwin)	莫淳
Liu Hsün	劉恂	Mo Hsiu-fu (Mak Hyou-byu)	莫休符
Liu Shih-cheng	劉士政	Mo Hsün (Mak Zyĕm)	莫潯
Liu Tsung-yüan	柳宗元	Mou Jung	牟融
Liu Yen	劉巖	Mu Hua	木華
Liu Yin	劉隱	Mu Hsüan-hsü	木玄虛
Liu Yü-hsi	劉禹錫	Nan-chao	南詔
Lo (La) [tribe]	羅	Nan-hai	南海
Lo (Lak) [nation]	駱,雒	Nan hsiang tzu	南鄉子
Lo-ch'a (La-tr'ăt)	羅剎	Nan-kung Yüeh	南宮説
Lo Ch'eng (La Zheng)	羅誠	Nan-p'ing	南平
Lo-ch'eng (La-zheng; Vietn. La-thanh)		Ning	寧
	羅城	Ning Ch'ang-chen	寧長真
		Ning Ch'un (Neng Zhwin)	寧純
Lo-fou (La-byou)	羅浮	Ning Hsüan (Neng Sywan)	寧宣
Lo-tzu	羅子	Ning Tao-ming (Neng Dau-mywăng)	
Lu [surname]	盧		寧道明
Lu Chia	陸賈	Niu Hsien-k'o	牛仙客
Lu Chih	陸贄	Niu Seng-ju	牛僧孺
Lu Chün	盧鈞	Nung (Nong)	儂
Lu Hsün	盧循	Nü Kua	女媧
Lu Kuei-meng	陸龜蒙	Ou [nation]	甌歐嘔
Lu-lu (Lu-luk)	盧鹿	Ou-yang Ch'ien	歐陽倩
Lu Mei-niang	盧眉娘	Ou-yang Chiung	歐陽炯
Lu Nan (Lu Nam)	盧南	Pa	巴
Lu Szu-kung	路嗣恭	P'an-hu	盤瓠

P'an-yü	畨禺	Ta-li	大禮
P'ang Chü-chao	龐巨昭	Ta yün szu	大雲寺
P'ang Hsiao-kung (Baung Hău-kyong)		Tan [people]	蜑
	龐孝恭	Tan-erh	儋耳
Pao Ku	鮑佑	T'ao Ch'ien	陶潛
Pao lin szu	寶林寺	T'ao Hung-ching	陶弘景
P'ei Hsing-li	裴行立	Teng Wen-chin	鄧文進
P'ei Huai-ku	裴懷古	Teng Yu	鄧祐
P'ei Tu	裴度	Ti Jen-chieh	狄仁傑
P'ei Yüan	裴淵	T'ien-wu (T'en-ngu)	天吳
P'ei Yüan-yü	裴元裕	To Hu-sang (Ta Ghu-sang)	多胡桑
P'eng-lai	蓬萊	T'o (T'a, Da) [people]	色
P'i Jih-hsiu	皮日休	Tou Ch'ün	竇羣
Pien [canal]	汴	Tou Shu-hsiang	竇叔向
Po Chü-i	白居易	Tou Ts'an	竇參
P'o-li (Ba-li)	婆利	T'ou-li (Dou-lei)	頭黎
P'o-lo	博羅	Ts'ai Ching	蔡京
Pu Chih	步隲	Ts'ai Hsi	蔡襲
P'u Ho-san (Pyu Ha-san)	蒲訶散	Tsang-ko (Tsang-ka)	牂柯
Shen Ch'üan-ch'i	沈佺期	Ts'ang-wu	蒼梧
Shen-hsiu	神秀	Ts'ang-hai	滄海
Shen Huai-yüan	沈懷遠	Ts'ao [stream]	曹
Shen T'ai-chih	申太芝	Ts'ao Sung	曹松
Shih-an	始安	Ts'ao Ta-tsung	曹大宗
Shih Hsieh (Dri Sep; Vietn. Si Nhiêp)		Ts'ao Yeh-na (Dzau Ya-na)	曹野那
	士燮	Tseng-ch'eng	增城
Shih-hsing	始興	Ts'en Shen	岑參
Shih Lu	史祿	Ts'uan	爨
Shu	蜀	Ts'ui Wei	崔煒
Shuang	瀧	Ts'ui Yen	崔郾
Shun	舜	Tu Fu	杜甫
Su Chien	蘇鑒	Tu Mu	杜牧
Su Kung	蘇恭	Tu Shen-yen	杜審言
Su O	蘇鶚	Tu Ying-han (Du Yăng-ghan)	
Sun Kuang-hsien	孫光憲		杜英翰
Sun Szu-miao	孫思邈	Tu Ying-ts'e	杜英策
Sung [river]	松	Tu Yu	杜佑
Sung Chih-wen	宋之問	T'u-lao	土獠
Sung Ch'ing-li	宋慶禮	Tuan Ch'eng-shih	段成式
Sung-p'ing (Vietn. Tông-binh)	宋平	Tuan Kung-lu	段公路
Sung Yai	宋崖	Wa (Ăăi, Wă)	娃
Sung Yü	宋玉	Wan Chen	萬震
Szu-lung	思籠	Wang Ch'ao	王潮
Szu-ma Hsiang-ju	司馬相如	Wang Chi	王績
Szu-ma Lü-jen	司馬呂仁	Wang Chien	王建
Ta chien ch'an shih	大鑒禪師	Wang Fan	王範
Ta Ch'ing	大慶	Wang Hung	王翃
Ta Hsi-t'ung	達奚通	Wang I-fang	王義方

Wang Ling-hsüan	王令寰	Yang Ch'ing (Yang Ts'yeng; Vietn. Dương Thanh)	楊清
Wang O	王鍔	Yang Fu	楊孚
Wang Shao-chih	王韶之	Yang Kuo-chung	楊國忠
Wang Sheng-chao (Ywang Shĕng-tyeu) 王昇朝		Yang Min	揚旻
Wang Shu-ho	王叔和	Yang Szu-hsü	楊思勖
Wang Wei	王維	Yang T'ao	楊濤
Wang yüan szu	王園寺	Yang Yen	揚炎
Wei (Wĕi) [tribe]	韋	Yang Yü-ling	楊於陵
Wei Cheng	魏徵	Yao	猺
Wei Cheng-kuan	韋正貫	Yeh Kuang-lüeh	葉廣略
Wei Kao	韋皋	Yen Chuan	嚴譔
Wei Tan	韋丹	Yen Kung-su	嚴公素
Wei T'ing-yün	溫庭筠	Yin shan	隱山
Wei Ying-wu	韋應物	Ying shan	螢山
Wu (Ngu)	吳	Yung-ch'eng	永城
Wu (Myu) [tribe]	武	Yung-k'ou	埔口
Wu-chen	悟真	Yung T'ao	雍陶
Wu Chün-chieh (Ngu Kywĕn-kăi) 吳君解		Yü [hero]	禹
Wu Ch'üan	吳權	Yü [pass]	庾
Wu hsing szu	悟性寺	Yü (Iwĕt) [river]	鬱
Wu-hu	烏滸	Yü [Kuei-chou mt.]	虞
Wu Hun	武渾	Yü [Kuang-chou mt.]	禺
Wu Jung	吳融	Yü Hsin	庾信
Wu ling	五嶺	Yü-lin	鬱林
Wu-lu	武陸	Yü Meng-wei	魚孟威
Wu Wu-ling	吳武陵	Yüan Chen	元稹
Wu-yang	武陽	Yüan Chieh	元結
Wu Yün	吳筠	Yüan Hung	袁宏
Yang Chih-ch'eng	楊志誠	Yüeh (Ywăt; Viet)	越
		Yüeh-ch'eng	悦城

GLOSSARY B

Words

Romanization	Characters	Romanization	Characters
a-lo-ho-chi-pa (a-la-ghwa-gyĕp băt)	阿羅和及拔	ch'ih (t'yi)	螭
a-mo-lo (a-mat-la)	阿末羅	ch'ih-mei (t'yiĕ-mi)	魑魅
an-lo (am-la)	菴羅	chin (kyĕn)	摼
an-mi-lo (am-miĕ-la)	菴弭羅	chin chü (kyĕm kywit)	金橘
an-mo-lo (am-mĕt-la)	菴没羅	ch'in chi liao (dzyin kyit-leu)	秦吉了
cha (tră)	鮓	ching [essence]	精
chan (dran)	棧	ching [wood]	荆
chan-po (chem-bĕk)	薝蔔	ching [deer]	麏
chang	樟	ch'ing fu	青蚨
chang-fu	章甫	chiu-mou (tsyou-mou)	蟗蝥
ch'ang [fish]	鯧	ch'iung (k'yung) [vault]	穹
ch'ang [pheasant]	鷩雉	ch'iung [gem]	瓊
che-ku (cha-ku)	鷓鴣	chou	州
chen (dyĕm)	鴆	chu	麈
ch'en (zhin)	脣	chu chin	朱槿
ch'eng (dyăng)	橙	chu-yü (chok-ngyok)	鸀瑁
chi mi chou	羈縻州	ch'u-man (t'yu-man)	貙猵
chi mu (ki myuk)	麂目	ch'u-meng (t'yu-măng)	貙氓
chi-ts'ai (kyit-dzai)	吉財	chü [typhoon]	颶
ch'i	氣	chü [tangerine]	橘
chiao (kău)	蛟	chü-na-wei (kyu-na-ywei)	俱
chiao hsiao	絞綃	chü-yü	鸀鳿
chieh-liao (ket-leu)	結遼	chü-yüan (kyo-ywen)	枸櫞
ch'ien	乾	e (ngak)	鱷
chih (dyi)	雉	fei-fei (pĕi-pĕi)	狒狒

345

fei-ts'ui	翡翠	kuan	管
feng (pyong)	犎	kuang-lang	桄榔
feng li	風貍	kuei	桂
fo-sang (bywĕt-sang)	佛桑	kuei mu (kwĕi myuk)	鬼目
fu [archive-office]	府	k'ung	空
fu [rhapsody]	賦	k'ung-t'ung	崆峒
fu-sang (byu-sang)	扶桑	kuo-jan (kwa-nhen)	果然
hai t'un	海豚	kuo-lo (kwa-la)	過羅
han hsiao hua	含笑花	lien	楝
han-p'eng (ghan-bĕng)	韓朋	lien-ch'an (lyen-zhen)	連禪
hou (ghou)	鱟	lien ch'üeh	練鵲
hsi-pi (ghei-pyek)	係辟	lin-ch'in	林檎
hsiao (syeu)	魈	ling	靈
hsien (ghăn) [pheasant]	鷳	ling-li	鯪鯉
hsien [township]	縣	ling mao	靈貓
hsien [transcendent]	仙	lu-chü (lu-kywit)	盧橘
hsien shu	仙鼠	mai tzu mu	賣子木
hsing-hsing	猩猩	man-t'ou (man-dou)	曼頭
hsiu-liu (hyou-lyou)	鷞鷜	mao (myou)	矛
hsü (hyo)	壚	mao-che (mou-cha)	茂遮
hsü-yeh (syo-ya)	屑斜	mei [apricot]	梅
hsün li	薰貍	mei [mildew]	黴
hu mao hsi	胡帽犀	meng-ch'ung (mung-ch'ong)	蒙衝
hu-san	虎散	meng-kuei	紫貴
hua li	花梨	meng-t'ung (mung-dung) [bird]	
hua ti	鏵鏃		艨艟
hua t'ung	花桐		
huan	鯇	meng-t'ung (mung-dung) [boat]	
huang chin	黃槿		艨艟
huang tan tzu	黃淡子		
hui (hwĕi)	翬	mi (myit)	蜜
hun-t'un (ghwĕn-dwĕn)	渾沌	mi-hou	獼猴
hung ts'ui	紅翠	mo-li (mat-li)	茉莉
i chih tzu	益知子	mou-li	牡蠣
jou kuei	肉桂	mu chin	水槿
kan (kam)	柑	mu fu-jung	木芙蓉
kan-lan [house]	干闌	mu-k'o	木客
kan-lan (kam-lam) [tree]	橄欖	mu-lien	木蓮
kao-liang	高良	mu-tan (mou-tan)	牡丹
kao-lu (kau-lu)	皋蘆	mu-wei (muk-wĕi)	木威
ko	柯	no (nak)	諾
ko-chieh (kap-kăi)	蛤蚧	nước măm (Vietn.)	浩鮸
kou-pi (kou-pek)	龜鼊	o (nga)	娥
ku	蠱	pa-chiao (pă-tseu)	芭蕉
ku-huo (ku-ghwak)	姑獲	pang	蚌
k'u-lung (k'wĕt-lung)	窟寵	p'ang-chiang	蟚蜞
kua	蝸	pao [treasure]	寶
kua-lu (kwă-lu)	瓜蘆	pao [tree]	枹
		p'ao	匏

pei-to (pai-ta)	貝多	tsung-lü	椶櫚
pei-tzu	貝子	tu (duk)	獨
p'i-li	薜荔	tu-chüan	杜鵑
pin-lang	檳榔	tu-hsien tzu (tu-ghăm tsi)	都咸子
po, pao [ox]	犦	t'u ching	圖經
p'o-so-mo (ba-sa-ma)	婆娑摩	tung [grotto]	洞
p'u-kuei (bu-gwi)	蒲葵	t'u-lin (du-lyĕm)	塗林
sao	矟	t'ung [ship]	舸
sha [tree]	桫	tzu-hsi (tsiĕ-ghwei)	蜻蟢
shan (srăm)	杉	tzu-jan	自然
shan-hu	珊瑚	tz'u	詞
shao tzu	韶子	tz'u ch'ou	廁籌
she (shă)	畬	tz'u shih	刺史
sheng	笙	tz'u t'ung	刺桐
sheng t'eng	省藤	wa [frog]	蛙
shih	使	wa [puddle]	窪
shih hu	石斛	wu [asterism]	婺
shih lang	師郎	wu–lo (mywĕt-la)	物羅
shih niang	師娘	wu tsei	烏賊
shu-yü	薯蕷	wu t'ung	梧桐
szu (zi)	兕	wu-yüan	烏員
szu hsi	兕犀	yang-mei (yang-mai)	楊梅
t'a (t'ap)	鰨	yao	瑤
tai-mei	瑇瑁	yao chüan	咬鵑
ti [theocrat]	帝	yeh ho hua	夜合花
ti (dek) [pheasant]	翟	yeh-ko	冶葛
tiao chang	釣樟	ying huo	熒惑
t'ien-chu kuei	天竺桂	yu (you)	柚
ting hsiang	丁香	yu t'ung	油桐
to-lo (ta-la)	多羅	yung [vegetable]	雍
t'o (da)	鼉	yung wu	詠物
tou-k'ou	豆蔻	yü (ywĕk)	蜮
tou men	斗門	yü (ywĕt)	鱖
tsao hua che	造化者	yüan	鵷
tsao wu che	造物者	yüan-chü (ywăn-kyo)	爰居
tse (trăk)	蚱	yüeh kuei	月桂
ts'ui ch'ai	翠釵	yün-tang	篔簹

347

GLOSSARY C

Nam-Viet Counties

KUANG ADMINISTRATION

Ch'ao (Dyeu) 潮
Chen (Chin) 振
Ch'in (Gyěn) 勤瓊
Ch'iung (Gyweng)
Ch'un (Ch'win) 春
En (En) 恩
Feng (Pyong) 封
Hsin (Syin) 新
Hsün (Zywin) 循
Kang[a] (Kang[a]) 康
K'ang (K'ang) 岡
Kao (Kau) 高

Kuang (Kwang) 廣
Lei (Lwai) 雷
Lien (Lyen) 連
Lo (La) 羅
P'an (P'an) 潘
Pien (Byen) 辯
Shao (Zheu) 韶
Shuang (Sraung) 瀧
Tan (Tam) 儋
Tuan (Twan) 端
Wan-an (Mywǎn-an) 萬安
Yai (Ngǎai) 崖

KUEI ADMINISTRATION

Chao (Cheu) 昭
Chih (Chi) 芝
Fu (Pyou) 富
Ho (Gha) 賀
Hsiang (Zyang) 象
Huan (Ghwǎn) 環
I[a] (Ngiě[a]) 宜
Jung (Yung) 融
Kang[b] (Kang[b]) 剛

Ku (Ku) 古
Kuei (Kwei) 桂
Kung (Kyong) 龔
Liu (Lyou) 柳
Meng (Mung) 蒙
Szu-t'ang (Si-dang) 思唐
Wu (Ngu) 梧
Yen (Ngyǎm) 嚴

349

Glossary C

Jung Administration

Hsiu (Syou)	繡		Shun (Jwin)	順
I[b] (Ngiĕ[b])	義		Tang (Tang)	黨
Jung (Yong)	容		T'eng (Dĕng)	藤
Lao (Lau)	牢		Tou (Dou)	竇
Lien (Lyem)	廉		Yen (Ngăm)	嚴
P'ing-ch'in (Bywăng-gyĕm) 平琴			Yü (Ngyu)	禺
Po (Băk)	白		Yü-lin (Iwĕt-lyĕm) 鬱林

Yung Administration

Ch'eng (Dyĕng)	澄		Luan (Lwan)	巒
Ch'in (K'yĕm)	欽		Pin (Pyin)	賓
Heng (Ghwăng)	横		T'ien (Den)	田
Hsün (Zyĕm)	潯		Yung (Iong)	邕
Kuei (Kwĕi)	貴			

Annam Administration

Ai (Ai)	愛		Fu-lu (Pyuk-luk) 福祿
Ch'ang (Dyang)	長		Huan (Hwan)	驩
Chiao (Kău)	交		Lu (Lyuk)	陸
Feng (P'yong)	峯		Yen (Yen)	演

Counties outside of Nam-Viet

Ch'ang (Zhang)	常		Hung (Ghung)	洪
Ch'en (T'yem)	郴		Jun (Nhwin)	潤
Chi (Kyit)	吉		K'un (K'wĕn)	昆
Ch'ien (Gyen)	虔		Lang[a] (Lang[a])	朗
Chih (Tyĭ)	智		Lang[b] (Lang[b])	閬
Ching (Kyăng)	荆		Mu (Myuk)	睦
Ch'u (Tr'yo)	楚		Ning (Neng)	寧
Ch'ü (Gyu)	衢		Pien (Byen)	汴
Ch'üan (Dzywen)	泉		Po (Pa)	播
Fu (Pyuk)	福		Su (Su)	蘇
Fu (Byou)	浯		Sung (Song)	宋
Hang (Ghang)	杭		Szu (Si)	泗
Heng (Ghăng)	衡		T'an (Dam)	潭
Hsiang (Syang)	湘		Yung (Ywăng)	永
Hsin (Syin)	信		Yü (Yu)	渝
Hsü (Zyo)	徐		Yüeh (Ywăt)	越

INDEX

Index

Amomum amarum, 193
Amomum globosum, 194
Amyda steindachneri, 215
An-ch'eng Mountain, 61
An ch'i sheng, 29
An Lu-shan, 63, 69
Anhwei, 16
Anna, 76
Annam, 5, 6, 19, 20, 27, 30–34 passim,
    36, 38, 39, 45, 57, 60, 63–71 passim, 74,
    81, 82, 85, 87, 90, 97, 98, 99, 105, 123,
    125, 126, 127, 137, 138, 141, 154, 162,
    163, 168, 172–175 passim, 177, 179,
    180, 181, 186, 191, 193, 194, 197, 198,
    201, 206, 210, 213, 214, 215, 220, 222,
    225, 226, 230–233, 236, 238, 241, 252,
    257. See also Vietnam
Anopheles maculatus, 131
Anopheles minimus, 131
Ant, 210, 251
Antares, 123
Antiaris toxicaria, 171
Anushirvan, 11
Ape. See Gibbon, Monkey
Apple, 183
Apricot, 127, 181, 192
Aquilaria, 197
Aquilaria agallocha, 197
Aquilaria sinensis, 197
Arab, Arabian, Arabic, 16, 28, 31, 49, 75,
    76, 77, 97, 124, 138, 163, 218, 227
Architecture, 73. See also Wall
Areca nut, 32, 72, 174, 175, 245
Arenga palm, 40, 41, 44. See also Sagwire,
    Sugar palm
Arenga saccharifera, 175
Argo, 123
Arisaema, 171
Arizona, 262
Armillary sphere, 92
Armor, 74, 132, 178, 227
Aromatics, 29, 77, 85, 134, 193–198. See
    also Incense, Perfume
Arrow, 50, 53, 72, 99, 103, 179, 225, 226,
    227, 231, 233
Arrowhead, 50, 154
Arsenic, 152
Artocarpus, 196, 197

Arum, 177
Asafoetida, 103
Asarum, 169
Asbestos, 158
Assam, 10, 167, 168
Au-lac. See Ou-lo
Augur, 236. See also Divination
Aurelia, 207
Aurochs, 223
Aurora, 259
Australasia, 235
Avataṁsaka, 118
Avocado, 183
Axe, 5, 54, 154; shouldered, 12
Aymonier, E., 75
Azalea, 260–261
Azurite, 157

Babbler, 235
Babbling thrush, 235
Babylonian, 80
Bactria, 78, 91
Bahnar, 256
Bali, 74, 222, 224
Balloon fish, 213
Bamboo, 25, 28, 31, 43, 48, 50, 54, 55,
    72, 84, 91, 109, 143, 168, 172, 177, 178–
    179, 215, 217, 218, 241, 249, 253, 254;
    shoot, 179, 250
Bamboo King, 53, 178
Banana, 30, 32, 54, 84, 85, 99, 132, 173,
    181, 186–188, 189, 199, 234, 252, 258
Banting, 75, 224
Banyan, 55, 204, 205, 216
Barbet, 234, 235
Barnyard fowl, 101. See also Chicken
Basic Herbal of Overseas Drugs, 83
Basketry, 177
Basra, 104
Bat, 142, 232–233; Harlequin, 222; Horse-
    shoe, 222; Tube-nosed, 222
Bates, Marston, 130
Bath, 147, 192, 198
Batik, 10
Baudelaire, Charles, 117
Bauhinia, 172
Bay of Bengal, 127
Bead, 169

Index

Ch'ang (-chou, County), 19, 22
ch'ang (fish), 213
Ch'ang (Mountain), 22
ch'ang (pheasant), 243
Ch'ang-an, 24, 28, 30, 36, 57, 58, 67, 68, 77, 78, 80, 88, 107, 119, 163, 169, 173, 185, 190, 200, 216, 221, 236, 243, 261, 262
Ch'ang ch'ing (reign), 66
Ch'ang-o (Zhang-nga), 125
Ch'ang-sha. *See* T'an (-chou)
Chao (-chou, County), 114, 140, 142, 229
Chao (Dyeu; tribe), 19, 49
Chao (warrior maiden), 81
Chao Ch'ang, 64, 149
Chao Kuo-chen, 71
Chao Te, 60
Chao T'o, 5, 9, 15, 25, 26, 28, 30, 38, 97, 159, 174, 179, 195, 208, 241
Ch'ao (-chou, County), 20, 30, 44, 60, 65, 95, 128, 145, 156, 158, 180, 185, 213, 214, 215, 217, 224
Charts of the Ten Circuits, 148
che-ku, 240
Chekiang, 13, 14, 24, 29, 45, 82, 85, 101, 148, 154, 182, 193, 196, 201, 221, 240
Chemistry, 87. *See also* Alchemy
chěmpaka, 199
Chen (-chou, County), 178, 215
chen (dyěm), 227, 245
Chen (River), 24, 25, 136
Chen Ch'ung-yü (Chin Dryung-iwět), 63
Chen-la (Chin-lap), 175
Ch'en (-chou, County), 25, 100
Ch'en (dynasty), 71
Ch'en Hsing-fan (Dyin Ghăng-bywăm), 63
Ch'en-liu, 22
Ch'en Szu-chi, 171
Ch'en T'an, 151
Ch'en T'ao, 131, 251
Ch'en T'ing-szu, 37
Ch'en Ts'ang-ch'i, 102, 133, 147, 153, 169, 212, 213, 230, 233
Ch'en Yen-ch'ien, 69
Cheng (River), 24
Cheng-ch'ang, 24
Cheng Ch'üan, 37

Cheng Erh (Tyěng Nhi), 81
Cheng Ho, 205
Cheng Szu-yüan, 228
Cheng Ts'e (Tyěng Tryěk, Vietn. Trung Trac), 81
Cheng-yang, 24
Ch'eng (-chou, County), 163
ch'eng (dyăng), 183
Ch'eng-tu, 58, 61, 190
Chert, 154
Chestnut, 183
Chi (-chou, County), 24
Chi Han, 148
chi-liao (kyit-leu), 244
chi mi chou. See Bridle and Halter Counties
chi mu (ki myuk), 192
chi-ts'ai, 171
ch'i (breath), 119
Ch'i-lao (Ngyět-lau), 48. *See also* Lao
Ch'i-t'ien (Pass), 25
Chiang (River), 22, 40, 119, 132. *See also* Yangtze
Chiang Chiao, 236
Chiang-nan, 4, 101, 127, 136, 140, 150, 151, 154, 163, 172
Chiang Tzu-lu (Kyang Tsi-lu), 62
Chiao (-chou, County), 5, 6, 19, 32, 33, 62, 65, 67, 68, 78, 124, 126, 175, 180, 186, 197, 228. *See also* Annam, Hanoi, Vietnam
chiao (kău)-dragon, 32, 128, 147, 217–221. *See also* Dragon, *kău*
Chiao-chih, 15. *See also* Chiao-chou
Chicken, 44, 56, 100, 102, 103, 111, 181, 222, 223, 240
chieh-liao (ket-leu), 72, 244
chieh tu shih. See Legate
Chien-chen, 191
Ch'ien (-chou, County), 21, 24, 36
Ch'ien Ch'i, 239
Ch'ien-chung, 15, 49, 71, 136. *See also* Kweichow
Ch'ien I, 38
Chignon, 81, 85. *See also* Coiffure, Hair
chih *(dyi),* 243
ch'ih (t'yi), 218
ch'ih-mei (t'yiě-mi), 112. *See also* Troll

Index

Index

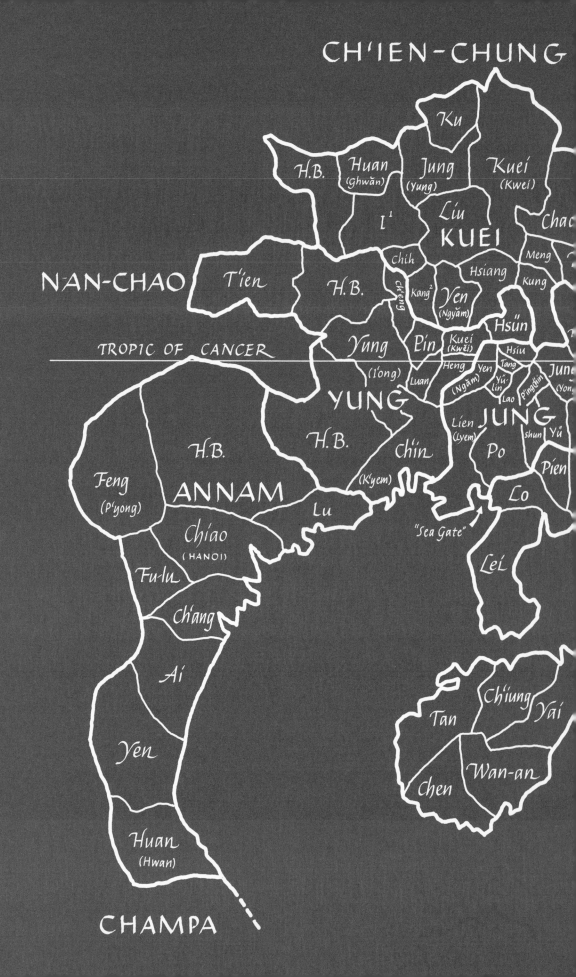

CH'IEN-CHUNG

Ku

H.B.   Huan   Jung   Kuei
        (Ghwǎn)   (Yung)   (Kwei)

                                        Chac
                        I¹   Liu
                                    KUEI

NAN-CHAO   T'ien   Chih   Meng
                              H.B.   Hsiang   Kung
                                              ch'eng Kang² Yen
                                                             (Ngyǎm) Hsün

TROPIC OF CANCER   Yung   Pin   Kuei   Hsiu
                                              (Kwěi) Tang
                                        (I'ong)   Heng Yen Yǔ- Jun
                                              Luan   (Ngǎm) Lao lin P'ingchin
                              YUNG   shun (Yon

                        H.B.   Chin   Lien JUNG   Yǔ
                                                    (Lyem)
Feng   (K'yem)   Po
(P'yong)   H.B.   Pien
            ANNAM   Lu   Lo

            Chiao   "Sea Gate"
            (HANOI)   Lei
Fu-lu

        Ch'ang

            Ai   Tan   Ch'iung Yai

        Yen   Wan-an
                                                    Chen

        Huan
        (Hwan)

CHAMPA